The Palgrave Handbook of Religion and State Volume II

Shannon Holzer
Editor

The Palgrave Handbook of Religion and State Volume II

Global Perspectives

Editor
Shannon Holzer
Houston Christian University
Houston, TX, USA

ISBN 978-3-031-35608-7   ISBN 978-3-031-35609-4   (eBook)
https://doi.org/10.1007/978-3-031-35609-4

Cover illustration: Godong / Alamy Stock Photo

This Palgrave Macmillan imprint is published by the registered company Springer Nature Switzerland AG.
The registered company address is: Gewerbestrasse 11, 6330 Cham, Switzerland

Paper in this product is recyclable.

Foreword to The Handbook of Religion and State Volume II: Theory and Practice in the Eastern Hemisphere

Religious practice and the political organization are both deeply rooted in human nature and manifest themselves throughout human history and human culture. Two of Aristotle's most famous claims about human beings are first "humanity is political by nature" and that politics encompasses all forms of sociability; and he claims second, that "humanity desires to know" and that such search for wisdom at the highest level is encompassed by metaphysics and theology. And yet religion and the political state take such a variety of forms and exhibit such diverse content, it is quite a challenge to understand and discuss their interactions and mutual influences. We must at the outset acknowledge this range of historical and cultural forms that each takes and that defines their interaction. This volume, *The Handbook of Religion and State*, edited by Shannon Holzer, gathers for the reader this wide diversity of phenomenon that emerge in human experience and history. The reader can then begin to search for common threads and to make judicious comparisons and contrasts.

We are grateful to the editor Shannon Holzer for supervising this wide-ranging project involving dozens of excellent scholars and arranging such a wealth of approaches to the topic. The chapters are well written and provide us with a wealth of date, useful analysis, and many insights into the reality of the mutual influence of religion and the state. The Handbook well prepares the student, traveler, statesmen, pastor, or any citizen of the world for a better understanding of the religious and political situation in the world today.

I commend the publisher, the editor, and the authors for taking on this work so that we may heed the words of Gandhi, "Those who believe religion and politics aren't connected don't understand either."

Houston, TX, USA   John P. Hittinger

CONTENTS

NOTES ON CONTRIBUTORS

Rodrigo Vitorino Souza Alves (LLB, LLM, PhD) is a professor of law at the Federal University of Uberlândia (Brazil), where he also serves as head of the Constitutional, International, and Human Rights Law Unit. He leads the Brazilian Center of Studies in Law and Religion, which focuses on religious freedom, protection of religious minorities, antidiscrimination norms and religion-state relations. Alves has been a visiting academic/fellow at the University of Oxford, the Autonomous University of Lisbon, and the ICLRS. He has been invited as a law and religion expert by national and international organizations such as the Office of the High Commissioner for Human Rights, the Organization of American States Permanent Council, and the International Development Law Organization. He has presented his research at events in various countries. Alves sits on the advisory board of the Advanced Program on Religion and the Rule of Law at Oxford and the editorial board for the book series Law and Religion in a Global Context.

Roberto Blancarte is Professor at the Center of Sociological Studies of El Colegio de México and holds a PhD in Social Sciences (1988) from the EHESS, in Paris, France. Blancarte has been a professor at Stanford University, Dartmouth College, École Pratique des Hautes Études, and the University of Paris-Diderot, counselor at the Mexican Embassy to the Holy See, and Chief of Staff at the Vice-ministry of Religious Affairs in the Mexican Government. Blancarte has written or edited 24 books on religion, laicity, and secularization.

Jeremy Bonner is Postgraduate Director of Studies at Lindisfarne College of Theology in the North East of England. He is the author of *The Road to Renewal: Victor Joseph Reed and Oklahoma Catholicism, 1905–1971* (2008) and *Called Out of Darkness Into Marvelous Light: A History of the Episcopal Diocese of Pittsburgh, 1750–2006* (2009), and co-editor with Mary Beth Fraser Connolly and Christopher Denny of *Empowering the People of God: Catholic Action Before and After Vatican II* (2013) and with Mark Chapman of *Costly Communion: Ecumenical Initiative and Sacramental Strife in the Anglican Communion* (2019).

Steele Brand is Assistant Professor of History at The King's College in New York City, where he teaches courses on the ancient Mediterranean world and medieval Europe. He holds a PhD from Baylor University, an MA from Southwestern Baptist Theological Seminary, and a BA from Texas A&M University. He previously served as the Director of Undergraduate Fellows for the Clements Center for National Security and as a tactical intelligence officer for the US Army.

Brand has authored the book *Killing for the Republic: Citizen-Soldiers and the Roman Way of War* (2019), and he has published articles in *USA Today*, *LitHub*, *The Washington Post*, and *The Hill* and in journals such as *Religions and Humanitas* about how this premodern ideal of citizen-soldiers has informed and inspired modern republics, particularly the United States.

Michael Brill his research focuses on modern Iraqi history, particularly during the Baʿthist period of 1968–2003. His topics of interest include militias under Saddam Hussein's regime, the last members of Iraq's Jewish community, Iran-Iraq relations, Iraq's foreign relations with the Arab world, and the Iraqi Muslim Brotherhood. Although his work is based primarily on the archives of Saddam's regime, during his research, he has also become very interested in the history of the various collections of documents in relation to the 1991 and 2003 wars. The history of the archives, in addition to being a valuable subject on its own, also has implications for historical memory of the Baʿthist period and politics in contemporary Iraq.

Janet Epp Buckingham is a professor at Trinity Western University and the Director of the Laurentian Leadership Centre, a one-semester public policy program in Ottawa, Canada. She also serves as Director of Global Advocacy for the World Evangelical Alliance. She is the Executive Editor of the *International Journal for Religious Freedom*. Buckingham previously served as Director, law and public policy, for the Evangelical Fellowship of Canada and Executive Director of the Christian Legal Fellowship in Canada. She was a religious freedom advocate at the UN in Geneva for the World Evangelical Alliance from 2003 to 2006. Her research area is religious freedom law in Canada and internationally. She published a book on the history of religious freedom in Canada, *Fighting over God*, in 2014.

Hoàng Văn Chung obtained his PhD in Sociology from La Trobe University (Australia) in 2015. He was a visiting fellow at ISEAS-Yusof Ishak Institute (Singapore) in 2017. He holds the position of the Head of the Department for Research on Theory and Policy on Religion at the Institute for Religious Studies and teaches about religious studies at the Graduate Academy of Social Sciences, all under the Vietnam Academy of Social Sciences. His main research interests are state-religion relationship, New Religious Movements, religious diversity, sacred spaces, and Protestantism in Vietnam. He has a number of edited books and journal articles published in English and Vietnamese, such as *New Religions and State's Response to Religious Diversification in Contemporary Vietnam* with Springer (2017); a chapter on religious diversity in Vietnam for the book *Religious Diversity in Asia* (2020) and a chapter on religion in Vietnam for the *Handbook of Contemporary Vietnam* (2022).

Daithí Ó. Corráin is an associate professor in the School of History and Geography at Dublin City University. He has published widely on Catholicism. He is the author of *Rendering to God and Caesar: The Irish Churches and the Two States in Ireland, 1949–73* (2006), contributions to the *Cambridge History of Ireland* (2018), the *Oxford History of British and Irish Catholicism* (2023), the *Oxford Handbook of Religion in Modern Ireland* (2023), and journal articles in *British Catholic History*. An expert on the Irish Revolution (1912–1923), he is co-author of landmark *The Dead of the Irish Revolution* (Yale, 2020) and *Cathal Brugha: 'An Indomitable Spirit'* (2022), and co-editor of the acclaimed *The Irish Revolution, 1912–1923* series.

David J. Davis is Associate Professor of History at Houston Baptist University, specializing in late medieval and early modern England. He is a fellow of the Royal Historical Society and writes for *The Wall Street Journal*, *The New Criterion*, and *The American Conservative*. His current book project is *The Culture of Revelation in England*.

Stephen M. Davis is an elder at Grace Church in Philadelphia (gracechurchphilly.org). He and his wife Kathy have been engaged in church planting in the US, France, and Romania since 1982. He holds a PhD in Intercultural Studies from Columbia International University, a DMin in Missiology from Trinity Evangelical Divinity School, and two French language diplomas. He is the author of several books including two on French history: *Rise of French Laïcité* in the Evangelical Missiological Society Monograph Series and *The French Huguenots and Wars of Religion*, selected by the National Huguenot Society for their 2022 Scholarly Works Award.

Julie deGraffenried is Associate Professor of History at Baylor University in Waco, Texas. A specialist in modern Russian history, her research interests include history of childhood, war, religion, and visual culture. Some recent publications include *Sacrificing Childhood: Children and the Soviet State in the Great Patriotic War* (2014), "Combating God and Grandma: The Soviet Anti-Religious Campaigns and the Battle for Childhood," in Dominic Erdozain's *The Dangerous God: Christianity and the Soviet Experiment* (2017), and *Voices of the Voiceless: Religion, Communism, and the Keston Archive* (2019) which she co-edited with Zoe Knox. Her current project explores the multiple meanings of a religious childhood in the Soviet and Cold War contexts.

Donald L. Drakeman is Distinguished Research Professor in the Program on Constitutional Studies at the University of Notre Dame. The Supreme Courts of the United States and the Philippines have cited his publications, which include *Church, State, and Original Intent, Church-State Constitutional Issues,* and *Church and State in American History.*

Joel S. Fetzer is Professor of Political Science and has received his bachelor's in English and Government from Cornell University in 1988 and his doctorate in Political Science from Yale University in 1996. Following postdoctoral studies in International Relations at the University of Southern California, he was Assistant Professor of Political Science at Central Michigan University for two and a half years before moving to Pepperdine University in 2001. Fetzer's research interests and publications are in the fields of international migration, ethnic relations, religion and politics, and indigenous rights in the regions of Western Europe, North America, and East Asia. He is the author or co-author of seven books: *Selective Prosecution of Religiously Motivated Offenders in America*

(1989); *Public Attitudes Toward Immigration in the United States, France, and Germany* (2000); *Muslims and the State in Britain, France, and Germany* (2005); *Luxembourg as an Immigration Success Story: The Grand Duchy in Pan-European Perspective* (2011); *Confucianism, Democratization, and Human Rights in Taiwan* (with J. Christopher Soper, 2012); *Open Borders and International Migration Policy: The Effects of Unrestricted Immigration in the United States, France, and Ireland* (Palgrave Macmillan, 2015); and *Religion and Nationalism in Global Perspective* (with J. Christopher Soper, 2018). He has also published numerous journal articles and book chapters on related topics. Fetzer teaches immigration politics and ethnic relations, comparative European politics, public opinion and voting, East Asian politics, modern Asian political philosophy, government and politics of developing areas, state and local governments, and Indigenous peoples of North America.

Bulus Galadima comes from Jos, Nigeria. He did his undergraduate studies at JETS (Jos ECWA Theological Seminary) and graduate studies at Wheaton Graduate School and Trinity International University. He is married to Rose Galadima, who did her doctorate in education at Trinity International University. They have been in theological education for nearly three decades. Together they started a ministry to widows and orphans called Almanah Rescue Mission in Jos nearly 30 years ago. They were also co-founders of MMD (More than a Mile Deep), an educational ministry to train pastors in Africa who are not able to go to seminary full time. Bulus was dean and later president of JETS and most recently dean of the Cook School of Intercultural Studies at Biola University, California.

Jörg Haustein is University Lecturer in World Christianities at the University of Cambridge and a Fellow of Selwyn College. Before coming to Cambridge, he was Senior Lecturer in Religions in Africa at the School of Oriental and African Studies and prior to that a Research and Teaching Fellow in Religious Studies and Intercultural Theology at the University of Heidelberg. He earned his PhD in Heidelberg with a historical study of the Ethiopian Pentecostal movement.

Haustein's research is centered on Christianity and Islam in Africa with a particular interest in Pentecostalism, the history of Christian missions, the colonial engagement with Islam, and the intersection of religion and development. He has published extensively on Pentecostalism in Ethiopia, Africa, and worldwide, and he has recently completed a major study on

Islam in German East Africa. He is a founding member of the European Research Network on Global Pentecostalism and serves as the editor of its journal *PentecoStudies*. He is also a founding member of the DSA study group "Religion and Development" and was co-investigator of the AHRC-funded research network studying the engagement of religious actors with the Sustainable Development Goals in Ethiopia, India, and the UK.

Radley Henrico matriculated top of his class with honors and went on to obtain his B Proc and LLB degrees from the University of the Witwatersrand in 1992 and 1994, respectively. He worked in the Department of Justice as a Public Prosecutor from 1993 to 1996. After completing pupillage, he commenced practice at the Johannesburg Bar of Advocates in July for a period of 14 years until 2010. He served as a member of the Johannesburg Bar Council Sub-Committee on Human Resources from 2007 to 2008 and while at the Bar also sat as a part-time commissioner of the Commission for Conciliation, Mediation and Arbitration (CCMA) for the period 1998–2001. While at the Bar, he developed a keen interest in labor dispute litigation, commercial matters, and High Court application proceedings. In 2010 he obtained his LLM degree in Labor Law (cum laude) from the University of Johannesburg and was awarded the SASLAW prize of excellence for obtaining the highest marks in such degree.

Radley is Associate Professor of Administrative Law in the Department of Public Law and Jurisprudence at the University of the Western Cape (UWC), South Africa. He started lecturing on a part-time basis in 2011 at the University of Johannesburg (UJ) and in 2012 his appointment was made permanent. In 2011, he lectured labor law to business law students and in 2012 began lecturing administrative law and criminal procedure and was also involved with lecturing labor law in the Postgraduate Diploma in Labor Law (PGDLL) program. From 2014, he was appointed course coordinator of the PGDLL. In 2017 he obtained his Doctoral Degree with his thesis titled "Religious Discrimination in the South African Workplace." At the end of 2019, Radley relocated to the Western Cape and was appointed Senior Lecturer in the Department of Public Law and Jurisprudence at UWC with effect from 01 January 2019. In 2020 he was NRF rated and promoted to associate professor. He has successfully supervised a number of Master of Law students and is supervising a Doctoral candidate. During his tenure at UJ and in 2018, Radley was invited to present a series of guest lectures to undergraduate and postgraduate students at the Symbiosis Law School in Pune, India (SLS). This culminated in the conclusion of an MOU between UJ and SLS. Radley has continued his relationship as a guest lecturer at SLS ever since. In 2019, a similar agreement was concluded between UWC and SLS to facilitate further research collaboration and the exchange of postgraduate students.

His research interests are mainly in administrative law and religious discrimination and labor law. Radley has presented papers at numerous national and international conferences. He has published extensively in journals and book chapters and co-authored books in the aforementioned disciplines. He has been authoritatively referred to by the South African Constitutional Court. He is the editor-in-chief of the *Law, Democracy and Development*, accredited law journal, and serves on various committees within the Faculty of Law and UWC, for example, the Academic Planning Committee and Tender Committee. Radley has been requested by various accredited law journals to peer-review submissions. He has reviewed applications on behalf of the NRF and has also acted as external examiner for numerous universities in South Africa. Since 2015, he has been the Treasurer of the Administrative Justice Association of South Africa (AdJASA), founded in 2012 by the late Arthur Chaskalson (first Judge President of the Constitutional Court). Since 2013, Radley has been the chief legal advisor of the standing legal committee (which is an international oversight body) to whom he renders legal advice (Pro Deo) on an ongoing basis in respect of corporate governance frameworks and systems to ensure proper compliance by the Old Apostolic Church.

John P. Hittinger is Professor of Philosophy at the University of St. Thomas, Houston, Texas, and the Director of the St. John Paul II Institute. He holds degrees from the University of Notre Dame (1974) and the Catholic University of America (1978, 1986). Hittinger has published articles on Thomistic political philosophy and the thought of Karol Wojtyła/John Paul II. He is author of *Liberty, Wisdom and Grace: Thomism and Modern Democratic Theory* (2002).

Shannon Holzer is Assistant Professor of Political Science at Houston Baptist University. He holds degrees in the areas of religion, philosophy, and religion, politics, and society. Holzer obtained his PhD in Religion, Politics and Society from Baylor University's J.M. Dawson Institute of Church-State Studies. He has published in the areas of philosophy, law, politics, and religion. Holzer is often heard on Houston's KTRH news commenting on religion, politics, and society.

Đỗ Quang Hưng obtained his PhD in History at Oriental Institute under the Soviet Academy of Science in 1986. He was the former Director of the Institute for Religious Studies at the Vietnam Academy of Social Sciences. At present, he is a professor teaching at the Faculty of Political Science, the School of Social Sciences and Humanities, Hanoi National University. He focuses on modern history, history of religions, Catholicism, religion-politics relationship, and religion and rule-of-law state in Vietnam. His key publications with publishing houses in Vietnam are: *The Issue of Religion in Revolutionary Vietnam* (2009); *Policy on Religion and the Rule-of-Law State* (2014); *State-Church Relationship and Policy on Religion* (2015); and *The Secular State* (2019).

Petra Kuivala conducts postdoctoral research in the fields of history, theology and religious studies, and Cuban studies. She received her doctorate from the University of Helsinki in 2019 and worked as a postdoctoral researcher at the University of Helsinki. She has also held an appointment as a Fulbright Visiting Scholar at the Cuban Research Institute, Florida International University (2016–2017). Besides her focus on religion and the Cuban revolution, Kuivala's broader research interests include Christianity in the Americas, contemporary Catholicism, and the questions of Catholicism and political power. Kuivala's research on the Cuban revolution draws on fieldwork on the island, combining archival and oral sources with ethnographic research. Particularly essential to her work are the previously unstudied archives of the Catholic Church in Cuba, in which Kuivala has conducted research since 2015. Her recent work includes articles on Cuban religious material culture and the histories of lived religion in revolutionary Cuba. Her current project focuses on the intersections of religious and revolutionary lifestyles in Cuban society.

Joachim Kwaramba is a Zimbabwean man who holds a Doctor of Philosophy in Practical Theology from the University of Pretoria, South Africa; Master of Arts—Systematic Theology from the University of Zimbabwe; Bachelor of Arts Honors in Religious Studies from the University of Zimbabwe. He is a grantee of Templeton Foundation under Nagel Institute (for Engaging African Realities). He is the Chairperson of the Department of Philosophy Religion and Ethics, University of Zimbabwe. He is a research fellow at the University of Pretoria, Department of Practical Theology and Mission Studies. His research interest focuses on pastoral theology, gender, systematic theology, child theology, feminism, and sexuality. He has published in local and international academic accredited journals and book chapters. He serves as a reviewer for AOSIS, *Journal of International Women's Studies* (JIWS), *ALTERNATION*, and SAGE Open. He is an external examiner for Theology for University of KwaZulu-Natal, University of Pretoria, and University of South Africa. He is a member of several academic associations which include the following: The Society of Practical Theology in South Africa (SPTSA), International Academy of Practical Theologians (IAPT), Circle of Concerned African Women Theologians (The Circle), African Association for the Study of Religions (AASR). He is also an ordained minister of the Word and Sacrament and a senior pastor in the Apostolic Faith Mission of Zimbabwe since 2007.

Ernils Larsson is a postdoctoral researcher at the Centre for Multidisciplinary Research on Religion and Society at Uppsala University and at the Organization for Advanced Research and Development, Kokugakuin University, Tokyo. His current research project examines how Shrine Shinto actors have negotiated the constitutional principle of secularism in postwar Japan. Larsson holds a PhD in the History of Religions from Uppsala University.

Joseph Tse-Hei Lee is Professor of History and Director of the Global Asia Institute, Pace University, New York City. His research focuses on the intersection of faith and politics in modern China. He is the editor of *Christianizing South China: Mission, Development, and Identity in Modern Chaoshan* (2018) and (with Lars Peter Laamann) *The Church as Safe Haven: Christian Governance in China* (2019).

Korey D. Mass (DPhil, University of Oxford) is Associate Professor of History at Hillsdale College in Hillsdale, Michigan. His publications include *The Reformation and Robert Barnes*, editorial prefaces for Luther's Works, and an introduction to the recent translation of Niels Hemmingsen, *On the Law of Nature*.

Charles McDaniel teaches in the Honors College at Baylor University and in the Baylor Interdisciplinary Core (BIC). McDaniel also teaches courses in the areas of church history, religion and law, and Christian social thought through Baylor's J. M. Dawson Institute. McDaniel has numerous publications in books and scholarly journals on subjects ranging from the Protestant Reformation to Christian and Muslim economic thought. His book, *God and Money: The Moral Challenge of Capitalism*, was published in 2007, and in 2016, his second book *Civil Society and the Reform of Finance: Taming Capital, Reclaiming Virtue* was published.

A. J. Nolte is Assistant Professor of Politics at Regent University's Robertson School of Government, and the chair of the Master of Arts in International Development program. Previously, he taught at Messiah College, George Washington University, Catholic University, and National Defense University. In Fall 2017, Nolte earned a PhD from Catholic University of America, with dissertation research focused on the relationship between Islam and the state in Turkey and Indonesia. Previously, he worked for the Religious Freedom Project at Georgetown University and the Center for Comhis plex Operations at National Defense University. Nolte's research interests include religion and politics, Christian and Islamic political thought, Christian minorities, international relations theory, comparative politics, tribalism, and globalization.

Eric Patterson serves as Executive Vice President of the Religious Freedom Institute. Patterson is scholar-at-large and past dean of the Robertson School of Government at Regent University and a Research Fellow at Georgetown University's Berkley Center for Religion, Peace & World Affairs, where he previously served full time. Patterson's interest in the intersection of religion, ethics, and foreign policy is informed by two stints at the US Department of State's Bureau of Political-Military Affairs, with work in Afghanistan, Pakistan, Congo, Angola, and elsewhere. He has significant government service, including over 20 years as an officer and commander in the Air National Guard and serving as a White House Fellow working for the Director of the US Office of Personnel Management.

Patterson is the author or editor of over a dozen books, including *Politics in a Religious World: Toward a Religiously Informed U.S. Foreign Policy* (2012), *Just American Wars: Ethical Dilemmas in U.S. Military History* (2019), *Ending Wars Well* (2012), *Ethics Beyond War's End* (2012), and *Military Chaplains in Iraq, Afghanistan* (2011). He has also published on religious freedom, democracy, and democratization in *International Studies Perspectives, Review of Faith and International Affairs, Public Integrity,* and the *International Journal of Religious Freedom*. In addition to articles in scholarly journals such as *Survival, Journal for the Scientific Study of Religion,* and *Security Studies* his work has been published in popular outlets like *The Washington Post* and *Washington Times.*

Patterson has provided briefings and seminars for multiple government agencies, including France's Ministry of Defense, US Department of State, US Central Command, US European Command, US Naval War College, US Naval Postgraduate School, the US military academies, and many others. Patterson holds a PhD in Political Science from the University of California at Santa Barbara and a Master's in International Politics from the University of Wales at Aberystwyth.

James Ponniah is Assistant Professor and the Head of the Christian Studies at the University of Madras. He was formerly the dean of the Faculty of Philosophy at Jnana Deepa Vidyapeeth, Pontifical Institute of Philosophy and Religion, Pune. He obtained both his MA (in Vaishnavism) and doctorate (on Sudalaimadan Cult) from the University of Madras. He was a visiting scholar in the University of California, Berkeley in 2008–2009.

He was a co-investigator with Chad Bauman (Butler University, US) for the Project on 'Christianity, Religious Freedom, and Religious Violence in Contemporary India' funded by Berkeley Centre for Religion, Peace and World Affairs, Washington. He was awarded Collaborative International Research Grant by American Academy of Religions (AAR) in 2015. He won best researcher award for the year 2018 in the University of Madras. In 2021, he was awarded 'Research Fellow of Religion and Culture' by CHRISTE (established by the intergovernmental charter of United Nations Treaty), Malaysia.

His publications include *The Dynamics of Folk Religion in Society: Pericentralisation as Deconstruction of Sanskritisation* (2011), *Dancing Peacock: Indian Insight into Religion and Redevelopment* (2010), *Identity, Difference and Conflict: Postcolonial Critique* (2013), *Committed to the Church and the Country* (2013), *Psycho-Spiritual Mentoring of Adolescents* (2019), and *Culture, Religion and Home-Making in and beyond South Asia* (2020).

Charles Ramsey holds a PhD in Islamic Studies from the University of Birmingham (UK), MA in the History of Religion from Baylor University, PGC in Poverty Reduction from the Centre for Development, Environment, and Policy at University of London (SOAS), and BA from Baylor University (University Scholar, Phi Beta Kappa). Prior to joining the faculty of Baylor University, Ramsey was Assistant Professor of Religion and Public Policy at Forman Christian College in Pakistan with dual appointments in the Department of Religion and the Center for Public

Policy and Governance. He is a senior fellow with the Religious Freedom Institute in Washington, DC. He has been awarded grants from the British Library's Endangered Archives Program, United States Institute of Peace, and the American Institute for Pakistan Studies. Ramsey is Editor, South Asia Section of the *Brill Encyclopedia of Christian-Muslim Relations* (CMR 1500–1900) and the author of *South Asian Sufis: Devotion, Deviation, and Destiny* (2012); *The Gospel According to Sayyid Ahmad Khan* (2020); and the forthcoming *God's Word, Spoken and Otherwise* (2021).

Rachel M. Scott is Professor of Islamic studies at Virginia Tech where she teaches comparative religion, Islam, Islamic political theory, religion and law, and religion and secularism. Her first book, *The Challenge of Political Islam: Non-Muslims and the Egyptian State* (2010), looks at contemporary Islamic thinking on pluralism and citizenship. Her second book, *Recasting Islamic Law: Religion and the Nation State in Egyptian Constitution Making*, was published in 2021.

Garrett Ward Sheldon is Professor Emeritus at the University of Virginia. He has been a visiting scholar at Oxford University; the University of Vienna, Austria; Moscow University; and Trinity College, Dublin, Ireland.

He has published ten books in the fields of political philosophy, American political thought, religion, and law, including *The History of Political Theory* and *The Political Philosophy of Thomas Jefferson* and · *A Memoir*.

Receiving a PhD in Political Theory from Rutgers University, he also pursued graduate studies at The New School for Social Research, New York City, and Princeton Theological Seminary.

Sheldon received The Outstanding Faculty in Virginia Award, the highest honor conferred on an academic by the Commonwealth, as well as the Bernard S. Rodey Award for Contributions to Education by his undergraduate alma mater, The University of New Mexico.

He has been an advisor to the White House and a delegate to the American-Israel Public Affairs Committee Policy Conference in Washington, DC.

An ordained Christian minister, he is retired and lives on a farm in Powell Valley, Virginia.

J. Christopher Soper is Distinguished Professor of Political Science at Pepperdine University, Malibu. He received his PhD from Yale University, Connecticut, and his MDiv from Yale Divinity School.

Karen Taliaferro is an assistant professor in the School of Civic and Economic Thought and Leadership at Arizona State University. She is the author of *The Possibility of Religious Freedom: Early Natural Law and the Abrahamic Faiths* (2019). Her research focuses on religion and the history of political thought with an emphasis on Islamic philosophy as well as liberalism, religion, and politics. Taliaferro has held fellowships at Princeton University's James Madison Program, Georgetown University's School of Foreign Service in Qatar and in Fez, Morocco through the Boren National Security Educational Program.

Steve Weidenkopf is an adjunct professor at the Christendom College Graduate School of Theology in Alexandria, Virginia. He is the author of *The Church and the Middle Ages: 1000–1378* (2020), *Timeless: A History of the Catholic Church* (2019), *The Real Story of Catholic History: Answering Twenty Centuries of Anti-Catholic Myths* (2017), and *The Glory of the Crusades* (2014), the creator and co-author of *Epic: A Journey Through Church History*, and the author and presenter of *The Early Church* adult faith formation studies. He is a member of the Society for the Study of the Crusades and the Latin East.

Allen Yeh is Associate Professor of Intercultural Studies and Missiology at Biola University. He earned his BA from Yale, MDiv from Gordon-Conwell, MTh from Edinburgh, and DPhil from Oxford. He is the author of *Polycentric Missiology* (2016) and co-editor (with Tite Tienou) of *Majority World Theologies* (2018).

CHAPTER 1

Introduction

Shannon Holzer

This book is Volume Two of the two-volume work *The Palgrave Handbook of Religion and State*. Whereas Volume One of this set examined religion and state philosophically, theologically, legally, and politically, this volume examines the subject historically and geographically. The relationship between religion and the state in the Western Hemisphere has been predominately between Christianity and differing forms of democracy, the relationship in the East is much more complex. Its history is longer, the plurality of religions is greater, and it is from all of this that the American Constitutional Experiment was conceived.

Volume Two's structure is simple. First, just as Volume One, Volume Two follows an interdisciplinary approach to this complex subject matter. The contributors are historians, political scientists, sociologists, missionaries, and legal theorists. The volume begins with a section on the History of Religion and State in Europe. It is this history in which the Americas find the roots of how they navigate the relationship between religion and state. Second, Volume Two addresses how individual countries from around the globe approach issues of religion and state.

S. Holzer (✉)
Houston Christian University, Houston, TX, USA
e-mail: sholzer@hbu.edu

© The Author(s), under exclusive license to Springer Nature Switzerland AG 2023
S. Holzer (ed.), *The Palgrave Handbook of Religion and State Volume II*, https://doi.org/10.1007/978-3-031-35609-4_1

By opening Volume Two with European history the contributors give attention to how religion and state have related to each other throughout the centuries. Specifically, the handbook covers how the differing Christian traditions approach the relationship between religion and state over time and geographical location. For example, the first several chapters of Volume Two address the relationship between the various forms of Christianity and various states in Europe and Russia. These chapters unpack how the conflict between differing Christian theological ideas came into conflict with the state throughout history.

This attention to European history is not merely the regurgitation of the first few centuries of the Christian Church up through the Middle Ages. It attends to the sensitive topics as to how the Church provided a prophetic voice to the Kings. In his excellent chapter, Steele Brand highlights how the domains of the sacred and secular were recognized, divided, and attended to by those who had jurisdiction over those particular realms.

Volume Two also gives an account of the crusading movement that is a little less damning than that which is usually presented in Hollywood box office smash hits. Steve Weidenkoph's outstanding chapter illuminates not only the origins of the crusading movement, but also the motivations of both the rulers and those who participated in them. This account will most assuredly give another picture than that of ignorant, intolerant, bloodthirsty warriors killing anybody whom they encountered.

From there, Korey Maas gives a brilliant assessment of the relationship between the Church and the State in Enlightenment Europe. In this, he shows the complex nature of the relationship between Church and State, and that the Enlightenment was not a "unitary phenomenon" as many believe it to be. David J. Davis uses the following chapter to show how religious tolerance developed in England. Given the emphasis on the importance of tolerance in contemporary society, Davis does a phenomenal job of showing that many of the roots of toleration were born from religious traditions.

In contrast to the development of toleration through the realm of religion, Julie de Graffenried shows how stripping the state of all religious ideas does not result in a peaceful and tolerant relationship between religion and state. Stripping all religiosity from a massive and diverse group of people is much more difficult than the Soviet Union imagined, indeed. De Graffenried also reveals that the level of antipathy the Soviet Union showed to religion was not as static as we in the West tend to believe it to be. De Graffenried's marvelous chapter is particularly important given the push by many in power to completely place religion into the private sphere.

For the sake of continuity, the next section covers religion and state in Europe. Like the previous chapters, the predominant religion is Christianity. This difference lies in how each of the countries differs in their government's relationship to the religions of their citizens. This becomes more important, especially as these countries are no longer religiously homogeneous. Chapters on England and Ireland are included in this section. On top of that, no volume on religion and state would be complete without a chapter on France's development of *laïcité*. Yet, along with the usual suspects, this volume also includes a chapter on Germany and Slovakia. Joel Fetzer and Chris Soper superbly compare and contrast how the relation between religion and state plays out in these two countries.

When discussing the subject of religion and state, Christianity often sucks up all the oxygen in the room. However, while the West's history and context is predominantly Christian, the East is extremely religiously pluralistic. This pluralism determined that the book would be titled "The *Palgrave Handbook of Religion and State*" rather than the "*Palgrave Handbook of Church and State*." Along with the attention given to the Christian experience in Europe and beyond, Volume Two attends to the pluralistic nature of the Eastern Hemisphere. In doing so, Volume Two breaks the discussion into various sections relating to geography and religion.

Volume Two has a section on religion and state in Asia. This is exciting in its complexity. There is a multitude of religious beliefs and attitudes toward religion and the state throughout Asia. This section includes two chapters on the Communist nation of China, and its relationship with Christianity. Joseph Tse-Hei Lee provides an excellently researched assessment of relationship between Christianity and China's government between 1949 and present while Allen Yeh dispels some of the myths in which we in the West have indulged concerning missionary work in China.

From there Ernils Larsson shifts our focus from China to the Japanese State's relationship to Shintoism. The concept of religion and state is an interesting one in the context of Japan. The reason for this is that there is no analogue for the word "religion" in the Japanese language. Thus, certain beliefs do not neatly fit into one category called religion as they do in the West. Yet, Larsson does an incredible job of showing how Shintoism fits the category as well as how the secular state of Japan has interacted with those who practice it.

The next chapter of this volume is important in that it is a rare find, indeed. It is difficult to find any scholarship on the relation of the Vietnamese state to religion, much less great scholarship. While most volumes come at the topic of religion and state in Vietnam from an outsider's perspective, Professors Hoàng Văn Chung and Đỗ Quang Hưng do so from the perspective of an insider.

Volume Two then shifts to Indonesia and the state's relationship to Islam and the Pancasila coalition. A.J. Nolte illustrates the balance between a state that is "neither fully secular nor fully Islamic." This chapter will certainly provide a picture that contrasts other Islamic nations' religion/state relations.

The following chapter shows that the development of religious liberty is not exclusively a Western idea. Professor James Ponniah provides this volume with a look at the development of religious liberty in India as it dealt with Muslim and Christian Imperial powers. From there he informs us about the recent debates between the differing secular, communist, anti-Brahminic Dravidian, and other regional parties.

Since 9/11, there has been heightened interest in Islam and the Middle East. Many assume that all Islamic cultures approach religion and the state the same way. Volume Two of the *Palgrave Handbook of Religion and State* stands out in its approach to the subject. This volume has several chapters on the subject of mosque and state. Moreover, it goes beyond a mere general approach to the subject. In this volume are chapters on religion and state in the Middle Eastern countries of Afghanistan and Iraq. Currently, the Taliban is back in control of Afghanistan and Saddam Hussein has long since been deposed. These are countries of great interest, especially in the realm of religion, from which much of their policies are derived.

Following this, Volume Two engages the continent of Africa. Just like Europe, Asia, and the Middle East, a volume could be dedicated to Africa alone. This being the case, Volume Two takes a sampling of countries that give a broad account of the history and ideas of religion and state in the various nations of this massive continent. Specifically, this section provides an exciting chapter on the multi-ethnic and multi-religious nation of Ethiopia. Jorg Haustein does a masterful job of walking his reader through the history of religion and state in modern Ethiopia.

Dr. Bulus Galadima then uses his contribution to describe the Nigerian situation of the sometimes-tense relationship between Christians and Muslims in a Majority Muslim state. Galadima laments that the Nigerian government and Christians have not been able to effectively respond to or mitigate attacks from the extremist Islamic group Boko Haram. While the interaction with this group is not the whole problem, it may be symptomatic of a greater issue. Specifically, Galadima highlights the ethnicization and religionization of politics in Nigeria along with the problems that doing so brings with them. From there the wise professor gives insight into what he believes an appropriate Christian response may be.

Volume Two also includes the African nations of South Africa, Zimbabwe, and Egypt. Without a doubt, these nations stand in stark contrast to each other. Radley Henrico's treatment of South Africa gives the reader the sense that this country is much like Western nations. And, in many ways it is like Western nations. While South Africa experiences much of the division and turmoil that other countries possess, Henrico shows that South Africa's "nuanced context-sensitive approach" balances competing interests that arise from religious liberties in a secular society.

Joachim Kwaramba provides another picture of Zimbabwe that other works on religion and state have overlooked. Pastor Kwaramba's chapter on religion and state in Zimbabwe points out how the melding of religion and state may corrupt pastors and politicians alike. The pastor points out that this is the case in his home country. This was especially the case during the Covid pandemic. Yet, given the pandemic, Kwaramba gives a brilliant argument for the relevance of the Church in general and the individual Churches specifically in their presence and activity during state-mandated lockdowns. Pastor Kwaramba highlights the healing power religious activity had among those who were sequestered and isolated by the lockdowns.

Rachel Scott closes out the section by examining the Egyptian state and its relation to the religious organizations of al-Azhar and the Coptic Orthodox Church. This chapter gives an example of what it means for a government to have the blessing of one or more religious groups. This was the case for both al-Azhar and the Coptic Church, in which both endorsed the ousting of President Muhammad Mursi and the majority Muslim Brotherhood parliament. Yet, in a turn of irony, the endorsement of the military's ousting of the previous government, which may imply that it is God's will that the new government has come to power, actually was the exchange of one limiter of religious freedom for another. Dr. Scott explains why this endorsement from the religious communities was important and how it affected the Coptic Orthodox Church's religious rights as well as the Islamic identity of the Egyptian state.

The Handbook of Religion and State Volume Two closes with religion and state in the Americas. It goes without saying that libraries can be filled with works on Church and State in the United States. This handbook also includes chapters covering religion and state in Canada, Mexico, Brazil, and Cuba. Each of these countries is different in their approach to the relationship between religion and state. This section displays a surprisingly broad spectrum of attitudes toward religion and state. America still possesses a large presence of those who value religious activities in the public square. Yet in Canada, there is a much greater political push toward secularism and privatization of the religious life. At the farthest end of the spectrum is Cuba, which is still under a communist regime. Reading this section alone will give the reader an appreciation for how different governments approach the intersection of religion and state.

As has been described, the *Palgrave Handbook of Religion and State* is quite comprehensive. Yet, in this, one can see how much more can be added to the conversation. Whether one argues that other countries may be added, or that certain philosophical or theological concepts were missed, one must admit that the *Palgrave Handbook of Religion and State* brings to light the importance of a subject about which many believe to be best left unspoken. Let the Palgrave Handbook be a reference guide from which one might start further academic studies on the subject. Let it also be a reminder of the complex nature of one of the most important questions facing all of us, "how should we then live?"

PART I

Religion and the State in European History

Christendom's Constitution: "The Clashing Swords of Church and State in History"

Steele Brand

THE GELASIAN CONSTITUTION

In the closing years of the fifth century, the Roman world was in crisis. After a century of military catastrophes and lackluster leaders, the last legitimate Western emperor, Julius Nepos, was deposed by his general Orestes in 475. Orestes then placed his own son on the throne, Romulus Augustulus, only to see him ousted by the barbarian general Odoacer the following year. Odoacer in turn was murdered and supplanted by the Ostrogoths 17 years later, ostensibly at the behest of the Eastern Roman emperor. Despite the high drama given to these events by historians such as Edward Gibbon, most Romans—and their Romanized barbarian rulers—who occupied the western portions of the aging Mediterranean empire were unaware that a major shift in world history had occurred. In their minds, the empire, with its laws, economic trade networks, and culture would survive the storm and continue to manage day-to-day affairs.

S. Brand (✉)
Politics, Philosophy, & History Program, Cairn University, Langhorne, PA, USA
e-mail: sbrand@cairn.edu

© The Author(s), under exclusive license to Springer Nature
Switzerland AG 2023
S. Holzer (ed.), *The Palgrave Handbook of Religion and State
Volume II*, https://doi.org/10.1007/978-3-031-35609-4_2

A greater crisis in many minds was the doctrinal schism tearing the Roman Christian world asunder. The Eastern emperor Zeno (474–491), who had "sent" the Ostrogoths to depose Odoacer, was attempting to find a compromise doctrine for his Christian subjects who disagreed over whether Christ had one nature (Monophysites) or had both a human and divine nature (Chalcedonians). Wading into the theological depths, Zeno, and then his successor Anastasius (491–518), desperately sought ideological uniformity in a Roman world that was slipping out of their control.

The bishop of Rome offered the most lucid opposition to the Eastern emperors. As imperial fortunes vacillated throughout the tumultuous fifth century, the power and prestige of the popes increased. Popes such as Leo I (440–461) had negotiated with barbarian captains, provided for Roman citizens in the wake of military depredations, and emerged as the only constant figurehead in a vacuum created by incompetent Western emperors and conquering chieftains. No less dangerous in the eyes of the popes were Eastern emperors who meddled in the doctrines that cultivated Christians throughout the world. When Pope Gelasius (492–496) succeeded to the See of Rome, he inherited his predecessor's strife with the emperors and the Chalcedonian-Monophysite schism. He wrote the emperor Anastasius a letter that has now become famous, explaining that the emperor must be cognizant that "there are two ways in which this world is chiefly ruled: the hallowed authority of the pontiffs (*pontificum*) and royal power" (Neil and Allen 2014, p. 74). The emperor was therefore neither supreme nor alone. His power was balanced by the bishops, with both bishops and emperors receiving their authority from God.

These two fifth-century ideas: that the empire lived on and that there were two separate and distinct powers within that empire would serve as the foundation of Christendom's constitutional order. Simply put, a constitutional order prefers a division and distribution of power over concentration and consolidation. It establishes this divided sovereignty by custom and law, thereby limiting the authorities that govern.

Gelasius' letter summarized the essential political idea for the period treated in this chapter. The chapter will begin by examining the long, slow growth of the Gelasian principle, firstly, out of the inheritances of the biblical and classical worlds, and secondly, within the Germanic kingdoms that emerged in the centuries following Gelasius. The chapter will then explore Christendom's constitutional climax in the high medieval period, especially as manifested in the Concordat of Worms and the Magna Carta. It will conclude by examining the derivations that emerged as the Gelasian order succumbed to attacks from both papal and royal apologists during the late medieval period, setting the intellectual stage for the irreparable fracture of Christendom during the sixteenth and seventeenth centuries.

ROMAN AND CHRISTIAN FOUNDATIONS

By the time Roman political power collapsed in the Western Mediterranean, Hebraic and classical political ideas had taken root. To varying degrees, medieval writers were aware of Plato and Aristotle's theorizing about the purpose of human government and the mixing of the pure forms of monarchy, aristocracy, and democracy. They were also aware of the historical legacy of the Roman Republic, with its government of checks and balances between the pure forms. Cicero's republican sentiments and political terminology lingered on in Latin Christendom. Shortly after the republic transitioned into the empire, Christianity brought in Hebraic conceptions of power, which included other countervailance forms such as the division between priests and kings, the legitimacy of the prophetic voice, the orientation of human government toward the Creator, and the human dignity inherent in every subject or citizen.

Christianity itself offered a new kind of community. The New Testament texts described this community as a people bound together by faith. Individual souls must express this faith but for the good of a mystical community jointly oriented toward the creator and redeemer Christ. The community of Christ Jesus reversed classical power structures by preferring and spiritualizing the poor. The title accorded to Jesus—the Christ—was also revolutionary, setting up a parallel "anointed one."[1] Christ's dominium, however, was misunderstood by both Jews and Romans. The gospel authors took pains to articulate how Christ was of the Davidic royal line but that Christ also masked his messianic mission. Moreover, Christ was not the conquering messiah desired by the Jews and feared by the Romans, for his domains did not immediately and obviously threaten earthly political power. Christ's origins were historic but humble, like the poor that he uplifted, and his "kingdom" was not "of this world."[2]

The church originated out of the historic person of Jesus, but the foundation of the institutional church followed his execution by the local Jewish and imperial Roman authorities. The biblical book of Acts traced the historical growth of Christianity from a small Pentecost community on the periphery to the arrival of its chief doctrinal formulator Paul into the capital of the empire. Paul articulated a community whose faith was not merely a subjective religious sentiment. Faith was a transformative process that created the mystical body of Christ on earth. Paul's letters instructed this new community, both in doctrines about the transcendent and in practical matters regarding day-to-day life. The New Testament thus moved from the gospel perfection of Christ to a Pauline compromise wherein Christ's community could operate within the societal order of the day. Although Christianity had emerged out of Judaism, it shed the Jews' exclusionary rituals and could operate on a grander scale akin to Rome's imperial order. Romans, Jews, and Greeks could all participate in Christ's otherworldly kingdom as they were unified by a transformative faith and new rituals such as baptism and communion.[3]

As an institution, Christianity was remarkably adaptive and started to map itself onto the empire itself, with urban concentrations of believers, episcopal jurisdictions, and erudite intellectuals blending into the empire as Christian theology altered or challenged Greco-Roman mores and ideologies. Rome's dominion had never been bound together by a broader framework beyond military power, engineering feats, and laws. Because Rome "was primarily a power apparatus, not the manifestation of the political will of a people," the spiritual power of Christianity for all peoples, regardless of wealth or status, eventually overtook the empire (Voegelin 1997a, p. 178). Pagan emperors labored for centuries to reinforce paganism as the binding ideology for society, but despite moments of intense persecution, this proved impossible. In this fearful and sometimes violent environment, the first Christian political thinkers attempted to negotiate the tension of living "in," but not "of" the world.[4]

Early authors such as Justin Martyr, Theophilus of Antioch, Clement, and Origen argued from biblical and classical sources that Christians made the best citizens of the empire, following the laws, praying for the emperor, and attempting to live peaceably within the established order. However, because they believed all authority stemmed from Christ, they were forbidden from pagan rites, particularly participation in the emperor cult. As Roman persecution intensified, authors such as Irenaeus, a bishop of Lyons in the late second century, stressed how human governments that attempted to usurp God's ultimate authority become the means for sin and organized rebellion against God.[5] It was natural, therefore, for a third-century author such as Tertullian to demarcate between Christ's kingdom and the world's. In *The Military Chaplet*, he paints a stark contrast between the evil, militaristic Roman domain of "chains and imprisonment and torture and punishment" and the suffering, sacrificial, peaceful, and sacramental world of the church (O'Donovan and O'Donovan 1999, p. 27).

This scenario shifted dramatically when the emperor Constantine (306–337) converted to Christianity. Constantine made it possible for Christianity to increase and become normalized by providing wealth, support, and peace. The result was that the church became a recognized power base in local communities. Lactantius and Eusebius, two intellectuals who served at the court of Constantine, lived through the last great persecutions and saw Rome transition to a position of official toleration. They contemplated justice, equality, and human dignity in a world where Christians could now directly and openly influence the imperial court and its governing framework. Eusebius adored the emperor and fashioned an "emperor-theology" that was particularly effusive in his praise of Constantine and his optimism for a Roman world that would be transformed into a Christian empire.

Doctrinal schisms, the politicization of theological debates, and barbarian incursions into the empire had tarnished such hopes by the end of the fourth century. Ambrose, the bishop of Milan, fought numerous battles against pagans, heretics, and emperors in a defense of the church that was construed as a sort of new martyrdom. When the imperial capital moved to Milan, he became locked in a dogged struggle against pagan senators over whether the Altar of Victory, a traditional imperial symbol and vessel for state rituals, should remain in the Senate house.[6]

Ambrose also retraced the church-world distinction with the power of his personality. In two legendary showdowns, Ambrose stood his ground against imperial demands. In 386 the court of Valentinian II insisted Ambrose share certain churches with Arian bishops. He refused and was called to account. With stirring rhetoric Ambrose defended his responsibility as a bishop to avoid bending to the court. He then heightened the drama by staging a sit-in during holy week when soldiers tried to take the churches by force. Four years later Ambrose humbled the powerful emperor Theodosius. After the latter brutally crushed a revolt in Thessalonica, Ambrose chastised the emperor for his unnecessary slaughter of thousands of citizens. He excommunicated the emperor, and, only after a period of repentance, did Theodosius regain his standing within the church. Such stories, even if they were staged or embellished, became powerful examples of episcopal power in the western half of the empire. Similar efforts by the Eastern Bishop John Chrysostom met with failure in

Constantinople, foreshadowing the different constitutional trajectories East and West would take.

Ambrose's charisma, personal kindness, and ideas deeply impacted the most influential thinker of the age, Augustine, bishop of Hippo. Augustine's rhetorical talents matched Ambrose and John Chrysostom, but he surpassed any thinker of the ancient world in the volume and sophistication of his writing. In relation to the emerging medieval order, Augustine's most important work was the *City of God*, a treatise written in response to accusations that Christianity had weakened the empire and prompted the success of barbarian incursions, particularly the sack of Rome by the Visigoths in 410. He turns the tables on critics by arguing that Rome's own history was merely filled with excellent vices rather than true virtues. In Book IV.4 he asks whether there really is much of a difference between a band of thieves and a kingdom. Is the first not merely a microcosm of the second? Rome, as an earthly city, was a flawed parallel for the heavenly realm that was perfectly ordered and virtuous. The terrestrial city of man, bound together not by justice but by what its people loved, would always succumb to its own imperfections and the pressures and punishment of external forces.[7]

Written from 411 to 426 and completed 5 years before Augustine's death in the Vandal siege of Hippo, his *City of God* was a "grandiose expression of Christian political existence" that revealed the complexity and maturation of Christian thought at the end of an age. Christianity had taken the mass of universal histories about particular peoples and created a conception of the political cosmos in a new history of humanity that began with God's creation and revelation. Augustine's spiritual community of Christians had expanded beyond the small Pauline community and overtaken an imperial political order. But changes were afoot. Earthly kingdoms would never endure, and the institutional church itself was vulnerable. It was not synonymous with the City of God, instead being its "militant representative on earth in history" that mediated the transcendent through its sacramental ministry (Voegelin 1997a, pp. 207, 214). Christians were observing undoubted changes and would need to enhance aspects of both church and state. Increasing numbers of barbarians became Romanized, but the process of full integration into the imperial structure did not occur before a systemic political collapse in the fifth century. As official political and military leadership faded, bishops and patron saints often rose in their place as sustainers of a way of life.

Augustine had constructed a complicated theopolitical foundation on which the medieval political power systems would be constructed. Tensions had not disappeared since the days of Paul; they had deepened. When Gelasius referenced the two powers delegated authority by God, he was attempting to navigate that tension as a new imperial order emerged.

The Sacrum Imperium

Gelasius picked up Augustine's theme of two loves, two societies, and two histories. In his letter to emperor Anastasius, Gelasius' framework presupposed continuity with the Roman imperial order. It transferred the ordering element, however, to the spiritual and the sacramental, which served and unified a new *sacrum imperium*, a sacred empire of the mystical body of the faithful. Gelasius' church, however, did not fully embody the order of the new age. It had survived Roman persecution, transformed Rome, and then emerged as a free and distinct institution after the termination of the Western Empire, but it was balanced by another institution, that of the royal office, first embodied by the emperor and subsequently by the Germanic warrior-kings.

Gelasius' terminology of the two powers has naturally drawn discussion, with scholars emphasizing the distinction Gelasius makes between episcopal "authority" (*auctoritas*) and the princely "power" (*potestas*). Three options emerge: the terms are differentiated to mean that the emperor's power is superior in practice, the terms are differentiated to mean that episcopal power is supreme over a delegated royal power, or the terms are mere synonyms, indicating a relative equality.[8]

This terminological ambiguity disappears in the context of the immediate paragraph and Gelasius' subsequent writings. Gelasius insists in the letter that he must confront Anastasius out of "obligation to the divine plan." He describes the *responsibilities* of the bishops as "so much greater" because their spiritual and sacramental ministry has a greater bearing on the "divine judgment." However, while the king bows his head regarding spiritual matters and must take advice on moral concerns, he "superintend[s] through high office of a human kind." The emperor's position has been "conferred ... by heavenly dispensation" and church leaders must not only acknowledge this, but submit themselves to the emperor's maintenance of public order. Royal power, conceived here in terms of the historic office and not merely the person of the emperor, has a temporal authority that must be respected, but this power must in turn defer to the spiritual and moral authority of the bishops. Moreover, the plural forms of "*pontificum*," "*sacerdotum*," "*praesulibus*," and "*antistites*" that describe episcopal leadership demonstrate Gelasius' inclusion of the episcopate as a whole, and not merely the papal hierarchy identified in later centuries (Neil and Allen 2014, p. 74).

Gelasius clarified matters further in the treatise *On the Bond of Anathema*, written c. 496. Taking up the Old Testament model of the priest-king Melchizedek, he warned how the Devil would prefer to keep these concentrated in order to usurp the divine order. Gelasius insists that only Christ was the true priest-king, and he saw fit to separate and distribute their powers:

> For Christ, mindful of human frailty, regulated with an excellent disposition what pertained to the salvation of his people. Thus he distinguished between the offices of both powers according to their own proper activities and separate dignities, wanting his people to be saved by healthful humility and not carried away again by human pride, so that Christian emperors would need priests for attaining eternal life and priests would avail themselves of imperial regulations in the conduct of temporal affairs. In this fashion spiritual activity would be set apart from worldly encroachments and the "soldier of God" would not be involved in secular affairs, while on the other hand, he who was involved in secular affairs would not seem to preside over divine matters. Thus the humility of each order would be preserved, neither being exalted by the subservience of the other, and each profession would be especially fitted for its appropriate functions. (Tierney 1988, pp. 14–15)

Gelasius leaves no doubt as to the balance of power and the reasons for that balance. Princes and bishops are sovereign regarding their own purposes and honors. They are intended to work together, but not to encroach on other realms of responsibility. Gelasius' clear theory of countervailing powers could—and would—be applied in many different institutional arrangements in the coming centuries, but the principle of balance between sacred and secular was unchanging. Satan's tyranny originated out of a desire to concentrate power. Obscure Old Testament examples were intended to foreshadow Christ. Christ's power as the sacrificing, mediating priest was separated from his power as the conquering king of the universe. The Gelasian constitutional order left little moral argument regarding the principle, but a great deal of flexibility—and ambiguity—in how it would function in the real world. The two orders must rule Christologically, but neither may fully embody the fullness of his power. They must work together to order Christendom.

THE FORMATION OF WESTERN CHRISTENDOM

The 200 years following Gelasius' pontificate saw East and West severed from one another as they pursued different visions of political order. More migrations by Germans, Avars, and Slavs coupled with the explosive conquests of Arabian Islam degraded or eliminated cultural and economic exchanges. In the East, the older Persian and Egyptian conceptions of a strict hierarchy under a divinized monarch overtook the Byzantine world. It is less surprising to find John Chrysostom arguing for subordination as a part of the natural order as compared to Irenaeus or Lactantius, who preferred "original equality" (O'Donovan and O'Donovan 1999, p. 90). John did stress the priest-king division of the Old Testament as carrying over into the Christian age, but later Eastern authors such as Agapetos (sixth cen) and Nikephoros Blemmydes (thirteenth cen.) strengthened the religious ideology of the emperor as the sacral mediator for his realm. The legal corpus of the emperor Justinian (sixth cen) does not envision two sovereigns, but instead only the all-powerful emperor who oversees both sacred and royal power. When John of Damascus (eighth cen.) opposed theological meddling as Gelasius had, his arguments did not include notions of countervailance.

In the West, where the Germanic kingdoms maintained degrees of continuity with Rome in terms of law, language, and the local populations, the Gelasian principle shaped political order. The old Roman aristocratic class worked with their Germanic warrior chiefs to create a new concept of sacral kingship. The Germanic kingdoms that emerged throughout Europe blended their kinship arrangements and tribal notions of heroic kingship with older and more sophisticated traditions from the empire. At the same time a tradition of ecumenical councils had emerged as the best means of sorting through doctrinal controversies. The universal council had been used by the first Christian Roman emperors to unify Christians within their realm, but by the eighth century councils had become independent, quasi-representative bodies that often checked royal machinations regarding the imposition of beliefs ranging from Arianism to Monophysitism and iconoclasm.

Kingship in Western Christendom did not take on absolutist forms until the late medieval period. Primitive kingship brought with it the ancient tribal councils and assemblies that Tacitus had described when the Romans first encountered the Germans. The Anglo-Saxon witan was a late survivor of such ad hoc aristocratic bodies. Christianity uplifted the countervailing episcopate but also transformed the purpose and ethical standards of the king. In the sixth and seventh centuries, Romano-Germanic kingship was transformed through the writings of those close to the new centers of power. Cassiodorus served the Ostrogothic court in Italy. Pope Gregory I lived through the ephemeral Byzantine reconquest of Italy before serving as an envoy to Constantinople and then being elevated to the papacy. Isidore, bishop of Seville, dedicated his career to establishing Visigothic power as a Christian kingdom. They drew from classical notions of republican leadership, particularly Cicero, and biblical models of humility to circumscribe the king. He may enjoy a position of authority, but he shared the sinful nature of his subjects and must be ever mindful that his judgments punishing sin should also orient his subjects to virtue and union with God.[9]

Cassiodorus was also instrumental in shaping the new monastic movements. Ascetics had existed since the pre-Christian period and some Christians were quick to adopt ascetic practices in both eremitic (isolated) and cenobitic (communal) settings. Christian monastic impulses coalesced around Benedict of Nursia, a contemporary of Cassiodorus. Benedict was only the most exemplary of numerous ascetics who fashioned a miniature constitutional order that others voluntarily joined. Spiritually charismatic, disciplined, and capable of structuring his own system based on a rule, or constitution, he created a new form of superior virtue within a new community. Plato's *polis* found a medieval reality in the monasteries that began proliferating throughout Christendom. Not only would these establish little polities within Christendom as a whole, but they would also be grafted into the spiritual fabric of the church and serve as models of virtue that others sought to emulate. Cassiodorus' great contribution to the nascent monastic orders was to incorporate into their daily labors the craft of studying, copying, illuminating, and elaborating on the great classical and patristic works of antiquity. When the Germanic kingdoms achieved stability, it was a mark of prestige when a king could harness these monasteries to develop libraries, circles of scholars, works of art, and other distinguished marks of culture.[10]

The most successful monarchs of the early medieval period attempted to reclaim the imperial glory of ancient Rome. When Byzantine power waned with the onslaught of the Arabs, the mid-eighth-century popes made a momentous decision to look to the kings north of the Alps for military protection. In doing so, they irrevocably altered the geographic orientation of Gelasius' two powers. Two kings, in particular, reinvigorated the imperial idea for the Franks: Charlemagne (768–814) and Otto I (936–973), with each identifying himself, with papal support, as a new Constantine over a spiritually homogenous, Christian populace. Like Cassiodorus for the Ostrogoths and Isidore for the Visigoths, Jonas of Orleans applied the Gelasian order in a theopolitical framework for the Franks in one of the earliest "mirrors of the prince." Charlemagne's dynasty proved unable to sustain the imperial vision, but Otto's successors enjoyed more success in East Francia, giving rise to the peculiar entity known as the Holy Roman Empire.

Charlemagne and Otto were able to transform the older model of a warrior king around whom a people found expression and identity into a sacral king who received his authority from God. The bishops, however, as seen in public coronation ceremonies like that of Pope Leo III's for Charlemagne on Christmas, 800, mediated this spiritual authority as officiators over royal rituals that borrowed heavily from consecrations. Sometimes the bishops were instrumental in identifying who succeeded to power. The kings themselves became jealous of their sacral powers and also sought to control the bishops. Pope John XII, for example, was deposed by Otto I, despite the fact that John had earlier bestowed titles on Otto and then crowned him Roman emperor. When the papacy responded to such overreaches in the eleventh century, a legal revolution occurred that threatened to unravel the Gelasian order.

The Climax: From Gregory VII to Magna Carta

As with all constitutional orders acted out in the real world, Gelasius' high ideals did not always materialize in an ideal fashion. The period from Gelasius to Gregory VII (1073–1085) was marred by some significant papal humiliations. Popes had been arrested by emperors, controlled by Italian aristocrats, caught up within their own papal schisms, and by the eleventh century were now increasingly threatened by Otto's successors in the Holy Roman Empire.

Reclaiming ecclesiastical independence began with a revitalized Benedictine monasticism. In 910 William I of Aquitaine deeded land to the Benedictines at Cluny in rural Burgundy. Most importantly, he granted the site immunity and independence from outside control. Cluny rapidly became the center of a reform movement that swept other monasteries in Western Christendom. Cluny created its own network of daughter houses through which the abbots intended to restore the Benedictine rule and spiritual purity. Several eleventh-century popes emerged within this Cluniac context and sought to apply a similar enthusiasm for order and independence on behalf of the episcopate. The Cistercian order followed the Cluniacs and took matters further, with one Cistercian even producing a "mirror of the popes." In this conception, the popes held both the spiritual and temporal swords, graciously delegating the temporal sword to the princes. Reforms during the period included a return to ascetic ideals and the elimination of simony and clerical marriage, which created little stir among princes. Freeing the bishops from princely investment or interference was a different matter.

Starting in the mid-eleventh century, the papacy loosened the grip of the Holy Roman Emperors, created a more regularized and independent method of selecting the bishop of Rome via the cardinalate, and began challenging the secular investment of power to bishops. Pope Gregory VII issued the definitive statement of the papal reform movement, *Dictatus Papae*, which claimed, among other things, that "the Roman Pontiff alone is rightly to be called universal," that "he may depose Emperors," that the pope "may be judged by no one," that "the Roman Church has never erred, nor ever, by the witness of Scripture, shall err to all eternity," and that "the Pope may absolve subjects of unjust men from their fealty" (O'Donovan and O'Donovan 1999, p. 242).

Gregory thus issued a challenge on two fronts: an increasing consolidation of episcopal power into the monarchy of the papacy and a claim to superiority over the European princes. The concept had emerged of the papacy's *plenitudo potestatis*, that they exercised the fulness of power, and all others were legally, politically, and spiritually subordinate. Gregory's doctrine of papal supremacy was already undergirded by several decades of intellectual activism on the part of men such as Humbert of Silva Candida, who was instrumental in the formation of the elective cardinalate and the assertion of the pope's supremacy over the Byzantine patriarchs. Other theologians would follow, such as Honorius Augustodunensis and Bernard of Clairvaux. The century and a half from 1050–1200 increasingly saw the elevation and consolidation of the papacy over the pope's supposed subordinates, whether bishops, princes, or Eastern patriarchs. In the coming years imperial pamphleteers responded in favor of the emperor, refuting the papalist arguments and establishing a rival theory that the emperor was supreme.

Always one to practice what he preached, Pope Gregory promptly acted on his dictates and excommunicated the Holy Roman Emperor for the lay investiture of bishops. Gregory had overcompensated and the result was civil war in Germany between the emperor and his nobles. In a flamboyant gesture of repentance, the emperor Henry IV made a penitential pilgrimage to the pope who was residing at Canossa. Barefoot and adorned in sackcloth, he begged for absolution from Gregory, which was granted. Despite the theatrics, the civil war in Germany raged on. Henry regained the upper hand when he restored order at home, marched on Rome, and exiled Gregory into Norman territory in southern Italy, where the feisty old pope perished. Nonetheless, the reform movement had begun in earnest, empowering a far more vigorous papacy that was supported by a growing administrative structure and a system of canon law. Some have rightly described the period as a "papal revolution" that "altered the course of Western political, legal, and social history."[11] It should be no surprise that this invigorated papacy was motivated and capable of marshaling the military forces of Western Europe for the Crusades, complete with military orders modeled on the monastic reform movements.

The Gelasian principle had not yet been overthrown, as demonstrated by the two greatest constitutional testaments of the age: the Concordat of Worms and the Magna Carta. The Investiture Controversy Gregory had launched was eventually ended with a compromise that reinforced the Gelasian order. At Worms in 1122, both parties reaffirmed the Gelasian principle by granting that the emperor and the pope were responsible for the episcopate within a principality. Pope Calixtus II and Emperor Henry V conceded the authority of the other, with the pope retaining the right to invest a freely and canonically elected bishop with the "ring and staff" and the emperor being granted the right to intervene in disputed elections and invest with the "scepter." Each power must furnish aid and support to the other (Tierney 1988, p. 91). Worms was undoubtedly a compromise, and it restored the old Pauline view of the necessity of the church's granting concessions in the practical governance of the world. Meanwhile, the intellectual forces agitating for royal or papal supremacy had been set aside for the peace of Christendom.

Affairs in England were just as tumultuous. England produced one of the first responses to the claims of papal supremacy. In 1066 the Normans conquered Anglo-Saxon England and established the first consolidated national order in Europe, leading to what some would describe as the first nation-state. The reforming papacy sanctioned the conquest, ostensibly to reign in an English church that was enjoying too many liberties. The Norman monarchy, however, disappointed the popes by proving even more difficult to control. In support of the monarchs, an anonymous Norman prelate, possibly the Archbishop of York, wrote the *York Tracts*, which made the king's reception of Christ's power superior to that of the bishops. The king ruled all of his Christian subjects, including the bishops, as a reflection of Christ's full divine powers. Sacral kingship was turned on its head. Bishops did not crown kings until they were first invested with power by the king.

Henry II (1154–1189), great-grandson of William the Conqueror, acted on such ideas as he sought to use royal law against the increasing legal jurisdiction of the church. The vigorous monarch, whose holdings by inheritance and marriage made him the most powerful king in Europe, believed he found an ingenious solution by appointing his friend Thomas Becket as England's leading prelate, the Archbishop of Canterbury. This time the king suffered disappointment. Becket became the church's most ardent defender against royal encroachment and a dramatic struggle ensued that only ended when the king's nobles unofficially murdered the archbishop in December 1170. The king himself was stunned by the event, and he only regained his standing within Christendom through several public humiliating acts of penance. In his martyrdom, Becket defeated royal depredations of church power in the most fantastic and unexpected of ways.

Henry's misfortunes were lost on his youngest son, John, who became king in 1199. History has not been kind to John, whom nearly all acknowledge as one of the worst kings in English—and probably European—history. John managed to alienate his nobles, bishops, and people while simultaneously losing the empire Henry had arduously cobbled together. In the process he clashed with the most potent pope of the age, Innocent III. In a letter from 1198 that was later reshaped into a canon of the 4th Lateran Council, Innocent opened with God's creation of the heavenly lights to describe papal and royal power. Using the metaphor of the sun and the moon, he described Christendom as a whole being ruled by the light of these two bodies, but the royal power, as the moon, derived all of its light from the papal power, which was the sun (Tierney 1988, p. 132). John played his role in the metaphor well and eventually conceded defeat to Innocent, ceding all of England to the pope as a fief. Innocent now envisioned himself as more than a spiritual king of kings. He was also a great feudal lord of an entire principality. John, on the other hand, finally had an ally with which he could battle his own barons at home. Both John and Innocent were thwarted in their alliance by the political coup of Magna Carta.

Initially designed as a treaty between the failed King John and his agitated barons, over the course of the next centuries, it became a foundation of English constitutional thought. In 1215, however, both king and pope disapproved of its concessions to English subjects and its conception of balanced power. Most of the clauses related to negotiations between the beleaguered king and his barons. But Magna Carta also drew on Anglo-Saxon constitutional traditions and the Coronation Charter of Henry I in its insistence that kings were bound by the law and that even the lowliest of subjects deserved basic political and legal protections. The famous clauses 39 and 40 pledged the protection of the law to all and that "to no one will We sell, to none will We deny or delay, right or justice." More important was the broader constitutional conception that guaranteed such protections, as stipulated in the first and final clauses. These were probably additions by Stephen Langton, the Archbishop of Canterbury, who had lifelong republican sympathies that stemmed from his study of the Old Testament. Both clauses linked the liberties of Englishmen with the independence of the church. Clause 63 closed the charter with language similar to how it had opened: "the English Church shall be free, and that all men in our kingdom shall have and hold all the aforesaid liberties, rights, and concessions, well and peaceably, freely, quietly, fully, and wholly, to them and their heirs of Us and Our heirs, in all things and places forever" (Howard 1998).

Regardless of the high-toned pledges, John repudiated the charter at the first available moment, and Innocent III, acting as his loyal sovereign, promptly nullified the document. Nonetheless, with the assistance of nobles still loyal to the crown, and of Langton, seen now as a rogue element by the pope, the charter prevailed and was reissued several times by later kings throughout the thirteenth century, enshrining a doctrine within the realm that English liberties were best secured by a free and independent church that could advise and balance the royal power. This principle held until Henry VIII's Act of Supremacy over three centuries later. Despite the irony that in the short-term both king and pope despised the document, Magna Carta could rightly be viewed as the culmination of the Gelasian order, where the royal and episcopal sovereignties buffeted one another and eventually cooperated for the benefit of the subjects within their domains.

DISINTEGRATING TOWARD EARLY MODERN CONSTITUTIONALISMS

The century following Magna Carta opened with absolutist claims that evoked entirely different orders as Christendom's constitutional compromise was threatened by both external and internal forces. As already seen, the Gelasian order had been fully articulated and applied, but radical wings within papalist and royalist camps had entrenched positions. These disagreements were empowered by the introduction of Aristotle's natural philosophy as mediated through Averroës and an Islamic tradition that unleashed new tensions. Among the most important was that between "faith" and "reason." Rivalries also intensified between the parallel and competitive jurisdictions of canon versus civil law. Ecclesiastical and secular authorities experienced an explosion of jurisprudence, inviting more showdowns like Becket's with Henry II. Still another tension was created by the newly formed Mendicant orders, particularly the Franciscans, who represented a trend toward absolute poverty. It did not take long for critics, both ecclesiastical and secular, to apply such ascetic strictures in criticisms of the growing Roman *ecclesia*, with its ever-expanding corporate infrastructure, legal jurisdiction, landed property, and moveable wealth.

Two Dominicans, Thomas of Aquinas and John of Paris, critically integrated the new trends without overthrowing the Gelasian balance. Throughout his writings, Thomas argued for a harmony between reason and revelation and in *On Kingship* he used analogies such as God's rule over the universe and reason's rule over the body to advocate for a monarch limited by virtue and the aim of Christian peace. Undergirding all of Thomas' thought was an intense spiritualism and a belief that the faithful Christian citizen exercised freedom within the commonwealth of Christendom, which must be oriented toward a communal love of God. John of Paris defended Thomas' integration in the wake of the ecclesiastical condemnations in 1277 that included some of Thomas' ideas. John's *On Royal and Papal Power* asserted royal and episcopal freedom from papal domination. The pope might head the sacred sphere, but he was also limited by the objectives of his office. Moreover, the episcopacy derived its authority from God and popular consent. Guided by the example of the incarnation, John reminds prelates that the church is bound to the world in a Christological compromise and division of power. It must not usurp secular rule.[12]

Most of the influential thinkers in the fourteenth century tended toward papal or royal absolutism. Published the same year as *On Royal and Papal Power*, Giles of Rome's *On Ecclesiastical Power* argued for papal supremacy. Not only did the pope hold both swords, but he was above positive law, political order, and temporal jurisdiction (O'Donovan and O'Donovan 1999, pp. 374–375). Boniface VIII's 1302 papal bull *Unam Sanctam* dogmatized such sentiments. Boniface declared that the papacy exercised judgment over kings and lesser bishops, but "if the supreme spiritual power errs it can be judged only by God not by man." In Boniface's construction, only one power directly represented Christ and ordered Christendom. He closed the bull assertively, stating: "we declare, state, define and pronounce that it is altogether necessary to salvation for every human creature to be subject to the Roman Pontiff" (Tierney 1988, p. 189).

Royalist responses were equally bold. Dante Alighieri's *De Monarchia* uplifted a universal and absolute monarch in the mold of Caesar who brought peace, purpose, and order to the communal Christian soul. The court of the Holy Roman Emperor Louis of Bavaria harbored intellectuals exiled by the papacy, including Marsilius of Padua, William of Ockham, and Michael of Cesena, all of whom attacked claims of papal absolutism. Marsilius of Padua went further, launching a "'radical', 'pivotal,' and 'revolutionary'" turn toward "secular political monism" (O'Donovan and O'Donovan 1999, p. 423).[13] On the eve of the Reformation, absolutist trends on behalf of papal and royal authority set the stage for the great power struggles that would harness the new spiritual impulses of the Reformation.

Late medieval absolutism found an opponent with the reemergence of republicanism. Marsilius of Padua and William of Ockham articulated a finer understanding of natural rights for the king's subjects and the necessity of popular consent. Urban communes throughout Europe, and especially in northern Italy, were revitalizing small-scale republicanism, often motivated by classical works such as Aristotle and Cicero. Machiavelli's prince later emerged as a pagan, republican alternative to Dante's Christian absolute monarch. In Switzerland, the cantons used imperial concessions from the last several centuries to create a confederation of smaller sovereignties. English kings increasingly incorporated parliament in the government of the realm. These various forms of republicanism would vie with European monarchs in the coming centuries, but all of them were tinged with *national* absolutism. When constitutional government finally triumphed in the West in the modern period, the secular nation was sovereign.

Republican convictions also sought to restrain the overmighty popes. As the towns had done with royal power, the little mendicant communities became more potent examples of Benedict's monastic *poleis*. The fourteenth and fifteenth centuries also saw the rise of conciliarism, the belief that the ecumenical council was more representative of Christendom than the papacy. Conciliarism found a range of advocates, but they all agreed that, at the very least, the pope was answerable to a countervailing power that was both aristocratic, with relation to the doctors and prelates, and representative, with relation to Christianity as a whole.

But these were all internal arguments *within* each of the two orders. The old *sacrum imperium* with its sacred and secular powers had perished as a constitutional order. Countervailance remained. It was more nuanced and developed but on a smaller scale. The grand vision of a mystical commonwealth spiritually unified under princes and bishops had transitioned to a conception of the world as merely a series of fragmented national powers that ruled the souls and bodies of their citizens and jealously guarded their territory from outside interference. It was a world that Gelasius would not have recognized and probably would have loathed.

Related Topics

Christendom, constitutionalism, countervailance, Gelasian principle, Investiture Controversy, Magna Carta, republicanism.

Notes

1. On the priorities of the sermons, see Matthew 5:1–7:29, Luke 6:17–49; see also Voegelin 1997a, pp. 154–166. Barnett explores Christ as the "anointed one" (Barnett 1999, pp. 27–46).
2. The gospel of Matthew in particular, starting with his genealogy, stresses Christ's descent from King David. The "secret messiah" is a particular theme throughout the gospel of Mark. The quote is from John 18:36.
3. Galatians 3:26–29. See also Voegelin 1997a, pp. 166–173.
4. John 14:16–17; 1 John 2:15–17.

5. For excerpts and the context of their writings, see Rahner 1992, pp. 1–38; O'Donovan and O'Donovan 1999, pp. 1–22, 30–45.
6. For excerpts and their contexts, see Rahner 1992, pp. 97–119, 123–132; Dales 1995, pp. 13–25; O'Donovan and O'Donovan 1999, pp. 46–88.
7. See *City of God*, Book 19, especially chapters 24–27. See also Dales 1995, pp. 36–39; O'Daly 2004.
8. Tierney has a good survey of the discussion (Tierney 1988, pp. 10–11).
9. Kern discusses the constitutional strictures of early European kingship (Kern 1970). Brown and O'Donovan survey the contributions of Cassiodorus, Gregory, and Isidore (Brown 2013, pp. 190–215, 364–368; O'Donovan and O'Donovan 1999, pp. 195–211). On early papal power as exhibited during the pontificates of Leo I and Gregory I, see Neil 2009 and Demacopoulos 2015.
10. On the monastic orders and the contribution of Cassiodorus, see Vessey 2004; Brown 2013: 217–266.
11. Such was Berman's assessment. On the Investiture Controversy and the Gregorian reform as a revolution, particularly with regard to legal and political terminology, see Berman 1983; Blumenthal 1991.
12. Numerous works on Thomas' theology exist, but suitable introductions to his political thought can be found in Sigmund 1988; Voegelin 1997b, pp. 207–232; O'Donovan and O'Donovan 1999, pp. 320–361.
13. An introduction to these developments can be found in Carstens 1992, pp. 13–36; O'Donovan and O'Donovan, 1999, pp. 389–475.

FURTHER READING

Brown, P. 2013. *The Rise of Western Christendom*. Chichester: Wiley-Blackwell.
  Brown's history of Christendom is a fine introduction to the ideas, personalities, and events in the opening centuries of Christendom.
O'Donovan, O., and J.L. O'Donovan. 1999. *From Irenaeus to Grotius: A Sourcebook in Christian Political Thought 100–1625*. Grand Rapids: William B. Eerdmans Publishing Company.
  Oliver and Joan O'Donovans' sourcebook is an indispensable resource that provides the historical context, scholarly debates, and key selections for many of the intellectuals from the early Christian period to the early modern period.
Tierney, B. 1988. *The Crisis of Church and State 1050–1300*. Toronto: University of Toronto Press.
  Tierney wrote several works on the medieval political order over the course of decades of scholarship. This is the best introduction to the themes and controversies at work in the early and high medieval periods, including a number of source selections not found in O'Donovan.

Voegelin, E. 1997–1998. *History of Political Ideas, Volumes I–III*. Columbia: University of Missouri Press.
  Voegelin's magisterial History of Political Ideas series provides a nuanced and detailed account of the animating ideas and systems of thought and demonstrates his commitment to understanding the historical events that surrounded those ideas. These volumes trace western political thought (including some selections from non-western thought) from ancient Greece through the late medieval period.

References

Barnett, P. 1999. *Jesus & the Rise of Early Christianity*. Downers Grove: InterVarsity Press.

Berman, H.J. 1983. *Law and Revolution: The Formation of the Western Legal Tradition*. Cambridge, MA: Harvard University Press.

Blumenthal, U.-R. 1991. *The Investiture Controversy: Church and Monarchy from the Ninth to the Twelfth Century*. Philadelphia: University of Pennsylvania Press.

Brown, P. 2013. *The Rise of Western Christendom*. Chichester: Wiley-Blackwell.

Carstens, R.W. 1992. *The Medieval Antecedents of Constitutionalism*. New York: Peter Lang.

Dales, R.C. 1995. *The Intellectual Life of Western Europe in the Middle Ages*. New York: E. J. Brill.

Demacopoulos, G.E. 2015. *Gregory the Great: Ascetic, Pastor, and First Man of Rome*. Notre Dame: University of Notre Dame Press.

Howard, A.E.D. 1998. *Magna Carta: Text and Commentary*. Charlottesville: University of Virginia Press.

Kern, F. 1970. *Kingship and Law in the Middle Ages*. New York: Harper Torchbooks.

Neil, B. 2009. *Leo the Great*. New York: Routledge.

Neil, B., and P. Allen. 2014. *The Letters of Gelasius I: Pastor and Micro-Manager of the Church of Rome*. Turnhout: Brepols.

O'Daly, G. 2004. *Augustine's City of God: A Reader's Guide*. Oxford: Oxford University Press.

O'Donovan, O., and J.L. O'Donovan. 1999. *From Irenaeus to Grotius: A Sourcebook in Christian Political Thought 100–1625*. Grand Rapids: William B. Eerdmans Publishing Company.

Rahner, H. 1992. *Church and State in Early Christianity*. San Francisco: Ignatius Press.

Sigmund, P.E. 1988. *St. Thomas on Politics and Ethics*. New York: W. W. Norton & Company.

Tierney, B. 1988. *The Crisis of Church and State 1050–1300*. Toronto: University of Toronto Press.

Vessey, M. 2004. *Cassiodorus: Institutions of Divine and Secular Learning and On the Soul*. Liverpool: Liverpool University Press.

Voegelin, E. 1997a. *History of Political Ideas Volume I: Hellenism, Rome, and Early Christianity*. Columbia: University of Missouri Press.

———. 1997b. *History of Political Ideas Volume II: The Middle Ages to Aquinas*. Columbia: University of Missouri Press.

CHAPTER 3

The Interaction of Church and State During the Crusading Movement: Cooperation, Control, Indifference

Steve Weidenkopf

The year 1095 witnessed the birth of a unique movement in European history. It was a movement initiated by the papacy, undertaken by Catholic warriors, and consumed nearly six centuries of European attention and resources. The structure of European society and the interaction between Church and State allowed for the creation of the movement, its support, and, eventually, as the Church-State relationship changed, brought about its end.

At a field in the town of Clermont on November 27, 1095, Pope Urban II (r. 1088–1099) delivered one of the most significant speeches in history and inaugurated the crusading movement. Several months before, Urban received imperial representatives from the Eastern Roman Empire at a large meeting of ecclesial reformers at Piacenza. These envoys requested military aid from the West to counter Islamic incursions into imperial territory. Urban recognized the need for military assistance was great but

S. Weidenkopf (✉)
Christendom College Graduate School of Theology, Front Royal, VA, USA
e-mail: steve@ourcatholichistory.com

© The Author(s), under exclusive license to Springer Nature
Switzerland AG 2023
S. Holzer (ed.), *The Palgrave Handbook of Religion and State
Volume II*, https://doi.org/10.1007/978-3-031-35609-4_3

wondered how to motivate warriors to embark on such a perilous journey. He developed the idea of linking military assistance with participation in a pilgrimage, which provided spiritual benefits, and set the liberation of Jerusalem as the goal of the expedition. Urban's revolutionary decision to allow for *armed* pilgrimages prompted significant secular interest and participation. The crusading movement began with a partnership between ecclesial and secular rulers, reflecting the unique nature of medieval European society. However, as the movement progressed, ecclesial rulers sought control over the actions of lay warriors on campaign, which proved problematic. As the relationship between Church and State changed, so did the crusading movement. Secular focus on internal political agendas resulted in indifference to papal goals, which brought an end to the crusades. This chapter provides an overview of the crusading movement that dominated the attention of ecclesial and secular rulers from the eleventh through fifteenth centuries in European history. It explores the origins of the movement, the motivations for its beginnings and sustainment, and the evolving interaction of Church and State leaders during the movement. It briefly surveys the various major crusade campaigns illustrating the relationship between ecclesial and secular rulers during those expeditions and shows that changes in Church-State relations ended the crusading movement.

ORIGINS OF THE CRUSADING MOVEMENT

Medieval society consisted of a community of "those who prayed, those who fought, and those who worked" (Bloch, Vol. 2, 1961b, p. 291). The relationship between "those who prayed" and "those who fought" powered the crusading movement by giving it impetus, sustaining it through the centuries, and, ultimately, producing its end. Church and State relations in the medieval period were complex and vacillated between cooperation and conflict depending on the personalities and goals of ecclesial and secular rulers. The medieval warrior caste obtained a dominant role in European society as a result of the breakdown of central governing authority, which began in the late fifth century with the collapse of the Western Roman Empire. The invasions of Muslim, Magyar, and Viking warriors in the subsequent centuries elevated the European warrior to the status of protector and political ruler. However, no one warrior was powerful enough to control sufficient territory or resources alone, so, "a network of dependent ties" developed in many areas of Europe (Bloch, Vol. 1, 1961a,

p. 173). This mutual aid system was not uniformly practiced throughout Europe, (in fact, it was not practiced at all in some areas) but this societal structure produced a measure of stability and created the community in which the crusades originated.[1] A structured, hierarchical feudal society rooted in the holding and distribution of land via complex interpersonal relationships became the normative societal construct in many areas of Europe, especially in those areas with abundant participation in the crusades.[2]

The general cooperation between Church and State in medieval society is illustrated in the initiatives developed in the late tenth century in France to combat the rising violence between Christian warriors and, at times, inflicted on the Church. The "Peace of God" and "Truce of God" initiatives were not an attempt by the Church to control violent noble warriors by restricting the use of arms and then directing those violent energies elsewhere but, rather, were enterprises of mutual cooperation between secular and ecclesial rulers focused on societal and ecclesial reform (Cushing 2005, p. 43). The "Peace of God" movement in France focused on the protection of Church property and clerics from secular control. Church officials in France focused on mobilizing popular support for peace as a means of steadying their position in relationship to powerful noblemen (Cushing 2005, p. 47). The "Truce of God" initiative produced specific restrictions on the times allowed for martial activity. These two initiatives were part of larger reform and renewal efforts undertaken by the Church in the eleventh century to restore clerical discipline and free the Church from undue secular interference.

The reformers were concerned not only with clerical discipline but also with setting boundaries between ecclesial and secular spheres (Cushing 2005, 36). The problem of lay interference in papal elections was solved in the pontificate of Nicholas II (r. 1058–1061) with the establishment of the College of Cardinals as the normative and exclusive electoral body. The battle over secular control of the Church became the focus of Gregory VII's (r. 1073–1085) pontificate in the Investiture Controversy with King Henry IV (r. 1056–1105). Pope and king engaged in a battle of wills over the appointment of bishops and their symbols of office in German territory.[3] Despite the occasional setbacks, the papal reform initiatives in the eleventh century succeeded in re-instituting clerical discipline and establishing definitive boundaries between the ecclesial and secular spheres. Popes and prelates were aided by faithful laity in the tasks of reform and renewal, placing Christendom in a unique position at the end of the eleventh century to cooperate in a military/spiritual endeavor to liberate occupied Christian territory in the Holy Land from Islamic control.

The crusading movement initiated by Urban II at Clermont evolved over time in structure, practice, and conduct and embraced many forms.[4] There were campaigns against Muslim forces in the Holy Land and North Africa as well as endeavors against pagans in the Baltic regions, heretics in southern France, and enemies of the papacy. Even the term used to describe these events evolved over time. Contemporaries called the armed pilgrimages *passagia*, a term indicating a large military campaign waged against enemies of Christ wherein the participants, known as *crucesignati* (those signed with the cross), received spiritual privileges, namely an indulgence, for their participation.[5] The penitential armed pilgrimages undertaken by Catholic warriors involved several essential elements: papal endorsement, taking the cross publicly by vow, the granting of several temporal privileges (e.g., protection of family and property, immunity from arrest, exemption from tolls and taxes), and reception of the indulgence, which was the remission of the temporal punishment due to sin whose guilt was previously forgiven in the Sacrament of Penance (Riley-Smith 2002, pp. 2–4). The penitential and spiritual nature of these military campaigns is illustrated by the granting of the indulgence, an ecclesial action not associated with any other form of warfare. The indulgence was the central quality of the crusade and proved the campaigns were recognized as praiseworthy endeavors by the Church (Bysted 2015, p. 5). "The crusade indulgences were the institutionalization of the idea that fighting for Christ and the Church were meritorious in the sight of God, and thus worthy of a spiritual reward proclaimed by the Church" (Bysted 2015, p. 6).

The response to the Urban's call was overwhelming. Urban spent the year after Clermont traveling throughout France preaching the crusade. He also commissioned preachers throughout Christendom to urge warriors to take the cross. A high proportion of the participants came from areas visited by Urban on his preaching tour (Tyerman 2006, p. 75). Bishops and priests were charged with screening candidates and no married man could take the cross without wifely consent in an effort to prevent men from using the crusade as an opportunity for abandonment (Brundage 1969, p. 77).[6] The initiation of the crusading movement at Clermont and the subsequent recruitment campaign illustrated the close relationship between Church and State from the onset of the movement. Ecclesial officials created awareness and fervor for the campaigns through preaching and secular rulers participated in and encouraged others to join the endeavors. Urban's grand adventure produced a large response as medieval people understood the importance and uniqueness of the opportunity. Urban provided the medieval warrior class with a chance to use their martial skills in the service of Christ and the Church in a meritorious manner impacting their eternal salvation. Medieval piety stressed the difficulty of eternal bliss for the laity, due to the wickedness and sinfulness of the world in which they acted. The pope's call at Clermont afforded the laity a unique opportunity to perform a task "pleasing to God, for which they were especially equipped" (Riley-Smith 1980, p. 38).

Crusading was not only a penitential practice, but it was also an act of love. Crusaders were motivated by love for Christ and his Church, love for fellow Christians in danger in the Holy Land, and love for themselves and their eternal salvation. Charters, documenting the sale of property to finance the journey East, detail charity as a main motivation for crusaders as warriors expressed the desire to perform acts of penance (love for one's soul), protection (love of neighbor), and piety (love of God).[7] Although crusading was viewed differently than other forms of warfare, behavior on the campaigns did not always manifest the ideal. Participants were human beings subjected to emotions and temptations; reason and piety were not always demonstrated, despite the expectation. Armies were comprised of saints and sinners motivated by holy and selfish desires, but all understood the uniqueness of the pope's call to arms.

Although division of historical events into concrete periodization defies reality and belays the complexities and intersections inherent in human affairs, organizational constructs are helpful in understanding historical activities. The interaction between Church and State during the crusading movement can be characterized into periods of cooperation, control, and indifference. A period of cooperation existed from the beginning of the movement at Clermont to the Third Crusade in the late twelfth century. Experiences in the cooperation phase led to ecclesial efforts focused on controlling the armed pilgrimages after the fiasco of the Fourth Crusade in the early thirteenth century. The crusading movement faltered with the end of the Crusader States in the late thirteenth century and entered into a time of secular indifference in the years after the fall of Constantinople to the Ottoman Turks in the middle of the fifteenth century.

COOPERATION

The tale of the First Crusade (sometimes known as the "Prince's Crusade") is one of the most well-documented events of the medieval period. Several eyewitnesses wrote chronicles of their participation and many other authors produced later manuscripts of the deeds of the First Crusaders.[8] Although Pope Urban II may have desired royal participation in the armed pilgrimage to the East, the major monarchs at the time were either barred from participating due to an excommunicated status or were engaged otherwise in political struggles with the Church. So, military leadership fell to other noblemen who led regional forces. Bishop Adhemar of Le Puy was designated the overall leader and papal legate. Medieval armies did not possess a unified command structure, so decisions were made by debate, discussion, and compromise. Bishop Adhemar did not exercise total control over the expedition but rather served as a peaceful mediator between the competing leading noblemen. Although the bulk of forces came from France, the armies comprised warriors from other regions of Christendom. French forces were divided into a northern and southern element commanded, respectively, by Hugh of Vermandois, the brother of King Philip I, and Raymond of Toulouse. Raymond was an older crusader, a veteran of campaigns against Muslim forces in Spain, and a powerful and wealthy nobleman. He led the best-funded and largest army group and, unlike most of the crusaders, planned to retire to the Holy Land. Other French forces, which included relatives of William the Conqueror, traveled independently of the main bodies.[9] The other main army groups comprised a German contingent led by Godfrey de Bouillon and Norman troops commanded by Bohemond, son of the famous warrior Robert Guiscard. These army groups arrived separately in Constantinople during the fall of 1096 and into 1097. The Easterners were unprepared for such large groupings of Western military forces, expecting rather smaller groups of mercenaries. Emperor Alexius I Comnenus was concerned and feared the crusaders might unite and attack Constantinople and perhaps overthrow him, so he demanded oaths of loyalty from the leading Western nobles. The emperor's reaction illustrates the lack of unity between East and West at the beginning of the crusading movement, which perpetuated throughout its course. Despite requesting Western military aid, Easterners were confused by the presence of the army groups and unsure of their intentions, which led to half-hearted support, for fear of Turkish reaction should the crusade fail, and actions during the campaign that Westerners viewed as betrayal.

When the oaths of loyalty were secured from the crusade nobles, the armies were transported to Anatolia and assembled for the march to Nicaea, which was liberated in June 1097. Afterward, the crusades departed for Antioch and endured a brutal four-month march through Anatolia, which led to hundreds of deaths and desertions. The crusaders arrived finally at Antioch, in the fall of 1097. After the exhausting and devastating trek through Anatolia the crusaders were in no position to take the city, so a prolonged siege developed. As winter set in, food became scarce, and starvation became rampant. Panic developed in the crusader camp, which prompted Bishop Adhemar to institute penitential regulations and spiritual exercises to imbue hope and secular lords established strict temporal regulations to maintain order. The multilingual Norman warrior Bohemond bribed a captain of one of the tower guards, who allowed a small group of crusaders into his tower before dawn on the morning of June 3, 1098. The successful raid led to the entry of the crusader host into the city and its capture, which was fortuitous because a relief army led by Kerbogha, the atabeg of Mosul, arrived at the gates the next day. A few weeks later, Bohemond devised a brilliant tactical strategy and led the crusader host outside the city walls in battle against Kerbogha's relief army to an astounding victory.

Although beset by multiple setbacks, the First Crusade had liberated two ancient Christian cities and was poised to march on the ultimate objective of Jerusalem. After a period of reset and refit, the crusade armies reached the Holy City in the summer of 1099. Initial attacks were thwarted but in early July, the priest Peter Desiderius announced that he was the recipient of a vision of Bishop Adhemar, who had died of disease the previous summer, who told Peter Jerusalem could be taken only after the crusaders processed around the city in an act of penance. After three days of fasting, the armies walked barefoot and unarmed around the city singing and bearing relics while Muslim defenders mocked the spectacle. A week later, a final assault resulted in the liberation of the city and the accomplishment of Urban's goal.[10] Three years after leaving Europe, Christian warriors had traveled thousands of miles, overcome logistical hardships, disease, and ferocious combat to liberate three major cities and a 600-mile-long coastal strip of land. The completion of the armed pilgrimage to Jerusalem led to the departure of the majority of surviving warriors. The success of the First Crusade was attributed to divine intervention and part of God's divine plan of salvation (Housley 2008, p. 7). Sadly, Urban II, who launched the crusading movement, died before news of Jerusalem's liberation reached Rome.

The warriors who remained in the Latin East consolidated and expanded their land holdings in the years after 1099. Feudal territories, known as the Crusader States, were established in the other liberated areas.[11] Since crusading was episodic in nature, the Latin East suffered from a lack of manpower to defend its territory, so an intense castle-building program was initiated to construct strategic fortifications throughout the land. Additionally, the situation in the Latin East produced a unique development in ecclesial life as military religious orders were established to defend the holy places. Participating in an armed pilgrimage was normally a temporary act of devotion but the establishment of the military religious orders turned holy warfare into a devotional way of life (Riley-Smith 1997, p. 161).

The fragile foothold in the Latin East suffered a serious defeat on Christmas Eve 1144 when Zengi, the ruler of Aleppo, took advantage of dynastic issues in the Kingdom of Jerusalem and captured the County of Edessa, the northernmost Crusader State.[12] The fall of Edessa and the massacre of its Christian inhabitants produced the first major crusade in a generation. Pope Eugenius III (r. 1145–1153) issued a summons to King Louis VII and the knights of France in the bull *Quantum praedecessores* in December 1145. The bull was one of the most widely circulated papal documents of the medieval period and listed the spiritual and temporal privileges enjoined on *crucesignati* (Phillips 2007, pp. 50–58). The pope recalled the actions of the First Crusaders and highlighted that his hearers/readers were the progeny of those heroic warriors: "It will be seen as a great token of nobility and uprightness if those things acquired by the efforts of your fathers are vigorously defended by you, their good sons" (Phillips 2007, p. 281). Although the pope birthed what became known as the Second Crusade (1147–1149), the campaign came to life through the preaching of Bernard of Clairvaux. The Cistercian reformer was the most influential cleric of his time. The pope, a former pupil of Bernard, asked the well-respected monk to personally preach the crusade. Bernard recognized the allure of Jerusalem could not be used to urge warriors to participate since the Holy City was still in Christian control, but he utilized the well-known stories of the First Crusade to motivate warriors to take the cross. Bernard traveled hundreds of miles in the dead of winter preaching the crusade in German territory and eventually secured the participation of King Conrad III. The German contingent arrived in

Constantinople in the fall of 1147. On the march through Anatolia, in imitation of the route used by the First Crusaders, Conrad suffered a debilitating defeat near the site of the Battle of Dorylaeum. During the retreat, the king was wounded in the head by an arrow shot. What was left of the German host arrived in Nicaea a few weeks later. Conrad spent time in Constantinople convalescing and eventually made his way to Jerusalem.

The French King Louis VII did not hesitate like Conrad III to take the cross at the behest of Eugenius III. Bernard arrived at Vézaly at Easter in 1146 and preached the crusade to a large gathering. His preaching was so effective that the prepared cloth crosses made for the expected numbers of *crucesignati* ran out and Bernard was forced to tear his own habit to make more (Phillips 2007, p. 68). The king departed in June 1147. The French arrived in Nicaea and witnessed the return of the defeated and demoralized German army. Louis and his warriors left Nicaea but suffered a similar fate as the Germans. A Turkish attack on the spread-out French army on Mount Cadmus resulted in heavy casualties and the near-death of the king. Arriving in Antioch in the spring of 1148, Louis recognized his force was no longer sufficient to take Edessa, the primary objective of the campaign. Instead, Louis traveled to Jerusalem to link up with Conrad and the remnants of the German army.

At Jerusalem, Conrad and Louis were convinced by the local Christian nobility to join forces for an attack on Damascus. The combined Christian army arrived at Damascus in the summer of 1149 and achieved initial tactical successes. However, faulty intelligence and the pursuit of a quick victory led to the abandonment of their highly defensible position for the Eastern wall a few days into the siege. The new position was not favorable and coupled with news of relief armies on the march, the kings and local nobles retreated in defeat to Jerusalem. The Second Crusade began with such promise and ended in abject failure. The cooperation between Church and State was illustrated from the beginning of the expedition but even the participation of two major monarchs, something absent from the First Crusade, was not enough to ensure success. The defeat negatively impacted the crusading movement as Christians in Europe struggled to explain why the success of the First Crusade was not replicated. Despite pleas from the Latin East for assistance, and papal letters authorizing expeditions, no major campaign came to fruition for over forty years. The result of the Second Crusade foreshadowed the end of cooperation between Church and State, and the beginning of ecclesial control over the movement as ecclesial leaders struggled to maintain secular focus on the purpose of the campaigns.

The greatest fear of Christians in the Latin East was manifested in the late twelfth century with the solidification of Muslim power in the hands of Saladin. The ethnic Kurd became master of Egypt and launched a series of raids into the Kingdom of Jerusalem. King Guy de Lusignan responded to Saladin's invasion by assembling the largest Christian field army in the history of the Latin East. At a council of war, Guy initially agreed to a defensive strategy of waiting behind a fortified position for Saladin's supply lines to stretch and then attacking at an opportune time. However, he was later persuaded to abandon that sensible approach for a march in the summer heat to lift the siege at Tiberias. The Christian army marched in deplorable conditions without accessible water and were surrounded by Saladin's forces at the twin peaks of Hattin in early July 1187. The Battle of Hattin was a Christian disaster. The defeat shocked the kingdom and left its major towns exposed, which Saladin methodically captured. The Holy City surrendered to Saladin after a valiant defense and after only eighty-eight years was back in Muslim control.

The defeat at Hattin and the loss of Jerusalem sent shock waves throughout Christian Europe. Pope Urban III (r. 1185–1187) reportedly died of grief at the news. His successor, Pope Gregory VIII (r. 1187), issued the bull *Audita tremendi* exhorting the warriors of Christendom to once more take up arms to liberate Jerusalem. The shock of losing Jerusalem motivated the major monarchs of Europe to join the expedition. Frequently at war with the papacy, especially in Northern Italy, Holy Roman Emperor Frederick Barbarossa recognized the importance of the crusade and, despite his age, took the cross. Barbarossa, a veteran of the Second Crusade, assembled a large army and departed for the East in the spring of 1189. Frederick's army eventually reached Anatolia, but the aged emperor drowned while crossing a river and his demoralized army dispersed. The arrival of the armies of Philip II Augustus of France and Richard the Lion-hearted of England in the Latin East led to the liberation of the city of Acre. After the victory at Acre, Philip, claiming illness, left the crusade and returned to France amid much criticism. Richard continued the campaign, fought Saladin at the Battle of Arsuf, but was unable to secure a decisive military victory to liberate Jerusalem. Instead, the king of England entered into a diplomatic treaty that guaranteed Christian access to the Holy City for three years. The Third Crusade, known as the "Three Kings Crusade," was partially successful. The unexpected death of

Frederick Barbarossa and the jealous rivalry between Philip and Richard hampered the success of the expedition but, in totality, the crusade illustrated the ability of major Christian monarchs to cooperate with the Church in pursuing the shared goal of Christian control of Jerusalem. The next crusade, however, resulted in ecclesial recognition of the need for greater Church involvement in order to control the outcome of the holy expeditions.

The crusading movement experienced significant changes during the pontificate of Innocent III (r. 1198–1216), who called for more holy campaigns than any other pope. Innocent desired the restoration of Jerusalem to Christian control and described the crusade as *negotium crucis/crucifixi*, the business of the cross/crucified (Tyerman 2006, p. 480). The next major crusade began with a committee of nobility sent to Venice to secure the required naval transport to the Latin East. In the summer of 1202, crusaders assembled in Venice where their transport ships awaited but the stipulated numbers of warriors in the treaty (33,500 troops) did not materialize. Short on numbers and the required cash to pay the Venetians, the crusade seemed destined to fail but Venetian Doge Enricho Dandolo concocted a plan to recoup the shortfall. He requested crusader assistance in capturing the city of Zara (on the Dalmatian coast), a former Venetian territory now under Hungarian control. Since King Emeric of Hungary had taken the cross, the city was under ecclesial protection and any Christian attacker suffered excommunication. In a precarious position, the majority of crusaders agreed to attack Zara with the Venetians. News of the city's capture by the crusaders convinced Pope Innocent that the crusade was out of control, and he issued a stinging reprimand. The crusaders still required funds to continue the campaign and believed the appearance of envoys from the exiled Byzantine prince Alexius Angelus provided a unique opportunity. Alexius Angelus desired the crusaders' help in restoring his father, the deposed Isaac II, to the throne and promised to restore ecclesial union with Rome, join the crusade with a contingent of imperial troops, and provide the necessary cash for the expedition. The pope knew about Alexius Angelus and his quest for Western troops, so he wrote a strongly worded letter to the crusade leaders to ignore Alexius' offer. However, the crusade nobles ignored Innocent and accepted Alexius invitation to Constantinople. The crusaders arrived at the imperial capital in the summer of 1203 and were stunned to discover the lackluster response from the people for Alexius. Instead of the expected peaceful coup, the crusaders realized a violent siege was required for entrance into the city.

The subsequent attack resulted in a large fire in the city set by the Venetians and the fleeing of the usurper Alexius III. Isaac II was released from prison and crowned Alexius Angelus co-emperor (as Alexius IV). Alexius tried to fulfill his promises to the crusaders but was unable to acquire the pledged funds. The presence of Western troops and their rambunctious behavior angered many in Constantinople. Mourtzouphlus, Alexius IV's chief lieutenant, initiated a palace coup, imprisoned the boy emperor, and, eventually, ordered his murder in the spring of 1204. News of Alexius IV's death sparked the crusaders into action once more, and on April 13, 1204, they invested in the city and engaged in one of the most notorious sacks in history.[13]

The fiasco of the Fourth Crusade illustrated the need for greater ecclesial control over the holy expeditions and prompted Pope Innocent III to institute new policies and procedures in the crusading movement, which initiated a new phase in the interaction between Church and State during the crusading movement.

CONTROL

In his bull *Quia Maior* (1213) and the later Fourth Lateran Council document, *Ad Liberandam* (1215), Innocent produced "a set of coherent legal, liturgical, and fiscal provisions that brought together a range of previous expedients to form the basis and model for future crusades" (Tyerman 2006, p. 481). Innocent understood the need for greater ecclesial control over the crusades, so his bull and the conciliar document provided the foundation for the Church to manage and administer the expeditions. Among Innocent's innovations were a more concerted effort to finance the crusades by taxing the clergy of Christendom, providing papal funds for expenditure; the appointment of papal legates to oversee preaching missions; the enforcement of crusade vows through ecclesial censures and punishments; expansion of the indulgence to those who subsidized the cost of warriors to go on crusade (substitution payments) as well as those who went in the place of others and those who materially supported the defense of the Latin East (redemption payments); and viewing the crusade as a moral imperative for all in Christendom.[14]

In the campaign against heretics in southern France (the Albigensian Crusade), Innocent radically altered the understanding of the crusade by establishing a period of military service (forty days) rather than a location (Jerusalem) for the granting of the indulgence. As a result, the crusading movement embraced an expanded definition of purpose, duration, and participation. Innocent's eighteen-year pontificate was one of the most influential in Church history due to his ecclesial reform efforts, enforcement of papal jurisdiction and supremacy, and his crusading innovations. The lawyer pope died in the summer of 1216 and did not live to see the result of the Church-directed and -administered Fifth Crusade.

The combatants of the Fifth Crusade believed their expedition would return Jerusalem to Christian control; however, this First Crusade directly administered by the Church proved a tactical failure, despite being on the verge of success. The expedition began in Egypt, where it was believed that Christian control would provide a launching pad for a successful campaign for full control of the Holy Land. The warriors of the Fifth Crusade arrived at the strategic and heavily fortified city of Damietta at the mouth of the Nile River in the spring of 1218. Although John of Brienne (r. 1210–1225), the titular king of Jerusalem, was elected leader of the expedition, real authority rested with two papal legates, Cardinals Pelagius and Robert, who arrived in the fall of 1218. Cardinal Robert died soon after arrival, which proved calamitous for the campaign as the remaining prelate, Pelagius, was stubborn and failed to take advantage of situations that would have brought Christian victory. Sultan al-Kamil was not interested in protracted warfare, so he offered to restore substantial portions of former Christian territory and a thirty-year peace treaty for the return of Damietta and a crusader withdrawal. Pelagius declined the offer believing the crusaders were in a position of strength and greater gains were in the future. In the fall of 1219, the crusaders finally entered Damietta to the smell and sight of much death as tens of thousands of inhabitants perished in the prolonged siege. The crusade stalled over the next year as John of Brienne left Egypt for Acre, another diplomatic offer from al-Kamil was rejected by Cardinal Pelagius, and the hoped for and promised reinforcements under the command of Holy Roman Emperor Frederick II never materialized. In the summer of 1221, Cardinal Pelagius ordered the army into the field for a march on Cairo, but a poor tactical decision led the army to camp in an insecure defensive position, which cut the supply line to Damietta. Surrounded by Muslim forces with no relief in sight, Cardinal Pelagius sued for peace. Al-Kamil agreed to an eight-year truce for the return of Damietta and the withdrawal of Christian forces from Egypt. Innocent's grand vision that a centrally managed ecclesial enterprise, devoid of secular politics and temptations to pursue other objections, would produce favorable outcomes did not materialize.

The Fifth Crusade failed not because of Innocent's vision but due to poor leadership and the stalled response of Frederick II who took the cross in 1215 but never sailed for Egypt. However, unlike the failure of previous crusades, which demoralized Christendom and negatively impacted the crusading movement, the disappointment of the Fifth Crusade provided a learning experience that the Church and secular rulers took to heart. They learned "…the lesson that their efforts needed to be more sharply focuses in terms of logistic preparations, military organization and religious commitments. The Fifth Crusade met military defeat for itself while securing institutional success for its cause" (Tyerman 2006, p. 649). Through the efforts of Pope Innocent III, which were continued by his successors, the crusading movement had become firmly entrenched in the societal fabric of Christendom, which could suffer the defeat of one crusade while preparing for a subsequent one.

The remaining major crusades of the thirteenth century form a juxtaposition between uncooperative and cooperative secular rulers who participated in Church-administered crusades. The difficulty experienced by the Church in centrally managing and controlling crusades was exhibited clearly in the papal relationship with Frederick II. Although the idea of a Church-controlled crusade was sound, because of the fiasco of the Fourth Crusade and papal desire to codify elements of the past century of crusading experience, the reality reflected the immense struggle by the Church in modifying royal and secular behavior for the good of the crusade. Frederick II's repeated crusader vow and promise to support the Fifth Crusade led to its ultimate failure. Pope Honorius III (r. 1216–1227), the king's former tutor, allowed multiple extensions to Frederick's crusade vow. His successor, Gregory IX (r. 1227–1241), was not as patient and demanded the emperor fulfill the now eleven-year-old vow. Frederick prepared an army but as the troops assembled in Brindisi disease ravaged the camp infecting the emperor who called off the campaign. Angry at Frederick's decision, Gregory IX excommunicated the emperor and placed all lands he visited under interdict in September 1227. Frederick was a contentious soul and a man out of place in the Christian-dominated European society in which he lived and reigned. In constant external quarrel with the papacy over political matters, Frederick quarreled internally with his spiritual life and appeared more favorable to Islam than to his Christian Faith. Despite his excommunicated status, which technically prevented one from participating in the crusade, and explicit papal prohibition, Frederick, with a small army, left Europe and arrived in the Latin

East in 1228. The emperor negotiated with Sultan al-Kamil and early in 1229 signed the Treaty of Jaffa, which provided Christian control of Jerusalem for a decade. Frederick's presence was not welcomed by the Christians in the Latin East. Despite his self-coronation as king of Jerusalem in the Church of the Holy Sepulchre in March 1229, local Christians pelted him with animal entrails as he departed Acre later in May.[15]

The recalcitrant monarch achieved a long-sought crusade objective, control of Jerusalem, through diplomacy in the campaign known as the Sixth Crusade but his behavior illustrated the Church's struggle to control secular rulers on crusade. Again, the ideal of a Church-administered crusade met the hard reality of independently minded secular rulers focused on personal rather than ecclesial objectives. In the case of Frederick, the monarch displayed such animosity toward papal territory and authority that Gregory IX proclaimed a crusade against him. Frederick was eventually excommunicated (again) and deposed at the First Council of Lyons (1245).

In juxtaposition to the "Crusader without Faith" is the "Perfect Crusader," King St. Louis IX of France.[16] Louis was a dutiful son of the Church, one of the central figures of Christendom in the thirteenth century, and a consummate proponent of the crusading movement. The French king first embarked for the crusade after the Khwarazmians attacked Jerusalem in 1244. Louis provided generously from the royal treasury to subsidize the cost of the campaign for fellow crusaders. The king planned a re-enactment of the Fifth Crusade with an expedition directed to Egypt and arrived in the summer of 1249. Louis led the crusaders in an amphibious landing near Damietta, which was successful and unlike the Fifth Crusade, the king captured the city within hours of landing. Unfortunately, Louis made the same tactical mistakes as the Fifth Crusade by over-extending his supply line, maintaining a poor defensive position, and engaging in a dangerous retreat amid sickness, which led to surrender by the exhausted, demoralized, and ineffective crusade host. Louis remained in captivity until payment of a hefty ransom. Upon release, he spent several years rebuilding coastal fortifications in the Latin East, but news of his mother's death prompted Louis' return to France in 1254. The saintly crusader marched into the breach once more sixteen years later to stem the advances of the ruthless Sultan Baybars, ruler of Egypt and Syria.[17] The Second Crusade of St. Louis focused on Tunis in North Africa but a few weeks after arrival illness swept the camp killing a prince, the papal legate, and, on August 25, the king. Louis IX of France was the last monarch of Europe to go on crusade and his failed expeditions marked the end of the Church-controlled era of crusading. The king's two campaigns were the most well-funded and royally supported crusades in history and were undertaken by a loyal son of the Church, whose objective was identical with ecclesial goals, yet they failed and with their failure the crusading movement entered into a period of decline marked by secular indifference and eventual rejection.

INDIFFERENCE

Nearly a year after the death of the saintly French king, Teobaldo Visconti was elected pope taking the name Gregory X (r. 1271–1276). The new pope focused his efforts on the calling of a new crusade to liberate Jerusalem. At the Second Council of Lyons (1274), plans were made for the new expedition, and a clerical tax and a preaching mission were authorized. Gregory persuaded the leading monarchs of Christendom to participate in the campaign and set the departure date for April 1277. However, the pontiff died and with him the crusade. The intervening years witnessed no new crusades and even when the County of Tripoli fell to a Mamluk army from Egypt in 1289 no major crusade followed. The fall of the Crusader State caused panic among the remaining Christian territories in the Latin East. Pleas for help from Europe went unheeded. By the end of the thirteenth century, only a narrow coastal strip of territory remained in Christian control. An economically rich area, many Christians in the Latin East believed, despite lacking adequate military manpower, they were safe from harassment by the Mamluks, but that belief was foolhardy. In late 1290, a large Muslim army marched on Acre, the last remaining major Christian city in the Latin East. When they arrived, a massive artillery bombardment involving a large assortment of siege engines erupted. Although the Christian defenders were outnumbered, they were buoyed by the arrival of Henry II, the king of Jerusalem, with a small contingent of soldiers. Henry quickly realized the military situation was hopeless and sent envoys to the Mamluk commander, but they proved futile. The final assault in May 1291 resulted in the loss of the city. When news of Acre's fall reached Christendom, it produced shock and dismay and a change in the crusading movement. By the end of the thirteenth century, crusading had become a way of life for Christians in Europe and encompassed a worldview but the translation of that worldview into concrete military action proved difficult given the internal focus of secular rulers despite the pleadings of numerous Roman pontiffs. Pilgrimages to the Holy Land from Europe continued after the collapse of the Crusader States, and many still dreamed and hoped for another Christian liberation of Jerusalem but the crusading focus changed to protection of the European homeland in the fourteenth century with the rise of the Ottoman Turks.

The Ottomans posed a dangerous threat to Europe for 300 years. A strong, united, well-organized, militarily powerful, and imperialistic group, the Ottomans began incursions into Eastern Europe in the late fourteenth century. In the middle of the fifteenth century, a large Ottoman army under the command of Sultan Mehmet II succeeded in destroying the Eastern Roman Empire by capturing Constantinople (1453). The bulwark against deep Muslim advances into Europe had fallen and produced overwhelming shock but the reaction of secular rulers afterward illustrated indifference to the crusading movement despite papal attempts at marshaling new campaigns. Pope Nicholas V summoned a crusade to liberate Constantinople only months after the city's fall, but no European rulers responded positively. His successor, Callistus III took an oath upon his papal consecration to liberate the former imperial capital and sent cardinals on a preaching mission to numerous areas on Christendom. Although some rulers responded to the pontiff's call, the military focus shifted closer to home when Mehmet II's army arrived at the gates of Belgrade in 1456.

Pius II (r. 1458–1464) prioritized the liberation of Constantinople and called the secular rulers of Christendom to a meeting at Mantua in 1459 to discuss plans for the new crusade. Despite his urgent appeal no major secular rulers came to the congress. Pius issued several documents concerning the crusading movement including one asserting papal authority to levy taxes on the faithful, without temporal ruler approval, to finance crusades (*Adversus impiam*, 1460) and mandating a universal Christian obligation to support the crusade in person or through monetary contribution (*Ezechielis*, 1463).[18] Frustrated at the lack of temporal support for his crusade to liberate Constantinople, Pius II took the unprecedented step of becoming a crusader personally in the hope secular rulers would be ashamed to see the aged pontiff marching off to war. The pontiff arrived in Ancona to lead the crusade, but disease broke out in camp and Pius II died, ending the crusade before it launched. Despite the lack of concrete action by secular rulers to support papal demands, the crusading movement continued to generate interest and activity as twelve indulgence campaigns were authorized between 1444 and 1502 to finance crusades (Tyerman 2006, p. 872). However, secular monarchs were more concerned about internal affairs and checking the policies of fellow European rulers than liberating ancient Christian territory in the East.

The sixteenth century witnessed the height of Ottoman power, especially during the reign of Sultan Suleiman the Magnificent (r. 1520–1566), who added significant territory to the empire including large areas of Eastern Europe. The battle between the Cross and Crescent in the sixteenth century centered on controlling the Mediterranean Sea and witnessed coastal pirate raids, island sieges, and epic sea battles. Suleiman's forces achieved victory at Rhodes in 1522 but suffered an ignoble defeat against Christian forces at Malta in 1565. Although popes granted indulgences for the defense of the Christian areas under Ottoman assault, warriors did not respond in numbers reminiscent of the crusading past. At the end of the sixteenth century, Pope Pius V (r. 1566–1572) attempted to rally large numbers of Christian warriors to repel the impending Ottoman invasion fleet. Most European rulers ignored the pope's pleadings and only a coalition comprised of military manpower from Spain, Venice, and the Papal States was assembled in the Holy League that won victory at Lepanto in 1571. Sailors and soldiers of the League were granted the plenary indulgence for their participation, and the resultant victory was established as a memorial on the Church's liturgical calendar.[19] Victory at Lepanto stopped Ottoman seaward expansion and resulted in the shifting of Turkish military priorities to land conquests in Europe, especially the capture of Vienna.

The Ottomans believed the long-sought victory at Vienna was achievable at the end of the seventeenth century during the reign of Mehmet IV, who allowed Kara Mustafa to break the truce with the Hapsburgs and launch an invasion. Emperor Leopold I sent desperate pleas to his allies to come to the aid of the city now invested with Ottoman troops. A three-month siege resulted in much death and destruction in Vienna but the arrival of allied forces under the command of Polish king Jan Sobieski turned the tide. Pope Innocent XI (r. 1676–1689) promised the plenary indulgence for Christian warriors who participated in the campaign in accordance with previous crusading privileges. Sobieski's famed Winged Hussars broke the Ottoman defenses and secured a Christian victory in September 1683. The last Turkish siege of Vienna represented the farthest Ottoman incursion into Europe. The succeeding centuries witnessed the decline of the Ottoman Empire and its eventual disbandment after the First World War.

The crusading movement in this period centered mostly on secular indifference. While popes continued to proclaim crusades and offer spiritual incentives for warriors to participate in the campaigns, the internal focus of European secular rulers produced a general feeling of apathy toward crusading on a large scale. This feeling and the impact of events in the papacy during the fourteenth century produced significant changes in the relationship between Church and State, which produced the end of the crusading movement.

Conclusion

The complex interaction between Church and State was illustrated throughout the crusading movement and exhibited times of cooperation, control, and indifference. Crusading was a papal innovation and as the influence of the papacy on secular rulers waxed and waned through the centuries, there was a concomitant impact on crusading. As secular rulers became more independent of the Church and more concerned with internal matters and the consolidation of their political power, their desire to engage in crusading expeditions requested of the papacy decreased. The crisis in the papacy during the fourteenth century, with the Avignon Papacy and the subsequent Great Western Schism, spurred a change in Church-State attitudes as the papacy suffered a loss of prestige and political sway.[20] This papal crisis resulted in growing disinterest for the crusading movement in German territory and France in the fifteenth century. In the sixteenth century, central Europe and the papacy were consumed by the religious revolt of Martin Luther and other Protestant leaders, as well as Ottoman incursions into eastern and southern imperial territories. The seventeenth century witnessed a continued interest in crusading from the papacy and those regions that bordered Turkish-occupied areas. The rise of anti-religious intellectuals in the Enlightenment brought a change in perspective to the crusades. These campaigns were mocked and derided by anti-Catholic authors, such as Voltaire and David Hume, seeking to lessen the influence of the Church in European society by painting the crusades, as "wasteful, pointless, ruined by excessive papal ambition for worldly power, an example of the corrosive fanaticism of the Middle Ages" (Tyerman 2011, p. 67). Despite the growing criticisms, the crusades continued to attract attention and impacted European culture through published histories, art (in particular the nineteenth-century Crusade Rooms at Versailles by King Louis-Philippe I), and theater. Medieval saints who participated in crusades, such as Louis IX of France, drew popular devotion and national recognition. In the Muslim world, the crusades were forgotten events until the late nineteenth and early twentieth century with the decline of the Ottoman Empire and a change in Muslim perception of its history. That change in historical perception was influenced by European colonial efforts and the use of crusader imagery during them (Tyerman 2011, p. 150). Modern Islamic understanding of the crusades is an artificially constructed memory embraced initially by Arab nationalists in the 1970s and then by Islamic terrorist organizations as a means of recruitment (Madden 2005, pp. 217–222).

Ultimately, the crusading movement ended because the spiritual and political world in which it originated, flourished, and persisted, changed. Indeed, "the Crusade did not disappear from European culture because it was discredited but because the religious and social value systems that had sustained it were abandoned" (Tyerman 2006, p. 918). The crusading movement reflected the interaction between Church and State in Europe over the centuries moving through periods of cooperation, control, and indifference. Changes to the interaction between Church-State in the Western world brought forth the end of the unique crusading movement. Transformations in Western society as a whole moved attitudes about the crusades from indifference to rejection so that both Church and State, the main actors in the centuries-long crusading movement, now express guilt and shame for their creation and participation in these unique military religious expeditions.[21]

Notes

1. See Susan Reynolds, *Fiefs and Vassals: The Medieval Evidence Reinterpreted* (Oxford: Clarendon Press, 1994) for an alternative view and discussion of feudalism.
2. For a discussion of the definition and use of the term "feudalism," see Richard Abels, "The Historiography of a Construct: 'Feudalism' and the Medieval Historian," *History Compass* 7/3 (2009): 1008–1031.
3. An excellent study of the controversy is provided by Uta-Renate Blumenthal, *The Investiture Controversy: Church and Monarchy from the Ninth to the Twelfth Century* (Philadelphia: University of Pennsylvania Press, 1995 [1988]).

4. Historians debate what constitutes a crusade and how to describe the campaigns. A review of the debate and the various schools of thought is found in Giles Constable, "The Historiography of the Crusades" in A.E. Laiou and R.P. Mottahedeh, eds., *The Crusades from the Perspective of Byzantium and the Muslim World* (Washington, D.C.: Dumbarton Oaks Research Library Collection, 2001), 1–22. There are five schools of thought among historians concerning the question of what a crusade was: the generalists, popularists, traditionalists, pluralists, and the traditional-pluralists. See Norman Housley in *Contesting the Crusades* (Malden, MA: Blackwell Publishing, 2006).

5. Aeneas Sylvius Piccolomini (later Pope Pius II) in *Opera omnia* defined *passagium*. See Norman Housley, "Pope Pius II and Crusading," *Crusades* (Journal of the Society of the Study of the Crusades and the Latin East), vol. 11, 2012, 221.

6. The requirement for spousal consent was lifted in the thirteenth century by Pope Innocent III.

7. The example of the brothers Geoffrey and Guy, who sold property to the abbey of St. Victor in Marseilles, is provided in Christopher Tyerman, *God's War: A New History of the Crusades* (Cambridge, MA: The Belknap Press of Harvard University Press, 2006), 27.

8. Eyewitness accounts were produced by Fulcher of Chartres, Raymond of Aguilers, Peter Tudebode, and the anonymous author of the *Gesta Francorum*. Later authors include Robert the Monk, Guibert of Nogent, and Ralph of Caen.

9. William's eldest son, Robert Curthose, and son-in-law, Stephen of Blois, traveled in this group.

10. The so-called Massacre of Jerusalem is one of the modern myths embraced about the crusades. An excellent discussion of this event see Benjamin Z. Kedar, "The Jerusalem Massacre of 1099 in the Western Historiography of the Crusades," *Crusades*, vol. 3, The Society for the Study of the Crusades and the Latin East (Burlington, VT: Ashgate Publishing Company, 2004).

11. The capture of Tripoli in 1109 solidified the four territories known as the Crusader States: The Kingdom of Jerusalem, the County of Edessa, the Principality of Antioch, and the County of Tripoli.

12. King Baldwin II died in 1131 without male issue. Melisende, his daughter, was married to Fulk V of Anjou. When Baldwin II died, Fulk and Melisende ruled as monarchs until 1143 when Fulk died in a freak riding accident. Their son, Baldwin III, was not of maturity but was proclaimed king under the regency of his mother Queen Melisende. The County of Edessa was ruled by Joscelin II, a distant and distracted ruler who fought with

Raymond, the Prince of Antioch, and was absent during Zengi's siege and capture of Edessa.

13. The ramifications of the sack of Constantinople reverberate to the modern day and continue to hamper the relationship between Eastern and Western Christians.

14. See *Quia maior* and *Ad liberandam* in *Crusade and Christendom: Annotated Documents in Translation from Innocent III to the Fall of Acre, 1187–1291*, ed. Jessalynn Bird, Edward Peters, and James M. Powell (Philadelphia: University of Pennsylvania Press, 2013), 107–112 and 124–129.

15. Frederick's claim to the throne was through marriage to the daughter of King John of Brienne—although Frederick promised not to claim the throne and depose John.

16. See Régine Pernoud, *The Crusaders*, trans. Enid Grant (San Francisco: Ignatius Press, 2003 [1959]).

17. Louis took the cross again in 1267 but did not leave for the crusade until 1270.

18. See Norman Housley, "Pope Pius II and Crusading," *Crusades*, vol. 11, The Society for the Study of the Crusades and the Latin East (Burlington, VT: Ashgate Publishing Company, 2012), 209–247.

19. It was originally known as the Memorial of Our Lady of Victory but Gregory XIII changed the name to Our Lady of the Rosary in 1573. It is still celebrated on October 7.

20. The Avignon Papacy marks the time when popes resided in southern France for nearly seventy years from 1309–1378, and the Great Western Schism involved multiple claimants to the papacy from 1378–1417.

21. The crusades are frequently portrayed negatively in secular education and the media. Although there were positive usages of crusader imagery in the mid-twentieth century (e.g., General Eisenhower titled his memoir about the Second World War, *Crusade in Europe*), the more recent modern mindset involves rejection and repudiation of the crusades, as evidenced by scores of colleges and universities changing their crusade-themed mascots. The influential Catholic media personality (and now bishop), Rev. Robert Barron, condemned the crusading movement and the Church's involvement in his video series and book *Catholicism* (2010).

FURTHER READING

Housley, N. 2008. *Fighting for the Cross—Crusading to the Holy Land*. New Haven: Yale University Press.
Housley's fascinating tome is more than just a recitation of the history of the major crusades, it is a thematic work covering topics such as logistics, military

structure and strategy, spiritual preparations and focus on crusade, and the reality of daily life during the arduous campaigns.

Madden, T.F. 2005. *The New Concise History of the Crusades Updated Edition.* New York: Rowan & Littlefield Publishers, Inc.

Madden provides a succinct, yet detailed account of the crusading movement directed towards Muslims in the Holy Land and North Africa. The work includes the history of the campaigns as well as a discussion on the misrepresentation and myths in the modern world concerning the crusades.

Tyerman, C. 2006. *God's War—A New History of the Crusades.* Cambridge, MA: Harvard University Press.

An extensive and meticulous volume on the crusading movement. Tyerman discusses the origin of Christian holy war, the beginnings of the crusading movement, and provides detailed narratives of all forms of crusading including to the Holy Land, the Baltic regions, and against heretics and enemies of the papacy as well as describing life for Christians and Muslims in the Latin East.

REFERENCES

Bloch, M., 1961a. *Feudal Society, Volume I—The Growth of Ties of Dependence.* Translated by L.A. Manyon. Chicago: The University of Chicago Press.

———. 1961b. *Feudal Society, Volume II—Social Classes and Political Organization.* Translated by L.A. Manyon. Chicago: The University of Chicago Press.

Brundage, J.A. 1969. *Medieval Canon Law and the Crusader.* Madison: University of Wisconsin Press.

Bysted, A.L. 2015. *The Crusade Indulgence: Spiritual Rewards and the Theology of the Crusades, c. 1095–1216, in History of Warfare.* Vol. 103. Boston: Brill.

Cushing, K.G. 2005. *Reform and Papacy in the Eleventh Century: Spirituality and Social Change.* Manchester: Manchester University Press.

Housley, N. 2008. *Fighting for the Cross—Crusading to the Holy Land.* New Haven: Yale University Press.

Madden, T.F. 2005. *The New Concise History of the Crusades Updated Edition.* New York: Rowan & Littlefield Publishers, Inc.

Phillips, J. 2007. *The Second Crusade—Extending the Frontiers of Christendom.* New Haven: Yale University Press.

Riley-Smith, J. 1980. Crusading as an Act of Love. In *The Crusades–The Essential Readings,* ed. Thomas F. Madden, 2006. Malden: Blackwell Publishing, Ltd.

———. 1997. *The First Crusaders, 1095–1131.* Cambridge: Cambridge University Press.

———. 2002. *What Were the Crusades?* 3rd ed. San Francisco: Ignatius Press.

Tyerman, C. 2006. *God's War—A New History of the Crusades.* Cambridge, MA: Harvard University Press.

———. 2011. *The Debate on the Crusades.* Manchester: Manchester University Press.

CHAPTER 4

Church and State in Enlightenment Europe

Korey D. Maas

Immanuel Kant (1996, p. 62) famously remarked, 'If it is asked "Do we now live in an *enlightened age?*" the answer is "No, but we do live in an age of *enlightenment."'* If one understands the Enlightenment to have been an intellectual project revolving around the 'central value' of 'universal religious toleration' (Marshall 2006, p. 1), Kant was clearly correct that he did not, even in the late eighteenth century, live in an enlightened age. When he wrote in 1784, for example, Catholics were free neither to worship openly nor to hold public office in England, and the same prohibitions applied to Protestants in France. In Portugal, within Kant's adulthood, more than 50 people were burned as heretics over the course of a single decade. Even by the same definition of Enlightenment, however, Kant might also have been correct to suggest that his age was nonetheless undergoing enlightenment. Despite the continuing existence of various legal disabilities, and even sporadic episodes of active persecution, a general trend—though certainly not a linear progression—is discernible in the years from the conclusion of the Thirty Years' War through the French and American Revolutions. In greatly simplified schematic terms,

K. D. Maas (✉)
Department of History, Hillsdale College, Hillsdale, MI, USA
e-mail: kmaas@hillsdale.edu

© The Author(s), under exclusive license to Springer Nature
Switzerland AG 2023
S. Holzer (ed.), *The Palgrave Handbook of Religion and State
Volume II*, https://doi.org/10.1007/978-3-031-35609-4_4

the trajectory in church-state relations was from the principle and practice of an intolerant state establishment of religion, through tolerant establishment, toward tolerant disestablishment.

In contrast to Kant and others, however, the present chapter treats the Enlightenment not as a coherent intellectual program, but simply as the historical era delimited by the Peace of Westphalia and the French Revolution. Contrary, for example, to Peter Gay's (1966, p. 3) famous declaration that there was 'only one Enlightenment,' which rejected Christianity, recent historiography has emphasized multiple, concurrent Enlightenments, including a decidedly 'Religious Enlightenment' (Sorkin 2008), a more specifically 'Christian Enlightenment' (Rosenblatt 2006), and even a still narrower 'Catholic Enlightenment' (Lehner 2016). More obviously, and despite the use of singular terms in the title above, early modern Europe was of course comprised of multiple 'states,' most of which were home to more than one 'church.' A preliminary acknowledgment of the multiplicity of churches, states, and even Enlightenments coexisting in Europe through the seventeenth and eighteenth centuries thus allows important distinctions to be made between the oft-treated theories associated with the Enlightenment (understood as a philosophical movement) and the actual policies implemented by various states, with respect to various churches, throughout the Enlightenment (understood as a historical era).

Not only did the laws of each nation differently address the relationship between the state and its church(es), but even within individual states these relationships, and the motives informing them, were far from static through the seventeenth and eighteenth centuries. Of equal import, though, is the similar disparity evident among early modern theorists; even among those commonly identified as representative, it remains impossible to identify a singular 'Enlightenment theory' of church-state relations. It is this diversity in both theory and practice, therefore, on which the present chapter focuses, not least because later thinkers were well aware of it when contemplating possibilities for subsequent religious settlements, as, for example, in the nascent United States. As Enlightenment Europe provided the most immediate background and reference point for early Americans, the sheer variety of its ideas and practices presented them with what might be considered, from the early modern perspective, a number of 'live options' in church-state relations.

Intolerant Establishment

Often implicit in conventional dating of the Enlightenment from the year 1648 and the conclusion of the Thirty Years' War is the supposition that 'The Wars of Religion finally convinced Christians that it was time to live and let live' (Lewis 1995, p. 17). Their cessation thus signaled the advent of an enlightened 'political liberalism' (Fukuyama 1992, p. 260) exemplified by its 'modern, secularized concept of the State,' which would be 'divorced from the duty to uphold any particular faith' (Skinner 1978, p. 352). On one influential account, the notions of toleration that attended such convictions were in some places embraced so swiftly that they were the 'responsible opinion' of 'the mass of men' already by 1660 (Jordan 1940, pp. 9, 467). Complicating such conclusions, however, are subsequent events leading others to judge the 1680s, for example, 'one of the most religiously repressive decades in European history' (Marshall 2006, p. 17). Nor can the continuance, and even intensification, of religious persecution be downplayed simply by suggesting that 'practice lagged behind theory' (Kamen 1967, p. 217). As has been perceptively observed in response to some popular narratives, 'If we consider the separation of church and state as a feature of liberalism, it becomes even more obvious that Enlightenment was not necessarily liberal' (Domínguez 2017, p. 285).

Given the centuries-long norm of religious establishment, and the persecution of dissent that attended it, a rapid and widespread rejection of the status quo could hardly have been expected. Medieval justifications for intolerant establishment were deemed part of the church's legitimate patrimony and could not simply be dismissed by the Catholic faithful. Indeed, the oath taken by Louis XVI at his 1774 coronation as King of France simply fulfilled the mandate pronounced already by the Fourth Lateran Council of 1215, that all secular authorities 'take an oath that they will strive in good faith and to the best of their ability to exterminate in the territories subject to their jurisdiction all heretics' (Schroeder 1937, p. 243).

Catholic sovereigns were hardly alone in understanding this to be their solemn duty, however. Whatever other medieval doctrines Protestants had rejected with the Reformation, the magistrate's obligation to uphold the true faith and to suppress error and division was not typically among them. As Edward Gibbon (1788, p. 436) observed, they 'imposed with equal rigour their creeds and confessions; they asserted the right of the magistrate to punish heretics with death.' The 1647 Westminster Confession is representative in proclaiming among the duties of the magistrate to ensure 'that unity and peace be preserved in the Church, that the truth of God be kept pure and entire, that all blasphemies and heresies be suppressed'; the Larger Catechism composed at the same time specifically identifies the toleration of false religion as a sin against the second commandment (Beeke and Ferguson 1999, pp. 233, 141).

Among Protestants as well as Catholics, preserving unity in the faith was understood not only to be a religious obligation, however; it was also deemed a political imperative, necessary for the prevention of civil unrest. Already a century earlier, French Chancellor Michel de L'Hôpital had concisely articulated the consensus opinion when he declared it 'madness to hope for peace, repose and friendship among persons of different religion' (Knecht 2010, p. 102). Subsequent conflicts, culminating in the Thirty Years' War, ostensibly confirmed this conviction, and the Peace of Westphalia, rather than rejecting it, might just as easily be read as enshrining it. Effectively reiterating the 1555 Peace of Augsburg's principle of *cuius regio, eius religio* (whose the region, his the religion), Westphalia further legitimized state prescription and proscription of religion. The enforcement of a single faith across the Holy Roman Empire having proved impossible, however, the locus of establishment simply devolved to its constituent territories.

To be sure, specific terms of the Peace did limit magistrates' regulation of religion, but the effects of such stipulations should not be exaggerated. Minority confessions which had enjoyed limited toleration in a given territory before a specified year (typically 1624) were to retain tolerated status; this concession, however, applied only to the Catholic, Lutheran, and Reformed confessions, and their toleration did not extend to the public exercise of their faith. In Hegel's (1802, p. 192) pithy formulation, any further privileges were matters of 'grace contrary to the law.' Moreover, the law might regularly be contravened in less gracious ways, as in the early eighteenth century when Reformed churches in the Palatinate were seized for Catholic use, or when some 30,000 Lutherans were forcibly expelled from Salzburg. Finally, though, the terms of Westphalia, even when honored, applied only to the territories of the Empire, leaving sovereigns in France, England, and elsewhere a more or less free hand.

In Catholic France, where long asserted and frequently conceded Gallican rights resulted in what was effectively a 'royal church' (Aston 2006, p. 22), Protestants had nonetheless enjoyed, by royal edict, a toleration more liberal than that granted minorities across most of Europe. Just as it looked like the Peace of Westphalia might remake imperial territories in the French image, however, Louis XIV initiated a series of policies culminating in the revocation of that toleration afforded by the 1598 Edict of Nantes. Most notably, the quartering of dragoons in Protestant homes was intended to provoke either conversion or emigration. The policy's perceived effectiveness was remarked upon by the Marquise de Sévigné, who quipped that the dragoons made 'very good missionaries' (Kaplan 2007, pp. 339–340), as well by the king himself, who could assert that 'the larger portion of our subjects of the said R.P.R. [*Religion Prétendue Reformée*, 'so-called Reformed religion'] have embraced the Catholic Religion' (Maclear 1995, p. 5). That claim served to justify Louis' conclusion that the century-long policy of toleration was no longer necessary. From 1685, therefore, exercise of the Reformed religion, even privately, was again proscribed; children born to Reformed parents were to be baptized and raised in the Catholic faith; Reformed clergy were ordered into exile and, in a reversal of the *dragonnades'* policy aims, the prerogative of emigration was denied the laity. Giving the lie to Louis' earlier conversion estimates, the number of Huguenots who illegally exited France quickly dwarfed the number of Lutherans later exiled from Salzburg; approximately 200,000 fled over the first decade, with another 100,000 following in subsequent years.

Nor did the Crown's revived interest in the enforcement of religious unity end with the suppression of Protestantism. In the same year that he revoked the Edict of Nantes, Louis XIV turned his attention to the realm's more ancient Waldensian population, pressuring the Duke of Savoy into dealing with them no less severely than the King himself had dealt with the Huguenots. In the following century, even certain movements which could, with varying degrees of plausibility, claim fidelity to the Catholic Church were targeted for suppression by the Crown. The Jansenists, who had originally welcomed the proscription of French Protestantism, were themselves accused of crypto-Protestant theology and became the focus of consistent controversy through the latter half of the seventeenth century. Finally, in 1730 Louis XV declared that *Unigenitus*, a papal condemnation of Jansenist theology, was to be regarded not only as the law of the church, but also as that of the state. Following a 1724 edict strengthening the previous century's already severe anti-Protestant policy, the proscription of Jansenism has with some warrant been deemed the 'high tide of absolutism' with respect to the Crown's legislation of religion (Van Kley 1996,

p. 127). But the irony of the monarchy turning on those who had applauded the earlier suppression of the Huguenots was heightened a generation later when the French Jesuit Order—long Jansenism's most bitter foe—was itself dissolved, and its property confiscated, by government order. The royal justification remained the same: it was done 'for the sake of the peace of my realm' (Van Kley 1996, p. 158).

Given the upheavals contributing to and consequent upon French attempts to establish and maintain religious uniformity, it is perhaps unsurprising that some were tempted to idealize the confessional situation elsewhere. Voltaire, for example, looked optimistically across the channel, remarking that in England 'there are thirty [religions], and they live in peace and happiness' (Voltaire 1980, p. 41). Even at the time of his writing in 1733, though, that assessment could only have surprised England's Catholic minority; throughout the prior century it would have struck even most Protestants as absurd. Since the early sixteenth century, the Church of England had been a far more explicitly 'royal church' than that of France. From Henry VIII's formal break with the papacy in 1534, parliament repeatedly proclaimed Protestant monarchs to be 'the only Supreme Head in earth of the Church of England,' with the right and duty to 'repress and extirp all errors, heresies, and other enormities' (Bray 1994, p. 114); oaths acknowledging the same were required of any who would hold public office. Successive parliaments likewise promulgated Acts of Uniformity which not only proscribed rites other than those in the state-sanctioned Book of Common Prayer, but also compelled weekly attendance at Prayer Book services. Though clearly affecting the realm's Catholic populace, most statutes were equally applicable to Protestant dissenters, with Puritans often being explicitly targeted.

Through the early seventeenth century, however, and despite having themselves been persecuted by Tudor and Stuart governments, even Puritans remained unwilling to disavow the state's coercive power in religious matters. Not only did they maintain, as in the Larger Catechism, the entirely traditional view that toleration was a theological error; they affirmed the similarly traditional conviction that religious division breeds political division. Briefly gaining control of parliament in mid-century, they were thus equally eager to employ its machinery for legislating ecclesiastical policy. In addition to foreseeable acts to abolish the episcopacy and proscribe the Prayer Book, a Presbyterian majority in 1648 passed its own 'Ordinance for the Punishing of Blasphemies and Heresies,' prescribing death for any who denied the Trinity, and imprisonment even for the

Baptists whom the Crown had viewed as their fellow dissenters. Enforcement of the law was prevented only by the army coup of the same year; even under the resulting Protectorate, however, few parliamentarians proved willing to question the state's authority respecting religion (Coffey 2006b, pp. 48, 59).

Legislative sentiment remained similarly unchanged with the Restoration's return to the *status quo ante*. Not only were royal supremacy, episcopacy, and the Prayer Book again reaffirmed; the reinstituted Act of Uniformity was strengthened by new legislation. The Corporation and Test Acts required all public office-holders to be communicant Anglicans, while the Quaker and Conventicle Acts further proscribed non-established religious gatherings. That more than 10,000 English Quakers alone were imprisoned over the next quarter century partially informs John Coffey's (2006b, p. 60) conclusion that, contrary to sanguine proclamations about the 'mass of men' embracing tolerationist sentiment by 1660, the subsequent two and a half decades witnessed even a 'persecution of Protestants by Protestants without parallel in seventeenth-century Europe.' Persecution of Catholics by Protestants of course continued through the following century, with James II's attempt to procure their toleration precipitating instead his own deposition and exile, and further anti-Catholic legislation.

In practice, intolerant state establishment and legislation of religion clearly remained the norm through much of the Enlightenment, in Catholic and Protestant territories alike. As previously noted, however, the qualifying phrase, 'in practice,' cannot be blithely dismissed as if European practice were wildly out of step with predominate theory. To the contrary, a number of prominent representatives of Enlightenment thinking on church-state relations explicitly articulated their approval—even encouragement—of religious establishment, uniformity, and coercion. Thomas Hobbes is illustrative of the problems attending too simple an equation between the Enlightenment, liberalism, and the separation of church and state. One of the early architects of liberal political theory, Hobbes (1909, pp. 460, 132) was explicit in endorsing the notion that the civil sovereign was not only a kingdom's 'Supreme Pastor,' but even its 'Mortall God.' Rather than secularizing politics, as liberal theory is often understood to have done, Hobbes' own emphases served to sacralize the political in a fashion far more extreme than French Gallicanism or English royal supremacy had ever envisioned. The lesson Hobbes took from England's civil war was that the separation of power inevitably bred conflict, which could only be prevented by its concentration in a single sovereign authority; a kingdom divided, even by a distinction of temporal and spiritual authorities, could not stand (1909, pp. 139–140, 253). Indeed, he would assert (1909, p. 457), the divided loyalties inherent in Christian commonwealths were the 'most frequent praetext of Sedition, and Civill Warre.' A unified civil polity, therefore, 'ought also to exhibite to God but one Worship,' and 'It belongeth therefore to him that hath the Soveraign Power, to be Judge, or constitute all Judges of Opinions and Doctrines' (1909, pp. 283, 137). Unsurprisingly, therefore, Hobbes (1840, p. 167) took a dim view of those who 'declared themselves for a liberty in religion.'

Despite his reputation as an early champion of free speech and free thought, Baruch Spinoza's liberalism likewise made little room for the free exercise of religion. Any suggestion that religious authority ought to be separated from political authority, Spinoza (1891, p. 251) dismissed as 'too frivolous to merit refutation.' Instead, he insisted (1891, p. 249), like Hobbes before him, that 'Divine right is entirely dependent on the decrees of secular rulers' and that only 'sovereign rulers are the proper interpreters of religion and piety.' It is therefore 'the function of the sovereign only … to determine how we should obey God' (1891, pp. 249–250). Moreover, even the narrower freedom of opinion Spinoza otherwise advocated remains ominously qualified by his profession that the sovereign 'has the right to treat as enemies all men whose opinions do not, on all subjects, entirely coincide with its own,' and even 'to put citizens to death for very trivial causes' (1891, p. 258).

Similarly, Hobbesian sentiments were expressed well into the eighteenth century, with Jean-Jacques Rousseau (1923, p. 116) offering that, in Christian Europe, 'only Hobbes' had rightly discerned the necessity of unifying religion and politics under the authority of the state. Hobbes had nonetheless erred, Rousseau thought, in believing Christianity might be compatible with political unity since, in his announcement of a spiritual kingdom distinct from the political, Jesus himself had 'brought about the internal divisions which have never ceased to trouble Christian peoples' (1923, p. 115). Rousseau (1923, p. 121) therefore advocated the establishment of a 'purely civil profession of faith of which the Sovereign should fix the articles.' Indeed, he is willing to name such an establishment 'a form of theocracy, in which can be no pontiff save the prince,' and in which 'the State is the Church' (1923, pp. 117, 122). Not only could this princely pontiff therefore banish any who refused to accept the doctrines pronounced by him, Rousseau acknowledged, but if anyone, 'after publicly recognising these dogmas, behaves as if he does not believe them, let him be punished by death' (1923, p. 121).

TOLERANT ESTABLISHMENT

As evidenced above, Enlightenment philosophers were hardly univocal in advocating a 'secularized' state 'divorced from the duty to uphold any particular faith.' Neither, however, were temporal magistrates of one mind about the prudence of coercing religious unity. Indisputably, princely legislation of religion remained the norm well into the eighteenth century, and nowhere in that century was comprehensive toleration embraced by state authorities. Nonetheless, qualified toleration was afforded minorities in various places throughout the seventeenth and eighteenth centuries, and in fact even earlier. Rather than practice lagging behind theory, then, it was often the case that practice preceded it. That such toleration remained qualified, however, serves to highlight the problem of speaking of toleration in absolute terms. Indeed, the example of the Dutch Republic serves even to complicate attempts to speak absolutely about the concept of 'establishment.'

With respect to state toleration of religious pluralism, the United Provinces were recognized already in the early modern era as a source of that 'light which spreads over all the world' (Fitzpatrick 2000, p. 25). As early as 1579 the Union of Utrecht had brought an end to the heresy trials which had, in the previous half-century alone, led to at least 1500 executions in the Netherlands. The Union granted a broad freedom of religion, specifying that none were to be persecuted for their beliefs. Though never technically 'established,' the Reformed Church was, however, the only legally recognized 'public' church. It alone received public funding and was allowed public worship; likewise, only its members were eligible to hold public office. Despite such restrictions, the promise of non-persecution and the freedom to worship at least privately ensured that the Republic was often held up—both positively and negatively—as an example of tolerant pluralism.

Voltaire's previously quoted assessment is merely one example of the opinion that, by the end of the seventeenth century, England also evidenced the viability of a religiously pluralistic state. The legislation most immediately associated with that opinion, the 1689 Act of Toleration, is equally important, however, for what it reveals about the limited scope of pluralism even in a state then—and now—often held up as a model of early modern toleration. Catholics, Deists, Unitarians, atheists, and Jews (who had been allowed to resettle in England only a generation earlier) remained excluded from its provisions. Dissenting Protestants were granted the coveted right of public worship, provided their religious houses were licensed with the Crown; the Corporation and Test Acts remained in force, however, effectively excluding all but communicant Anglicans from holding public office. Indeed, as Benjamin Kaplan (2007, p. 348) observes, read 'literally,' the Toleration Act merely exempted dissenters from the penalties of statutes that themselves remained the law of the land.

The Act is further revealing, though, for the light its passage sheds on the rationale for its provisions. This is especially the case when comparing the 1689 Act with James II's 1687 Declaration of Indulgence. Similarly granting free exercise to dissenting Protestants, the Declaration had gone further in extending toleration to Catholics. Dissenters quickly embraced the freedoms granted to them, but with their erstwhile Anglican opponents objected to the privileges extended to Catholics, fearing they were merely a strategic step toward realizing James' explicitly expressed desire that 'all the people of our dominions were members of the Catholic Church' (Browning 1996, p. 387). The French Revocation of the Edict of Nantes only two years earlier merely heightened such suspicions. Though perhaps not blatantly *quid pro quo*, it is not difficult to discern in the 1689 Toleration Act a concession to those Protestants who, though dissenting from the established faith, allied with it in support of the Glorious Revolution and the return of a Protestant monarch to the throne. The sufficiently common interests of all the realm's Protestants thus became a staple of the new king's own rhetoric. Addressing parliament in 1701, for example, William III exhorted his hearers, 'Let there be no other distinction heard of amongst us for the future, but of those, who are for the Protestant Religion, and the present establishment, and of those, who mean a Popish Prince' (Cobbett 1809, p. 1331).

If England thus came to be perceived as paradigmatic of religious establishment coexisting with (limited) religious toleration, it likewise exemplifies the often pragmatic and political justifications for the latter. England was hardly unique in this respect, however. Despite the narrowly circumscribed concessions granted minority confessions by the Peace of Westphalia, it often remained the case that local edicts of toleration 'went far beyond what was technically permitted by the Peace' (Whaley 2000, p. 186). Just as often, such 'grace contrary to the law' was motivated by mundane political and economic factors. The dramatic reduction of

Brandenburg's population by the Thirty Years' War, for example, induced Elector Frederick William to welcome not only his co-religionists fleeing post-Revocation France, but also those Jews expelled from Vienna in 1670. The same motivation informed the similarly named (and similarly Reformed) Prussian King Frederick William I's welcoming of Lutherans exiled from Salzburg early in the next century. Nor were Protestant rulers alone in rationalizing toleration on such grounds. Sovereigns in Catholic territories could similarly be swayed, and economic factors certainly informed Emperor Joseph II's late eighteenth-century patents of toleration for Protestants, Orthodox, and Jews alike.

If the largely pragmatic considerations motivating such policies partially undermine the narrative of enlightened liberal theory being the primary motivator of increasing religious toleration, the popular reactions to such policies further call into question claims about the 'mass of men' being amenable to them. Many Catholics, for example, were dismayed by Emperor Joseph's concessions to Protestants—limited though they were, and applicable only to those first submitting to six weeks of instruction by a Catholic priest—and local nobles, bishops, and office-holders regularly attempted to obstruct their implementation. French Catholics of the same decade were no more welcoming of Louis XVI's 1787 edict of toleration, despite its terms being far less generous than those of the earlier Edict of Nantes, or even of Joseph's patent. While restoring certain civil rights to the Reformed minority—to marry and to own property, for example—it did not lift restrictions on public worship or holding public office. Clergy and laity alike protested nonetheless, and half the realm's regional *parlements* opposed the edict. A similar scenario had played out even more dramatically only a few years earlier among England's Protestants, when parliament finally granted a degree of relief to the realm's Catholics. As with the French edict of 1787, the 1778 Catholic Relief Act, though only minimally restoring civil rights and still prohibiting public worship and public office to Catholics, was vigorously opposed by the populace. The subsequent 'Gordon Riots' that engulfed the capital have with little exaggeration been called 'the bloodiest episode of religious violence in London's history' (Kaplan 2007, p. 354).

That even late eighteenth-century concessions of toleration tended to be pragmatically motivated, stringently qualified, and popularly opposed does not of course mean that principled theoretical arguments for even more expansive toleration were unheard of. Indeed, viewed especially in their early modern context, 'pragmatic' and 'principled' arguments could largely converge. This is the case most obviously because one of the principles long justifying the proscription of pluralism was itself pragmatic in nature. The state's coercive enforcement of religious uniformity was often predicated on the conviction that confessional pluralism precipitated civil unrest; confessional unity was therefore understood as a prerequisite to political harmony. Though events of the sixteenth and seventeenth centuries ostensibly lent some credence to that conviction, subsequent evidence increasingly allowed it to be called into question. Citing the evidence of London's Stock Exchange, for example, Voltaire (1980, p. 41) could observe that 'Jew, Mohammedan and Christian deal with each other as though they were all of the same faith.' By way of contrast, and with similar reference to economic activity, it could already be claimed in seventeenth-century London that religious intolerance was 'a mischief unto Trade' (Kaplan 2007, p. 351).

With regard to politics more specifically, Benjamin Kaplan (2007, p. 351) points to events of the mid-eighteenth century—the Jacobite Rebellion in Britain and France's involvement in the Seven Years' War—as important turning points for popular conceptions of the relationship between confessional and civic loyalties, when, despite fears to the contrary, British Catholics and French Protestants alike largely refrained from exploiting those conflicts. But similar evidence of political loyalty despite theological dissent had been acknowledged already a century earlier, when, for instance, Louis XIV commended the allegiance of his Huguenot subjects during the Fronde. Such examples, in addition to the relative peace and prosperity of confessionally mixed territories such as the Netherlands—and non-European realms which, Voltaire (1912, p. 23) insisted, provided ample evidence of both 'toleration and tranquility'—emboldened theorists to question the longstanding assumption that religious pluralism was an inevitable precipitant of civil discord.

Not only did such examples call into question the assumption of 'all former ages,' that religious diversity was 'dangerous, if not pernicious to civil government' (Hume 1983, vol. 5, p. 130); it further prompted the novel counter-claim that the real threat to civil harmony was the attempt to compel unity. Thus, Voltaire (1912, p. 25) could make the dual claim that 'toleration, in fine, never led to civil war; intolerance has covered the earth with carnage.' John Locke (2010, p. 60) forwarded the similar thesis that '[i]t is not the Diversity of Opinions, (which cannot be avoided) but the Refusal of Toleration to those that are of different Opinions, (which might have been granted) that has produced all the Bustles and Wars that have been in the Christian World, upon account of Religion.' In this light, Roger Williams (1963, vol. 1, p. 328) could bluntly denounce religious persecution as a 'State-killing doctrine,' and David Hume (1983, vol. 5, p. 130) would refer to the 'fatal experience' of this doctrine as critically informing the embrace of 'the paradoxical principle and salutary practice of toleration.'

Hume's interpretation is also echoed by those modern scholars who argue that the 'Enlightenment did not bring a more principled view of toleration, but rather diffused the conviction that allowing a certain degree of religious diversity was less dangerous for social cohesion and civil authority than pursuing religious uniformity' (Domínguez 2017, p. 279). In Protestant lands, however, a certain kind of 'principled' view of toleration was increasingly voiced in the seventeenth and eighteenth centuries. Those raised on Protestant martyrologies such as John Foxe's *Acts and Monuments*, and who imbibed the 'black legend' of anti-Catholic polemic, could be persuaded that, despite clear evidence of Protestant states being similarly persecutory, religious intolerance was an essentially Catholic phenomenon and therefore inherently incompatible with Protestant principles. The English dissenter Micaiah Towgood, for example, could rail against coercion in religion as 'the very ESSENCE of Popery' (Coffey 2013, p. 67), and Locke worked with the assumption that Catholics were doctrinally 'obleigd [*sic*] to propagate their religion by force' (Walmsley and Waldman 2019, p. 1114). Where such convictions were ingrained, there was little to prevent obvious implications being drawn even about Protestant magistrates. John Milton's (2007, p. 300) assessment of the 'new forcers of conscience' in mid-seventeenth-century England, that 'New *Presbyter* is but old *Priest* writ large,' is merely the best known of regular objections that Protestants were behaving as 'papists in principle' (Miller 2012, p. 69) by imitating 'popish tyranny of conscience' (De Roover and Balagangadhara 2009, p. 131). William Penn could thus denounce coercion as fundamentally 'anti-protestant' (Coffey 2006a, p. 170), and Locke would similarly theorize that persecution for aberrant theology could not be justified 'upon Protestant principles' (Walmsley and Waldman 2019, p. 1115).

Whatever influence arguments for increased toleration had, however, they were not necessarily calls for disestablishment. Indeed, defenses of both toleration and establishment were frequently combined. William Paley (1845, p. 276) could thus call for both a 'comprehensive national religion' and a 'complete toleration of all dissenters from the established church.' A half-century earlier his fellow Anglican William Warburton (1811, p. 250) had similarly argued that 'the obvious remedy' against the discord provoked by religious persecution was 'to *establish* one church, and give a *free toleration* to the rest.' Even the *enfant terrible* Hume, an advocate of the skepticism often assumed to undergird Enlightenment theories of toleration, could unabashedly argue for the maintenance of an established religion as 'advantageous to the political interests of society' (1983, vol. 3, p. 136).

The compatibility of religious establishment and religious toleration was, in fact, typically assumed—even if not always practiced—by early modern inheritors of a coherently literal medieval concept of toleration. In this understanding, toleration was predicated not on uncertainty or indifference, but rather on the conviction that tolerated behaviors or beliefs were in fact objectively evil, and therefore deserving of proscription and punishment. Nonetheless, prudence might dictate that they be allowed for the sake of preventing a greater evil (Bejczy 1997). Viewed in this light, tolerant establishment was less the result of novel Enlightenment principles than it was simply the broader application of pre-modern principles as necessitated by post-Reformation religious pluralism. This understanding, however, also illuminates the new objections raised at the very moment religious toleration had become increasingly common across Europe. These came not, as might have been anticipated, from old-guard champions of intolerant establishment, but from the 'enlightened' who resented the implications of tolerance as prudential forbearance. The Deist Thomas Paine (1984, p. 85), for example, objected that 'Toleration is not the *opposite* of Intolerance, but is the *counterfeit* of it. Both are despotisms. The one assumes to itself the right of withholding Liberty of Conscience, and the other of granting it.' Similarly, therefore, Goethe proclaimed that 'toleration should really only be a transitory attitude' (Whaley 2000, p. 191).

TOLERANT DISESTABLISHMENT

Though few magistrates were swayed by claims such as Goethe's, tolerance as traditionally understood did prove transitory at least in France and the Netherlands, both of which had formalized religious disestablishment before the close of the eighteenth century. In the context of ongoing religious strife attending the Revolution, the French Constitution of 1795 finally relieved the state of any obligation to privilege one confession or restrict the exercise of another; in the same year the French-influenced

Batavian Revolution effected the transition from the Dutch Republic to the Batavian, which in 1796 also followed the lead of France in formally separating church and state. Though these are the only examples of European nations embracing disestablishment in the eighteenth century (with neither arrangement surviving unrevised through the nineteenth century), arguments in favor of separating church and state had increasingly come to prominence. At least with respect to disestablishment, then, it might be warranted to speak of practice lagging behind theory. John Locke, whose famous *Letter Concerning Toleration* goes beyond simple toleration to implicitly advocate disestablishment, is perhaps representative. Though welcoming the new practice legislated by England's 1689 Toleration Act, he privately spoke of its provisions as merely 'beginnings' and 'foundations' on which a more expansive religious liberty might be built. (Locke 1978, p. 633).

That the practice of disestablishment was slow to match its defense in theory might be partially explained not only by the sheer novelty of such an arrangement, but also by the radicalism associated with its early advocates. In the same way that Magisterial Protestants could increasingly shun religious coercion as inherently 'papist,' so too could they be dissuaded from entertaining disestablishment as an essentially 'Anabaptist' principle. The Anabaptists had long been popularly associated with sedition and civil unrest in view of the Peasants' War and Münster Rebellion of the early sixteenth century, but also on account of the political theology expressed, for instance, in the Schleitheim Confession (Lindberg 2000, p. 133), which deemed Christianity incompatible with oath-taking, office-holding, or the exercise of political power. Though clearly supportive of church-state separation, the implications were far more extreme, entailing the complete separation of Christians from politics; in a society still overwhelmingly constituted of professing Christians, such a proposal could only be heard as disastrously anarchical. Unsurprisingly, then, even more modest proposals for disestablishment could be perceived as slippery slopes to the destabilizing politics associated with Anabaptism. The Irish cleric Philip Skelton is illustrative of such perceptions. His satirical *Proposals for the Revival of Christianity* (1736, p. 29) accurately summarizes the increasingly vocal claims of Baptists, Quakers, and others that 'the greater Part of the Mischiefs that have fallen out in Civil Society, has been owing to the Mistake of establishing some Religion, and mixing Government and that together.' However, he not only notes (1736, p. 9) that the obvious conclusion of such a premise would be 'to demolish the present

Established Church,' but further suggests (1736, p. 28) that 'The only safe Way' to prevent discord 'is to have Magistrates of no Religion.'

While such caricatures of disestablishmentarians as political and theological radicals might sometimes have confirmed prejudices against them, appeals to an etymologically literal 'radicalism' could also have the opposite effect. Given the shared conviction of Protestants, that the Reformation's aim was to restore the church to its roots (*radices*) by trimming away unwarranted medieval accretions, dissenting Protestants of various stripes could argue that the post-Constantinian entanglement of church and state was just the sort of 'Catholic' aberration that consistent Protestants ought to reject. Roger Williams (1963, vol. 3, p. 184) is representative in complaining that true Christianity 'fell asleep in *Constantines* bosome,' when 'the *Gardens* of *Christs Churches* turned into the *Wildernesse* of *Nationall Religion*' (1963, vol. 4, p. 442). Thus, long before Thomas Jefferson, Williams (1963, vol. 1, p. 392) could invoke the desirability of a 'wall of Separation,' and argue (1963, p. 3.384), as Locke later would, that the 'proper end of the *civill Government*' does not touch on affairs of the church, but merely 'the *peace* and *welfare* of the *state*.'

Though expressing a decidedly minority opinion, Williams' arguments were echoed by English dissenters and articulated, for example, in the parliamentary debates of the late 1640s. Among those embracing Williams' position was Sir Henry Vane the Younger, who had become familiar with Williams in America, and whose brother Walter would employ John Locke as a secretary. Vane's published opinions were subsequently repeated in the work of his assistant—and Locke's acquaintance—Henry Stubbe, who similarly maintained Williams' conviction that magistrates have no power to 'judge of *Spirituall* matters' (Stubbe 1659, p. 28). The similarities with and connections to Locke are almost certainly not coincidental. Locke's own argument, though often deemed representative of the 'secular' or 'Enlightenment' theory of church-state relations, not only differs dramatically from those of Enlightenment thinkers such as Hobbes or Spinoza; just as significantly, precisely where it does differ it appears indebted to the earlier positions articulated by devout (if dissenting) Protestants.

Though Locke does not invoke the language of disestablishment, Mark Goldie rightly concludes that his 'overriding case is for the separation of the church from the state' (Goldie 2010, p. xii). His 1689 *Letter concerning Toleration* is explicit, for example, in advertising his intention to 'distinguish exactly the Business of Civil Government from that of Religion, and to settle the just Bounds that lie between the one and the other,' and concludes that each should 'contain it self within its own Bounds' (Locke 2010, pp. 12, 61). As Williams had before him, then, Locke can assert (2010, pp. 42, 12) that 'there is absolutely no such thing, under the Gospel, as a Christian Commonwealth,' because the state's purview encompasses only '*Civil Interests.*' Thus, in the same vein as the mid-century dissenters who had taken up Williams' arguments, he (2010, p. 13) similarly makes the case that 'the Care of Souls is not committed to the Civil Magistrate.' Viewed in the light of such predecessors, then, it does indeed appear that Locke offers no 'new or unprecedented arguments' (Murphy 2001, p. 149); his significance, rather, is in synthesizing and popularizing existing arguments 'from a place of real influence in society, as part of a circle that included leading politicians and aristocrats, and as a member of the establishment Anglican church' (Miller 2012, pp. 78–79). That is, perhaps as much as the content of the *Letter* itself, it was Locke's status that allowed the argument for tolerant disestablishment to be heard as something other than the 'loser's creed' of disadvantaged religious minorities.

CONCLUSION

If the above is illustrative of an Enlightenment trajectory in church-state relations from intolerant establishment, through tolerant establishment, toward tolerant disestablishment, it also reveals that this process was 'fitful, contingent, and untidy' (Collins 2009, p. 610). Moreover, it was by no means universal. Despite late eighteenth-century experiments in France and Holland, therefore, as late as 1871 the American Presbyterian Robert Dabney (1976, p. 880) could say of the 'separation and independence of Church and State' that 'No Christian nation holds it to this day, except ours.' Indeed, though tolerant establishment had become increasingly common in the eighteenth century, intolerant establishment continued to remain the norm in many European territories, perhaps most notably on the Iberian peninsula. Clearly, then, there was in practice no single 'Enlightenment' relationship between church and state. Nor, again, was there a single, representative Enlightenment theory concerning such relations. Given the great diversity in both the theory and practice of Enlightenment Europe's church-state relations—and a similar diversity of motives and effects—intolerant establishment, tolerant establishment, and tolerant disestablishment all remained 'live options' well beyond the eighteenth century.

FURTHER READING

Coffey, John. 2000. *Persecution and Toleration in Protestant England, 1558–1689.* London: Longman.

  Coffey surveys early modern English theory and practice concerning state regulation and toleration of religious difference, defending a traditional view of the importance of the late seventeenth century as the turning point in popular Protestant understanding, while also emphasizing the earlier influence of radical dissenters.

Conyers, A.J. 2009. *The Long Truce: How Toleration Made the World Safe for Power and Profit.* Waco: Baylor University Press.

  Conyers provocatively argues that Enlightenment toleration, rather than diminishing the state's authority, was intended to expand its power by marginalising the influence of the church.

Grell, Ole Peter, and Roy Porter, eds. 2000. *Toleration in Enlightenment Europe.* Cambridge: Cambridge University Press.

  The essays here collected provide concise synthetic analyses together with a number of geographical case studies in seventeenth- and eighteenth-century thought and practice.

Kaplan, Benjamin J. 2007. *Divided by Faith: Religious Conflict and the Practice of Toleration in Early Modern Europe.* Cambridge, MA: The Belknap Press.

  Kaplan's social history contests the popular narrative of toleration progressing in the wake of Enlightenment ideals, emphasising instead the local and pragmatic phenomena of confessional coexistence.

REFERENCES

Aston, Nigel. 2006. Continental Catholic Europe. In *The Cambridge History of Christianity, vol. 7, Enlightenment, Reawakening and Evolution 1660–1815,* ed. Stewart J. Brown and Timothy Tackett, 15–32. Cambridge: Cambridge University Press.

Beeke, Joel R., and Sinclair B. Ferguson, eds. 1999. *Reformed Confessions Harmonized.* Grand Rapids: Baker.

Bejczy, I. 1997. *Tolerantia*: A Medieval Concept. *Journal of the History of Ideas* 58: 365–384.

Bray, Gerald, ed. 1994. *Documents of the English Reformation, 1526–1701.* Cambridge: James Clark & Co.

Browning, Andrew, ed. 1996. *English Historical Documents, 1660–1714.* London: Routledge.

Cobbett, William, ed. 1809. *Parliamentary History of England.* Vol. 5. London: R. Bagshaw.

Coffey, John. 2006a. Scepticism, Dogmatism and Toleration. In *Persecution and Pluralism: Calvinists and Religious Minorities in Early Modern Europe*, ed. Richard Bonney and D.J.B. Trim, 149–176. Oxford: Peter Lang.

———. 2006b. The Toleration Controversy during the English Revolution. In *Religion in Revolutionary England*, ed. Christopher Durston and Judith Maltby, 42–68. Manchester: Manchester University Press.

———. 2013. Church and State, 1550–1750: The Emergence of Dissent. In *T&T Clark Companion to Nonconformity*, ed. Robert Pope, 47–74. London: Bloomsbury.

Collins, Jeffrey R. 2009. Redeeming the Enlightenment: New Histories of Religious Toleration. *Journal of Modern History* 81: 607–636.

Dabney, Robert L. 1976. *Lectures in Systematic Theology*. Grand Rapids: Zondervan.

De Roover, Jakob, and S.N. Balagangadhara. 2009. Liberty, Tyranny and the Will of God: The Principle of Toleration in Early Modern Europe and Colonial India. *History of Political Thought* 30: 111–139.

Domínguez, Juan Pablo. 2017. Introduction: Religious Toleration in the Age of Enlightenment. *History of European Ideas* 43: 273–287.

Fitzpatrick, Martin. 2000. Toleration and the Enlightenment Movement. In *Toleration in Enlightenment Europe*, ed. Ole Peter Grell and Roy Porter, 23–68. Cambridge: Cambridge University Press.

Fukuyama, Francis. 1992. *The End of History and the Last Man*. New York: Free Press.

Gay, Peter. 1966. *The Enlightenment: An Interpretation. The Rise of Modern Paganism*. New York: W.W. Norton.

Gibbon, Edward. 1788. *The History of the Decline and Fall of the Roman Empire*. Vol. 5. Dublin: Luke White.

Goldie, Mark. 2010. Introduction. In *John Locke: A Letter Concerning Toleration and Other Writings*, ed. Mark Goldie, ix–xxiii. Indianapolis: Liberty Fund.

Hegel, G.F.W. 1802. *The German Constitution*. In *Hegel's Political Writings*, trans. T.M. Knox, 143–242. Oxford: Clarendon, 1964.

Hobbes, Thomas. 1840. Behemoth: The History of the Causes of the Civil Wars of England. In *The English Works of Thomas Hobbes*, ed. William Molesworth, vol. 6, 161–418. London: John Bohn.

———. 1909. *Hobbes's Leviathan: Reprinted from the Edition of 1651*. Oxford: Clarendon.

Hume, David. 1983. *The History of England, 6 vols*. Philadelphia: Liberty Fund.

Jordan, W.K. 1940. *The Development of Religious Toleration in England*. Vol. 4. Cambridge, MA: Harvard University Press.

Kamen, Henry. 1967. *The Rise of Toleration*. New York: McGraw-Hill.

Kant, Immanuel. 1996. An Answer to the Question: What Is Enlightenment? In *What Is Enlightenment? Eighteenth-Century Answers and Twentieth-Century Questions*, ed. James Schmidt, 58–64. Berkeley: University of California Press.

Kaplan, Benjamin J. 2007. *Divided by Faith: Religious Conflict and the Practice of Toleration in Early Modern Europe*. Cambridge, MA: The Belknap Press.

Knecht, R.J. 2010. *The French Wars of Religion, 1559–1598*. 3rd ed. London: Routledge.

Lehner, Ulrich L. 2016. *The Catholic Enlightenment: The Forgotten History of a Global Movement*. Oxford: Oxford University Press.

Lewis, Bernard. 1995. *Cultures in Conflict: Christians, Muslims, and Jews in the Age of Discovery*. Oxford: Oxford University Press.

Lindberg, Carter, ed. 2000. *The European Reformations Sourcebook*. Oxford: Blackwell.

Locke, John. 1978. In *The Correspondence of John Locke*, ed. E.S. de Beer, vol. 3. Oxford: Clarendon.

———. 2010. A Letter Concerning Toleration. In *John Locke: A Letter Concerning Toleration and Other Writings*, ed. Mark Goldie, 1–67. Liberty Fund: Indianapolis.

Maclear, J.F., ed. 1995. *Church and State in the Modern Age: A Documentary History*. Oxford: Oxford University Press.

Marshall, John. 2006. *John Locke, Toleration and Early Enlightenment Culture*. Cambridge: Cambridge University Press.

Miller, Nicholas P. 2012. *The Religious Roots of the First Amendment: Dissenting Protestants and the Separation of Church and State*. Oxford: Oxford University Press.

Milton, John. 2007. On the New Forcers of Conscience under the Long Parliament. In *Milton: The Complete Shorter Poems*, ed. John Carey, Rev. 2nd ed., 298–300. London: Longman.

Murphy, Andrew R. 2001. *Conscience and Community: Revisiting Toleration and Religious Dissent in Early Modern America*. University Park: Pennsylvania State University Press.

Paine, Thomas. 1984. In *Rights of Man*, ed. Henry Collins. London: Penguin.

Paley, William. 1845. *Paley's Moral and Political Philosophy*, ed. A.J. Valpy. Philadelphia: Uriah Hunt & Son.

Rosenblatt, Helena. 2006. The Christian Enlightenment. In *The Cambridge History of Christianity, vol. 7, Enlightenment, Reawakening and Revolution 1660–1815*, ed. Stewart J. Brown and Timothy Tackett, 283–301. Cambridge: Cambridge University Press.

Rousseau, Jean-Jacques. 1923. The Social Contract. In *The Social Contract and Discourses by Jean-Jacques Rousseau*, ed. G.D.H. Cole, 3–123. London: J.M. Dent and Sons.

Schroeder, H.J., ed. 1937. *Disciplinary Decrees of the General Councils: Text, Translation and Commentary.* St. Louis: Herder.

Skelton, Philip. 1736. *Some Proposals for the Revival of Christianity.* London: Globe.

Skinner, Quentin. 1978. *The Foundations of Modern Political Thought.* Vol. 2. Cambridge: Cambridge University Press.

Sorkin, David. 2008. *The Religious Enlightenment: Protestants, Jews, and Catholics from London to Vienna.* Princeton: Princeton University Press.

de Spinoza, Benedict. 1891. Theologico-Political Treatise. In *The Chief Works of Benedict de Spinoza*, ed. R.H.M. Elwes, vol. 1, 1–266. London: George Bell and Sons.

Stubbe, Henry. 1659. *An Essay in Defence of the Good Old Cause.* London: n.p.

Van Kley, Dale. 1996. *The Religious Origins of the French Revolution: From Calvin to the Civil Constitution, 1560–1791.* New Haven: Yale University Press.

Voltaire. 1912. On Toleration. In *Toleration and Other Essays by Voltaire*, ed. Joseph McCabe, 1–87. New York: G.P. Putnam's Sons.

———. 1980. *Letters on England.* Leonard Tancock, trans. London: Penguin.

Walmsley, J.C., and Felix Waldman. 2019. John Locke and the Toleration of Catholics: A New Manuscript. *The Historical Journal* 62: 1093–1115.

Warburton, William. 1811. The Alliance between Church and State. In *The Works of the Right Reverend William Warburton*, ed. Richard Hurd, vol. 7, 21–296. London: T. Cadeli and W. Davies.

Whaley, Joachim. 2000. A Tolerant Society? Religious Toleration in the Holy Roman Empire, 1648–1806. In *Toleration in Enlightenment Europe*, ed. Ole Peter Grell and Roy Porter, 175–195. Cambridge: Cambridge University Press.

Williams, Roger. 1963. *The Complete Writings of Roger Williams*, 7 vols. New York: Russell and Russell.

CHAPTER 5

Royal Supremacy and Religious Tolerance in Early Modern England

David J. Davis

In 1689, the Toleration Act granted freedom of worship to nonconformists in England, though it maintained the superior position of the Church of England as not only the established church but also the only church granted special privileges (e.g., mandatory tithes, representation in government, etc.). John Locke, in the same year, published *A Letter Concerning Toleration*, which went even further in separating the church and the state from one another. In the *Letter* Locke wrote,

> the whole Jurisdiction of the Magistrate reaches only to these Civil Concernments; and that all Civil Power, Right and Dominion, is bounded and confined to the only care of promoting these things; and that it neither can nor ought in any manner to be extended to the Salvation of Souls, these following Considerations seem unto me abundantly to demonstrate ... [and then later on] I cannot be saved by a Religion that I distrust, and by a Worship that I abhor. It is in vain for an Unbeliever to take up the outward shew of another mans Profession. (Locke 1689, pp. 7–8, 27)

D. J. Davis (✉)
Department of History, Houston Christian University, Houston, TX, USA
e-mail: ddavis@hbu.edu

© The Author(s), under exclusive license to Springer Nature   77
Switzerland AG 2023
S. Holzer (ed.), *The Palgrave Handbook of Religion and State Volume II*, https://doi.org/10.1007/978-3-031-35609-4_5

Although Locke's idea of separating church and state had many detractors, notably the outspoken Anglican cleric Jonas Proast, the Toleration Act and Locke's *Letter*, taken together, represent for many scholars the beginning of religious tolerance in an England that had been strapped with legislated state interference in ecclesiastical affairs since the establishment of the Act of Supremacy (c.1534) by Henry VIII. For historians like Perez Zagorin in *How the Idea of Religious Toleration Came to the West*, the breakthroughs of the seventeenth century were among the first forays against the oppressive and corrosive relationship of the church and the state, which had plagued Europe for centuries (2003, p. 7). The following two centuries, with key works like Voltaire's *Treatise on Tolerance*, witnessed a nearly complete separation in many European kingdoms and principalities.

Fortunately, this triumphant, and misleading, narrative of religious tolerance's slow development out of the bloodshed and chaos of the Reformation and the Wars of Religion has been challenged by many scholars over the past two decades (Grell and Scribner 1996). It is evident from much of this scholarship that there certainly was during the early modern period a slow redefining of religious tolerance, particularly at the macroscopic level of religions' relationship to the state, and this process of redefinition continues to this very day. Tolerance in medieval and early modern Europe was seen almost as a necessary evil, a recognition that human corruption limits our ability to recognize and/or comprehend the truth. As such, society is forced, for the sake of peace and charity, to permit certain intractable differences of theology and philosophy to persist, and the boundaries in which these differences were permitted to persist were patrolled by ecclesiastical and political authorities. That being said, even within the most circumscribed contexts of pre-1700 Europe, there were important and profound expressions of religious tolerance from the early official decrees of religious tolerance like the Peace of Augsburg to the fact that some Catholic Parisians rescued their Protestant neighbors from the mob violence of the St. Bartholomew's Day massacre in 1572 (Kaplan 2007, p. 251).

This chapter highlights some of the ways that religious tolerance operated in early modern England. Although royal supremacy is not often regarded as a context for successful religious tolerance, the religio-political context that was created by Henry's power grab did at least provide, if not consciously create, space for kinds of religious tolerance. Of course, it is easy to dismissively conclude with Joseph Lecler that royal supremacy simply resulted in 'The dissolution of the monasteries, the confiscation of their properties by the crown, the substitution of royal for episcopal visitation to control clerical discipline, all this completed the thorough occupation of the ecclesiastical domain by the civil power' (Lecler 1960, p. 334). Not exactly the most opportune context for religious tolerance. However, recent scholarship on the evolution of ideas of tolerance in Western Europe throws this sweeping and bleak conclusion into doubt. The fact that the king took control of the English Church is not in doubt, but the mere *de jure* establishment of civil supremacy over religion can overshadow the much more complicated terrain upon which this authority was worked out. This chapter intends to highlight some of the more apparent complications surrounding church-state relations in early modern England, in particular the spaces that existed for degrees and kinds of religious toleration that, although not fitting into Locke's grand scheme of tolerance, regarded other belief systems with charity, if not official permission.

ROYAL SUPREMACY AND ITS CRITICS

Undoubtedly, one of the most circumscribed contexts for religious tolerance in the early modern period was England following the Act of Supremacy. Henry VIII's break with the Roman Catholic Church in the 1530s, in his efforts to secure a divorce from Katherine of Aragon and marry his mistress Anne Boleyn, is not normally associated with tolerant practices. In fact, shortly after legislating his reformation and marrying Anne, Henry had his friend and former Lord Chancellor Thomas More along with one of England's most celebrated clerics, Cardinal John Fisher, executed for their opposition to Henry's schemes. Of course, Henry already was well-learned in the art of religious oppression, having executed Lutherans in the 1520s, and following More and Fisher, he proceeded to execute many others of various creeds, including a leading Catholic nobleman Sir Thomas Percy, the Franciscan John Forrest, and an outspoken, young Protestant woman named Anne Askew. Needless to say, Henry was not shy about carrying out the language of the Act of Supremacy, to which he required all public officials swear an oath:

> the king, our sovereign lord, his heirs and successors, kings of this realm, shall be taken, accepted, and reputed the only supreme head in earth of the Church of England, called *Anglicana Ecclesia*; and shall have and enjoy, annexed and united to the imperial crown of this realm, as well the title and

style thereof, as all honors, dignities, preememinences, jurisdictions, privileges, authorities, immunities, profits, and commodities to the said dignity of the supreme head of the same Church belonging and appertaining; and that our said sovereign lord, his heirs and successors, kings of this realm, shall have full power and authority from time to time to visit, repress, redress, record, order, correct, restrain, and amend all such errors, heresies, abuses, offenses, contempts and enormities, whatsoever they be, which by any manner of spiritual authority or jurisdiction ought or may lawfully be reformed, repressed, ordered, redressed, corrected, restrained, or amended, most to the pleasure of Almighty God, the increase of virtue in Christ's religion, and for the conservation of the peace, unity, and tranquility of this realm; any usage, foreign land, foreign authority, prescription, or any other thing or things to the contrary hereof notwithstanding. (Gee and Hardy 1896, p. 243)

Henry's arguments for supremacy did not rest solely upon legislative/jurisdictional grounds. Defenders of royal supremacy pointed to biblical models of church-state relations in the Old Testament kings. The most devout rulers of Israel and Judah (e.g., Kings David, Josiah, and Hezekiah) played central roles in the development of the religion (e.g., returning the Ark of the Covenant to Jerusalem, building the Temple, etc.) and were active in instituting religious reforms, often returning the people to the worship of Yahweh. In this vein of looking backward for inspiration, defenders argued that Henry's Act restored an ancient rite of the English monarchy, which had been stripped from them by the papacy in the middle ages. Both indigenous British kings, like King Lucius in the second century, and the later Anglo-Saxon kings in the seventh century established the religion of their respective dominions. The civil authority, not that in Rome, held the power to determine religion in the realm. Following this logic, defenders of Royal Supremacy drew upon Lutheran propaganda about the Bishop of Rome's abandonment of Christian truth and discipline, and therefore in order to follow Christ, England must break with Rome. England, it was argued, cannot serve two masters: the Pope and Christ. The essence of this argument was visually depicted on the title page of Henry's first authorized English Bible, the Great Bible (c.1538). In the frontispiece woodcut, the king is depicted receiving the Word of God from Christ who reaches down from heaven, directly above Henry who sits upon his throne, receiving scripture as the true, earthly head of the English Church. Henry hands copies of the *Verbum Dei* to his closest advisers, Thomas Cromwell and Thomas Cranmer, who distribute it to the nobles and the clergy (Ferrell 2008, p. 76).

Royal supremacy, however, was not without its detractors, despite the arguments put forward in works like Thomas Starkey, *An exhortation to the people instructing them to unity and obedience* (c.1536). Although the idea that the civil authority should govern the church was not entirely foreign, the immediacy and sweeping nature of royal supremacy alarmed many people. Perhaps the most significant, and personal, critic of Henry's actions was his cousin, Bishop Reginald Pole in his book *Pro Ecclesiae Unitatis Defensione* (c.1536). Pole argued that Henry's actions were not only criminal but also would undoubtedly sow strife and sedition in England. Pole went on to compare Henry to the Roman emperors Nero and Domitian (both of whom were known for their persecution of Christianity) and to warn Henry by reminding him of the fate of their shared ancestor Richard III, who seized power that was not properly his own (Bernard 2005, p. 220). Later Catholic critics like Nicholas Sander in *De Visibili Monarchia Ecclesiae* (c.1571) went further to subjugate the role of all civil authority beneath the ecclesiastical authority, arguing that the latter is a purer expression of God's will, whereas the former exists only because humans are corrupted by sin. Although English Protestants were much more hesitant to question the monarch's authority in matters of religion, puritans and Presbyterians under Queen Elizabeth I, taking their lead from continental voices like Theodore Beza, were not afraid to declare that the monarchy had not reformed sufficiently the English church. Later in the seventeenth century, nonconformist groups like the Quakers, Muggletonians, and others followed the puritan lead in criticizing the status quo of royal supremacy.

Even those that wholeheartedly supported royal supremacy did not think that the monarch possessed *carte blanche* authority over the English religion. First, the text of the Act made the power invested in the king contingent upon 'the pleasure of Almighty God,' and as W.J. Torrance Kirby has pointed out, this means 'The Civil Magistrate's ecclesiastical power is derived from Christ's, but must be viewed as subordinate to his, limited in the extent or degree of its sway, and finally, distinct from Christ's power in kind' (Kirby 1990, p. 124). The Elizabethan cleric Richard Hooker's highly influential *The Lawes of Ecclesiastical Polity* framed this authority structure as two realms, one spiritual and one temporal, with Christ as the head of the spiritual and the monarch as head of the temporal. However, the monarch's power and authority found their source in

Christ. Subordinating the monarch under the authority of Christ became even more important when Elizabeth I ascended in 1558. Not only did Elizabeth exchange the title of 'head' of the Church for 'supreme Governor,' in order to avoid ruffling the patriarchal feathers of her Parliament and episcopal hierarchy, but also her Act of Supremacy, as Daniel Eppley explains, 'invalidated any sort of arbitrary doctrinal canons emanating solely from the will of the prince' (Eppley 2007, p. 145).

RELIGIOUS PLURALISM UNDER ROYAL SUPREMACY

In examining royal supremacy, it is easy to neglect the grassroots reality of early modern England. Far from a homogenous, or even relatively homogenous, religious society, deep doctrinal and ecclesiological divides emerged in England beneath the seamless unity asserted by the 1534 Act. Beyond the theoretical critics of Henry's authority, by the middle of the seventeenth century, almost two dozen distinct religious groups were on offer in England. A Presbyterian minister Thomas Edwards carefully cataloged 16 distinct dissenting sects in his book *Gangraena* (c.1645). Edwards did not even bother including the different Roman Catholic groupings in England or the growing Deist sect. Edwards was a preacher at London's Christ Church in Newgate Street, which was just down from St. Paul's Cathedral, and in his ministry to the people of the capital, Edwards became alarmed at the increasingly powerful drift toward sectarianism that many of the population were taking. However, these divides were not as novel as Edwards seems to have thought. Even 20 years before Edwards's book, when Charles I became king in 1625, there were already puritans, Presbyterians, conformists, non-conformists, anabaptists, Familists, Arminians, and Calvinists under the 'Protestant' umbrella. There were Jesuit, Carthusian, and Dominican clergy being hidden away by Catholic recusant families, along with a large population of quietly conforming Catholics known as 'church papists,' who attempted to balance a recognition of both the authority of the monarch and the bishop of Rome. The smorgasbord of religious groups in early modern England highlights the importance of G.R. Elton's comment that 'The realm as a whole was never sworn to the supremacy' (Elton 1972, p. 229). Although church attendance was required (punishable by a fine, which was inconsistently enforced) and churches were required to employ the Book of Common Prayer in the weekly parish services, outside of Sunday services the average English person's religion was very much his/her own.

What Royal Supremacy stressed much more than individual conformity to the state religion, beyond the basic expression of church attendance, was peace and stability within the kingdom. Alexandra Walsham has argued, 'compromise was to be preferred above the evils of schism,' an attitude which on the whole 'fostered a kind of de facto pluralism and toleration' (Walsham 2006, pp. 201–2). This principle held true even in industries like the print trade, which seemingly would have been under much greater scrutiny than other areas of society. That is not to say the print trade lacked regulation, but in terms of their personal beliefs, printers were treated, on the whole, like other tradesmen (Watt 1994, p. 43). For example, printers like John Cawood who served as the royal printer for the Roman Catholic Queen Mary I were permitted to continue doing business after the restoration of Protestantism under Elizabeth. Cawood also served as secretary to Nicholas Harpsfield (a Catholic apologist who was imprisoned for refusing to swear the oath of supremacy to the Queen), confirming Cawood's own religious leanings. Nevertheless, in the 1560s, Cawood printed editions of the Elizabethan homilies as well as the Book of Common Prayer and the New Testament, without impediment from royal censors. In the next century, a similar example can be seen in the career of the printer Henry Hills, who was able to successfully serve as a printer for the republican government under Oliver Cromwell as well as the restoration monarchies of both Charles II and his Catholic brother James II.

Likewise, one of Cawood's apprentices, Thomas East, was suspected throughout his long and successful career of having papist sympathies. In 1600, several of East's own apprentices sounded the alarm that a Jesuit conspiracy was being organized in East's printing house; however, no charges were filed and East's reputation suffered not a bit from the accusation. Other printers were even more brazen, wearing their private beliefs out in public by printing obviously Roman Catholic books. Between 1575 and 1580, a Catholic printer William Carter issued about a dozen blatantly papist texts by medieval writers like Thomas Kempis and Henry Suso, along with English translation of the Jesuit Gaspar de Loarte's devotions, the English Catholic Gregory Martin's *A treatise of schisme* (c.1578), and an edition of Bishop Fisher's *A spirituall consolation* (c.1578) (Davis 2013, pp. 81–3).

Although publications from Carter's London presses halted abruptly in 1580, the books themselves were not prohibited or hunted down and destroyed. Much more concerning to the authorities were publications like the Marprelate tracts that directly challenged ecclesiastical authority, and by extension, royal supremacy. Printed by the puritans John Penry and Robert Waldegrave between 1588 and 1589, the handful of pseudonymous tracts by 'Martin Marprelate' attacked the episcopal hierarchy with sweeping condemnation, as well as personal insults (Black 2008). While the authorship of the tracts is still debated by scholars, the Elizabethan government went to much greater lengths to squash these tracts, which smacked of schismatic sentiment, than any devotional or other religious literature that did not align with Anglican thought. Published works that inspired private religion, even if the content tended to more traditional modes of devotion, were much less threatening than direct challenges to the ecclesiastical status quo.

Recusancy and the Limits of Tolerance

Elsewhere, scholars have identified certain degrees of tolerance extending to some of the established Catholic recusant families around the kingdom. In *Catholicism and Community in Early Modern England*, historian Michael Questier has unearthed incredibly detailed networks of Catholic communication, exchange, and loyalty that crossed generations and international borders in the early modern world. Recusants could present a simple nuisance to the parish priest intent upon seeing his village committed to true religion. The popular preacher George Gifford exemplified a typical complaint among many ardent, reforming clergy, complaining that in his parish of Maldon he found it nearly impossible to overcome the papist sentiments of many of the locals, who were committed to the old religion (Walsham 2006, pp. 100, 112). Other traditional parishes were fortunate enough to have like-minded clergies like the conforming Catholic minister Christopher Trychay in Morebath, Devonshire, or Robert Parkyn in Adwick-le-Street, Yorkshire (Duffy 2001, p. 157). Nevertheless, recusants could present even more substantive challenges, beyond the local context. At Cowdray House, a large recusant network was organized by Anthony Browne, 1st Viscount Montague, who fostered a variety of social and religious connections that reached from the English government to the centers of Catholic reform in Europe (Questier 2006).

Unlike many other more traditionally minded English who conformed to the mandates of royal supremacy, while quietly maintaining their own beliefs outside of church, Catholic recusants refused to attend the Protestant service and many actively encouraged Roman Catholicism in

England by purchasing and distributing Catholic works, sending their sons to the English Catholic colleges in Europe, importing prayer beads, crucifixes, and other such devotional paraphernalia, and housing (and hiding) Catholic clergy in England. In October 1623, a church service of some 300 Catholics, worshipping in a room adjacent to the French embassy in London, was disastrously upset when the floor to the makeshift chapel collapsed, killing untold numbers of people. Although the Protestant presses pointed to the disaster as a sign of divine judgment against Catholicism, it is interesting that such a large gathering of Catholics in London was even possible almost a century after Henry VIII's break with Rome. Moreover, while their presence was frustrating to many and a serious concern to some, it does not seem to have come as a surprise to anyone in the city (Walsham 1994).

A pamphlet titled *A newyeares gifte dedicated to the Popes Holinesse* (c.1569) by Bernard Garter provided anti-Catholics with a visual aid to help identify dangerous objects. At the front of the short work, a foldout woodcut illustrated 15 different kinds of objects that typically indicate papist beliefs, including amulets with the Agnus Dei or the Virgin, prayer beads, and icons with pictures of kneeling saints (Davis 2013, p. 110). These activities, more than non-attendance at church, could find a recusant in hot water with the state. The greatest fear was not only of Catholic missionaries infiltrating the countryside but also the threat of a plot to upset the government (Milton 1995, p. 43). The gentleman Thomas Wilford was imprisoned in the 1580s after his London house—a meeting place for recusants in the city—was searched and papist books were found. Similarly, Thomas Vaux, 2nd Baron Vaux of Harrowden, was imprisoned for harboring the Jesuit priest Edmund Campion; however, his family continued to support English recusants at home and abroad.

A final consideration in this context is the relationships between different religious groups with one another. In other words, how did (if at all) Catholics and Protestants, recusants and Presbyterians, interact with one another in their everyday lives? While further research is needed to examine particular counties, parishes, and so on and at particular times—as certain moments in history tend to be much less tolerant than others—most recent scholarship identifies a much more powerful sense of charity and neighborliness than what one might expect. Certainly, Protestants reported on suspected recusants and Catholic conspirators (as we saw in the case of Thomas East's apprentices), as Catholics reported on reformers in other regions in Europe, the culture of local neighborhoods, as Ben

Kaplan reports, 'had the capacity to promote toleration' (Kaplan 2007, p. 251). Unlike the witchcraft craze of the same period, there never seems to have been a widespread appetite with the vast majority of the English to go heretic hunting. Other than a few historical moments of national crisis—the Gunpowder Plot, the English Civil War, and the Popish Plot—English neighbors tended to tolerate more than report upon one another. At the local level, people seem to have held in tension the deeply held theological differences with the practicalities of living in society and loving (and/or needing) many of those people with which they fundamentally disagreed about things like ecclesiastical authority, the nature (and number) of the sacraments, devotion given to saints and the Virgin, and so on.

THE MONARCHY AND CLERICAL DISSENT

If royal authority in matters of religion had a need to accommodate and compromise with the people of England, there was an equally powerful need for the monarch to tolerate his/her own ecclesiastical leaders, who often found the monarch's expression of royal supremacy unsatisfactory. Although the clergy was held to a higher standard of conformity than the English laymen, simple verbal assent to royal supremacy in the form of an oath was the norm. Only in exceptional circumstances was a minister's personal theology scrutinized any further. Nor was a cleric's family, or even personal history, necessarily held against them. John Donne, the renowned poet and dean of St. Paul's Cathedral from 1621 to 1631, was born to a family of recusants in Elizabeth's reign. Donne's family harbored priests and generally supported the Catholic cause in England. Donne was even refused a degree by both Oxford and Cambridge, because he refused to swear the oath of supremacy (Stubbs 2006, pp. 8–9). However, sometime around the end of the sixteenth century, Donne converted to the Anglican Church and quickly rose to prominence in James I's reign for his religious poetry and his sermons, after he was ordained in 1615. Although scholars today wonder if Donne ever fully shook off the creed of his family, these suspicions in his own day never amounted to anything more than rumor.

Disagreements between the church and state abound, demonstrating the fact that the reality of royal supremacy in England was never straightforward when it came to the institution of ecclesiastical policy. As Walsham points out, 'it would be wrong to imply that the Church meekly relinquished its role in the making of ecclesiastical policy,' after 1534 (Walsham

2006, p. 51). Indeed, almost every Tudor and Stuart monarch found themselves on tumultuous terms with at least some of their clergy at one point or another. Elizabeth's Archbishop Matthew Parker deprived many puritanical ministers in London of their positions for refusing to wear the appropriate clerical vestments, as required by the Book of Common Prayer. In 1604 at the Hampton Court Conference, King James I was given a petition signed by 1000 ministers, requesting further reforms of the English Church, including the abolition of Confirmation, the use of vestments, and using the sign of the cross during Baptism. The king rejected these requests entirely. Then, in 1662, Charles II shortly after the restoration of the monarchy ejected over 2000 ministers for refusal to conform to the Book of Common Prayer.

These examples, however, should not blind us to the large space of tolerance within which the clergy and the monarchy worked with one another. One potentially explosive example illustrates that not all disagreements led to utter discord. In the early 1560s, Queen Elizabeth's private chapel became a sore spot for monarchy-clergy relations, because the Queen had restored the traditional cross and candlesticks to the chapel's altar. The fact was so well known that John Martiall, an English Catholic living on the continent, dedicated his *A Treatise of the Crosse* (c.1564) to the Queen. The cross as a symbol often was lumped together with many other images and objects as too corrupted by Catholic worship to be permitted inside churches. Many churches already had removed crosses and crucifixes from their altars, rood screens, and windows, and even Elizabeth's clerical leaders like John Jewel, the bishop of Salisbury (an otherwise stout defender of royal supremacy), was critical of the cross. In fact, when the dean of St. Paul's cathedral Alexander Nowell preached against the image of the cross in 1565, the Queen who was among Nowell's audience shouted him down; however, the Queen never punished Nowell for his impertinence (Collinson 1983, pp. 130–1). In the following decade, the soon-to-be Archbishop of Canterbury, John Whitgift, warned the Queen to avoid making the mistake her father had made in seizing church property, which was lawfully protected by Magna Carta (Thompson 1948, p. 405). Even though it was an ill-advised move for Whitgift, it does not seem to have impeded his role in the church whatsoever.

CONCLUSION

Perhaps it is easy to dismiss such examples of forbearance and compromise as insignificant and paltry compared to the institution of religious liberty that slowly develops in the eighteenth and nineteenth centuries. It is equally easy to allow the violence of martyrdom to dominate the historical narrative of the period, as indeed many people in the early modern world did. John Foxe's martyrology *Actes and Monuments* was, after all, one of the bestselling folio books in early modern England. However, that would be to miss the point that despite the fervor with which religious beliefs were held and despite the importance they played in the larger socio-political milieu of the age, spaces and contexts remained available for religious tolerance. Their notion of tolerance was certainly different from ours, but that is not to say that it was entirely wrongheaded. As the philosopher John Gray writes, 'On this older view, toleration is a precondition of any stable *modus vivendi* among incorrigibly imperfect beings. If it has become unfashionable in our time, the reason is in part to be found in the resistance of a post-Christian age to the thought that we are flawed creatures whose lives will always contain evils' (Gray 1995, p. 18).

FURTHER READING

Eppley, Daniel. 2007. *Defending Royal Supremacy and Discerning God's Will in Tudor England*. New York: Ashgate.
    This book provides a recent study of royal supremacy in Tudor England. Eppley focuses upon the work of two theorists, Christopher St. Germain and Richard Hooker, examining not only the motivations and reasoning behind royal supremacy but also the subsequent efforts to defend it against its many critics.
Torrance Kirby, W.J. 1990. *Richard Hooker's Doctrine of Royal Supremacy*. Leiden: Brill.
    This book remains a profound analysis of perhaps the most influential early modern Anglican theologian's exposition on royal supremacy. Kirby's assessment approaches Hooker's ideas from both the political and theological contexts, from which they were born, offering a comprehensive analysis of the doctrine in the sixteenth century.
Walsham, Alexandra, and Charitable Hatred. 2006. *Tolerance and Intolerance in England, 1500–1700*. Manchester: Manchester University Press.
    This book is a magisterial analysis of mentalities and practices of religious tolerance in early modern England. Examining a variety of perspectives, Walsham sheds insight into the viewpoints of both those at the center of religious hegemony in England to those on the outskirts of its periphery. It remains a necessary starting point for any research on religious tolerance in the period.

REFERENCES

Bernard, G. 2005. *The King's Reformation: Henry VIII and the Remaking of the English Church*. London: Yale University Press.

Black, J., ed. 2008. *The Martin Marprelate Tracts: A Modernized and Annotated Version*. Cambridge: Cambridge University Press.

Collinson, P. 1983. *Godly People: Essays on English Protestantism and Puritanism*. London: Hambledon Press.

Davis, D. 2013. *Seeing Faith, Printing Pictures: Religious Identity During the English Reformation*. Leiden: Brill.

Duffy, E. 2001. *Voices of Morebath: Reformation & Rebellion in an English Village*. London: Yale University Press.

Elton, G. 1972. *Policy and Police: The Enforcement of the Reformation in the Age of Thomas Cromwell*. Cambridge: Cambridge University Press.

Eppley, D. 2007. *Defending Royal Supremacy and Discerning God's Will in Tudor England*. New York: Ashgate.

Ferrell, L. 2008. *The Bible and the People*. London: Yale University Press.

Gee, H., and W. Hardy. 1896. *Documents Illustrative of English Church History, Compiled from Original Sources*. London: Macmillan.

Gray, J. 1995. *Enlightenment's Wake: Politics and Culture at the Close of the Modern Age*. London: Routledge.

Grell, O., and B. Scribner, eds. 1996. *Tolerance and Intolerance in the European Reformation*. Cambridge: Cambridge University Press.

Kaplan, B. 2007. *Divided By Faith: Religious Conflict and the Practice of Toleration in Early Modern Europe*. London: Harvard University Press.

Kirby, W.J. Torrance. 1990. *Richard Hooker's Doctrine of Royal Supremacy*. Leiden: Brill.

Lecler, J. 1960. *Toleration and the Reformation, Vol. II*. Translated by T.L. Westow. London: Longmans.

Locke, J. 1689. *A Letter Concerning Toleration: Humbly Submitted, Etc*. London: Printed for Awnsham Churchill.

Milton, A. 1995. *Catholic and Reformed: The Roman and Protestant Churches in English Protestant Thought, 1600–1640*. Cambridge: Cambridge University Press.

Questier, M. 2006. *Catholicism and Community in Early Modern England: Politics, Aristocratic Patronage and Religion, c. 1550–1640*. Cambridge: Cambridge University Press.

Stubbs, J. 2006. *John Donne, a Reformed Soul: A Biography*. London: W.W. Norton and Company.

Thompson, F. 1948. *Magna Carta: Its Role in the Making of the English Constitution, 1300–1629*. Minneapolis: University of Minnesota Press.

Walsham, A. 1994. "The Fatal Vesper": Providentialism and Anti-Popery in Late Jacobean London. *Past and Present* 144: 37–87.

————. 2006. *Charitable Hatred: Tolerance and Intolerance in England, 1500–1700*. Manchester: Manchester University Press.

Watt, T. 1994. *Cheap Print and Popular Piety, 1550–1640*. Cambridge: Cambridge University Press.

Zagorin, P. 2003. *How the Idea of Religious Toleration Came to the West*. Oxford: Princeton University Press.

CHAPTER 6

Religion and Politics in the USSR: The Cold War Era

Julie deGraffenried

According to Marxist-Leninist principles, religion had no place in the Soviet Union. Born of ignorance, bred by superstition and the irrational, and characteristic of those suffering in economic slavery, religious belief was seen as an obstacle to progress. Institutionalized religion obliged the oppressor rather than rousing the oppressed, dulling the masses into a senseless subordination to the status quo—hence Karl Marx's famed "opium of the people" phrase. Many in the Bolshevik Party viewed religion as simply irrelevant to their project of revolution and modernization, launched via the October Revolution in 1917, trusting that religion would simply "wither away" once the transformation of economic conditions occurred (Wanner 2012, p. 5).

What to do until that day, though, with the millions of believers, tens of thousands of houses of worship, dozens of faiths, and centuries of deeply rooted spiritual traditions? Vladimir Lenin and the Bolsheviks "imagined Communism as a world without religion" (Smolkin 2018, p. 2). This fundamental conflict shaped decades of Soviet religious policy

J. deGraffenried (✉)
Baylor University, Waco, TX, USA
e-mail: julie_degraffenried@baylor.edu

S. Holzer (ed.), *The Palgrave Handbook of Religion and State
Volume II*, https://doi.org/10.1007/978-3-031-35609-4_6

and church-state relations in the Soviet Union from its inception. Thus, the relationship between religion and state remained contentious, though inconsistently so, as both could lay claim to authority and the regulation of social mores. Religion is inherently political given its obligatory connection to a historical context; under communism, religion's political character is compounded as the church may be the only independent institution competing with the state (Ramet 1992, p. 5). In the USSR, that threat to power and perceived "existential alternative to the Soviet order" led to the first attempt to eliminate all religion (Kuromiya 2012, p. 188). Though it was clear it had failed by the late 1930s, the underlying contradiction between faith and ideology persisted until the late 1980s, unevenly influencing the various shifts in religious policies beginning in the 1940s until the Soviet Union's demise in 1991.

The Cold War (1945–1991) was the global clash between competing ideologies, economies, politics, and technologies of the communist and non-communist worlds led by post-World War II superpowers the Soviet Union and the United States. Since the late 1990s, New Cold War historians have explored the role of ideas, ideology, and culture in shaping the Cold War as a counterbalance to decades of geopolitical, Great-Power-style analysis. One consensus emerging is this: the Cold War had a religious dimension (Kirby 2018, p. 1). The United States' postwar conception of itself as righteous and God-fearing locked in a battle of good versus evil against a godless communism led to the intertwining of politics and a particular version of Christianity in the West (Kirby 2003a, p. 3, b, p. 78; Rotter 2000, p. 606). The Soviets offered the world a model of revolutionary liberation that cast off the old and traditional ways in favor of the new (Smolkin 2018).

Despite this, religious policy was not at the forefront of Soviet policymakers' thoughts during the Cold War, nor at any other point in the twentieth century (Ellis 1993, p. 85). Once it became clear that it could not be eradicated, Soviet authorities viewed religion as a tool, subordinated to state needs and aims. As Tatiana Chumachenko notes, "the single highest priority in church-state relations was the position of the regime" (2002, p. 193). Marxism-Leninist ideology dictated that religion would disappear; in the meantime, religious policy could be used for and remained dependent upon prevailing political, economic, social, or ideological considerations (Walters 1993, p. 3; Ellis 1993, p. 85). However secondary, religious policy affected both institution and individual: convictions were not a private matter in the Soviet system nor were churches provided any legal safeguards against government intervention (Luehrmann 2011, p. 9; Ellis 1996, p. 257). While freedom of conscience appeared on paper, it did not and could not exist (Chumachenko 2002, p. 194). And though this chapter will focus primarily on policymakers and institutions, it is worth remembering that "individuals, whether they were believers or not, were not passive ... it is their very reactions to the secularizing policies that prompted the state to respond in particular ways" (Wanner 2012, p. 4).

What follows is a chronological survey of religious policy in the Soviet Union, concentrating on the Cold War era and the implications of that conflict for the church-state relationship. Though many faith communities are a part of this story, the Russian Orthodox Church receives primary focus proportionate to its outsized role in Russia, the largest of the Soviet socialist republics. A final section considers legacies of this set of policies in the post-Soviet space. To begin, a brief summary of pre-war developments in religion and politics sets the scene.

Religion in the Soviet Union to 1939

The Russian Empire, on the eve of revolution in 1917, was a 200-year-old, multi-ethnic, multi-confessional empire. The Russian Orthodox Church, the national faith since 988 and state church of the empire from 1721, though stripped of its Patriarch and incorporated into the state bureaucracy, still held a great deal of wealth and allegiance from the overwhelming majority of Russian subjects. The 1897 census results revealed that about 70 percent of the estimated 175 million imperial subjects identified as Russian Orthodox, while smaller numbers of peoples—many on the borders of empire—adhered to Islam (about 11 percent), Catholicism (about 9 percent), Judaism (about 4 percent), and a variety of Protestant denominations (about 3 percent), with small communities of Buddhists, Apostolic believers, and traditional religionists. European secularization was slow to reach the empire, its landscape dotted with over 80,000 places of worship (including 50,000 churches), hundreds of monasteries, hundreds of thousands of clergymen, monks, nuns, and churchmen and its culture saturated with religious referents (Davis 2003, p. 12). Alongside class, gender, language, and residence, religious confession was a determining factor in a person's legal rights and obligations in the Russian Empire until the October Revolution of 1917 (Luehrmann 2011, p. 4).

The Bolshevik Party, distinguished by its Marxist-Leninist ideology and plan to construct the first communist society, seized power in October

1917 and held it despite a devastating civil war. An early 1918 decree separated church and state and challenged the Russian Orthodox Church's privileged position. Some believers may have welcomed this move, believing it would free faith communities from state interference, but the Bolsheviks perceived this differently—as freedom for the state from church intervention and freedom for society from reactionary religious irrationality (Sawatsky 1992, p. 238). The Bolshevik Revolution did not "end religion" or "outlaw God" in the Soviet Union; in fact, the Soviet constitution always provided for freedom of conscience. Though Lenin declared freedom of religion (and freedom of unbelief), he believed it unnecessary: according to Marxism, proper socioeconomic conditions would soon obviate the need for bourgeois belief systems. In the interim, belief in the wrong things hampered the creation of the New Soviet Man. Within the Bolshevik Party (or Communist Party, as of 1918), two approaches toward religion predominated: the ideologues who sought to hasten the demise of belief in the supernatural and the pragmatists who preferred to control and manage religious institutions.

Institutionalization followed revolution as the Party consolidated power. From 1918 until the war, the implementation of religious policy was divided among several state agencies in at least three departments (or commissariats)—the Department of Cults in the Commissariat of Justice, later replaced with the Secretariat for the Affairs of Cults; state security (the Cheka/NKVD) in the Commissariat of Internal Affairs; and the Department for Agitation and Propaganda in the Commissariat of Enlightenment—in addition to *ad hoc* committees (Walters 1993, p. 4). Broadly, Soviet policy objectives included pursuit of the "withering away" of religions, the expansion of administrative control over religious organizations and activities, the protection of leaders willing to collaborate, and the use of submissive churches for regime ends (Bociurkiw 1986, pp. 427–428) with three general, long-range strategies: interruption of the religious organizations' ability to regenerate, confinement of religious activities to "rites out of sight," and atheist indoctrination (Davis 2003, pp. 6–9). Leaders' shifting initiatives and state goals determined which objectives and which strategies were most visible. Bohdan Bociurkiw notes these "operative principles" woven into Soviet religious policy: only Soviet authorities could define freedom of religion; known believers could not be proper Soviet citizens, therefore they could not be selected for positions of responsibility; Soviet authorities discriminated among faiths or faith groups as it suited them; coercion was always an option; all religion was detrimental but usable; state manipulation and infiltration of religious organizations was a given; antireligious propaganda was also a given, though religious propaganda could be utilized as needed (1986, p. 438).

From 1917 to 1920, the Party's attack was confined primarily to the Russian Orthodox Church (ROC). By January 1918, the ROC had been stripped of its legal standing, its property and right to own property, its right to run schools for children, and its state subsidies for clergy, leaving it with only the right to perform its liturgy in churches over which it no longer had control (Walters 1993, p. 5; Garrard and Garrard 2008, p. 7).

Beginning in 1921, a public defamation campaign against the church during a national famine led to the seizure of nearly all the ROC's relics and treasures and the imprisonment of Patriarch Tikhon. The Party fanned schism in the church, and when Tikhon died in 1925, the ROC was left split and the patriarchate vacant. Other churches, such as the Georgian Orthodox Church and the Armenian Apostolic Church, were subject to similar attacks at this time (Jones 2010, p. 104; Corley 1992, p. 8). Calls for increased atheist activism occurred after the civil war ended in 1921, and anticlerical literature and posters abounded as a publishing house dedicated to antireligious/atheist production was established. Party activists in the League of the Militant Godless offered up derisive public critiques of spiritual beliefs, and the Party itself sought to offer a counter-faith replete with Soviet holidays (Electrification Day, anyone?), rituals, sacred spaces, moral language, and devotional cults eventually built around socialist heroes and political leaders (Steinberg and Wanner 2008, p. 6). In the 1920s, Jews faced a massive secularization campaign, their synagogues, schools, and seminaries shut, rabbis harassed, and publications outlawed (Weinberg 2008, p. 120). Persecution of Protestant groups such as Baptists, Lutherans, and Adventists began around 1925, while Muslim persecution began in 1927 (Walters 1993, p. 13). By 1928, representatives of nearly all the major religious communities had signed declarations of loyalty to the Party, hoping to preserve their shrinking privileges.

The hope was in vain, as a wave of religious persecution accompanied the collectivization drive in the late 1920s, culminating in the terror of the late 1930s. Philip Walters calls the decade of 1929–1939 "the most savage persecution of religion in the entire Soviet period" (1993, p. 13). A set of religious laws enacted in 1929 set precedents remaining in place until 1990. Tax rates for clergy were set at the highest levels, bell ringing was prohibited, and the education system was to integrate atheist education in the curriculum. The most significant, the Law on Religious Associations, limited the rights of believers to services in registered buildings, outlawing evangelism or proselytism, religious education (except privately in the home), religious literature and publications, group activities for the faith community, charity work, public projects such as playgrounds or libraries or spas, and ecclesiastical bank accounts.

The process of "registration" was of utmost importance; it was the key to both state regulation and church existence. To function legally in the Soviet Union, an "association" of at least twenty believers (the *dvadt-satka*) was to apply to local district or city authorities for permission to form a religious association and to use a registered building for worship. That application wended its way through city, district, region, and provincial committees before ending up in Moscow for a final decision. Registration was no formality, but an obligation that created juridical relationship between that specific religious association and the local soviet (or administrative council) and could get delayed or denied at any point in the process if anti-Soviet or illegal religious activity was detected (Bourdeaux 1968, pp. 3–4; Davis 2003, p. 69). After registration, the next crucial step related to acquisition of or permission to renovate a building, whether that was the local church or otherwise, via a lease from the local authorities. A religious association without a building had no place to legally worship (Walters 1993, p. 14). Registration could be lost if rules were not followed. To be an unregistered faith community was to be illegal. Further, the registered religious association—or parish—was the only unit to have legal standing in the Soviet Union. Neither the monasteries, the seminaries, nor the ROC episcopacy had any place in the published legislation. Nothing in Soviet legislation prevented authorities from persecuting the infrastructure of any church, including that of the ROC (Ellis 1996, p. 257).

A violent campaign of repression against clergy and destruction of worship sites led by atheist activists broke out in 1928, often resulting in a vigorous backlash, especially from rural dwellers. With collectivization declared a success by the early 1930s, this wave of persecution receded, as did the influence of League of the Militant Godless, especially once the results of the 1937 census were revealed. The census demonstrated the remarkable staying power of religious identity: over half the adult population over sixteen years old self-identified as believers, with about two-thirds of rural inhabitants and one-third of urban inhabitants claiming a faith. In response, Soviet authorities unleashed an enormous church closure campaign as well as the mass repression of believers and clergy (Davis 2003, p. 10; Kuromiya 2012, p. 36). Coinciding with the Stalinist Great Terror (1936–1938) aimed at alleged political enemies, the pump was already primed for victims. Across the USSR, mosques were closed en masse, imams repressed, and the last medresseh was shuttered in the late 1930s (Troyanovsky 1991, p. 169; Conquest 1968, p. 73). Protestants' numbers had already dropped to a fraction of their 1917 membership, and with the arrests and imprisonment of clergy in 1937–1938, a few groups such as the Lutherans collapsed entirely (Sawatsky 1992, p. 242). All Buddhist temples were closed, the lamas persecuted, and the monasteries destroyed; in 1938, the Leningrad temple became a sports arena (Troyanovsky 1991, p. 178). Only thirty-four of Armenia's 491 Apostolic Churches remained open, while the state shut down the Echmiadzin seminary, its library having already been seized by the Party in 1931. The Catholicos, Khoren I, was executed in 1938 and so many priests repressed that the church "effectively ceased to exist" (Corley 1992, p. 8, 2010, p. 190).

Even the largest of the churches, the Russian Orthodox Church, stood on the brink of total destruction. Reduced to 200–300 open churches with slightly over 100 actively functioning, 25 of the 90-some regions of the Soviet Union in 1939 were "churchless" and most regions had only 1 church functioning (Davis 2003, pp. 12–13; Chumachenko 2002, p. 4). All 1025 Orthodox convents, both monasteries and nunneries, had been closed, and at least 80,000 clergy and monastics executed (Davis 2003, p. 11, 164), a fact especially significant when one understands that the hierarchs of the ROC—all four ranks of the episcopate: patriarch, metropolitans, archbishops, bishops—must be drawn from the monastic clergy. By 1939, only 2 metropolitans and 2 archbishops remained, with some 300–400 priests remaining (of 50,000 pre-1917). The church had no financial base, no patriarch or Holy Synod, no publishing presence, no training institutions, and no hermitages. And then the war happened.

RESCUE: WAR, RELIGION, AND POLITICS TO 1953

It is no understatement to say that World War II—or the Great Patriotic War (1941–1945), as it is known in Russia—saved organized religion in the Soviet Union. Circumstances brought on by the terrible crisis of invasion, defense, and liberation led to a rapprochement between state and church made formal on 4 September 1943. On Joseph Stalin's initiative, a two-hour meeting between the head of state and the hierarchs of the Russian Orthodox Church signaled a dramatic shift in their relationship, with a patriarch, Sergi (Stragorodskii) elected only days later. The ROC was immediately granted financial resources, patriarchal housing, and official standing. Churches and convents were opened, and ROC priests preached to the Red Army. By August 1945, the Russian Orthodox Church had "legal personhood," property rights, the ability to manufacture and sell candles, a 70-strong hierarchy, thousands of priests and churches, a journal, over one hundred convents and seminaries functioning, government publication and distribution of church leaflets, and working bank accounts with which the church collected hundreds of millions of rubles in donations to the State Defense Fund. Very little antireligious literature was published by the state and the phrases "antireligious struggle" and "obscurantist churchmen" disappeared from the press in the 1940s (Corley 1996, p. 89; Chumachenko 2002, pp. 4–5, 82; Davis 2003, p. 20, 129, 161). Similar concessions were made to Muslims in Central Asia, the Georgian Orthodox Church, the Armenian Apostolic Church, and most Protestant groups (Tasar 2017; Jones 2010, p. 106; Corley 2010, pp. 190–191). Given the devastation wrought on religious communities in the 1930s, the war, ironically, provided a respite and a chance to start again for nearly all.

Stalin explained the shift in a 1944 conversation with Polish-American priest Fr. Stanislaus Orlemanski this way: "The war eliminated the contradictions between the church and the state. The believers abandoned their positions of rebellion, and the Soviet government abandoned its own militant position toward the religion" (Record of a Conversation 1944). Scholars have provided a number of additional explanations for Stalin's change of direction. Gleb Yakunin suggested that Stalin wished to channel the patriotic activity of the churches, particularly that of the ROC, toward official war ends. Sergi's open letter on 22 June 1941 inspired many of the faithful to defend the Motherland (Chumachenko 2002, p. 7). Nathaniel Davis and others note that the liberal religious policies of the Germans in occupied territory necessitated some permissiveness on Stalin's part. As the Nazis allowed priests to operate churches behind their advance in 1941–1942, fears that the Orthodox Church could be weaponized *against* the Soviets by the enemy were real (Davis 2003, p. 16, 23). "Occupied territory" included the lands acquired by the Soviets in the 1939 Molotov-Ribbentrop Pact: the eastern third of Poland, Bessarabia and Bukovina, and the Baltics. These newly annexed areas added to the Soviet Union over 6 million Orthodox adherents, 3500–4000 Orthodox churches with priests, monasteries and nunneries, church hierarchs, and seminaries (Davis 2003, p. 15), along with sizable Catholic, Greek Catholic (or Uniate), and Protestant communities. To avoid a large-scale uprising or underground movement—because believers could potentially be anti-Soviet—and reassert control over the regions eventually liberated from the Germans, the pragmatic move was to work more indirectly through a resurrected Russian Orthodox Church. Reviving the ROC provided opportunities not only to enlarge the Moscow patriarchate's influence but also to deal with religious communities perceived to have collaborated with the enemy when the opportunity arose (Dickinson 2003, pp. 29, 32–33). Finally, the potential for the church to play a key role in foreign policy influenced Stalin's decision. Stalin learned that religion could be a bargaining chip in diplomacy when it became part of the negotiations over the United States' recognition of the Soviet Union in the early 1930s (Kirby 2018, p. 3). The religious persecution of the 1930s had not played well abroad, and Stalin needed allies. The church-state concordat occurred immediately before the Big Three first met in Teheran, and the Soviets banked on positive reception from the Allies and smoother negotiations. Further, the church itself could become an instrument of state foreign policy, not only in the winning of loans and goodwill from the Allies, but in "taming" believers in Eastern Europe after the war, rejoining the Orthodox *oikumene*, and projecting Soviet influence abroad (Lupinin 2010, p. 20; Chumachenko 2002, p. 7, 20, 189; Davis 2003, p. 18; Pospielovsky 1984).

Church leaders of a variety of faiths, including those of the ROC, acted in cooperation with state interests out of multiple motivations: self-preservation for individual and institution; anticipation of reviving international connections cut off in the 1920s and 1930s; self-interest and career-building; eschatological reasoning; or a skewed sense of *symphonia* (Dickinson 2003, p. 24, 29; Leustean 2010a, p. 1, 7). New state institutions were created to serve as the intermediary between religious hierarchies and the Soviet government. In October 1943, a government resolution established the Council for the Affairs of the Russian Orthodox Church (CAROC/*Sovet po delam Russkoi Pravoslavnoi Tserkvi*), attached to the Council of People's Commissars (Sovnarkom), to facilitate contact between the ROC patriarchate and state, ensure adherence to religious laws and handle registrations, serve as a neutral decision-maker in cases of local conflict, and provide information on the ROC to state agencies.

Working through a network of regional commissioners, CAROC became a policy instrument through which control might be exerted over believers. The first head of the Council was Georgii Karpov, formerly of the NKVD's "Church Department," who saw his role not as interference in ROC workings but as management of church-state relations. Thus, the Council sometimes found itself defending the rights of believers against abuses of enthusiastic antireligious actors while simultaneously restricting the acts of overeager faith communities (Luchterhandt 1993, p. 57; Lupinin 2010, pp. 21–22; Chumachenko 2002, p. 8, 190). A second institution, the Council for the Affairs of Religious Cults (CARC/*Sovet po delam religioznykh kul'tov*), founded in May 1944, served the same purposes for all other religious groups. To ease management of non-Orthodox sects without traditional hierarchical structures, the state invented them. Four Muslim muftiates (or spiritual boards) based on geographical regions appeared, as did the All-Union Congress of Evangelical Christians-Baptists (AUCECB) for Protestants in 1944 (Tasar 2017, p. 2; Sawatsky 1993, p. 324). In addition to easing the state's efforts to regulate such disparate, non-hierarchical movements, the boards were to assist in rebuilding internal denominational structures and facilitate registrations of local congregations. Communities failing to participate with these supervisory boards remained unregistered and their rights unrecognized; this was the case for some Sufic followers and independent groups of Pentecostals, Mennonites, Lutherans, Adventists, and Baptists (Sawatsky 1992, p. 239, 243; Bourdeaux 1968, p. 6; Ramet 1992, pp. 3–4). These institutions lasted in various forms for the period under review.

Rising tensions over postwar world systems near the war's conclusion led to the onset of hostilities soon coined the Cold War. Despite the devastating toll of the Great Patriotic War, the Soviet Union emerged as one of two superpowers at its conclusion. Soviet leadership of the communist world depended on its ability to project power globally, to maneuver skillfully in its diplomacy, and—Stalin believed—to defend itself from an inevitable war with the capitalist West. The church became an instrument with which to wage Cold War. Despite the public collaboration between religious leaders and an ideologically antireligious regime, the underlying ideological contradiction immensely complicated the church-state relationship (Leustean 2010a, p. 1).

The ROC created a Department of External Church Relations in 1946 to travel abroad representing the church, meet with foreign tourists and religious delegations, and serve as a public relations front for the Soviet state. Its one hundred staff members constituted the largest of the patriarchate's offices, and its representatives were invariably well-educated, well-heeled types. Jane Ellis called the department "an extension of the state's foreign affairs apparatus" (1986, pp. 266, 269–270). This quid pro quo relationship made the Church useful to Stalin, providing some protection and cover. Even before the formal establishment of the External Relations office, the patriarchate had sent delegations to Bulgaria and Yugoslavia (April 1945), Romania (May 1945), and Serbia (1946) and the Russian diaspora in London (June 1945), Paris (August 1945), and the United States (September 1945). Patriarch Aleksii himself traveled to Syria, Palestine, and Egypt (1945) in an attempt to win over the Oriental Orthodox communities (Leustean 2010a, pp. 2–3; Pospielovsky 1984, pp. 302–303). Stalin and Aleksii, for different reasons, hoped to bring all possible Orthodox churches, including the émigré churches, into the Moscow patriarchate's sphere of influence. In fairly short order, the Ukrainian Autocephalous Orthodox Church, Belarus Orthodox Church, Estonian Orthodox Church, Latvian Orthodox Church, and Lithuanian Orthodox Church were absorbed into the Russian Orthodox Church (Wasyliw 2010, p. 156; Leustean 2010b, p. 205, 208, 210, 212). ROC religious diplomacy worked beyond the borders as well, as Soviet-friendly governments gained power in the postwar years. For example, Aleksii pressured the Finnish Orthodox Church to "return to communion" with the ROC, finally settling the issue in 1948 when their governments concluded the "special relationship" of the Soviets and Finns; the Finnish Church kept its independence in exchange for allyship with Moscow (Laitila 2010, p. 284, 286). Émigré churches in Eastern and Central Europe as well as the Orthodox Church in Czechoslovakia accepted the jurisdiction of Moscow and the ROC held great influence in the Balkans (Kalkandjieva 2015, p. 307). Lucian Leustean argues that "the Cold War redesigned the map of Eastern Christianity" due to the proliferation of new émigré churches, smaller churches being subsumed into larger ones, and the appearance of new national churches in the immediate postwar era (Leustean 2010a, p. 9). After a failed 1947 bid by the Russian Orthodox Church and CAROC to convene a council affirming the Moscow Patriarchate as supreme, a step on the road to Stalin's dream of an "Orthodox Vatican," Moscow settled instead for a political statement. At the 1948 Pan-Orthodox Conference in Moscow, Orthodox representatives of the people's democracies together celebrated the 500th anniversary of ROC autocephaly and their own self-proclaimed freedom of worship. Karpov spoke openly of a world divided into two camps, and the delegates sent Stalin a telegram hailing him as global peacemaker (Kalkandjieva 2015, chap. 9). In the face of Moscow's pretensions to power, Ecumenical Patriarch Athenagoras, naturalized U.S. citizen and friend of Truman, sought to unify Orthodox polities in non-communist lands and pursued reconciliation with Rome (Leustean 2010a, p. 6).

In the mid-twentieth century, any move toward the Pope smacked of anti-Soviet sentiment. Catholicism, in the Party's eyes, caused both internal and external problems for them. Any religious group with ultimate spiritual authority beyond the borders siphoned off commitment, while the Vatican had proven itself to be staunchly anti-communist. In 1937, Pius XI issued the encyclical *Divini Redemptoris*, declaring that "bolshevistic and atheistic Communism" threatened to "undermin[e] the very foundations of Christian civilization," partly in response to religious persecution in the Soviet Union (Pius XI 1937). In the context of the Cold War, opposition from Rome acquired an additional layer of politicization. Not only had the Soviet Union gained significant Roman Catholic populations in the Lithuania and Poland, but also additional Uniate communities in addition to already-sizable numbers in Ukraine. Established in 1596, the Uniates, or Greek Catholics, celebrated Eastern Orthodox liturgy but recognized papal supremacy. As the war wound down, Stalin determined to rid the Soviet Union of the Uniate Church once and for all, labeling its members Nazi collaborators and persecuting its priests. The Russian Orthodox Church had long favored the revocation of the Union of Brest and dissolution of the Uniate Church, working alongside the state to accomplish a shared goal. After years of anti-Vatican speechifying by Karpov and the ROC hierarchy, centering primarily around a papal plot to dominate the world and accusations of pro-Hitler sentiment, the Uniate churches of Ukraine, Poland, Czechoslovakia, and Romania were abolished and forcibly reunited with the Russian Orthodox Church in the fall of 1949. In response to Vatican interference in Eastern European affairs, the Soviets—through the ROC and its state institutions—deprived Rome of its second largest particular church. Thus, the Greek Catholic Church in Ukraine became the "largest faith group in the world to be denied the right to exist" (Kirby 2018, p. 6, 9; Chumachenko 2002, p. 46; Dickinson 2003, pp. 29–30; Leustean 2010a, p. 4, b, p. 213; Wanner 2012, p. 16).

The Soviets' negative perception of Catholics in the postwar era affirms Catherine Wanner's contention that "after 1945, religious groups were evaluated individually in terms of their potential to pose a challenge to the

Soviet state and its official ideology" (2012, p. 16). Rather than blanket attacks on "religion," the postwar era is characterized by intense persecution for some groups and relative relaxation for others. Any religious group with foreign ties was suspect in the days of the Soviet anti-cosmopolitanism campaign, which began with anti-Western/anti-foreign feelings inspired by the early days of the Cold War and concluded with full-blown anti-Semitism by the late 1940s. Catholics fell into this category because of their ties to Rome. Baptists and Adventists found themselves smeared as agents of U.S. imperialism due to their missionary origins (Kuromiya 2012, pp. 11–12). Jehovah's Witnesses, with their Brooklyn, New York, headquarters and insular communities, were declared an anti-Soviet organization and accused of warmongering due to their dedication to immanent apocalypse (Knox 2018, p. 258). Nearly all 10,000 Witnesses and their families were exiled in two secret operations in 1949 and 1951 (Baran 2014, p. 3). Jewish identity had already been stripped of its religious content via assimilation efforts in the 1920s and 1930s, yet Jews remained a separate nationality. In the postwar era, an all-out assault on Yiddish culture began, and Jewish artists, public figures, and intellectuals were accused of "rootless cosmopolitanism," "kowtowing to the West," and Zionism (Wanner 2012, p. 14, 16). With U.S. support thrown firmly behind Israel by 1949, the latter charge could label one a security risk or anti-patriotic. Anti-Semitic attacks continued both in the Soviet Union and in the eastern bloc until Stalin's death in 1953.

For the Russian Orthodox Church, on the other hand, the immediate postwar years may have marked the climax of its institutional strength in the Soviet era (Davis 2003, pp. 20–21). Those who remained had survived the 1930s, the church had been renewed with an influx of parishes and resources via annexations, over a thousand new churches had been opened in Russia, the episcopacy was stable, the Moscow patriarchate had restored longstanding international preeminence, and dozens of seminaries, academies, and monasteries once again trained up new clergy. The state awarded the Red Banner of Labor for the Defense of Leningrad to Patriarch Aleksii (Simanskii), who succeeded Sergi in 1945, and an ROC delegation stood on the platform at a postwar victory parade. Nearly 12,000 priests and deacons served, according to CAROC reports for 1948. The center had shifted west, as half the churches at that time were not in Soviet territory pre-1939 and a full two-thirds of the 14,421 parishes were in Ukraine by the late 1940s (Davis 2003, p. 23; Dickinson 2003, p. 25; Chumachenko 2002, p. 51). The ROC stood at the forefront of the world peace movement by mid-1949, seeking to rally public opinion against the United States. Soviet propaganda consistently portrayed the United States as aggressive, immoral, racist, and neo-fascist, a task made easier by the Korean War in 1950. Traveling widely, Soviet ecumenical representatives to world peace events commended their own government and allies while condemning those of West (Pospielovsky 1984, pp. 312–313; Chumachenko 2002, p. 120; Ellis 1986, p. 271; Leustean 2010a, p. 4).

The relative prosperity came at a price. No change had been made to the 1929 laws on religion, so the concessions granted were based solely on instructions from Stalin and various government bodies. All church communication with foreign churches or clergy had to go through official channels and meetings reported in full. Church leaders had not only to stay within bounds of permissible acts, but also to "continually thank the Soviet regime … and to consciously spread an obvious lie by exaggerating the church's well-being in the country" (Chumachenko 2002, p. 52; Dickinson 2003, p. 25). ROC clergy used their sermons to share scriptural meditations, but also to encourage voting in the 1946 elections, to exhort increased labor discipline, and to explain the significance of May 1. The local priest sometimes provided financial help to the village soviet. Karpov and CAROC controlled the composition of the student body in all seminaries and theological academies by screening applicants for suitability; hired, fired, and transferred faculty; set the curriculum and censored the libraries; and monitored the social lives of pupils. By 1949, the Council also directed the patriarchate whom to appoint to the episcopacy and where, retiring or transferring energetic bishops in the Soviet Union while retaining a few cultured and educated men to represent the church abroad (Chumachenko 2002, pp. 68, 73, 115–116). Believers submitted thousands of petitions to open churches between 1944 and 1948, but only a small percentage were approved due to clergy shortages, decrepit or dismantled church buildings, procedural errors, or opposition at the local level (Chumachenko 2002, pp. 59–62).

Provincial toleration for religious revival had ended with the war, and the ideologues within the Party had never abandoned it. The Communist Party's Central Committee revived antireligious work in 1947, creating a new agency called the All-Union Society for the Dissemination of Political and Scientific Knowledge, simply known as *Znanie* (Knowledge). Local officials, with no resolutions to guide them, resorted to their own tactics: excessive taxes, threats of unemployment, even kidnapping of priests, insults and violence, or public defamation (Tasar 2017, pp. 92–93). By

1950, zero petitions for registration reached CAROC, and it remained zero through 1953; the lower-level committees rejected them for "inexpediency" or held them indefinitely. CAROC commissioners, vulnerable to removal by regional party committees, received complaints from believers about local decision-making but criticism from local authorities for attempting to uphold the law. Similarly, the Central Committee frequently complained that CAROC and CARC were being partial to clergy, insufficiently forthcoming with information, and too soft on believers. Agit-Prop, in particular, pressured Karpov to reconsider CAROC's role and motives, successfully reorienting the agency's work away from legal processes and toward ideology. When segments of the party attempted to ram through new limits on the ROC and CAROC in 1949, however, Stalin personally intervened to stop it (Chumachenko 2002, pp. 87, 100–103, 108–109, 121).

The relative relaxation of church-state relations in the high Stalinist era (for most faith communities) depended entirely on Stalin himself. The church had proved valuable in the war effort, its collaboration with the state had contributed an additional source of legitimacy, and it had played a beneficial role in foreign policy, especially with the onset of the Cold War. In fact, the key for the ROC had been its continual efforts to show itself useful and submissive to the state; it owed its existence to Stalin (Lupinin 2010, p. 20). Every wartime concession or change in the church-state relationship resulted from dozens of decrees and instructions, many of which contradicted the 1929 laws on religion. They had no legal basis, only the power of Stalin's personal authority. Chumachenko contends that as the government became less involved in religious policy in the early 1950s, Party ideologues prepared to move into the void; everyone— church, state, party—understood that the relative calm would last only as long as Stalin did (Chumachenko 2002, p. 85, 124, 191).

ATTACK: THE ANTIRELIGIOUS STRUGGLE OF THE KHRUSHCHEV ERA, 1954–1964

By the early 1960s, church-state relations in the Soviet Union had been, once again, radically redefined and Stalin's entente repudiated. If Stalin's death in 1953 did not make a new assault on religion "predetermined and unavoidable," it at least made it a distinct possibility (Chumachenko 2002, p. 149). Party ideologues had pushed for a more aggressive stance against faith communities since the late 1940s, and the lack of formal legal action on religious policy at that time meant that the 1929 law still stood. In addition, the new leader, Nikita Khrushchev, appeared to support an uncompromising stance toward religion.

Khrushchev's motives for this round of antireligious campaigns are not entirely clear. The most common reason accepted is his sincere belief that religion and communism were incompatible: if full communism was to be achieved by his target date of 1980, faith in the supernatural had to be overcome (Davis 2003, p. 33; Chumachenko 2002, p. 149). A more nuanced version of this explanation suggests that Khrushchev wished to modernize rural life and viewed religious belief as an obstacle to that goal (Stone 2008). Less satisfying are speculations about Khrushchev's personal life, seeking some deep-seated hatred of religion. Combined with the enthusiasm for antireligious work among ideologues (particularly the Department of Agit-Prop) and Party concerns about growth in the church, especially among youth, Khrushchev's backing—whatever the motive—unleashed an assault not seen since the pre-war era.

Despite a limited campaign of repression in 1954, the period from 1953 to 1957 remained fairly quiet as the power struggle for leadership, related domestic issues, and the Cold War took center stage (Chumachenko 2002, pp. 128–135, 156). In 1957, however, turnover in CAROC membership and fresh discussions about religion in the Party's Central Committee, likely a response to Khrushchev's denunciation of Stalin at the 20th Party Congress in 1956, began laying the groundwork for a comprehensive change in religious policy. After all, any supporter of hardline religious policy could safely argue that "Stalinist-style toleration of faith" needed to be corrected. New drafts of laws affecting believers began circulating and antireligious training of activists accelerated. Central Committee resolutions beginning in the fall of 1958 targeted church finances, structures, clergy, registration procedures, and ultimately, CAROC. In 1959, the Council and its work was declared "a deformation of ecclesiastical policy of the socialist state" that had led only to the strengthening of religion, and the previous decade-and-a-half was denounced as a "manifestation of Stalinism" (Chumachenko 2002, pp. 148–149, 153). Using Khrushchev's recent revelations about injustices during the Stalinist Terror as cover, the Central Committee removed Karpov as chair of the Council "for the violations of socialist legality committed from 1937 to 1938" (Corley 1996, p. 204), in reality punishing him for attempting to uphold law over ideology. His replacement, Party apparatchik Vladimir Kuroedov, oversaw the conversion of CAROC's mission—and by extension, that of CARC as well—from one of possible mediation/assistance to one of simply upholding the party line as defined by the ideologues (Luchterhandt 1993, p. 58; Tasar 2017, p. 211). The Council relinquished its role as advocate-adjudicator and took a more domineering stance. It removed governance of the ROC from the episcopacy entirely, working only through hand-selected hierarchs to carry out party instructions (Chrystostom 1966, p. 31; Pospielovsky 1984, p. 343). CAROC commissioners were instructed to form "public assistance commissions" of volunteers willing to assist in enforcement of new restrictions by collecting data on church attendees or reporting on co-workers who missed work for religious reasons, and to ensure that each *dvadtsatka* was sufficiently "reliable"/compliant (Bourdeaux 1968, pp. 15–16; Davis 2003, p. 41). Registration, previously used to control the number of congregations, was used by CAROC to impose conditions on congregations (Walters 1993, p. 21).

On 3 March 1961, all the Central Committee resolutions of the previous three years became law via the Council of Ministers, creating a "political war" on religion with a legal basis. This government action formalized a return to full enforcement of the 1929 laws. In response, CAROC and CARC distributed instructions to all church leaders interfering with their operations and to all Council commissioners directing them to limit the influence of the church on the population (Chumachenko 2002, p. 187). Khrushchev affirmed these actions at the 22nd Party Congress in October when he called for liberation from religious prejudices and superstitions via scientific-atheist education. The Party adopted a new charter which required every member to participate in the antireligious struggle. Antireligious activists and their sympathizers were set loose, and a campaign of ferocious propaganda and no holds barred administrative pressure swept the Soviet Union for the next several years.

A distinct surge in atheist education and propaganda production, led by Agit-Prop's stable of activists and *Znanie* members, began in the late 1950s. A flood of antireligious features in the press appeared. Some were scholarly or scientific treatments of spiritual topics, but many fell back on longstanding stereotypes, depicting priests as drunk or corrupt, religion as a con game, believers as duped ignoramuses, and sacraments or religious holidays as superstitious nonsense. A number of famous apostates shared their stories. A new Atheist publishing house churned out hundreds of thousands of copies of antireligious materials (Pospielovsky 1984, p. 330).

The monthly journal *Nauka i religiia* (*Science and Religion*) was launched in 1959, and its content was dedicated to debunking religion. School textbooks beefed up the scientific-atheist content, and teachers were encouraged to facilitate age-appropriate discussions of science's supremacy over faith. The 1961 Moral Code for the Builder of Communism, adopted at the 22nd Party Congress, presented twelve humanist-inspired precepts of communist morality that could be easily incorporated into school lessons. For youth and adults, *Znanie* lecturers made the rounds in clubs, workplaces, and civic centers, offering lectures such as "Religion—The Enemy of Science," "Science Refutes Religion," and "Reasons for the Preservation of Religious Vestiges in the USSR and Ways to Overcome Them" (Karpushin 1965).

Overwhelmingly, however, the campaign consisted of a variety of rules, regulations, and procedures designed to make religious practice difficult or impossible. New taxes on candles, sales of which comprised by far the largest portion of the ROC budget, decreased church revenue by millions of rubles (Chumachenko 2002, p. 168; Davis 2003, p. 206). Clergy paid 81–83 percent income tax on income over 7000 rubles a year (Pospielovsky 1984, p. 345). The 1961 decree prohibited financial aid from central church administrations to local parishes that were not self-sustaining and required struggling parishes to combine with others (Davis 2003, p. 39).

Approval of registration applications came to a standstill, while an enormous wave of worship site closings, or deregistrations, occurred, gathering speed after 1961. While some actions, such as the closure of folk shrines or arrest of wandering clerics, met with the approval of ROC hierarchy and the Muslim Spiritual Boards, most did not. Hundreds of mosques, temples, and churches were closed or retasked by local authorities. Confiscation of prayer houses for local or state purposes was legalized by the 1961 decree, as was a one-church-per-village rule (Lupinin 2010, p. 25). A CARC report from Kyrgyzstan claimed that over one hundred unregistered mosques had been closed in Osh province alone in 1960 (Tasar 2017, p. 211). By 1960, no Buddhist temples in Tuva and only two datsans in Buryatia remained open (Conquest 1968, p. 120). One-third of the forty-eight Armenian Apostolic Churches in the USSR were shut down by 1964, with only three churches serving Armenia's capital, Yerevan (Corley 1992, pp. 10–12, 2010, p. 190). Hardest hit was the Russian Orthodox Church: authorities deregistered over 6000 churches—44 percent of the churches open in 1958—by the mid-1960s (Corley 1996, p. 184; Davis 2003, p. 42). Moldova and Belarus lost approximately half of their churches (Leustean 2010b, pp. 213–214). The state closed bishops' cathedrals in Orel, Kishinev, Vinnytsia, and Riga in 1962, with the Riga cathedral refit as a planetarium and coffee shop (Davis 2003, p. 41; Leustean 2010b, p. 206). Orthodox layperson Boris Talantov described a church closing in Korshik, Kirov region, in Russia in which icons were torn down; chandeliers, screens, and vessels smashed; books burned; vestments, linens, and candles confiscated; church wine drunk; and crosses sawed off. To top it off, the village Soviet chairman took the church's roof paint and painted his house with it (Davis 2003, p. 44). In all, authorities closed the doors of about one-third of all places of worship.

The Party enacted new restrictions on monasteries beginning in 1958. As traditional centers of spiritual life, focal points of pilgrimage, and critical points of contact between laity and clergy, these institutions drew the ire of ideologues. The tax exemption gifted in 1945 was withdrawn, and additional penalties included a reduction in land for food production, new lease agreements with local authorities, a ban on pilgrims and hostels in monasteries, and a prohibition on receiving financial support from parish or diocesan funds. As the consequences of these restrictions reduced the income of convents, authorities could prosecute or close them for tax evasion (Pospielovsky 1984, pp. 345–346). Seizure of such an institution could happen quickly: at the Ovruch convent in Zhitomir region, Ukraine, sixty-two resident nuns were packed up and sent away on 25 June and the Ovruch Interdistrict Children's Hospital opened in the convent the very next day (Chumachenko 2002, p. 170). Even Kiev's historic Monastery of the Caves was shuttered in 1960, converted a few years later into a museum (Wasyliw 2010, p. 159). By 1964, only eighteen of the one hundred Orthodox monasteries open in 1946 remained so, occupied by fewer than three hundred and fifty monastics—less than 2 percent of the pre-revolutionary number in the Russian Empire (Davis 2003, p. 161, 166).

Clergy, ridiculed and attacked in the press, faced daily pressure in their roles. The Councils enacted a plan to reduce the number of clerics through retirement, pressure, and promises of alternate employment. It worked: four of every ten priests working in 1958 were retired, deceased, or defrocked by 1964 (Davis 2003, p. 42). Church hierarchy was of little assistance: a mild protest by Patriarch Aleksii in 1960, for example, led to public criticism and charges against several of the bishops in the ROC (Davis 2003, pp. 36–37). By the early 1960s, over one-third of rural village churches had no priest (Davis 2003, p. 131). To make matters worse for Orthodox clergy, a 1961 Holy Synod instruction removed all financial and administrative authority from the parish priest, placing it in the hands of a lay council (the *dvadtsatka*). The council could exclude him from meetings, leave him out of disputes or budget decisions, and avoid church discipline. For all practical purposes, the priest became the employee of the laity, with no control over decision-making in his parish. The *Journal of the Moscow Patriarchate* reported that in one parish in Pskov, a senior churchwarden had run off twenty-five priests (Davis 2003, p. 40, 68; Bourdeaux 1968, p. 17; Pospielovsky 1984, pp. 337–339).

Laws banning the religious instruction of minors and their presence in places of worship, in place since 1929, were more strictly enforced (Pospielovsky 1984, p. 342; Davis 2003, p. 42). CAROC sent oral instructions that priests were not to begin services with children under eighteen present nor could they give communion to a minor (Lupinin 2010, p. 25). In 1961, a local CARC commissioner posted Communist Youth League and Young Pioneer members at the entrances of the four mosques in the southern capital of Kyrgyzstan to stop boys from attending prayers with their fathers (Tasar 2017, p. 235). Ideological justifications for deprivation of the parental rights for believers who "subjected" their children to religion abounded in the press. One school threatened Adventist parents with deprivation of parental rights for refusing to send their children to school on Saturdays (Sapiets 1990, p. 148). In 1963, thirty-two Evangelical Christians from Siberia sought asylum at the U.S. Embassy in Moscow, claiming that their children had been removed to children's homes after a dispute over atheist education in school (Bourdeaux 1968, p. 17). In fact, a divisive schism in the AUCECB occurred in large part due to the Congress's acquiescence with newly enforced restrictions on religious education for children. A large contingent of Baptists left the group, formed their own organizing committee, wrote their own revised statute, and became some of the most prominent—and most persecuted—religious dissidents of the era (Sawatsky 1992, pp. 245–246).

Ironically, the international profile of religious groups in the Soviet Union expanded dramatically while the situation at home deteriorated. Paralleling the post-Stalin foreign policy of Khrushchev who eschewed isolation in favor of peaceful coexistence, Soviet religious delegations attended the first meeting of Josef Hromádka's Christian Peace Conference (1958), helped found the Conference of European Churches (1959), and sent observers to Vatican II. In November 1961, the Russian Orthodox Church was voted into membership at the 3rd Assembly of the World Council of Churches (WCC), becoming the largest single-member church in the largest ecumenical association (Hebly 1993, p. 105; Ellis 1986, p. 270). In later years, the Armenian Apostolic Church, the Georgian Orthodox Church, and the AUCECB joined the WCC as well. After a Soviet Muslim delegation attended the 1962 World Islamic Conference in Baghdad, CARC ordered the creation of a Department of Foreign Relations of the Muslim Organizations of the USSR to coordinate future contacts. In the context of Khrushchev's anti-imperialist message about national liberation, Soviet Muslims played a key role for Third World audiences. A series of international pro-Soviet Islamic conferences began in the early 1960s, chiefly to "demonstrate the existence of Muslims' freedom of conscience in the Soviet Union" and expand religious diplomatic opportunities (Tasar 2017, pp. 248–251). Thus, Khrushchev continued Stalin's use of religion as a tool of soft diplomacy during the Cold War. Ecumenical and peace organizations were venues to advance positive images of socialism, deflect charges of human rights abuses, oppose Western imperialism, and build alliances (Hebly 1993, p. 113). The churches' international work largely insulated the Soviets from sanctions (Walters 1993, p. 23). Unlike the postwar era, however, Soviet religious figures conducted their outreach efforts knowing that the situation for believers at home was not improving.

The Khrushchev Era was described by one clergyman as a time "when it appeared that the string would break any time" (Pospielovsky 1984, p. 340, n25). The revival of the 1929 law and renunciation of the concessions of the 1940s and early 1950s, coupled with an intensive atheist propaganda and education campaign, wrought destruction in faith communities. Even foreign communists expressed their concerns about Soviet excesses. Religious policies embittered believers and undermined rule of law, pushed some religious groups underground, increased sympathy for believers amongst the public, and damaged Soviet reputation abroad (Warhola 1992, p. 19; Davis 2003, p. 42; Tasar 2017).

ATTRITION: CHURCH-STATE RELATIONS TO 1985

The collective leadership that ousted Khrushchev in 1964 determined to do damage control for his erratic acts. Led by Leonid Brezhnev (1964–1982), then by Yuri Andropov (1982–1984) and Konstantin Chernenko (1984–1985), the Soviet Union settled into a period of stability, characterized by global power, détente, and loss of revolutionary zeal. Church-state relations, in many ways, mirrored the nation. Large-scale church closings and splashy antireligious campaigns disappeared, but neither were the losses of the Khrushchev era reversed or redressed—as Lupinin puts it, continuity minus the excesses (2010, p. 27). Stability meant acceptance of a "hostile state supremacy over the churches" and the "slow erosion of the church's institutional resources" (Sawatsky 1992, p. 249; Davis 2003, p. 47). With the acknowledgment that developed socialism could continue indefinitely, the ideological imperative to eliminate religion evaporated. Explaining away the persistence of faith as an issue of backwardness, pernicious imperialist influence, and anti-Sovietness, the state chose control over eradication (Ellis 1986, p. 252; Baran 2014, p. 173).

The primary institution through which the state exercised control was the Council for Religious Affairs (CRA/*Sovet po delam religii*), created in 1965 by combining CAROC and CARC. This seven-department council with Union-wide authority over religious communities answered to both government (Council of Ministers) and party (the Central Committee). Kuroedov, previously chairman of CAROC, led the CRA. Designed to "put the politics of the Soviet state into action in terms of the religions," the CRA dispatched representatives to union, republic, region, and district-level committees, with the express tasks of liaising between Moscow and the provinces, managing clergy, and exerting control over congregations. The CRA worked with state security, the KGB, to suppress illegal sects, deal with outspoken clerics or dissidents, and manage foreign contacts for intelligence-gathering purposes. The Council also observed and gathered information, sponsoring large-scale sociological studies of religious belief and practice as well as regular reports on the minutiae of parish activities. Finally, the CRA actively directed religious communities through suggestions to church leadership on everything from personnel decisions to permissible days for baptisms to renovations to clerical discipline to censorship of the patriarchate's journal. No part of spiritual life was too insignificant for regulation as the state centralized power in the CRA (Luchterhandt 1993, pp. 59–62, 64, 67–73; Ellis 1986, p. 258). Yet, it is important to note that local officials influenced the experiences of faith communities as well; as James Warhola reminds us, the arbitrariness of local officials' actions was systemic in Soviet governance, creating a "gap between formal authority and actual power" (1992, p. 32). A lenient local soviet might mitigate the effects of CRA directives while a council unsympathetic to a particular religious group might harass it mercilessly by shutting off electricity or water, disconnecting phones or heat, confiscating license plates or whole buildings (Chumachenko 2002, p. 107). As local officials often had little connection to the communities they served and little incentive to practice toleration of religious life, they often not only executed but exceeded the wishes of the CRA commissioner (Warhola 1992, pp. 34–35).

A new pattern emerged whereby officially registered religious organizations, operating in the open where they could be monitored, received moderate concessions while unregistered, underground religious groups bore the brunt of the state's pressure. The ROC, headed by its carefully selected and submissive episcopate, experienced few forcible church closings and the arbitrary persecution of clergy and prohibition on inter-diocese travel ended (Davis 2003, pp. 48–49). Simply through attrition, however, it lost dozens of parishes per year; by 1986, about 6700 registered Orthodox communities existed serving about 5 million parishioners, or just under 2 percent of the Soviet population (Davis 2003, pp. 55–56). The clergy declined by about 1000 from 1966 to 1985, but the average age of priests had dropped to the 30s (Pospielovsky 1984, p. 402). Annual church revenue fell by half over this period, but it was sufficient for the circumscribed role of the church in Soviet society (Davis 2003, pp. 208–209). Registered Baptists gained a few more registrations each year, slightly increased journal circulation, a license to import Bibles, and progress toward religious materials for children (Sawatsky 1992, p. 249).

Unregistered Baptists, however, became a prime target for the CRA. Together with over a thousand known underground communities of Pentecostals, Muslims, Adventists, Catholics, Jehovah's Witnesses, and Uniates, they faced surveillance, physical abuse, arrest and imprisonment, psychiatric commitment, deprivation of parental rights, and harassment at work (Bociurkiw 1986, p. 426). A 1966 set of laws, inspired by the unregistered Baptists but applicable to all, levied fines on members of unregistered associations and financial penalties for unauthorized meetings, processions, or youth activities, and it criminalized evangelism, work with children under eighteen, and informal meetings such as seminars or study circles (Davis 2003, p. 48). By Brezhnevian logic, choosing to opt out of the system merited harsher treatment.

Consistent with a "more civilized" approach to church-state relations, the government announced revisions to the 1929 Law on Religious Associations in 1975. The revisions were not new: the amendments simply made public the early 1960s laws of the Khrushchev era that had never been formally publicized. Though there was little substantive change, publication of "the rules" for church-state relations at least made believers aware of their content. The Brezhnev Constitution of 1977 "guaranteed" instead of "recognized" the freedom of conscience, pledged respect for human rights, and prohibited hatred on "religious grounds" (Baran 2014, pp. 174–175).

In part, increased dissident activity inspired these actions by the state. Religious dissent, as a response to unjust treatment of the Khrushchev Era, multiplied in the 1960s and 1970s. Open letters to the patriarchate and government appealed to the WCC and United Nations, and lists of political prisoners circulated underground and made their way to the West. Laity and priests critical of the hierarchy's seeming corruption and complaisance complained of division within the church. Arrests, clerical transfer, and communication disruption all but quashed open dissent. The Soviet government's signature on the Helsinki Accords in 1975, however, inspired new Helsinki Watch Groups and contacts with international human rights groups. Though prominent dissidents still experienced harassment, loss of position, surveillance, and arrest, their activity likely had "some restraining influence" on the state because of their success in contradicting the Soviet line about freedom of speech and in making their plight known via foreign media (Bociurkiw 1986, p. 435). If nothing else, open dissent was an embarrassing lever to provide the United States in the Cold War.

The state relied on official religious organizations to counter dissident perspectives through continued soft diplomacy and affirmations of religious freedom in the Soviet Union. In one expression of détente, the WCC helped the AUCECB arrange import licenses for Bibles and seminary exchange programs that won approval from the Soviet government (Sawatsky 1992, p. 248). The ROC did manage to keep meaningful discussion of human rights issues off the agenda at the WCC, but exerted no Marxist influence on the organization, even holding liberation theology at arm's length (Hebly 1993, pp. 114–115). In some cases, the church plugged a vital hole in Soviet Cold War foreign policy. The Central Asian muftiate, for example, served as Soviet representative to Arab countries, especially Saudi Arabia, where the USSR lacked formal diplomatic ties. Central Asian international outreach not only served the state's diplomatic purposes, but strove to find "common moral ground on the basis of religion" that transcended the Muslim world (Tasar 2017, p. 293).

Atheist activists had hoped to provide a substitute "moral ground" as well, but as the educators of the Khrushchev era aged, efforts became less energetic and more perfunctory. Despite one last crackdown on unofficial and unregistered Muslim groups around 1979 (the beginning of the Soviet-Afghan War), the admission that religion was around to stay sucked the dynamism out of antireligious propaganda. Unexpected pockets of conversion to Orthodoxy and Protestantism among urban intellectual youth perplexed activists, who expected urbanization and education to "cure" religiosity. Populations of citizens who self-identified as "Soviet and Orthodox" or "Soviet and Muslim" seemed to contradict claims about the natural subversiveness of religion. Above all, atheist cadres found themselves contending with indifference: the ideological fervor of communism waned in the late Soviet period, stifled by cronyism and careerism within the Party and shinier objects of affection beyond ideology (Smolkin 2018; Davis 2003, p. xxii).

By the mid-1980s, church-state relations appeared to have settled into a pattern of predictable, if not comfortable, sameness. Regulated and managed, the church had shrunk, playing little role in society outside its walls. The state reigned supreme over faith, but the rules of engagement had been clarified. Only those who chose to live outside the lines needed to live in fear of reprisal. No signs of change appeared on the horizon.

REVIVAL: SOVIET CHURCH AND STATE TO 1991

Three times as many churches and places of worship were open in 1953 than when Mikhail Gorbachev came to power in 1985 (Lupinin 2010, p. 30). With perestroika, however, came a complete turnaround in Soviet church-state relations and a revitalization of religious life. By 1991, the revalidation of religion was complete, outlasting Gorbachev, his reforms, and the Soviet Union itself.

What explains this about-face? Though Gorbachev was a committed communist, he was unafraid to jettison ideology when pragmatism seemed the better choice; apparently this held true for his views on religion as well. Gorbachev hoped to build a social consensus to legitimize radical changes in foreign and domestic policy. His plan to revive the USSR via reform needed allies in society. Further, glasnost had revealed the depth of corruption and ethical malaise among the population, and Gorbachev believed the country needed a "moral awakening" to fix everything from work habits to family life. Finally, an enhanced role for the church couldn't hurt foreign relations, as Gorbachev sought to reach out to the West, end the arms race, and defuse the Cold War (Ramet 1993, p. 32; Ellis 1993, p. 87; Davis 2003, pp. 61–62).

Change did not happen immediately; Ramet argues that it is "doubtful that Gorbachev knew from the beginning exactly where religious policy was heading" (1993, p. 46). As late as 1986, he was still publicly advocating firm antireligious struggle. At the same time, however, the ROC was sponsoring conferences in preparation for the 1988 Millennium Celebration, a few hundred religious dissidents had been pardoned or released from jail, and the press began to write sympathetically of believers. By early 1988, CRA officials publicly admitted "past errors" in dealing with believers. And on 29 April 1988, Gorbachev received Patriarch Pimen and five Metropolitans for a 90-minute meeting in Kremlin, the first reception given to a patriarch since Stalin in 1943, at which Gorbachev acknowledged past mistakes and offered a new relationship in exchange for ROC support of perestroika (Davis 2003, pp. 62–66). He promised a new law on freedom of conscience, and declared, "Believers are Soviet people, workers, patriots, and they have the full right to express their convictions with dignity" (Bourdeaux 1995, p. 114).

The events surrounding the celebration of 1000 years of Christianity in Russia marked a turning point. The Millennium Celebration in June 1988 not only brought hundreds of dignitaries and visitors to Moscow, it put the pageantry of the Russian Orthodox Church front and center on every media outlet across the country. As part of the ceremonies, the 1961 church statute removing priestly authority from the parish was revoked, and the Soviet government decorated ROC hierarchs with state awards. The new liberal attitude extended beyond Orthodoxy: in conjunction with the Millennium, Protestant denominations received permission to import hundreds of thousands of Bibles and commentaries, doubling the number available since 1945, foreign evangelists were invited to speak in the USSR, and public baptisms occurred (Sawatsky 1992, p. 260).

Gorbachev's promised legislation appeared in the fall of 1990 with the Freedom of Conscience and Religious Organizations Act. Though it retained the Soviet practice of registration, the law decreased the critical mass needed to ten people and provided legal standing. Religious associations of all sorts gained the rights to property, industry, free worship anywhere, import/export of religious literature, philanthropic work, free travel, evangelism, and religious instruction for children. Income tax rates for clergy were reduced to that of workers, and churchmen gained the rights to contracts, unions, and benefits. Seminary students acquired draft deferment. The state dropped its support for atheism entirely, and the CRA's mission was to be redefined as an interfaith representative body (Davis 2003, pp. 88–89; Sawatsky 1992, p. 267; Luchterhandt 1993, p. 79). Several republics, including Russia, passed their own freedom of conscience legislation prohibiting state interference with worship around the same time, which served as the primary laws on religion upon the collapse of the USSR in 1991 (Luchterhandt 1993, p. 78; Sawatsky 1992, p. 268).

The religious recovery was dramatic. Over 4000 new parishes were registered over the next 3 years, at a rate of 100 to 200 a month. Church bells rang again, monasteries reopened, religion courses were offered in schools, and public discussion of rehabilitation of repressed believers commenced. New institutes for choir directors, psalmists, and church administrators sprang up, religious processions took to the streets, and the ROC initiated a new Youth Movement. An explosion of religious literature appeared, and Easter liturgy was broadcast live on television in 1991 (Davis 2003, pp. 70, 78, 96–97; Ramet 1993, p. 38). Following Pimen's death and the election of a new patriarch in 1990, Gorbachev received Aleksi II two days after his enthronement. Not all proceeded without dispute between the ROC and Soviet state. One year earlier, Gorbachev had met with Pope John Paul II to discuss Roman and Greek Catholic affairs. He agreed to legalize the Uniate Church, a process which began in 1990, much to the dismay of the ROC hierarchy (Davis 2003, p. 77). In addition, the Ukrainian Autocephalous Orthodox Church broke away from the ROC and elected its own patriarch in the summer 1990 (Davis 2003, p. 74).

Protestant groups enjoyed newly granted freedoms as well. A quarter-million German Lutherans in the USSR received an ordained bishop, Adventists obtained full recognition for the first time, and a number of groups—among them, Pentecostals, Mennonites, and Lutherans—were granted permission to emigrate (Sawatsky 1992, pp. 265–266, 269). Hundreds of parachurch organizations started missions work, and by 1990, Protestant groups had fully embraced charity work, opening clinics, orphanages, meal programs, prison ministries, rehab centers, elder homes, disability programs, and hostels (Sawatsky 1993, p. 344). New opportunities proliferated, but freedom also splintered the Protestants into far smaller denominational groups and reduced their numbers through emigration. Other faith communities dealt with similar consequences.

Religious perestroika brought unintended effects as well. While some sought to recover lost traditions, others became uneasy with the introduction of "non-traditional" faiths (Balzer 1993, p. 238). An increasingly pluralism made the Hare Krishna movement the fastest-growing faith in the late 1980s, and the Baha'i and Mormon ventures expanded quickly as well. A new permissiveness in spiritual seeking led to a swelling tide of faith healers, astrologists, clairvoyants, ESP experts, and UFO interest groups (Ramet 1993, pp. 45–46). Of greater concern was the sharp rise in anti-Semitism associated with Russian nationalism, anti-sectarian violence led by the Georgian Orthodox Church, and conflict between Orthodox and Catholics in Ukraine. A few right-wing neofascist and monarchist groups began appropriating the ROC for their purposes, to Aleksii's alarm, and may have even murdered two prominent Orthodox priests (Davis 2003, pp. 90–91, 94; Ramet 1993, p. 48). A number of the "ethnic churches" made common cause with emerging nationalist movements. The Latvian Lutheran Church and Lithuanian Catholic Church endorsed their republics' bids for independence, and dramatic resurgence of national-religious identity surprised many (Corley 1992, pp. 21–22). The Central Asian muftiate, for example, began disintegrating on national lines, and mosques separated by ethnic group (Tasar 2017, p. 366).

Unsurprisingly, the line between religion and politics remained blurred. In elections to the newly formed Congress of People's Deputies (CPD), three ROC clergy—including Metropolitan Aleksii of Leningrad—won seats, as did several Muslim clerics (Ellis 1996, p. 122). The Orthodox hierarch spoke in full vestments during the televised CPD sessions, once using his speech to criticize Uniates for seizing Orthodox churches. By late 1990, 192 ROC priests had been elected to office at some level (Davis 2003, p. 134). Aleksii took his pledge to Gorbachev seriously. As the Soviet Union began to unravel, the patriarch met with delegates to encourage a yes vote on the Union Treaty. Hedging his bets, perhaps, he also attended Boris Yeltsin's inauguration as Russian President in July 1991 (Davis 2003, pp. 94–95). During the August attempted coup, a number of noted Orthodox priests and former dissidents circulated in the crowds of protestors, as did the imam of the Moscow mosque, providing food and prayer. Aleksii made public statements against the coup and reportedly worked behind the scenes to shore up support with the military (Ellis 1996, p. 130; Garrard and Garrard 2008, p. 26).

By the time the Soviet Union collapsed in December 1991, little remained of the church-state relationship first conceived by the Bolsheviks in 1917. In an extraordinarily brief period of time, Gorbachev had broken entirely with atheism and restored religion to public life.

LEGACIES FOR THE POST-SOVIET CHURCH AND STATE

Seventy years of imposed secularization have complicated church-state relationships, religion's role in society, and religious identity in the post-Soviet region. Though a significant degree of atheization occurred, scholars were surprised by the persistence of religious belief and practice and the rebound in religious self-identification. Catherine Wanner argues that, in addition to the tenacity of genuine belief, the state's appropriation of sacred language, spaces, and rituals in the name of communism kept alive a spirituality that has been channeled back into more traditional faiths (2007, p. 2). The Soviet experiment helps us to understand more about the religious change engendered by secularization, especially as it relates to power and the state (Wanner 2012, p. 8).

Each of the major religious traditions has its own unique post-Soviet story. Ukraine has become known as the Bible Belt of the (former) USSR, home to the largest Baptist community in Europe and the largest megachurch in Europe, the charismatic Evangelical Christian Embassy of the Blessed Kingdom of God for All Nations. Evangelicals in Ukraine have managed to build strong international ties in the post-Soviet world while still maintaining robust local community through church groups, schools, and social services (Wanner 2007, p. 1, 5). The Russian Orthodox Church, however, has struggled to find its place in post-Soviet society, sparring with elements of the Orthodox world, failing to develop any kind of comprehensive social engagement program (and thus depending fully on local initiatives), and resisting calls to become both more relevant and more missional (Kenworthy 2008, p. 49; Davis 2003, p. 235; Ellis 1986, p. 90, 279). Despite the fact that the ROC emerged as the "largest actor within Russian civil society," close connections and secretive financial dealings with the Russian state have led to widespread distrust of its hierarchy (Papkova 2008, p. 56; Davis 2003, p. 212, 244). As it jealously tries to protect its favored status, the ROC episcopate has supported government moves to discourage religious pluralism, a step back toward Soviet-style management of the religious landscape.

In some parts of the former Soviet Union, a revived nationalism has fused religious and ethnic identities, stripping them of spiritual meaning. Such religio-ethnonational melding suggests that religion is "inherited and inalienable" (Wanner 2012, p. 7), thus it is common to meet people in the former Soviet space who claim no faith but identify as Orthodox or Muslim (Luehrmann 2011, p. 19). Political leaders in some of the former

Soviet republics frequently use religious language and solicit the approval of faith communities for political acts or to win over constituencies (Steinberg and Wanner 2008, pp. 2, 7; Ramet 1993, p. 49). Most former republics of the Soviet Union declare separation of church and state, guarantee freedom of worship as a human right, and practice some degree of religious tolerance, yet in practice are still working out the church-state relationship in light of the Soviet past.

FURTHER READING

Davis, Nathaniel. 2003. *A Long Walk to Church: A Contemporary History of Russian Orthodoxy*. Boulder: Westview.
    Combining thirty years of diplomatic experience in Russia with archival research and interviews, Davis' history of Russian Orthodoxy is the most reliable and up-to-date survey available. Besides being beautifully written, it includes enormous amounts of data and anecdotal evidence.
Smolkin, Victoria. 2018. *A Sacred Space Is Never Empty: A History of Soviet Atheism*. Princeton: Princeton University Press.
    The first history of atheism in the Soviet Union from 1917 to 1991, Smolkin's nuanced and fascinating book makes a significant contribution to our understanding of religion, ideology, and the collapse of the Soviet Union.
Tasar, Eren. 2017. *Soviet and Muslim: The Institutionalization of Islam in Central Asia*. New York: Oxford University Press.
    A multifaceted look at Islam in Central Asia during the postwar Soviet era drawing on deep archival work in multiple languages, Tasar's work provides a view of religious institutions that decenters Moscow and Orthodoxy.

REFERENCES

Balzer, Marjorie Mandelstam. 1993. Dilemmas of the Spirit: Religion and Atheism in the Yakut Sakha Republic. In *Religious Policy in the Soviet Union*, ed. Sabrina Petra Ramet, 231–251. Cambridge: Cambridge University Press.
Baran, Emily B. 2014. *Dissent on the Margins: How Soviet Jehovah's Witnesses Defied Communism and Lived to Preach About It*. Oxford: Oxford University Press.
Bociurkiw, Bohdan R. 1986. The Formulation of Religious Policy in the Soviet Union. *Journal of Church and State* 28 (3): 423–438.
Bourdeaux, Michael. 1968. *Religious Ferment in Russia: Protestant Opposition to Soviet Religious Policy*. London: Macmillan.
———, ed. 1995. *The Politics of Religion in Russia and the New States of Eurasia*. Armonk, NY: M.E. Sharpe.

Chrystostom, P. John. 1966. *Church and State in Soviet Russia: The Fate of the Moscow Patriarchate, 1917–1960*. Translated by George J. Undreiner. Taunas, West Germany: Haus der Begegnung.

Chumachenko, Tatiana A. 2002. *Church and State in Soviet Russia: Russian Orthodoxy from World War II to The Khrushchev Years*. Translated by Edward E. Roslof. Armonk, NY: ME Sharpe.

Conquest, Robert, ed. 1968. *Religion in the USSR*. London: The Bodley Head.

Corley, Felix. 1992. *Armenia and Karabakh: Ancient Faith, Modern War*. London: CTS Publications.

———. 1996. *Religion in the Soviet Union: An Archival Reader*. Washington Square, NY: NYU Press.

———. 2010. The Armenian Apostolic Church. In *Eastern Christianity and the Cold War, 1945–91*, ed. Lucian N. Leustean, 189–203. London: Routledge.

Davis, Nathaniel. 2003. *A Long Walk to Church: A Contemporary History of Russian Orthodoxy*. Boulder: Westview.

Dickinson, Anna. 2003. Domestic and Foreign Policy Considerations and the Origins of Post-war Soviet Church-State Relations, 1941–6. In *Religion and the Cold War*, ed. Dianne Kirby, 23–36. New York: Palgrave Macmillan Ltd.

Ellis, Jane. 1986. *The Russian Orthodox Church: A Contemporary History*. London: Croom Helm.

———. 1993. Some Reflections About Religious Policy under Kharchev. In *Religious Policy in the Soviet Union*, ed. Sabrina Petra Ramet, 84–104. Cambridge: Cambridge University Press.

———. 1996. *The Russian Orthodox Church: Triumphalism and Defensiveness*. Houndmills: Macmillan.

Garrard, John, and Carol Garrard. 2008. *Russian Orthodoxy Resurgent: Faith and Power in the New Russia*. Princeton: Princeton University Press.

Hebly, J.A. 1993. The State, the Church, and the Oikumene: The Russian Orthodox Church and the World Council of Churches, 1948–1985. In *Religious Policy in the Soviet Union*, ed. Sabrina Petra Ramet, 105–122. Cambridge: Cambridge University Press.

Jones, Stephen F. 2010. The Georgian Orthodox Church. In *Eastern Christianity and the Cold War, 1945–91*, ed. Lucian N. Leustean, 99–120. London: Routledge.

Kalkandjieva, Daniela. 2015. *The Russian Orthodox Church, 1917–1948: From Decline to Resurrection*. New York: Routledge.

Karpushin, V.A., ed. 1965. *Populiarnye lektsii po ateizmu*. Moskva: Izd-vo polit. lit-ry.

Kirby, Dianne. 2003a. Religion and the Cold War—An Introduction. In *Religion and the Cold War*, ed. Dianne Kirby, 1–22. New York: Palgrave Macmillan Ltd.

———. 2003b. Harry Truman's Religious Legacy: The Holy Alliance, Containment and the Cold War. In *Religion and the Cold War*, ed. Dianne Kirby, 77–102. New York: Palgrave Macmillan Ltd.

———. 2018. The Roots of the Religious Cold War: Pre-Cold War Factors. *Social Sciences* 7: 56. https://doi.org/10.3390/socsci7040056.

Kenworthy, Scott M. 2008. To Save the World or to Renounce It: Modes of Moral Action in Russian Orthodoxy. In *Religion, Morality, and Community in Post-Soviet Societies*, eds. Mark D. Steinberg and Catherine Wanner, 21–54. Bloomington: Indiana University Press.

Knox, Zoe. 2018. *Jehovah's Witnesses and the Secular World: From the 1870s to the Present*. London: Palgrave Macmillan.

Kuromiya, Hiroaki. 2012. *Conscience on Trial: The Fate of Fourteen Pacifists in Stalin's Ukraine, 1952–53*. Toronto: University of Toronto Press.

Laitila, Teuvo. 2010. The Finnish Orthodox Church. In *Eastern Christianity and the Cold War, 1945–91*, ed. Lucian N. Leustean, 282–298. London: Routledge.

Leustean, Lucian N. 2010a. Eastern Christianity and the Cold War: An Overview. In *Eastern Christianity and the Cold War, 1945–91*, ed. Lucian N. Leustean, 1–16. London: Routledge.

———. 2010b. Other Orthodox Churches Behind the Iron Curtain. In *Eastern Christianity and the Cold War, 1945–91*, ed. Lucian N. Leustean, 204–218. London: Routledge.

Luchterhandt, Otto. 1993. The Council for Religious Affairs. In *Religious Policy in the Soviet Union*, ed. Sabrina Petra Ramet, 55–83. Cambridge: Cambridge University Press.

Luehrmann, Sonja. 2011. *Secularism Soviet Style: Teaching Atheism and Religion in a Volga Republic*. Bloomington: Indiana University Press.

Lupinin, Nickolas. 2010. The Russian Orthodox Church. In *Eastern Christianity and the Cold War, 1945–91*, ed. Lucian N. Leustean, 19–39. London: Routledge.

Pius XI. 1937. Divini Redemptoris. The Holy See, March 19. https://www.vatican.va/content/piusxi/en/encyclicals/documents/hf_p-xi_enc_19370319_divini-redemptoris.html.

Papkova, Irina. 2008. The Freezing of Historical Memory? The Post-Soviet Russian Orthodox Church and the Council of 1917. In *Religion, Morality, and Community in Post-Soviet Societies*, 85–114. Bloomington: Indiana University Press.

Pospielovsky, Dimitry. 1984. *The Russian Church Under the Soviet Regime, Vols I & II*. Crestwood, NJ: St. Vladimir's Seminary Press.

Ramet, Sabrina Petra. 1992. Protestantism and Communism: Patterns of Interaction in Eastern Europe and the Soviet Union. In *Protestantism and Politics in Eastern Europe and Russia: The Communist and Postcommunist Eras. Christianity Under Stress, Vol. III*, ed. Sabrina Petra Ramet, 1–10. Durham: Duke University Press.

———. 1993. Religious Policy in the Era of Gorbachev. In *Religious Policy in the Soviet Union*, ed. Sabrina Petra Ramet, 31–52. Cambridge: Cambridge University Press.

"Record of a Conversation between I. V. Stalin and the Roman Catholic Priest Stanislaus Orlemanski about the Feelings of the Polish Nationals in the United States toward the USSR." 1944. History and Public Policy Program Digital Archive, *Vostochnaia Evropa*, vol. 1, edited by G.P. Murashko, et al., 36–42 (AVPRF, f. 6, op. 6, p. 42, d. 548, 1. 9–15). Translated by Svetlana Savranskaya. April 28. https://digitalarchive.wilsoncenter.org/document/123130.

Rotter, Andrew J. 2000. Christians, Muslims, and Hindus: Religion and U.S.-South Asian Relations, 1947–1954. *Diplomatic History* 2 (4): 593–613.

Sapiets, Marite. 1990. *True Witness: The Story of Seventh Day Adventists in the Soviet Union*. Kent: Keston College.

Sawatsky, Walter. 1992. Protestantism in the USSR. In *Protestantism and Politics in Eastern Europe and Russia: The Communist and Postcommunist Eras. Christianity Under Stress, Vol. III*, 237–275. Durham: Duke University Press.

———. 1993. Protestantism in the USSR. In *Religious Policy in the Soviet Union*, ed. Sabrina Petra Ramet, 319–349. Cambridge: Cambridge University Press.

Smolkin, Victoria. 2018. *A Sacred Space Is Never Empty: A History of Soviet Atheism*. Princeton: Princeton University Press.

Steinberg, Mark D., and Catherine Wanner, eds. 2008. *Religion, Morality, and Community in Post-Soviet Societies*. Bloomington: Indiana University Press.

Stone, Andrew B. 2008. "Overcoming Peasant Backwardness": The Khrushchev Antireligious Campaign and the Rural Soviet Union. *The Russian Review* 67 (2): 296–320.

Tasar, Eren. 2017. *Soviet and Muslim: The Institutionalization of Islam in Central Asia*. New York: Oxford University Press.

Troyanovsky, Igor, ed. 1991. *Religion in the Soviet Republics: A Guide to Christianity, Judaism, Islam, Buddhism, and Other Religions*. San Francisco: HarperCollins.

Walters, Philip. 1993. A Survey of Soviet Religious Policy. In *Religious Policy in the Soviet Union*, ed. Sabrina Petra Ramet, 3–30. Cambridge: Cambridge University Press.

Wanner, Catherine. 2007. *Communities of the Converted: Ukrainians and Global Evangelism*. Ithaca: Cornell University Press.

———, ed. 2012. *State Secularism and Lived Religion in Soviet Russia and Ukraine*. New York: Oxford University Press.

Warhola, James W. 1992. Central vs Local Authority in Soviet Religious Affairs 1964–89. *Journal of Church and State* 34 (1): 15–37.

Wasyliw, Zenon V. 2010. The Ukrainian Autocephalous Orthodox Church. In *Eastern Christianity and the Cold War, 1945–91*, ed. Lucian N. Leustean, 156–172. London: Routledge.

Weinberg, Robert. 2008. Demonizing Judaism in the Soviet Union during the 1920s. *Slavic Review* 67 (1): 120–153.

PART II

Religion and the State in Europe

CHAPTER 7

France's Long March from State Religion to Secular State

Stephen M. Davis

For centuries of French history, secular authority was at the service of ecclesiastical authority with restraints on personal liberty. Christianity existed as a politico-religious system present in the daily life of subjects. The dominant physical presence of churches and monuments served as a constant reminder that people lived in a Christian nation. The beginning of official Christianity in Europe is dated to the conversion of Constantine (272–337) in the fourth century AD. The distinction between church and state was erased with privileges accorded to the Roman Church and the intervention of the emperor in the affairs of the church. In 498 AD, following victory in the battle of Tolbiac, Frankish King Clovis (466–511) received Christian baptism on Christmas Day from the bishop of Reims along with 3000 followers (Chaunu and Mension-Rigau 1996, p. 10). This event is regarded as the beginning of Christian France, or Christendom, a fusion of the political and religious spheres, and "the first of the Germanic nations to espouse the orthodox Christianity of the empire" (Walker et al. 1985, p. 150).

S. M. Davis (✉)
Grace Church, Philadelphia, PA, USA
e-mail: sdavisgcp@gmail.com

© The Author(s), under exclusive license to Springer Nature Switzerland AG 2023
S. Holzer (ed.), *The Palgrave Handbook of Religion and State Volume II*, https://doi.org/10.1007/978-3-031-35609-4_7

127

With the Church's ascendancy, "'Christendom' appeared—a single society with two expressions of power. The coronation of Charlemagne by Pope Leo III in 800 made the question of who governed Christendom less clear" (Lillback 2017, p. 678). The monarchy by divine right (*droit divin*) was installed in power through the coronation and by the consecration of the Church. The king supported the Church in establishing pontifical states with financial and military participation. During these early periods of Christian France there was no religious pluralism. "In the medieval West one had no choice but to be born into the (essentially unique and indivisible) Church.... In the Middle Ages the Church's affairs were matters of State, but only for the elite who made the decisions" (Cameron 1991, p. 198). The configuration of church and state structures ensured that the form of Christianity held by those in power was rarely transformed into anything resembling biblical Christianity (Delumeau 1977, pp. 22–23).

CHRISTIAN FRANCE?

Wessels asks a probing question concerning the nature of Christianity in French history: "How Christian was Europe really? To what extent has it been de-Christianized today?" He responds that Europe was largely Christianized by 750 AD if one uses the marks of baptism and other religious rituals, yet he questions "how deeply this Christianization had really penetrated in the so-called Christianized areas" (1994, pp. 3–4). Many associated with the Christian faith were attached to the religious form as such, but the content, the message of love, was hardly evident in the reality of human relations (Ferry 1996, p. 245). The Christianization of Europe in medieval times was unsuccessful. Both Protestant Reformers and their Catholic adversaries viewed the peasantry, which constituted the vast majority of Europeans, as ignorant of Christianity, given to pagan superstitions and to vices (Delumeau 1977, p. 90). Delumeau asserts that one can speak of medieval Christianity only by an abuse of language or by holding to the myth of a golden age, and that those living during that period often lived as if they had no moral code (1977, p. 29). Christianity was a project or a dream that was wrongly taken for a reality (1977, p. 41). In a pre-revolutionary context, with the union of church and state, it was necessary that everyone belong, willingly or not, to the cultural and moral framework established by the Roman Church. For many it was simply conformism, resignation, and forced hypocrisy (1977, p. 73).

CHRISTIAN UNITY FRACTURED

At the dawn of the sixteenth century there were elements in place to fracture the coercive unity of the Christian religion in France and challenge the growing absolutism of the monarchy. For centuries Europe had endured disaster after disaster, and the Catholic Church had experienced division and contestations to her authority. The Black Plague from 1346 to 1353 had taken over 25 million lives; the Hundred Years' War finally ended in 1453; and Constantinople was captured by the Ottoman Turks that same year. Haunted by death and the prospect of final judgment, people turned to the Church and to her saints for protection. The dogma of purgatory was promulgated as an intermediate place between heaven and hell and led the Church to offer indulgences to shorten the period of suffering. The sale of indulgences by the Dominican monk Johann Tetzel in Germany provoked Luther's ire and led to his protest in posting Ninety-Five Theses on the door of the Castle Church in Wittenberg on October 31, 1517. He had seen the corruption of the Church firsthand during a visit to Rome, and his eyes were soon opened to the wondrous biblical and apostolic truth of justification by faith. As a faithful Catholic monk, Luther initially sought the reform of the Church from within. In time he would understand the Church's intransigence and the impossibility of significant reform (Bost 1996, p. 28).

Prior to the Reformation, the monarchy and the Roman Church in France were wedded without religious competition. The Church communicated to the faithful only fragments of Scripture interpreted by the Church in Latin which the common people did not understand. Belief in the Church had replaced belief in the gospel of Jesus Christ. The pope claimed to represent Jesus Christ as the Vicar of Christ on earth, and the decrees of popes were placed on the same level of authority as Holy Scripture. Rather than accepting criticism or attempting reformation, the Church condemned and silenced her critics (Bost 1996, pp. 17–18). Scholars uniformly look to the Reformation as the beginning of religious, social, and political turmoil in France which would destabilize both the monarchy and the Church. In its wake, "the Reformation manifestly split the ecclesiastical structure of the Middle Ages and thereby shattered the framework of that society called Christendom" (Bainton 1952, p. 4). This religious and political foment of the sixteenth century challenged the status quo and brought significant changes. The emergence of a religious minority in a kingdom of Catholic religion and culture led to confessional and political confrontation (Garrisson 2001, p. 11).

The Catholic Church had been in decline for centuries long before the Reformation, and "the disintegration of this stupendous structure of theocracy and theology had already set in" (Bainton 1952, p. 12). There was a widespread spiritual crisis throughout Europe with multiple causes. The venality of the pontifical court and the debasement of the clergy were themes for satirists. Many Christians began to consider Rome as Babylon and the Pope as the Antichrist. Until this time, religious revolts, often complicated by national interests, led only to local movements and peasant uprisings followed by brutal suppression and suffering. Above all, at the root of the spiritual crisis was the Church's "total inability to bring peace and solace to troubled generations in an era of dissolving certainties .... The consolations of the Church failed to satisfy" (Elton 1999, p. 11).

Luther's early writings were eagerly received in France before being condemned by the Sorbonne in 1521 (Diefendorf 1991, p. 49). His writings had spread widely and were soon censured and publicly burned. It was at this time that those who spoke about the Reformation, or were designated for persecution by the inquisitors, were called "Lutherans" regardless of their connection with Luther (Elton 1999, p. 81). The first "Lutheran" was burned alive at the stake in Paris in August 1523, an Augustinian monk named Jean Vallière. By the simple fact of their existence, Protestant teachings challenged the authority of the king and the principle of ecclesiastical privilege in their attack against the first privileged order, the Church of France (Bost 1996, p. 29). Early on in France it became clear that the Catholic Church wanted no part in a Reformation which threatened both the privileged Church and the increasingly authoritarian state on the path to absolute monarchism.

There were non-schismatic priests and bishops within the Church who sought reform, ashamed of the corruption of the papacy which sacrificed spiritual authority for material interests. Historians are not in agreement on whether to call these attempts at reform from within the Church a Counter-Reformation or Catholic Reform. They do largely concur "that there were traditions of protest and renewal that went back well into the fifteenth century and in themselves owed nothing to the Protestant revolution" (Elton 1999, p. 125). Followers of Erasmus like Lefèvre d'Étaples (1455–1536) sought reform from within the Church to address the shocking state of affairs. Other clergy, not tempted by internal reform, were attracted nonetheless to novel ideas which often condemned them to the same fate as heretics. The monk Jean de Caturce was burned to death at Toulouse in 1532, and a former inquisitor, Louis Rochette, was executed in 1538 for proclaiming his new-found faith (Miquel 1980, pp. 154–155). These early attempts at reform were ultimately unsuccessful, their advocates identified as Lutherans, and they were swiftly condemned as traitors to the state and heretics in the eyes of the Church (Elton 1999, p. 75). The Council of Trent (1545–1563) would mount a Counter-Reformation to the Protestant Reformation to establish Catholic dogma and attempt a reform of the pervasive moral laxity and indiscipline among the clergy (Baubérot and Carbonnier-Burkard 2016, p. 16).

Jonathan Bloch considers it an error to imagine that Christianity in France was united and strong at the dawn of the Reformation and maintains that pagan elements were present in the various expressions of Catholicism. He explains that this situation permitted Protestantism to progressively gain a foothold without meeting the resistance that a united Catholicism would have provided (2015, p. 7). Elton asserts that "Luther did not assail a well-ordered society but one in the throes of moral decay and spiritual doubt; and he was not alone in recognising these weaknesses" (1999, p. 125). The Church appeared too closely tied to the nobility, too distant from the issues confronting common people, and blind and deaf to the need for spiritual reformation and socioeconomic reform. Skepticism and criticism grew toward the Church's authority and dogmatic assertions. Superstition abounded in the diverse expressions of Catholicism, advances in adult literacy led to contempt for untrained priests, and "fiscal privileges enjoyed by the clergy were a source of particular irritation" (McGrath 1990, p. 9). This instability and disenchantment of the times permitted Protestantism to progressively gain a foothold without meeting the resistance that a united and respected Catholicism would have provided (Bloch 2015, p. 7). Gallican and Ultramontane factions and infighting within the French Church heightened tensions and suspicions between Rome and France. The division and quests for power provided fertile soil in diverse intellectual and religious milieux, at least initially, for the new religious ideas which came from Germany (Baubérot and Carbonnier-Burkard 2016, p. 13).

These challenges to Rome's religious hegemony led to increasing hostilities and repression and were foreboding precursors to the Wars of Religion. The tyrannical tendencies of the powerful French monarchy and complicit Church were unmistakably seen in their united response to *l'affaire des placards* in 1534 and 1535. Placards smuggled in from

Switzerland were posted on walls around Paris to denounce the mass as sorcery. The leaders of the Sorbonne persuaded François I (1494–1547) that Protestants wanted to provoke an uprising in France. From this moment on, François I consented to brutal measures to suppress the heretics with widespread persecution. In response to the placards, an elaborate procession against the heretics was organized in January 1535 during which at least twenty heretics were burned to death and scores of others fled the city (Bost 1996, p. 44). The procession advanced throughout the city with royal princes, numerous relics, and reliquary caskets including those of Saint Marcel and Saint Geneviève. *L'affaire des placards* "marked the termination of Lutheran success in France and, despite the later Calvinist explosion, the end of any hope that the Reformation might conquer that country" (Elton 1999, p. 80).

In a few decades, the Reformation's influence in France "not only shattered the unity of religion, but it led to the contesting of the monarchy itself" (Holt 2002, p. 23). This new religion became known as Calvinism and its followers were called Huguenots. Carter Lindberg states that "the French Calvinists preferred the term *Réformés*, the Reformed. Catholic satires of the time called them *la Religion Déformée*" (1996, p. 282). By 1561–1562 Calvinism became a considerable power in the kingdom with about two million adherents or one out of ten French people. Among them were academics and former religious workers, bourgeoisie from legal and commercial professions, and representatives of high and low nobility, whose conversions led to the conversion of entire cities and villages. Their strength and determination frightened the Catholic hierarchy and constrained the authorities to seek a solution. The growth of this new faith raised fears and concerns that needed to be addressed by the royal family since the converts to Protestantism "were simply too numerous to suppress" (Holt 2002, p. 25).

WARS OF RELIGION

The Wars of Religion and persecution of Protestants from the sixteenth to eighteenth centuries cannot be divorced from political, socioeconomic, and military efforts to gain or retain power. Prior to the Wars of Religion there was little organized Protestant resistance to the state. The politics of both Protestants and Catholics involved calling on foreign powers: Spain, Germany, Italy, and Switzerland for Catholics; mostly England and Lutheran princes in Germany for Protestants. The royal houses of

France—Valois-Angoulême, Bourbon, Guise (branch of the house of Lorraine), and Montmorency—were often in competition and made alliances according to political expediency. The house of Guise in France was the most implacable archenemy of Protestants, and its members became the architects of the Saint Bartholomew's Day massacre. Political intrigues, self-serving machinations, assassinations, and executions were never far from religious questions. François de Lorraine (1519–1563), also known as François de Guise, commander of French Catholic forces, was assassinated in 1563; Henri de Guise had Gaspard de Coligny assassinated in 1572; Henri de Guise and his brother Charles, the cardinal of Guise were assassinated by Henri III (1551–1589) in 1588, who himself was assassinated by a monk in 1589; Henri IV was assassinated in 1610 by a Catholic fanatic; kings Charles IX and Louis XIV had their subjects massacred, and they declared outlaws and traitors all those who did not embrace their Catholic faith. Louis XVI and his family were executed in 1793 by their subjects, and priests of the formerly triumphant Catholic confession fled into exile. In all this some saw the hand of God; others the hand of man (Stéphan 1945, p. 146).

The cost of wars weakened the French state, yet the construction of an absolute monarchy begun under Louis IX (1214–1270) continued unabated. Whatever internal and external struggles were endured, the French monarchy continued to reinforce its powers during the first half of the sixteenth century at the expense of clergy, nobles, privileged cities, and provincial states with crushing taxes. Calvin's influence would soon eclipse that of Luther with the publication of his *Institutes*, in Latin in 1536 and in French in 1541. In a short time, the majority of French provinces were profoundly saturated by Calvinism. The first synod of the Reformed Church took place in 1559, the same year as the Treaty of Cateau-Cambrésis which marked the end of the struggle between France and Spain for the control of Italy (Elton 1999, p. 193). The royal power in France lost two battles at the same time: the battle against foreign adversaries and the battle against heresy. The kingdom was besieged from within by a foreign religion that could not be tolerated and thus must perish. A heavy price would be paid by those who dared resist (Miquel 1980, pp. 28–29).

EARLY COMPROMISES

Challenges to the concept of the inseparability of church and state eventually led to compromises under Catherine de Médicis (1519–1589). The Edict of January 1562 accorded Protestants partial rights to privately practice their religion in government-approved places. According to Lindberg, "Huguenot public worship was allowed in private homes in towns and outside the towns' walls. This was the watershed for French Protestantism" (1996, p. 289). The authorities of the Church considered Catherine's edict in contradiction with the Council of Trent (1545–1563) which had anathematized the heresy of Luther and Calvin. She soon became aware of the dangerous situation in which the edict placed her and sought to side with and placate the Catholic faction.

The massacre of Protestants in Vassy in March 1562 by the Duke of Guise foreshadowed the bloodshed which would follow in the Wars of Religion for almost forty years. At stake was the status of the Reformed religion in the kingdom (Carbonnier-Burkard 2012, pp. 14–15). At Vassy, the Duke, with 200 armed men, came across a large congregation of Huguenots gathered in a barn for worship and set upon them. Some seventy Huguenots were killed and many more wounded. The incident sparked more massacres, and the religious wars were on. The result was tragic and "only after four decades of civil war would the nation re-emerge with any semblance of community, imagined or otherwise" (Holt 2002, p. 25). The landscape of post-Reformation France was permanently altered. Under the then-present structures of government there could be no peaceful coexistence between two competing religions. However, Catherine's Edict of January 1562 had broken with the past and "made France the first Western European kingdom to grant legal recognition to two forms of Christianity at once" (Benedict 2002, p. 147).

In short order, the inability of two incompatible faiths to live peacefully side-by-side led to the massacre on St. Bartholomew's Day on August 24, 1572, which then spread from Paris to other cities. The massacre "precipitated a massive wave of defections from the Protestant cause. In the wake of the killing, Charles IX forbade the Reformed believers from gathering for worship—to protect them against violence, his edict proclaimed, but also because he undoubtedly realized that the massacre might end the Protestant problem once and for all" (Benedict 2002, p. 157). One Catholic historian reports that Pope Gregory XIII (1502–1585), upon receiving the news of the massacre, decreed a jubilee of thanksgiving, struck a commemorative medal, and commissioned Italian artist Vasari to immortalize the event by a fresco on the walls in the Vatican *Sala Regia* (Delumeau 1977, p. 32). Protestants and Catholics were both prisoners of a system of thought that considered heresy the greatest enemy and mutual extermination an act of justice in the name of God (Delumeau 1977, p. 35). One major consequence of the massacre was "a flurry of publications about the limits of obedience to royal authority that made the years after 1572 one of the most fertile periods of political reflection in all of French history" (Benedict 2002, p. 159).

EDICT OF NANTES

The Edict of Nantes in 1598 was conceived by Henry IV to end the civil and religious torment which plunged France into chaos. His conversion to Catholicism and the Edict of Nantes brought the Wars of Religion to an end. The state became the guarantor of civil peace and liberty of conscience for the two religions. The edict's import lay in considering individuals in two ways. First, as political subject, the individual was expected to obey the king, regardless of confession. Second, as a believer, the subject was free to choose his religion which was now considered a private matter. The edict opened access for Protestants to universities and public offices. Protestants were allowed garrisons in several towns, most notably the port city of La Rochelle. The Edict of Nantes survived almost a century before its revocation, during which time French Catholics and Protestants cohabitated in relative calm (Dusseau 2006, p. 13). However, as early as 1629 with the Edict of Nîmes under Louis XIII, Protestants experienced the loss of some gains. Their pastors had the right to preach, celebrate the Lord's Supper, baptize, and officiate at marriages only in villages and cities authorized by the Edict of Nantes. Louis XIV, grandson of Henry IV, governed as an absolute monarch and claimed the divine right as God's representative on earth. Under pressure from the Catholic clergy, the king enacted the Revocation of the Edict of Nantes on October 17, 1685, also known as the Edict of Fontainebleau. The king's subjects were compelled to adopt the religion of the one who ruled by divine right. Protestant worship was forbidden in France and the edict led once again to the departure of thousands of French Protestants (De Montclos 1988, pp. 67–69). Protestants lost the right to have separate cemeteries and were compelled to receive the sacraments of the Church. The banned religion became officially designated R.P.R, *religion prétendue réformée* (Carbonnier-Burkard 2012, p. 9).

WAR OF THE CAMISARDS

The Catholic Church welcomed the Revocation, aligned herself with the monarchy, and rejected religious liberty and freedom of conscience (Gaillard 2004, pp. 21–22). The Revocation sheds light on the religious, regional, and historic collective memory of the Cévenol region of France and the war of the Camisards, waged by Calvinist insurgents during the persecutions which followed the Revocation of the Edict of Nantes. The Camisards owe their name to the white shirt they wore over their clothing for recognition among themselves in battle (*Petit Robert* 2007, p. 335). They fought to defend and to reclaim their religious rights obtained under the Edict of Nantes in 1598. They fought above all for the freedom of conscience to worship God according to Protestant teaching. The war, triggered by the desire of Louis XIV to impose one law and one faith, tore apart the Cévennes from 1702 to 1705. Thousands of men were imprisoned, deported, sent to the galleys, and tortured, and more than 500 villages were burned to the ground (Chamson 2002, p. iii). The power of the Church and the exclusion and exile of hundreds of thousands of Protestants would harden antagonisms for the next century. Yet, according to De Montclos, the idea of tolerance was born (1988, p. 69).

THE FRENCH REVOLUTION

The eighteenth century was marked by the Enlightenment (*le siècle des Lumières*), known also as the Age of Reason and extended from the death of Louis XIV in 1714 to the French Revolution in 1789. The secularization of the state in France finds its origins in the philosophy of Enlightenment thinkers in opposition to religion and the power of the Catholic Church (Jeantet 2006, p. 29). Enlightenment philosophy created the conditions for the recognition of *laïcité* as a principle of a society open to religious freedom and philosophical thinking, whether agnostic or atheistic, detached from religion (Dusseau 2006, pp. 36–37). Voltaire advocated for an enlightened monarchy, Rousseau chose the Republic, but both condemned the obscurantism of the Church (Dusseau 2006, p. 13). With their critique of religious superstition, they considered that a rupture with religion would birth a democratic universe (Ferry 1996,

p. 37). These times have been described as a blast of knowledge in constant movement, like a steady tide against the cliffs of dogma. When the insatiable thirst for change met the aspirations of the enlightened nobility, of the dynamic bourgeoisie, and of the miserable commoners, the result was the Revolution (Gaillard 2004, p. 22).

The French Revolution serves as the starting point of the secularization of French society and her institutions. The term *laïcité* was not yet in use at the time and first appeared as a neologism in the nineteenth century in the context and struggle of removing the Church's influence over public education (Ducomte 2001, p. 3). The arrival of the Revolution broke with the past model of governance by the Ancien Régime with its societal divisions and the mingling of church and state in the affairs of the citizenry. Economically, the nation was dominated by the feudal system: its class structure revolved around a three-tiered hierarchy, and its political system was one of absolutism, the divine right of kings consecrated by the Church. The pre-revolutionary social hierarchy in France was composed of three orders or estates (*les trois états*): clergy, nobility, and peasantry (*le tiers-état*). The first two groups were largely exonerated from the crushing taxes imposed on the peasantry. The monarchy reached its zenith under Louis XIV and was greatly weakened beginning in 1774 under the mediocre Louis XVI (1754–1793). The king remained the living symbol of a system in which the Roman Church was the state religion (Vovelle 2006, pp. 6–9). It comes as no surprise that the peasantry welcomed the Revolution, at least in principle. The atrocities of the Revolution and the Reign of Terror which followed are well-known and in hindsight rightly criticized. Less well-known is the oppression endured by the French people under the nobility and under the clergy which wielded secular power. In 1789, France had a population of 26 million and over 100,000 clergy. The clergy, representing a tiny fraction of the population, possessed large swaths of territory in the kingdom (Delumeau 1977, pp. 46–47).

The removal of the Catholic Church from public influence and the overthrow of the monarchy were among the objectives achieved by the Revolution. In August 1789, Catholic clergy lost its position as the first of the three orders in France, and the tithe, the Church's principal source of revenue, was eliminated. In November 1789, all the possessions, property, and holdings of the Church became property of the nation. In 1794, all exterior manifestations of worship were forbidden and the Church was confined to the private sphere (Gastaldi 2004). The National Assembly elaborated what would become part of the future Constitution concerning the organization of the Church of France. Priests were required to take an oath of allegiance to the nation, to the king, and to the Constitution. Many clergy refused to obey this law. Their refusal was at the origin of political conflict which led revolutionary France toward a civil war (Bruley 2004, pp. 40–41). The Revolution was well received in many Protestant quarters. Protestants received limited civil status rights in 1787 with the Edict of Toleration and welcomed their emancipation from the intolerance and persecution at the hands of the Church. Then in 1789 they were granted equal rights and the liberty of worship. The Assembly tacitly authorized them to organize at their discretion, which they did notably in opening places of worship in cities where that had been previously forbidden (De Montclos 1988, p. 106).

Louis XVI was executed after being found guilty of treason on January 21, 1793. Two groups, *la Gironde* and *la Montagne*, disputed his fate. The former group, a political entity formed in 1791 by several deputies from the region by the same name, argued for clemency. The latter group, among whom was Robespierre, referred to elevated places at the Convention where the political left sat led by Robespierre and Danton (*Petit Robert* 2007, p. 1154; 1630). They demanded the king's death. According to Robespierre, the Revolution required virtue and terror, "virtue, without which terror is harmful; and terror, without which virtue is powerless" (Robespierre 1967, p. 357).

NAPOLEON BONAPARTE AND THE CONCORDAT

A religious crisis occupied France for ten years before Napoleon (1769–1821) came to power in 1799 to reverse many of the gains of the Revolution. He became the founder of the First Empire which lasted until his defeat at the Battle of Waterloo in 1815, and he died in exile on the island of Saint Helena in 1821. The arrival of Napoleon threw revolutionary, separatist projects into confusion when he seized the initiative to bring religion into his service. Yet the future would reveal that many people freed from obligatory religious duties and rituals would soon fall away from an organized religion which no longer wielded political power.

Napoleon was a man without strong religious leanings. He recognized, however, that the majority of French people were Roman Catholic and he sought to bring the Church under his control for political purposes. The state needed the Church to assume tasks, such as education, that the state did not wish to administer. Pope Pius VII (1742–1823) was elected in

1800 and desired to restore the unity of the Church in the most powerful Catholic nation at the time. The Concordat, signed in 1801 between Napoleon and Pius VII, "was to rule the relations between France and the papacy for more than a century" (Walker et al. 1985, p. 669). The Concordat recognized that the Catholic, Apostolic, and Roman religion was the religion of the majority of French citizens (Cabanel 2004, p. 21). To the Catholic Church's consternation, three other religious confessions—Lutheran, Reformed, and Jewish—received protection of their religious rights and were brought into the service of the state in 1802 with the Organic Orders (Roberts 2014, p. 274). Protestants generally welcomed the Concordat which gave them access to most public positions. Pastors swore an oath of loyalty and became paid employees of the state. Churches were reorganized into consistories which called pastors followed by government confirmation (Baty 1981, pp. 1–2). Although the Concordat offered a level of religious pluralism, Napoleon's objective was the control of religion for societal submission. The head of state appointed bishops while those bishops previously loyal to Rome (*réfractaires*) were forced to resign. The state retained possession of Catholic property seized after the Revolution and assured the upkeep of certain properties. In December 1804, Napoleon Bonaparte was crowned as emperor in Notre-Dame Cathedral in the presence of Pius VII (McManners 1972, p. 4).

The restoration of the Bourbon dynasty followed the fall of Napoleon in 1814. It was accompanied by a spirit of religious retaliation and the return of exiled supporters of the monarchy. Louis XVIII (1755–1824) made it known that he did not want to be king of two peoples. The Charter of 1814 reestablished Catholicism as the state religion. The Concordat remained in force, but the throne and altar were once again united (Ducomte 200, p. 12). A Parisian revolution overthrew the Bourbon monarchy in 1848 which set the stage for the short-lived Second Republic (1848–1851) and the election of its only president, Louis-Napoleon Bonaparte, the nephew of Napoleon Bonaparte. Under Louis-Napoleon, later known as Emperor Napoleon III during the Second Empire (1852–1870), state relations with the Catholic Church became more cordial with a corresponding loss of religious liberty and repression of non-concordataire churches (Pédérzet 1896, p. 132).

On July 18, 1870, bishops of the Church from around the world gathered at Saint Peter's Basilica in Rome to vote their approval of the dogma of the infallibility of the Pope. In speaking *ex cathedra*, the Pope would be preserved from error in faith and practice. With this proclamation, the

Church effectively put an end to papal opposition from the French Gallican wing of the Church. The Council also "gave the final authoritative and irrevocable endorsement of the Augustinian axiom by affirming that no one can be saved outside the church" (Kärkkäinen 2003, p. 71). One day after the papal proclamation of infallibility, France declared war on Prussia and suffered a humiliating defeat in a mere six weeks. Following the resounding rout of the French army at the Battle of Sedan on September 1, 1870, the emperor abdicated his throne after an uprising in Paris which ended the Second Empire. From a religious viewpoint, the defeat in 1870 and the constitutional uncertainty provoked by the fall of the Second Empire resulted in a crisis of conscience. Many were nostalgic for the Ancien Régime which was idealized with the image of a legendary Middle Ages. They looked for a form of government more favorable to the Church which gave birth to a spirit of mysticism (Dansette 1951, p. 37).

Nineteenth-Century Clericalism and Anticlericalism

Throughout the nineteenth century, a battle was waged between anticlericalism, favorable to the ideals of the Revolution, and clericalism which kept alive the dream of a return of the Church in union with the state. The anticlericalism of the nineteenth century did not arrive in a vacuum. It was an attack on religion, on tradition, on the aristocracy, and reflected the philosophical changes that had been in operation since the sixteenth century. To be able to change religion, and to profess atheism or agnosticism without suffering the consequences meted out for centuries, constituted a transformation of the status of religion in secularized societies (Monod 2007, p. 49). The secular Republic and the Catholic Church entered into conflict with alternating periods of extreme tension and of rapprochement (Grévy 2005, p. 9). The anticlericals were described as free thinkers and rationalists, attached to the independence of civil society, advocates of the separation of church and state, and hostile to the interference of the clergy in private life or in community activities. Their clerical adversaries considered anticlerical all those who did not share their beliefs, their conception of church and state relations, or the relation between religion and common life (Rémond 1999, p. 8). Anticlericalism was considered a natural response to the Church's resistance to the idea of a new world order detached from religious certitudes. Under the pontificates of Gregory XVI (1831–1846) and Pius IX (1846–1878), the Church, according to its critics, revealed its incapacity to accept the modern world and the prevailing emphasis on the autonomy of the individual. The anticlericals looked to the Revolution which had freed the people from the tyranny of the Church, removed the repressive tithes to the Church, and restored lands to the dispossessed. The Declaration of the Rights of Man and of the Citizen was viewed as the epitome of liberty from oppression. There was no turning back to the times of religious domination.

One of the most fascinating historical events preceding the Law of Separation in 1905 was the Dreyfus Affair in the 1890s. It is considered a major trigger for the movement which led to the law (Rognon and Weber 2005, p. 41). This event shook France to its core and led to widespread reexamination of its republican values. It may be difficult to properly appreciate the importance of *l'Affaire* more than one hundred years after its occurrence. The details of *l'Affaire* mesmerized not only the French public but reverberated internationally. Émile Zola "denounced the framing of Dreyfus by the military hierarchy [and] constructed the affair as a struggle between liberty and despotism, light and darkness" (Gildea 1994, p. 105). The condemnation, degradation, and exile of Dreyfus set in motion his defense by the Republicans. The enormous influence of Zola contributed to Dreyfus's eventual exoneration and later provided support for the rationale and the defense of the law of 1905 separating the Roman Catholic Church from the state. The Antidreyfusards had the support of the Church and the army, and they were persuaded of the existence of a syndicate grouping anti-France, Jewish, Protestant, and Freemasonry forces (Boyer 2005, p. 72). The Dreyfusards had the support of writers, artists, scientists, radicals, and free thinkers who denounced the alliance of the Church and the army. According to Barzun, "the incredibly long-drawn-out Dreyfus Affair aroused passion and prejudice throughout the world. In France the chain of misdeeds—treason, coercion, perjury, forgery, suicide, and manifest injustice—re-created the cleavage of the 'two Frances,' always reoccurring at critical moments" (2000, p. 630). These critical historical events and the acrimonious debates over the place of religion in France were fundamental to the formal introduction of the principle of *laïcité* in France in 1905.

1905 Law of Separation of Churches and the State

The beginning of the twentieth century announced the first step taken against the Church with the 1901 Law of Associations which required governmental authorization for religious teaching orders. The refusal of authorization led to the closure of teaching institutions and confiscation of property, and many religious workers were forced into exile. It was only a matter of time before the Church came under more intense pressure. President Émile Combes applied the law of 1901 with a vengeance. Parliament rejected most of the requests by religious congregations for authorization, and diplomatic relations with the Vatican suffered (Gaillard 2004, p. 32). Finally, in 1905, the Law of Separation was voted on by the legislature. The vote was preceded by the rupture of diplomatic relations with the Holy See. The rupture rendered the maintenance of the Concordat status quo impossible. Owing to historical factors the Concordat survives today in the region of Alsace-Moselle. These departments were annexed by Germany in 1871 after France's defeat in the Franco-Prussian War and were returned to France following World War I and Germany's defeat in 1918. A condition of their reintegration into France was the continuance of the Concordat (CNEF 2013, p. 14).

Through the Law of Separation, the situation of ecclesiastical institutions throughout France was turned upside down. Often presented as an agreement, the law was in fact an act of force which destroyed the 1801 diplomatic convention. In exchange for an independence the Church was not seeking, the law deprived the Church of its patrimony and resources (Machelon 2012, p. 19). The law was opposed and condemned by Pope Pius X (1835–1914), and was perceived as an aggression against the Catholic Church. Protestants and evangelicals largely welcomed the Law of Separation which granted them legal standing alongside the Catholic Church. Protestant leaders played an important role during this period, including historian Gabriel Monod, Raoul Allier, dean of a Protestant school of theology, and Francis de Pressensé, son of a Protestant pastor and author of the first draft of the Law of Separation in 1903. Louis Méjan, son and brother of pastors, wrote the final version of the law and had the task of applying it as the last director of the Ministry of Religions (Boyer 2005, pp. 74–75). Although presented in a pacifying form deemed beneficial for the institution targeted, the law's application led to violent confrontations. In time the law would undergo amendments to facilitate cohabitation between the separated institutions in a country with an overwhelming Catholic majority. Among these modifications was the creation of chaplain services in hospitals and the armed forces and the return of property to dispossessed institutions (Machelon 2012, p. 20).

Early in the twentieth century there were modifications of the law and new laws to clarify the law of 1905, followed by a period in which the

Church accepted and adapted to its new status, and a later period in which the rise of Islam began to contest established principles of the separation of church and state. However, there was no turning back to the former state of affairs. The battle for a secular state had been won. The Roman Church would never again share power with the state. Rulers would never again rule by divine right. The Republic would control the public education of its youngest citizens. The Third Republic (1870–1940) achieved the ideals of the French Revolution in establishing a new form of religion with its belief in the progress of humanity, intellectual and social freedom, and the formation of young citizens in public schools (Cabanel 2006, pp. 177–179).

Religious confessions responded differently to the law of 1905. The first half of the twentieth century was certainly a time where the freedoms to believe and speak were formally accepted, but great obstacles remained to the expression of these freedoms (Carluer 2015, p. 40). The separation of church and state had little impact on evangelical French Protestant churches who saw an act of Providence in the law. These churches, few in number, emphasized conversion and a regenerate church membership and were distinct from concordataire Reformed churches which had a "*sensibilité évangélique*" (Fath 2005, pp. 151–152). For Judaism, there was no opposition to the law and no conflict with French secularism. During World War I, Jews paid with their blood the debt owed to France for according them citizenship in 1791 (Korsia 2006, pp. 80–82). The law's application, however, would create a tumultuous state of affairs and encounter opposition from the Catholic Church for several years while issues were addressed and eventually resolved. The change of status for the Church and its political defeat had left wounds that many believe began healing during World War I (1914–1918) in what has been called the "*fraternité de tranchées*" between clergy and civilians (Gaillard 2004, p. 36). The war turned people's attention to more serious external threats and served to unite the country as the French clergy supported national unity. French people of all political persuasions fought alongside one another to protect and preserve the Republic. The vast majority of Catholic bishops sided with the patriotic cause. The defense of the nation came first and helped extinguish, at least for a time, ancient quarrels (Prévotat 1998, pp. 13–14). A period of pacification would follow as the nation adapted to the changes.

The twentieth century experienced persistent challenges in the application of the law of 1905 as French society became less homogeneous with the arrival of immigrants of religions which were not present in 1905 or not considered in the law. Practical changes included urban cemeteries with confessional sections where burials took place according to religious confession and kosher and halal meals served in the armed forces (Cabanel 2004, p. 18). The end of the twentieth century would witness a reemergence of debates on the separation of church and state corresponding to demographic changes and the rise of Islam's influence. The legislators in 1905 did not foresee the sociological upheavals which transformed France in the twentieth century. Yet the law of 1905 continues to occupy a fundamental place in the relation of religion and state in France (Boussinesq 1994, p. 57).

DEVELOPMENT OF THE CONCEPT OF *LAÏCITÉ*

French society accommodated itself to religious changes in the twentieth century following the disestablishment of concordataire state churches. The law was both a law of rupture and a law of conciliation. The rupture was considered justified by many since the Church was seen as a threat to the Republic. The conciliation was a guarantee of the free exercise of religion and freedom of conscience (Rognon and Weber 2005, p. 91). French *laïcité* has been deemed a necessary response to confrontations between the Catholic Church and political powers to end several centuries of religious quarrels which profoundly marked and bloodied French society, and was an attempt to battle the imperialism of the Catholic Church of France (Bélorgey 2006, p. 53).

Since 1905, and especially toward the latter half of the twentieth and early twenty-first centuries, the meaning of *laïcité* has evolved and remains a subject of intense debate. There are many who admit the principle of *laïcité* with the condition that they redefine the sense (Pena-Ruiz 2003, p. 17). In official documents, the Conseil d'État recognizes that the term *laïcité* is untranslatable outside of Latin languages and defines *laïcité* as both a juridical concept and a political philosophy (Schrameck 2004). English-language writings often speak of secularism or the secular state. There is general consensus among French writers that *laïcité* is particular to France and linguistically captures a specificity inseparable from its historical context. They see a distinction between secularization as a phenomenon of society that does not require any political implementation, and *laïcité* as a political choice which defines the place of religion in society in an authoritative and legal manner (Roy 2005, pp. 19–20). Gauchet

illustrates this point in making a distinction between a Europe of laicization in Catholic countries characterized by a confessional unicity, and a
Europe of secularization which prevailed in Protestant lands, where following a break with Rome, national churches continued their influence in
the political sphere (1998, pp. 19–20). The former required a political
intervention to release society from the grip of the Catholic Church; the
latter often has a place for a state religion. In general, laicization is associated with countries of Catholic tradition and secularization is more characteristic of Protestant countries. In other words, secularization took place
as a phenomenon of evolving societies in Protestant nations apart from
state intervention. *Laïcité*, however, required an act of legal intervention
from the state in order to force the separation of religious and state
domains (Haarscher 1998, p. 45). In whatever way the nuanced concepts
of secularization and *laïcité* may be viewed, Baubérot makes the stunning
observation that "contrary to the fears of many, secularization and laicization have not led to the disappearance of Christianity" (2008, p. 76).

One of the principal and generally accepted characteristics of *laïcité* in
France is the emancipation from religion. In the first stage of emancipation, religion retained the notion of duty according to Kantian and republican patriotic traditions. The notion of duty was completed with the ideas
of self-sacrifice and anticlericalism and an element of religiosity was preserved. In effect, moral obligations toward God were transferred to moral
obligations toward others in human spheres. This phase, characterized by
the obligations of duty and sacrifice, lasted into the 1950s when the "it is
necessary" yielded to the spell of happiness, the categoric obligation of the
stimulation of the senses, and the right to be true to oneself, freed from all
imposition of values outside of oneself (Ferry 1996, pp. 115–117). This
emancipatory separation was considered necessary since the state serves all
the people (*laos*), and religious conceptions are considered affairs of the
conscience which cannot be imposed on others (Haarscher 1998, p. 9).

Twenty-First-Century Challenges

In twenty-first-century France, *laïcité* remains virtually uncontested as a
concept, value, or principle. The ongoing struggle resides in the meaning
and application of *laïcité* according to each disputatious voice. The resurgence of interest in *laïcité* is unquestionably linked with the emergence of
Islam as the second-largest religion in France (Fontenay 2006, p. 45).
Islam presents the problem of *laïcité* in a different manner to French and

European society. The problem is not the long presence of Muslims in France, but the radicalization of Islam in the 1990s (Cesari 2004, p. 23). The issues now include employees in the public sector who are obligated to be neutral in religious matters, hospitals where women refuse to be treated by male doctors, school debates on displaying religious symbols in dress and accessories, and traditional Nativity displays on municipal property. A critical and unanswered question remains: "How can Islam and Muslims be integrated into Western culture while still maintaining the latter's principles of equality and individual freedoms?" (Cesari 2004, p. 63).

Another emerging area of concern and tension regarding Islam is the rise of anti-Semitism in France. This was highlighted in March 2018 by thousands of French marching in the streets of Paris following the brutal murder of an elderly Jewish woman (Schnapper 2018). Among those who marched were Muslim imams who confessed that Islamic anti-Semitism was the greatest threat that weighs on Islam in the twenty-first century. In turn, the imams were placed under police protection in fear of retaliation by extremists. A month later over 250 politicians, intellectuals, and artists signed a manifesto calling on Islam to denounce as obsolete those texts in the Quran calling for violence against Christians and Jews. Among the signatories were former president Nicholas Sarkozy, three former prime ministers, and a former mayor of Paris (Georges 2018). France faces the challenge of remaining neutral toward religions which refuse to accept the values of the Republic—liberty, equality, and fraternity. Many of the challenges to *laïcité* and their resolution are being decided case-by-case in the legal system. If history is any guide in these matters, there should be little expectation that opposing perspectives will arrive at a consensus.

CONCLUSION

When we understand the history of religion in France, it should be unsurprising to discover that many French people harbor resentment, indifference, or opposition toward religion. It is undeniable that religious memory is full of wounds and that images from the past continue to present obstacles to a good understanding of the gospel. Even more, these negative images feed prejudices against religion today (Coq 2003, p. 305). It can be argued that religion as experienced in France for centuries needed to be removed from its place in the political sphere. As a consequence, however, religion in general declined, became a private affair, and competing ideologies rushed in to fill the void. These ideologies lacked the power to sustain and satisfy, and some led to untold suffering and loss of life (Coq 2003, p. 310). *Laïcité* has been described as a dying religion which once filled France with certitudes, where the emphasis on rights prevailed over duties and where the god of progress was dethroned in the crises of the twentieth century. Other gods, secular and religious, offer guaranteed rights for all differences, fulfillment for all sexual desires, and reparations for seemingly universal victimhood (Cabanel 2006, pp. 177–179).

Tensions exist in France today as secularizing forces push religion into the private sphere and religions raise their claims to be heard in a democratic society. The balance is no longer between a dominant religion and an independent state, but about equality among different religions in the midst of a secular Republic which still bears the strong imprint of Catholicism (CNEF 2013, p. 18). While the nation remains nominally Roman Catholic, many French have rejected the institutionalized church. French resistance to religion and to perceived foreign expressions of religion (i.e., evangelical faith) makes perfect sense when viewed from a historical standpoint. The battle for different visions of religion and its place in the Republic continues to occupy an important place in French society. It is too soon to predict which vision will prevail.

REFERENCES

Bainton, Roland H. 1952. *The Reformation of the Sixteenth Century*. Boston: Beacon Press.

Barzun, Jacques. 2000. *From Dawn to Decadence (1500 to the Present): 500 Years of Western Cultural Life*. New York: Harper Collins.

Baty, Claude. 1981. Les Églises Évangéliques Libres de France: Leur Histoire à Travers la Genèse et l'Évolution de Leurs Principes jusqu'en 1951. Maîtrise en Théologie, Faculté Libre de Théologie Evangélique de Vaux-sur-Seine.

Baubérot, Jean. 2008. *Petite Histoire du Christianisme*. Paris: Éditions Librio.

Baubérot, Jean, and Marianne Carbonnier-Burkard. 2016. *Histoire des Protestants: Une Minorité en France (XVIe–XXIe siècle)*. Paris: Éditions Ellipses.

Bélorgey, Jean-Michel. 2006. Terroirs de la Laïcité. *Revue Politique et Parlementaire* 1038: 52–59.

Benedict, Philip. 2002. The Wars of Religion, 1562–1598. In *Renaissance and Reformation France, 1500–1648*, ed. Mack P. Holt, 147–175. New York: Oxford University Press.

Bloch, Jonathan. 2015. *La Réforme Protestante, de Luther à Calvin: La Réponse aux Abus de la Religion Catholique*. Namur, Belgium: Lemaitre.

Bost, Charles. 1996. *Histoire des Protestants de France*. 9th ed. Carrières-sous-Poissy, France: Éditions La Cause.

Boussinesq, Jean. 1994. *La Laïcité Française: Mémento Juridique*. Paris: Éditions du Seuil.

Boyer, Alain. 2005. *La Loi de 1905: Hier, Aujourd'hui, Demain*. Lyon: Éditions Olivetan.

Bruley, Yves, ed. 2004. *1905, La Séparation des Églises et de l'État: Les Textes Fondateurs*. Paris: Éditions Perrin.

Cabanel, Patrick. 2004. *Les Mots de la Laïcité*. Toulouse: Presses Universitaires du Mirail.

———. 2006. La 'Question Religieuse' et les Solutions en France (XVI–XXI siècle). In *La Laïcité: Une Question au Présent*, ed. Jean Birnbaum et al., 165–184. Nantes: Éditions Cécile Defaut.

Cameron, Euan. 1991. *The European Reformation*. 2nd ed. Oxford: Oxford University Press.

Carbonnier-Burkard, Marianne. 2012. *La Révolte des Camisards*. Rennes: Éditions Ouest-France.

Carluer, Jean-Yves. 2015. Liberté de Dire, Liberté de Croire: Deux Siècles de Défi Évangélique, 1815–2015. In *Libre de le Dire: Fondements et Enjeux de la Liberté de Conscience et d'Expression en France*, 35–73. Marpent, France: BLF Éditions.

Cesari, Jocelyne. 2004. *When Islam and Democracy Meet: Muslims in Europe and in the United States*. New York: Palgrave Macmillan.

Chamson, André. 2002. *Suite Camisarde*. Paris: Éditions Omnibus.

Chaunu, Pierre, and Eric Mension-Rigau. 1996. *Baptême de Clovis, Baptême de la France: De la Religion d' État à la Laïcite d'État*. Paris: Éditions Balland.

CNEF. 2013. *La Laïcité Française: Entre l'Idée, l'Histoire, et le Droit Positif.* Marpent, France: Éditions BLF.

Coq, Guy. 2003. *Laïcité et République: Le Lien Nécessaire*. Paris: Éditions du Félin.

Dansette, Adrien. 1951. *Histoire Religieuse de la France Contemporaine sous la Troisième République*. Paris: Éditions Flammarion.

De Montclos, Xavier. 1988. *Histoire Religieuse de la France*. Paris: Presses Universitaires de France.

Delumeau, Jean. 1977. *Le Christianisme va-t-il Mourir?* Paris: Hachette Édition.

Diefendorf, Barbara B. 1991. *Beneath the Cross: Catholics and Huguenots in Sixteenth-Century Paris*. New York: Oxford University Press.

Ducomte, Jean-Michel. 2001. *La Laïcité*. Toulouse: Milan Presse.

Dusseau, Joëlle. 2006. L'Histoire de la Séparation: Entre Permanences et Ruptures. *Revue Politique et Parlementaire* 1038: 13–22.

Elton, G.R. 1999. *Reformation Europe: 1517–1559*. 2nd ed. Malden, MA: Blackwell.

Fath, Sébastien. 2005. De la Non-Reconnaissance à une Demande de Légitimation? Le Cas du Protestantisme Évangélique. *Archives de Sciences Sociales des Religions* 50: 151–162. http://www.jstor.org/stable/30128895.

Ferry, Luc. 1996. *L'Homme-Dieu ou le Sens de la Vie*. Paris: Éditions Grasset.

Fontenay, Élisabeth de. 2006. Un Enseignement sur les Religions à l'École. In *La Laïcité: Une Question au Présent*, ed. Jean Birnbaum, et al., 37–45. Nantes: Éditions Cécile Defaut.

Gaillard, Jean-Michel. 2004. L'Invention de la Laïcité (1598–1905). In *1905, La Séparation des Églises et de l'État: Les Textes Fondateurs*, ed. Yves Bruley, 19–36. Paris: Éditions Perrin.

Garrisson, Janine, ed. 2001. *Histoire des Protestants en France: De la Réforme à la Révolution*. 2nd ed. Toulouse: Éditions Privat.

Gastaldi, Nadine. 2004. Le Concordat de 1801. *Histoire par l'Image*. http://www.histoire-image.org/etudes/concordat-1801.

Gauchet, Marcel. 1998. *La Religion dans la Démocratie: Parcours de la Laïcité*. Paris: Éditions Gallimard.

Georges, Guillaume. 2018. Manifeste Contre le Nouvel Antisémitisme. *Le Parisien*. http://www.leparisien.fr/societe/manifeste-contre-le-nouvel-antise mitisme-21-04-2018-7676787.php.

Gildea, Robert. 1994. *The Past in French History*. New Haven: Yale University Press.

Grévy, Jérôme. 2005. *Le Cléricalisme? Voilà l'Ennemi! Un Siècle de Guerre de Religion en France*. Paris: Armand Colin.

Haarscher, Guy. 1998. *La Laïcité*. 2nd ed. Paris: Presses Universitaires de France.

Holt, Mack P., ed. 2002. The Kingdom of France in the Sixteenth Century. In *Renaissance and Reformation France, 1500–1648*, 5–26. New York: Oxford University Press.

Jeantet, Thierry. 2006. L'École et la Laïcité. *Revue Politique et Parlementaire* 1038: 29–38.

Kärkkäinen, Veli-Matti. 2003. *An Introduction to the Theology of Religions: Biblical, Historical and Contemporary Perspectives*. Downers Grove, IL: InterVarsity Press.

Korsia, Haïm. 2006. La Laïcité: Valeur du Judaïsme Français. *Revue Politique et Parlementaire* 1038: 80–84.

Lillback, Peter A. 2017. The Relationship of Church and State. In *Reformation Theology*, ed. Michael Barrett, 675–719. Wheaton, IL: Crossway.

Lindberg, Carter. 1996. *The European Reformation*. Oxford: Blackwell.

Machelon, Jean-Pierre. 2012. *La Laïcité Demain: Exclure ou Rassembler?* Paris: CNRS Éditions.

McGrath, Alister E. 1990. *A Life of John Calvin*. Oxford: Blackwell.

McManners, John. 1972. *Church and State in France, 1870–1914*. London: SPCK.

Miquel, Pierre. 1980. *Les Guerres de Religion*. Paris: Fayard.

Monod, Jean-Claude. 2007. *Sécularisation et Laïcité*. Paris: Presses Universitaires de France.

Pédérzet, J. 1896. *Cinquante Ans de Souvenirs Religieux et Ecclésiastiques.* Paris: Librairie Fischbacher. https://archive.org/stream/eglisesreformees00pede#page/n7/mode/2up.

Pena-Ruiz, Henri. 2003. *Qu'est-ce que la Laïcité?* Paris: Éditions Gallimard.

Petit Robert de la Langue Française, Le. 2007. Paris: Le Robert.

Prévotat, Jacques. 1998. *Être Chrétien en France au XXe Siècle: De 1914 à Nos Jours.* Paris: Éditions du Seuil.

Rémond, René. 1999. *L'Anticléricalisme en France: De 1815 à Nos Jours.* Paris: Fayard.

Roberts, Andrew. 2014. *Napoleon: A Life.* New York: Penguin Books.

Robespierre, Maximilien. 1967. *Œuvres de Maximilien Robespierre. (July 27, 1793–July 27, 1794).* Paris: Presses Universitaires de France. https://archive.org/stream/oeuvrescomplte10robe#page/n5/mode/2up.

Rognon, Évelyne, and Louis Weber. 2005. *La Laïcité: Un Siècle Après:1905–2005.* Paris: Éditions Nouveaux Regards.

Roy, Olivier. 2005. *La Laïcité Face à l'Islam.* Paris: Éditions Stock.

Schnapper, Dominique. 2018. Mort de Mireille Knoll: 'L'Antisémitisme est un Signe Inquiétant de l'Affaiblissement de la Démocratie.' *Le Monde.* http://www.lemonde.fr/societe/article/2018/03/29/mort-de-mireille-knoll-l-antisemitisme-est-un-signe-inquietant-de-l-affaiblissement-de-la-democratie_5278257_3224.html.

Schrameck, Olivier, ed. 2004. Un Siècle de Laïcité. In *Études et Documents du Conseil d'État,* 241–402. Paris: La Documentation Française.

Stéphan, Raoul. 1945. *L'Épopée Huguenote.* Paris: La Colombe.

Vovelle, Michel. 2006. *La Révolution Française:1789–1799.* Paris: Armand Colin.

Walker, Williston, Richard A. Norris, Davis W. Lotz, and Robert T. Handy. 1985. *A History of the Christian Church.* 4th ed. New York: Charles Scribner's Sons.

Wessels, Anton. 1994. *Europe: Was It Ever Really Christian? The Interaction Between Gospel and Culture.* London: SCM.

CHAPTER 8

From National Church to State Anglican Multifaithism: Church and State in England and Wales Since 1829

Jeremy Bonner

INTRODUCTION

In the Brexit referendum of June 2016, the United Kingdom witnessed a popular reaffirmation of the principle of English exceptionalism. The disproportionate enthusiasm displayed by members of the Church of England for leaving the European Union affirmed the persistence of what Smith and Woodhead have termed 'English Anglican cultural-ethnic pride'. That the bishops of the Church of England, long derided as detached from the concerns of ordinary worshippers, declined to take an institutional position on Brexit demonstrated their awareness of the need for the national church to acknowledge the concerns of both the pro-Leave and the pro-Remain camps. It has even been suggested that the divided world of post-Brexit Britain presents an unprecedented opportunity for the established

J. Bonner (✉)
Lindisfarne College of Theology, North Shields, UK
e-mail: jeremy.bonner@durham.ac.uk

© The Author(s), under exclusive license to Springer Nature
Switzerland AG 2023
S. Holzer (ed.), *The Palgrave Handbook of Religion and State
Volume II*, https://doi.org/10.1007/978-3-031-35609-4_8

church to rediscover its historic role as a force for community upbuilding and reconciliation (Smith and Woodhead 2018, Brown 2020).

A singular feature of English public life over the past 200 years has been the enduring relationship between the established church and the English state, a phenomenon without parallel in continental Europe and far removed from the form of church-state separation that shapes the United States. Because the English Reformation of the sixteenth century was less the establishment of a national church *de novo* than the replacement of papal supremacy with royal supremacy, the transformation of the Church *in* England to the Church of England meant that the established church, though closely entwined with the state, was far from being its creation. The so-called Elizabethan Settlement—interrupted by the English Civil War but revived in 1660—presumed the existence of an established church that laid more stress on outward conformity than inward belief. To be a conforming Anglican (a member of the Church of England) was a prerequisite for participation in the political life of the nation and Anglicanism was generally understood as the religious expression of English identity. Though dissenting forms of Christianity (often described in the collective as Nonconformity) enjoyed a degree of toleration in the seventeenth and eighteenth centuries, their sectarian identity disqualified them from active involvement in the public sphere (Bogdanor 1997).

While it might be argued that Anglicanism has much in common with the Scandinavian folk church model, the comparatively early English embrace of limited religious toleration ensured that the Church of England never enjoyed the dominant position of Lutheranism in the Scandinavian nations. In both France and Germany, by contrast, strong and weak forms of church-state separation prevail and yet, paradoxically, they benefit far more from their interactions with the state than does the Church of England. Where the German Länder levy church taxes on behalf of state-recognized religious communities, the Church of England is self-supporting, and where even the forcefully secularist French state assumes responsibility for the maintenance of church buildings, the Church of England relies upon charitable donations and the financial support of its own members. The established church has thus undergone a process of what Bogdanor calls 'progressive attenuation' over the past 200 years, as an increase of its autonomy and corresponding decline of its privileges have combined to diminish—but not completely extinguish—the conception of the Church of England as the nation at prayer (Bogdanor 1997; Morris 2009).

For reasons of space and coherence, the present chapter is concerned with church-state relations in England and Wales, which—at least until 1920—both featured an Anglican establishment in a Protestant majority nation. The historically Presbyterian established church in Scotland has enjoyed a greater degree of separation from the state than its southern neighbor, while the island of Ireland had no established church after 1871 and Northern Ireland (which remained a British jurisdiction in 1922) is evenly divided between Catholic and Presbyterian constituencies. Notwithstanding the disestablishment of the Church of England in Wales in 1920, developments in church-state relations in England and Wales have traversed a common path for much of their history that distinguishes them from the rest of the Celtic Fringe.

The decline of the established church in the nineteenth century can be traced to the failed attempt to restore it to the status of a truly national church, not merely in England and Wales but in Catholic-majority Ireland, which had been incorporated into the United Kingdom under the Act of Union of 1801. Political concessions to Irish Catholics and to English Nonconformists in the first half of the nineteenth century led even members of the Church of England to question whether there remained a constitutional justification for preserving the established church's connection with the state. The expansion of the British Empire during the nineteenth century also saw no general reproduction of the established church model, with many of its new colonial dependencies preferring to embrace religious pluralism. Thus, the Church of England increasingly accepted by the late nineteenth century that it was merely *primus inter pares*, acknowledging the growing influence of Nonconformity while still proclaiming itself to be the guardian of England's Protestant heritage (Brown 2001; Carey 2011).

In the decades following the First World War, the established church pursued a much greater degree of autonomy from the state. The creation of the Church Assembly (later the General Synod), a legislative body for the Church of England elected only by baptized Anglicans, reflected the established church's partial embrace of the sectarian principle. Until the 1960s, however, Church of England still presented itself as the defender of Christian (rather than Protestant) Britain and a voice of conscience for the entire nation, although the expansion of the Welfare State in 1945 led to a diminution of its active involvement in political life. Closer ties with the state would only resume in the late 1990s, when growing interest in the contribution of non-governmental organizations to community regeneration presented the established church with the opportunity no longer to be the voice of Christian Britain but to embrace what Bonney calls 'state Anglican multifaithism', or the use of Church of England structures to help promote the involvement of both Christian and non-Christian faiths in the revivification of local communities (Grimley 2004; Green 2010; Bonney 2016).

Religious Demographics

Since the constitutional revolution of the 1830s there has been a singular change in the patterns of religious practice (and nonpractice), which for the first time in 150 years was recorded in the national censuses of 2001 and 2011. Not formerly a preoccupation of the state (beyond compilation of statistics relating to children in religious education), the decision to include a (voluntary) census question on religious profession owed much to pressure from representatives of non-Christian faiths, the growing tendency of many Britons to identify themselves in terms of religion rather than race and the accompanying interest of recent Labour and Conservative governments in the ability of faith-based organizations to promote social cohesion. This was despite continued evidence of the steady decline of organized Christianity evident in a significant fall in the proportion of those in England and Wales identifying as Christian between 2001 and 2021. While the number of those professing a non-Christian faith increased (the number of Muslims rose from 1.5 million to 3.8 million and the number of Hindus from 0.5 million to 1.0 million), the most significant gain was among those professing no religious affiliation. An apparent decline of roughly fourteen million Christians between 2001 and 2021 was matched by a parallel gain of sixteen million among the unaffiliated. In 2021, self-identifying Christians for the first time constituted less than half the population. Nevertheless, despite clear regional variations, including a concentration of Muslims and Hindus in London and the West Midlands and higher levels of Christian affiliation in northern England compared to southern England (outside London) and Wales, such figures suggest that while Christianity may be on the wane in Britain it seems unlikely to be supplanted by a non-Christian alternative in the foreseeable future. The implications for the state's approach to organized religion (and church establishment) are a different matter entirely (Allen 2011; Field 2021; Office for National Statistics 2021) (Table 8.1).

Table 8.1 Religious identification as a percentage of the population in England and Wales

	Christian	No religion/religion not stated	Muslim	Hindu	Sikh	Jewish
2001	71.8	15.0	2.8	1.0	0.6	0.5
2011	59.3	32.3	4.8	1.5	0.7	0.5
2021	46.2	43.2	6.5	1.7	0.9	0.5

Sources: Field 2021, Office for National Statistics 2021

THE CROWN

While the United Kingdom is far from alone in Europe in preserving a constitutional monarchy, it is unique in its proclamation of the monarch as the 'Supreme Governor' of the established church. Over the past two centuries that role has been defined by the reigns of Victoria (1837–1901) and Elizabeth II (1952–2022), both of whose relationships to the Church of England reflected the changing religious character of the kingdom over which they ruled. Erastianism (the supremacy of the state over the church) was Victoria's guiding principle and she made clear her opposition to all efforts to disestablish the church over which she presided (including the calls of Welsh Nonconformists to disestablish the minority Church of England in Wales). Her hostility to the 'High Church' wing of Anglicanism led her to endorse state-mandated efforts to suppress ritualistic innovations in Anglican liturgy through the Public Worship Regulation Act of 1874, while royal favor was extended to members of the 'Broad Church' party, which viewed church and nation as constituting an organic whole, embracing Christians beyond its ecclesiastical jurisdiction, and emphasized the responsibility of the established church to cooperate with the state to strengthen the moral life of the nation and promote social reform (Brown 2011; Ledger-Lomas 2021).

In the early twentieth century, Victoria's immediate successors found themselves obliged to acknowledge the increasing religious diversity of the nations of which they ruled. Symbolic of that shift was a change in the wording of the royal Declaration of Accession, which until 1910 included an explicit denunciation of the Catholic doctrine of Transubstantiation. Edward VII's pronouncement of this formula in 1901 provoked a chorus of protest (not least from many of the imperial dominions), as offensive to the religious beliefs of loyal Catholic subjects. By 1910, when George V succeeded his father, the then government was obliged to devise a formula that acknowledged these concerns while still affirming the commitment of the Crown to the Protestant constitutional order. The debate served further to expose the fault lines within the Protestant majority and the diminished ability of the Church of England to function in a comprehensive manner (Wolffe 2010; Fewster 2011; Bonney 2016).

The revision of the Declaration of Accession would prove prophetic for the role played by the monarchy between the wars, as it evolved from the upholder of England's Protestant patrimony to the focal point of a more diverse Christian community. The ceremonial anointing of the monarch and the celebration of Holy Communion at the coronation of George VI in 1937 were widely portrayed as evidence of the enduring power of the Christian state in contemporary British life. That the new king's coronation oath was modified such as to limit his commitment to maintaining the 'Protestant Reformed Religion' to the United Kingdom alone, though ostensibly an acknowledgment of the autonomy granted to the Dominions by the Statute of Westminster (1931), marked a further attenuation of the state's commitment to religious establishment, although it attested more to the growing *Christian* diversity of the Empire than to the plurality of non-Christian religions under its jurisdiction. The interwar era was also one marked by increased cooperation between the Church of England and the monarchy, building upon a pattern established during the First World War of seeking royal support for trans-denominational national days of prayer, a model that subsequently informed the royal announcement of the two-minute silence on Armistice Day. George VI's radio broadcasts during the Second World War—noted for their religious references— served to present the Crown as, though still undeniably Anglican, nevertheless embodying a wider commitment to the religious values of a much broader Christian nation (Grimley 2004; Bonney 2016; Wolffe 2010; Williamson 2020).

Such a model of national Christianity was still evident at the 1952 coronation of George VI's daughter. Notwithstanding the limited involvement of Nonconformist and Catholic representatives in the ceremony, the coronation sought to present a vision of an inclusive postwar social consensus that transcended class, religion, and race and was broadly Christian in its appeal. That the new queen invited prayers from people throughout the UK and the Commonwealth 'whatever your religion', however, implicitly acknowledged a looming religious pluralism that would increasingly characterize her reign. Elizabeth II's experience of the diversity of religious practice across the New Commonwealth prefigured an altered role for the

Supreme Governor of the Church of England that in the late twentieth century prompted her to acknowledge the multifaith reality of modern Britain, expressed in the growing number of royal visits to non-Christian places of worship and the inclusion of 'world faith representatives' at her Golden Jubilee celebrations. In contrast with her predecessors, she would make much of the Church of England's contribution to ecumenical and interfaith dialogue in sustaining the significance of religious values in the public sphere (Bonney 2016; Wolffe 2010).

For the Church of England, the religious rituals connected with the monarch and the Royal Family (including the Royal Wedding in 2011 and the Diamond Jubilee in 2012 and the Queen's funeral in 2022) have provided opportunities to reaffirm the presence of the established church at the heart of the nation. Such rituals, its leaders argue, serve the needs of the unchurched majority and promote social consensus, themes reflected in instructions issued to congregations of the Church of England on the death of Elizabeth II, which stated that they would 'play a key role in the life of the nation at that time' and included advice on the provision of areas of mourning and books of condolence for members of the public, as well as the procedure for the tolling of church bells on the day of the state funeral. The religious rituals that will attend the coronation of King Charles III in 2023 are likely to be even more reflective of the multifaith culture of contemporary Britain than those of 1953, but the monarch will remain the Supreme Governor of the Church of England, a position requiring that the incumbent be 'in communion' with the Church of England (a provision that excludes not only atheists and non-Christians but also Roman Catholics). In an echo of past practice, the king's accession proclamation was issued by the Privy Council and the Lords Spiritual and Temporal, including bishops of the established church, and invoked divine blessing on the new monarch. It also declared him to be Defender of the Faith, a title that—as Prince of Wales—Charles III had previously called into question in arguing that 'Defender of Faith' would be more in keeping with contemporary religious pluralism (Morris 2009; Bonney 2016; Church of England 2022).

Parliament

When the Cavalier Parliament adopted the Act of Uniformity in 1662, prompting the 'Great Ejection' of Puritan ministers from the Church of England parishes in which they had ministered for more than a decade, they set the seal on what for more than 150 years would be the norm of Anglican conformity and the holding of public office. Even after the repeal of the Test and Corporation Acts in 1828 and passage of the Catholic Emancipation Act in 1829, which permitted the election of both Nonconformists and Roman Catholics to the House of Commons, the predominance of members of the established church was slow to erode (even more so in the House of Lords which, until the adoption of the Life Peerages Act in 1958, was composed largely of hereditary peers). The belief that Parliament served as a last line of defense for members of the established church was reflected in the Public Worship Regulation Act of 1874 (which resulted in the imprisonment of certain Anglican clergy who defied efforts by the state to restrict their liturgical practices) and could still be seen in the parliamentary debates concerning the future of the Book of Common Prayer in both the 1920s and the 1980s.

For supporters of the established church, the record of nineteenth-century Parliaments was increasingly perceived as one of benign neglect (or worse). Four-fifths of the 217 church bills proposed between 1880 and 1913 were not even debated and only thirty-three became law. Worse still, exterior political realities had led to the formal disestablishment of the Church of Ireland in 1871 and the approval of Welsh disestablishment in 1914, further demonstrating the weakness of the church-state connection across the United Kingdom. In 1919 Parliament adopted the Enabling Act, which created the National Assembly of the Church of England (the Church Assembly), elected by baptized Christians who declared themselves to be members of no religious organization not in communion with the Church of England (Podmore 2019).

While the existence of the Church Assembly ostensibly marked the termination of the notion that all citizens—regardless of religious affiliation—shared in the national church, the parliamentary playing field remained contested. A dramatic demonstration of Parliament's continued role came in 1928, when a proposed revision of the Book of Common Prayer suffered defeat in the House of Commons at the hands of trans-denominational coalition united in the belief that the new form of worship was insufficiently Protestant and that Parliament had not completely surrendered its right to speak for Protestant Britain, which retained a share in the Anglican patrimony. In general, however, Parliament tended to accept most Church Assembly measures without opposition, even those that granted the Church increasing freedom to manage its finances, land, and buildings or to reform its system of theological colleges. Matters concerned with worship and doctrine (that which touched the ordinary worshipper most deeply) have been the most likely to provoke controversy, as was shown during the late 1970s when the Church of England contemplated another replacement for the 1662 Book of Common Prayer. Despite Parliament having accorded the General Synod (established in 1969 as a successor to the Church Assembly) the authority to revise its liturgy in 1974, a rearguard action was waged—mainly in the House of Lords—to secure to ordinary parishioners the right to continue use of the 1662 Prayer Book if they so wished. As in 1928, opponents of change included non-Anglicans who viewed the traditional liturgy as the embodiment of an English identity and who sought to maintain the principle that an established church enjoying the privileges that it did could not expect absolute autonomy from the oversight of Parliament. More recently, it was suggested that the General Synod's initial rejection of women bishops in 2012 might provoke Parliament to amend canon law to compel their appointment, a constitutional crisis averted by a second Synod vote (Grimley 2004; Cranmer 2012; Podmore 2019; Webster 2020; Pattenden 2021).

The model established by the Enabling Act continues to govern the relationship between Parliament and the established church to the present day. Although legislative initiative on church matters rests with the General Synod (the Church Assembly's successor) and the so-called Measures that it adopts cannot be modified in Parliament, although they can be rejected in toto, and there is nothing to prevent Parliament from passing legislation affecting the Church of England (although it is generally disinclined to do so). Scrutiny of church legislation falls to an Ecclesiastical Committee composed of fifteen members from each of the House of Commons and House of Lords. A singular parliamentary office is that of the Second Estates Commissioner who serves as the official spokesman for the Church Commissioners who administer the financial affairs of the Church of England (Morris 2009; Baldry 2015).

If Parliament has withdrawn from the business of the Church of England it might plausibly be argued that the reverse is not the case. There are twenty-six members of the Lords Spiritual (bishops of the Church of England) who sit in the House of Lords. While the Lords Temporal have included two Chief Rabbis and the Methodist Donald Soper (all appointed as life peers), the representation of religious leaders greatly favors the established church, a problem identified by the Wakeham Commission of 2000. Despite this, the bishops are rarely all in attendance at the same time and do not tend to vote as a bloc. One analysis revealed that the bishops' vote changed the outcome in only three of 806 votes, and it was less their vote than their ability to influence the votes of others that is decisive (Russell and Sciara 2007; Morris 2009).

It is of course the presence of Church of England bishops that has long justified the involvement not only of the Crown but of the prime minister of the day in their appointment. Some of these appointments (such as Ramsay Macdonald's selection of E. W. Barnes as bishop of Birmingham and Margaret Thatcher's choice of George Carey as archbishop of Canterbury in 1990) have involved political priorities, but the process also reflects the fact that the appointees may—at least at some point in their career—enjoy voice and vote in the House of Lords. The process of appointment has undergone modification both in the 1970s, when much of the selection process was devolved to a church-led commission, and more recently in 2007 when the then prime minister stated that he and his successors would abide by the commission's first choice (Medhurst 1991; Merricks 2012; Coleman 2017).

The Church of England also continues to set the tone for the spiritual life of the mother of parliaments. An Anglican chaplain is assigned to the House of Commons, whose responsibilities include a weekly Eucharist in Parliament's chapel and pastoral support for members of the House of Commons, while in the House of Lords one of the twenty-six Anglican bishops is charged with offering daily prayer in the Upper House according to a traditional formula. Such tokens of religious establishment are conspicuously absent from the National Assembly of Wales (established as a form of devolved government in 1999), which has no chapel and does not offer daily prayer, although it has developed a relationship with a local Anglican chaplain in recent years. Conscious of the declining influence of Christianity and the growth of non-Christian religions in Wales, the Senedd has preferred to focus its attention on interfaith activities and make its buildings available for a diverse array of religious festivals (Morris 2009; Bonney 2016).

The Established Church

Anglican theologians have long endeavored to argue the case for a form of establishment that understands church and state to co-exist within a framework of mutual recognition and obligation. Thus Paul Avis, in rejecting the prevailing paradigm of the secular state, insists that the state's relationship with the diversity of faiths that characterize contemporary Britain need not be impaired by its affirmation of a single faith that affirms the common good and which is willing to put itself at the service of all, whether within the Anglican context or beyond it. Michael Turnbull (a former bishop) argues that the established church's presence in every community (a legacy of its historic network of geographically defined parishes and dioceses) and its status as the upholder of the nation's religious heritage enables the established church to exercise a uniquely prophetic role both in helping define to national character and challenging received wisdom within the political establishment (Avis 2008; Turnbull and McFayden 2012).

Avis and Turnbull both constitute a twenty-first-century Anglican realism in the face of the weak establishment that today prevails only in England. In the early nineteenth century, by contrast, the established church reacted with profound hostility to the state's assault on its prerogatives, with its bishops resisting the Great Reform Act of 1832 and denouncing government willingness to abandon the cause of the Church of Ireland. That the creation of the Ecclesiastical Commission in 1835 to implement reforms of the established church was accompanied by no additional pledges of state funding for church extension served to confirm that the governments of the day were unwilling to alienate newly enfranchised Nonconformist voters. Such a subordination of the structures of the established church to the wishes of the British state fatally undermined the principle of a single Protestant establishment and prompted a reevaluation of the state-church connection and the increasing conviction that disestablishment of the Church of England might be necessary to preserve its spiritual integrity. Church leaders proved increasingly unwilling to treat the Church of England as a creature of the state, where its clergy were civil servants, and its dioceses were mere administrative divisions (Brown 2001; Taylor and Huzzey 2018).

The second half of the nineteenth century only served further to erode the sense of church-state partnership. At home, the struggle against 'Anglo-Papalism' prompted an unprecedented—at least by nineteenth-century standards—drive on the part of the state to compel liturgical uniformity within the state church which succeeded only in making religious martyrs of a subset of the clergy. Abroad, the spread of imperial power, though accompanied by an ever-increasing commitment to missionary activity, was not limited to the established church but extended to a variety of Protestant denominations. While the establishment of the Lambeth

Conference (a decennial gathering of Anglican bishops from across the globe) in 1867 might have been understood in some quarters as embodying a sense of 'Greater Britain', it was also a pan-Anglican initiative that owed little to the initiatives of the British state. The view that Christianization and civilization went hand in hand nevertheless remained a common feature of both political and religious discourse, reflected in the general observance of Empire Day after 1904. However, the colonies themselves increasingly manifested a tendency toward religious pluralism that militated against the reproduction of Anglican establishment outside England (Wolffe 1994; Maughan 2003; Carey 2011; Cruickshank 2020).

In such a setting it was perhaps inevitable that the trend toward self-governance was not long delayed. In the mid-nineteenth century the state raised no objection to the revival of the Convocations of Canterbury and York, which had been suspended by King George I in 1717. These assemblies of clergy and bishops from the two provinces of the Church of England would serve as the first step toward the establishment of the Church Assembly. Spurred by the finding of the Archbishops' Committee on Church and State (1916), practicing Anglicans formed the Life and Liberty Movement to press for a body that would have the time and expertise to debate ecclesiastical legislation and would, by its democratic and representative character, render the established church less prone to external criticism. The new Church Assembly functioned as a legislature of first resort, with Parliament's role being limited to one of veto. Very revealing, however, was the Church of England's reaction to the parliamentary defeat of the revised Book of Common Prayer in 1928. With certain notable exceptions, the bishops, rather than embrace disestablishment, chose to defy the state by publishing the book with a note to the effect that it was not to be considered authorized for use. Not until adoption of the Worship and Doctrine Measure in 1974 was the principle formally conceded that such issues were a matter of ecclesiastical jurisdiction (Brown 2001; Grimley 2004; Podmore 2019).

If the post-1919 Church of England sought to carve out for itself a sphere apart from the state, it did not surrender its right—as a faith community—to speak to the appropriate role of the state in contemporary society. Noteworthy in this respect was William Temple (bishop of Manchester and successively archbishop of York and of Canterbury between 1921 and 1944) who, in such writings as *Christianity and the Social Order* (1942), championed a pluralist understanding of nationhood in which such values as voluntarism, localism, and religious toleration were privileged. Temple insisted that the national community was grounded in shared Christian values and a national church free to govern itself in purely internal matters. The advantage for Temple and others like him, as compared with the experiences of Anglicans in the Victorian and Edwardian eras, was that post-1919 England had undergone a process of what Simon Green has termed political 'desacralization'. Abroad, the disappearance of the 'Irish problem', consequent upon the independence of southern Ireland and the departure of Catholic Nationalist MPs from Parliament greatly reduced sectarian tensions. At home, the declining influence of Nonconformity and rise of a Labour Party, which—unlike many of its continental counterparts—boasted no tradition of anticlericalism, allowed the Church of England to present itself as a spokesman for all the churches and so enhance the moral authority of its pronouncements. The decline of political Nonconformity and the greater willingness of the Free Churches to identify areas of common ground with the established church only reinforced the capacity of the interwar Church of England to transcend class and political divides and affirm a sense of universal citizenship in which Anglicanism was increasingly identified with Britishness. The new style of politics was most dramatically embodied in the person of the Anglican priest Charles Jenkinson who, in the 1930s, became Labour Party leader of Leeds city council and championed a policy of slum clearance that helped create the new model settlement of Quarry Hill (Lloyd 1966; Grimley 2004; Green 2010).

It was consequently ironic that the postwar rise of the English welfare state also marked a decline in the political profile of the Church of England. As the scope of voluntary service gave way to the cult of the professional, the established church was increasingly sidelined, although a marginal presence was still evident, within the BBC or in hospital chaplaincy, where Anglicanism still reflected a sense of English religious identity. Increasingly, however, as the 1960s wore on, the established church was more identified in the public mind with the pronouncements of its more liberal members on the cultural revolution of the 1960s from capital punishment to divorce and homosexuality. Relations between the established church and the state reached a nadir in the early 1980s, when the discomfort of much of the leadership of the Church of England with what was perceived as the excessively individualistic policies of Margaret's Thatcher's administration was reflected in such church-sponsored policy documents as *Faith in the City* (1986), which criticized the state's failure to address urban poverty. Archbishop Robert Runcie's emphasis on repentance and reconciliation at service held at St. Paul's Cathedral to mark the conclusion of the Falklands War in 1983 also demonstrated that the Church of England's historic identification with the nation in time of war had become greatly attenuated and Anglican bishops—including those in the House of Lords—were increasingly seen as a 'surrogate political opposition', despite the fact that self-identified Conservatives (including one sitting cabinet minister) formed the largest bloc. In such a climate, support for the government's approach to deregulation and privatization came increasingly from evangelical Christians (within and beyond the established church) and was reflected in Thatcher's appointment of the more conservative George Carey as Archbishop of Canterbury in succession to Runcie (Medhurst 1991; Loss 2017).

Whatever vestiges of cultural Anglicanism survive within the corridors of Westminster, it remains the case that the approach to religion (or, as it now tends to be termed, faith) in politics is no longer framed through an explicitly Anglican lens. The championing of the virtues of faith-based organizations as 'compassionate communities' by the opposition Conservative leader in 2001 was echoed by the Labour government of Tony Blair, which appointed a 'faith czar' the same year and subsequently made material commitments to the upbuilding of 'faith infrastructure' amounting to £13.8 million, with a further £50 million allocated to interfaith initiatives. For all its implicit approval of the faith sector, however, these initiatives were intended to empower religious moderates (particularly in a Muslim context) at the expense of extremists and reframe religion as faith, all too evident in Labour efforts to treat clergy (of all faith traditions) as potential 'development workers' (Harris et al. 2003; Allen 2011; Bonney 2016).

The Conservative-led governments that have been in power since 2010, by contrast, have resorted much more to the language of Britain as a 'Christian country' and the contribution of faith to the preservation of public morality. Former prime minister David Cameron went so far as to insist that minority faiths were better tolerated under a system of weakly established Christianity than they would be within the framework of French *laicité*. The new political commitment to 'state Anglican multifaithism' reflects a growing concern that since multiculturalism has produced radicalized immigrant communities unconnected to the wider society, the established church still has a role to play as the centerpiece of a new civil religion that encourages interfaith initiatives. While Labour governments sought to 'do God', therefore, Conservative governments have been more concerned to 'do Christianity'. Many Conservative initiatives have reflected a commitment to *religious integrity*, be they the right to hold prayers at local council meetings or the promotion of sharia-compliant mortgages and start-up loans. Much greater emphasis has also been placed on the Church of England as a deliverer of faith initiatives, for example, in the requirement that applications for the Near Neighbours project must be counter-signed by the local Anglican priest (Allen 2018; Bonney 2016).

The established church has thus ostensibly enjoyed a renewed role in public life (although it is an open question how such church-state partnerships affect its ability to criticize the state), but it has also been affected in recent years by legislative changes in employment practices—some prompted by EU legislation prior to Brexit—which threaten to alter how religious organizations employ and discipline their clergy and the full implications of such measures as the Human Rights Act (1998) and the Equality Act (2010) have yet to be determined. Ecclesiastical courts do still exist at both the diocesan and provincial (Canterbury and York) level, together with the Court of Ecclesiastical Causes Reserved (which addresses cases of doctrine and ritual) and the Judicial Committee of the Privy Council, which serves as a final court of appeal. While canon law remains part of the law of the land, the jurisdiction of such courts since 1963 has extended only to the fabric and contents of churches and clergy discipline, but ecclesiastical courts nevertheless have the same power to examine witnesses and inspect documentation as their civil counterparts and their judgments are enforceable (Morris 2009; Hunt 2013).

With the final abolition of church tithes in 1936, the Church of England became an entirely self-supporting religious body, the bulk of whose income is derived from loyal churchgoers. The Church Commissioners, who administer the established church's principal assets, are an independent corporation and not an office of state. Most public benefits accruing to the Church of England are those available to any registered charity (religious or secular), most notably the practice of Gift Aid which since 2000 has permitted charities to reclaim the tax that was paid on any donation. The maintenance of church buildings—particularly the major cathedrals—derives from a variety of sources but less than a third of it can be attributed to the state (consisting mostly of grants from English Heritage and the National Lottery, neither of which are discriminate based on religion). The principal source of state-derived church income—and the most enduring institutional presence—is that provided by clergy of the Church of England in public sector chaplaincies in healthcare, schools, prisons, and the armed forces. While none of these are restricted to Anglican clergy (or in some cases to clergy) the established church accounts for three-quarters of hospital chaplains, three-fifths of military chaplains and a third of prison chaplains (Morris 2009).

RELIGIOUS FREEDOM

If the nineteenth century constituted a long struggle for the equal treatment of non-established Christian churches, the late twentieth century has been more characterized by the struggle to preserve a sphere of religious expression from state compulsion. It is therefore appropriate to consider these two eras from the perspective, on the one hand of Protestant Nonconformity and, on the other, of non-Christian faiths, notably Islam. The rise of Nonconformity to full equality was not assured by the repeal of the Test and Corporation Acts in 1828 but required a steady process of revision of different articles of legislation that privileged Anglicanism, including abandonment of the religious tests governing admission to the universities of Oxford and Cambridge and the extension of authority for legally recognized marriages to be performed in religious buildings owned by denominations other than the Church of England. Resentment toward the privileges of the established church, however, led to the formation of the Liberation Society in 1844 to press the case for disestablishment. English Nonconformists increasingly took their cue from the Scottish Disruption of 1843 during which the evangelical wing of the Church of Scotland had repudiated state control of the Kirk and formed the Free Church of Scotland. In Wales the intimate association of Welsh culture with the network of Nonconformist chapels caused the Church of England in Wales to increasingly be perceived as a foreign institution. Establishing a position of influence within the Liberal Party after 1867, Welsh Nonconformists demanded that similar legislation to be applied to Wales and were championed in this endeavor by future prime minister David Lloyd George. With passage of the Welsh Church Act in 1914 (not implemented until 1920), Anglicanism in Wales was reduced to the status of a mere denomination (Wolffe 1994; Brown 2001; Husselbee and Ballard 2012; Evans 2021).

While the first half of the twentieth century experienced little in the way of struggles over religious liberty, the onset of mass migration from Southeast Asia and the Caribbean introduced ethnoreligious elements into the English body politic that have become increasingly assertive in their expression of enclave religiosity and have frequently sought to take advantage of the new understanding of religious identity as a protected category. Since 2009, with the establishment of the Supreme Court, the United Kingdom has moved closer to American jurisprudence in articulating more express judicial reasoning in respect of cases of religious freedom. Though it has demonstrated a willingness to consider an affected group's self-understanding of its beliefs, judges still distinguish between freedom of belief and freedom to manifest such a belief and pay particular deference to the decisions of educational authorities. Thus in 2006 the Law Lords ruled that a female student's religious objections to the dress code instituted by her school—which were intended to be inclusive of different faiths and had been endorsed by the local Muslim community—did not rise to the level of religious discrimination. Two years later, however, a case involving the prohibition of a Sikh wearing a bangle as a religious symbol was decided in the student's favor based on the enhanced protections accorded religious belief by the Equality Act of 2006. Issues of religious freedom took on a peculiar significance in 2020 given challenges to the proportionality of state restrictions on mass gathering in the context of religious worship during the COVID-19 pandemic, although most legal challenges were ultimately dismissed of the grounds of mootness and because the temporary nature of such restrictions carried more weight than the fact that similar restrictions were not applied to some secular activities (Eberle 2011; Sarrouh 2020; Baldwin 2021).

Of particular concern to many faiths—including the Church of England—has been how the provisions of the Equality Act (2010) apply where the beliefs of religious bodies run counter to certain protected characteristics. It was in consequence of expressions of concern from an ecumenical (and multifaith) coalition that included bishops of the established church that a proposal that religious organizations be required to employ persons whose manner of living ran counter to the teaching of the faith was defeated in the House of Lords. Ironically, the determination of the Church of England not to be compelled to solemnize same-sex civil partnerships on church premises (despite the desire of many Anglicans for this to happen) led to a legislative compromise that prohibited such ceremonies in congregations of the established church while permitting them for those religious traditions that so desired (Hunt 2013).

Perhaps the most dramatic turn in church-state relations occurred in 2001, when the perceived disengagement of British Muslims from mainstream political life began to preoccupy the then Labour government. Ironically these concerns arose in the context of a nation in which Muslim schools had been receiving state funding (in the same manner as their Christian and Jewish counterparts) since 1997, with no fewer than twenty-seven operating in 2020, and where—in contrast with Europe—there was no legal proscription on wearing the headscarf (or even the niqab) in public. Muslim groups with whom British governments have chosen to cooperate in the 2000s and 2010s, however, are increasingly those willing to support the state's anti-radicalization strategy. This has imposed a statutory duty on state and local government agencies, including faith schools and university chaplains (but not places of worship, including those of the Church of England), to discourage citizens from being drawn into terroristic acts, particularly those inspired by Islamist extremism. The Coalition Government elected in 2010 also established an anti-Muslim Hate Working Group, although this was later criticized for confining its work to a purely theoretical level (Sarrouh 2020; Riedel 2021).

In 2008, Rowan Williams, then archbishop of Canterbury, sparked controversy by inviting discussion of whether a pluralist court system in which religious tribunals were involved might better contribute to communal harmony. While Williams spoke at a time of public preoccupation with Muslim Sharia councils, Jewish Beth Din courts have been in operation in the UK since the early eighteenth century. The willingness of the British legal system to recognize the latter's decisions with respect to family and dietary law could be said to offer a precedent for similar acknowledgment of their Muslim counterparts, notably the Muslim Arbitration Tribunal, which includes a lawyer qualified in English law and is concerned with divorces and commercial disputes. The belief in Muslim (and Jewish) law that family matters are essentially private and that reconciliation in domestic disputes is the preferred outcome has nevertheless prompted concern that religious courts will fail to address appropriately (or refer to the secular courts) offenses such as spousal abuse that they cannot effectively arbitrate. No religious court can grant a civil divorce or make determination of child custody arrangements, however, and the Arbitration Act (1996) precludes state sanction of unlawful rulings. Interestingly, the Divorce (Religious Marriages) Act of 2002 requires that any religious divorce be finalized before a civil divorce is granted to prevent the women involved being pressured to accept unreasonable financial or custodial demands, but this does not apply to Muslim marriages, many of which lack a civil component, and efforts to prevent 'jurisdiction creep' within Islamic courts have failed to become law (Griffiths 2014, Zee 2014).

EDUCATION

The persistence of a religious dimension in English public education owes much to its nineteenth-century origins. Prior to 1870, the provision of education had been almost exclusively a concern of the churches, overseen by the Nonconformist British and Foreign School Society and the Anglican National Society for the Promotion of Education. Efforts to establish tax-payer-funded elementary schools were opposed by the Free Churches who feared that it would serve to confirm the ascendancy of the established church and undermine the voluntary schools. Altered political priorities within the new Liberal Party led to the adoption of the Forster Education Act in 1870, which made provision for publicly funded and compulsory state-run elementary education, with new schools in areas not yet served by the voluntary system. Free Church reservations nevertheless ensured both that religious instruction would be of a nondenominational character and that parents would enjoy the right to withdraw their children from such instruction, principles that continued to inform educational practice in later decades. Thirty years later, the Balfour Education Act, in providing for universal secondary education, altered the so-called dual system of state and voluntary (religious) schools by extending state funding to the latter. The fact that the majority of such schools were either Anglican or Catholic provoked further Free Church criticism and provoked a campaign of passive resistance under the slogan 'No Rome on the Rates'. Even though the state asserted a primary responsibility for educational provision, therefore, it proved much less hostile to the involvement of religious partners (including Catholics) in the process than would have been the case in either France or the United States (Brown 2001; Prochaska 2008; Husselbee and Ballard 2012).

More than forty years would elapse before a Conservative education minister and an archbishop of Canterbury would together attempt to reverse the perceived de-Christianization of the educational sphere that had occurred in the years following the Balfour Act. The Butler Education Act of 1944 can in many ways be seen as a triumph for the established church insofar as embodied the vision of Archbishop William Temple for a form of religious education that promoted Christian morality on a non-sectarian basis. In its introduction of a category of 'voluntary aided school', which permitted denominational schools to retain their religious ethos, the Butler Act brought most Catholic schools under state oversight, even as most Church of England schools became 'voluntary controlled', transferring responsibility for maintaining their physical plant to the state. More importantly, the Butler Act's commitment to daily corporate worship in schools and an agreed syllabus for nondenominational religious instruction involved oversight by local education authority committees, which enjoyed guaranteed representation from the established church and local denominations, and favored unanimous consent over majority decision-making (Bradney 2009; Green 2010; Loss 2017).

The framework of the Butler Act continues to inform religious instruction today, notwithstanding legislation adopted in 1988 requiring that schools of a non-religious character offer a daily act of worship 'wholly or mainly of a broadly Christian character', from which parents retain a right to withdraw their children and teachers the right to decline to participate. At the same time, religious education syllabi are expected not to treat Christianity in isolation, but to examine all the major faith traditions within the UK, most notably Buddhism, Hinduism, Islam, Judaism, and Sikhism. Oversight of religious education in state-run schools is provided by local education authorities through a standing advisory council on religious education, which must include a representative of the Church of England, and use of denominational formularies (though not their study) is prohibited. It has been argued that it is precisely the Church of England's enduring participation in the dual system that has ensured the survival of religious education in the state sector (Bradney 2009; Parker and Freath 2020).

Beyond this state-mandated form of religious education can be found the voluntary religious schools whose faith-based character the state acknowledges. While most voluntary schools are Anglican or Catholic (and either state-aided or state-controlled), recent policy debates have inevitably focused more upon the much smaller numbers of Muslim schools (eighteen of which were state-funded by 2015) which in recent years have been accused of perpetuating an enclave mentality (a similar criticism of independent Orthodox Jewish schools). Twenty-first-century governments have sought to address these concerns by promoting twinning arrangements between state and independent schools, while some state schools have endeavored to promote policies that take account of cultural sensibilities within a local community. It has nevertheless been noted that many independent Muslim schools have been more open to hiring non-Muslim teachers than have Catholic and Evangelical Christian schools to hire those who are not co-religionists (Ahdar and Leigh 2013; Flint 2009; Sarrouh 2020).

WELFARE

In retrospect it is remarkable how rapidly faith-based organizations in England and Wales were displaced from areas of social provision (other than education) in the decades following the advent of the welfare state in 1945. Church leaders who had celebrated an enhanced role of the state in the 1920s and 1930s soon discovered that it came with an inevitable cost to the vitality of community life that had once underpinned by religious voluntarism. Charitable hospitals and philanthropy in general were increasingly dismissed by successive governments as amateurish and undemocratic and residual civic voluntarism played a minor role from the 1950s to the 1980s. Even the early phase of the Thatcherite reversal of state power was accompanied by a disinclination on the part of the state to invite the voluntary sector to fill the void (Prochaska 2008).

Interest in the potential of faith-based organizations has subsequently undergone a renaissance, initially inspired by the so-called Third Way promoted by the 'New Labour' governments of the 2000s. Dinham has argued that an early precedent for this can be found in the 'Faith in the City' report produced by the Church of England in 1985, which, despite its redistributive arguments, still accepted a role for the market in alleviating poverty. Under New Labour the state sought to promote faith communities as positive agents of social transformation. The perception that the Church of England, through its geographic system of parishes is peculiarly suited to engage with such a project is reinforced by a case study of the English town of Darlington, where the established church has been identified as playing an 'in-between' role in relation to the state and the local community. This is particularly evident in the expectation of civil authorities that it will serve as 'neutral holy ground' in the provision of welfare, the fact that the Church of England facilitates community upbuilding (church halls are often the only communal space in a residential area), and its clergy frequently mediate between government agencies and members of the public (Dinham 2008; Middlemiss Lé Mon 2010).

The British model of faith-based welfarism that has emerged in the twenty-first century differs both from France, with its antipathy to intermediary institutions between the state and the citizen, and from Germany, with its long-established integration of churches into its state welfare system. The Third Way—and, indeed, Conservative-led governments since 2010—encouraged faith-based organizations to fill an expanding void in social provision by participating in policy decisions and competing for government funding and service contracts. The idea that clergy might be seen as potential 'development workers' offers the potential for enhanced church-state cooperation but also presents a challenge to the integrity of criticism that a faith-based organization might express in relation to government policy. One study of the Jewish voluntary sector identified a problem with excessive state reliance on faith-based organizations, namely that much of their charitable focus is necessarily focused on their co-religionists rather than the wider community, a failing more common to sectarian religions than to the established church (Harris et al. 2003; Prochaska 2008; Göçmen 2013).

For many of these reasons there has been an increasing predisposition on the part of the state to favor partnerships with interfaith organizations. The creation of the Inner Cities Religious Council in 1992 (replaced by the Faith Communities Consultative Council in 2006) represented a significant increase in the involvement of faith-based organizations in urban regeneration and the promotion of community cohesion, and there has been considerable state investment in interfaith programs and faith participation in urban public life. Nevertheless, many religious organizations—particularly those without defined authority structures or characterized by an evangelistic mindset—prefer to keep the state at arm's length and the Anglican and Catholic faith communities tend to be overrepresented in such bodies. At the local level, faith-based organizations are viewed as enhancing or even legitimating public policy objectives within minority populations, a role that often speaks less of an equal partnership than of a reduction of the churches to a subservient role. Those faith organizations who desire to be partners often feel a need to conform to such state-determined requirements as charitable status and fiscal accountability and interfaith organizations have proved increasingly attractive partners because they free the state from the dangers of picking and choosing among competing faith traditions (Chapman 2009; Weller 2009; Prideaux and Dawson 2018).

CONCLUSION

The death of Queen Elizabeth II in September 2022 marked not merely the passing of a second Elizabethan age but the final eclipse of the religious establishment of which she had for seventy years been the embodiment. There are many points at which the Church of England might be said to have taken steps along the road to denominational identity, most notably in its embrace of self-government in 1919, but its alignment with successive heads of the House of Windsor served to preserve the notion that the established church was still the fundamental religious expression of English national identity. It is ironic, given the contribution of so many Anglican clergy and laypeople—Archbishop William Temple not the least—to its establishment, how much the postwar Welfare State accelerated the desacralization of the public sphere that had begun in the 1920s. Although the postwar churches aspired to articulate a prophetic vision, they found their contributions to public discourse increasingly scorned or disregarded. In a world where, as Grace Davie has put it, the aspiration of the vast majority is 'believing without belonging', the state could afford to disregard the pronouncements of religious leaders, a state of affairs that reached its apogee in the age of Margaret Thatcher. While the twenty-first century has witnessed a resumption of the church-state relationship, it is no longer a partnership of equals, nor is it grounded in the vision of a broadly Christian nation of which the established church is the custodian. Rather it reflects an essentially functionalist vision of religion that treats the established church as merely another agency for the putting into practice of government policy and one—moreover—increasingly expected to conform its belief system to the prevailing winds of culture. The Church of England may not yet be the Lutheran Church of Sweden, but it can no longer be considered the nation at prayer (Davie 1994).

REFERENCES

Ahdar, R., and I. Leigh. 2013. *Religious Freedom in the Liberal State*. Oxford University Press.

Allen, C. 2011. We don't do God': A critical retrospective of New Labour's approaches to 'religion or belief' and 'faith. *Culture and Religion* 12 (3): 259–275.

————. 2018. 'Cameron. *Conservatives and a Christian Britain: A Critical Exploration of Political Discourses about Religion in the Contemporary United Kingdom' Societies* 8 (1): 5.

Avis, P. 2008. Church, State, and Establishment in the United Kingdom. *Studies in World Christianity* 8 (2): 228–243.

Baldry, T. 2015. Parliament and the Church. *Ecclesiastical Law Journal* 17 (2): 202–214.

Baldwin, G. 2021. The Coronavirus Pandemic and Religious Freedom: Judicial Decisions in the United States and United Kingdom. *Judicial Review* 26 (4): 297–320.

Bogdanor, V. 1997. *The Monarchy and the Constitution*. Oxford: Oxford University Press.

Bonney, N. 2016. *Monarchy, Religion and the State: Civil Religion in the United Kingdom, Canada, Australia and the Commonwealth*. Manchester: Manchester University Press.

Bradney, A. 2009. *Law and Faith in a Sceptical Age*. Taylor and Francis.

Brown, S.J. 2001. *The National Churches of England, Ireland, and Scotland, 1801-1846*. Oxford University Press.

————. 2011. The Broad Church Movement, National Culture, and the Established Churches of Great Britain. In *Church and State in Old and New Worlds*, ed. W. Janse et al., 99–128. Brill.

Brown, M., 'Brexit-Shaped Britain and the Church of England: Looking Back to Look Forwards' In J. C. Bradstock and A. Bradstock, *The Future of Brexit Britain: Anglican Reflections on National Identity and European Solidarity*. SPCK, 2020, 149-156.

Carey, H. 2011. *God's Empire: Religion and Colonialism in the British World, c.1801–1908*. Cambridge University Press.

Chapman, R. 2009. Faith and the voluntary sector in urban governance: Distinctive yet similar? In *Faith in the Public Realm: Controversies, Policies and Practices*, ed. Adam Dinham et al., 203–222. Policy Press.

Church of England, 'Guidance for parish churches following the death of Her Majesty Queen Elizabeth II' 8th September 2022.

Coleman, S. 2017. The Process of Appointment of Bishops in the Church of England: A Historical and Legal Critique. *Ecclesiastical Law Journal* 19: 212–223.

Cranmer, F., 'Women as bishops: the House of Commons debate' 15 December 2012   https://lawandreligionuk.com/2012/12/15/women-as-bishops-the-house-of-commons-debate

Cruickshank, D. 2020. Debating the Legal Status of the Ornaments Rubric: Ritualism and Royal Commissions in Late Nineteenth- and Early Twentieth-Century England. *Studies in Church History* 56: 434–454.

Davie, G. 1994. *Religion in Britain since 1945: Believing without Belonging.* Blackwell.

Dinham, A. 2008. From Faith in the City to Faithful Cities: The 'Third Way', the Church of England and Urban Regeneration. *Urban Studies* 45 (10): 2163–2174.

Eberle, E.J. 2011. *Church and State in Western Society: Established Church. Cooperation and Separation:* Routledge.

Evans, G.R. 2021. *Crown, Mitre and People in the Nineteenth Century: The Church of England. Establishment and the State:* Cambridge University Press.

Fewster, J. 2011. The Royal Declaration Against Transubstantiation and the Struggle Against Religious Discrimination in the Early Twentieth Century. *Recusant History* 30 (4): 555–572.

Field, C.D. 2021. *Counting Religion in Britain, 1970-2020: Secularization in Statistical Context.* Oxford University Press.

Flint, J. 2009. Faith-based schools: Institutionalising parallel lives? In *Faith in the Public Realm: Controversies, Policies and Practices,* ed. Adam Dinham et al., 163–182. Policy Press. John Flint.

Göçmen, I. 2013. The Role of Faith-Based Organizations in Social Welfare Systems: A comparison of France, Germany, Sweden, and the United Kingdom. *Nonprofit and Voluntary Sector Quarterly* 42 (3): 495–516.

Green, S.J.D. 2010. *The Passing of Protestant England: Secularisation and Social Change, c.1920–1960.* Cambridge University Press.

Griffiths, C. 2014. Sharia and Beth Din courts in the UK: Is legal pluralism nothing more than a necessary political fiction? *Studia Iuridica Toruniensia* 15: 39–52.

Grimley, M. 2004. *Citizenship, Community, and the Church of England: Liberal Anglican Theories of the State Between the Wars.* Oxford University Press.

Harris, M., et al. 2003. A Social Policy Role for Faith-Based Organisations? Lessons from the UK Jewish Voluntary Sector. *Journal of Social Policy* 32 (1): 93–112.

Hunt, S. 2013. Negotiating Equality in the Equality Act 2010 (United Kingdom): Church-State Relations in a Post-Christian Society. *Journal of Church and State* 55 (4): 690–711.

Husselbee, L., and P. Ballard. 2012. *Free Churches and Society: The Nonconformist Contribution to Social Welfare 1800-2010.* Bloomsbury.

Ledger-Lomas, M. 2021. *Queen Victoria: This Thorny Crown.* Oxford.

Lloyd, R. 1966. *The Church of England, 1900-1965.* SCM Press.

Loss, D.S. 2017. The Institutional Afterlife of Christian England. *The Journal of Modern History* 89 (2): 282–313.

Maughan, S. 2003. Imperial Christianity? Bishop Montgomery and the Foreign Missions of the Church of England, 1895–1915. In *The Imperial Horizons of British Protestant Missions,* ed. A. Porter, 32–57. Eerdmans.

Medhurst, K. 1991. Reflections on the Church of England and Politics at a Moment of Transition. *Parliamentary Affairs* 44 (2): 240–261.

Merricks, P.T. 2012. God and the Gene': E.W. Barnes on Eugenics and Religion. *Politics, Religion & Ideology* 13 (3): 353–374.

Middlemiss Lé Mon, M. 2010. The "In-Between" Church: Church and Welfare in Darlington. In *Configuring the Connections - Welfare and Religion in 21st Century Europe*, ed. A. Backstrom et al., 113–128. Taylor and Francis.

Morris, R. 2009. *Church and State in 21st Century Britain: The Future of Church Establishment*. Palgrave Macmillan UK.

Office for National Statistics, 'Religion, England and Wales: Census 2021, The religion of usual residents and household religious composition in England and Wales, Census 2021 data.' https://www.ons.gov.uk/peoplepopulationand-community/culturalidentity/religion/bulletins/religionenglandandwales/census2021#religion-england-and-wales-data

Parker, S., and R. Freath. 2020. The Church of England and religious education during the twentieth century. In *The Church of England and British Politics since 1900*, ed. T. Rodger et al., 199–221. Boydell & Brewer.

Pattenden, H. 2021. The Prayer Book Controversy, c.1974–c.2000: Liturgy, Church, and Parliament in Late Twentieth Century England. *Journal of Religious History* 45 (2): 211–232.

Podmore, C. 2019. Self-Government Without Disestablishment: From the Enabling Act to the General Synod. *Ecclesiastical Law Journal* 21: 312–328.

Prideaux, M., and A. Dawson. 2018. Interfaith activity and the governance of religious diversity in the United Kingdom. *Social Compass* 65 (3): 363–377.

Prochaska, F. 2008. *Christianity and Social Service in Modern Britain: The Disinherited Spirit*. Oxford University Press.

Riedel, R. 2021. Religion and Terrorism: The Prevent Duty. *Ecclesiastical Law Journal* 23: 280–293.

Russell, M., and M. Sciara. 2007. Why Does the Government get Defeated in the House of Lords?: The Lords, the Party System and British Politics. *British Politics* 2: 299–232.

Sarrouh, B.T. 2020. Protected and Precarious: Muslims in the United Kingdom. In *State, Religion and Muslims Between Discrimination and Protection at the Legislative, Executive and Judicial Levels*, ed. M. Saral et al., 553–597. Brill.

Smith, G., and L. Woodhead. 2018. *Religion and Brexit: Populism and the Church of England*.

Taylor, S., and R. Huzzey. 2018. From Estate under Pressure to Spiritual Pressure Group: The Bishops and Parliament. *Parliamentary History* 37: 89–101.

Turnbull, M., and D. McFayden. 2012. *The State of the Church and the Church of the State*. Longman and Todd: Darton.

Webster, P. 2020. Parliament and the law of the Church of England, 1943–74. In *The Church of England and British Politics since 1900*, ed. T. Rodger et al., 182–198. Boydell & Brewer.

Weller, P. 2009. How participation changes things: "inter-faith", "multi-faith" and a new public imaginary. In *Faith in the Public Realm: Controversies, Policies and Practices*, ed. Adam Dinham et al., 63–81. Policy Press.

Williamson, P. 2020. Archbishops and the monarchy: leadership in British religion, 1900–2012. In *The Church of England and British Politics since 1900*, ed. T. Rodger et al., 57–79. Boydell & Brewer.

Wolffe, J. 1994. *God and Greater Britain: Religion and National Life in Britain and Ireland, 1843-1945*. Routledge.

———. 2010. Protestantism, Monarchy and the Defence of Christian Britain 1837–2005. In *Secularisation in the Christian World*, ed. M. Snape, 57–74. Routledge.

Zee, M. 2014. 'Five Options for the Relationship between the State and Sharia Councils: Untangling the Debate on Sharia Councils and Women's Rights in the United Kingdom' (January 15, 2014). *Journal of Religion and Society* 16: 1. Available at SSRN: https://ssrn.com/abstract=2380066.

CHAPTER 9

Of Faith and Fatherland: Churches and States in Ireland from the Act of Union to the Belfast Agreement, 1800–1998

Daithí Ó. Corráin

For centuries Catholicism and Protestantism have been defining elements of identity in Ireland. The churches surveyed in this essay are the Anglican Church of Ireland and the Roman Catholic Church and the term 'church' refers to the institutional churches, especially their episcopal leaderships, rather than the broader communities of believers. The Church of Ireland was the established or state church between 1537 and 1869. Although never numbering more than about one-sixth of the population, it enjoyed a privileged position and dominated social and political life as well as land ownership. That status became increasingly untenable during the nineteenth century. Anglicanism was not the only Protestant denomination in Ireland with Presbyterians, concentrated in the north-east, forming the largest dissenting tradition. By the outbreak of the French Revolution in 1789, the Catholic revival in Ireland was well advanced, having benefitted from relief acts in 1778 and 1782

D. Ó. Corráin (✉)
School of History and Geography, Dublin City University, Dublin, Ireland
e-mail: daithi.ocorrain@dcu.ie

179

S. Holzer (ed.), *The Palgrave Handbook of Religion and State Volume II*, https://doi.org/10.1007/978-3-031-35609-4_9

which removed most of the penal law restrictions on religious practice. The 'state' with which the churches interacted until the early 1920s was the British state. In response to the rebellion of the United Irishmen in 1798 and the threat of French invasion, the Act of Union, which came into effect on 1 January 1801, created the United Kingdom of Great Britain and Ireland. Under its terms, the Irish parliament was abolished, and Ireland was given 100 MPs at Westminster while the Irish peerage was represented in the House of Lords. During the nineteenth century there was an increasing political and religious alliance between all Protestants in defense of the Union and the protestant character of the state in the face of a resurgent Catholicism to which the vast majority of the population adhered. The Act of Union defined the relationship between the British state and Ireland until 1920 when the Government of Ireland Act partitioned the island and created a predominantly Protestant unionist six-county Northern Ireland. The following year the Anglo-Irish Treaty granted the Catholic nationalist Irish Free State dominion status on the same footing as Canada. One other state—the Vatican—will feature briefly in this account. For the purpose of clarity, a broadly chronological approach is taken to some of the key developments in church-state relations. Generally, this period of momentous political change witnessed the steady decline in the status, influence, and demographic strength of the Church of Ireland and the reconstruction, consolidation, and then ascendancy of the Catholic Church.

The Catholic Church Before the Great Famine, 1820s–1840s

A census in 1834 revealed that of an Irish population of 8 million, 6.5 million were Catholic, 853,000 were Anglican, and 665,000 were dissenters (mainly Presbyterians). Although Catholics occupied all social grades, the vast majority lived in poverty. Visitors to Ireland such as the political scientist and historian de Tocqueville and the novelist Thackeray commented on the strength of popular Catholic religious devotion. Ministering to such a large flock posed significant difficulties for the Catholic hierarchy which faced the challenge of an insufficiency of clergy and church buildings. The British state alleviated this by providing funds for the establishment of a national seminary at Maynooth in 1795 which was supported by an annual grant. There were significant regional variations but there was about one priest for every 3000 people. Mass attendance, estimated at about 40 percent, was a fraction of what it would become in the post-Famine decades (Miller 2000).

During the nineteenth century, the Catholic hierarchy emerged as a powerful body and its annual meetings became a means of coordinating policy. Unlike other European countries, the British state had no say in episcopal appointments and there was no nuncio in Ireland as the church was directly under the Congregation of Propaganda Fide until 1908 (Kerr 2002). From the 1820s, Irish Catholic bishops were increasingly trained in Maynooth rather than in the Irish colleges in Europe as had been necessary during the penal restrictions of the eighteenth century. This cohort of younger bishops was more forceful in demanding an end to Catholic grievances. When Catholic emancipation—in particular the removal of the oaths that prevented them becoming MPs—did not accompany the Act of Union, Britain's Catholic question was transformed into an Irish question (Bartlett 1992). The bishops and clergy supported the campaign of Daniel O'Connell's Catholic Association which became a non-violent mass movement. The achievement of emancipation in 1829 earned O'Connell the title 'the Liberator'. It was a symbolic and psychological victory for Irish Catholics. Emancipation allowed them to assume most public offices and sit in parliament. Fittingly, O'Connell became the first Irish Catholic MP to take his seat at Westminster. The example of a clerical-nationalist alliance became a template for future political movements.

The 1820s witnessed the new reformation—a crusade to accomplish what the first reformation had not achieved. This led to an intensification of religious antagonisms. Catholic churchmen were alarmed by Protestant missionary endeavor. All the Irish churches underwent significant reform and religious revival in the early nineteenth century. The pace of Catholic reorganization and the introduction of Tridentine reforms increased after emancipation. In 1844, the *Irish Catholic Directory* reported that within the previous thirty years some 900 Catholic churches had been built or refurbished (Kerr 2002, p. 176). There was also an upsurge in the provision of schools and welfare for the poor and underprivileged by religious orders such as the Sisters of Mercy (founded by Catherine McAuley) and the Sisters of Charity (established by Mary Aikenhead). In addition, foreign missionary activity by the Catholic and Protestant churches increased and remained prominent for over a century.

O'Connell's second great campaign to repeal the Act of Union was not successful but it did compel the British government to allow some concessions to Catholics such as a larger grant to Maynooth in 1845. Plans to give the Catholic Church a form of concurrent establishment with the Established Church by Lord John Russell, the Whig prime minister, were opposed by his political party and overtaken by the catastrophe of the Great Famine (1845–9) which altered Ireland profoundly: 1.25 million died, another 1.5 million emigrated, the cottier class who lived at a subsistence level were eliminated, and the Irish language and popular religious practice were largely destroyed (Delaney 2012; Gray 1998). Clergy of all denominations did much to relieve suffering but accusations, often exaggerated, of the use of food ('souperism') as an inducement to convert abounded and left a bitter legacy. By the time of the 1861 census, which was the first to include a question on religious profession, of a total population of 5.76 million, Roman Catholics comprised almost 4.5 million (78 percent), Anglicans 678,661 (11.7 percent), Presbyterians 528,992 (9.2 percent), and Methodists 44,532 (0.77 percent).

THE DEVELOPMENT OF A DENOMINATIONAL EDUCATION SYSTEM

Throughout the period under review, education was the most significant area of interaction between the churches and state. In the 1820s, several bishops joined with O'Connell to press the British government in vain for an educational system acceptable to Catholics. The Whig government in 1831 introduced the National System of Education whereby a state-supported primary school was established in each parish. The system was under the auspices of a state board of commissioners which replaced a multiplicity of ad hoc educational agencies and controlled the management of school buildings, curriculum, textbooks, teacher training, and a system of inspection. The state's desire to create a non-denominational system was opposed by the main churches because religious formation was regarded as a fundamental element of a child's education. The Catholic bishops were bitterly divided, and two opposing factions emerged. Archbishop Daniel Murray of Dublin and eighteen other bishops supported the initiative because they believed it was the best the government could provide. They were opposed by Archbishop John MacHale of Tuam and ten fellow prelates who feared the state schools could be used to convert Catholic children to Protestantism. In 1841 the pope ruled that each bishop could decide how schools were run in his own diocese.

The primary school network spread rapidly and became increasingly denominational in character. By 1900 almost 65 percent of the 8644 schools, which catered for 770,622 pupils, were denominationally homogeneous and 80 percent had clerical managers (Walsh 2016, pp. 10–11). As the number of schools increased, so did the need for trained primary school teachers. Of almost 8000 Catholic teachers in 1883, three-quarters had no training (McElligott 1966, p. 7). Between the 1860s and 1883 an arduous campaign was waged by the Catholic hierarchy to obtain state support for denominational training colleges as was the norm in England. To increase pressure on the government, the bishops banned Catholics from attending an interdenominational and co-educational training college at Marlborough Street established after 1831. The Church of Ireland's Kildare Place training college also demanded state support. Grant-in-aid was provided by the state to teacher training colleges under local management from 1883 (Parkes 2016, p. 74).

PAUL CULLEN AND THE TRANSFORMATION OF THE IRISH CATHOLIC CHURCH

The dispute between the Murray and MacHale factions in the 1840s also extended to charitable bequests, a proposal to establish secular higher education, and the succession as archbishop of Armagh. In late 1849 Pius IX chose the Irish-born and Rome-educated Paul Cullen as the new archbishop. He was charged with bringing unity to the Irish church and was determined to make it conform to the fullest extent with the Roman model. A national synod at Thurles in 1850, the first since 1642, 'laid the foundations of Cullen's transformation of Irish Catholicism' (Barr 2009). Four broad areas of decision merit a brief comment. First, the Vatican ruling on primary schools was upheld and under Cullen's leadership the Catholic hierarchy grew more united on the education question. A paramount concern was to resist any increase in state control, particularly at second level. In this domain Cullen introduced a number of teaching orders. Secondly, restoring ecclesiastical discipline among clergy and episcopal authority over them was emphasized. In addition, Cullen used his influence in Rome to reshape the bench of bishops in his likeness over time. Third, sacraments such as baptism and marriage could only be administered in church. Lastly, greater religious practice among the laity was encouraged amid fears of proselytism by evangelical Protestants.

During Cullen's tenure there was a boom in church building and clerical recruitment. The number of Catholic clergy relative to the size of their flock, severely diminished by the Famine, and relative to the number of Protestant clergy grew dramatically. In 1851 there was 1 priest to approximately 2000 lay people; by 1911 there was 1 per 1000. Emmet Larkin devised the term 'devotional revolution' to describe these changes in Irish Catholicism (Larkin 1972). This idea has been contested by other historians who have maintained that the changes were part of a longer process of modernization of Irish religious life (Connolly 1985).

The University Question

In 1845 the British government created three non-denominational queen's colleges to cater for Catholics and Presbyterians. Anglicans traditionally attended Trinity College, established in Dublin by royal charter in 1592. In 1848 Pope Pius IX condemned the colleges as dangerous to faith. Cullen responded by establishing the Catholic University in Dublin in 1854 with John Henry Newman, the distinguished Oxford convert to Catholicism, as first rector. Cullen's hopes that the university would become Europe's leading English-speaking Catholic institution were not realized because it lacked a charter and could not award degrees or attract enough students.

In 1873 William Gladstone's proposal for a single comprehensive secular national university that would include every university institution in Ireland foundered. The gradual secularization of university education was anathema to the Catholic hierarchy. In 1879 the British government established the Royal University which had the power to grant degrees to all students who passed its examinations. Although the Catholic University (renamed University College Dublin in 1882) was not recognized as a teaching institution in its own right, its students could at least now obtain degrees. The university question remained vexatious as the Catholic majority were denied a publicly endowed university. At the same time, Ulster pushed for its own university. The demand for higher education increased because the 1878 intermediate education act expanded the second level sector. Under this measure, secondary education was promoted by holding public examinations, awarding exhibitions and certificates, and payment of fees to school managers based on results.

During the 1890s the idea of two non-denominational universities alongside Trinity gained popularity. In 1908 Augustine Birrell, the Irish chief secretary, introduced the Irish Universities bill which envisaged two new state-funded and non-denominational universities. The National University of Ireland, with constituent colleges in Cork, Galway, and Dublin, accommodated Catholic concerns, while the Queen's University Belfast catered for non-conformists. The legislation included legal protections against interference in religious beliefs. By the early twentieth century, Ireland had three secular universities each with its own religious atmosphere. For the Catholic Church, the 1908 act was a crowning achievement because it now had effective control over all levels of a denominational educational infrastructure that was financed by the British state.

THE DISESTABLISHMENT OF THE CHURCH OF IRELAND

Disestablishment was the most significant nineteenth-century example of constitutional reform. It was the first breach of the Act of Union by which the Church of Ireland and Church of England had been joined 'as by law established' under article five (Vaughan 1989). At the November 1868 general election, Gladstone rallied the Liberal Party behind the cause of disestablishing the Church of Ireland. Somewhat incongruously, Irish Catholic bishops and clergy helped him to secure sixty-six seats in Ireland or half his overall majority in parliament. In general, Cullen believed that the church should concern itself with politics only when religious issues were at stake. In the 1850s he had withdrawn clerical support from the Independent Irish Party which hastened its demise, and he vigorously condemned Fenianism in the 1860s which sought Irish independence by military means. The Catholic hierarchy rejected a proposal to level up referred to as concurrent endowment. The alternative was leveling down or disendowment of all churches, thereby putting them on an equal footing, free of legal links with the state. The Church of Ireland was disestablished and disendowed with remarkable speed. A bill was introduced in parliament in March 1869, received the royal assent in July 1869, and the Church ceased to be established on 1 January 1871. Henceforth, it was a voluntary body, its ecclesiastical law was no longer part of the law of the land, and bishops were no longer Crown appointees but would in future be chosen by an electoral college.

Disestablishment came as a shattering blow to most churchmen. The Church of Ireland faced challenges in terms of finance, church government, doctrine, and relations with the Church of England (McDowell

1975; Shearman 1995). The Representative Church Body was created to act as trustee of money and property at the church's disposal. Places of worship no longer in use passed into the care of the Board of Works, and in this way many ancient ecclesiastical sites became public monuments. The Church of Ireland adopted a synodical structure of governance by bishops, clergy, and laity that was modeled on Westminster with a House of Bishops and a House of Representatives. It retained Dublin as its administrative capital. The crisis drew out reserves of ability, self-reliance, and cohesion that proved a credit to the Church of Ireland.

Disestablishment also had a range of wider social and economic implications. Ireland became the only component part of the United Kingdom where there was no established church and where Catholics were in an overwhelming majority. The act was almost entirely concerned with various arrangements for the transfer and dispersal of property. In essence, it was the first in a series of Irish land acts which over time occasioned a revolution in land ownership. The Irish Church Act also served as a precedent for developments in Wales, where disestablishment was introduced in 1919 (Bell 1969). Lastly, it united Protestants of all denominations against the perceived threat from Catholicism.

THE LAND QUESTION AND THE PURSUIT OF HOME RULE, 1870–1893

The established church, land, and control of local government were the tripod on which the Protestant ascendancy rested. Each aspect was undermined during the nineteenth century. Between the 1870s and the early twentieth century, the land question and the demand for home rule or an autonomous Irish parliament were the dominant Irish political issues. In the 1870s, landlords of 1000 acres or more owned four-fifths of all Irish land. Half of the total number of tenants farmed less than fifteen acres and the vast majority were on insecure annual leases. The agitation associated with the Land War (1879–82) differed from earlier economic crises because the Land League created a mass movement and transformed an economic issue into a political problem for the British state. The ultimate aim of the league was the establishment of a peasant proprietorship. Crucially, the involvement of Catholic clergy in large numbers made it difficult for the British state to proscribe the league. The hierarchy was more circumspect. Archbishop Thomas Croke of Cashel recognized the dangers of alienating the laity. By contrast, Edward McCabe, who succeeded Cullen as archbishop of Dublin in 1879 and cardinal in 1882, opposed the league, the involvement of priests in political agitation, and the campaign for home rule. While McCabe's stance found favor in Rome, it was condemned in Ireland. The land agitation led Gladstone to introduce the 1881 land act which granted tenants fair rent, fixity of tenure, and free sale (the 3Fs). The legislation did not resolve the Irish land question, but, by providing a mechanism for purchase, it ushered in the beginnings of a social revolution in terms of land ownership.

The land war catapulted Charles Stewart Parnell to the forefront of politics in Britain and Ireland during the 1880s when home rule became an aggressive political campaign. Parnell's ascendancy was the product of three factors: the development of a powerful party machine in the shape of the National League; exploiting the Franchise and Redistribution Acts of 1884–5, which trebled the size of the electoral register; and the cultivation of an informal but high effective alliance with the Catholic Church. He supported the hierarchy's demand for Catholic control of education at all levels and in return their lordships formally supported the National League (Larkin 1975). The Catholic Church was not neutral and hoped for the emergence of a Catholic nation state (Miller 1973). In June 1885, the politically adept William Walsh became the new archbishop of Dublin. Under his leadership the Catholic bishops endorsed the Irish Parliamentary Party's (IPP) position on home rule and the system of purchase as a solution to the land question. Following the 1885 general election, the price of Irish support for Gladstone and the Liberal Party was the introduction of the first home rule bill in April 1886 which was predictably defeated in the House of the Commons. In Ireland, opposition to home rule quickly developed sectarian overtones, particularly in predominantly unionist Ulster which rejected any notion of an Irish government in Dublin. There was a determination to maintain the union with Britain and the political status quo under which the north-east had prospered economically. Strong resistance was mobilized in 1886, in 1893 during the second home rule crisis, and in 1912–14. In Britain, it was feared that Irish self-government would lead to the dismemberment of the empire.

Land agitation resumed with the Plan of Campaign of 1886–91, an effort at collective bargaining on individual estates. An alarmed Pope Leo XIII dispatched Monsignor Ignatius Persico to Ireland in July 1887 to investigate ecclesiastical involvement in agrarian agitation. The papal envoy did not grasp the intricacies of the land issue or Walsh's motivations in supporting the tenantry. His report regarded the arch-bishop of Dublin 'as much too politically-minded, too closely involved in public affairs through his association with the parliamentary party, the National League and Plan of Campaign and less committed to his pasto-ral work than he should have been' (Macaulay 2002, p. 355). By con-trast, Persico admired the moderate nationalism and prudence of Michael Logue, who had been appointed archbishop of Armagh in December 1887. Walsh was summoned to Rome and while there a papal rescript was issued condemning the Plan. This was the product not simply of Persico's report but of the divisions within the Irish hierarchy and strong lobbying by the British government. In Ireland, there was intense anger at perceived papal interference in domestic political matters. Walsh reas-sured the pope that the decree would be obeyed by all good Catholics. However, he dexterously finessed the distinctions between pronounce-ments on moral and political matters to comply with the decree, keep violent agitation in check, preserve nationalist unity (both lay and cleri-cal), and maintain the church's influence (both religious and secular) in Ireland. Historians have tended to dismiss the dour Logue and depict Walsh as the *de facto* leader of the Irish Catholic Church. In fact, as Logue's biographer makes clear, over two decades they maintained a strong friendship and an effective collaboration (Privilege 2009). Logue generally left the political direction of the hierarchy and the campaign for Catholic university education to Walsh while he retained responsibil-ity for ecclesiastical discipline.

The papal rebuke was overshadowed by the downfall of Parnell, fol-lowing revelations of a ten-year liaison with Mrs. Katharine O'Shea, and the consequent schism in the IPP in 1890. A political crisis was provoked not by the stance of Irish Catholic hierarchy but by the opposition of English non-conformists. This forced Gladstone to signal that Parnell's continued leadership imperiled the alliance with the Liberal Party which was poised to win the next election. Effectively, the choice was between Parnell and home rule. In December 1890, the IPP split with 45 MPs opting for home rule and 27 supporting Parnell. The anti-Parnellite majority seemed justified when in 1893 Gladstone's second home rule bill negotiated the House of Commons but was defeated in the House of Lords. On his death in October 1891, Parnell's immediate legacy was a shattered political party. The myth of a leader sacrificed by his own people and the Catholic Church rather than as a result of his own actions proved enduring. The church continued to play an important role in home rule politics. Many churchmen were also involved in the extraordinary cultural revival of the Irish language and sport at the end of the nineteenth century.

THIRD HOME RULE CRISIS (1912–14) AND EASTER 1916 RISING

The home rule question lay in abeyance, despite the reunification of the IPP in 1900, until the second decade of the twentieth century. A constitutional crisis in Britain over the rejection by the House of Lords of the 'People's Budget' of 1909 led to two general elections in 1910. The IPP found itself holding the balance of power. Once again, the price of Irish political support was home rule. In April 1912, Prime Minister H.H. Asquith introduced the third home rule bill. It provoked a crisis that verged on civil war in Ireland between unionism and nationalism. The situation differed from earlier home rule crises because the Parliament Act (1911) replaced the veto of the House of Lords with delaying powers for a maximum of two years. The Catholic bishops shared in the general air of expectancy that nationalist aspirations would therefore be fulfilled by 1914. The national question overshadowed other political concerns for church leaders such as preaching the dangers of socialism and labor agitation in the 1910s. While Logue and Walsh deemed the IPP leadership too secularist, too reliant on the British Liberals, and too inclined to accept an attenuated version of home rule, a large episcopal middle ground was determined not to interfere in politics and was supportive of the national cause. For the Ulster Catholic bishops, the specter of partition and the creation of a unionist government in Belfast imperiled their religious and educational interests. Conversely, Protestants of all shades feared that home rule would amount to Rome rule. Religious tensions were exacerbated, particularly in Ulster, by the *Ne Temere* decree (1908). For the main Protestant churches, religious and political fears proved mutually reinforcing. At the root of this was a lack of confidence in an Irish government to maintain civil and religious liberties for all. The General Synod of the Church of Ireland denounced *Ne Temere* which was raised frequently at anti-home rule protests. The bogey of religious intolerance proved impossible to quash.

In 1913, as tension rose in Ireland with the formation of unionist and nationalist paramilitary forces, the British government proposed partitioning Ireland to exclude the predominantly unionist north-east from home rule and compelled the IPP to accept this approach. Edward Carson, the Ulster Unionist leader, initially sought the exclusion from home rule of the entire nine-county province of Ulster but was willing to settle for six counties. John Redmond, leader of the IPP, articulated the Irish nationalist position by declaring 'the idea of two nations in Ireland is to us revolting and hateful'. Exclusion raised several intractable questions: what area was involved, would exclusion be temporary or permanent, and what jurisdiction would be retained by Westminster (Jackson 2003). Conflict over home rule was averted by the outbreak of the First World War. Although home rule was placed on the statute book in September 1914, it was immediately suspended for the duration of the war and accompanied by an unspecified provision for the special treatment of Ulster.

The length of the war had profound consequences for Redmond and home rule. Equally, it had significant consequences for a small group of republican separatists who were determined to organize a rebellion while Britain was engaged in a major international conflict (Townshend 2005). The Easter 1916 Rising proved a watershed in the subsequent trajectory of Ireland. The British response in the form of martial law, executions, arrests, and internment worked a sea change in Irish public opinion. Accurately judging the public mood, the Catholic hierarchy followed the lead of Archbishop Walsh and made no public pronouncement on the 1916 Rising. The British government made an ill-fated attempt in the summer of 1916 to introduce a home rule settlement based on partition. With the exception of Patrick O'Donnell of Raphoe, a confidante of the IPP leadership, the northern bishops publicly disavowed the proposals. Famously, Cardinal Logue declared that it would be 'infinitely better to remain as we are for fifty years to come under English rule than to accept these proposals' (*Irish Catholic Directory* 1917, p. 517). In May 1917, an appeal against partition was organized by Bishop Charles McHugh of Derry and was signed by sixteen Catholic and three Church of Ireland bishops. McHugh later made clear that he would never submit to the Catholic community becoming 'serfs in an Orange [unionist] Free State carved out to meet the wishes of an intolerant minority' (*Irish Independent*, 18 Feb. 1920).

Transition to an Independent Irish State, 1916–23

Repudiation of political violence but not the goal of Irish independence, obeisance to the legally constituted government, advocacy of majority rule, hostility toward partition, and a desire for order and social stability characterized the stance of the Irish Catholic hierarchy between 1916 and 1923 (Keogh 1986; Murray 2000). This required considerable political and theological dexterity. While the political influence of Catholic bishops and clergy during this traumatic period should *not* be overstated, the church was sensitive to the shifting political landscape and determined not to alienate the laity. By the time of the December 1918 general election, home rule had been jettisoned in favor of a popular demand for an Irish republic. Championed by Sinn Féin, which annihilated the IPP at the polls, that goal was pursued politically and militarily during the War of Independence (1919–21). An underground counter-state in the form of Dáil Éireann challenged British rule and claimed public allegiance. At the same time the Irish Republican Army (IRA) engaged in guerrilla warfare, principally against the overwhelmingly Catholic Royal Irish Constabulary. The Catholic Church's alignment with majority nationalist opinion was cemented during the massive protest campaign against conscription in April 1918 which the bishops declared 'an oppressive and inhuman law' which the Irish people had a right 'to resist by all the means that are consonant with the law of God' (*Irish Times*, 19 Apr. 1918). The wholehearted involvement of the church prevented widespread disorder and scuppered any prospect of conscription being applied in Ireland.

During the War of Independence, the Catholic hierarchy was fearful of lending moral sanction to either side in the deepening conflict. In their statements in 1920 and 1921, they denounced violence, blamed failed British policy for the disturbed state of the country, called for an undivided Ireland to be allowed choose its own form of government, and increasingly drew attention to the excesses of the Crown forces. Just one bishop excommunicated members of the IRA. The Catholic hierarchy did not formally recognize the Dáil, however. The bishops were greatly perturbed by the conditions endured by beleaguered northern Catholic nationalists. Between July 1920 and July 1922, communal violence claimed over 450 lives in Belfast, its epicenter, two-thirds of whom were Catholic. In addition, thousands of nationalists lost their jobs and homes, and hundreds of nationalist-owned businesses were destroyed (Parkinson 2004; Feeney 2021). In June 1921, the hierarchy delivered a scathing condemnation of the Government of Ireland Act, which made partition and a Northern Ireland government a reality, for facilitating a 'campaign of extermination' against the Catholic community (*Irish Catholic Directory* 1922, p. 595). Bishop Joseph MacRory of Down and Connor was in the invidious position of seeking to end sectarian violence while at the same time being unwilling to give formal recognition to the Northern Ireland government.

Once the Anglo-Irish truce was declared in July 1921, the bishops bestowed moral sanction on Sinn Féin as the Irish government in waiting. This was a pragmatic move ahead of peace negotiations which produced the Anglo-Irish Treaty in December 1921. Unsurprisingly, the bishops welcomed the settlement. As Bishop Michael Fogarty of Killaloe put it: 'The terror is gone and with it the foreign power that held our country in destructive grip for seven hundred years. … Ireland is now the sovereign mistress of her own life' (*Irish Catholic Directory* 1922, p. 553). Enthusiasm for the settlement among northern bishops was tempered by anxiety about partition—'the big blot on the Treaty'—as Bishop McKenna of Clogher put it (Murray 2000, p. 356). The northern bishops reluctantly concluded that the Treaty offered the best hope of all Ireland unity. The Church of Ireland bishops had no desire for a change of constitution but pledged their loyalty to the new political dispensation (Seaver 1963, p. 119). A majority of Catholic Ireland supported the Treaty which granted a significant measure of self-government but not a republic. The settlement was approved by the Dáil on 7 January 1922.

In the months that followed, the Catholic bishops attempted through word and deed to avert the disaster of civil war. When that conflict began in June 1922, the hierarchy unequivocally upheld the authority of the provisional government in Dublin, sustaining and reinforcing the authority of an *Irish* state (Murray 2000, p. 34). This extended to producing a partisan pastoral on 10 October 1922 to coincide with an amnesty offer to republicans by the government before the imposition of a draconian public safety act. The pastoral rejected the legitimacy of the anti-Treaty republican campaign because 'no one is justified in rebelling against the legitimate Government … set up by the nation and acting within its rights', an argument reinforced by the overwhelming endorsement of the Treaty at the June general election (*Freeman's Journal*, 11 Oct. 1922). The hierarchy threatened to deprive those engaged in unlawful rebellion of the sacraments of Eucharist and confession, and to suspend priests who gave spiritual aid to the anti-Treaty IRA (in the event neither was stringently applied). Lastly, the pastoral enjoined republicans to pursue grievances through constitutional action. Outraged republicans appealed to Pope Pius XI who dispatched Monsignor Salvatore Luzio to report on the Irish situation in 1923 by which stage the civil war was almost over. Cold-shouldered by church and state authorities, the government petitioned the Vatican to recall the envoy for endeavoring 'to interfere in the domestic affairs of the country' (Laffan 2014, p. 123). The October pastoral may have emboldened the government to take a sterner stance against republicans. Two manifestations of this were the policy of executions and the toleration of often gruesome reprisals. This was matched by an anti-Treaty IRA campaign of arson, intimidation, and assassination. Private appeals by individual bishops against executions, such as that of Erskine Childers, went unheeded. However dismayed the bishops were at the excesses of the Irish state during the civil war, no public condemnation was issued. In this, there was an element of pragmatic self-interest. The creation of Northern Ireland under a unionist government inimical to Catholic interests filled the Catholic bishops with foreboding. That strengthened their determination to secure the Irish Free State and the opportunities that it promised.

A Partitioned Ireland and Its Legacies

The traumas and legacies of the early 1920s shaped church-state relations in significant ways. First, all the main Christian churches continued to operate on an all-island basis despite contending with two political jurisdictions. Some Catholic bishops refused to accept partition. In his consecration address as bishop of Derry in 1926, almost a year after the boundary between north and south had been confirmed, Bernard O'Kane referred to the 'anomaly and absurdity' of having one part of his diocese 'in one kingdom and the remainder in another state' and pledged to work for a united Ireland (*Irish Catholic Directory* 1927, p. 615). There was never any question that the political border would compromise the religious unity of the Catholic Church or Church of Ireland whose map image remained an all-Ireland one. Second, partition proved deeply traumatic for the Catholic Church given the appalling civil strife between 1920 and 1922, the number of its adherents in Northern Ireland, its conviction that the Unionist government was hostile to the nationalist community which it regarded as a security problem, and the church's overwhelming desire to safeguard Catholic education. Unsurprisingly, resentment and political aloofness lingered. The northern Catholic experience before the 1960s was marked by a sense of being in but not of the state, where, as Marianne Elliott suggests, 'their religion was their politics' (Elliott 2015, p. 177). Third, partition reinforced the association of political allegiance and religious affiliation on both sides of the border. It produced a remarkably homogenous population in the Irish Free State. In 1926, Catholics accounted for almost 93 percent of the population. This had a significant bearing on the political and public culture and the status enjoyed by the church. It also facilitated the depiction of a unionist and Protestant Northern Ireland in contrast to a Catholic nationalist south. There was little reflection on the relationship between the Protestant churches and unionism before the 1960s.

State-Building in the Irish Free State and Catholic Ascendancy

The Catholic Church was uniquely well placed to contribute to the state-building project in the Irish Free State in terms of enhancing national unity and self-definition, providing an unmatched institutional presence, and controlling policy areas, none more so than education. Catholicism helped bind some of the wounds inflicted by the civil war. There was remarkably little republican resentment toward the church, no anti-clerical party developed, and de Valera and his Fianna Fáil party (on the losing side of the civil war) could demonstrate their devout Catholicism. This facilitated a remarkable level of continuity and harmony in church-state relations when Fianna Fáil took office in 1932. Denominational homogeneity facilitated a Catholic habitus—a way of thinking and acting in conformity with a systematic view of the world—that permeated all social classes (Inglis 1998). Therefore, during the first fifty years of independence, both church and state leaders, irrespective of political party, shared a desire to develop the state according to a philosophy of Catholic nationalism. Catholicism also differentiated the new Irish state culturally from its former British master. The centenary of Catholic emancipation in 1929 and the 31st Eucharistic Congress in 1932, an international showpiece of global Catholicism, were symbolic expressions of a triumphant Catholic nationalism. They allowed the Irish Free State 'to proclaim its permanence, its separate identity from England, and to give a high profile to its image as a Catholic nation' (McIntosh 1999).

The Catholic Church provided the new state with continuity, stability, and an extensive infrastructure. In return, a financially bankrupt government was content to see the church consolidate and extend its institutional presence in the realms of education, health, and welfare with minimal interference—a pattern that continued until the 1960s. As various commissions of enquiry have revealed, the status enjoyed by the church contributed to inadequate state oversight. During the first four decades of independence, the Catholic Church was more secure and more confident than at any previous time and enjoyed close links with the southern state. While an informal consensus between political and religious leaders was often evident, ministers did not always submissively dispose as the bench of bishops proposed. For example, diplomatic relations were established with the Vatican in 1929 despite the known opposition of the hierarchy, and the Dunbar-Harrison case in 1931 demonstrated the resolve of the W.T. Cosgrave government to reject the imposition of religious tests against non-Catholics. There was a commitment to retain the support of the Protestant minority which dominated business, banking, and insurance.

In the 1920s and 1930s, significant elements of the Catholic moral code were enshrined in law, particularly in the areas of sexual morality (other forms of morality were largely ignored) and family relations. Conservatism defined most aspects of Irish life between the 1920s and 1950s. For this reason, the censorship of films (1923) and publications (1929), the abolition of the right to divorce by private member's bill in 1925 and a constitutional prohibition in 1937, and a ban on the importation and sale of contraceptives (1935) were broadly favored by all the Christian churches. Too much has been read into W. B. Yeats's celebrated defense in the Free State Senate in June 1925 of divorce facilities as inflicting a wrong on his co-religionists (Whyte 1971, pp. 59–60; Regan 1999, p. 254; Foster 2003, pp. 293–300). His argument was not representative of either the Church of Ireland or other Protestant churches. The Church of Ireland was markedly reticent about divorce and remarriage which featured in just one of its pre-Second World War public statements in 1944. Measures such as censorship were not unique to Ireland. What differed was the stringency and longevity of Irish moral protectionism. For instance, the censorship of publications was not relaxed until 1967. Between the 1920s and the 1950s, the institutional Catholic Church was at its most dominant and devotional practices by a devout and deferential laity, in addition to weekly attendance at Mass, were at their most visible and numerous. Nevertheless, after the Second World War, the hierarchy unsuccessfully lobbied the government on aspects of the moral law not deemed rigorous enough! For example, in 1952 the Catholic bishops wanted all dancehalls closed at midnight and in 1958 the government was urged to have the police and censorship of publications board clamp down on foreign evil literature. Such requests were declined by the Irish state.

Many commentators have suggested that Catholic social teaching had a significant influence on de Valera's 1937 constitution (Bunreacht na hÉireann). The 1922 constitution was secular and did not mention the Catholic Church at all. While Bunreacht na hÉireann guaranteed religious pluralism, Article 44.1.2 conferred a special position on the Catholic Church 'as the guardian of the faith professed by the great majority of citizens'. Recent legal-historical scholarship has downplayed the Catholic influences on the 1937 constitution and emphasized its secular values, the extent to which the conceptualization of the state was greatly enlarged, and the degree to which it borrowed heavily from European constitutions, such as Weimar Germany, before later being supplemented by Catholic teaching on natural law (Hogan 2005; Kissane 2020; Coffey 2018). The 1937 constitution did not establish the Catholic Church or describe it as the one true church and recognized other churches in Article 44.1.3, to the chagrin of Cardinal Joseph MacRory, Catholic archbishop of Armagh and primate of all-Ireland from 1928 to 1945. Article 45, listing the 'directive principles of social policy', drew heavily on Catholic teaching but was intended only for the 'general guidance' of parliament. The 'special position' clause was deleted with minimum fuss in a constitutional referendum in 1972 under the shadow of the Northern Ireland Troubles. Despite their disquiet at the economic and cultural policies pursued by the Free State and alarm at widespread Protestant emigration, the Church of Ireland received the new constitution with quiet acceptance. The most notable effort to incorporate Catholic social teaching into the Irish state's administrative system was the Commission on Vocational Organisation between 1939 and 1943, chaired by Bishop Michael Browne of Galway. Its 300,000-word report proposed a vocational board composed of employers and workers for each trade or craft. The Fianna Fáil government (and the opposition parties in the Dáil) simply ignored it, having no appetite for a non-party center of power in Irish life (Lee 1979).

CONTROL OF EDUCATION AND HEALTH

Until the Second Vatican Council, Pius XI's *Quadragesimo Anno*, which developed the concept of subsidiarity, was frequently cited by the Irish Catholic bishops, who remained suspicious of state activity, even though in an Irish context the state 'stepped in not too much but too little' (Ryan 1979, p. 6). The most significant areas of policy interaction between church and state before the 1960s were the sensitive areas of education, and to a lesser extent health. Control of education (its ethos, school management, and teaching appointments), wrested from the British government in the nineteenth and early twentieth centuries, was regarded as essential if Catholic faith and values were to be transmitted to future generations. The same was true for the Church of Ireland. After 1922, the department of education had limited power over the management of primary and secondary schools, which remained vested in the Catholic and Protestant clergy. The state paid the salaries of teachers, but its influence was largely restricted to control of the curriculum and an inspection system to ensure minimum teaching standards (Ó Buachalla 1988). The Catholic Church's priority, which was facilitated by the state, was to maintain the status quo. For the Church of Ireland, schools were of particular importance in the south in terms of preserving community identity and that church was treated generously by the Irish state (Ó Corráin 2006).

In the 1960s, it was belatedly recognized that the extension of educational opportunity was a central aspect of national economic development. In 1965 *Investment in Education*, an OECD study of Ireland's long-term educational needs, revealed that just one-quarter of those leaving primary education continued to second level. This prompted the introduction of free post-primary education from the 1967 school year. John Walsh has revised the cordial characterization of church-state interaction in this period put forward by earlier studies. Although the denominational character of schools remained unaltered, a new balance of power in education had been achieved, in which the enhanced influence of the state in education was accepted with varying degrees of reluctance (Walsh 2012).

During the 1990s and 2000s, there was a flurry of new policies in education by an increasingly interventionist and secular Irish state. For example, under the new primary school curriculum, introduced in 1999, there was a greater separation of secular and religious instruction than ever before. Under the 1998 Education Act, for the first time the state recognized a variety of non-denominational schools such as Gaelscoileanna

(Irish-language schools) and multidenominational schools (which from 1984 came under the umbrella of Educate Together). The Catholic Church still exerts immense influence on the education system through its patronage, management, and ownership of 90 percent of primary schools; in addition, about half of post-primary schools are under denominational control.

In the domain of health and welfare there was also significant continuity with patterns established in the nineteenth century. Following emancipation, a number of Catholic voluntary hospitals were founded by religious orders, particularly in the cities. After the 1898 Local Government Act, religious orders also began to extend their influence into the poor law or workhouse system. When this was abolished in the mid-1920s many workhouses were closed, some became county hospitals, and others became county homes to care for the infirm, the elderly, the intellectually disabled, and unmarried mothers (Cox 2018). With plentiful vocations, religious orders increased their involvement in county homes and hospitals which were financed by local rates.

By the late 1920s, the voluntary hospitals, both Catholic and Protestant, faced grave financial challenges due to rising operational and treatment costs, a fall in the value of their endowment funds following the First World War, and a reduction in income from charitable donations. Increasingly, hospitals relied on income from patient fees as their debts mounted. To meet this, in 1930 the Public Charitable Hospitals (Temporary Provisions) Act permitted sweepstakes on horse racing (Coleman 2009). The proceeds of this remarkably popular venture went into a Hospitals Trust Fund which was increasingly controlled by the minister for local government. To benefit from the fund voluntary hospitals had to reserve at least one-quarter of their beds for non-paying patients. The sweepstakes ensured the survival of a large number of voluntary hospitals which otherwise would have been forced to close or amalgamate (Barrington 2003). From the late 1940s, the fund was used for capital investment in the State hospital sector.

After the Second World War, expanded medical services in Western Europe and the establishment of the National Health Service in Britain prompted the Irish government to address the pressing issues of tuberculosis, wider access to medical care, and improved ante and postnatal care. When a comprehensive health service was mooted in the mid-1940s, the medical profession feared socialized medicine and the end of private practice. The Catholic bishops were anxious about state control of voluntary hospitals and a dilution of Catholic medical ethics. Opposition to greater state involvement in healthcare by doctors and the hierarchy was at the root of the Mother and Child controversy in 1951, on which much has been written (Barrington 1987; McKee 1986; Horgan 2000). This cause célèbre has often been portrayed simplistically as a clash of church and state, with the latter coming off second best. In fact, it was a three-cornered tussle involving the state, the Catholic Church, and the powerful medical profession. Ultimately, the doctors secured concessions on retention of a means test and private practice. The 1953 Health Act ended any prospect of a health service on British lines. Free medical care of mothers before and after birth, and of their infants until the age of six weeks was permitted along with free health clinics for schoolchildren to the age of six. The pattern of hospital consultants using voluntary hospitals for private medical practice in return for treating the poor for free became entrenched. The voluntary hospitals retained their independence as they did after the 1970 Health Act established eight regional health boards, even though they were largely funded by the exchequer.

A Changing Irish Republic, 1960s–1990s

In a survey of Dublin Catholics in 1962, a remarkable 87 percent of respondents disagreed that if there was a conflict between the church and the state, the state should prevail (Biever 1976). However, the context of church-state relations was soon altered due to transformations at home and within the universal church. From the 1960s, the state began to prioritize economic growth over the simpler Catholic nationalist vision of society that had prevailed since independence. In addition, legislative and constitutional support for a Catholic ethos was undermined by a variety of societal developments. These included the establishment of a national television service in 1961 which reinforced a growing questioning of church and state authority; the transformative extension of educational opportunity at second and third level; the changing position of women which challenged the patriarchal nature of Irish society and traditional church teaching; the relaxation of censorship; the *aggiornamento* of the Second Vatican Council of which the Irish Catholic bishops were unenthusiastic lest it undermine their magisterium; and the onset of the Northern Ireland Troubles. Furthermore, previously plentiful vocations went into steady decline from 1968 onward with obvious implications for maintaining the Catholic Church's institutional presence in traditional areas of activity such as education and health. From the 1970s, the church developed a more critical view of the Irish state's social policy shortcomings, particularly in relation to inequality, poverty, and unemployment.

The first papal visit to Ireland in 1979, when an estimated 2.7 million people greeted John Paul II, is often regarded as a celebration of Catholic Ireland. It is more accurately understood as an unsuccessful attempt to slow down the inroads made by materialism and secularism, and an increasing detachment from the institutional church (Ó Corráin 2021). For much of the twentieth century, Ireland was unique among Western countries in not permitting abortion, contraception, or divorce. The Catholic hierarchy held the traditional line on these issues, but for the first time in November 1973 it openly acknowledged that the state should not be the guardian of private morality. In Britain and the United States, change in this sphere occurred over a century but in Ireland this was telescoped into a much shorter time span. Seven bruising 'moral issue' constitutional referenda on abortion and marriage were held between 1983 and 2002. They were preceded by the legalization of contraception in 1979 with further extensions in 1985 and 1992. Accompanying these campaigns, even before the full revelations of a litany of clerical sex abuse scandals, was 'a growing coolness between the government and the hierarchy' and little prior church-state consultation, something unimaginable in earlier decades (Nic Ghiolla Phádraig 1995, pp. 611–12).

NORTHERN IRELAND, THE TROUBLES, AND THE BELFAST AGREEMENT

Between 1921 and 1972 Northern Ireland was effectively a one-party unionist state. The Unionist Party was a diverse coalition held together by a trenchant stand on the union and constant fears of enemies within, chiefly the nationalist community and labor. Antagonism initially characterized relations between the Catholic Church authorities, who had a political importance as spokesmen for the minority, and the Northern Ireland administration (Harris 1993; Rafferty 1994). After the Second World War the opportunities occasioned by the welfare state saw the northern Catholic bishops adopt a more pragmatic approach, as they moved from highlighting the injustice of the state to injustices within it (Ó Corráin 2006, pp. 43–69). The government's readiness 'to pander to sectarian pressures was influenced by fear of the rise of cross-community, working-class support for Labour' (Holmes and Biagini 2017, p. 101). In 1969, unionism splintered under the impact of the civil rights movement and Northern Ireland was plunged into three decades of conflict which cost over 3700 lives. Throughout the Troubles, which promoted inter-church rapprochement and a reassessment of church-state relations, the Catholic Church was indefatigable in condemning violence (whether paramilitary or state-sanctioned), disassociating the vast majority of the nationalist community from the IRA campaign, and calling for cross-community dialogue (Power 2021; Scull 2019). At the New Ireland Forum in 1984, the Catholic hierarchy made clear that the Catholic Church ardently sought peace and justice in Northern Ireland and that it rejected the concept of the confessional state. The leaders of the main Christian Churches supported the peace process during the 1990s and welcomed the Belfast Agreement in 1998 which went further than just providing political institutions. It also addressed the issue of equality between the two traditions in the economic, social, and cultural domains. The agreement was approved by simultaneous referenda north and south in May 1998 and won the support of 94 percent of those voting in the Republic and 71 percent in Northern Ireland. Whereas the Catholic nationalist community was overwhelmingly in favor, only about half of the Protestant community was.

CONCLUSION

For most of the period covered in this survey, there was a clear intertwining of religion and political allegiance in Ireland. Both the Catholic Church and Church of Ireland feared the implications of new political arrangements for their religious freedom and key interests. In some respects, the experience of the Church of Ireland at the time of disestablishment when it lost its privileged status and links with the British state has been mirrored in the closing decades of the twentieth century by the Catholic Church. For a variety of economic and social reasons, it lost the hegemonic status it had enjoyed since Irish independence. Once above public scrutiny, scandal has engulfed the Catholic Church in Ireland since the 1990s. More than any other factor, that accelerated the recalibration of church-state relations that had been in train since the 1960s.

REFERENCES

Barr, Colin. 2009. Cullen Paul. In *Dictionary of Irish Biography*. https://doi.org/10.3318/dib.002281.v1.

Barrington, Ruth. 1987. *Health, Medicine and Politics in Ireland, 1900–1970*. Dublin: Institute of Public Administration.

———. 2003. Catholic Influence on the Health Services, 1830–2000. In *Religion and Politics in Ireland at the Turn of the Millennium*, ed. James P. Mackey and Enda McDonagh, 152–165. Dublin: Columba Press.

Bartlett, Thomas. 1992. *Fall and Rise of the Irish Nation: The Catholic Question in Ireland, 1691–1830*. Dublin: Gill & Macmillan.

Bell, P.M.H. 1969. *Disestablishment in Ireland and Wales*. London: SPCK.

Biever, Bruce. 1976. *Religion, Culture and Values: A Cross-Cultural Analysis of Motivational Factors in Native Irish and American Irish Catholicism*. New York: Arno Press.

Coffey, Donal. 2018. *Drafting the Irish Constitution, 1935–1937: Transnational Influences in Interwar Europe*. Basingstoke: Palgrave.

Coleman, Marie. 2009. *The Irish Sweep: A History of the Irish Hospitals Sweepstake, 1930–87*. Dublin: University College Dublin Press.

Connolly, Seán. 1985. *Religion and Society in Nineteenth-Century Ireland*. Dundalk: Dundalgan Press.

Cox, Catherine. 2018. Institutional Space and the Geography of Confinement in Ireland, 1750–2000. In *Cambridge history of Ireland Vol. IV*, ed. Thomas Bartlett, 673–707. Cambridge: Cambridge University Press.

Delaney, Enda. 2012. *The Curse of Reason: The Great Irish Famine*. Dublin: Gill & Macmillan.

Elliott, Marianne. 2015. Faith in Ireland, 1600–2000. In *The Oxford Handbook of Modern Irish History*, ed. Alvin Jackson, 168–192. Oxford: Oxford University Press.

Feeney, Brian. 2021. *Antrim: The Irish Revolution, 1912–23*. Dublin: Four Courts Press.

Foster, R.F. 2003. *W. B. Yeats: A Life, II: The Arch-Poet*. Oxford: Oxford University Press.

Freeman's Journal. 1922, October 11.

Gray, Peter. 1998. *Famine, Land and Politics: British Government and Irish Society, 1843–1850*. Dublin: Irish Academic Press.

Harris, Mary. 1993. *The Catholic Church and the Foundation of the Northern Ireland State*. Cork: Cork University Press.

Hogan, Gerard. 2005. De Valera, the Constitution and the Historians. *Irish Jurist* 40: 293–320.

Holmes, Andrew, and Eugenio Biagini. 2017. Protestants. In *The Cambridge Social History of Modern Ireland*, ed. Eugenio F. Biagini and Mary E. Daly, 88–111. Cambridge: Cambridge University Press.

Horgan, John. 2000. *Noel Browne: Passionate Outsider*. Dublin: Gill & Macmillan.
Irish Independent, 18 Feb. 1920.
Inglis, Tom. 1998. *Moral Monopoly: The Rise and Fall of the Catholic Church in Modern Ireland*. Dublin: University College Dublin Press.
Irish Catholic Directory. 1917.
———. 1922.
———. 1927.
Irish Times. 1918, April 19.
Jackson, Alvin. 2003. *Home Rule: An Irish History, 1800–2000*. London: Weidenfeld and Nicolson.
Keogh, Dermot. 1986. *The Vatican, the Bishops, and Irish Politics, 1919–39*. Cambridge: Cambridge University Press.
Kerr, Donal. 2002. The Catholic Church in the Age of O'Connell. In *Christianity in Ireland: Revisiting the Story*, ed. Brendan Bradshaw and Dáire Keogh, 164–185. Dublin: Columba Press.
Kissane, Bill. 2020. Catholicism and the Concept of 'the State' in the Irish (1937) Constitution. *Oxford Journal of Law and Religion* 9: 508–528.
Laffan, Michael. 2014. *Judging W. T. Cosgrave*. Dublin: Royal Irish Academy.
Larkin, Emmet. 1972. The Devotional Revolution in Ireland, 1850–75. *The American Historical Review* 77 (3): 625–652.
———. 1975. *The Roman Catholic Church and the Creation of the Modern Irish State, 1878–1886*. Dublin: Gill & Macmillan.
Lee, J.J. 1979. Aspects of Corporatist Thought in Ireland: The Commission on Vocational Organisation 1939–43. In *Studies in Irish History*, ed. Art Cosgrave and Donal McCartney, 324–346. Dublin: University College Dublin.
Macaulay, Ambrose. 2002. *The Holy See, British Policy and the Plan of Campaign in Ireland, 1885–93*. Dublin: Four Courts Press.
McDowell. R.B. 1975. *The Church of Ireland, 1869–1969*. London: Routledge and Kegan Paul.
McElligott, T.J. 1966. *Education in Ireland*. Dublin: Institute of Public Administration.
McIntosh, Gillian. 1999. Acts of "National Communion": The Centenary Celebrations for Catholic Emancipation, the Forerunner of the Eucharistic Congress. In *Ireland in the 1930s: New Perspectives*, ed. Joost Augusteijn, 83–95. Dublin: Four Courts Press.
McKee, Eamonn. 1986. Church-State Relations and the Development of Irish Health Policy: The Mother-and Child Scheme, 1944–53. *Irish Historical Studies* 25 (98): 159–194.
Miller, David W. 1973. *Church, State and Nation in Ireland, 1898–1921*. Dublin: Gill & Macmillan.
———. 2000. Mass Attendance in Ireland in 1834. In *Piety and Power in Ireland 1760–1960: Essays in Honour of Emmet Larkin*, ed. S.J. Brown and David

W. Miller, 158–179. Belfast and Notre Dame: Queen's University of Belfast, Institute of Irish Studies and the University of Notre Dame Press.

Murray, Patrick. 2000. *Oracles of God: The Roman Catholic Church and Irish Politics, 1922–37.* Dublin: University College Dublin Press.

Nic Ghiolla Phádraig, Máire. 1995. The Power of the Catholic Church in the Republic of Ireland. In *Irish Society: Sociological Perspectives*, ed. Patrick Clancy et al., 593–619. Dublin: Institute of Public Administration.

Ó Buachalla, Séamus. 1988. *Education Policy in Twentieth Century Ireland.* Dublin: Wolfhound Press.

Ó Corráin, Daithí. 2006. *Rendering to God and Caesar: The Irish Churches and the Two States in Ireland, 1949–73.* Manchester: Manchester University Press.

———. 2021. Why Did Pope John Paul II Visit Ireland? The 1979 Papal Visit in Context. *British Catholic History* 35 (4): 1–24.

Parkes, Susan M. 2016. 'An Essential Service': The National Board and Teacher Education, 1831–1870. In *Essays in the History of Irish Education*, ed. Brendan Walsh, 45–82. Basingstoke: Palgrave Macmillan.

Parkinson, Alan. 2004. *Belfast's Unholy War: The Troubles of the 1920s.* Dublin: Four Courts Press.

Power, Maria. 2021. *Catholic Social Teaching and Theologies of Peace in Northern Ireland: Cardinal Cahal Daly and the Pursuit of the Peaceable Kingdom.* London: Routledge.

Privilege, Michael. 2009. *Michael Logue and the Catholic Church in Ireland, 1879–1925.* Manchester: Manchester University Press.

Rafferty, Oliver P. 1994. *Catholicism in Ulster, 1603–1983: An Interpretative History.* London: Hurst & Co.

Regan, John M. 1999. *The Irish Counter-Revolution, 1921–1936.* Dublin: Gill & Macmillan.

Ryan, Liam. 1979. Church and Politics. The Last Twenty-Five Years. *The Furrow* 30 (1): 3–18.

Scull, Margaret. 2019. *The Catholic Church and the Northern Ireland Troubles, 1968–1998.* Oxford: Oxford University Press.

Seaver, George. 1963. *John Allen Fitzgerald Gregg, Archbishop.* London: Faith.

Shearman, Hugh. 1995. *Privatising a Church: The Disestablishment and Disendowment of the Church of Ireland.* Lurgan: Ulster Society.

Townshend, Charles. 2005. *Easter 1916: The Irish Rebellion.* London: Allen Lane.

Vaughan, W.E. 1989. Ireland c. 1879. In *A New History of Ireland, Vol. V*, ed. W.E. Vaughan, 726–800. Oxford: Clarendon Press.

Walsh, John. 2012. Ministers, Bishops and the Changing Balance of Power in Irish Education 1950–70. *Irish Historical Studies 38* (149): 108–127.

Walsh, Tom. 2016. The National System of Education, 1831–2000. In *Essays in the History of Irish Education*, ed. Brendan Walsh, 7–43. Basingstoke: Palgrave Macmillan.

Whyte, John H. 1971. *Church and State in Modern Ireland, 1923–1970.* Dublin: Gill & Macmillan.

CHAPTER 10

Religion and the State in Germany and Slovakia: Convergence and Divergence of a Western Versus Central European Case

Joel S. Fetzer and J. Christopher Soper

Although most of Western and Central Europe became one political confederation after the fall of the Berlin Wall and the addition of most Central European states into the European Union in 2004, the political histories, institutional arrangements, and political mobilization around religion shapes current religion-state practices in the two regions. Using Germany and Slovakia as case studies, we document the institutional and legal similarities between these two countries. Both guarantee religious freedom and have adopted a form of multiple religious establishment. Nevertheless,

We are grateful to Pepperdine University for funding language study and field work for the first writer, to Alena Batson and the late Owen V. Johnson for insightful comments on an earlier draft of this chapter, and to Rev. Kyle Svennungsen for helpful advice on research strategies. All errors of fact or judgment remain our own, however.

J. S. Fetzer (✉) • J. C. Soper
Pepperdine University, Malibu, CA, USA

on the ground, these two states diverge markedly in how religious actors and institutions engage in politics and in the role that religion plays in national identity. This chapter provides an overview of the historical and institutional context that continues to shape contemporary interactions between religion and politics, and also looks at specific recent examples of the varying interplay between these two factors in debates over abortion, immigration, same-sex marriage, and the role of Christianity in public life.

INTRODUCTION

The fall of the Berlin Wall in 1989, the political independence of Central European countries, and the eastward expansion of the European Union in 2004 led many people to assume that Central European countries would mirror their western counterparts on a host of political arrangements, including issues of religion and the state. Using Germany and Slovakia as case studies for their respective regions of Europe, we argue that there has been a good deal of convergence between these European countries on church-state matters. Both countries are religiously pluralistic, liberal democracies with strong constitutional protections for the rights of religious believers. Germany and Slovakia also share a multiple establishment church-state model where the government works closely with recognized religious groups on various policy areas. Despite these areas of convergence, however, there are also significant and increasingly salient points of divergence in the social and political role of religion in the two countries. As with much of Central Europe, religious practice is much higher in Slovakia than it is in Germany, which leads to greater political salience for religion on such issues as abortion, same-sex marriage, and the role of Christianity in public life. The countries (and their respective regions) also diverge in the link between religious (Christian) identity and national identity. One consequence of this different pattern of identity is that the countries differ dramatically in how they have responded to Muslim immigration. This twin story of convergence and divergence is a result of sociological, cultural, and historical factors unique to each country. We begin this chapter with the historical development of religion-state arrangements first in Germany and then in Slovakia.

Historical Background

The concept of the "two-swords" or two authorities—church and civil rulers—took deep root in the various German Kingdoms and principalities very loosely tied together during the Holy Roman Empire. Under this concept, the people were under two rulers, the prince and the church, and both worked for the stability and prosperity of society. The doctrine held in theory—even if it was often not followed in practice—that the church and the state, the two swords, were coequal institutions, each with rights and responsibilities. In theory at least, the church was not an arm of or subservient to the state.[1]

While the Protestant Reformation shattered the unity of European Christendom, it reinforced the two swords ideal. Most of the German territories followed the practice of *cuius regio, eius religio* (the religion of the ruler is the religion of the state). The 1648 Peace of Westphalia, which ended the devastating Thirty Years' War, reaffirmed the right of rulers to determine the religion to be followed in their territories. In each region, the prince determined whether his people were to be Roman Catholic, Lutheran, or Calvinist. Given the relatively small size of many of the German principalities, this practice created areas almost totally committed to one of these religious traditions within Christianity. The practice of *cuius regio, eius religio* perpetuated the "two swords" concept, although in practice the secular authority came to dominate the spiritual authority. With the church (Protestant or Roman Catholic) usually dependent on the civil rulers for its existence, this result is not surprising.

It was from out of this time period that the tradition of a church-state partnership emerged. The well-being of society rested on the two pillars of church and state, or throne and altar, as it is often put. They were seen as united in a common cause. Thus, cooperation and mutual support came to be the norm. The religious uniformity within the separate principalities made church-state cooperation and mutual support possible, for the most part, without raising charges of religious discrimination and favoritism.

The establishment of the Second Reich (1871–1918) under the leadership of Otto von Bismarck unified the nearly fifty principalities into a single German state. The various regional governments provided direct financial subsidies to the church, and the church became an important

---

[1] Portions of this section are based on the second author's related publication (see Chap. 7 of Soper, den Dulk, and Monsma 2017).

unifying force for the newly formed nation. At the time of German unification, the new nation was clearly Protestant. Its moving force was Prussia,
which was strongly Protestant. For a period of time in the 1870s, Bismarck
launched what came to be called the *Kulturkampf* (culture war), a series
of oppressive and discriminatory measures which aimed to advance the
political power of the state and to neutralize the political power of
Catholicism. Doing so had the opposite effect of what was intended, however, as Catholics rallied behind their leaders, and the Catholic Center
Party developed into a powerful political force. Most of the discriminatory
measures were repealed in the early 1880s, but the Center Party retained
its political influence (Conway 1992; Gould 1999; Kalyvas 1996).

The second empire ended following the defeat of Germany in World
War I and was replaced by the Weimar Republic. Given the crisis created
by the German defeat, the spirit of revolution that was in the air, and the
generally liberal nature of the new constitution, one might suppose that
the Weimar Constitution would break with past church-state practices.
The Weimar Constitution for the first time formally adopted the principle
of church-state separation, declared there was to be no state church, and
provided that "civil and political rights and duties shall be neither dependent on nor restricted by the exercise of religious freedom." It thereby
recognized the basic principle of governmental neutrality on matters of
religion, as well as the earlier principle of autonomy. The significance of
the Weimar Constitution for religious freedom can be seen in the fact that
the current constitution ("Basic Law"), adopted after World War II, incorporated by reference the basic articles establishing religious freedom found
in the Weimar Constitution. Nonetheless, a variety of subsidies and privileges were kept by the Roman Catholic and Protestant *Evangelische*[2]
churches under this new regime.

Most of the Protestant and Roman Catholic leadership opposed the
Weimar Constitution, a view that seemed to be vindicated when Germany
experienced a series of severe economic reversals and political difficulties
during the Great Depression. Thus, when Adolf Hitler and his National
Socialists promised stability, prosperity, freedom for the churches, and
greatness for the Fatherland, the churches, for the most part, initially

---

[2] In Germany, *Evangelische* refers to the historically dominant Lutheran-Reformed Church.
Although it translates literally to evangelical, this term is not synonymous with American-
style evangelicalism, the closest German equivalent of which would be *Freikirche*, or Free-
Church Protestant.

rallied in support. The Catholic Center Party unanimously supported the Enabling Act in 1933 that gave Hitler dictatorial powers. In the same year the Vatican signed the infamous *Reichskonkordat* with the Nazi regime, which assured the Roman Catholic Church certain rights but also helped the Nazis consolidate their power. Within the *Evangelische* Church, a "German Christian" movement emerged that enthusiastically supported Hitler's rise to power and thoroughly wedded German discipline and greatness with a form of Christianity (Spotts 1973).

The Roman Catholic Church never fully supported the Nazi regime. It was more concerned with protecting its own institutional autonomy and maintaining a semblance of normal church life in the midst of political upheaval and war than either supporting or opposing Nazism (Goldhagen 2003; Spicer 2004). Within the more culturally powerful *Evangelische* Church—after initial enthusiasm for Hitler—the theologian Karl Barth developed a "Confessing Church" based upon a confession of faith in the supremacy of Scripture which might not be changed to suit prevailing ideological or political convictions. This Confessing Church, while a minority in the larger Protestant community, nonetheless competed with the pro-Nazi German *Evangelische* Church. During the Hitler regime, 3000 pastors were arrested, at least 125 were sent to concentration camps, and 22 were executed, including the famous pastor and theologian Dietrich Bonhoeffer (Spotts 1973: 9).

The postwar era witnessed the rise of the Christian Democratic move-ment in West Germany, the most powerful political force in the country and the intellectual successor of the Center Party. This new party was interconfessional—including both Catholics and Protestants under the same political roof for the first time—and was firmly committed to liberal democracy and to learning from the bitter experiences under the Weimar Republic and the Third Reich (Warner 2000, chapter 9). The party also actively supported the movement toward European integration later in the twentieth century (Nelsen and Guth 2015). The *Evangelische* Church reinforced this democratic commitment by adopting the Stuttgart Declaration, which acknowledged the churches' and the nation's guilt in supporting the Nazi regime. By firmly linking Christianity to the powerful democratic impulses sweeping postwar Germany, it made possible the continued cooperation or partnership of the state with religion. Religion and Christianity came to be seen as positive, democratizing forces and as bulwarks against the reemergence of Nazism and as agents for the promo-tion of democratic political principles. Church-state cooperation was thereby seen not as a danger to be avoided, but as an asset to be used in the search for democracy (Elcott et al. 2021, chapter 2).

The situation in the communist-controlled German Democratic Republic (GDR) after the Second World War was quite different. Although the outright opposition of the Communist authorities waxed and waned during the forty years of their rule, even in the best of times East German parents were pressured not to baptize their children, church-going young people were often unable to obtain a college education, and active Christians were frequently denied government and business promotions. At the same time, an uneasy détente between the state and the churches emerged that was marked by pragmatism and accommodation by both sides. The state tolerated churches so long as they were not critical of regime policies, while the churches acquiesced to the state so long as it gave them some measure of control over their internal affairs. Nevertheless, both the Protestant and the Catholic churches played a significant role in the demise of the East German government (Schaefer 2010; Tyndale 2010; Doellinger 2013). Among the few institutions that were at all autonomous from the state, the churches provided the space and the opportunity to mobilize opposition to the regime.

The history of what would become Slovakia is inextricably tied to the Kingdom of Hungary (1000–1918) and the Austro-Hungarian Empire (1867–1918). Roman Catholicism was the official state religion of both of these monarchies, and a close partnership developed between the church and the state. Nonetheless, both the Kingdom of Hungary and the Austro-Hungarian Empire were remarkably diverse along linguistic, cultural, ethnic, and religious lines. Slovaks were one of countless groups of people who gradually developed a sense of their unique identity based on their shared language, history, and their Christian faith, to which the vast majority of Slovaks adhered (Kirschbaum 1995:61–154; Baer 2010).

As in Germany, the intersection of religion and politics developed in part as a reaction to attempts by Hungarian political leaders to curtail the temporal power of the Roman Catholic Church. Catholicism was the official state religion of the Empire, and most Hungarian political elites were themselves practicing Catholics. For centuries, church and state formed a partnership working toward common ends, but monarchs and state officials increasingly interfered in church life (Moravčíková 2010: 616). In the nineteenth century, the governing Liberal Party in Hungary advanced political reforms in education, family law, and church-state practices that attacked the political privileges of the Roman Catholic Church. Like its

German counterpart, however, this Hungarian *Kulturkampf* had the paradoxical effect of encouraging the mobilization of Roman Catholic Slovaks into political organizations and parties that defended Roman Catholic political prerogatives and conservative Catholic social values (Lorman 2019: 9–27).

While their respective *Kulturkampf* similarly led to new forms of political engagement by Roman Catholics in both Germany and Slovakia, the latter was distinctive in the degree to which this newly formed Slovak People's Party (*Slovenská ľudová strana*) led by Roman Catholic priest Andrej Hlinka became the vehicle for Slovak nationalism and cultural autonomy. Slovak identity, for the party, merged linguistic, religious, and ethnic (Slovak) distinctiveness. In its nascent form in the early twentieth century, in short, Slovak nationalism fused national and religious identity in a way that was not as apparent for the Catholic Center Party in Germany. As we will see later in this chapter, a lingering point of divergence between the two countries is the degree to which national and religious identities are linked. Slovak nationalism hewed more closely to religion than its German counterpart for various reasons. National identity is forged by crafting and/or manipulating cultural and social boundaries among groups of people. As noted above, while Hungary was also predominantly Roman Catholic, Slovak Catholics had a reputation for being particularly devout and conservative, perhaps because the locus of traditional Slovak culture and the home of most Slovaks until World War II has been the village in the countryside. Thus, liberal movements, political parties, and elites—even if they were Catholic—were often portrayed as alien and as a threat to Slovak cultural and religious values.

The fusion of religion and Slovak nationalism became even more pronounced with the disintegration of the Austro-Hungarian Empire at the end of the First World War and the establishment of the first Czechoslovak Republic in 1918. Czechoslovakia, as the country's name suggested, hoped to unite two groups of people within one nation. But Slovaks remained an ethnic minority in the newly formed state (17 percent), and many Slovak Roman Catholics continued to rail against what they perceived to be liberal, anti-clerical policies that were being pursued by Czech-oriented political officials in Prague. Moreover, many Slovaks resented being viewed as "backward country bumpkins" living in a "province" of an essentially "Czechoslovak nation." After assuming power, the governing socialist party intensified efforts toward church-state separation by nationalizing church properties, banning priests from serving in politics, and further limiting the church's role in education (Johnson 1985; Stan and Turcescu 2011: 151; Sekerák 2018:9–30). Leaders of the Slovak People's Party (SPP), many of whom were themselves Catholic clerics, presented Czech political leaders as no better than their Hungarian counterparts, and the party increasingly pushed for independence from their Czech cousins. During the interwar period, conservative Catholic identity continued to be a key foundation of Slovak nationalism.

Slovakia seceded from Czechoslovakia in 1939 and became a de facto client state of Nazi Germany. The pro-German government was led by President Jozef Tiso, a Catholic priest, and his Prime Minister Vojtech Tuka, who was instrumental in planning the deportation of 70,000 Slovak Jews to German concentration camps and the imprisonment of 40,000 co-religionists in Slovak "labor camps." The new government became an ally of Nazi Germany out of conviction and for strategic reasons. Some SPP party leaders were enthusiastic fascists, and all were willing to acquiesce in proto-fascist policies to win German support for Slovak independence. The clerico-fascist state that emerged from this Faustian bargain reaffirmed the social and political privileges of the Roman Catholic Church and abolished all forms of church-state separation (Stan and Turcescu 2011: 151–152; Sekerák 2018: 31–44). While the Catholic Church was an ally of fascism in Slovakia, Catholic leaders in the German-occupied Czech lands were active in anti-Nazi resistance movements.

Slovakia lost its nominal independence after World War II as Czechoslovakia was reconstructed as a single state in 1945. Following a Communist coup three years later, the country became a satellite of the Soviet Union. After the coup, the Communist Party of Czechoslovakia (*Komunistická strana Československa*, or KSČ) instituted various antireligious policies during its nearly half century in power. In fact, few states in the Soviet sphere witnessed as comprehensive an antireligious campaign as did Czechoslovakia (Stan and Turcescu 2011: 32). All clergy were required to take on oath of loyalty to the state, seminaries and monasteries were closed, the Greek Catholic Church was dissolved, and thousands of priests, nuns, monks, and laypersons were imprisoned or sent to labor camps on account of their faith (Doellinger 2013: 21–25; Sekerák 2018: 58–71). Opposition to the regime was especially strong in the Roman Catholic Church, whose leaders increasingly looked for inspiration to Poland as a model of how to promote democratic and religious values. Ironically, five decades of systematic oppression helped the Roman Catholic Church regain the credibility it had lost during its support of Slovak fascism. In

1987, furthermore, the Slovak Cardinal Ján Chryzostom Korec apologized on behalf of his church for its role in the deportation of Slovak Jews to death camps during the Holocaust (Katolícka Cirkev na Slovensku 1998).

The Velvet Revolution in 1989 that led to Czechoslovakia's democratization and independence from Soviet control was followed closely thereafter by the Velvet Divorce, which—despite public opinion among both ordinary Slovaks and Czech—split the Czechoslovak Federation once again into the two separate countries of the Czech Republic and Slovakia. The Slovak leader who helped manufacture this split, Vladimír Mečiar, alluded to the long-developing idea that Slovak national identity was separate from that of Czechoslovakia. And religion was once again a significant factor in driving the 1993 split between the more urban and largely secular Czechs and the more rural and much more devout Slovaks. As we noted above, ethnic and religious differences had been pronounced during the First Czechoslovak Republic (1918–1939), and those cleavages were just as significant 75 years later.

CONSTITUTIONAL CONTEXT

The constitutional and legal status of religion in Germany and Slovakia reinforces the narrative of convergence and divergence on issues of religion and politics. The German constitution, or "Basic Law," went into effect in May 1949. Its preamble begins with a recognition of God: "Conscious of their responsibility before God and Humankind." The first nineteen articles constitute a bill of rights, with Article 4 assuring that "(1) Freedom of faith and conscience as well as freedom of creed, religious or ideological, are inviolable," and "(2) The undisturbed practice of religion shall be guaranteed." Its third section provides for conscientious objectors to be exempted from military service. It is helpful to note that ideological as well as religious freedom and both conscience-driven beliefs and actions are safeguarded. Article 3 is also relevant to church-state issues. It provides that "All people are equal before the law" and that "Nobody shall be prejudiced or favoured because of their sex, birth, race, language, national or social origin, faith, religion or political opinions." The provisions of Articles 3 and 4 are supplemented by Article 140, which incorporates the basic religious freedom provisions of the old Weimar Constitution into the current Basic Law. Among the provisions thereby included in the Basic Law are a ban on the existence of a state church and several provisions with implications for religious establishment issues (Basic Law of the Federal Republic of Germany 1995).

In many respects, the 1992 Constitution of the Slovak Republic mirrors the German Basic Law. The preamble acknowledges the country's Christian heritage by referencing "the spiritual bequest of Cyril and Methodius" (eighth-century missionaries to the Slavs). The First Article describes Slovakia as a "sovereign, democratic state governed by the rule of law." That same article rejects the idea of any one established church by noting that the Republic "is not bound by any ideology or religion." The convergence with liberal international norms is made explicit in that same article which affirms that "The Slovak Republic acknowledges and adheres to general rules of international law, international treaties by which it is bound, and its other international obligations." This category would presumably include such documents as the Universal Declaration of Human Rights. Article 24 makes explicit a commitment to religious freedom as it guarantees "freedom of thought, conscience, religion and belief," along with the related right "to change religion or belief and the right to refrain from a religious affiliation." And in words nearly identical to the German Basic Law, the Constitution of Slovakia grants conscientious objector status on religious grounds: "No one shall be forced to perform military service if it is contrary to his or her conscience or religion" (Slovakia's Constitution of 1992 with Amendments through 2017).

There is also a fair amount of overlap on issues concerning state aid to or recognition of religion. In Germany, the concept of a church-state partnership has done much to frame questions related to various forms of state cooperation with or support for religion. Church and state are seen as having different responsibilities, but they both have public obligations and are important for society as a whole. Thus, cooperation between the two bodies benefits public welfare. This focus on cooperation results in the government supporting and helping the religious communities in a number of ways. One way is by granting the three main, historical religious communities—Evangelische, Catholic, and Jewish—status as a corporation under public law (PLC or *Körperschaft des öffentlichen Rechts*; see Hofhansel 2013; United States Department of State 2019). Practically speaking, this provision helps assure these religious bodies of their legal autonomy, gives them the right to levy taxes on their members, allows them to offer religious instruction in the public schools, enables them to work with the government to appoint prison, hospital, and military chaplains, and provides funds for faith-based social welfare organizations. The legal basis for the church tax is found in Article 137(6) of the Weimar Constitution, which has been incorporated into the current Constitution. It reads: "Religious communities that are public corporations shall be entitled to levy taxes in accordance with Land [state] law on the basis of the civil taxation."

The decision to grant PLC status is made at the state level based on certain requirements, including an assurance of permanence, the size of the organization, and an indication that the organization is not hostile to the constitutional order or fundamental rights. There has been some political debate about granting this status to new religious groups such as Muslims. Some groups such as Scientologists have failed to gain PLC status, and well-placed observers claim that the system benefits religious traditions that are hierarchically organized and thereby better able to negotiate with government officials. However, German states in recent years have eased the process and expanded the number of groups within the system. An estimated 180 religious groups have PLC status in one or more states, including Roman Catholics, *Evangelische*, Baha'is, Baptists, Christian Scientists, Jehovah's Witnesses, Jews, Mennonites, the Church of Jesus Christ of Latter-day Saints, the Salvation Army, and Seventh-day Adventists, to name a few. Ahmadi Muslim groups have PLC status in the states of Hesse and Hamburg, and more progressive Aleviten gained this benefit in 2020 in North Rhine Westphalia; no other Muslim communities have PLC status (Lehnhoff 2019; United States Department of State 2019; RP Online 2020).

Best known and most important of the privileges granted to religious groups that have qualified as public corporations is the church tax (*Kirchensteuer*). Under the church tax, all members of recognized religious groups are assessed a fee set by the organizations' leaders that amounts to about 8 or 9 percent of what is owed the federal government in income taxes. This money is added to one's income tax bill—in fact, it is deducted from one's paychecks by employers along with the income taxes that are owed—and is forwarded to the churches by the government after the state deducts a small fee. In the case of Catholics and *Evangelische*, membership comes automatically with baptism and follows that person the rest of his or her life. The only way a member can avoid the church tax is to resign his or her membership in the church, which, due to the public corporation nature of the churches, involves a formal, legal process and an appearance before the civil authorities. While more and more Germans are opting out of the system, overall support for the church tax remains high, with nearly three out of every four Germans paying it (Pew Research Center 2019a). In 2011, income from the church tax amounted to 9.2 billion Euros (about US$12 billion) to the Catholic and *Evangelische* churches, which totaled around 70 percent of their total income. The money is used to finance both the pastoral activities of the churches and wide-ranging charitable and educational activities (Robbers 2005; Soper et al. 2017: 205).

A similar system of church-state partnership exists in Slovakia. Article 24 of the 1992 Constitution grants "churches and ecclesiastical communities" the right to administer their own affairs. As in Germany, religious bodies that are formally recognized by the government are eligible for various government benefits and programs, including salaries for clergy, money for religious schools, the teaching of religion in public schools, the right to appoint clerics in state-run prisons and hospitals, and access to public broadcasting, to name some of the most evident benefits. While the process of granting official status to new religious groups has liberalized in Germany in recent decades, the opposite has occurred in Slovakia where the number of recognized religions has hardly increased and the process for gaining that status has become more onerous. Under the terms of a 1991 Act on religious societies (308/1991 Z. z.), the Slovak Republic (then as part of Czechoslovakia) officially recognized 14 religious communities. By 2017, that number had increased to 18 in the now independent Slovak Republic (Schwarz 2005; Vokálová 2009; Moravčíková 2010: 623; Stan and Turcescu 2011:156–157; United States Department of State 2019).

In 2016, however, the National Council (or parliament) passed a measure that significantly raised the bar for new religious groups seeking state recognition. According to this bill, applicants needed to present a petition with the signatures of at least 50,000 adherents, which was more than double the previous requirement of 20,000. The Slovak president, Andrej Kiska, vetoed the bill, saying that it violated the constitutional commitment to religious freedom. In 2017, however, Parliament easily overrode the veto by a more than a two-thirds majority vote. The ultra-nationalist Slovak National Party had drafted the bill, and leaders of this party made no attempt to hide that the law was intended to prevent the estimated 5000 Slovak Muslims from gaining official recognition. The party's chairman, Andrej Danko, asserted that "Islamisation starts with a kebab, and it's already under way in Bratislava. Let's realise what we can face in five to ten years.... We must do everything we can so that no mosque is built in the future" (Reuters 2016). According to data from the 2011 census, half of the currently registered churches and religious societies have fewer than 5000 members, though none is in danger of losing its status. In fact, only the four largest denominations (Roman Catholics, Lutherans, Greek Catholics, and Reformed Christians) would still meet the much higher, 2017 numeric cut-off, and some of the smallest approved groups (e.g., Jews, Mormons, and Jehovah's Witnesses) remain thousands shy of meeting this hurdle (Havelková 2018; United States Department of State 2018; Grančayová and Kazharski 2020).

There are fiscal, legal, and spiritual implications to gaining official recognition (as one of the "Registrované cirkvi alebo náboženské spoločnosti"). In 2019, the government allocated 48 million Euros (US $57 million) to recognized religious organizations, and obviously no money to those that were not registered. In that same year, more than ninety percent of the funding went to the five largest religious groups. Moreover, unregistered groups have reported difficulty getting permits to build places of worship, religious leaders from those traditions do not have the right to perform weddings or to minister to co-religionists in prisons or government hospitals, and they cannot offer religious education in public schools as can their registered counterparts.

RELIGION AND EDUCATION

Convergence and divergence is also the common motif in a comparison of religion in public schools in Germany and Slovakia. Article 7 of Germany's Basic Law (1995) guarantees religious groups the right to establish private schools and requires the government to provide religious instruction in state-run schools: "Religious instruction shall form part of the curriculum in state schools." The operative word here is "shall," not "may." Students and their parents in a particular Federal state, however, usually choose among several related versions, including Catholicism, Protestantism, Judaism, and often Islam or Ethics. It is also important to note that the religious bodies themselves, not the public school authorities, control the content of the religious courses of study. Classes have always been available to members of the historically dominant Catholic or *Evangelische* churches, and most states have similarly accommodated the small but growing Jewish community.

The educational situation in Slovakia mirrors that in Germany. A 2000 Concordat with the Vatican (Ministry of Foreign Affairs of the Slovak

Republic 2001) specified that "The Slovak Republic creates conditions for the [Roman] Catholic education of children in schools and school facilities in accordance with the religious beliefs of their parents." This commitment includes an "obligation to meet the demands of parents to enable Catholic religious education at all levels of primary schools and at all types and types of secondary schools and school facilities." As in Germany, the churches also have the power to "authorize"—or select—the person who is teaching religious education. These schools are described as an "inseparable and equivalent part of the educational system of the Slovak Republic." Since they "have the same status as state schools and school facilities," they are fully funded by the government. A parallel contract signed two years later with the other "registered churches and religious societies" established a virtually identical framework for the other approved religious groups (Slovak Republic 2002).

Where the two countries' educational systems diverge most notably is in how—or if—they have expanded to include more religious groups within the system of religious instruction. Starting in 2010 in the state of North Rhine Westphalia, where one-third of Germany's Muslims live, 150 schools for the first time offered Islamic studies classes to 13,000 children in grades 1 through 10. Four years later, Islamic instruction was available in all the former Western German states, though nowhere in the former Deutsche Demokratische Republik (DDR), or East Germany, where relatively few Muslims live. After decades of hesitancy by public officials, Islamic instruction in the schools is now on the same footing as Catholic, Protestant, and Jewish religious education in much of the country. There are also now four university-based Centers for Islamic Theology in Germany and a Jewish school of Theology to complement the various Protestant and Catholic seminaries. All are funded by the federal government. The most important cause for this shift has been the realization among German authorities that Muslim religious instruction can be a way to counter radical teaching and to encourage the successful integration of the nation's growing Muslim minority into the liberal-democratic values of the larger society. Working with Islamic leaders, educational officials have designed curriculums that emphasize Islamic teachings on tolerance and acceptance of differences (Fetzer and Soper 2005).

In contrast, Slovakia has not seen a corresponding shift toward greater ecumenism. Religious communities that have not been officially recognized, including Muslims, are not able to offer religious instruction in public schools. While the policy is ostensibly neutral (at least among the recognized churches), in practice only five groups officially teach Religious Education: the Roman Catholic, Greek Catholic, Orthodox, Lutheran, and Reformed Churches (Soltesova and Pleva 2020). At the university level, the state funds religious universities, such as the Catholic University in Ružomberok, and supports a Protestant theological program at Matej Bel University and Roman Catholic and Evangelical Lutheran faculties of theology at the country's largest and most prestigious school, Comenius University.

DEMOGRAPHICS

Convergence and divergence also mark the religious demographics of these two nations. Germany and Slovakia are predominantly Christian and religiously pluralistic, and both have a fast-growing non-religious sector. Germany's 80 million inhabitants are nearly evenly divided among Roman Catholics (30 percent), *Evangelische* (29 percent), and those who are religiously unaffiliated or have no religion (36 percent). A scattering of Protestant churches that are not part of the Evangelische Kirche in Deutschland (EKD) and Orthodox Christians represent two percent of the population. With somewhere between five and six million adherents, Islam is the largest non-Christian religion in Germany, representing an estimated six percent of the country's total population. The other reasonably large non-Christian groups are Buddhists (200,000) and Jews (100,000). The percentage of Germans claiming no religious affiliation has nearly quadrupled over the last few decades, rising from 9 percent in 1981 to 36 percent in 2017. There has also been a corresponding decline in church attendance in recent years. According to data from the *Evangelische* church, only 4.2 percent of church members attend services weekly, and less than half (38 percent) do so on the most attended service of the year, Christmas Eve (Evangelical Church in Germany 2016a; Pew Research Center 2017).

Like Germany, Slovakia is religiously diverse (particularly by the standards of Central Europe), and is increasingly secular, especially among young urbanites. According to government data, 62 percent of Slovakia's 5.4 million population are Roman Catholic, 6 percent are Lutherans, 4 percent are Greek Catholics, and another 4 percent are affiliated with various Protestant denominations or are Eastern Orthodox. The non-Christian population in Slovakia is very small, with an estimated 5000 Muslims and 2000 Jews representing the largest of that miniscule population.

One-quarter of the population is religiously unaffiliated or "undetermined" (likely secular). In a ten-year period between 2001 and 2011, the religiously affiliated percentage of the population declined from 84 to 76 percent (Ministry of Culture of the Slovak Republic 2021; United States Department of State 2018).

Another significant contrast between the two counties is that Germany's expanded borders post-reunification made the country as a whole more secular, while the narrowed boundary of post-independence Slovakia led the country to be much more religious. From 1961 to 1989 the West German Evangelische Church lost 15 percent of its membership, but the East German Evangelische Church lost over 50 percent. When East and West Germany reunited in 1990, nearly two-thirds of the East German population was without any church affiliation (Elf and Rossteutscher 2011). Thus, the reunification of Germany meant that German society as a whole became more secular than it had been when West Germany existed as a separate state. The situation on the ground was much different in Slovakia. According to a 2019 survey, three-quarters of Czech respondents indicated that they were religiously unaffiliated, while 63 percent of Slovaks reported that they identified as Roman Catholic. Slovaks were also more than three times as likely to say that they attended religious services monthly, that religion was very important in their lives, and that they prayed daily (Starr 2019). When it was part of Czechoslovakia, Slovakia's relative religiosity was overwhelmed by the much more secular and numerous Czech population and the more Czech-oriented government in Prague. After Slovak independence in 1993, however, the Roman Catholic elements of Slovak identity were able to play a more direct, open role in Slovakia's politics.

RELIGION AND POLITICS

These demographic differences are part of the reason for a growing divide in how religion interacts with politics in Germany and Slovakia, and we will consider those numerical factors in the pages below. But the historical context is just as salient for the politics around such issues as abortion, same-sex marriage, immigration, and national identity. As we noted above, Slovak independence in 1993 altered the country's religious make-up. When Slovakia was part of the larger Czechoslovakia, it was either under the thumb of the atheist USSR (1948–1989) or dominated by a more secular, Czech-oriented Czechoslovakia (1918–1938 and 1989–1992).

Throughout the twentieth century, Roman Catholicism was a decisive factor defining Slovak identity. The overall tendency in recent years in Slovakia, as one observer notes (Tížik 2017: 162), is "that of the increasing symbolic importance of (mainly Christian) religion as a source of symbolic capital and constituent power." The Concordat signed with the Vatican and the subsequent contract with the other recognized religious groups (virtually all of whom are some sort of Christian) personify this movement toward a de facto religious establishment at the institutional level.

Equally important at a symbolic level is the attempt by the church to link Slovak identity with that of the Roman Catholic Church specifically and with Christianity more generally. A 2002 resolution from the Conference of Bishops in Slovakia asserts that "The history and culture of our nation, as well as of the whole of Europe, are based on the Christian foundation laid by Saints Cyril and Methodius. It is natural that, as people with a particular culture, we want to know and further develop this spiritual wealth" (Katolícka cirkev na Slovensku 2002). In a 2004 Pastoral Letter on the Elections to the European Parliament, the bishops urged the faithful to "sanctify our European house with our religious identity. Even in Europe, we must not be ashamed of being Christians.... It would not be good if those who do not respect Christian values make decisions on behalf of us believers" (Katolícka cirkev na Slovensku 2004). On the occasion of Slovakia assuming for the first time the Presidency of the Council of the European Union in 2016, the bishops affirmed that "as believers, we want to remind ourselves and Europe of our Christian roots at this time.... Let us present Slovakia as a country that remembers its spiritual and cultural identity and can use it with courage for the benefit of the whole community of the European nations" (Katolícka cirkev na Slovensku 2016a).

The historical record of the church in defending the nation (particularly during the Communist period) provides it with moral authority within society and among politicians. Each of the four documents from the Bishop's History Council recalls the painful memories of Communist rule and the heroic efforts by the church to oppose them. Among the most notable of those events was the nonviolent "Candle Demonstration" in 1988, which was organized by politically active Roman Catholics and violently suppressed by the authorities (Doellinger 2013:158–165; Slovakia Today 2020). A 2015 statement by the Bishops on the 50th Anniversary of the Death of Bishop Ján Vojtaššák hints at how the church presents this history. As the commemorative document notes, Vojtaššák "unequivocally opposed the Communist regime" and "remained faithful to his convictions and the magisterium of the Catholic Church." As a consequence of his principled views, Vojtaššák was "sentenced to 24 years in prison" and died a martyr to the cause. The document urges readers to learn more about this Catholic bishop who "positively affected the whole of Slovakia." The church has also spearheaded an effort to canonize Vojtaššák (Katolícka Cirkev na Slovensku 2015a). What is glossed over in the 2015 statement is that Vojtaššák, along with several other church leaders, held a government position in the First Slovak Republic during World War II and did not oppose the deportation of Slovak Jews during the Holocaust (Hutzelmann 2018).

The historical memory for the churches in Germany is far different. The churches responded to their complicity in the rise of German fascism by rejecting any right-wing politics and providing unconditional support for democratic practices and institutions. The churches and the closely related Christian Democratic movement played major roles in the rise of Germany after the devastation of the war during 1945–1960. The Christian Democratic Union (CDU) has dominated the postwar political landscape. While the CDU uses the word "Christian" to describe itself, it has as much to do with the churches giving their imprimatur to democracy than with a narrow or particularistic Christian vision of public policy. In its most recent manifesto, for instance, the party notes that "the basis of our global political action is and will remain the Christian image of man." The concrete examples provided in the manifesto for what constitutes a "Christian image of man" include "social diversity," "religious freedom, including for religious minorities," "the preservation of Creation and stewardship of the environment," and a dual commitment to "individual freedom and collective responsibility." For the CDU, ostensibly the party of Christians in the country, Christian values uphold democracy and pluralism (CDU/CSU 2021).

Catholic and *Evangelische* church leaders similarly go to great lengths to disassociate their churches, or even Christianity, from German identity or German nationalism. On the occasion of Germany assuming the Presidency of the Council of the European Union in 2020, Bishop Bedford-Strohm of the EKD and Bishop Bätzing, chair of the German Catholic Bishops' Conference, put out a joint statement. Unlike their Slovak counterparts on the same occasion, however, they did not call on politicians to remember Europe's Christian heritage, but instead these religious leaders reaffirmed their churches' commitment to the European project: "We are convinced that the future of all of us lies not with nation states but in Europe. We therefore call on German politics, in the context of Germany's Council presidency in 2020 and beyond, to shape the future of our common European home with responsibility for European cohesion" (Evangelical Church in Germany 2020). The EKD, in a 2018 Position Paper on Christian–Islamic Dialogue, affirms that it "opposes all efforts to counteract the existing religious diversity and to create a religiously or culturally homogeneous society. Precisely because Christian history, and notably that of Protestantism, is not free from violence towards those of other faiths, the EKD here recognizes a special responsibility and task for itself" (Evangelical Church in Germany 2018). Not to be outdone, In July 2018, Cardinal Reinhard Marx, head of the Catholic bishops in Germany, said in an interview, "As a church, we should stand up for a society of responsible freedom.... People should be free to choose a political party, for—or against—a religion. In any case, I would like to live in a society in which freedom of opinion, conscience, and religion prevail— even a society where people do not agree with me or my religious convictions." In that same interview, Cardinal Marx also noted that "You cannot be a nationalist and a Catholic" (Witte and Dudek 2018). The strength of these convictions supports the conclusion of one analysis that "German democracy rests on the assumption that nationalism leads ineluctably to Nazism" (Krastev and Holmes 2018: 120).

These differences in political symbolism and national identity are further reinforced in how Germany and Slovakia have responded to the issue of Muslim immigration and settlement. The Muslim story in Germany is especially linked to migration from Turkey. In the midst of postwar labor shortages, Germany signed bilateral agreements with Turkey, among other countries, that sent laborers to Germany as "guest workers." The policy assumed that these workers would stay for a period of time and then go back to Turkey; they were not seen as immigrants who had come to make Germany their home. Yet many of them did stay, their families joined them, and these migrant families had children and grandchildren. As we previously noted, Islam is now the third largest religion in Germany, and it has grown rapidly over the past several decades (Fetzer and Soper 2005).

Many Germans still see Muslims as foreigners living in Germany, rather than as persons who have become Germans and share in the economic and cultural life of the country. More than half of the respondents (53 percent) in a 2011 Pew survey reported that there were too many immigrants in

Germany, and 54 percent said that immigration had a fairly or very negative effect on the country (Pew 2011). However, a more recent 2019 Pew
Survey found that 69 percent of German respondents had a favorable
impression of Muslims in their country (Pew Research Center 2019b).
And this survey was conducted after Chancellor Merkel opened the
German borders in 2015 to asylum seekers from war-torn Syria,
Afghanistan, and Iraq. According to a German Federal ministry, 1.1 million migrants, most of whom were Muslim, came to Germany in 2015 and
registered for asylum. Under political pressure from the right, Merkel later
rescinded this policy and negotiated a treaty that required tens of thousands of refugees to stay in Turkey. Popular opposition to immigration
intensified in the aftermath of her welcoming policy, including increasing
support for the radical right-wing, anti-immigrant party Alternative for
Germany (AfD). As the only party officially to oppose all Muslim immigration to Germany, the AFD did reasonably well in the 2016 state elections in Baden-Württemberg, Rhineland-Palatinate, and Saxony-Anhalt,
winning 15.1 percent, 12.6 percent, and 24.2 percent of the vote, respectively, in the three federal states (Soper et al. 2017).

The AfD remains the only significant party that categorically opposes
Muslim immigration and state efforts to accommodate Muslim religious
practices. In its 2017 party manifesto, the AfD boldly announced that
"Islam does not belong in Germany. Its expansion and the ever-increasing
number of Muslims in the country are viewed by the AfD as a danger to
our state, our society, and our values." The party promised to reject any
application "to grant the status of a public body [Körperschaft des
öffentlichen Rechts] to Islamic organizations," opposed the minaret as "a
symbol of Islamic supremacy," and vowed to abolish the "theological chairs
for Islam studies at German universities" (Alternative for Germany 2017).

While the AfD presents itself as the only true Christian party in Germany,
Catholic and *Evangelische* church leaders have firmly and consistently
rejected the party's nativism and Islamophobia. Thomas Sternberg, president of the Central Committee of German Catholics, the Roman Catholic
Church's lay organization, recently urged people not to vote for the right-
wing Alternative for Germany. The Vicar-General of the Münster Diocese,
Klaus Winterkamp, announced a ban in his diocese on AfD party members
from holding Church leadership roles (Doody 2020). In the midst of the
refugee crisis the EKD called for "solidarity with refugees as one consequence of Christian faith committed to working towards a just and compassionate society." The church further asked that all EU member states

"establish a common European asylum system with uniformly high standards of protection. The European response to the refugee question must not be reduced to deterrence and minimum standards" (Evangelical Church in Germany 2016b). The willingness of German church leaders to speak out against right-wing populism and in favor of the rights of asylum seekers is particularly significant in a country like Germany where the two largest churches (Roman Catholic and *Evangelische*) represent nearly 95 percent of the country's religious population. Public statements from religious leaders do not necessarily determine the views of those in the pews, but they can define what are acceptable and unacceptable viewpoints and in turn have an electoral impact. It is worth noting, for example, that support for the AfD in German elections is concentrated among non-religious voters rather than among the religiously devout (Elcott et al. 2021: 59).

The situation is far different in Slovakia, where the number of Muslims (an estimated 5000) pales by comparison to Germany. Yet elite opposition to Muslim immigration is often stronger in Slovakia than in Germany, the political rhetoric is harsher, and religious leaders are much more likely to express identification with the nation's Christian identity and remain silent on the rights of religious minorities such as Muslims. On the surface these attitudes are particularly surprising as the very small Slovak Muslim community is well-integrated and economically and socially successful (Grančayová and Kazharski 2020:260). The negative attitude toward Muslims is most evident in how Slovakia responded to the European migration crisis. Along with the other three countries of the Visegrád Four (a cultural and political alliance of the Czech Republic, Poland, Hungary, and Slovakia), Slovakia rejected the recommendation of the European Commission that all EU countries share responsibility for asylum seekers by accepting migrants in a quota-based system. The Prime Minister during the crisis, Robert Fico, said that "Islam has no place in Slovakia" and that as a "Christian country, we cannot tolerate an influx of 300,000–400,000 Muslim immigrants who would like to start building mosques all over our land and trying to change the nature, culture and values of the state" (Tharoor 2016). Slovakia later agreed to take in some migrants, but only those that were Christian. An Interior Ministry spokesman, Ivan Netik, reasoned that "we could take 800 Muslims, but we don't have any mosques in Slovakia, so how can Muslims be integrated if they are not going to like it here?" (O'Grady 2015).

Statements and documents from the Conference of Catholic Bishops of Slovakia during the Migrant Crisis focus mainly on the persecution of

Christians rather than on how best to respond to the millions of Muslim refugees streaming into Europe. In a 2015 Declaration of the Persecution of Christians, the bishops noted "with great concern the growing persecution of Christians and other religious groups in the Middle East and in some African countries" (Katolícka Cirkev na Slovensku. 2015b). At a plenary session of the bishops the following year, "the issues of the migration crisis were touched on by the bishops," and the bishops "praised the [government] initiative to receive 149 Iraqi Christians" (Katolícka Cirkev na Slovensku. 2016b).

Politicians were more than happy to exploit the issue of Muslim immigration for political gain even though there was no actual influx of Muslims into Slovakia and the "fear" was a manufactured one. As in Germany, one of the electoral beneficiaries of the anti-Muslim sentiment was the extreme right, in this case the neo-Nazi People's Party Our Slovakia (Ľudová strana Naše Slovensko) of Marian Kotleba. Although not formally tied to the Roman Catholic Church, the party celebrates the legacy of the Slovak State, the 1939–1945 clerico-fascist regime, and is openly and virulently anti-Roma, anti-LGBTQ, anti-European Union, and particularly xenophobic and Islamophobic. For the first time in the party's history, it won parliamentary seats (14) in the 2016 national elections, and the party increased its number of seats to 17 in the 2020 elections (Walter 2019; Garaj et al. 2021). Where Slovakia differed from Germany, however, is that many of the mainstream parties also ran on an anti-Muslim and anti-immigrant agenda. Former Prime Minister Robert Fico, for example, was the leader of the nominally left-leaning, social -democratic SMER party, but it too adopted a much more nationalistic and anti-Islam/anti-immigrant agenda in both the 2016 and 2020 elections (Grančayová and Kazharski 2020). His party won the largest percentage of the vote in the 2016 elections. While the parties are certainly guilty of manufacturing a so-called Muslim crisis where none existed, there is some evidence that there was a market for their xenophobia. Only about half of Slovak respondents (47 percent) said that they would be willing to accept Muslims as members of their family, which was actually significantly more accepting than the 12 percent of Czechs who were similarly open-minded (Starr 2019). However, in a different survey more than three-quarters of Slovak respondents indicated that they had an "unfavorable opinion of Muslims in their country," compared to only 24 percent of Germans (Pew 2019b).

One even observes the differing roots of nationalism in each country's popular patriotic songs. In Germany, such folk staples as Die Wacht am

Rhein, Argonnerwaldlied, and Westerwaldlied tend to focus on the glories of pointing guns at or killing the citizens of neighboring countries (especially the French). A typical stanza from the original version of the first song reads, "As long as a drop of blood still shines, as long as a fist holds a sword, and an arm still grips a rifle, no enemy will step onto your shore! [Solang ein Tropfen Blut noch glüht, noch eine Faust den Degen zieht, und noch ein Arm die Büchse spannt, betritt kein Feind hier deinen Strand!]" (Schneckenburger 1900; von Gordon 1915; Münker 1938 [1932]). The first version of Germany's historically troubled national anthem (Deutschlandlied) contains phrases that now appear sexist and debauched and expressions linked to the Nazi regime, but God is entirely absent (Hoffmann von Fallersleben 1841). Not so the equivalents in Slovakia. Perhaps the most telling example is the still-popular "My Slovakia, My Fatherland [Slovensko moje, otčina moja]." After praise for the natural wonders of Slovakia, the original text quickly moves into standard God-and-country fare (Rataj and Machajdík 1943):

> Yes, I have another fatherland, where my God and Lord forever reigns. There the Lord Jesus will call and lead His own from all directions. There all griefs and laments will disappear. There I will live forever.... Until that time comes, ... I want to live in dedication to God and country. [Hej mám otčinu, ja, ešte inú, kde večne vládne môj Boh a pán. Tam si povolá tam si privedie pán Ježiš svojich zo všetkých strán. Tam zmiznú žiale aj náreky, tam budem bývať až naveky. ... Kým ten čas príde ... chcem Bohu, vlasti žiť oddane.]

Some more secular Slovaks appear uncomfortable with the original Christian lyrics, but today's center-right party the Christian Democratic Movement (Kresťanskodemokratické hnutie) still uses it as their official hymn (KDH 2014). Another popular tune, used by both the clerico-fascist Slovak State and modern Slovak nationalists, is "Hey, Slovaks [Hej, Slováci]." Penned by the Slovak Lutheran pastor Samo Tomášik, the narrative asserts that the Slovak language is a "gift entrusted to us by almighty God [Jazyka dar zveril nám Boh, Boh náš hromovládny]." Quoting the Apostle Paul in Romans, the author also declares that "God is with us; who can be against us? [Boh je s nami: kto proti nám?]" (Tomášik 1839). Religion therefore seems to undergird Slovak national identity much more than it does German nationalism.

Given the different levels of religiosity in the two countries, it is not surprising that the issues of abortion and same-sex marriage have more political salience in the Slovak Republic than in Germany. Abortion has not been on the political agenda in Germany for several decades. As in much of Western Europe, abortion is legal in Germany up to twelve weeks of pregnancy and is also permitted beyond that time under certain circumstances. The CDU/CSU historically opposed the legalization of same-sex marriages, but in 2017 German Chancellor Angela Merkel allowed the question to come to a vote in Parliament, where it passed by a nearly two-thirds majority. All of the churches that are part of the EKD bless same-sex marriages. The Roman Catholic church opposes same-sex unions, but in a sign of just how progressive the German Catholic Church is, more than a hundred German priests said that they would defy the Vatican ban by blessing same-sex couples (Anarte 2021). To some degree, these churches are simply reflecting the near-universal acceptance of same-sex relationships among the German population. A Pew (2020) survey reported that 92 percent of the religiously unaffiliated said that "homosexuality should be accepted by society," while even 84 percent of the religiously affiliated affirmed the same view.

The Roman Catholic Church in Slovakia has been much more visibly active in trying to shape public policy on both abortion and same-sex marriage. The Slovak Republic inherited an abortion policy that legalized abortion for up to twelve weeks of the pregnancy. The leadership of the Catholic Church has been very involved in the pro-life movement, from organizing the annual National March for Life and promoting it to the faithful, to cooperating with policy makers who wish to restrict access to abortion. Nonetheless, the legal framework on abortion has not been substantially changed since Slovak independence, and popular support for the current abortion policy remains high. As one analyst notes (Beláňová 2020:402) there is a "Polish nostalgia" among the Slovak Bishops who have not yet been able to replicate the success of the Polish Catholic Church in criminalizing abortion or even in limiting the conditions under which it is allowed. The failure suggests that there are barriers to overt politicization on religious lines on the abortion issue, not just because abortion rates appear slightly higher in the more religious Slovakia (UNdata 2007).

The bishops and other conservative Christians have had greater success (though still mixed) on same-sex marriage. Bills have been introduced on several occasions in the National Council to recognize same-sex partnerships, but have failed each time. In response to an attempt in 2012, the church put out a statement which asserted that "homosexual partnership cannot be equated with a natural marital bond between a man and a woman. Homosexual acts are inherently unnatural and are in stark contrast to the sanctity of the sexuality of a man and a woman in marriage" (Katolícka Cirkev na Slovensku 2012). While same-sex marriage has never been legal in the Slovak Republic, opponents of the practice wanted to cement the existing framework through a national referendum in 2015. Led by the Catholic Church, a coalition of some one hundred mostly Christian organizations secured more than 400,000 signatures and got the referendum before the voters. The referendum sought to codify the definition of marriage as a union between a man and a woman, deny to same-sex couples the opportunity to adopt children (rights already denied to them), and allow parents the right to opt out of the compulsory sex education classes (Smrek 2015). The church raised funds for the campaign, and the bishops put out several statements unequivocally supporting each of the three questions on the referendum. One typical statement noted: "We express our support for the referendum on family protection.... We turn to believers and all people of good will to actively exercise their right to vote in February and to comment positively on the issues raised. We express our conviction that family and marriage support should be at the heart of our society" (Katolícka Cirkev na Slovensku 2014). The result of the referendum was mixed. To be legally binding, fifty percent of eligible voters needed to participate, and opponents urged a boycott of the election. That strategy, along with likely voter apathy, led to a turnout rate of just over twenty percent, well below the necessary turnout to make the vote binding. Of those who did vote, however, more than ninety percent supported each of the three questions. Thus, the referendum failed, but it nonetheless demonstrated that there is more of a market for conservative moral policies in Slovakia than in Germany, and that church is central to that effort.

Following the collapse between 2018 and 2020 of the corrupt government of Robert Fico and his associates, a new pro-transparency coalition led by Igor Matovič came to power in Bratislava (even if Fico himself remains politically active in the opposition as a member of the National Council). While arguably much less corrupt than its predecessors, the current government parties are either explicitly pro-Roman Catholic (e.g., Christian Union) or at a minimum fellow-travelers (e.g., We Are Family). Given such a "Parish Republic" (a term dating back to the era of the clerico-fascist Slovak State), Slovakia today continues to illustrate the electoral opportunities for mobilizing relatively religious voters around such social issues as abortion and gender (Vašečka 2020).

CONCLUSION

When Slovakia and other Central European countries joined the European Union in 2004, many analysts assumed that these "junior" partner states would gradually adopt the political norms and practices of their more "senior" colleagues on various policy issues. Twenty years later, the story is much more complex as various Central European states are charting their own path on a variety of issues, including those related to religion and politics. Populist politicians in Central European countries have chafed at what they portray as the imposition of "Western" secular values and have called instead for a reaffirmation of their country's' Christian roots.

Using Slovakia and Germany as ideal types for their respective regions of Europe, we have found that there is a good deal of convergence at an institutional level on various church-state issues. Both countries have strong constitutional protections for religious freedom, which are generally upheld by state institutions, both have adopted a church-state model that formally recognizes numerous churches and religious societies, and in both countries this recognition comes with various state benefits. Germany and Slovakia are also religiously pluralistic by the standard of their region of Europe and both have a large and a growing percentage of their population that is not religious.

Yet the differences between these European near-neighbors are as notable as the similarities. This divergence is a function of sociological, cultural, and historical factors that are unique to each country. While Slovakia is more religiously pluralistic than most Central European countries, its diversity is almost entirely within the Christian family of traditions. In contrast with Germany with its large and growing Muslim community, Slovakia has only a miniscule Islamic presence. While Slovakia has a growing secular population, the proportion of non-affiliated citizens remains smaller there than in Germany, and the fraction of the population that is religiously active is much higher in Slovakia than in Germany. A larger market for religiously based electoral strategies and public policy therefore exists in the former than in the latter. There is little value in German politicians using religion to mobilize a largely secular population, and it is almost unheard-of for candidates to tout their religious bona fides in the

Federal Republic. With 62 percent of the Slovak population claiming an affiliation with the Roman Catholic Church and another 14 percent affiliated with various other Christian churches, Slovak politicians contrastingly have every reason to seek votes in the pews and to affirm their spiritual connection with the voters.

The two countries also have unique religious histories which shape contemporary norms and practices. Arguably the key historical event for German churches was their complicity in the rise of Nazism and their subsequent postwar commitment to democracy. That value plays itself out in various forms, not the least of which is a strong aversion to any discourse among religious leaders that links national and religious identity. This reticence by the church to bless any conflation of nationalism and Christianity is one reason, among many, that German nationalism is largely secular and based on the idea of a social compact of equals rather than on ethnic or religious ties. This perspective also helps explain why the German churches have largely been allies with Muslims, who are gradually being incorporated into Germany's religion-state model.

The Slovak Roman Catholic Church was deeply implicated in the clerico-fascist state during World War II. During the Cold War, however, the Church and the other officially recognized churches in the country suffered mightily at the hands of the oppressive state and were virtually the only major institutions that openly stood against the Communist regime. This legacy, which the Church is proud to promote, provides it with a good deal of political legitimacy. Moreover, Roman Catholic or Christian identity has become a prominent feature of Slovak nationalism as Slovaks increasingly define themselves against secularism and Islam. Slovak national identity, therefore, hews more closely than its German counterpart to ethnic and religious ties rather than to secular values. As Ondrej Prostredník (2021), former Dean of the Evangelische Theological Faculty at Comenius University and previous General Secretary of the Ecumenical Council of Churches in Slovakia put it, "The majority of the population in Slovakia ... perceives their Christianity as a sign of cultural identity, which distinguishes them from the other two major world monotheistic religions (Islam and Judaism)." This impulse helps explain why Slovakia, without a Muslim population to speak of, passed a law making it more difficult for any Islamic group legally to be recognized and made certain that the country would not be party to a European Union treaty that required Slovakia to take in any Muslim refugees.

Religion has greater political salience in Slovakia than in Germany, yet Slovakia is not as religiously fervent as Poland, and its future might point to greater convergence with Germany. As one well-placed Slovak religious leader summarized the situation, "The trend of secularization in Slovakia is clear" (Prostredník 2021). Young Slovaks are much less likely to practice their religion than are their elders, and actual theological knowledge is declining substantially (Baláková and Kováčová 2017:25–26). But these trends hardly portend the disappearance of a Christian-nationalist discourse; as Aneta Világi (2021; see also Garaj et al. 2021) has documented, Slovak nationalists over the past generation have exchanged an ethnicity-based identity for one that is rooted in Christian affiliation. Because most citizens continue to identify as Roman Catholic or Christian, politicians will probably still have some motivation to continue religio-nationalistic appeals to "Slovak Christians" even if voters do not support public policies put forward by the actual Roman Catholic Church. And as the Muslim population in Germany continues to grow, politics in the Federal Republic may start looking remarkably similar that in Slovakia. Culturally Christian voters such as the socially conservative wing of the CDU/CSU may begin to emphasize the importance of their religious identity, and amenable German politicians may take electoral advantage of this constituency.

REFERENCES

Alternative for Germany. 2017. "Manifesto for Germany: The Political Programme of the Alternative for Germany." https://www.afd.de/wp-content/uploads/sites/111/2017/04/2017-04-12_afd-grundsatzprogramm-englisch_web.pdf. Accessed September 17, 2021.

Anarte, Enrique. 2021. "German priests defy Vatican ban by blessing same-sex unions." *Reuters.* https://www.reuters.com/article/us-germany-religion-lgbt/german-priests-defy-vatican-ban-by-blessing-same-sex-unions-idUSK-BN2CR1QC. Accessed December 3, 2021.

Baer, Josette. 2010. *Revolution, Modus Vivendi or Sovereignty? The Political Thought of the Slovak National Movement from 1861 to 1914.* Stuttgart: ibidem.

Baláková, Dana, and Viera Kováčová. 2017. *K výskumu biblickej frazeológie [Research on Biblical Phraseology].* Ružomberok: Verbum.

Basic Law for the Federal Republic of Germany. 1995. Bonn: Press and Information Office of the Federal Republic of Germany.

Beláňová, Andrea. 2020. Anti-abortion activism in the Czech Republic and Slovakia: 'nationalizing' the strategies. *Journal of Contemporary Religion* 35 (3): 395–413.

CDU/CSU. 2021. "Das Programm für Stabilität und Erneuerung." https://www.csu.de/common/download/Regierungsprogramm.pdf. Accessed September 17, 2021.

Conway, John S. 1992. The Political Role of German Protestantism, 1870–1990. *Journal of Church and State* 34 (4): 819–842.

Doellinger, David. 2013. *Turning Prayers into Protests: Religious-based Activism and its Challenge to State Power in Socialist Slovakia and East Germany.* Budapest: Central European University Press.

Doody, Cameron. 2020. "Münster diocese bans far-right AfD members from Church leadership roles." https://novenanews.com/afd-munster-diocese-bans-far-right-leadership/

Elcott, David M., C. Colt Anderson, Tobias Cremer, and Volker Haarman. 2021. *Faith, Nationalism, and the Future of Liberal Democracy.* Notre Dame: Notre Dame University Press.

Elf, Martin, and Sigrid Rossteutscher. 2011. Stability or Decline? Class, Religion and the Vote in Germany. *German Politics* 20 (2011): 111–131.

Evangelical Church in Germany. 2016a. "The Evangelical Church in Germany: Facts and Figures", https://www.ekd.de/english/download/facts_and_figures_2016.pdf.

———. 2016b. "On the Situation in Europe." https://www.ekd.de/en/On-the-situation-in-Europe-831.htm

———. 2018. "EKD Position Paper on Christian – Islamic Dialogue." https://www.ekd.de/en/EKD-Position-Paper-on-Christian-Islamic-Dialogue-1341.htm. Accessed September 17, 2021.

———. 2020. "Statement by the chairs of the German Bishops' Conference and the Council of the Evangelical Church in Germany on Germany's Council presidency (July-December 2020)." https://www.ekd.de/ekd_en/ds_doc/Statement_on_Germanys_Council_presidency_2020_06_17.pdf. Accessed September 17, 2021.

Fetzer, Joel S., and J. Christopher Soper. 2005. *Muslims and the State in Britain, France, and Germany.* Cambridge: Cambridge University Press.

Garaj, Michal, Jakub Bardovič, and Jaroslav Mihálik. 2021. Vplyv sociologicko-demografických charakteristík obce na volebné správanie a podporu M. Kotlebu [The Impact of Municipal Sociological-Demographic Characteristics on Electoral Behaviour and Support of M. Kotleba]. *Politické vedy / štúdie* 24 (1): 153–180.

Goldhagen, Daniel Jonah. 2003. *A Moral Reckoning: The Role of the Catholic Church in the Holocaust and Its Unfulfilled Duty of Repair.* New York: Vintage.

von Gordon, Hermann Albert. 1915. "Pionerlied." https://ingeb.org/Lieder/argonner.html. Accessed September 23, 2021.

Gould, Andrew C. 1999. *Origins of Liberal Dominance: State, Church, and Party in Nineteenth Century Europe*. Ann Arbor, Michigan: University of Michigan Press.

Grančayová, Michaela, and Aliaksei Kazharski. 2020. 'The Slovakebab': Anti-Islam Agenda in Slovak Parliamentary Elections and Beyond. *Politologický časopis* 27 (3): 259–277.

Grzymata-Busse, Anna. 2015. *Nations under God: How Churches Use Moral Authority to Influence Policy*. Princeton: Princeton University Press.

Havelková, Mária. 2018. The Amendment of the Religious Registration Law and Its Impact on Freedom of Religion in the Slovak Republic. *Public Governance, Administration and Finances Law Review* 3 (2): 36–45.

Hoffmann von Fallersleben, Heinrich. 1841. "Das Lied der Deutschen." https://ingeb.org/Lieder/deutschl.html. Accessed September 23, 2021.

Hofhansel, Claus. 2013. Recognition Regimes for Religious Minorities in Europe: Institutional Change and Reproduction. *Journal of Church and State* 57 (2013): 90–118.

Hutzelmann, Barbara. 2018. Einführung: Slowakei. In *Slowakei, Rumänien und Bulgarien: Die Verfolgung und Ermordung der europäischen Juden durch das nationalsozialistische Deutschland 1933-1945*, ed. Barbara Hutzelmann, Mariana Hausleitner, and Souzana Hazan, vol. 13, 18–45. Institut für Zeitgeschichte: Munich.

Johnson, Owen V. 1985. *Slovakia, 1918-1938: Education and the Making of a Nation*. New York: East European Monographs/Columbia University Press.

Kalyvas, Stathis N. 1996. *The Rise of Christian Democracy in Europe*, 1996. Ithaca, New York: Cornell University Press.

Katolícka Cirkev na Slovensku. 1998. "Vyhlásenie KBS k vatikánskemu dokumentu o holokauste [KBS statement on the Vatican document on the Holocaust]." https://www.kbs.sk/obsah/sekcia/h/dokumenty-a-vyhlasenia/p/doku-menty-kbs/c/vyhlasenie-kbs-k-vatikanskemu-dokumentu-o-holokauste-50. Accessed December 3, 2021.

———. 2002. "Vyhlásenie Konferencie biskupov Slovenska k vyučovaniu pred-metu náboženská výchova na školách [Declaration of the Conference of Bishops of Slovakia on the Teaching of Religion in the Schools]." https://www.kbs.sk/obsah/sekcia/h/dokumenty-a-vyhlasenia/p/dokumenty-kbs/c/vyhlasenie-kbs-k-vyucovaniu-predmetu-nabozenska-vychova-na-skolach-50. Accessed September 17, 2021.

———. 2004. "Pastoral Letter of the Bishops of Slovakia on the Elections to the European Parliament - June 2004." https://www.kbs.sk/obsah/sekcia/h/dokumenty-a-vyhlasenia/p/pastierske-listy-konferencie-biskupov-slovenska/c/pastiersky-list-biskupov-slovenska-k-volbam-do-europskeho-parlamentu-jun-2004. Accessed October 12, 2021.

————. 2012. "Statement on the draft law on registered partnership." https://www.kbs.sk/obsah/sekcia/h/dokumenty-a-vyhlasenia/p/dokumenty-komisii-a-rad-kbs/c/vyhlasenie-k-navrhu-zakona-o-registrovanom-partnerstve. Accessed on October 12, 2021.

————. 2014. "Declaration of the Conference of Bishops of Slovakia on the referendum on family protection." https://www.kbs.sk/obsah/sekcia/h/dokumenty-a-vyhlasenia/p/dokumenty-kbs/c/vyhlasenie-konferencie-biskupov-slovenska-k-referendu-o-ochrane-rodiny. Accessed October 12, 2021.

————. 2015a. "Vyhlásenie Rady KBS pre cirkevné dejiny k 50. výročiu smrti spišského biskupa Jána Vojtaššáka [Statement of the KBS Council for Church History on the 50th Anniversary of the Death of Bishop Ján Vojtaššák of Spiš]." https://www.kbs.sk/obsah/sekcia/h/dokumenty-a-vyhlasenia/p/dokumenty-komisii-a-rad-kbs/c/vyhlasenie-k-50-vyrociu-smrti-spisskeho-biskupa-jana-vojtassaka. Accessed September 17, 2021.

————. 2015b. "Declaration of the Conference of Bishops of Slovakia on the PersecutionofChristians."https://www.kbs.sk/obsah/sekcia/h/dokumenty-a-vyhlasenia/p/dokumenty-kbs/c/vyhlasenie-konferencie-biskupov-slovenska-k-prenasledovaniu-krestanov (accessed on September 21, 2021).

————. 2016a. "Vyhlásenie k predsedníctvu SR v Rade EÚ [Declaration on the Slovak Presidency of the Council of the EU]." https://www.kbs.sk/obsah/sekcia/h/dokumenty-a-vyhlasenia/p/dokumenty-kbs/c/vyhlasenie-k-predsednictvu-sr-v-rade-eu. Accessed September 17, 2021.

————. 2016b. Report from the 83rd Plenary Session of KBS in Bardejovské lázně. https://www.kbs.sk/obsah/sekcia/h/konferencia-biskupov-slovenska/p/plenarne-zasadania/c/plenarne-zasadanie-kbs-29-2-1-3-2016-83. Accessed September 21, 2021.

KDH (krestanskidemokrati). 2014. "Slovensko moje, otčina moja (Hymna KDH) [My Slovakia, My Fatherland (Anthem of the KDH Party)]." Video. https://www.youtube.com/watch?v=BA_t4-MhapE. Accessed September 9, 2021.

Kirschbaum, Stanislav J. 1995. *A History of Slovakia*. 2nd ed. New York: St. Martin's Press.

Kissová, Lenka. 2018. The Production of (Un)deserving and (Un)acceptable: Shifting Representations of Migrants within Political Discourse in Slovakia. *East European Politics and Societies and Cultures* 32 (4): 743–766.

Krastev, Ivan. 2017. The Refugee Crisis and the Return of the East-West Divide in Europe. *Slavic Review* 76 (2): 291–296.

————. 2020. The Fear of Shrinking Numbers. *Journal of Democracy* 31 (1): 66–76.

Krastev, Ivan, and Stephen Holmes. 2018. Explaining Eastern Europe: Imitation and Its Discontents. *Journal of Democracy* 29 (3): 117–128.

Lehnhoff, Brigitte. 2019. "Körperschaftsstatus für Islamverbände?." *NDR Kultur,* January 18. https://www.ndr.de/kultur/sendungen/freitagsforum/ Koerperschaftsstatus-fuer-Islamverbaende,lehnhoffkoerperschaftsstatus100. html. Accessed September 3, 2021.

Lorman, Thomas. 2019. *The Making of the Slovak People's Party: Religion, Nationalism and the Culture War in Early 20th-Century Europe.* London: Bloomsbury Academic.

Ministry of Culture of the Slovak Republic. 2021. "Počet veriacich podľa sčítania obyvateľov [Number of Believers According to the Censuses of Residents]." Bratislava: https://www.culture.gov.sk/wp-content/uploads/2020/02/ veriaci.pdf. Accessed September 10, 2021.

Ministry of Foreign Affairs of the Slovak Republic. 2001. "Basic Agreement between the Slovak Republic and the Holy See." 326/2001 Z. z. Bratislava: Ministry of Foreign Affairs.

Moravčíková, Michaela. 2010. "Religion, Law, and Secular Principles in the Slovak Republic." Pp. 615-627 in Martínez-Torrón J., Durham Jr., and Cole W., eds. *Religion and the Secular State: National Reports / La religion et l'État laïque: Rapports nationaux.* The International Center for Law and Religion Studies, Provo, Brigham Young University Publications. https://www.strasbourgcon-sortium.org/content/blurb/files/Slovak%20Republic%202014%20FINAL. pdf. Accessed July 21, 2021.

Münker, Willi. 1938 [1932]. "61. Westerwaldlied." P. 70 in J. Breuer, ed. *Das neue Soldaten-Liederbuch: Die bekanntesten und meistgesungenen Lieder unserer Wehrmacht.* Mainz: Schott. https://de.wikipedia.org/wiki/Westerwaldlied#/ media/Datei:Westerwaldlied_(Das_neue_Soldaten-Liederbuch_1938).jpg. Accessed September 23, 2021.

Nelsen, Brent F., and James L. Guth. 2015. *Religion and the Struggle for European Union.* Georgetown: Georgetown University Press.

O'Grady, Siobháhn. 2015. "Slovakia to EU: We'll Take Migrants — If They're Christians." *Foreign Policy,* August 19. https://foreignpolicy. com/2015/08/19/slovakia-to-eu-well-take-migrants-if-theyre-christians/

Pew Research Center. 2011. "Muslim-Western Tensions Persist", Pew Research Center, http://www.pewglobal.org/2011/07/21/muslim-western-tensions-persist/

———. 2017. *The Growth of Germany's Muslim Population.* https://www. pewforum.org/essay/the-growth-of-germanys-muslim-population/. Accessed on September 8, 2021.

———. 2018. *Eastern and Western Europeans Differ on Importance of Religion, Views of Minorities, and Key Social Issues.* Report, Pew Research Center. https://www.pewforum.org/2018/10/29/eastern-and-western-europeans-differ-on-importance-of-religion-views-of-minorities-and-key-social-issues/. Accessed July 21, 2021.

————. 2019a. *In Western European Countries With Church Taxes, Support for the Tradition Remains Strong.* https://www.pewforum.org/2019/04/30/in-western-european-countries-with-church-taxes-support-for-the-tradition--remains-strong/. Accessed September 1, 2021.

————. 2019b. *European Public Opinion Three Decades after the Fall of Communism.* https://www.pewresearch.org/global/2019/10/14/minority-groups/. Accessed September 17, 2021.

————. 2020. *Religiously unaffiliated people more likely than those with a religion to lean left, accept homosexuality.* https://www.pewresearch.org/fact-tank/2020/09/28/religiously-unaffiliated-people-more-likely-than-those-with-a-religion-to-lean-left-accept-homosexuality/. Accessed October 11, 2021.

Prostredník, Ondrej. 2021. Email interview with first author, August 13, Bratislava.

Rataj, Ján, and Ján Machajdík. 1943. "Slovensko moje, otčina moja [My Slovakia, My Fatherland]." P. 107 in *Nová pieseň*. Bratislava: Modrý kríž.

Reuters. 2016. "Slovakia toughens church registration rules to bar Islam." https://www.reuters.com/article/us-slovakia-religion-islam/slovakia-toughens-church-registration-rules-to-bar-islam-idUSKBN13P20C

Robbers, Gerhard. 2005. *State and Church in the European Union.* 2nd ed. Baden-Baden, Germany: Nomos Verlagsgesellschaft.

RP Online. 2020. "Aleviten erhalten Körperschaftsstatus in NRW." *RP Online* December 10. https://rp-online.de/nrw/kultur/islam-aleviten-erhalten-koerperschaftsstatus-in-nrw_aid-55131677. Accessed September 3, 2021.

Rupnik, Jacques. 2018. Explaining Eastern Europe: The Crisis of Liberalism. *Journal of Democracy* 29 (3): 24–38.

Schaefer, Bernd. 2010. *The East German State and the Catholic Church: 1945-1989.* New York and Oxford: Bergbahn Press, translated by Jonathan Skolnik and Patricia C. Sutcliffe.

Schneckenburger, Max. 1900. "No. 25. Die Wacht am Rhein." Canada: International Music Score Library Project. https://imslp.org/wiki/File:Wilhelm_%26_Schneckenburger_-_Die_Wacht_am_Rhein.pdf (accessed September 23, 2021).

Schwarz, Karl. 2005. Das Recht der Religionsgemeinschaften in der Slowakei. In *Das Recht der Religionsgemeinschaften in Mittel-, Ost- und Südosteuropa*, ed. Wolfgang Lienemann, Hans-Richard Reuter, and Iris Döring, 443–471. Nomos: Baden-Baden.

Sekerák, Lukáš. 2018. *Historický pohľad na vzťah štátu a Katolíckej cirkvi na Slovensku v XX. storočí [A Historical View of the Relationship between the State and the Catholic Church in Slovakia in the 20th Century].* Ružomberok: Verbum.

Slovak Republic. 2002. "Contract between the Slovak Republic and Recognized Churches and Religious Societies." 250/2002 Z. Z. Bratislava: Slovak Republic.

Slovakia Today. 2020. "Velvet Revolution holiday edition -- stories of life under Communism." *Slovakia Today,* podcast, November 17. https://www.rtvs.sk/radio/archiv/1487/1456123. Accessed September 17, 2021.

Slovakia's Constitution of 1992 with Amendments through 2017. https://www.constituteproject.org/constitution/Slovakia_2017.pdf?lang=en

Smrek, Michal. 2015. "The Failed Slovak Referendum on 'Family': Voters' Apathy and Minority Rights in Central Europe." *Baltic Worlds.* http://balticworlds.com/the-failed-slovak-referendum-on-%E2%80%9Cfamily%E2%80%9D/. Accessed on October 12, 2021.

Soltesova, Victoria, and Matus Pleva. 2020. The Influence of Religious Education on the Religiosity of Roma Children in Slovakia. *Religious Education* 115 (5): 536–548.

Soper, J. Christopher, and Joel S. Fetzer. 2018. *Religion and Nationalism in Global Perspective.* Cambridge: Cambridge University Press.

Soper, J. Christopher, Kevin den Dulk, and Stephen V. Monsma. 2017. *The Challenge of Pluralism: Church and State in Six Democracies.* 3rd ed. Lanham, Maryland: Rowman and Littlefield Press.

Spicer, Kevin P. 2004. *Resisting the Third Reich: The Catholic Clergy in Hitler's Berlin.* DeKalb: Northern Illinois University Press.

Spotts, Frederic. 1973. *The Churches and Politics in Germany.* Middletown, Connecticut: Wesleyan University Press.

Stan, Lavinia, and Lucian Turcescu. 2011. *Church, State, and Democracy in Expanding Europe.* Oxford: Oxford University Press.

Starr, Kelsey Jo. 2019. "Once the same nation, the Czech Republic and Slovakia look very different religiously." Flash Briefing, Pew Research Center. https://www.pewresearch.org/fact-tank/2019/01/02/once-the-same-nation-the-czech-republic-and-slovakia-look-very-different-religiously/. Accessed July 21, 2021.

Tharoor, Ishan. 2016. "Slovakia's leader said Islam has 'no place' in his country. Now he's taking a leadership role in the E.U." *The Washington Post,* June 21. https://www.washingtonpost.com/news/worldviews/wp/2016/06/21/the-next-e-u-president-says-islam-has-no-place-in-his-country/

Tížik, Miroslav. 2017. Slovakia: Secularization of Public Life and Desecularization of the State. In *Religion and Secularization in the European Union: State of Affairs and Current Debates,* ed. Jan Nelis et al., 161–167. Bern: Peter Lang.

Tomášik, Samo. 1839. "Hej, Slováci." Text and background at http://webarchive.loc.gov/all/20011128160810/http%3A//www.iarelative.com/nss1946/slovaci.htm. Accessed September 23, 2021.

Toscer-Angot, Sylvie. 2017. Germany: The Challenge of Religious Pluralism and Secularization. In *Religion and Secularization in the European Union: State of Affairs and Current Debates,* ed. Jan Nelis et al., 75–80. Bern: Peter Lang.

Tyndale, Wendy R. 2010. *Protestants in Communist East Germany: In the Storm of the World*. Burlington, Vermont: Ashgate.

UNdata. 2007. "Abortion rate." New York: United Nations Statistical Division. http://data.un.org/Data.aspx?d=GenderStat&f=inID:12&c=1,2,3, 4,5,6&s=crEngName:asc,sgvEngName:asc,timeEngName:desc&v=1. Accessed December 3, 2021.

United States Department of State. 2018. "Slovak Republic 2018 International Religious Freedom Report." https://www.state.gov/wp-content/uploads/2019/05/SLOVAKIA-2018-INTERNATIONAL-RELIGIOUS-FREEDOM-REPORT.pdf

———. 2019. "International Religious Freedom Report for 2019, Germany". https://www.state.gov/reports/2019-report-on-international-religious--freedom/germany/

Vašečka, Michal. 2020. "From Mafia State to "Parish" Republic." https://publicseminar.org/essays/from-mafia-state-to-parish-republic/. Accessed October 21, 2021.

Világi, Aneta. 2021. "Od Slováka ku kresťanovi -- posun nacionalistickej rétoriky politických stán v Slovenskej republike" [From "Slovak" to "Christian": the shift in the nationalistic rhetoric of political parties in Slovakia]. *Studia Academica Slovaca* 50: 318–335.

Vokálová, Emília. 2009. "Smerovanie cirkevnej politiky na Slovensku po roku 1989" [The Trend of Church Politics in Slovakia after 1989]. *Almanach: Aktuálne otázky svetovej ekonomiky a politiky* 4 (1): 65–75.

Walter, Aaron. 2019. "Islamophobia in Eastern Europe: Slovakia and the Politics of Hate." *Connections*. https://www.connections.clio-online.net/article/id/artikel-4705. Accessed September 22, 2021.

Warner, Carolyn M. 2000. *Confessions of an Interest Group: The Catholic Church and Political Parties in Europe*. Princeton: Princeton University Press.

Witte, Leticia and Bartosz Dudek. 2018. "Catholic Church should fight for 'responsible freedom' in Europe, says cardinal." Deutsche Welle, September 1. https://www.dw.com/en/catholic-church-should-fight-for-responsible-freedom-in-europe-says-cardinal/a-45313840. Accessed September 17, 2021.

PART III

Religion and the State in Asia

CHAPTER 11

Missionary Work in China: Benign Ministry or State Subversion?

Allen Yeh

When the topic of China and missionaries is mentioned, a series of images and associations inevitably come to mind, many of which are negative. Often people think about expulsion of missionaries, arrest of Christians, raids on house churches, governmental control, persecution, tearing down of crosses and churches, and censorship. However, China is arguably the second-most Christian nation on earth today by absolute number (though not by percentage) after the United States, though definitive numbers are hard to come by.[1] Although this does not mean the persecution isn't real, it also means that there is good news for Christianity in China amidst all the hardship. Certainly the faith could not survive and thrive there without a lot of positive things going for it.

However, some might argue that the persecution is what *makes* Christianity thrive in China. John Stott in *Christianity Today* (October 2006, p. 96) said:

A. Yeh (✉)
Intercultural Studies, Biola University, La Mirada, CA, USA
e-mail: ALLEN.YEH@BIOLA.EDU

S. Holzer (ed.), *The Palgrave Handbook of Religion and State Volume II*, https://doi.org/10.1007/978-3-031-35609-4_11

[W]hen I was ordained in the Church of England, evangelicals were a despised and rejected minority. ... Over the intervening 60 years, I've seen the evangelical movement in England grow in size, in maturity, certainly in scholarship, and therefore I think in influence and impact. We went from a ghetto to being on the ascendancy, which is a very dangerous place to be. Pride is the ever-present danger that faces all of us. In many ways, it is good for us to be despised and rejected. I think of Jesus' words, 'Woe unto you when all men speak well of you.'

Certainly when one compares China with Taiwan, it seems to bear out the theory that Christianity grows amidst persecution,[2] because the latter is a democracy with religious freedom but is smaller in percentage of Christians than mainland China (Johnson and Ross 2010, p. 139).[3] But Philip Jenkins also cautions against leaning on that assumption too heavily. In *The Lost History of Christianity* (2008, p. 141), he says that Christianity has shown itself to collapse under the weight of persecution many times in history. So, what is the truth? It is not as simple as the situation of North Korea (the state has absolute control in mandating atheism) or Saudi Arabia (the state's official religion trumps—or at least drives under-ground—Christianity). There is quite a complex reality today of Christianity—in particular missionaries—and their relationship to China. To have a full-orbed understanding of the situation, at least three major players need to be taken into consideration: Chinese Christians them-selves, foreign missionaries and their history, and the Chinese government.

DISPELLING MYTHS ABOUT CHRISTIANITY IN CHINA

Although this chapter is mainly dealing with missionaries and their rela-tionship to China, it is worth unpacking some popular misconceptions about Christianity in China to start:

1. Christianity is illegal in China. This is absolutely not true. Although China is officially an atheist state under Communist rule, Christianity is actually tolerated and sanctioned[4] through certain official chan-nels, most notably the Three-Self Patriotic Movement (TSPM), the China Christian Council (CCC),[5] the State Administration for Religious Affairs (SARA), and the 22 seminaries of which Nanjing Union Theological Seminary is the flagship. What is illegal is pros-elytization and underground churches. What the Communist gov-

ernment is afraid of is not Christianity itself. They are afraid of what people are saying or doing that is outside their surveillance, because more than anything they simply want to hold on to power.

2. The Three-Self Church is a bad thing, because the Chinese government does not allow real Christianity. Actually, the term "Three-Self" originated with an American and a British missiologist—Rufus Anderson and Henry Venn, respectively—in the nineteenth century. The idea of missionaries wanting the "target" cultures to eventually become self-governing, self-propagating, and self-sustaining was actually quite a progressive idea at the time (some might even argue that it still is!). And the idea that missionaries need to work themselves out of a job and eventually turn it all over to the locals is, overall, a positive idea. Just because the TSPM—aka the Chinese governmental church—appropriated the name for themselves does not make the "three selves" negative. In many ways, it should still be the goal. Paul Hiebert (1994, p. 58) mentions an additional "fourth self" that he hopes for indigenous churches: self-theologizing.

3. The TSPM churches and the underground house churches are at odds with one another, with the former being the "bad guys" and the latter the "good guys." It is not as simple as that. Both have authentic Christians within them. The TSPM itself is even sometimes persecuted by the Communist government even though they fall under its purview. And many times, Christians attend both TSPM *and* house churches, so there is significant overlap between them. There is also a third category of church: expatriate churches like Beijing International Christian Fellowship (BICF) which exists for foreigners but not for nationals (passport proof needs to be shown at the door to gain admittance). The expat churches have much more freedom to worship as they like, and preach whatever they want. But expats sometimes also attend TSPM and house churches.

4. Christianity is the most persecuted religion in China. In fact, Christianity has it quite easy compared to most other religions. Falun Gong (aka Falun Dafa),[6] an offshoot of Buddhism and Taoism, is far more persecuted,[7] as are Uyghur Muslims in Xinjiang province and Tibetan Buddhists.[8] The level of religious persecution across China is not uniform; rural areas and urban areas experience it differently, as do the East (majority ethnic Han Chinese) versus the West (mostly ethnic minorities) (Hattaway 2000).

5. The Bible is illegal in China. That may have been true once upon a time (e.g., Brother David 1981, p. xiv), when missionaries would have to smuggle Bibles into the country, but actually today China itself is the biggest printer of Bibles in the world, via the Amity Foundation in Nanjing which established its printing press in 1987. The growth in Bible printing is staggering: between 1980 and 1986, only three million Bibles had been printed in China. By 2012, the number grew exponentially and had reached 100 million (now the number is approaching 200 million)! The Bible today can be purchased openly in sanctioned bookstores everywhere. They even have it available in Braille, in ethnic minority languages, in bilingual translations, and in both simplified and traditional characters. Amity also prints hymnals and theological books. Their facility's "footprint" spreads out over 85,000 square meters.

History of Missionary Work in China

In order to properly understand the relationship of missionaries to China today, it is helpful to briefly outline the four historical stages of Christianity coming to China: the Nestorians, Catholics, Protestants, and indigenous churches. Tracing the development of ministry and thought clarifies how Christianity today in China is manifested.

The Nestorians are often credited with being the first to bring Christianity to China, in the year 635 A.D. during the Tang Dynasty. They become known as *Jing Jiao* (the "Resplendent Religion"). Their leader was a certain Bishop Alopen, about whom not much is known. Nestorianism, interestingly, is often associated with (in Western theological circles), an understanding of Christ's two natures that was condemned as heretical in the third and fourth Ecumenical Councils, namely Ephesus in 431 and Chalcedon in 451 A.D. Unlike the classic Chalcedonian understanding of Christ's two natures being fully human and fully divine (hypostatic union), Nestorius believed in a radical dyophysitism, that the two natures were linked but did not overlap as such. Interestingly, this split in the church caused Nestorians to become far-flung missionaries.[9] Because they were "kicked out" of the Mediterranean church, they took their teachings East—initially to Persia but eventually all the way to China.

Despite the Nestorians' radical attempts at contextualization (Palmer 2001),[10] it did not last more than 200 years in China. It is not that their message was initially ineffective. However, a major reason for the lack of longevity was a change in leadership, a "Pharaoh that did not know Joseph" (Exodus 1:8).[11] Similar to the Japanese having a healthy indigenous church at one point, and then an imperial reign of terror expelled them from the land,[12] China lost its first church through changing leadership. Unlike Japan, however, China would be destined to recover, multiple times. It seems that Christianity "takes" naturally to Chinese soil, and will not be denied.

However, it is important to understand why Nestorianism did not survive as well as later forms of Christianity: because it was overly tied to the center of power. Under such a model, as goes the emperor so goes Christianity. It failed because it was not owned by the people. Also, some people have criticized it as leaning too heavily on Daoism, to the point of syncretism. However, Nestorian Christianity is not to be dismissed simply as a trivial piece of history; ironically today it is seen as a powerful symbol of Christianity being "indigenous" to China and thus it inspires the Chinese people to own it as a part of their history. The most "concrete" (literally!) lasting evidence of the beginnings of Christianity in China is the famous Nestorian cross found in the Forest of Steles Museum in Xi'an, China.[13] This stylized cross engraved atop the Nestorian stele has become China's very own symbol of The Way and continues to be appropriated as a source of national pride.

The second type of Christianity to sweep through China would be Roman Catholicism. The most radical and effective of the contextualizers would be the Jesuits, led by Matteo Ricci (1552–1610) (Bays 2012, pp. 21–22) from Italy. He was a polymath who not only was an evangelist but also a mathematician, cartographer, engineer, astronomer, and creator of the first-ever European-Chinese dictionary (Portuguese-Chinese). He even dressed like a Buddhist monk, and later a Confucian scholar, which made him a target of a lot of criticism by many of his fellow Catholics for taking contextualization too far. His parallel was Robert de Nobili, his fellow contemporary Jesuit laborer in India. The two employed several of the same tactics like reaching the educated upper-class with secular learning and adopting local mannerisms and styles.

Matteo Ricci would be an itinerant through his 28 years in China (1582–1610), starting in Macau (then Romanized as Macao) eventually ending up in Beijing (then Romanized as Peking) and dying there. This was during the late Ming and early Qing dynasties, which had made Peking their capital city. His main contribution to Christianity in China was not using Daoist concepts like the Nestorians, but finding the proper equivalent indigenous Chinese words to express Christian theology. Though his goal was never to translate the Bible in its entirety due to Latin rather than the vernacular being favored by Catholics, he wrote numerous catechisms and instructions like *Ten Commandments of the Lord of Heaven*, as well as works of apologetics like *The True Meaning of the Lord of Heaven*. He used his extensive learning for evangelization toward the literati, and adapted Roman Catholicism for the Chinese, especially the Mass. Where things got extremely fraught was when it came to the name of God. The Pope had decreed the acceptability of Ricci's assertation that *Tian Zhu*[14] is the proper word for God in Chinese, but Emperor Kangxi of China was miffed that a foreign power had decided that on the behalf of his nation, thus ensued the infamous Rites Controversy (Bays 2012, pp. 28–32). Even more, it was one thing to employ a Chinese word for the Christian God, but to adapt ancestral veneration for Christianity felt like a bridge too far for some.

Some later Jesuits attempted to translate portions of Scripture, such as the Frenchman Louis de Poirot (1735–1813) who managed to do the entire New Testament and a portion of the Old Testament. Despite this remarkable achievement, it was never granted papal permission and thus the manuscript was subsequently stored in a vault and then destroyed. It literally never saw the light of day, which left it up to the next wave of missionaries to accomplish this.[15] The main contribution of the Catholics therefore was to introduce catechetical works to China, bring other kinds of learning to the educated elite, and setting up Roman Catholicism. Their downfall, however, was that China was hungry for their own indigenous church leadership, not one ruled by a foreign power (the Pope). Despite all the Jesuits' attempts at being contextual, they (unlike the Nestorians) were never accepted as being indigenously Chinese.

The third wave of Christianity in China was the arrival of the Protestants in the eighteenth and nineteenth centuries. Although J. Hudson Taylor (1832–1905) (Steer 1990) is arguably the most well-known, the first Protestant missionary was actually the English Presbyterian Robert Morrison (1782–1834) (Hancock 2008). When Morrison first set out, he was challenged by a fellow Englishman: "Do you expect to make an impression on the idolatry of the great Chinese Empire?" to which he famously replied: "No sir, but I expect God will!"

Taylor was well-known for faith missions (Tucker 2004, p. 197),[16] and moving mission beyond the coast to the inland areas—both incredibly important contributions that leapt Christianity forward in China—but

Morrison was the first to complete an entire translation of the Bible into Chinese,[17] as well as the very first Chinese-English dictionary and the establishment of the Anglo-Chinese College (Cook and Pao 2011, p. 39). Though he barely converted anyone during his lifetime, and his base of operations for much of his ministry was outside China in the city of Malacca in the Malay Peninsula, the lasting legacy of Morrison was his Bible, assisted by his printer friend William Milne. This translation is still largely intact and is still the main base for most modern translations in China today.

The biggest question in Bible translation was The Term Controversy: how does one translate the name of God? Although Ricci and his fellow Catholics wrestled with this, Morrison (and other Protestant missionaries like the Scotsman James Legge and the American William Boone) had a more difficult time of this issue because of numerous disagreements among them (Pfister 2004), and no papal authority to settle the matter. Words like *Shang Di* and *Shen* were considered, along with the Catholic contribution *Tian Zhu*. The one thing all could agree on: it had to be an indigenous word for God, not a foreign transliteration like *Yehehua* (Yahweh).

Eventually the Protestant work grew to expand not just Bible translation but all sectors of life, for example: Hudson Taylor did some of the greatest mass evangelism ever,[18] and opposed the opium trade; Welsh Baptist Timothy Richard[19] (1845–1919) did social justice efforts such as earthquake and famine relief, and social contributions such as science, technology, and newspapers; and the Student Volunteer Movement (SVM), whose most famous representative was cricketer C.T. Studd (1860–1931) and the Cambridge Seven[20] (Pollock 2006) who spurred on the movement of university students to abandon secular careers for the mission field, expressed well by this sentiment: "If Christ be God and died for me, then no sacrifice can be too great for me to make for him." Protestants were effective in large part because, unlike the Nestorians and the Catholics, they appealed to the working classes and common people (Tucker 2004, p. 120). Their bottom-up (as opposed to top-down) model was extremely effective at spreading the faith far and wide.

The fourth and final movement of Christianity in China is the indigenous churches, in which the nationals rather than foreigners are the missionaries. Unlike the three previous eras of Christianity in China, which all had a clean break between them (i.e., each was independent of the one that preceded it), the third and fourth eras overlapped, forming a kind of Venn diagram. Ironically, the transition from Protestants to indigenous was both violent and not exactly Christian: the Taiping Heavenly Kingdom was a cult led by Hong Xiuquan who claimed to be the brother of Jesus Christ. He fomented his Taiping Rebellion (1850–1864) against the foreign-ruled Qing dynasty[21] which was equal parts religious uprising as ethnic uprising. This was the bloodiest civil war in Chinese history, with tens of millions of deaths, with the Taiping Heavenly Kingdom eventually losing the war. Still, this set some important things in motion, most notably the beginning of the fall of the Qing Dynasty.

The Taiping Rebellion was later followed by the Boxer[22] Rebellion (1899–1901) which had almost the exact reverse priorities: instead of being a religious (purportedly Christian) movement which fought against the foreign Qing rulers, this was anti-Christian, pro-Qing, and anti-Western. During this time, an eight-nation alliance of foreign powers started pressing in on China as the Qing empire (the last of the dynasties) started to crumble, and there was much paranoia from the imperial throne. Foreign missionaries were expelled from China and Chinese Christians were hunted down and killed. Ultimately, however, despite all its efforts at resistance, the Qing fell to European and American powers, which gave way to Japanese puppet rule through the last emperor, Puyi.

Out of this arose Sun Yat-sen (1866–1925), the "George Washington of China" (Bergere 1998). He successfully ousted the imperial Qing/Japanese powers, securing China as its own democratic Republic for the first time in its history, and becoming its first President. Importantly, Sun was a Christian. The conditions of this Republic of China (under which Christianity was freely welcomed back into the country) did not last long, as Mao Zedong (1893–1976) established the Communist People's Republic of China which tried to eradicate Christianity. However, Mao—despite catastrophes such as the Great Leap Forward (1958–1961) and the Cultural Revolution (1966–1976)—inadvertently created conditions in which Christianity would eventually thrive in China. First, he unified the country under one language: Mandarin Chinese. This made evangelism much easier, as only one language and one Bible translation was needed to reach over a billion people. Second, he eradicated competing religions such as Buddhism and Daoism and even Confucianism, creating a spiritual hunger that the Chinese people have since been trying to satisfy—and millions turned to Christianity. Third, communism bred egalitarianism and grassroots leadership, opening the way for female leadership[23] which has been one of the backbones of the house churches.

Mao's successor, Deng Xiaoping (1904–1997), introduced an "Open Door" policy. Under these guidelines, the clamps were loosened. Church attendance was allowed, Bibles could be purchased openly, and people could openly question pastors or priests about theology. This led to the strong influence of Bishop K.H. Ting of the TSPM churches, and later the rise of prominent house church leaders like Watchman Nee, Brother Yun ("The Heavenly Man") (Yun 2002), and the Back to Jerusalem movement (Yun et al. 2003) in which Chinese are attempting to take the Gospel "full circle" around the world across the Silk Road back to its place of origin.[24] However, given that many of these groups still had to operate under government restrictions, this led to factions and divisions, with many distrusting each other. Not only was this the case between the house churches and the TSPM, but even different house churches grew suspicious of each other: some called Nee's "Little Flock" a cult; some disbelieved Yun's prison deliverance story or that he fasted for more days than Jesus did. In short, more openness led, ironically, to less unity.

CHINA AND ITS GOVERNMENT TODAY

Each successive leader of the PRC, including Jiang Zemin and Hu Jintao, loosened the clamps even more—until the current President, Xi Jinping. President Xi represents a return to Mao-style leadership, ruling with an iron fist and censorship and religious persecution. Under his leadership, Western social media is not allowed, replacing Google, Twitter, Facebook, YouTube, and so on with their Chinese equivalents: Baidu, Weibo, WeChat, and Youku, respectively. Of course, many people try to circumvent these firewalls with VPNs (Virtual Private Networks), but it is not as if the Chinese government is unaware of such things. In addition, they have massive video surveillance, which purportedly can locate anybody in the entire country within minutes, using closed-circuit television (CCTV) cameras operating on all streets, highways, and in buildings. They have digital technology that can scan data from anyone's laptops as they travel through airports. And the "coded emails" that missionaries send to their supporters in prayer letters are easily decipherable by the government. And of course, there is now less tolerance of religious groups—as mentioned earlier in the chapter, not just of Christians but even more of Muslims, Buddhists, and Falun Gong, among others.

Outside of China, there is a different type of tightening of the clamps. This is called the Belt and Road Initiative (BRI), also referred to as the

"New Silk Road." China is attempting to extend its dominance economically worldwide by making both overland and maritime commercial channels. The scope of this includes some 60-plus countries, setting up Special Economic Zones[25] (modeled after Shenzhen which is Hong Kong's neighbor city), and involves an exchange of goods: China's infrastructure help (e.g., building highways and such) in exchange for access and natural resources. The problem is, any country which agrees to this may be signing up for a Faustian deal: short-term gain but long-term indebtedness to China. Some countries have attempted to either rebuff the BRI or extricate themselves from the deal, but sometimes it is inevitable if that is the only way forward. The combination of President Xi's internal clamping and the external BRI could prove to be a tension: how to truly keep tight control on mainland China's population while also going global. There is really no way to dominate the world while keeping the people insular. For example, the rise of Alibaba (their version of Amazon), and Dalian Wanda's foray into sports[26] and the purchase of AMC cinemas,[27] are part of China's economic expansion as well, even if they are private enterprises. All this means, not only will Chinese people need to go out into the world, but China has to let the world in.

The case of Hong Kong is the example *par excellence* of this tension between trying to be open and also closed to the world: when that island territory was handed back to China after a 99-year lease by the British in 1997, there was a promise that there would be "One Country, Two Systems," as Hong Kong was designated an SAR (Special Administrative Region). This meant that, supposedly, it would be left well enough alone, to carry on as before without government interference. The idea was that Hong Kong is the "goose that lays the golden egg," so there is no need to change things, as long as they keep up economic production. Yet, having a democratic system underneath a Communist umbrella proved to be a tricky balance to maintain. For example, many Westerners could enter Hong Kong without a visa, but mainland Chinese had to have a passport to enter Hong Kong—even though it was technically part of their own country! However, Beijing was hoping that they could do to Hong Kong as the proverbial frog in the kettle experience: if you turn up the heat one degree at a time, the frog does not notice that it is slowly being boiled to death. Unfortunately for Beijing, Hong Kongers noticed, as their rights were gradually being taken away. This led to protests culminating in the Umbrella Movement led by teenager Joshua Wong starting in 2014, and really coming to a head in 2019[28] with daily clashes and street blockades as a response to Governor Carrie Lam's extradition bill. Social media highlighted these things in a way that was not available in 1989 with Tiananmen Square. But this was only possible because Hong Kong did not have the same internet restrictions (popularly known as the Great Firewall of China) as the mainland does, which made the Communist government rethink their strategy of letting Hong Kong alone.

Beijing's answer, over the course of the last quarter century, has been to try to minimize Hong Kong as the country's financial center, and replace it with Shanghai. In the last decade, Shanghai has built three of the world's tallest skyscrapers,[29] and become also a major tourist destination (Shanghai Disneyland far outshadowing Hong Kong Disneyland is just one prominent example, as well as having Asia's first-ever Starbucks Roastery Reserve). There is also an attempt to replace Hong Kong's movie industry—once the world's third-largest after Hollywood and Bollywood—by moving most of the studios to Qingdao[30] (a city formerly famous mostly for their beer, Tsingtao, which is the city name spelled in the Wade-Giles fashion).

The Chinese government has a quandary: to be open or not? They can't accomplish their global dreams without being open, but if they let in the outside world, their version of Arab Spring is going to happen (Hong Kong would be just the beginning). They can't afford to do another Tiananmen Square for fear of bad global PR, but they can't just let Hong Kongers "win" because that will set a precedent for this happening again (an analogy: Beijing sees themselves as the parent and Hong Kong as the child. One principle of parenting is that the parental discipline must always be consistent—that is, always do what you say you will—otherwise the child quickly learns what they can get away with). This exploration of China's government today, combined with the history of the four waves of Christianity in China, and the current multifaceted state of Christianity, leads us to consider how missionaries are viewed by Beijing.

Missionaries: Triangulating Chinese Christianity, Missionary History, and the Chinese Government

With regard to the question of trust between missionaries and mainland China, what can we learn from the current state of Christianity in China, the four waves of missionary history in China, and the restrictions and allowances by the Chinese government today? There are at least five factors to consider, with both descriptive and prescriptive lessons to be gleaned from each.

1. Post-denominationalism: Descriptively, denominations were abolished by the China Christian Council (CCC) in 1958, because the Chinese Communist Party (CCP) does not like to share power. Christianity is allowed as long as it is under the watchful eye of the government, and it is truly rooted in indigenous Chinese soil. Denominations suggest foreign powers (whether it is the Vatican, or the Church of England, or even small Protestant denominations). Prescriptively, foreign missionaries ought to do as the Presbyterian missiologist Lesslie Newbigin did when he went to India: leave aside his Western denomination, seek out local ecumenism, and submit to their leading (in Newbigin's case, it was the Church of South India). Of course, the reality in China is further complicated by the fact that there are two faces of the local Chinese church—the house churches, as well as the TSPM churches—and they themselves do not necessarily even trust each other.[31] But suffice it to say, to earn the trust of Chinese Christians, foreign missionaries must contextualize and indigenize, which brings us to the next point.

2. Sinicization: Descriptively, Christianity has thrived in China as long as it is heavily contextualized. This could either be the Nestorian or Catholic way which is more top-down, or the Protestant or house church way which is bottom-up. This was even why the Taiping cult thrived: the shape of the religion was indubitably Chinese above all else. Today, in the TSPM churches and seminaries, a style of theology known as *Zhong Guo Hua* (Sinicization) is taking place, where indigenous theology is *de rigueur*. Some people are suspicious of it, much in the same way that Watchman Nee or Bishop Ting or Brother Yun has been looked askance at times. Prescriptively, the dangers of heresy or syncretism notwithstanding, Christianity *must* be articulated in local terms like Daoist or Buddhist language, or the foreign missionary movement has to be seen as so indigenous to Chinese history that they "own" it as their own.[32] One example of the latter is the new chapel (built in 2016) of their flagship seminary, Nanjing Union Theological Seminary, sports a Nestorian cross outside the door. In Africa, the question of whether or not Islam or Christianity—the two giant foreign religions—really does hold sway over ATRs (African Traditional Religions) has been one which has

been debated extensively. The two major theories come from Robin Horton (1971) who posited the Intellectualist Theory, and Humphrey Fisher (1973) who rebutted with the Juggernaut Theory.[33] Prescriptively, it can be argued that Chinese Christianity must be understood with the Intellectualist Theory. Missionaries must not only be structurally Chinese (post-denominational), but theologically Chinese (Sinicization).

3. Discipleship: Descriptively, the Christianity in China is "a mile wide and an inch deep." This is how the authors of the *Africa Bible Commentary* (Adeyemo 2010, p. viii) also described Christianity in their own continent. As sub-Saharan Africa and East Asia are arguably the two centers of gravity of Christianity in the world today, it is no surprise that there is a parallel. The numbers of Christians in these two regions are staggering, but there is often a lack of depth in training, biblical literacy, and spiritual maturity. In China, obviously the TSPM has a great network of state-sponsored seminaries as described above, but the house churches have no such apparatuses in place. Therefore, leadership development is of the utmost priority. With the egalitarianism of communism which tore down the traditional Confucian patriarchy, we are now seeing mostly women leading the Chinese churches, especially as they are the majority of the Christian demographic in that country. There is a Chinese proverb: "Women hold up half the sky," and it is said (though difficult to confirm) that up to 80% of house church members in China are women. The World Council of Churches (oikoumene.org) writes:

Pastoral work of the Chinese churches has been expanded during the last twenty-five years. More than 60,000 churches and meeting places have been opened, 70% of which are newly built. Of the more than 26 million Protestant Christians 70% live in the rural areas. Lay training, theological formation, and Bible distribution are among the top priorities of the CCC. From 1980 to 2014, 70 million Bibles were printed and distributed in China. Social service has developed in recent years. There are currently 22 theological seminaries and Bible schools and hundreds of lay training centers throughout China. The theological institution at the national level, Nanjing Union Theological Seminary, grants M.Th. and M.Div. degrees.

Yet, despite this progress, there are not enough ordained pastors or even educated ministers. Lay pastors are the most common kind, especially in rural areas. Prescriptively, this means that the job of missionaries in China should not be evangelism/proselytization. This does not mean foreign missionaries call a moratorium on engaging with China, however. Training, instead, should be the goal. Chinese have enough numbers to evangelize themselves, not to mention the linguistic and cultural know-how that foreigners might lack. But especially in the house churches, they need resources, whether that be books (though not Bibles!), or mentoring, or online educational resources.

4. Shift in strategy: Descriptively, the old model included foreign missionaries coming into China in the guise of English teachers, doing "faith" support raising. It used to be that places like Hong Kong would serve as a strategic missionary jumping-off point for ministry in mainland China. And it used to be that foreigners held all the theological knowledge. Most of these are not necessarily true anymore. Prescriptively, it might be wiser to employ ethnic Chinese as the missionaries. These could be mainland nationals, or they could be overseas Chinese who are an often-overlooked hugely untapped resource. These overseas Chinese could be from the West, but often are actually more from Southeast Asia, places like Taiwan, Singapore, Indonesia, Malaysia, the Philippines, Vietnam, and Thailand (Yeh 2014, p. 92). These ethnic Chinese could come as scientists, engineers, computer programmers, university professors, and other highly skilled and highly educated contributors to society. This is not just about reaching the literati as it would have been in days gone by; now China's global reach is so expansive that they need all the intellectual resources they can muster in order to accomplish their global ambitions. Also, relief workers and health workers and social workers are needed, as the pressures and physical dangers and mental health concerns of the modern world mount. The headquarters for missionaries would have to be in those diaspora countries like Thailand or Singapore, or perhaps in Special Economic Zones like Shenzhen or even major metropolises like Shanghai. And the encouragement now would be for nationals to take over the ministries, produce their own theologies, and foreign missionaries would gradually divest themselves of being the primary drivers of mission. It is time for Chinese nationals to come into their own and become the apostles (the ones sent out), not just the disciples (followers/

learners), such as in the case of the Back to Jerusalem Movement. This is truly the vision of Venn and Anderson with the three- (or four-) self church.

5. Be wise as serpents but innocent as doves: Descriptively, there are a lot of parallels between the People's Republic of China and the Roman Empire, especially the unifying effect of a massive land mass into one culture, language, and technology.[34] This kind of empire has impact far beyond just its own continent, and requires global thoughtfulness of how to engage with such political behemoths. Prescriptively, there is a way to be Christian in China without being a political dissenter. Consider how Jesus and Paul interacted with Rome and its emperor: they paid taxes, appealed to citizenship when needed, even leveraged the legal path to go before the governor or even the Emperor. In modern-day China, a similar creativity is needed. For example, the house churches are not the only venue for Christianity; the TSPM churches can be too. There is no need to smuggle in Bibles anymore, as Amity and the CCC can print and distribute them legally. There are ways to not tarnish the witness of the church or generate suspicions. That being said, don't be naïve: China is not fooled by VPNs or coded messages, and don't leave your laptop lying around if you do not want your information being read. And finally, pray for China. There are books like *Operation China* which gives data and prayer points on every ethnic group in the country.

As the coronavirus originated in China, perhaps this is an apt illustration: the situation of Christianity in China may follow a similar trajectory—that things may get worse before they get better. Three times in history, Christianity came and died. And three times, it came back to life. This gives hope for places like Europe, that there could be a revival again. Things may come in waves, which is different from lacking permanence.

The situation of foreign missionaries in China is ever in flux, and there are no easy answers. Leaning on stereotypes is not helpful, nor is irrational fear. Caution must always be exercised, and nuances and complexities must be sussed out. In truth, China is willing to use foreigners as much as foreigners are willing to use China. What this means is, despite President Xi's clamps, China will never return to being truly a closed country. And what it means for Christian missionaries is, there will always be a place and space for them, though the means of access may ever be changing.

Notes

1. The estimates have ranged anywhere between 5% and 10% of the population of China being Christian. With a total population of 1.3 billion, this means the upper end of the estimate has China with 130 million Christians, and the lower end has China with 65 million Christians. Even the minimal number has the absolute number of Christians in China exceeding the total population of most countries in this world!

2. There are estimates of the Chinese church growing at the rate of 16,500 new converts per day.

3. According to the *Atlas of Global Christianity*, China's Christian population numbered 115,009,000 in 2010, making it 8.6% of the country. This is in contrast to Taiwan which is 6% Christian.

4. China officially recognizes five religions, which are all legally allowed to function. They are: Taoism (aka Daoism), Protestant Christianity, Chinese Catholicism, Buddhism, and Islam.

5. Rev. Dr. Gao Feng is the President of the CCC (making him the highest-ranking government official in the Chinese church), as well as the President of Nanjing Union Theological Seminary.

6. The globally popular Chinese performing arts group, Shen Yun, is a Falun Gong affiliate.

7. In front of every Chinese embassy in the world, you will find Falun Gong protestors demonstrating for their religious freedom.

8. It is well known that the Dalai Lama, leader of Tibetan Buddhists, is in exile in India, as he is seen as a threat to power in China. This is a case-in-point about it being less about religion than about political power. This politics-disguised-as-religion is seen all over the world, for example, the battle between Catholics and Protestants in Northern Ireland is really more about Republicans versus Monarchists rather than anything actually religious.

9. In much the same way, Protestant women outnumbered men 2:1 on the mission field in history, due to—ironically—complementarianism. When women were prohibited from serving/preaching in churches in the West, they took their ministry overseas.

10. The Nestorians used Taoist imagery and language to convey Christianity to the Chinese.

11. Emperor Taizong warmly received Alopen and his coterie; some two centuries later, Emperor Wuzong (who reigned from 840 to 846 A.D.), a devout Taoist, was relatively successful in stamping out Christianity. Actually his goal was to eradicate Buddhism, but all foreign religions—including Manichaeism and Zoroastrianism—also were expunged.

12. This story is powerfully recounted in historical fiction form in Shusaku Endo's novel, *Silence* (1969).
13. Xi'an, aka Chang'an, is the long-time capital of China. Though China has had many capital cities, Beijing is a relatively recent development (just in the last two dynasties—the Ming and the Qing—and in the modern era). Xi'an is where China was unified (thus the Terracotta Warriors) under the first emperor Qin Shi Huang in the third century B.C., and remained as capital until the tenth century A.D.
14. In fact, the word for Roman Catholicism in Chinese took its name from this—*Tian Zhu Jiao*.
15. Eventually, Catholics did complete their own full translation of the Bible into Chinese, but not until the twentieth century. This was the work of Father Gabriele Allegra (1907–1976) from Italy, who finished it in 1922.
16. He mandated certain financial principles from all missionaries who served through the China Inland Mission: no debt; no guaranteed income; dependence on God alone; no solicitation.
17. Actually, the first was one of the members of the Serampore Trio, William Carey's compatriot Joshua Marshman. When Marshman and Morrison heard that the other was attempting to be the first translator of the Bible into Chinese, the race was on. Marshman technically "won" the race but his was a shoddy translation as he did it while stationed in India. So, Morrison is generally credited as the first, given the quality of his work, even if chronologically he came in second place. Both translations were completed in 1822.
18. It is the estimation of Ruth Tucker (p. 186) that "Few missionaries in the nineteen centuries since the apostle Paul have had a wider vision and have carried out a more systematic plan of evangelizing a broad geographical area than did James Hudson Taylor."
19. According to Ruth Tucker (p. 201), he is regarded by the Chinese as *the* greatest missionary to their country!
20. Similarly, in Scotland, Alexander Duff and the St. Andrews Seven (Piggin & Roxborough 1995) were university students who went out into the mission field and made a huge impact. Alexander Duff's particular mission was to reach high-caste Indians via Western education.
21. Only two dynasties in Chinese history were foreign-ruled, namely the Yuan Dynasty (1271–1368) which was by the Mongols, and the Qing (1644–1911) which was by the Manchus.
22. Boxers referred to the vast number of people involved who were trained in Chinese martial arts.
23. In Chinese seminaries, more than 60% of the students enrolled are women and in Churches an equal number of pastors are women. This is very unique in China. Nowhere else do we find such involvement

24. This phrase was coined by Luis Bush, chairman of the AD 2000 movement and who also coined 10/40 window phrase.

25. Since the establishment (by Deng Xiaoping) of Shenzhen as China's first SEZ, there have been six others set up: Zhuhai, Shantou, Xiamen, Kashgar, Hainan Province, and Khorgas. Now, China is setting them up overseas as well, notably in Africa.

26. The owner of Wanda, Wang Jianlin, is the richest man in China. They just purchased Ironman and Rock 'n Roll marathons, and became a co-sponsor with Abbott of the World Marathon Majors. They also struck a deal with FIFA to launch the China Cup, an Asian international football competition.

27. The Chinese cinema holdings of Wanda, combined with AMC, make it the largest movie theater company in the world.

28. Who knows how long the stalemate between the pro-democracy protestors and Beijing would have lasted (in many ways it was like "the irresistible force meets the immovable object"), if not for the coronavirus (COVID-19) bringing Hong Kong—and the entire world—to a standstill.

29. The Jin Mao Tower, the Shanghai World Financial Center aka the "Bottle Opener," and the Shanghai Tower which is the second-tallest building in the world.

30. The Oriental Movie Metropolis, built in 2018, is the largest movie studio and film production company in the world, with the effect of Qingdao becoming known as the "Hollywood of the East."

31. The reality is similar in Latin America: the Catholics and the Protestants are so at odds with each other, with the former calling the latter a cult and the latter thinking of the former as oppressors, but both can be considered truly local forms of Latino ecclesiology.

32. The Nestorian cross for China Christians is similar to the Star of David for Jews; this was not a symbol they came up with, it was given to them at best and foisted on them at worst, but they soon chose to adopt it as if it were their own, even putting it on the flag of the State of Israel.

33. Fisher's claim is that the "juggernauts" of Islam and Christianity, when they came into Africa, "trumped" the ATRs and wiped out their cosmology. Horton, however, said that underlying the veneer of these major world religions was an African worldview—a three-tiered diffused monotheism—that is so strong that foreign religions are forced to adapt to it. It has since been proved that Horton was more correct in his understanding.

34. In fact, there is a lot of similarity between the U.S. and Rome as well, as the former modeled itself after the latter, with the architecture of Washington D.C. being markedly Greco-Roman, the symbol of the eagle and the structure of the Senate being borrowed from Rome, the Presidential monuments resembling temples to the gods, and so on.

FURTHER READING

Aikman, David. 2003. *Jesus in Beijing: How Christianity is Transforming China and Changing The Global Balance of Power.* Washington, DC: Regnery.

Covell, Ralph R. 1995. *The Liberating Gospel in China: The Christian Faith among China's Minority Peoples.* Baker: Grand Rapids.

Lambert, Tony. 2000. *China's Christian Millions: The Costly Revival.* Grand Rapids: Monarch Books.

REFERENCES

Adeyemo, Tokunboh, ed. 2010. *Africa Bible Commentary.* Nairobi: WordAlive Publishers.

Bays, Daniel H. 2012. *A New History of Christianity in China.* Chichester: Wiley-Blackwell.

Bergere, Marie-Claire. 1998. *Sun Yat-sen.* Stanford: Stanford University Press.

Cook, Richard R., and David W. Pao, eds. 2011. *After Imperialism: Christian Identity in China and the Global Evangelical Movement.* Pickwick: Eugene.

David, Brother. 1981. *God's Smuggler to China.* Hodder and Stoughton: Suffolk.

Endo, Shusaku. 1969. *Silence.* Tokyo: Monumenta Nipponica.

Fisher, Humphrey. 1973. Conversion Reconsidered: Some Historical Aspects of Religious Conversion in Black Africa. *Africa: Journal of the International African Institute* 43 (1): 27–40.

Hancock, Christopher. 2008. *Robert Morrison and the Birth of Chinese Protestantism.* London: T&T Clark.

Hattaway, Paul. 2000. *Operation China: Introducing All the Peoples of China.* Piquant: Pasadena.

Hiebert, Paul G. 1994. *Anthropological Reflections on Missiological Issues.* Baker: Grand Rapids.

Horton, Robin. 1971. African Conversion. *Africa: Journal of the International African Institute* 41 (2): 85–108.

Jenkins, Philip. 2008. *The Lost History of Christianity: The Thousand-Year Golden Age of the Church in the Middle East, Africa, and Asia—and How It Died.* New York: HarperOne.

Johnson, Todd M., and Kenneth R. Ross, eds. 2010. *Atlas of Global Christianity.* Edinburgh: Edinburgh University Press.

Palmer, Martin. 2001. *The Jesus Sutras: Rediscovering the Lost Scrolls of Taoist Christianity.* New York: Wellspring/Ballantine.

Pfister, Lauren. 2004. *Striving for the Whole Duty of Man: James Legge and the Scottish Protestant Encounter with China.* Berlin: Peter Lang.

Piggin, Stuart, and John Roxborogh. 1995. *The St. Andrews Seven.* Banner of Truth: Edinburgh.

Pollock, John. 2006. *The Cambridge Seven: The True Story of Ordinary Men Used in No Ordinary Way*. Christian Focus: Fearn.

Stafford, Tim. 2006. Evangelism Plus. *Christianity Today*, October 13.

Steer, Roger. 1990. *J. Hudson Taylor: A Man in Christ*. Milton Keynes: Authentic.

Tucker, Ruth A. 2004. *From Jerusalem to Irian Jaya: A Biographical History of Christian Missions*. Zondervan: Grand Rapids.

World Council of Churches. China Christian Council. https://www.oikoumene.org/en/member-churches/china-christian-council.

Yeh, Allen. 2014. The Chinese Diaspora. In *Global Diasporas and Mission*, ed. Chandler H. Im and Amos Yong. Oxford: Regnum.

Yun, Brother. 2002. *The Heavenly Man*. London: Monarch.

Yun, Brother, Peter Xu Yongze, and Enoch Wang. 2003. *Back to Jerusalem: Three Chinese House Church Leaders Share Their Vision to Complete the Great Commission*. Milton Keynes: Authentic.

CHAPTER 12

Christian God and Hostile State: Church-State Relationship in China

Joseph Tse-Hei Lee

INTRODUCTION

Historian Wang Gungwu once commented on the different patterns of the Church-state relationship: "Unlike the West, which had to deal with a powerful Church for centuries, the Chinese had begun with a secular outlook that ensured that no Church could be established to challenge political authority" (Wang 2004, p. 126). Whereas in Europe, the power of the Catholic Church and the unity of Christendom generated tensions between the ecclesiastical and political authorities, the Confucian rulers proclaimed to uphold the heavenly mandate (*tianming*) on earth, monopolizing people's access to the transcendent. This ideological foundation enabled the Chinese imperial dynasties to place Daoist, Buddhist, and popular religious institutions in service of the state. Yet, the phenomenal growth of Christianity in contemporary China has disrupted this accommodating relationship between state and religion.

J. T.-H. Lee (✉)
Pace University, New York City, NY, USA
e-mail: jlee@pace.edu

This chapter provides a historical assessment of the Church-state relations in the People's Republic of China (1949–Present), concentrating on two parallel phenomena. The first concerns the transformation of Christianity from a heavily persecuted and marginalized belief system in the Maoist era (1949–1976) into a deeply indigenized religious movement. Both Catholics and Protestants not only survived decades of persecution under Mao's rule but have also flourished in a relatively liberalizing environment. The second phenomenon is the emergence of an indigenous Christian spirituality that provides people with strong spiritual, psychological, and material resources to cope with the multiple overlapping challenges of inequality, and the uncertain encounters with the state that is still hostile toward religious ideas and practices.

Recent scholarship has rejected the simplification of China's Church-state encounters into "state control" and "religious resistance" paradigms (Ashiwa and Wank 2009; Lee 2007, 2009). The rapidity of China's liberalization during the period from the 1990s to 2010s has enabled scholars to trace the development of both officially registered and unofficially recognized churches from bottom up, delving deeper into the variations of their encounters with the socialist state (Chan 2019). Outlasting Soviet communism, China's durable one-party state has adjusted institutional mechanisms to stabilize the spiritual domain, permitting local officials to offer Catholics and Protestants limited autonomy in order to retain their loyalty (Reny 2018). Carsten T. Vala (2018) highlights the proactive role that the state has played in the training of patriotic clergy. Cao Nanlai's (2011) widely cited ethnography of fast-growing Protestant churches in eastern China's Wenzhou focuses on the boss Christians' ability to negotiate with the municipal authorities, asserting their influence inside and outside the church. Meanwhile, growing numbers of conscientious Christians consider the state-managed religious patriotic organization to be a broken system. Proclaiming the Church to be a spiritual body outside the state's control, many Catholics and Protestants have devised innovative strategies to weaken the state's monopoly on the religious sphere.

Methodologically, any study of China's Church-state relationship must address a terminological problem. The conventional categories that describe Chinese Christians as "open churches" (*dishang jiaohui*), "underground [Catholic] churches" (*dixia jiaohui*), and "[Protestant] house churches" (*jiating jiaohui*) are problematic. The Communist state requires places of worship to register with the local bureau of religious affairs, whether they are churches, temples, monasteries, or mosques. An "underground church" is not underground literally. Neither does a "house church" necessarily meet in someone's home. The terms "underground church" and "house church" refer to an unregistered faith community that rejects the state's surveillance for doctrinal and ecclesiastical reasons. Yet, the official treatment of both registered and unregistered churches varies temporally and spatially. For the purposes of discussion, this study employs "Christianity" as a generic word to refer to both Chinese Catholics and Protestants. It uses "unregistered church" or "autonomous church" to describe a congregation not legally recognized, even though tactically acknowledged, by the authorities. The term "pro-Vatican Church" refers to those Catholics loyal to the Holy See.

Beginning with an overview of Church-state interactions in China, this chapter evaluates the profound challenges facing China's registered and unregistered churches, and the strategies that Christians employ to cope with, circumvent, and overcome organizational constraints imposed by the state. It concludes with some comments on the future prospects of Church-state encounters in the twenty-first century.

CHURCH-STATE RELATIONSHIP IN CHINA

After the Communists seized power in 1949, they manipulated the old "Three-Self" evangelistic slogan into the "Three-Self Patriotic Movement" (*sanzi aiguo yundong*), legitimatizing the state's takeover of the Protestant Church. The term "Three-Self," originally coined by Rufus Anderson, of the American Board of Commissioners for Foreign Missions, and Henry Venn, of the Church Missionary Society, in the nineteenth century, describes a mission policy designed to organize native Christians in Africa and Asia into self-supporting, self-governing, and self-propagating churches. Yet, calling for the indigenization of Chinese churches, the state-controlled Three-Self Patriotic Movement imposed a coercive assimilation of the foreign mission institutions into the socialist order.

The outbreak of the Korean War on June 25, 1950, worsened the situation for Chinese Christians. In the name of purging Western imperialism, the Communists launched mass denunciations of church leaders, forcing them to denounce foreign missionaries, some of whom they had known for years. The Communists expelled Western Catholic and Protestant missionaries, confiscated mission church properties, and forced local Christians to cut ties with foreigners, marking the end of foreign imperialism in China (Ling 1999, pp. 148–80). The persistent wave of party propaganda

against the U.S. military intervention in Korea incited anti-foreign sentiment. Under tremendous pressure for absolute loyalty to the Maoist state,
political neutrality was not an option, and Protestants were compelled to
betray each other and show submission to the socialist order (Lin 2017).
While prominent Protestant leaders like Wang Mingdao and Watchman
Nee drew on the Bible to oppose the Communist's interference in the
spiritual affairs of the Church, pro-government thinkers like Wu Yaozong
(Y. T. Wu) and Bishop Ding Guangxun (K. H. Ting) appropriated biblical
passages to accommodate Protestant Christianity with socialism. Despite
the state's seemingly totalitarian rule, clandestine evangelistic activities
existed beneath the surface of the Maoist regime.

The Communists used a similar top-down policy of coercive intimidation against Catholics, demanding "not only the public obedience of key
Church figures, but also their sincere total allegiance" (Hanson 1980,
pp. 36–7). In 1951, the state launched the Catholic Three-Self Movement
to eliminate the Vatican's influence. In 1957, it created the Chinese
Catholic Patriotic Association, rejecting the Pope's ecclesiastical authority
over the Chinese faithful. In 1958, this state-controlled Catholic institution consecrated new bishops without Rome's approval, and Pope Pius
XII condemned the body as rebellious.

Political conditions for Catholics and Protestants deteriorated between
1958 and 1962, a period referred to by them as the "elimination of
Christianity" (*miejiao*) (Chow 2021). Because the Maoist state restruc-
tured all rural settlements into mutual aid teams, with militarized discipline, during the campaign of agricultural collectivization in 1953, the
redrawing of village boundaries merged Christian households with non-
Christian neighbors. This, in turn, put non-Christian cadres in charge of
Catholic and Protestant villagers, and replaced the existing Christian
power structure with a socialist one (Lee 2009). Rural congregations
ceased to function, when village officials forcibly converted chapels into
schools, warehouses, factories, and government offices. Then, Mao
launched the Great Leap Forward (1958–1961), a mass campaign
designed to mobilize all citizens to join in collective industrial production.
Whenever the production activities conflicted with Christians' weekly congregational activities, non-Christian cadres accused the former of not
doing their share to support the Great Leap campaign.

The most hostile period for Christians took place during the Socialist
Education Movement (1962–1965), as illustrated in the surviving
accounts of some Christian religious prisoners, such as Lin Zhao in

Shanghai. As with the ancient desert patriarchs and matriarchs, Lin Zhao contextualized her prison ordeal as a spiritual battle and practiced contemplative silence to focus intensely on God. Rejecting socialist values and norms, she recounted biblical verses, prayers, and devotional hymns as "imaginary bricks," constructing an imagined "chapel in her prison cell for weekly 'grand church worship'" (Lian 2018, p. 19). In the same Shanghai prison were Watchman Nee, founder of the Christian Assembly (or Little Flock Movement), Ignatius Pin-Mei Kung, the local Catholic Bishop, and many Little Flock church leaders and Seventh-day Adventists (Mariani 2011; Lee 2017). Charged with the task of remolding Christian political prisoners into new socialist citizens, the prison regime relied on harsh and brutal interrogation techniques to reshape prisoners' religious commitment into an absolute devotion to the state. The mighty Communist state demolished countless physical churches, but what sustained the faithful was an invisible spiritual fortress around their hearts and minds. These prisoners' experiences highlight the characteristics of a historically grounded spirituality that emerged in China as a theology of defiance or a gospel of suffering.

During the Cultural Revolution (1966–1976), Red Guards attacked religious activities in the name of destroying the four olds (old customs, old culture, old habits, and old ideas). Ironically, factional rivalries among the Red Guards, workers, students, and armies paralyzed provincial, municipal, and district authority. The intensity of religious suppression decreased, and some Christians resumed covert congregational activities during the early 1970s. In cases of ordained leadership absence, laity and former church leaders launched clandestine and decentralized house gatherings to support each other. By reinventing their congregational, kinship, and cross-regional networks as conduits for evangelization, they kept faith alive and conversion followed the social hierarchy; that is, the Christian patriarchs, mostly older men and women, instructed younger relatives in the faith. When Christianity became a family religion, Jesus Christ replaced ancestors as the focus of worship and became part of a collective identity to hold different generations of a Christian family together. Christian patriarchs saw conversion, baptism, and church affiliation as essential filial duties for their children (Lee 2003, pp. 29, 83). One intriguing feature of this conversionary process is the lack of individual consciousness. The Christian family is a strong social unit that discourages individual choice, thereby maintaining group cohesiveness. Such findings confirm Richard

Madsen (1998)'s view that strong kinship ties held Catholics together and prevented the church from falling apart under Mao's rule.

Furthermore, Catholics and Protestants employed a wide range of survival strategies. One major strategy was to shift the center of religious operation from urban to rural areas in order to avoid confrontation with the state. In previous centuries, the center of Christianity was the countryside, and the success of rural evangelization inspired church leaders to return to their roots. Another strategy was to proselytize among victims of Mao's policies, such as landholders, capitalists, and officials of the Nationalist regime, because Christians could appeal to them with a promise of salvation. Equally important was the strategy to help children of the Christian families to hold onto their faith, organizing them into youth groups in support of each other. Because the state monopolized the educational sphere, church leaders sought to counter the state's indoctrination of youth. The final strategy was to rely on overseas Chinese Christians for support. Remittances sent by churches in Hong Kong and Southeast Asia proved beneficial to Christians in coastal provinces throughout the Maoist era. Besides material resources, Christian radio broadcasting enterprises in Hong Kong aired programs in Mandarin and local dialects, creating an electronic platform for isolated Christians to form a listening community of believers, seeking spiritual guidance from the outside. Listening to these programs became an important part of the faith practice when the state closed places of worship and prohibited public religious activities.

Ignoring what they could not change, while making use of the situation to preserve their strength, many Protestants and pro-Vatican Catholics kept a low profile and organized diffuse worshiping communities according to their needs, despite persistent interference and systematic control from the state (Cheng 2003). Many elderly believers use the word *chiku*, literally translated as "having tasted bitterness," to characterize their experience of persecution. One Catholic clergy recalls, "When we were bombarded with the anti-Christian propaganda, we had tasted the bitterness. We did not swallow it. We survived" (Carbonneau 2005, 2006). To him, the memory of suffering has a sacramental aspect as it reveals the power of the resurrected faith in a crisis moment. When the Maoist state forced Christians into a suffering mode, it transformed religious persecution into a unique opportunity to gain heavenly rewards. This narrative of suffering brings Christians together, and enables them to sympathize with other victims of socialist policies and to face persecution bravely.

MODERNIZATION WITHOUT LIBERALIZATION SINCE THE 1980s

Deng Xiaoping's economic reform and "open door" policies, after 1978, departed from the anti-religious ideology of the Maoist period. Catholic and Protestant clergy released from labor camps and prisons cautiously took advantage of the new political climate to organize religious activities. They received visitors from Hong Kong and the West, answered questions from faith-seekers, and provided pastoral services. An explosive growth of Christianity was reported nationwide, especially in areas not previously visited by missionaries (Lambert 1994).

Coinciding with the "Christianity fever" of the 1980s, newly released church leaders expressed much suspicion toward the state-controlled patriotic churches. The state founded two parallel ecclesiastical structures with offices at the national, provincial, and district levels to regulate religious activities. In 1978, the Bureau of Religious Affairs supported pro-government Catholics to revive the Chinese Catholic Patriotic Association. In 1980, the government created the National Administrative Commission of the Catholic Church in China and the Chinese Bishops' College to handle pastoral concerns. Pro-Vatican Catholics reached out to Rome and continued their own activities without the state's approval.

To control Protestants, the Bureau of Religious Affairs appointed Bishop K. H. Ting, in 1980, to revive the Three-Self Patriotic Movement. Bishop Ting was instrumental in forming the China Christian Council to manage the internal affairs of the Church. Both the Three-Self Patriotic Movement and the China Christian Council under Bishop Ting's leadership, from 1981 to 1996, served as the state's support for ecclesiological affairs (Hunter and Chan 1993, pp. 139–40). Jointly called "two associations" (*lianghui*), these state-controlled bodies were tasked with rebuilding the Protestant communities the regime could trust. In the following decades, the two associations reinstated the former Three-Self patriotic church leaders of the 1950s (*lao sanzi*), elected and ordained new officially approved pastors, rebuilt the regime-sponsored seminaries, and reclaimed numerous confiscated mission properties.

The Protestants' responses to the top-down policy of co-optation exhibited adverse patterns. The influx of visitors, funding, and religious materials aroused the Communist state. Starting in the late 1980s, the government widened its crackdown on religious printing, church-run bible training programs, and the circulation of imported biblical literature.

Despite these obstacles, believers were relatively free to gather and worship at home until the 1990s. Since there was no formal regulation of religious gatherings outside designated venues, the status of house churches was ambiguous in the eyes of local officials (Human Rights Watch 1992, pp. 55–67).

The 1980s and 1990s saw the proliferation of autonomous house churches that refused to join the Three-Self Patriotic Movement. Despite their conservative theological orientation, these autonomous churches took the Bible seriously, treating it as "a revelatory text inspired by the Holy Spirit and accordingly an authoritative scripture" (Yeh 2010, p. 905). The Ark Church (*Fangzhou jiaohui*) and Watchers Church (*Shouwang jiaohui*) in Beijing attracted disillusioned intellectuals, after the Communist crackdown on the pro-democracy student movement in Tiananmen Square in June 1989, offering them a biblical worldview of personal struggle and social engagement. In 1998, several urban house church networks issued a faith statement to reassert their belief in the Bible and the universal principle of religious liberty, and their efforts to expand Christian spiritual sovereignty to the secular domain, putting them at odds with the Communist state. In response, the government stepped up its grip on religion, fearing foreign infiltration, which was what had happened with the Catholic-supported Solidarity Movement in Poland (Hunter and Chan 1993, pp. 56–7; Dunch 2008, pp. 168–9). The religious crackdown was implemented through a meticulous local registration procedure that targeted independent churches. The rhetoric of "adapting religion to socialist society," advocated by the then-Communist Party Secretary Jiang Zemin, was predicated on an alignment of Protestantism to the socialist state. The regulations of church registration were "temporary" or "draft" ordinances and administrative orders which would later be consolidated in China's first comprehensive "Regulations on Religious Affairs" in 2005 (Yang 2011, p. 76). These policies, further revised in 2017 under the current Communist Party Secretary Xi Jinping, became templates for patriotic religious institutions and local authorities to curb church growth. The registration requirement came with a concerted effort led by the Three-Self Patriotic Movement and the China Christian Council to construct a Protestant orthodoxy in response to the many new Protestant groups that had popped up in the mid-1990s (Dunn 2015, pp. 163–95). In constructing an orthodox Protestant discourse to distinguish proper from improper faith practices, patriotic Christian institutions advocated the discourse of "better church management (*banhao jiaohui*)." The most important document was the 1991 "Trial Document of the Chinese Protestant Church Order for Local Congregation," which states that congregations not violating the Three-Self principles can manage their church affairs based on their "original tradition" (*yuanyou chuantong*), a term referring to former denominational background the Chinese believers have (Chow 2021). The document instructs Christians to respect different denominational heritages and take care of those with unique beliefs. The ecclesiology spelled out in the document recognized, for the first time, Protestant denominationalism in practice.

From the 1990s onward, the new policy context has widened the scope of autonomy for believers. There is a mixture of the diverse traditions of Protestant liturgy within the patriotic churches. Members of the pre-1949 independent Chinese churches, such as the Little Flock, the Jesus Family, and the True Jesus Church, often worship in officially registered churches. The Little Flock still practices the breaking of bread on Sunday evenings and requires women to cover their heads during services (May 2000). The Three-Self Patriotic churches, with many members from the Little Flock tradition, often hold separate Sunday night services. Members of the True Jesus Church and Seventh-Day Adventists observe the Sabbath on Saturday.

Today's Chinese Christianity covers a wide range of groupings, from the Catholic Church and Euro-American Protestant denominations to the pre-1949 Chinese independent churches and newly emerged sectarian movements that borrow loosely and selectively from Christianity. These indigenous churches have adapted Christianity to local cultures and traditions. They see Jesus Christ as holy and fearsome, as one who heals the sick, casts out demons, and performs miracles. Using Christianity as a key to physical recovery and spiritual salvation is common in many parts of the world. At the other end of the theologian spectrum, some Christian apocalyptical groups have organized themselves around charismatic leaders of different house churches. Unfamiliar with the growth of Christian-inspired sectarianism, the state has labeled and persecuted these groups as "evil cults" (*xiejiao*), a political stigma imposed by the state and a religious brand subject to criticism by officially registered patriotic churches and unofficially recognized house churches (Dunn 2015; Kupper 2007). Although the state does not intend to turn the clock back to the Maoist control on religious activities, it has criminalized new Christian groups. The punishment of two leaders of a fundamentalist group called the South China Church in December 2001, and the arrest of a Hong Kong entrepreneur who smuggled 33,000 Bibles to a house church reveal the state's intolerance of unsanctioned church growth (Edelman and Richardson 2005, p. 254).

The most famous Christian sectarian group is probably the Lightning of the East, also known as "Eastern Lightning," in reference to Matt 24:27: "For as the lightning comes from the east and flashes as far as the west, so will be the coming of the Son of Man" (NRSV). Rejecting the doctrine of the Trinity and having renamed the God of Christianity as Lightning, this group denotes China as the exact location where the Almighty God was born. Widely called "the Church of Almighty God" today, it is believed to be founded by Zhao Weishan in his homeland of Heilongjiang Province in northern China. Faced with the state's suppression that followed the criminalization of Falun Gong in 1999, Zhao Weishan left China for the United States in 2000. This movement is primarily "Sinocentric," placing China at the heart of Christian salvation in the end time. Criticizing China as the land of the "great red dragon," an apocalyptic symbol of Satan in the Book of Revelation, it proclaims that the Almighty God has become an incarnate Chinese woman named "Deng," who strives to recruit Chinese believers to save all nations. The movement is probably the most innovative and ambitious indigenous Christian sectarian group, and its success has to do with its publication program that has produced a wide range of sacred scriptures and hymns. Whenever expanding into a specific locality, it often engages local church leaders in a theological discussion and impresses them with its eschatological interpretation of human destiny. Besides recruiting converts from registered and unregistered churches, these Christian sectarians often compete with each other for membership and territory, as shown in a publicized incident of confrontation between the Three Ranks of Servants and the Church of Almighty God in Shandong Province in 2004 (Kahn, November 25, 2004).

Since taking refuge in the United States in 2000, its leader, Zhao Weishan, has made use of his newfound freedom to spread the Almighty God's dispensationalist anti-state eschatology. Previously known for pronouncing the Chinese Communist Party as the anti-Christ and the red dragon, metaphorically depicted in the Book of Revelation, the Church of Almighty God has deepened its theological message to reach out to both Chinese and non-Chinese speakers worldwide. The globalization of this homegrown Chinese Christian sectarian group should not come as a surprise. In fact, the Church of Almighty God follows in the footsteps of some pro-democracy dissidents and other officially banned religious syncretic movements such as Falun Gong and Zhonggong (Practice of Life Preservation and Wisdom Accretion) to adopt "decidedly high-tech, extremely mobile and multifaceted" organizational strategies (Thornton 2003, p. 249). Rebuilding themselves abroad and shifting much of their operations to the online sphere, the group has waged an impressive multi-front campaign against Chinese human rights abuses, using the Internet to pressure Chinese authorities and lobbying national governments and global organizations for help. In the online realm, it positions itself as an open, peaceful, and independent house church movement, and makes use of human rights discourse to enhance its legitimacy. It has coordinated international evangelistic efforts among the Chinese diaspora, circulating the Church's sacred texts in multiple languages, adopting online news formats to provide information about activities, and commenting on Chinese politics on social media. The ease with which their members collaborate with international human rights organizations, and reposition themselves as a persecuted community such as Falun Gong, Tibetan Buddhists, and Uyghur Muslims, has legitimated the Church of Almighty God as a normal Christian movement, empowering its ability to outwit Chinese authorities. Under the human rights banner, the Church of Almighty God has modernized its image, ameliorated the exclusivity of its doctrines, and above all, normalized itself as a socially acceptable Christian religion. Embracing the universal human rights and fundamental freedoms of other faith communities and pro-democracy dissidents, they have found much common ground with victims of Chinese human rights abuses and have crossed the religious boundary to engage in political lobbying and activism.

FUTURE PROSPECTS

As China's economy progresses in this fast-changing era of globalization, people seek prosperity and security. A group of "boss Christians" (*laoban jidutu*) has emerged in major cities like Wenzhou, Shanghai, and Hangzhou. They attribute business success to their faith in Jesus Christ, proclaiming to work for God in the commercial sector. Defending the status quo, they are less concerned with the division between the Three-Self Patriotic churches and unregistered Christian groups. They often mediate between the churches, local authorities, and non-Christians in religious property disputes (Chen and Huang 2004).

Equally significant is the growth of Protestant intellectuals, writers, artists, publishers, lawyers, professionals, and scientists in metropolitan cities such as Beijing, Shanghai, and Guangzhou. Since the 1990s, a number of "cultural Christians" (*wenhua jidutu*) in universities have used Christianity to criticize traditional values for lacking a transcendental understanding of the world. Through the introduction of Christian theology and values to academia, they believe that Christianity is useful in creating a new ethical system for modernization. The younger generation of Christians strives to explore the public role of the Church. Besides participating in charitable works and social services, church leaders are keen on safeguarding the constitutional rights of Christians, opposing the state's harsh policies toward religious minorities and marginalized groups. Some intellectuals and lawyers have even appropriated Christianity as a new political force, using it to reconnect with the West against their own authoritarian state.

In addition, young Christians have taken advantage of social media to proselytize. As social media unites people, it confirms the state's suspicion of the Internet's liberalizing tendencies. A notable example is an immensely popular Christian-run Heymen WeChat public account launched by Zhang Zhenpan in May 2016 in Guangdong Province (Xi 2019, pp. 1016–20). Majoring in architecture at Shantou University, Zhang underwent a journey of soul-searching and decided to assert his Christian identity in the digital sphere, connecting with like-minded believers outside the patriotic churches. With a rich history of Protestant Christianity, Shantou continues to be a hotbed of evangelism (Lee 2018). With the financial support of Hong Kong's Li Ka-Shing Foundation, Shantou University worked with the divinity school of the Chinese University of Hong Kong to find the Center for Christian Studies in the mid-2000s, introducing faith-based life education for undergraduates. This relatively liberal campus enabled tech-savvy Christians to form online networks, addressing moral and social issues through the lens of Christian social ethics.

The popularity of the Heymen WeChat owes much to Beijing's relative tolerance of social media collectivity among Christians. Subsequently, young Christians can implicitly tell the authoritarian state to keep out of their private, spiritual affairs—while challenging the pervasive narratives of state control. Their virtual Christian discourse, framed in theological terms, legitimates grievances against ideological hegemony and reimagines communal space online. Despite its vitality, virtual space remains vulnerable to the state's aggressive censorship. In late 2018, different security and propaganda agencies of the Chinese state countered moves by the

Early Rain Covenant Church in Chengdu, Sichuan Province, and elsewhere with more restrictive regulatory measures. In late December 2019, the state sentenced Pastor Wang Yi, founder of the Early Rain Covenant Church, to nine years in prison for incitement to subvert state power and managing an illegal business operation. The timing of the trial is of great significance, as it marks the end of ecclesiastical autonomy for unofficially registered Protestant house churches. Beijing has completely rejected Wang's efforts to preach and practice the principle of Christian spiritual sovereignty in society.

For nearly three decades, independent house church movements have given Pastor Wang, or people with a similar theological background, a social space to reconcile piety with activism. Moving away from focusing exclusively on spiritual cultivation, the taking up of civic duties signals an attitudinal change among today's Christians. Seeing themselves as God-chosen individuals with a providential destiny, they have dropped the long-held distaste for politics and regard community engagement as a sacred calling to serve God and country. Unfortunately, this moderate form of religious activism is vulnerable to state repression. Beijing has reacted harshly, fearing these Christian activities might challenge the state, in an increasingly diverse environment that is troubled by corrosive class tensions and rapid technological change.

Since assuming power in 2012, Xi Jinping has worried about the spread of Western values and norms amid an economic slowdown. He has revived the teachings of Mao Zedong and Marxism to enforce ideological uniformity and political stability at all levels. The mid-2010s witnessed a tightening control over public religious activities. There was a consistent pattern of church and cross demolitions in Wenzhou, known as China's Jerusalem due to its high concentration of Protestants. Thousands of both patriotic and autonomous churches were targeted, signifying a change in the state's religious policy, from co-opting sympathetic church leaders to suppressing Christian activities at the grassroots level (Chow 2016; Ying 2018). Reluctant to characterize the cross-removal campaign as a national policy, Cao Nanlao (2017) suggests that the campaign should be placed in the larger context of the central government's efforts to control the local culture, renew Confucianism, and Sinicize Christianity. Fenggang Yang, however, criticizes the campaign as "a political experiment to suppress Christianity in the name of non-religious causes," arguing that Xi Jinping actually emboldened the operation after hearing Zhejiang's party secretary report on "Three Rectifications, One Demolition" (Yang 2018, pp. 6,

12). What matters is how ordinary congregants felt about the mistreatment of the churches. The violence afflicted upon the cross—the most sacred Christian symbol—alienated the authorities from the believers. Human rights lawyers who dared to challenge the legality of the campaign were criminalized, a pronounced case being the Christian lawyer Zhang Kai, in Beijing, who was detained in Wenzhou for opposing the legality of cross-removal and was only released after he publicly confessed to the crime of "disturbing the public order" (Wong, March 24, 2016; Chow 2021). Mark McLeister (2018) captures a sense of crisis among some Protestants who have drawn on a body of millenarian beliefs to respond to the persecution policies. Believing in the absolute sovereignty of God in this world, they have striven to be prepared spiritually for coping with the hardship, and turning this hostile moment into a time of great tribulation for the faithful.

The same fear of losing their religious liberty is widespread among pro-Vatican Catholics. Even though China and the Vatican reached a provisional agreement on the appointment of Chinese bishops on September 22, 2018, there has been a mounting degree of unwarranted control and harassment of church activities at the grassroots level. Similar to Protestant churches in Wenzhou, some local authorities tore down the crosses of Catholic patriotic churches and stopped minors from attending Mass. Having conceded to the Chinese state's approval in reviewing candidates for bishop, the Vatican has shown an expansive and complacent signal to China (Criveller 2020, p. 24). Yet, the Sino-Vatican agreement appears to give the state a convenient legal pretext to subdue and take over some underground churches. Several pro-Vatican bishops and priests have allegedly experienced growing oppression by the local authorities, and ordinary Catholics who attend Mass in the patriotic churches feel troubled by these restrictive policies and intimidation measures (Ticozzo 2020, p. 40).

Hopeful Signs of Church-State Encounters

Even though China is taking a more authoritarian turn under Xi's rule, there are some encouraging signs of Church-state interactions in other parts of the Chinese world. In postcolonial Hong Kong and Macau, Catholics and Protestants are indispensable partners for the local authorities in pursuing social services. Their extensive networks of mission schools and hospitals have produced many professionals and government officials. The longstanding Church-state partnership benefits Hong Kong and

Macau, but it discourages Christians from engaging in social and political activism. In a time of rapid change and uncertainty, many Christians have become frustrated with the failure of clergymen to address the public's worries about governance. They can no longer tolerate their church leaders who regard political reflection and civic engagement as taboo. One way to resolve this conflict between church affiliation and personal commitment has been to develop the faith-based NGO as "an alternative way of experiencing Christianity" (Nedilsky 2014). Some prominent Christians organized the Occupy Central with Love and Peace Campaign, an act of civil disobedience that demanded direct democracy in the election of the territory's chief executive and lawmakers, laying the foundation for the Umbrella Movement, the two-and-one-half-month-long peaceful occupation of Hong Kong's commercial districts in late 2014. One of the organizers was the well-known Baptist minister and pro-democracy activist Rev. Chu Yiu-Ming, who pastored a congregation in the working-class district of Chai Wan. This wave of political awakening has prompted Hong Kong Christians to take part in the recent pro-democracy struggle of 2019–2020. The most notable youth activist is Joshua Wong, who sees Christianity as a matter of personal conscience rather than as an instrumental tool with which to appeal to other people yearning for comfort in uncertain times. Wong has said, "Christianity motivates me to care about politics and society. But I am not saying that I am pushing for self-determination because God or Jesus gave me a signal. I don't want religion to become the instrument for me to gain some support and social capital" (Bland 2017, p. 33). In neighboring Macau, the Catholic Diocese expressed its displeasure over images of socialist China being projected at the ruins of the historic Church of the Mother of God, also known as Ruins of St. Paul's, during the celebration of China's National Day on October 1, 2019. These examples suggest that Christians in these former colonies have considered religious piety as compatible with civic engagement (Chow and Lee 2016).

It is in democratic Taiwan where Christians and state officials can engage with each other on an equal basis. The Presbyterian Church in Taiwan played an indispensable role in advancing the country's transition from authoritarianism to democracy. During the martial law era, from 1949 to 1987, Presbyterians partnered with churches in the United States and Europe, utilizing transnational Christian networks to support Taiwanese struggles for democracy. The Presbyterians not only defended the right to self-determination in Taiwan, but also sheltered the *dangwai* ("outside the Nationalist Party") opposition, which later became the pro-independence Democratic Progressive Party. This development eventually brought about the end of one-party rule in Taiwan with the presidential election of March 2000.

CONCLUSION

After several centuries of proselytization, Catholicism and Protestantism have transformed themselves from alien faiths into Chinese religions. In Mainland China, this process of indigenization is characterized by the coexistence of state-controlled patriotic churches and autonomous Christian groups, the growth of Christian-inspired sectarians, and the appeal of Christianity as a new moral-ethical system among the citizenry. The failure of the Communist state to control Christians has given rise to a truly self-supporting, self-governing, self-propagating, and self-theologizing Church. This development has made Christians less vulnerable to state persecution and has allowed them to respond quickly and be flexible to changes.

The Christian expansion in today's China points to the failure of the state to exercise absolute control in the religious sphere. Pro-Vatican Catholics and unregistered Protestant churches are reluctant to accept the subservient role that the Chinese Catholic Patriotic Association and the Three-Self Patriotic Movement have assigned them. They have made use of the hostile situation to preserve their strength, defending the Church's independence from state control. They have liberated themselves from official religious institutions and established autonomous and widespread worshiping communities to cater to their spiritual needs.

Taking into account churches in other Chinese cultural zones, the temporal and spatial variations of Church-state relationships reveal that Chinese Christians are not passive recipients of an ideological conformity that secular authorities have imposed on them. What they have in common, inside and outside Mainland China, is their efforts to make moral conscience an integral part of their societies. When Christians in Hong Kong, Macau, and Taiwan find their secular rulers to be in conflict with their religious and political convictions, they challenge the established elites. Such a contest for moral and spiritual power is key to understanding the evolving patterns of Church-state collaboration and conflict in the Chinese world.

FURTHER READINGS

Chan, K.K. 2019. *Understanding World Christianity: China*. Minneapolis, MN: Fortress Press.

This book offers a concise, informative, and balanced account of the development of Christianity in China today, highlighting the spiritual lessons of the Chinese church growth for the world.

Dunn, E. 2015. *Lightning from the East: Heterodoxy and Christianity in Contemporary China*. Leiden: Brill.

This is the finest case study of the Eastern Lightning, also known as the Church of Almighty God, which proclaims that Jesus Christ has returned to earth as a Chinese woman to judge humankind. This homegrown Christian-inspired movement reveals the complexity of Church-state encounters in Reform China.

Lian, X. 2018. *Blood Letters: The Untold Story of Lin Zhao, A Martyr in Mao's China*. New York: Basic Books.

This biography tells the story of Lin Zhao, a female progressive Christian and Communist activist, who joined the socialist revolution during the 1940s but who ended up as a prisoner of the Maoist state. It documents the violence of persecution facing Christians and dissidents, and reveals the importance of faith and agency in a seemingly hopeless environment.

Mariani, P.P. 2011. *Church Militant: Bishop Kung and Catholic Resistance in Communist Shanghai*. Cambridge, MA: Harvard University Press.

This insightful study of the Church-state conflicts in Shanghai challenges the misconception that the mighty Communist regime was able to consolidate its control with little resistance in the 1950s. It throws light on the resilience of Catholicism at the grassroots level.

Yang, F.G. 2011. *Religion in China: Survival and Revival Under Communist Rule*. Oxford: Oxford University Press.

This account draws on the historical, sociological, and demographic data to explore the resurgence and consolidation of a wide range of Christian communities in post-Maoist China. It highlights the diversity and vitality of fast-growing Chinese churches in urban and rural areas.

REFERENCES

Ashiwa, Y., and D.L. Wank, eds. 2009. *Making Religion, Making the State: The Politics of Religion in Modern China*. Stanford, CA: Stanford University Press.

Bland, B. 2017. *Generation HK: Seeking Identity in China's Shadow*. London: Penguin.

Cao, N. 2011. *Constructing China's Jerusalem: Christians, Power, and Place in Contemporary Wenzhou*. Stanford: Stanford University Press.

————. 2017. Spatial Modernity, Party Building and Local Governance: Putting the Christian Cross-Removal Campaign in Context. *The China Review* 17 (1): 29–52.

Carbonneau, R.E. 2005. Yuanling, Hunan, China: Peace. *The Passionist Heritage Newsletter* 12 (1): 1–3.

————. 2006. Resurrecting the Dead: Memorial Gravesites and Faith Stories of Twentieth-Century Catholic Missionaries and Laity in Western Hunan, China. *U.S. Catholic Historian* 24: 19–37.

Chan, K.K. 2019. *Understanding World Christianity: China.* Minneapolis, MN: Fortress Press.

Chen, C., and T. Huang. 2004. The Emergence of a New Type of Christians in China Today. *Review of Religious Research* 46 (2): 183–200.

Cheng, M.M.C. 2003. House Church Movements and Religious Freedom in China. *China: An International Journal* 1 (1): 16–45.

Chow, C.C.C. 2016. Demolition and Defiance: The Stone Ground Church Dispute (2012) in East China. *The Journal of World Christianity* 6 (2): 250–276.

————. 2021. *Schism: Seventh-day Adventism in Post-Denominational China.* Notre Dame, IN: University of Notre Dame Press.

Chow, C.C.C., and J.T.H. Lee. 2016. Almost Democratic: Christian Activism and the Umbrella Movement in Hong Kong. *Exchange: Journal of Missiological and Ecumenical Research* 45 (3): 252–268.

Criveller, G. 2020. An Overview of the Catholic Church in Post-Mao China. In *People, the Communities, and the Catholic Church in China*, ed. C.Y.Y. Chu and P.P. Mariani, 9–27. New York: Palgrave Macmillan.

Dunch, R. 2008. Christianity and 'Adaptation to Socialism'. In *Chinese Religiosities: Afflictions of Modernity and State Formation*, ed. M.M.H. Yang, 155–178. Berkeley, CA: University of California Press.

Dunn, E. 2015. *Lightning from the East: Heterodoxy and Christianity in Contemporary China.* Leiden: Brill.

Edelman, B., and J.T. Richardson. 2005. Imposed Limitations on Religion in China and the Margin of Appreciation Doctrine. *Journal of Church and State* 47 (2): 243–267.

Hanson, E.O. 1980. *Catholic politics in China and Korea.* Maryknoll, NY: Orbis.

Human Rights Watch. 1992. *Freedom of Religion in China.* New York: Human Right Watch/Asia Watch.

Hunter, A., and K.K. Chan. 1993. *Protestantism in Contemporary China.* Cambridge: Cambridge University Press.

Kahn, J. November 25. 2004. Violence Taints Religion's Solace for China's Poor. *The New York Times.*

Kupper, K.K. 2007. Images of Jesus Christ in Christian Inspired Spiritual and Religious Movements in China Since 1978. In *The Chinese Face of Jesus Christ,* ed. Roman Malek, vol. 3b, 1365–1375. Sankt Augustin: Institut Monumenta Serica and China-Zentrum.

Lambert, T. 1994. *The Resurrection of the Chinese Church*. Wheaton, IL: Harold Shaw.

Lee, J.T.H. 2003. *The Bible and the Gun: Christianity in South China, 1860–1900*. New York: Routledge.

———. 2007. Christianity in Contemporary China: An Update. *Journal of Church and State* 49 (2): 277–304.

———. 2009. Politics of Faith: Christian Activism and the Maoist State in Chaozhou, Guangdong Province. *The China review* 9 (2): 17–39.

———. 2017. Faith and Defiance: Christian Prisoners in Maoist China. *Review of Religion and Chinese Society* 4 (2): 167–192.

———., ed. 2018. *Christianizing South China: Mission, Development, and Identity in Modern Chaoshan*. New York: Palgrave Macmillan.

Lian, X. 2018. *Blood Letters: The Untold Story of Lin Zhao, a Martyr in Mao's China*. New York: Basic Books.

Lin, J. 2017. *Shanghai Faithful: Betrayal and Forgiveness in a Chinese Christian Family*. Lanham, MD: Rowman and Littlefield.

Ling, O.K. 1999. *The Changing Role of the British Protestant Missionaries in China*. London: Associated University Presses.

Madsen, R. 1998. *China's Catholics: Tragedy and Hope in an Emerging Civil Society*. Berkeley, CA: University of California Press.

Mariani, P.P. 2011. *Church Militant: Bishop Kung and Catholic Resistance in Communist Shanghai*. Cambridge, MA: Harvard University Press.

May, G.Y. 2000. *Watchman Nee and the Breaking of Bread: The Missiological and Spiritual Forces that Contributed to an Indigenous Chinese Ecclesiology*. Unpublished Th.D. dissertation, Boston University.

McLeister, M. 2018. Chinese Protestant Reactions to the Zhejiang 'Three Rectifications, Ono Demolition' Campaign. *Review of Religion and Chinese society* 5 (1): 76–100.

Nedilsky, L.V. 2014. *Converts to Civil Society: Christianity and Political Culture in Contemporary Hong Kong*. Waco, TX: Baylor University Press.

Reny, M.E. 2018. *Authoritarian Containment: Public Security Bureaus and Protestant House Churches in Urban China*. New York: Oxford University Press.

Thornton, P.M. 2003. The New Cybersects: Resistance and Repression in the Reform Era. In *Chinese Society, Change, Conflict, and Resistance*, ed. E.J. Perry and M. Selden, 247–270. New York: RoutledgeCurzon.

Ticozzo, S. 2020. The Development of the Underground Church in Post-Mao China. In *People, the Communities, and the Catholic Church in China*, ed. C.Y.Y. Chu and P.P. Mariani, 29–41. New York: Palgrave Macmillan.

Vala, C.T. 2018. *The Politics of Protestant Churches and the Party-State in China: God Above Party?* New York: Routledge.

Wang, G.W. 2004. Secular China. In *Diasporic Chinese Ventures: The Life and Works of Wang Gungwu*, ed. G. Benton and H. Liu, 23–45. London: Routledge.

Wong, E. March 24, 2016. Chinese Lawyer Who was Detained While Defending Churches is Released. *The New York Times*.

Xi, J. 2019. Christian New Media in China: The Gospel Via WeChat. *Asian Survey* 59 (6): 1001–1021.

Yang, F.G. 2011. *Religion in China: Survival and Revival Under Communist Rule*. Oxford: Oxford University Press.

———. 2018. The Failure of the Campaign to Demolish Church Crosses in Zhejiang Province, 2013–2016. *Review of Religion and Chinese Society* 5 (1): 5–25.

Yeh, J.Y.H. 2010. The Bible in China: Interpretations and Consequences. In *Handbook of Christianity in China, Vol.2: 1800–Present*, ed. R.G. Tiedemann, 891–913. Leiden: E.J. Brill.

Ying, F.T. 2018. The Politics of Cross Demolition: A Religio-Political Analysis of the 'Three Rectifications and One Demolition' Campaign in Zhejiang Province. *Review of Religion and Chinese Society* 5 (1): 43–75.

CHAPTER 13

Public Shrine Ritual or Private Religion? Yasukuni Shrine and the Precarious Secularism of Modern Japan

Ernils Larsson

INTRODUCTION

The invention of "religion" as a category in Japan coincided with the rapid modernization during the second half of the nineteenth century, which saw the country transform from an isolated feudal state into an imperial nation-state. Through the Meiji Restoration of 1868, whereby the samurai leadership of the former state was replaced by a civilian government dominated by the wealthy merchant class, the emperor was granted the position as the nation's supreme political and spiritual leader. According to the mytho-historical narrative of the nation, Japanese emperors ruled by virtue of their status as descendants of the sun goddess Amaterasu

E. Larsson (✉)
Centre for Multidisciplinary Research on Religion and Society (CRS),
Uppsala Universitet, Uppsala, Sweden

The Organization for the Advancement of Research and Development,
Kokugakuin University, Tokyo, Japan
e-mail: ernils.larsson@teol.uu.se

© The Author(s), under exclusive license to Springer Nature
Switzerland AG 2023
S. Holzer (ed.), *The Palgrave Handbook of Religion and State
Volume II*, https://doi.org/10.1007/978-3-031-35609-4_13

283

Ōmikami, through an unbroken line stretching back to the first emperor, Jimmu (Hardacre 2017, 323–354). When Japan enacted its first modern constitution in 1890 (the "Meiji Constitution"), this narrative was reflected in the legal text through the preamble, which made clear that the document was a gift from the emperor to his imperial subjects. The constitution established that as the sovereign of the nation, the emperor was "sacred and inviolable," and through his office he was granted supreme command over the nation's military and naval forces. Thus, although the reinvented Japanese nation-state of the Meiji period (1868–1912) was established as a bicameral parliamentary democracy, supreme leadership rested with the divinely sanctioned emperor (Shimazono 2017, 33–35).

Despite the imperial institution's preeminent role in the nascent nation-state, Japan under the Meiji constitutional system was a secular state. The constitution of 1890 established a distinct sphere of social life designated for religion, and the state was formally separated from this sphere. The new constitution of 1947, introduced during the occupation of Japan after World War II, did not signal a move from "state religion" to "secularism," so much as it indicated a change in *how* religion was understood as a legal and social category in Japan. Both constitutional systems contained provisions for distinguishing between the two distinct spheres of "religion" and "not-religion," with the key difference being how the boundaries of these spheres were understood (Thomas 2019, 17–21). This chapter will explore how religion has been framed under Japan's two modern constitutional regimes. The discussion will focus on the central question of whether Shinto is a *public* expression of nationhood or a *private* belief of individual citizens; a question widely debated in Meiji era society and of continuing relevance to this day. I will use the case of Yasukuni Shrine to illustrate how this question has manifested under both regimes, as well as to show why the definition of religion continues to be a topic of significant political importance in contemporary Japan.

THE MEIJI RESTORATION AND THE UNITY OF RITUAL AND GOVERNMENT

The Meiji Constitution represented the outcome of several decades of negotiation regarding the category of religion in Japan. As the country opened up for trade and diplomatic relations with the Western powers, demands for freedom to practice Christianity soon followed (Maxey 2014, 58–72). While these demands originally focused on the rights of Westerners stationed at trade posts around the country, they were soon expanded to include the general freedom to proselytize in Japan. This forced Japanese lawmakers and statesmen to not only negotiate the limits of these freedoms, but also to decide what exactly freedom of religion would mean in a Japanese context (Josephson 2012, 71–78). As Helen Hardacre has put it, in pre-Meiji Japan "there existed no concept of religion as a general phenomenon, of which there would be local variants like Christianity, Buddhism, and Shintō," and "no word existed to designate a separate sphere of life that could be called 'religious,' as opposed to the rest of one's existence" (Hardacre 1991, 18). While it was eventually agreed that the Sino-Japanese compound *shūkyō* would be used as the equivalent of the Latinate term *religion*, the question of what was to be included in this category and how such entities should relate to and be regulated by the state proved more complex.

The opening of Japan for trade and diplomatic interaction with foreign powers in the mid-nineteenth century coincided with the rise to prominence of a school of thought known as "National Learning" (*kokugaku*). While the roots of National Learning can be found in a philological method for studying the Japanese language developed in the seventeenth century, by the late Tokugawa period (1603–1868) it had developed into a nativist movement concerned with reinvigorating the original essence of the Japanese people (Hardacre 2017, 323–354). A significant part of this endeavor was the introduction of new interpretations of Shinto as representing the *original* beliefs of Japan, understood in stark contrast to the *foreign* teachings of the Buddha. As the Japanese leadership began to reinvent and modernize the state after 1854, they did so based both on Western forms of modernity and with inspiration from National Learning. Significantly, ideas about a Japanese *essence* that could be found in the writings of scholars of National Learning coincided with current trends in Western thinking, most importantly with the paradigm of nationalism. As Japan was gradually remolded into a nation-state, a process which culminated in the 1868 Meiji Restoration, Shinto became firmly intertwined in the new notion of Japanese national identity (Isomae 2012, 184–189).

While the question of when exactly "Shinto" arrived as a meaningful category remains a divisive issue in the scholarly community, it is hard to deny that the five decades of the Meiji period saw a significant transformation of the heterogeneous myths, shrines, and rites that constituted pre-Meiji Shinto (Breen and Teeuwen 2010, 7–13; Zhong 2016, 182–185). Of particular importance was the government edict issued in 1868 that ordered the separation of Buddhas from gods (*kami*), thereby creating the two distinct discursive spheres of "Buddhism" and "Shinto" in Imperial

Japan (Hardacre 2017, 368–371). The edict was followed by a large-scale purge of Buddhist iconography and architecture from what was now understood to be *Shinto* shrines all across the country, as what Kuroda Toshio has described as the "secular face" of Buddhism (Kuroda 1981) was reinvented as its own theological entity. Although the question of whether or not there exists a Shinto orthodoxy is still up for debate (Rots 2017, 25–29), the rise of Shinto to the forefront of national identity in the second half of the nineteenth century saw a number of ideas gain prominence, many of which continue to play a significant role in contemporary understandings of Shrine Shinto.

One example of this can be found in the intimate ties between Shinto and the imperial institution (Shimazono 2017, 98–105). Whereas the emperor has historically played the dual role of mediator between gods and people and protector of the Buddha's law (Kuroda 1996), the Meiji Restoration saw him shred of any Buddhist associations and reinstated as a figurehead of the nation, intimately tied to the increasingly dominant idea of Shinto as an aspect of the Japanese national essence. In support of this transformation, many rites related to the imperial system that had reflected the emperor's syncretic position were reimagined as exclusively Shinto in nature. This included the *daijōsai* ceremony, during which the emperor shares a ritual meal with Amaterasu Ōmikami, that continues to be carried out whenever a new emperor ascends the throne (Breen and Teeuwen 2010, 184–193). Related to the transformation of the emperor into the head of the Japanese "family state" (*kazoku kokka*) (Morris-Suzuki 1998, 84–85), garbed exclusively in Shinto apparel, were the debates on what gods and, consequently, shrines would hold paramount significance for the nation. While the god Ōkuninushi-no-mikoto, with his main shrine at Izumo, had been a strong competitor for this position (Zhong 2016, 165–182), by the 1870s it was clear that it was the sun goddess Amaterasu Ōmikami who would gain preeminence in the national narrative, in large part due to her role as primogenitor of the imperial family (Hardacre 2017, 380–381). As a consequence, her main shrine at Ise was granted the status of highest shrine in the nation, to "which all Japanese were putatively connected by a tie of common descent from the imperial house and a concomitant obligation of obeisance" (Hardacre 1991, 84).

Despite some early advocates for the establishment of Shinto as a "state religion" in Japan (Maxey 2014, 25–32), such a system was never implemented. Instead, a policy was enforced which separated "teachings" (*kyō/oshie*) from "ritual" (*sai*) by essentially establishing the former as "private" and the latter as "public." While the origins of this policy can be found in various schools linked to late Tokugawa period National Learning, it became official policy in March of 1868, three months after the Meiji Restoration. Through the state directive known as *saisei-itchi* ("the unity of ritual and government"), ritual was positioned in a fundamentally separate social sphere from "teachings." The state and its representatives were concerned with ritual, which was viewed as a means of uniting the Japanese people in common morals and ideals, whereas teachings were eventually moved entirely to the private sphere (Isomae 2012, 191–193; Teeuwen 2017). By the time the Meiji Constitution came into effect in November of 1890, Shinto was understood to form the basis for state ritual and, consequently, was excluded from the legal category of religion. Ritual served to unite the people through various compulsory expressions of adherence to the state, including revering the imperial institution, worshiping at state shrines, and participating in public shrine rituals. While this system was at times described by outside observers as the "state religion" of Imperial Japan, this was in fact not the case. The Meiji Constitution contained no clause for the establishment of a state religion (Maxey 2014, 185–193).

Having said that, religion was still a legal category under the Meiji constitutional system. Article 28 of the Meiji Constitution stipulated that "Japanese subjects shall, within limits not prejudicial to peace and order, and not antagonistic to their duties as subjects, enjoy freedom of religious belief" (quoted in Larsson 2020, 116). It is worth noting that the text in the constitution did not rely on the neology *shūkyō* to denote "religion" in "freedom of religion," instead using the term *shinkyō*. Jason Josephson has argued that this choice was quite deliberate, as *shinkyō* (literally "belief in teachings") emphasizes that the guarantee is primarily aimed at private belief and does not necessarily extend to "a freedom of association, political action or indeed anything that could be externalized in public" (Josephson 2012, 232). This again comes back to the divide noted earlier: whereas Shinto ritual was situated in the public sphere, *religion* was a matter of individual belief and practice, conditioned on the subject's adherence to state norms. Josephson has suggested that religion under the Meiji constitutional system should be understood as a "paradoxically optional set of beliefs between state truths and banned delusions" (Josephson 2012, 260), with Shinto inhabiting the space of state-sanctioned reality.

It could be argued that the modern understanding of religion as a concept in Japan was modeled on Western Christianity (Josephson 2012,

76–77). While this is hardly unique to Japan, it is significant for the current discussion, as it also had a major effect on the other traditions that were eventually reimagined as Japanese religions. Christianity is in many ways the main reason for why Japanese lawmakers had to negotiate the category of religion to begin with, as the opening of Japan in 1854 brought with it demands from the Western powers for the implementation of freedom of religion. While these demands primarily concerned the freedom of Christianity, through an intellectual and political debate spanning decades, the contours of the Japanese term *shūkyō* eventually took form (Maxey 2014, 232–238). Although much of these debates are beyond the scope of this chapter (see Josephson 2012, 164–223), the end result was that by the turn of the twentieth century, religion was generally understood as including three major traditions: Christianity, Buddhism, and Sectarian Shinto (*kyōha shintō*). All three main denominations of Christianity had established a foothold in Japan soon after the country's opening, and the subsequent two decades saw a gradual ease of restrictions until, in the 1870s, general proselytization was eventually allowed. When the Religious Organizations Law was introduced in 1939, which put pressure on religious actors to join together into larger organizations, the Catholic Church had fifteen dioceses in the Japanese mainland and there were hundreds of independent and semi-independent Protestant congregations (Krämer 2011).

Japanese Buddhism underwent a fundamental transformation during the second half of the nineteenth century. Following the forced separation of Buddhas from the gods, it became clear that Buddhism would no longer enjoy the position of state-endorsed teaching which it had commanded during the Tokugawa period, and was instead relegated to the private sphere of religion. With this came pressure to adapt to the limits set on what a recognized and tolerated religion was allowed to teach, something which contributed to a purge from the tradition of anything that could be considered a "superstition" (*meishin*), in order for it to better correspond to the supposedly rational ideals of Western modernity (Josephson 2006). A similar effect played a role in the transformation of the various heterogeneous forms of *kami* worship in Japan that eventually resulted in the establishment of thirteen legally recognized Shinto sects (*kyōha*). While some of these were based on a founder's revealed teachings and others on earlier local forms of worship, under the heading of Sectarian Shinto they were tolerated by the state, as long as they accepted their position as purveyors of *teachings*, not of national *ritual* (Hardacre 2017, 381–387).

This distinction is also echoed in the debates surrounding the use of the term "shrine" (*jinja*) and "church" (*kyōkai*), with the general idea being that the former was limited to institutions of state ritual, whereas the latter could be used by religious organizations (Zhong 2016, 188–189).

While there is some debate regarding the applicability of the term "secular" in Japan (see Teeuwen 2017), it is hard to deny that from a purely legal point of view, Imperial Japan was a secular state. Religion was firmly situated in the private sphere, separated from the state and from the public, and religion was clearly distinguished from "not-religion" under law. As Jolyon Thomas has argued, however, the problem is that "not everyone agreed on where to draw the line" (Thomas 2019, 20). This somewhat ambiguous model, whereby shrines were situated in the public sphere and religion in the private, has been referred to as "the Shinto secular" by Josephson (2012, 255), but it is more commonly referred to as "State Shinto" (*kokka shintō*). While the origins of the term can be traced back to scholars in Imperial Japan (Mullins 2021, 10–13), it has been argued by Jolyon Thomas that State Shinto was primarily created by American policymakers as a way of conceptualizing a Japanese state religion at a time when the country formally did not have one (Thomas 2019, 141–165). As a concept, State Shinto became widely used by academics in the postwar period to denote the pre-1945 ideological order in Imperial Japan. It was popularized in the Japanese scholarly vocabulary through the works of Murakami Shigeyoshi (e.g., Murakami 1970), and has since been further developed as an academic category by, among others, Shimazono Susumu, who uses State Shinto to refer to a range of practices related to the imperial institution, shrine ritual, and theories on "national polity" (*kokutai*) (e.g., Shimazono 2017).

While State Shinto remains popular among scholars both in and outside of Japan, the term has become somewhat divisive (Hardacre 2017, 355–357). It is often used in a manner echoing the definition presented in the December 15, 1945, Directive for the Disestablishment of State Shinto ("the Shinto Directive"), in which it was described as "that branch of Shinto which by official acts of the Japanese Government has been differentiated from the religion of Shrine Shinto and has been classified as a nonreligious national cult" (quoted in Larsson 2017, 228). As used in the directive, State Shinto can be seen as essentially referring to "bad" Shinto, whereas the disestablished form of Shinto, today commonly known as "Shrine Shinto" (*jinja shintō*), becomes "good" Shinto (Thomas 2019, 144–150). This understanding can be used as a rhetorical tool to claim that State Shinto is a thing of the past and to argue against those who worry that state interactions with Shinto shrines signal a return to the pre-1945 ideological order. Since State Shinto was disestablished under the Allied occupation, it becomes fully relegated to the past, as an ideology only present during the period 1868–1945 and supposedly with no relevance in today's society (e.g., Larsson 2020, 243–252). As Shimazono has argued, however, many of the variegated ideological trends which are grouped together under the heading State Shinto, including emperor worship and various ideas of Japanese uniqueness, continue to have a lingering appeal in contemporary society (Shimazono 2017, i–ix).

However, the perhaps most damning issue with State Shinto as a category is that it perpetuates the notion that pre-1945 Japan had an established state religion. It must be emphasized again that this was not the case. The legal framework prior to 1945, including the Meiji Constitution of 1890 and the Religious Organizations Law of 1939, clearly established the boundaries for religion under law, and fully distinguished between religion and not-religion. While it is possible to take a functionalist approach to the matter and argue that State Shinto constituted a *de facto* "state religion," when seeking to understand the complexities of postwar debates about the role of shrines in public society, one must recognize that shrine ritual in pre-1945 Japan was not part of the discursive field of *religion*. What took place at shrines across the empire was not conceptualized as expressions of private *belief*, but as public manifestations of *nationhood*.

Yasukuni Shrine and the Public Veneration of Heroic Spirits

Yasukuni Shrine was founded in 1869 as *Tōkyō Shōkonsha*, or "Tokyo shrine to welcome the spirits," as a place where the "heroic spirits" (*eirei*) of those who gave their lives for the new Meiji regime could be enshrined. It was built on Kudan hill in central Tokyo, a location chosen specifically for its proximity to the imperial palace (Takenaka 2017, 23–24). Behind the initiative to erect the shrine was Ōmura Masujirō, a military commander who led the imperial forces to victory in the civil war that led to the ousting of the feudal regime, and who has since become revered as the founder of Japan's modern army (Nelson 2003, 447). The first enshrinement ritual took place over five days in June and July of 1869, when the spirits of

3588 imperial soldiers were enshrined at Tōkyō Shōkonsha (Takenaka 2017, 24). This enshrinement was symptomatic of a new trend in Japanese religious life, where the responsibility for venerating and pacifying the spirits of certain dead shifted from the Buddhist clergy to the Shinto priesthood. The first modern rituals aimed at comforting the war dead were conducted by both Shinto and Buddhist priests, but as the new regime demanded the construction of *shōkonsha* throughout the nation, these rituals became the exclusive domain of the Shinto priesthood. This also indicated a significant shift in which the practice of pacifying the spirits of all those who died in battle, which had been common throughout the Tokugawa period, was replaced by a practice where only those who fell on the imperial side were enshrined (Nelson 2003, 446–450). As one postwar critic of Yasukuni Shrine has argued, this was a clear break with Japan's "traditional view of the dead," which was characterized by postmortem "equality of friend and foe" (*onshin byōdō*) (Anzai 1998, 199–201).

Over the next decade, the number of enshrined spirits increased, as those who fell in the civil war were joined by soldiers who died in Imperial Japan's first overseas adventure in Taiwan in 1874, as well as by those who fought for the imperial regime during the rebellions of 1874 and 1877. In 1879, the government announced that Tōkyō Shōkonsha would be renamed Yasukuni Shrine (*Yasukuni-jinja*, "land at peace shrine"), while also granting it the status of special state-funded shrine (*bekkaku kanpeisha*) (Hardacre 1991, 84–85). As Takenaka Akiko has argued, through this designation "the rituals and physical structures associated with the use of the war dead for political purposes were institutionalized" (Takenaka 2017, 45). While Tōkyō Shōkonsha had originally been a rather minor site of worship and veneration, by the time it was granted its new name and status it had become a major cultural institution in the rapidly growing imperial capital. Besides the major festivals that took place in the spring and autumn, the shrine grounds also hosted various sports events, horse races, and cultural activities. In February of 1882, the *Yūshūkan* war museum opened on the shrine grounds, dedicated to informing the imperial subjects about Japan's military victories, and in 1893 the first Western-style bronze statue made by a Japanese artist was erected on the shrine grounds—an imposing statue of Ōmura placed at the center of an open plaza close to the shrine gates. By the late 1800s, Yasukuni Shrine had become a central institution of public life in the Japanese capital, dedicated to the nation's military but at the same time a site of pleasure and celebration (Takenaka 2017, 54–67).

Yasukuni Shrine stood at the center of what Helen Hardacre has called the "cult of the war dead" (Hardacre 1991, 79–80). Rituals surrounding the war dead were situated in the public sphere more or less from the outset, clearly distinguished from the field of private religious belief. Already in 1872, at a time when the relationship between Shinto shrines and the state had not yet been formalized, Yasukuni Shrine was placed under the direct control of the army and navy ministries. Two years later, the emperor visited the shrine for the first time to pray for the spirits of the war dead, marking the first time that a Japanese emperor paid his respects to fallen commoners and nobility alike (Nelson 2003, 450). It is worth noting that this first visit coincided with the start of the emperor's more "public" role, as a visible father figure for the people of the nation. Shedding his traditional garb, beginning in September of 1872 the emperor would be seen wearing a formal military uniform during his recurring tours (*junkō*) of the empire (Kim 2011, 73–75). This was in stark contrast to the role the emperor had prior to the Meiji Restoration, when he had lived in seclusion in Kyoto, communicating only with a few select court nobles. In his new role, the emperor was supreme commander of Japan's military forces, father of the Japanese people, and a manifest god. It was in this capacity that the Meiji emperor made his seven visits to Yasukuni Shrine, the Taishō emperor his two, and Hirohito, the Shōwa emperor, his twenty visits prior to the Japanese defeat in 1945 (Hardacre 2017, 395).

While nominally a shrine, by the turn of the twentieth century Yasukuni and the cult of the war dead had become a matter of national significance, as closely integrated with the modern conception of Japanese nationalism as the emperor system. As Japan turned toward authoritarianism and militarism after the brief period of Taishō era (1912–1926) democracy, Yasukuni came to play an even more significant role in the public narrative of the nation. By 1879, the number of enshrined spirits was still relatively low, but as Japan's imperial ambitions increased, these numbers rose dramatically. Following the First Sino-Japanese War in 1894–1895, more than 13,000 fallen soldiers were enshrined at Yasukuni. Ten years later, the hard-fought victory in the Russo-Japanese War added another 88,000 fallen to this number. These numbers pale in comparison to the more than 2.3 million soldiers who were enshrined during and after the Second Sino-Japanese War and World War II (Takahashi 2005, 81–82). At the time of Japan's surrender on August 15, 1945, most imperial subjects had friends or family enshrined at Kudan hill, as well as at one of Yasukuni's many subsidiary shrines throughout the empire. Each prefecture and colonial holding had a designated "nation-protecting shrine" (*gokoku-jinja*), in which the heroic spirits of local soldiers could be enshrined. On the village level, the most common expressions of this national ritual system were the war memorials (*chūkonhi*) raised in public sites, often school grounds, at which residents could pay their respect to the spirits of local soldiers (Hardacre 1991, 92–93). As war became a project of the nation-state, the process of mourning and honoring became a national duty.

It is important to keep in mind that enshrinement was never optional. The national cult surrounding the war dead was a public matter, not affected by private belief. Regardless of what faith a soldier might have practiced in life, in death his spirit merged with those of all the empire's war dead as a single divine form (Takenaka 2017, 93). This was true of imperial subjects from the Japanese mainland as well as from the colonies, as thousands of soldiers and conscripts from Okinawa, Korea, and Taiwan were enshrined as heroic spirits at Kudan hill (Tanaka 2007, 219–231). Since enshrinement at Yasukuni was never part of the discursive field of *religion*, it created an equality in death for all the nation's fallen soldiers that trumped any private beliefs of individual subjects. Thus, while the family of a Christian soldier would be at liberty to hold a Christian memorial service following his death in battle, the state would ensure that his spirit was also enshrined at Yasukuni. Takahashi Tetsuya has described this paradigm as the separation of religion from "national ritual" (*kokka no saishi*) (Takahashi 2005, 138–139). Subjects had the freedom to believe in teachings and practice religion as a private matter, but the rituals of the state were compulsory for all imperial subjects. The rituals for the war dead at Yasukuni Shrine are a prime example of how this system manifested in the daily lives of the people.

Religious freedom was always conditional under the Meiji constitutional system, yet as the nation turned to militarism and as the number of fallen soldiers increased, pressure to comply with national ritual increased. Christian churches and Buddhist denominations had to find ways to accommodate the Shinto rituals endorsed by the state, or risk persecution under increasingly draconian laws. Before the turn of the twentieth century, most controversies focused on the question of the sacred nature of the imperial institution, but after the introduction of the Peace Preservation Law in 1925, the state struck down with greater force on any dissenting movement. While the main targets of the law were the political opponents of the governing order, in particular socialists and communists, the law also targeted those religious groups that questioned the ideological foundation of the state (Thomas 2019, 125). This included Japanese new religious movements such as Ōmotokyō and Hito-no-michi Kyōdan (PL Church) as well as Western churches such as Jehovah's Witnesses. The latter was effectively eliminated in the country after the introduction of the Peace Preservation Law in 1933, since the Witnesses' position on matters of nationalism, military service, and emperor worship was incompatible with the ideology of Imperial Japan (Wah 2002).

As a result of increasing government pressure, most religious organizations found ways to compromise with state ritual. Beginning in the 1910s, the state began to put increasing pressure on educational institutions to include proper veneration of the imperial institution and participation in shrine rites in the curricula (Hardacre 2017, 418–422). While many Christian educational institutions were originally defiant in the face of these directives, as the period of Taishō democracy ended and the state turned to authoritarianism, the major congregations adapted. The Catholic Church had attempted to resist many of the new initiatives, but following a major dispute in 1932 with government authorities about student participation in rituals at Yasukuni Shrine, the Vatican issued the 1936 Propaganda Fide, declaring that shrine rites had "only a purely civil value" and were therefore not at odds with the Christian faith (Wildman Nakai 2017, 115). By the 1940s, the leadership of both the Catholic Church and the Protestant United Church of Christ in Japan (UCCJ, formed in 1940 following the introduction of the Religious Organizations Law) was generally compliant with state directives to partake in public rituals at national shrines, while also accepting the emperor's position within the divinely sanctioned family state (Takahashi 2005, 133–139).

The same was true for other major denominations that might have had theological reasons for distancing themselves from state ritual. The major Buddhist denominations had adapted to the Meiji constitutional system after 1868, often accommodating the compulsory shrine rites without major friction on an institutional level (Takahashi 2005, 139–145). This included the widely practiced non-monastic Shin Buddhism. Despite the fact that the denomination's founder, the thirteenth-century Buddhist sage Shinran, had taken a clear position against the worship of spirits, the major branches of Shin Buddhism became early supporters of the imperial state and of the enshrinement of military dead at Yasukuni. While individual actors within the denomination would voice dissent and even face imprisonment for their opposition to state practices, it was only several decades into the postwar period that Shin Buddhist institutions began to pivot on the issue. Today, Shin Buddhists are often at the forefront of opposition to state patronage of Yasukuni Shrine, while many are also struggling with the denomination's history of compliance with a militarist state (Larsson 2020, 262–306).

Yasukuni Shrine was a public space of national significance under the Meiji constitutional system. The shrine maintained a special relationship with the state from the time of its founding and operated under the direct supervision of the army and navy ministries. After 1874, when the disparate memorials dedicated to fallen soldiers that had been constructed across Japan were redesignated as *shōkonsha*, the government took full responsibility for the financing and maintenance of these institutions (Takenaka 2017, 45–50). This relationship became even clearer after 1939, when the prefectural *shōkonsha* were rebranded as nation-protecting shrines. The cult of the war dead was thus closely intertwined with the Japanese state, as a central aspect of modern national identity. While the cult of the war dead took its inspiration from older customs concerned with how to deal with untimely death (Takenaka 2017, 27–36), the practices that developed around Yasukuni Shrine were, like the imperial institution, in many ways examples of "invented traditions" of the modern nation-state (Shimazono 2017, 23–29). Yasukuni filled a role similar to national war cemeteries in other nation-states, as a place where everyone from the supreme leadership of the nation to the families of fallen soldiers could pay their respect to the spirits of those who gave their lives for Japan. It was a site veiled in a shroud of post-restoration Shinto symbolism, but also an institution assumed to inhabit a secular space of national importance for all imperial subjects, irrespective of their individual private beliefs.

Shrine Shinto as a Postwar Religion

On August 15, 1945, Emperor Hirohito announced that Japan would accept the terms of the Potsdam Declaration, effectively ending World War II in Asia. Japan thereby accepted an unconditional surrender and became subject to occupation by the victorious Allied powers following the formal surrender on September 2. For the next seven years, until Japan regained independence on April 28, 1952, the country was thoroughly reshaped by what John Dower has called a "neocolonial military dictatorship" (Dower 2000, 80–81). Under the leadership of the Supreme Commander for the Allied Powers (SCAP), General Douglas MacArthur, for much of its first year the nominally allied occupation was dominated by the United States (Dower 2000, 73). Many of the major reforms were carried out during this period of American leadership, including the complete rewrite of the constitution. SCAP originally wanted the occupied government to carry out this work, but it soon became apparent that the Japanese statesmen had little interest in implementing the thorough democratic amendments demanded by the occupation. As a consequence, in February of 1946, SCAP assembled a small workgroup of predominately American servicemen, who were given the task of writing a new Japanese constitution in little over a week. Originally written in English, the draft was then translated into Japanese and presented to Prime Minister Shidehara Kijūrō on March 6, 1946. After a brief period of negotiations and some minor amendments, the constitution was approved by the diet and came into effect on May 3, 1947 (Dower 2000, 346–404).

To understand the effects the new constitution would have on how religion has been understood in postwar Japan, it is important to note how hostile the occupying powers were to the idea of state-promoted shrine rituals (Mullins 2021, 35–41). As far as SCAP was concerned, Shinto was a religion, and as such should be treated in exactly the same way as other religions. The first formal step toward ensuring such equality was the December 15, 1945, Shinto Directive. Building on findings established in a memorandum published two weeks prior, the directive was issued through the Allied headquarters and aimed to ensure that Shinto would immediately be fully separated from the state (Hardacre 1991, 133–139). This essentially meant that all Shinto institutions that had previously been publicly funded suddenly found themselves on their own and without any source of income, as the "heretical secularism" of State Shinto was replaced with a new form of secularism, building on American understandings of what constituted religion and not-religion (Thomas 2019, 141–165). At the same time, the Shinto Directive also signaled a new role for Shinto, as it was proclaimed that "Shrine Shinto … will be recognized as a religion if its adherents so desire and will be granted the same protection as any other religion" (quoted in Larsson 2020, 135).

The rights and restrictions of religion in Japan were codified under Articles 20 and 89 of the new constitution (Hardacre 2017, 449–451). Article 20 ensured that unconditional religious freedom was guaranteed to all citizens and that religious organizations were fully separated from the state:

- Freedom of religion is guaranteed to all. No religious organization shall receive any privileges from the State, nor exercise any political authority.
- No person shall be compelled to take part in any religious act, celebration, rite or practice.
- The State and its organs shall refrain from religious education or any other religious activity.

This was complemented through Article 89, which prohibits the use of public money for the support of religious organizations:

No public money or other property shall be expended or appropriated for the use, benefit or maintenance of any religious institution or association, or for any charitable, educational or benevolent enterprises not under the control of public authority.

Through these two articles a clear wall of separation was erected between religion and the state, yet it is worth noting that the articles do not define "religion" (*shinkyō, shūkyō*) or "religious" (*shūkyō-teki, shūkyō-jō*). The Allied servicemen drafting the constitution assumed an understanding of religion in line with the principles of the Shinto Directive, according to which Shrine Shinto would be fully understood as a religion, but they did not articulate this in the text (Tanaka 2007, 11–13). Instead, they relied on Japanese courts of law to interpret religion in a way that prevented renewed ties between shrines and state. The constitution also did not specify the term "religious organization" (*shūkyō-dantai*), but this was done through the new Religious Juridical Persons Law that was drafted over a period of eighteen months in 1949–1951 by a group consisting of religious leaders, Japanese government officials, and representatives of the occupation forces. The law came into effect on April 3, 1951, and provided detailed provisions for how organizations could organize as religions as well as what their rights and duties would be (Woodard 1972, 93–102). Like the constitution, the law did not provide a general definition of religion, but it established that a "religious organization" is "an organization with the principal objective of spreading a religious teaching, conducting ceremonial events, and promoting the indoctrination of believers" (quoted in Larsson 2020, 155–156). What this means is that in general, any association formally registered as a religious juridical person (*shūkyō-hōjin*) constitutes a "religious organization" in legal terms. The question of whether actions conducted by a religious organization should count as "religious activity," however, has proved more complex.

As it was clear from the outset of the occupation that Shinto would be separated from the state, shrine leadership immediately began planning for how to organize under the new regime (Mullins 2021, 62–67). While there were some initial discussions about whether shrines should agree to organize as religious associations, following the Religious Juridical Persons Directive of December 28, 1945, a number of leaders from various major shrines filed an application to register the National Association of Shinto Shrines (*Jinja Honchō*, NASS) as a religious juridical person. This status was confirmed after the introduction of the Religious Juridical Persons Law in 1951 (Woodard 1972, 190–193). During the occupation NASS served primarily as an organization monitoring the interests of the shrine world vis-à-vis the occupation authorities, in particular with regard to issues of land ownership, but as Japan regained independence in 1952, the organization gradually shifted gears to focus on reviving the ties between Shinto and the Japanese state. NASS and its political branch, the Shinto Association for Spiritual Leadership (*Shintō seiji renmei*), have been key players in the movement to reintroduce practices that were ended during the occupation, in what John Breen and Mark Teeuwen have described as an attempt to "replicate the imperial 'form' of prewar society, so far as the Constitution allows" (Breen and Teeuwen 2010, 200). This has mani- fested in the involvement of Shrine Shinto organizations in the successful campaigns to reinstate the National Foundation Day (*Kenkoku kinen-hi*) as a national holiday in 1966, to legislate the imperial reign name system under the Era Name Law in 1979, and to grant the national flag and anthem official legal status in 1999 (Mullins 2021, 80–82). Since the 1990s, NASS has been increasingly concerned with the question of consti- tutional reform (Larsson 2017).

Under the postwar constitutional system, NASS is organized as a com- prehensive religious juridical person, with approximately 80,000 individ- ual affiliated shrines. This includes major institutions of national significance under the pre-1945 regime, such as Ise Shrine, but also a majority of the minor shrines that exist in towns and villages throughout Japan. Yasukuni Shrine is not organized under NASS, however, but is registered as a fully independent religious juridical person (Larsson 2020, 157–162). It could be argued that the term Shrine Shinto when used in a postwar context broadly refers to NASS and its affiliated shrines, but it is important to note that all shrines maintain a high degree of independence. While Shrine Shinto priests generally receive their formal training at one of two Shinto universities, Kokugakuin University or Kōgakkan University, where much of the teaching is informed by scholars and priests affiliated with NASS, each shrine is an independent institution. Most shrines do not receive any financial support from NASS, but are often expected to contribute financially to the national organization. Instead, shrines in the postwar era rely on worshipers' offerings, festivals, payment for rites, and sales of amulets for their income. For major shrines this income is enough to maintain a large staff, but in depopulated rural regions many shrine priests struggle to make ends meet (Breen and Teeuwen 2010, 202–203).

Postwar Japan is for all intents and purposes a secular society under law, where religion and not-religion are effectively compartmentalized and where the state is strictly prohibited from interfering with or promoting any religion. Having said that, there is still little societal consensus with regard to how religion should be understood as a category. As Horii Mitsutoshi has shown, when used in popular discourse the category of "religion" can be understood in a multitude of ways, including as ethics and morals, cultural tradition, and as restricted to new religious movements (Horii 2018, 87–122). While often used negatively about the dogmatism of others, Horii argues that the term can also produce positive connotations with regard to one's own family practices. In short, "*shūkyō* [religion] is an important rhetorical tool in Japanese popular discourse" (Horii 2018, 120). The power of religion as a rhetorical tool is also reflected in legal debates on state-religion relations, where different definitions of religion are often employed when arguing for or against the legality of public participation in shrine practices. After all, the question of whether a ritual taking place at, for instance, Yasukuni Shrine should fall under the constitutional concept of "religious activity" or not depends entirely on how one defines *religion* (Larsson 2017, 2020).

Yasukuni Shrine in the Postwar Period

Yasukuni Shrine found itself in a precarious situation during the Allied occupation. The shrine had been founded as an institution of public significance, dedicated to the Shinto rituals of the Japanese nation-state and fully distanced from the sphere of private religion. Yet in order to survive the purge of all elements of militarism and ultra-nationalism that took place at the hands of the victorious Allies, Yasukuni Shrine had to distance itself from its role in state ideology and emphasize the religiousness of shrine rituals (Mullins 2010). While there was initially some pressure to abolish the shrine along with its subsidiary shrines across the empire due to their intimate links to Japanese militarism, the occupation authorities soon realized that this would be impossible to do while also implementing complete freedom of religious belief in the country (Woodard 1972, 66–67). As the Shinto Directive posited, once Shrine Shinto had been "divorced from the state and divested of its militaristic and ultra-nationalistic tendencies," it would be considered a religion like all others, free for Japanese citizens to practice. Yasukuni was therefore allowed to register as an independent religious juridical person in February of 1946, a status that was later confirmed in 1951 (Mullins 2021, 63–67).

Yasukuni belongs to a group of shrines that have a particularly close relationship to notions of modern Japanese nationhood, along with Meiji Shrine in Tokyo, dedicated to the deified Meiji emperor, and Ise Shrine, where Amaterasu Ōmikami is venerated. In fact, some scholars have assigned Yasukuni a primary role within postwar Japanese nationalism, with Mark Mullins suggesting that "although Ise Shrine is widely acknowledged as the main shrine for [NASS], it is Yasukuni Shrine that actually functions as the symbolic headquarters [...] for the neonationalist movement today" (Mullins 2021, 26). Based on this observation, Mullins has opted to refer to the postwar movement of Shinto-based nationalist politics as "Yasukuni fundamentalism," notwithstanding the fact that Yasukuni is not formally affiliated with the dominant representative of organized Shrine Shinto, NASS, nor that political patronage of Yasukuni occurs less frequently than patronage of other former imperial shrines. For instance, since 1965, Japan's prime ministers have maintained the practice of holding the first press conference of the new year in Ise, following the prime minister's first prayer of the new year (*hatsumōde*) at Ise Shrine (Tanaka 2007, 114). Unlike the deeply divisive visits by representatives of the state to Yasukuni, these prayer visits by the nation's top political leaders generally cause little debate in Japan (Larsson 2020, 405–410).

There are various reasons for why Yasukuni Shrine remains a more divisive site than other shrines with ties to the pre-1945 ideological system. In a seminal work on the "Yasukuni problem," Takahashi Tetsuya has suggested that Yasukuni Shrine is linked to a number of rather distinct issues, of which the question of secularism is but one. Yasukuni in the postwar period is intertwined with complicated questions of mourning, history, culture, remembrance, and diplomacy (Takahashi 2005). As the national institution for honoring those who gave their lives for the Empire of Japan, Yasukuni must be understood both as a place where many families go to grieve for lost loved ones, but also as a contentious site that constantly reminds Japan's neighboring countries of their suffering at the hands of the imperial army (Takahashi 2005, 80–96). Among the first soldiers to be enshrined at Yasukuni after the civil conflicts had been resolved were twelve soldiers who had participated in the 1874 punitive expedition to Taiwan. Enshrined in February of 1875, these were but the first of thousands of soldiers who, after falling in battle on foreign soil, would be enshrined at Kudan hill as heroic spirits of the nation (Takahashi 2005, 91–92). For people in the lands that bore the brunt of Imperial Japan's expansionist zeal, Yasukuni Shrine is not only a symbol of the pre-1945 imperial order, but an institution glorifying Japan's brutal history as a colonial empire.

While the different "Yasukuni problems" identified by Takahashi are all worthy of more detailed study, for the purposes of this chapter the question of how the shrine navigates the secular law of postwar Japanese society is of greatest relevance. Although Yasukuni was formally registered as a religious juridical person during the occupation, this was seen by many as nothing more than a temporary acceding to the will of the occupation authorities. Significantly, the shrine never lost its central position in the national narrative (Mullins 2021, 117–118). Once the occupation ended, the shrine's relationship with the state and the imperial institution quickly resumed, "at least superficially" (Takenaka 2017, 136–137). Starting on October 16, 1952, Emperor Hirohito, in his new constitutional capacity as "symbol of the state and of the unity of the people," returned to the pre-1945 custom of visiting the shrine to pray for the spirits of fallen soldiers. Despite the emperor clearly being an "organ of the state" and Yasukuni maintaining the status of religious organization, the constitutionality of these visits was never widely debated (Tanaka 2007, 31–33). It was only after the enshrinement of fourteen convicted Class A war criminals in 1978 that the emperor discontinued this practice (Tanaka 2007, 147–157). Yasukuni has also maintained a complicated relationship with the political leadership of Japan throughout the postwar period. Prime ministerial visits to Yasukuni have been common for much of the period (Tanaka 2007, 113–116), although these have often been framed as "private" in order to evade the constitutional separation of religion and state. Until the 1980s the controversies surrounding these visits were largely domestic, but since the complaints raised by Chinese dignitaries at the time of Nakasone Yasuhiro's visit in 1985, they have been framed more as an issue of international significance (Takenaka 132–134). It is perhaps telling that it was only after visits to Yasukuni became enmeshed in diplomatic controversies with Japan's major trade partners in Asia that the practice became less regular.

While NASS has remained an ideological ally of Yasukuni Shrine throughout the postwar period, the major lobby group arguing for renewed ties between Yasukuni and the state is the Japan War-Bereaved Families Association (*Nippon izokukai*). The association was originally founded soon after the Japanese surrender as a welfare organization with the purpose of supporting families who had lost their breadwinners in the war (Seraphim 2006, 60–85). It reorganized after Japan regained independence and has since developed into a major support base for the Liberal Democratic Party (LDP), lobbying for closer ties between the state and Yasukuni Shrine (Tanaka 2007, 20–23). The association was intimately involved in the campaigns to renationalize Yasukuni in the 1950s and 1960s, during which they used their broad grassroots base to petition Diet members to support the so-called Yasukuni bills. The first bill aiming to reinstitutionalize government support for Yasukuni Shrine was presented in the Diet in 1969, and although it was defeated, it had the support of many politicians, especially from the LDP. Four subsequent bills were defeated over the next five years, after which the proponents of renationalization gave up these attempts. A significant problem for the bills was the growing consent in Japan about Yasukuni's status as a religious institution. As long as Yasukuni was religious, it was argued that public support for the shrine would not be possible under the 1947 constitution (Hardacre 1991, 145–149). While many politicians, including several LDP prime ministers, have continued to visit the shrine in private or in their public capacity since the 1970s, the campaign to formally reconnect Yasukuni to the state has stagnated.

The question of how to interpret religion under the Japanese constitution has been the subject of several lawsuits. While religious freedom is generally granted to any organization registering as a religious juridical person, the question of what constitutes "religious activity" under Article 20 Paragraph 3 is more controversial (Larsson 2017; Takahata 2007). The first landmark ruling on this issue was handed down by the Supreme Court in 1977, when the Tsu Groundbreaking Ceremony case was resolved. The justices behind the majority ruling concluded that while Shrine Shinto should be viewed as a religion, this did not necessarily mean that all activities carried out by shrine priests constituted "religious activity" under the constitution. The groundbreaking ceremony (*jichinsai*) at the center of the lawsuit was allowed because it was assumed that "common people" viewed it as a "secular event" or "social ritual," rather than as a religious activity (Larsson 2020, 164–214). Based on this ruling, over the next two decades a number of subsequent lawsuits were resolved in favor of those who advocated a closer relationship between the state and Shrine Shinto, essentially establishing a precedent that NASS and other lobbyists on the political right could accept. This changed in 1997 when the Supreme Court handed down a ruling in the Ehime Tamagushiryō case, which essentially placed Shrine Shinto on equal footing with other religious organizations. The case concerned ritual offerings made at Yasukuni Shrine and the local nation-protecting shrine in Ehime prefecture, and while the defendants claimed that these offerings were simply customary acts, the justices argued that the legal status of the institution should be more important than an evaluation based on the assumed views of common people. Essentially, if a Shinto shrine was responsible for the rituals, they should be considered religious (Larsson 2020, 215–261). Based on this precedent, even shrines with claims to national significance such as Yasukuni would be placed on equal footing with other formally religious institutions in Japan.

CONCLUSION

Since the Supreme Court ruling in the Ehime Tamagushiryō case, proponents of a closer relationship between Shinto and the state have become increasingly active in campaigns to revise the 1947 constitution (Larsson 2017; Mullins 2021, 167–193). On the political right, various lobby groups have joined forces to support the LDP in their long-standing goal to write a new constitution "by Japanese hands," as former Prime Minister Abe Shinzō has expressed it (Abe 2013, 32–33). One of the major groups pushing for constitutional reform today is the Japan Conference (*Nippon kaigi*), a broad and loosely structured association in which actors with different backgrounds unite behind a few shared goals, including the vision to see Japan return as a "proud country" (Larsson 2017, 227–228). Although the Japan Conference is not registered as a religious organization, it maintains links to a number of religious groups. These include NASS as well as other independent Shrine Shinto institutions, including Yasukuni Shrine, whose former head priest Tokugawa Yasuhisa is an affiliated member (Mullins 2021, 102–106). It is difficult to evaluate the grassroots support for the "nationalist turn" in Japanese politics, but the influence of these organizations on party politics is easily observable. Since the second Abe cabinet was inaugurated on December 26, 2013, a majority of ministers have been affiliated with both the Japan Conference and the Diet group representing the interests of NASS.

Postwar Japan is governed under a strictly secular constitution, but at the same time the limits of Japanese secularism are nebulous. One reason for this is the continued reliance on religion as a legal category in a country where the term has a short and divisive history. While religious minorities and many liberals in Japan tend to agree with the occupation-era assumption that religion as a category should include Shrine Shinto in all its forms, many conservatives and nationalists disagree with this interpretation. In the discourse of Japan's Shinto-nationalist right, the nonreligious Shinto of pre-1945 imperial Japan is often idealized. While there are few voices calling for a full return to the former system of state shrines, there are many who wish to see Yasukuni returned to its prominent position within the Japanese nation. No bill for the renationalization of Yasukuni has been submitted to the Diet since 1974, yet political patronage of the shrine remains strong. The last prime minister to visit while in office was Abe Shinzō, who made a private visit in December of 2013, but every year a number of leading politicians from the LDP make publicized visits to the shrine. Current (2021–) Prime Minister Kishida Fumio has not visited the shrine since taking office, but has instead opted to send ritual offerings on the occasion of major festivals. Through these actions, Kishida reflects the current relationship between Yasukuni Shrine and the state, a relationship that is constantly renegotiated as the precarious secularism of postwar Japan continues to be the topic of legal and political controversies.

REFERENCES

Abe, Shinzō. 2013. *Atarashii kuni e, utsukushii kuni e: kanzenban*. Tokyo, Japan: Bungei shunjū.
Anzai, Kenjō. 1998. *Jōdo no kaifuku: Ehime tamagushiryō soshō to shinshū-kyōdan*. Tokyo, Japan: Kinohana-sha.

Breen, John, and Mark Teeuwen. 2010. *A New History of Shinto*. Hoboken, NJ: Wiley-Blackwell.

Dower, John. 2000. *Embracing Defeat: Japan in the Wake of World War II*. New York, NY: W.W. Norton & Co.

Hardacre, Helen. 1991. *Shintō and the State, 1868–1988*. Princeton, NJ: Princeton University Press.

———. 2017. *Shinto: A History*. Oxford, UK: Oxford University Press.

Horii, Mitsutoshi. 2018. *The Category of 'Religion' in Contemporary Japan: Shūkyō & Temple Buddhism*. London, UK: Palgrave Macmillan.

Isomae, Jun'ichi. 2012. *Shūkyō-gainen arui wa shūkyōgaku no shi*. Tokyo, Japan: Tōkyō Daigaku shuppankai.

Josephson, Jason. 2006. When Buddhism Became a 'Religion': Religion and Superstition in the Writings of Inoue Enryō. *Japanese Journal of Religious Studies* 33 (1): 143–168. https://nirc.nanzan-u.ac.jp/nfile/2889.

———. 2012. *The Invention of Religion in Japan*. Chicago, IL: The University of Chicago Press.

Kim, Kyu Hyun. 2011. The Mikado's August Body: 'Divinity' and 'Corporeality' of the Meiji Emperor and the Ideological Construction of Imperial Rule. In *Politics and Religion in Japan: Red Sun, White Lotus*, ed. Roys Starrs, 54–83. London, UK: Palgrave Macmillan.

Krämer, Hans Martin. 2011. Beyond the Dark Valley: Reinterpreting Christian Reactions to the 1939 Religious Organizations Law. *Japanese Journal of Religious Studies* 38 (1): 181–211. https://nirc.nanzan-u.ac.jp/nfile/3040.

Kuroda, Toshio. 1981. Shinto in the History of Japanese Religion. *The Journal of Japanese Studies* 7 (1): 1–21. https://doi.org/10.2307/132163.

———. 1996. The Imperial Law and the Buddhist Law. *Japanese Journal of Religious Studies* 23 (3/4): 271–285. https://www.jstor.org/stable/30233575.

Larsson, Ernils. 2017. Jinja Honchō and the Politics of Constitutional Reform in Japan. *Japan Review* 30: 227–252. https://doi.org/10.15055/00006740.

———. 2020. *Rituals of a Secular Nation: Shinto Normativity and the Separation of Religion and State in Postwar Japan*. PhD diss., Uppsala University.

Maxey, Trent. 2014. *The "Greatest Problem": Religion and State Formation in Meiji Japan*. Cambridge, MA: Harvard University Press.

Morris-Suzuki, Tessa. 1998. *Re-Inventing Japan: Time, Space, Nation*. London, UK: M.E. Sharpe.

Mullins, Mark. 2010. How Yasukuni Shrine Survived the Occupation: A Critical Examination of Popular Claims. *Monumenta Nipponica* 65 (1): 89–136. https://doi.org/10.1353/mni.0.0109.

———. 2021. *Yasukuni Fundamentalism: Japanese Religions and the Politics of Restoration*. Honolulu, HI: University of Hawai'i Press.

Murakami, Shigeyoshi. 1970. *Kokka shintō*. Tokyo, Japan: Iwanami Shinsho.

Nelson, John. 2003. Social Memory as Ritual Practice: Commemorating Spirits of the Military Dead at Yasukuni Shinto Shrine. *The Journal of Asian Studies* 62 (2): 443–467. https://doi.org/10.2307/3096245.

Rots, Aike P. 2017. *Shinto, Nature and Ideology in Contemporary Japan: Making Sacred Forests.* London, England: Bloomsbury.

Seraphim, Franziska. 2006. *War Memory and Social Politics in Japan, 1945–2005.* Cambridge, MA: Harvard University Asia Center.

Shimazono, Susumu. 2017. *Kokka shintō to nihonjin.* Tokyo, Japan: Iwanami Shinsho.

Takahashi, Tetsuya. 2005. *Yasukuni-mondai.* Tokyo, Japan: Chikuma Shinsho.

Takahata, Eiichiro. 2007. Religious Accommodation in Japan. *Brigham Young University Law Review* 2007 (3): 729–750. https://digitalcommons.law.byu.edu/lawreview/vol2007/iss3/7.

Takenaka, Akiko. 2017. *Yasukuni Shrine: History, Memory, and Japan's Unending Postwar.* Honolulu, HI: University of Hawai'i Press.

Tanaka, Nobumasa. 2007. *Yasukuni no sengoshi.* Tokyo, Japan: Iwanami Shinsho.

Teeuwen, Mark. 2017. Clashing Models: Ritual Unity vs Religious Diversity. *Japan Review* 30: 39–62. https://doi.org/10.15055/00006732.

Thomas, Jolyon. 2019. *Faking Liberties: Religious Freedom in American-Occupied Japan.* Chicago, IL: The University of Chicago Press.

Wah, Carolyn. 2002. Jehovah's Witnesses and the Empire of the Sun: A Clash of Faith and Religion During World War II. *Journal of Church and State* 44 (1): 45–72. https://www.jstor.org/stable/23919700.

Wildman Nakai, Kate. 2017. Between Secularity, Shrines, and Protestantism: Catholic Higher Education in Prewar Japan. *Japan Review* 30: 97–127. https://doi.org/10.15055/00006735.

Woodard, William P. 1972. *The Allied Occupation of Japan 1945–1952 and Japanese Religions.* Leiden, the Netherlands: Brill.

Zhong, Yijiang. 2016. *The Origin of Modern Shinto in Japan: The Vanquished Gods of Izumo.* London, UK: Bloomsbury.

CHAPTER 14

An Overview of State-Religion Relationship in Vietnam

Hoàng Văn Chung and Đỗ Quang Hưng

INTRODUCTION

To discuss religion in Vietnam today or in the past, one should include the imported world religions and a variety of indigenous folk religions. Since Vietnam is a multi-religious and multi-ethnic country, in many aspects, it is a minimized world of religious beliefs and traditions. Over the times, the most popular religious traditions in the world have found ways to enter and establish communities of followers in Vietnam. Besides major traditions such as Buddhism, Catholicism, Protestantism, and Islam, nowadays one can see the existence of smaller communities of followers of Hinduism, Baha'i faith, Orthodox Christianity, Jehovah's witnesses, I-kuan Tao, Jesus Christ's Church of Latter-Day Saints, and so on. Meanwhile, folk religions have been diversified over time as various ethnic groups residing in the land such as the Kinh, the Chăm, the Khmer, the Chinese Vietnamese, the

H. V. Chung (✉)
Institute for Religious Studies, Vietnam Academy of Social Sciences, Hanoi, Vietnam

Đ. Q. Hưng
Hanoi National University, Hanoi, Vietnam

Bahnar, the Mường, the Tai, and the like increased their social and cultural integrations along with the long formation of the nation-state of Vietnam as we know today.

The Vietnamese's religious mindset is basically polytheistic oriented. Upon acceptance of multiple-religious worldviews, they worship a wide range of spirits, gods, deities, and other forms of supernatural entities. The Vietnamese are comfortable living in a world simultaneously occupied by human and non-human yet invisible forces (Cadière 1989 [orig. 1944]; Condominas 1987; Hue-Tam Ho Tai 1987). Therefore, rituals are performed for different purposes during one's lifetime. Besides, the diversity of worshipped objects results in the diversity of sacred spaces erected for worship activities.

Although historical political regimes and the modern state have been very aware of the people's polytheistic mindset, for the sake of nation-building, they developed different policies on religion. Consequently, the state-religion relationship has been subjected to change over the years. What are the prominent patterns of state-religion relationship in Vietnam at different historical periods? In today social context conditioned by international integration and modernity, what are remarkable changes and the main drives for such changes in the relationship between the secular Socialist state and religion?

This chapter seeks to shed light on these issues. It first provides an overview of the relationship between religion and politics in Vietnam through its history. It then analyzes typical models of state regulations of religion and the religious engagement in politics during its historical course, but then will focus in on the recent decades since Renovation took place in 1986. The authors employ a concept of religion in its broad meaning, thus including institutional and non-institutional (or folk) religions.

STATE-RELIGION RELATIONSHIP UNDER MONARCHIES

From the Beginning of Ancient States to the Sixteenth Century

Ancient states in Vietnam were believed to emerge from the seventh century BC. Archeological evidence, especially the surface of bronze drums of the Đông Sơn culture, revealed forms of a tribe state's worship of the natural forces such as the sun and animals.

During the Chinese domination which lasted for over a millennium (207 BC–905 AD), the Chinese mandarins who were sent to govern the occupied land in Southern China (now Vietnam) sought to adapt their administrations with the indigenous people's customs (Keith Weller Taylor [orig. 1983] 2020, p. 102). Reception of Buddhism took place in around the second century AD, as evidenced in the building of four ancient Buddhist temples in Luy Lâu—the first Chinese colonial headquarters. Many centuries later, Buddhism was brought to Vietnam from China via the introduction of distinctive Buddhist schools known as Pure Land, Zen (Lin Chi, Cao Dong), and Tantra. These schools greatly contributed to the development of Buddhism in Vietnam. Taoism was also received by the Vietnamese during this period, but only some parts of it were practiced. Confucianist doctrines, meanwhile, were first used by Chinese mandarins for the teaching of behaviors for the indigenous people and the diffusion of Chinese culture.

Since the Vietnamese proclaimed their independence with the rise of the Ngô dynasty (939–968 AD), religious philosophies were used by monarchs for ruling the nation and its people. The Vietnamese did not differentiate major religious traditions but sought to syncretize them. Thus, the paradigm of Three teachings (Tam giáo) was gradually formed and became dominant. Certain elements of Buddhism, Taoism, and Confucianism were blended and mixed into a body of beliefs associated with ritual practices. Kings of monarchy states issued royal decrees to allow certain forms of ritual practices at the court and among the masses. The kings themselves mastered some key religious rituals around the year for the nation's prosperity and peace (see, e.g., Dyt 2015).

At different times, however, certain religious traditions were granted the dominant position. The Đinh dynasty (968–980 AD) favored Buddhism in many ways. Monk Ngô Chân Lưu was assigned the title of Great Tutor who supervised the king in almost every aspect of governance of the people and national defense. At the same time, the king financed the building and maintenance of many Buddhism temples. Buddhist doctrines and monks were used for the ruling of the nation in successive dynasties including Early Lê (980–1009 AD), Lý (1009–1225 AD), and Trần dynasties (1400–1407 AD). Buddhism's influence under the Trần dynasty can be seen through the fact that many kings and mandarins became Buddhists. These Buddhist elites, however, neither engaged deeply in politics nor made Buddhism the religion of the nation. Instead, they withdrew from political life when they got older. For example, King Trần Nhân

Tông (1258–1308 AD) dedicated his life to Buddhism after he ceded the throne to his son. He spent the rest of his time developing a Zen Buddhist school for the Vietnamese which is still preserved until today, known as Bamboo Buddhist school (Phật giáo Trúc Lâm).

At the beginning of the monarchies, Confucianism was mainly utilized for education of the royal family members and the formation of the class of elites in the society. The first national civil service examination, aimed at the selection of talents to be mandarins, was held in 1075 under the Lý dynasty. During the Lý and Trần dynasties, the examination was named the "Three-teachings examination" (thi Tam giáo) at which examinees had to demonstrate excellence in understanding Taoism, Confucianism, and Buddhism. This kind of examination lasted from 1195 to 1247 (see Nguyễn Khắc Viện 1974; Kelly 2006). Since the late Trần dynasty, Confucianism was promoted for the education of the people and for the selection of talents to serve the government apparatus. When the Hồ dynasty (1400–1407) arose in the fifteenth century, King Hồ Quý Ly began to downgrade the role of Buddhism in politics while leveling up Confucianism. This could be seen in the rise of Confucian scholars along with their critics against Buddhism, the building of literature temples to worship Confucius and his disciples, and the Confucian doctrines were made the sole foundation of national education. When Lê Lợi (Late Lê dynasty, 1428–1527) got to the throne in 1423, he made Confucianism the dominant religion and this continued until the last feudal dynasty (Nguyễn dynasty 1902–1945).

There is evidence that the feudal states had managed to regulate religion. The Lê codes (issued in 1483) had articles regulating national rites and family's rituals; the requirement of authority certification for Buddhist monks over 50 years' old and Taoist practitioners; punishment for destructive actions on temples for kings. This is to say that the Late Lê dynasty respected the people's freedom in ritual practices, but also had intention to limit certain religious activities.

In short, upon acceptance of the Confucian model of the state in China, the feudal states in Vietnam asserted the state's position which was higher than religion. In combining political and spiritual powers, the states began to build laws to regulate people's religious activities, including ritual practices. During this period, Confucianism "became a political doctrine in the hands of ruling class" (Pham Duy Nghia 2005, p. 82) rather than a religion for the masses. Buddhism, meanwhile, gradually withdrew from the royal court and was largely practiced among the masses while very few studied or practiced Taoism (see Trần Văn Toàn 2010, p. 314). Importantly, the Vietnamese neither fought each other nor engaged into social uprisings against the ruling class because of religious reasons. For many centuries, the religious sphere constituted by Three teaching models was quite stable until the infusion of the Western monotheistic religious tradition of Catholicism in the sixteenth century.

From the First Encounter with Christianity in 1533 to 1862

From 1533 to 1862, the states to monopolized Confucianism. Under the influence of Confucian doctrines on the mandate of Heaven and Heaven-mankind interactions, Vietnamese kings also saw themselves as a son of Heaven, thus they would stand below the Heavenly emperor only and above all the rest. Starting in the sixteenth century, the court began the documentation and classification of spirits and gods worshipped throughout the nation. The kings granted royal titles for these supernatural entities, regularly reviewed their rankings, and asked them to protect the nation and the people (see Trần Văn Toàn 2010, p. 312). This act continued until the last monarchy in 1945. Inherently, the court reaffirmed its position of the determiner of which and how spirits and gods would be worshipped.

As the Vietnamese encountered the promulgation of Christianity, the religion-state relationship became complicated. In 1533, Catholicism was first introduced into Vietnam by Portuguese and Spanish missionaries. Later, the Missions Ètrangère de Paris (MEP) sent their missionaries to Vietnam. Gia Long (1762–1820), the first king of the Nguyễn dynasty (1802–1945), first allowed for the practice of Catholic missionary work. However, his son, King Minh Mạng (1791–1841) did not like the presence of Western missionaries on the land. He saw foreign missionaries as an aid to Western colonialism in Cochinchina and that the Christianization of his kingdom could undermine or sweep out the indigenous religious beliefs and traditional customs. He issued hard-line royal decrees to prohibit Catholic missionary work. His successors such as King Thiệu Trị and King Tự Đức also continued this policy. Thus, foreign Catholic missionaries were hunted down, put into prison, and even persecuted. This anti-Catholic policy pushed the Vietnamese Catholics into opposition with the court.

Upon receiving information about the dangers missionaries faced, the French imperial state intensified their pressure on the Nguyễn court. For the protection of their missionaries, the French military opened fire in 1858 to start the French Empire's colonization of Vietnam. The arrival of French Catholicism put an end to the long-lasted paradigm of Three teachings in Vietnam.

From 1862 to 1945

By 1862, the weakened Nguyễn dynasty had to sign in the Treaty of Saigon. King Tự Đức ceded Saigon and three provinces in the South to the French. The treaty's second term allowed everyone to practice Catholicism or not. In 1865, King Tự Đức via a decree stated that Western missionaries were free to promulgate the Christian faith and the Vietnamese were allowed to follow this religion without fear of discrimination. For the first time, a Vietnamese state legally recognized religious liberty much like the secular state model in the West.

Yet, many intellectuals, most of them who were Confucian scholars, still showed their own ways to react to the Western presence. They led a grass-roots movement called Văn Thân to fight the French colonialism. Their motto was clear, to "exclude the Westerners and kill the Catholics" (bình tây, sát tả). At first, they received strong support, and their grassroots movement became widespread. Later, the Nguyễn Court that had surrendered to the French Empire suppressed the movement. The movement, though it ended after some 20 years in failure, for the first time showed the tension and violent conflicts in the relationship between the state and the people over their religious beliefs.

In short, since independence and prior to the arrival of Catholicism, the state and religions enjoyed peace and harmony in their relationship. No serious confrontation or conflicts between the state and religions occurred and both sides even cooperated on common interests. Monarchies in Vietnam had developed a flexible mechanism to adapt to the presence and operation of three major religious traditions. But the last monarchy encountered big challenges put forth by the introduction of the Western theological tradition of Catholicism. In many circumstances, the monarchies always made themselves higher than religion.

Under the French colonial regime (1884–1945), the Vietnamese state was influenced by the French-Laïcité model which was characterized by the separation of church and state. During this time, religions could enjoy religious liberty. Among them, Christianity was well protected and given the most favorable conditions to develop. In the case of Catholicism, missionaries were free to convert indigenous people, Catholic organizations were allowed to purchase land, build churches, monasteries, schools, hospitals, charity houses, and so on. New parishes were opened up one after another and the Catholic population increased. Protestantism came later in 1911, thanks to the efforts of missionaries from Christian and Missionary Alliance (C&MA) which was based in North America. After overcoming some difficulties early on, missionaries were given freedom to promulgate their faith. Consequently, new churches were built in major cities in the north, as well as the middle and the south, and the Protestant Christians began to increase in number.

FROM THE BIRTH OF THE REVOLUTIONARY STATE IN 1945 TO 1975

The modern state rose in 1945 and replaced the last weakened feudal state, which marked the turning point of the political regime in Vietnam. The revolutionary government led by Hồ Chí Minh soon declared its official stand toward religion via affirmation of its secular nature plus its neutrality before religion. At the same time, it called for unification among all religions and between the non-religious and the religious adherents for national interests. Religious leaders were mobilized to participate in the revolutionary government apparatus and encouraged to contribute to the construction of Socialism.

However, France attacked Vietnam again in 1945. The Vietnamese stood up and fought the second resistance war against the French. Nine years later, the Geneva Accord (signed in 1954) temporarily divided Vietnam into the North and the South. The North continued its vision of Socialism while the South adopted Capitalism. In that context, the relationship between religion and state became very different in the two regions. The religious adherents throughout the nation were confused about their stance before confronting political regimes pursuing different political agendas and had different approaches to religion.

Many religious practitioners stayed away from the political conflict and focused on the protection of the faith (Phi-Vân Nguyen 2018, pp. 745–747). From the years 1937–1947, the Roman Catholic Church heavily criticized those who supported Communism. In Vietnam, the new state's declaration of Communist ideology was interpreted by a number of Catholic clergymen as a real threat to Catholics. Rumor had it that

Catholicism would be terribly suppressed by the Communists. Because of this, by 1954, around a million of Catholics migrated from the North to the South (Hansen 2009, pp. 179–181). This movement actually deepened the hatred between Catholics and non-Catholics, and many years later it continued to widen the gap between the Communists and the Catholics.

Only when the Second Vatican Council (1962–1965) declared the Church's changes of its attitude, the church in Vietnam began to show that it would stand by the nation and cooperate with the Government. The relationship between the two sides gradually improved. Unlike the mainstream Chinese Catholics who established their own national Church that was independent from the Vatican, the Catholic church in Vietnam saw itself as an integral part of the universal Catholic church. Thus, they maintained their direct relationship with the Vatican. In 1980, the Vietnam Bishop Council (the representative organization of Catholics in Vietnam) announced its Common Letter which determined how the Catholics would be with the nation: (1) to protect and build the nation with all compatriots and (2) to build a Church with a style and expression of the faith in accordance with the national tradition. Overall, the motto for all Catholics was set as: "Live the Gospel in the heart of the nation to serve the happiness of the compatriots." As can be seen from the motto, the Catholics stressed their loyalty with the people and the nation, rather than specifying a political regime. Given this, these directions resolved problems with Catholics' relationship with the state and opened up possibilities for them to have friendly dialogue and develop better cooperation with the state and non-Catholics.

Meanwhile, the Protestants, most of the time, chose to stay away from politics. They did not take sides during wartime. Instead, they focused on the protection of the faith in Jesus Christ and maintained their small communities.

A part of the religious population, however, sought to pursue their own political agenda. For example, the inner-born religion known as Hòa Hảo Buddhism (1939) in the South under the leadership of master Huỳnh Phú Sổ sought to liberate the nation from the French colonialist and to implement a social revolution. Huỳnh Phú Sổ established the Vietnam Social Democratic Party (Việt Nam Dân chủ xã hội Đảng) in 1946 along with a military force to realize his own vision.

The other part of the religious population, typically the Catholics, the Buddhists, and the Caodaists chose to support the revolutionary government and contributed to the fight for national unification and independence. There also appeared patriotic movements established and joined by followers of Buddhism, Catholicism, or Caodaism. During the war of resistance against the French colonial regime, in the North, the Việt Nam Công giáo cứu quốc (Vietnam Catholics Association for Saving Nation) was established in 1950s, along with Ủy ban liên lạc những người Công giáo Việt Nam yêu tổ quốc, yêu hòa bình (Connecting Committee of Vietnamese Catholics who love the nation and peace). In the South, Liên đoàn Công giáo Nam Bộ (Alliance of Southern Catholics) or Hội đồng Công giáo Kháng chiến Nam Bộ (the Catholic Committee of the War of Resistance in the South) were built up almost at the same time. In 1941, Hội Phật giáo cứu quốc (the Vietnam Buddhist Association for saving the nation) was established in Hanoi. In the Middle and South, similar Buddhist associations were born. In the North in 1947, there appeared a movement called "put off Buddhist costumes and wear the soldier's uniform" in which all members were monks. They abandoned the life of self-cultivation, joined the Vietnamese People's army, and fought on the battlefields. These Buddhist monks' acts of love for the nation inspired generations of Buddhists later. In 1946, the leader of Caodaist church in Hậu Giang province, Cao Triều Phát, declared the church's motto: "Be loyal to Hồ Chí Minh's regime and fight for national independence and unification." One year later, a Caodaist Association for saving the nation was established, with the participation of 12 different Caodaist branches. All these organized religious groups were established and led by the clergymen and they joined the Mặt trận Việt Minh (The Việt Minh front) under the leadership of Hồ Chí Minh.

In another context, monks and nuns in the Middle and the South of Vietnam stood up to criticize the Southern political regime for discrimination and suppression of Buddhism. They indicated that Ngô Đình Diệm's government (1955–1963) favored Catholicism while it discriminated against other religions. During the 1960s, Buddhist monks organized public protests, from the Middle to the Southern regions of Vietnam asking the Government for equal treatment of all the religions and freedom of religious promulgation. At the climax of this violent suppression by the Southern regime over the protesters, monk Thích Quảng Đức burned himself to death on June 11, 1963. After this groundbreaking event, Ngô Đình Diệm's government had to announce a reform in its policy over religion.

In the North, during 1945–1975, the relationship between religion and state was mainly unchanged, all under the influence of two factors. The first was the Leninist-state model which was imported and applied by the communists. The anti-religious struggle became intense at this time. Consequently, various forms of religious practices were condemned as manifestations of superstition. Many religious buildings were destroyed, neglected (Roszko 2012, p. 28), or turned into structures for secular purposes. The second was the Hồ Chí Minh's thoughts which were more nationalistic than communist. Hồ Chí Minh also set out foundations for the building a secular state with reference to the French-Laïcité experiences. In that sense, religion was meant to be separated from politics rather than suppressed (Chung Van Hoang 2017, p. 40; Đỗ Quang Hưng 2019, p. 552).

Meanwhile, in the South, in 1954 the relationship between religion and the state had a major change. The pre-1945 French state model was replaced by the American state model. Under the Second Republic, constitution and laws allowed the state to legally recognize religious associations. Religious organizations were able to accumulate property, open schools, hospitals, orphanages, printing houses, and so on.

In 1975, after the Fall of Saigon, Vietnam became unified again. The Northern state model was applied nationwide. The rush of building a Socialist nation was accompanied by an anti-religious struggle which viewed all forms of religious belief and ritual practices as hindrances to social progress (see Taylor 2007, p. 10; Claire Trần Thị Liên 2013, p. 234). Besides, the Party-state was aware of any acts by rivalry forces that manipulated religion to destroy the great national unity block (khối đại đoàn kết dân tộc). Upon the fear of facing discrimination, religious people often chose not to declare their religious affiliation when preparing CVs. Christian churches, Buddhist temples, shrines for indigenous spirits and deities, communal houses for village tutelary gods, and so on were technically closed and rituals were seldom performed. Various religious properties, especially lands, were nationalized or borrowed by the authorities for secular purposes. Besides, many religious clergymen in the South were put into re-education camps for several years before they could participate in society again (Chung Van Hoang 2017, p. 41). This period would be the hardest time for all religions in Vietnam.

RELIGION-STATE RELATIONSHIP IN RENOVATION CONTEXT

From 1976 to 2003

During this time, Vietnam experienced great difficulty in many aspects. The centrally planned economy did not work while the U.S trade embargo was applied to all of Vietnam. This began in 1975 and lasted for 19 years. Poverty became a national issue. International relations were limited while the Soviet bloc began weakening before it finally collapsed in late 1990s. For the sake of political stability, the state even enhanced its control of the religious sphere (see Bouquet 2010, pp. 90–91).

At the same time, the Communist Party promoted the education for the masses of nationalism and of the great national unity in which religious organizations were considered an important force. Decrees or resolutions were issued which tended to interfere with the various religious organizations' internal affairs. Resolution No.26, issued on April 19, 1999, was typical for the mechanism called "asking for and giving permission." In this way, the religious organizations felt stressed and angry because they had to seek authorities' permission for most of their major activities within their private spaces.

Since 1990s, Vietnam began to witness a strong revival of religion. This phenomenon can be observed from the restoration of ritual practices, festivals, meetings, and so on to the renovation and resacralization of places of worship, re-organization of religious communities, and the re-establishment of educational and training bases. Further, religious practitioners have intensified their engagement in social life via charity work and improvement of social welfare. On the one hand, this process in Vietnam resembles the universal phenomenon of religious revival at the turn of the third millennium. Inside the country, people have come back to their religious beliefs and practices as a way to cope with unprecedented challenges from international integration and the negative impacts of the market economy (see Pham Quynh Phuong 2009, p. 171). On the other hand, this revival was possible because of the Party-State's renovation policy and laws on religion (Claire Trần Thị Liên 2013, p. 239) which will be further analyzed here.

Along with the renovation policy, Vietnam declared that it "wants to be a friend and trustworthy partner of the international community." But this came with a price. Vietnam had to follow international standards of religious freedom (see Claire Trần Thị Liên 2013, p. 233). For decades, international NGOs and governments placed great pressure on the Vietnam government to improve religious freedom (see Gillespie 2014). Yet, the guarantee of religious freedom could only be slightly improved because of the lack of up-to-date policy and detailed legal regulations. All of these issues led to the Party-state's decision to change its views and treatment of religion. Accordingly, new policies were introduced since 1990s. Especially, the introduction of the Central Committee of the Communist Party of Vietnam's Resolution No.25 dated March 12, 2003, on religious works was seen as a "breakthrough" in the official view of religion. The Resolution made three major points: (1) it recognized that religion was a need of a part of the population and it would exist with the nation during the construction of Socialism; (2) the Party-state would consistently implement the policy of building a great national unity in which religious community was an integral part; and (3) any acts that used religion to break the laws and to infringe upon national security were prohibited. Along with this, the Resolution set out a routine for the building of a specific law to regulate religious activities.

From 2003 to Present

Following Resolution no.25, the Ordinance on belief and religion was issued in 2004. This was the first detailed legal framework for religious activities. Twelve years later, in 2016, the National Assembly passed a law called the Law on beliefs and religion. The law and its detailed instructions for implementation basically resolved existing issues relating to the promulgation of religious beliefs, management of emerging Protestant groups, religious properties, ordainment of the clergy, registration for religious activities, recognition of religious organizations, rights, interests, and opportunities to engage in civil activities in secular sectors, and the like.

When the law was in preparation, several versions of draft were sent to religious organizations for opinions. The majority of religious organizations gave positive feedback to the drafts. They supported the idea of building a rule-of-law in accordance with the resolution of the 11th Communist Party National Congress in 2011. For them, it was essential that to fairly deal with problems that emerged from religious activities in the new social context, the state and the religion would interact with each other only on a legal basis. Religious adherents and organizations would be able to do whatever was stated in the laws and would be fully responsible for any unlawful activity. Meanwhile, if a state official did not seriously follow the laws as resolving religious organizations' requests or applications, he could be punished as well.

So far, there had been no serious disagreement between religious organizations and the government about the building and approvement of the Law on beliefs and religion. The government is happy to show that the Law has basically resolved long-term problems in management of religious activities, thus improving the relationship between religion and the state. Yet, the public still doubts that the Law will actually resolve problems in religious life. By prosecuting a religious person or organization for crimes associated with their religion, the government reveals the ever politically sensitive issue of religious freedom. Further, there is a big problem with the ability of local state officials who are responsible for state management of religious activities. For decades, they have revealed the lack of ability to correctly and consistently interpret the Party-State's policy on religion and to apply legal regulations on specific, local-based religious issues.

One should also consult the Constitutions to examine the matter of religious freedom. Article 70 of the 1992 Constitution asserted that "citizens have the right to freedom of belief and religion." In the newest Constitution passed by the National Assembly in 2013, the same Article has been amended as follows: "everyone has the right to freedom of belief and religion." This is an important expansion of the scope of the right, since even the non-citizen can still enjoy the full right to religious freedom. However, in Vietnam, there still exists a real gap between the law as it is written and the law in its implementation and practice. Therefore, the government has to resolve this problem at all costs to retain the support and cooperation of the religious community.

Another State action has also made religious communities feel that they are being taken care of. In recent decades, the State has boosted the heritagization of the religious legacies. Thus, a great deal of state budget has been spent for documentation, classification, and preservation of sacred spaces of religions that are said to be imbued with precious historical and cultural values. Other forms of religious heritage, such as rituals, festivals, relics, music performance, and so on, also receive protection via legal tools. The religious communities find this heritagization helpful and meaningful. However, there are complaints about how the state factor has again interfered into the community's worship activities and separated them from the legacies left for them by the previous generations.

From what has been presented above, in many ways, renovation in the Party-state's approach to religion is undeniable. International researchers expressed different views about the renovation, but their common assessment was that it in a certain way had relaxed the state control of religions, thus improving the state-religion relationship. Philip Taylor was reasonable to argue that in post-Renovation Vietnam "the realms of religion and politics are not reducible to each other, just as they are not necessarily in competition with each other" (2007, p. 15). According to Pascal Bourdeaux and Jean-Paul Willaime, renovation policy "has notably favoured the objective re-evaluation of religion as an ethic and a social practice, allowing Vietnam's current religious reconfigurations to be better considered in a national and global perspective" (2010, p. 307). Mathieu Bouquet (2010) points out that the state-religion relationship had been redefined since 1990. As a result of the ideological shift of the role of religion, the official discourse on religions had been renovated, thus a rapprochement between the Party-state and religious organizations had taken place (2010, p. 95). But looking at this relaxation of the control of religion from other angle, one may see that the State is actually developing more sophisticated tools to regulate religious activities, either via building a more complex legal framework or heritagization of religious legacies (see Oscar Salemink 2010; Edyta Roszko 2012; Claire Trần Thị Liên 2013). Further, the assertion of the state's will in effective regulation of religious activities can be interpreted as the effort to reinforce the state's legitimacy and political power over the society.

CONCLUSION

During the history of Vietnam, the relationship between religion and the state experienced ups and downs. Although no religion had ever been made a national religion, at times one religion would be favored by the state over others. Since the twentieth century, all religions in Vietnam have experienced different state models which varied in ideologies and approaches to religion (Đỗ Quang Hưng 2014). This explains the differing attitudes and reactions of religious adherents toward the state.

In post-Renovation context, changes in policy have significantly improved the relationship between the State and religion. Both sides are building trust and seeking more opportunities to collaborate with each other. Moreover, positive changes are being made as Vietnam has planned to build a Socialist rule-of-law state. Basically, the state continues to better protect religious freedom, endorse religious diversity, and facilitate religions to co-exist in harmony. As more favorable conditions have been created, religious organizations are pushing state-defined boundaries further so as to obtain greater autonomy and become more socially present.

Practically, religious organizations will cooperate with the state if they are enabled to legally pursue their own objectives. Meanwhile, the state needs the religious communities' support and contribution for the building of the nation. The sustainability of the state-religion relationship in the future thus depends on how the principle of mutual benefit is maintained.

References

Bouquet, Mathieu. 2010. Vietnamese Party-State and Religious Pluralism since 1986: Building the Fartherland? *Sojourn: Social Issues in Southeast Asia* 25 (1): 90–108.

Bourdeaux, Pascal, and Jean-Paul Willaime. 2010. Introduction: Religious Reconfiguration in Vietnam. *Social Compass* 57 (3): 307–310.

Cadière, Léopold. 1989 (orig. 1944). *Religious Beliefs and Practices of the Vietnamese*. Trans. Jan W. Mabbett. Melbourne: Monash University.

Chung Van Hoang. 2017. *New Religions and State's Response to Religious Diversification in Contemporary Vietnam: Tension from the Reinvention of the Sacred*. Springer.

Claire Trần Thị Liên. 2013. Communist State and Religious Policy in Vietnam: A Historical Perspective. *Hague Journal on the Rule of Law* 5 (2): 229–252.

Condominas, George. 1987. Vietnamese Religion. In *The Encyclopedia of Religions*, ed. Mircea Eliade, 256–260. New York: Collier Macmillan Publishers.

Dyt, Kathryn. 2015. "Calling for Wind and Rain" Rituals: Environment, Emotion, and Governance in Nguyen Vietnam 1802–1883. *Journal of Vietnamese Studies* 10 (2): 1–42.

Gillespie, John. 2014. Human Rights as a Larger Loyalty: The Evolution of Religious Freedom in Vietnam. *Harvard Human Rights Journal* 47 (1): 107–149.

Hansen, Peter. 2009. Bắc Di Cư: Catholic Refugees from the North of Vietnam, and Their Role in the Southern Republic, 1954–1959. *Journal of Vietnamese Studies* 4 (3): 173–211. https://doi.org/10.1525/vs.2009.4.3.173.

Hưng, Đỗ Quang. 2014. *Nhà nước - Tôn giáo - Luật pháp*. Hanoi: Công an Nhân dân publishing house.

Hưng, Đỗ Quang. 2019. *Nhà nước thế tục [The Secular State]*. Hanoi: National Politics Publishing House.

Kelly, Liam C. 2006. "Confucianism" in Vietnam: A State of the Field Essay. *Journal of Vietnamese Studies* 1 (1–2): 314–370.

Nghia, Pham Duy. 2005. Confucianism and the Conception of the Law in Vietnam. In *Asian Socialism and Legal Change*, ed. John Gillespie and Pip Nicholson. ANU Press.

Nguyễn Khắc Viện. 1974. *Tradition and Revolution in Vietnam*. Indochina Resource Center.

Nguyen, P. 2018. A Secular State for a Religious Nation. The Republic of Vietnam and Religious Nationalism, 1946–1963. *The Journal of Asian Studies* 77 (3): 741–771.

Pham Quynh Phuong. 2009. *Hero and Deity: Tran Hung Dao and the Resurgence of Popular Religion in Vietnam*. Chiang Mai: Mekong Press.

Roszko, Edyta. 2012. From Spiritual Homes to National Shrines: Religious Traditions and Nation-Building in Vietnam. *East Asia* 29 (1): 25–41.

Salemink, Oscar. 2010. Ritual Efficacy, Spiritual Security and Human Security: Spirit Mediumship in Contemporary Vietnam. In *A World of Insecurity: Anthropological Perspectives on Human Security*, ed. T.H. Eriksen, E. Bal, and O. Salemink. Pluto Press.

Tai, Hue-Tam Ho. 1987. Religion in Vietnam. Accessed at: Religion in Vietnam | Asia Society. Accessed 11 November 2022.

Taylor, Keith W. (2020 [orig. 1983]). *Việt Nam thời dựng nước*. Hanoi: Dân Trí publishing house.

Taylor, Philip. 2007. Modernity and Re-enchantment in Post-revolutionary Vietnam. In *Modernity and Re-enchantment: Religion in Post-revolutionary Vietnam*, ed. P. Taylor, 1–56. Singapore: ISEAS Publishing.

Trần Văn Toàn. 2010. A Breath of Atheism in Religious Vietnam. *Social Compass* 57 (3): 311–318.

CHAPTER 15

The Indonesian Difference: Nationalism, Islam, and Pancasila Pluralism from State Formation to the Present

A. J. Nolte

INTRODUCTION

When asked to identify the world's most populous Muslim country, few casual observers of the Islamic world would immediately think of a sprawling archipelago in Southeast Asia. Yet Indonesia holds this distinction, among many others of significance to this volume. It is a relatively stable democracy, having undergone a series of peaceful transfers of power since 1998. It is also one of the very few Muslim countries that have embraced neither state-enforced secularism nor state-enforced Islam. Indonesia's unique framework of multiple religious establishments has created a stable environment of bounded tolerance, in which religious communities operate with relative freedom, while individuals' freedom to pursue their personal religious conscience has been more circumscribed. Perhaps most intriguingly, Indonesia has witnessed a kind of Islamic revivalism and

A. J. Nolte (✉)
Regent University, Virginia Beach, VA, USA
e-mail: anolte@regent.edu

© The Author(s), under exclusive license to Springer Nature
Switzerland AG 2023
S. Holzer (ed.), *The Palgrave Handbook of Religion and State
Volume II*, https://doi.org/10.1007/978-3-031-35609-4_15

resourcement that might, in due course, open the door for even more substantive religious freedom both in the world's largest Muslim country and around the world.

The Ideational Context: Nahdlatul Ulama and Indonesian Nationalism

Key to Indonesia's unique balance between religion and state is the relationship between two intellectual and institutional currents. First, Indonesian nationalism has been shaped by a kind of religious and ideological syncretism, with a goal of preserving a national unity that is multi-interpretable and flexible enough to account for the country's natural diversity. Second, a strand of Indonesian Islam, represented by Nahdlatul Ulama, has sought to preserve the local character of Indonesia's Islamic tradition by aggressively combating Islamist tendencies. Taken together, these intellectual currents of thought have forged institutions that support one another while maintaining enough critical distance to keep either from being co-opted.

To understand the impact of Nahdlatul Ulama, it is useful to contrast it with two organizations founded around the same time: Muhammadiyah and Persatuan Islam. Muhammadiyah was founded first, at the instigation of a former student in Mecca named Ahmed Dahlan, and advocated for modernist Islam (Menchik 2016, ch. 1). Nahdlatul Ulama (hereafter NU) and Persatuan Islam (hereafter Persis) were both formed in reaction to Muhammadiyah. NU, which would eventually eclipse its rivals in size, represented what it perceived to be traditional Javanese Islam and reverence for the four schools of jurisprudence, against the individual ijtihad of groups like Muhammadiyah (Menchik 2016, introduction). It would be inaccurate to describe NU as a champion for the "abangan" or nominal Muslims, for the core of NU was, and remains, the Pesantren led by respected Kyai that are spread throughout East Java (Van Bruinessen 1999). At first glance, the traditionalism of NU might lead an observer to suspect NU of a kind of reactionary conservatism. In practice, however, NU has often issued fatwas that are more progressive than those of Muhammadiyah or Persis. To a degree, this results from the practice of collective *ijtihad* within NU. As Nadirsyah Hosen (2004, pp. 8–9) elucidates, this process has many benefits when issues touching on modernity are addressed:

By performing *ijtihad* collectively, Nahdlatul Ulama can invite opinions from, or consult with, "secular" scholars. For example, before they make ijtihad on such matters as family planning or banking, they tend to discuss medical aspects with medical scholars and economic aspects with economists. Since there are many situations that are not mentioned in the *Qur'an* and the *Sunnah*, particularly where social problems are concerned, Indonesian *'ulama* have realized that they have to work together with other *'ulama* and scholars. This, in effect, is the spirit of collective *ijtihad*.

NU saw Wahhabism as a particular threat. In his introductory speech given at the founding meeting of NU in 1926, NU co-founder and the first chairman of its Supreme Council, Hadratus Shakyh Hasyim Asy'ari (1926, introduction), described Wahhabis as a class of people who create strife and division and "pervert the truth in order to suit themselves, enjoining evil as if it were good and forbidding good as if it were evil." Further, he argues Wahhabis have "founded organizations to systematically propagate their deviant teachings and amplify their manifest error" (Asy'ari 1926, introduction). This may have been a direct reference to Persis, which had Wahhabi and Salafi roots (Federspiel 2001, preface). Persis rejected the nation-state and demanded a pan-Islamic Caliphate and strict orthodoxy (Federspiel 2001, preface). It is significant, therefore, to note that NU remains incredibly influential a century after its establishment, while Persis no longer exists.

In his seminal work describing nationalism, *Imagined Communities*, Benedict Anderson (2006, ch. 2) emphasizes the importance of constructing a common discourse of nationhood experienced universally by all members of the nation. For Indonesian nationalists, united more by colonial boundaries than common ethnic or religious characteristics, this task was quite complicated, for to fully acknowledge the colonial roots of the nation would be to provide no common bond, beyond oppression. In such a context political Islam, which possessed a deeper shared vision but narrower appeal to the people at large, might well usurp the place of nationalism. Thus, it was incumbent on Sukarno and the other Indonesian secular nationalist leaders to both powerfully evoke some element of shared history and, at the same time, create a national narrative sufficient to bind together Indonesia's diverse population in the modern world. To do so, they drew heavily on the work of Mpu Tantular, a court poet living in the pre-Islamic Hindu-Buddhist kingdom of Majapahit (Ismail 1995, introduction). Thus, the national motto of Indonesia, *Bhinneka Tunggal*

Ika (roughly translated by Faisal Ismail as "unity in diversity"), came from Tantular's works (Ismail 1995, introduction). So also Pancasila, a fusion of two Sanskrit words meaning five principles, was derived from a similar concept of five ethical principles elaborated by Empu Tantular and with echoes in Buddhist ethics (Ismail 1995, introduction). In hearkening back to Majapahit, Sukarno and the Indonesian nationalists claimed a glorious pre-colonial and even pre-Islamic past for their nation and, at the same time, reinterpreted that past to meet the challenges of modernity. It was a brilliant strategy, not only due to its clever use of history, but also because it was classically Javanese, echoing the syncretistic Islamic, Hindu-Buddhist, and traditional Javanese spiritual legitimation strategies of Mataram.

THE JAKARTA CHARTER: A CRITICAL JUNCTURE FOR INDONESIA'S RELIGIOUS REGULATORY ENVIRONMENT

The first area in which these two important currents of thought were to collectively shape Indonesia's balance between church and state was the whiting of Indonesia's post-independence constitution of 1945. As nationalists sought to frame this new national compact on the five principles of Pancasila, it was "belief in God" that caused the most controversy and touched most directly on the conflict between Muslim and secular nationalists. In Sukarno's original formulation, this principle was sparingly expressed as "belief in God" without any further elaboration and was placed last in the list of Pancasila principles (Ismail 1995, ch. 1). Such an amorphous declaration was deemed insufficient by Muslim nationalists, and so a committee of nine, four Muslim nationalist leaders and five secular nationalists—of whom one was Christian—met to hash out a compromise between Sukarno's generic divine invocation and the more specific desires of the Muslim groups. The result of this process was the so-called Jakarta Charter, which moved belief in God to first position in the Pancasila and added the clause "with the obligation to practice the sharia for its adherents" (cited in Ismail 1995, p. 51). According to Ismail (1995, p. 51):

> With this Islamic clause, the Indonesian Muslims gained a strategic position which would enable them to implement the sharia for their community in an independent Indonesia, even though they had to accept the Pancasila rather than Islam as the basis and ideology of the state … Nevertheless, the sentence "with the obligation to practice the sharia for its adherents," from

the Muslim point of view, would apply only to Indonesian Muslims, and not to other religious groups in the country. They felt this sentence was logical since it would not offend or violate the rights of non-Muslim groups in the country.

By no means was this a full victory for the Muslim forces; such an outcome could not have been expected with a committee on which their voices were outnumbered by secular nationalists. Yet neither was it a total defeat, and it departed sharply from the desired principle of the minorities that all religions should be treated equally.

As the Jakarta Charter was proposed, two main sources of opposition emerged: traditional and syncretistic Muslims from Java on one hand and Christian minorities, in particular those in Eastern Indonesia, on the other. The argument of the minorities revolved around equal treatment, but for more traditional and syncretistic Muslims, the fear was that sharia would be imposed according to the views of the modernists, thereby leading the Muslim community away from traditionalism and toward fundamentalism (Ismail 1995, ch. 1). On the other hand, Muslim nationalists, despite the Jakarta Charter, still argued in favor of an Islamic state, claiming that Islam itself was sufficient protection of religious freedom and equal treatment for minorities and emphasizing the 90 percent Muslim demography of the country at the time (Ismail 1995, ch. 1). Yet it seemed, until the middle of August at least, as though the Jakarta Charter would hold.

What happened next is still a matter of debate. According to Muhammad Hatta, the man responsible for drafting the constitution and a close ally of Sukarno at the time, a mid-ranking Japanese naval officer told him that the Catholic and Protestant populations of Eastern Indonesia were sufficiently dissatisfied with the Jakarta Charter that they were considering remaining outside the republic if the seven words remained (Ismail 1995, ch. 1). According to Hatta, he consulted with four prominent Muslim leaders about this very serious matter, implying that he received permission from them to reformulate the first principle of the Pancasila (Ropi 2017, ch. 5). Some Muslim leaders and their descendants have disputed this claim, and no evidence can actually be found that a Japanese naval officer ever spoke to Hatta on the issue (Ropi 2017, ch. 5). Nevertheless, secular nationalist fears of secession from parts of Eastern Indonesia do seem to have been genuine, as Sukarno and others expressed fear of alienating Christians, Hindus, and other religious minorities as an argument to minimize the Islamic character of the state (Ismail 1995, ch.1).

In exchange for the removal of the Jakarta Charter, the Muslims received two very important concessions. The vague formulation "belief in God" was replaced with a more explicit "belief in the one and only god" (Ropi 2017, pp. 57–78). This language echoes, at least in part, the language of Islamic monotheism (Ismail 1995, ch. 1). In his history of Islam in Indonesia, B.J. Boland asserts that "the first principle of the Pancasila … must be understood as a multi-interpretable formula and must be appreciated as providing a real possibility for people to agree while disagreeing" (Boland 1982, p. 39). Ismatu Ropi (2017, p. 73) concurs in part but emphasizes the importance of the Muslim nationalist interpretation: "*Ketuhanan Yang Maha Esa* (belief in the one and only God) could be seen to be a pivotal principle, signifying a substantial acknowledgment of God in the state system, so that the state would not be closed to the use of Islamic principles."

The second major concession was the creation of a Ministry of Religious Affairs. In theory, the purpose of this ministry was to administer government benefits to all religions equally (Ropi 2017, ch. 8). In practice, Ropi (2017, p. 97) argues, "It was, from the beginning, a safe haven for Muslim activists to channel their Islamic aspirations following their defeat in their Islamic state proposal in 1945." This is perhaps not entirely surprising since Indonesia was a Muslim-majority country. Nor has the Indonesian government failed to support those religions it recognizes. Yet, as will be discussed further in the chapter, recognition or non-recognition of a religion often became a political football in Indonesia, as failure to achieve recognition for one's faith could well result in severe penalties from the state. Thus, to a degree, while the seven words were omitted from the Pancasila, a bit of their spirit would survive through the power to support and recognize religions wielded by the Ministry of Religious Affairs.

With these concessions in hand, and given the widespread assumption that the 1945 constitution was a necessary but temporary expedient in the face of possible Dutch reconquest, Muslim nationalists accepted the amended Pancasila formation without the Jakarta Charter. As subsequent events demonstrate, the "temporary" compromise of 1945 proved far more enduring than either secular or Muslim nationalists could have guessed. In hindsight, Muslim nationalists' bargaining power would never again be as formidable as it was in 1945, at which point independence was not yet assured. In prioritizing independence over an Islamic state, Muslim nationalists both guaranteed the former and effectively prevented the latter. The secular nationalists, by contrast, got almost everything they wanted at the cost of vaguely monotheistic language and a ministry of religious affairs that might serve as a redoubt for eventual expansion of Islam's political role.

It was in this period of 1945, then, characterized by declining Japanese rule and declaring independence, that Indonesia experienced its critical juncture in the relationship between Islam and the state. In short, the choices made in this short period of time, and subsequently reified by two authoritarian regimes and the present consolidating democracy, define the relationship between political Islam and the Indonesian state. The longevity of the ideological compromise established in 1945 to resolve the debate over the seven words is in and of itself quite a remarkable achievement. Like all compromises, it has been imperfect and inconsistent in its application, with considerable room for negotiation and interpretation. Yet what resulted was neither entirely secular, in either the aggressive or passive sense, nor fully Islamic. What is even more remarkable is just how narrow the path was to this generally stable compromise. Had the state pushed too far in either a secular or a political Islamic direction, it is entirely possible secession and/or serious civil war might have been the result. Had the seven words been included, as they were in the initial draft, rather than omitted, as they were in the final version, it is no exaggeration to say that both the nature of religion's relationship to the state and the very future of the Indonesian project itself might have been drastically different.

RELIGIOUS REGULATION UNDER SUKARNO AND SUHARTO

Of course, 1945 by no means definitively ended attempts by political Islamic parties to advocate for an Islamic state (Ismail 1995, ch. 1–2). Initially, their efforts played themselves out against the backdrop of two new constitutions, produced in 1949 and 1950. Taken together, these two documents tell us a great deal about the balance between religion and the state as imagined by the founding generation post-independence. By far the most extensive guarantees of religious freedom came in the 1949 constitution, which was written to appease the majority-minority population of East Indonesia that remained under Dutch control during the war for independence. The 1949 constitution included language allowing the right to convert from one religion to another, the right to religious self-education, and other religious freedom language very much reminiscent of the UN Declaration on Religious Freedom (Ropi 2017, ch. 6). The major innovation in this constitution was the phrase "recognized religions" (*agama yang diakui*), which explicitly limited, for the first time, those religions to which the government would provide protection and support (Ropi 2017, ch. 6). Thus, a tension was introduced between the government's supervisory role with respect to religion and its guarantees of freedom of religion. The 1950 constitution, by contrast, was a post-independence document designed specifically to eliminate some of the Western and federalist influences of 1949. Due to the efforts of Muslim parties, the balance in this second constitution shifted away from religious freedom and toward government supervision in particular by excluding the right to change one's religion guaranteed in previous texts (Ropi 2017, ch. 6). According to Ropi (2017, p. 83), this omission was "a result of compromise after heated debates in the parliament when some Muslim members of parliament voiced strong objection to any religious conversion." These activists argued conversion

> ... went against Islamic teaching ... Negative Islamic sentiment over the issue of conversion was evident in the parliamentary discussions, and it was due to strong pressure from Muslim parties that the clauses, particularly on the right for conversion (together with remaining clauses such as the right to manifest religious/belief expression in public and the right of religious education for children previously found in the 1949 Federal Constitution) were removed. (Ropi 2017, p. 83)

It is quite clear that Muslim objections were targeted at Christian missionaries, the group most likely to seek conversion of Muslims, and was part of a broader discourse popular in Muslim anti-colonial circles arguing that religious freedom is equivalent to imperialism (Menchik 2016, introduction). We may reasonably conclude, however, that this argument was somewhat suspect, at least on the part of Muslim nationalists, since their argument against Dutch colonial rule was that it impeded their religious freedom to practice Islam (Ropi 2017, ch. 5). Through this lens, it is clear that Muslim parties benefited from the harmony of their notion of religious freedom with the integralist tendency among Indonesia's secular nationalists, whereby group rights were privileged over those of the individual. Thus, if a group, Muslims, would be offended by the decision of an individual to change his religion, the rights of the individual would give way for the good of the whole.

Even as Muslim nationalists won a qualified victory in the 1950 constitution, events elsewhere in the Archipelago served to complicate the picture. Most notable of these was the split between Masyumi, the unified political party of Muslim nationalists, and NU. Arguably, this split marks the beginning of NU's shift toward its eventual staunch defense of Pancasila, even against its perceived abridgment by the government (Ramage 1995). In many ways, the split had been a long time coming. While Masyumi's formation papered over the long-standing cleavages in Indonesian Islam, the increasing concentration of power in the hands of Muhammadiyah-style modernist Muslims and central Javanese business elites cannot have sat well with NU, with its base in the traditional pesantren of Central and East Java (Boland 1982, ch. 1). Yet B.J. Boland also points out an increasing difference in the political programs of the two Muslim parties:

> The resolutions and the action programme of the NU drawn up in 1952 give the impression that its religio-political formulations were less clearly Islamic than those of the Masyumi. Probably it was easier simply to quote available formulas, for example, those of the Pancasila and the 1945 Constitution. For instance, the NU wanted "to press the government to intensify instruction in the Pancasila to be given in an orderly and fundamental way, in particular instruction concerning the (first) pillar of Belief in God, to which clearly too little attention is being paid". (Boland 1982, p. 51)

NU hinted here at a strategy of seeking to promote Islamization of the Muslim population through Pancasila, which would be followed to great effect by Muslim activists in the future. These political differences combined with the traditional fear of NU leaders that modernist fundamentalism would erode traditional Islam were probably sufficient to cause the split. Notwithstanding this division, Islamic forces were able to consolidate their control over the Ministry of Religious Affairs during this time, denying recognized religious status to traditional Indonesian mysticism or *kebatinan*, in the process (Ropi 2017, ch. 7). While practitioners of *kebatinan* argued that *ketuhanan yang maha esa* was actually a formulation unique to their tradition that pre-dated Islam, Muslim activists were able to prevent *kebatinan*'s recognition by the state and gain authority from the Ministry of Religious Affairs to favor a more Islamic interpretation of the Pancasila (Ropi 2017, ch. 7). In short, under Sukarno, the bureaucratic and societal influence of political Islam actually increased even as, politically, it faced serious setbacks.

In September 1965, a coup was launched against the Sukarno government by elements that, at a minimum, sympathized with the Communist Party of Indonesia (PKI) (Ropi 2017, ch. 3). The PKI, in a tactical blunder from which it would never recover, announced its support for the new "revolutionary government," only to see it brutally and efficiently crushed by the military in early October 1965 (Ropi 2017, pp. 135–156). General Suharto, the head of the military, assumed control of the country shortly after the suppression of the coup and engaged in what may fairly be described as a systematic politicide against the PKI and its supporters. Fearing ideological divisions caused by what he saw as the totalizing ideologies of communism and political Islam, Suharto sought to create "a notion of a 'national consensus' which involved 'a total change of the old political structure', and through which competition would involve managed contests over means rather than over ideologies and ultimate ends, and technocratic in impulse" (Elson 2008, p. 247). Pancasila was to be transformed from a temporary compromise that was "good enough" for all sides, into a framework on which a new and, it was hoped, enduring national project could be built (Elson 2008, p. 247). This integralist approach to Pancasila was at the heart of the New Order and would have significant implications for the relationship between Islam and the state.

The early stages of the New Order, running roughly from 1966 to the mid-1970s, would prove critical to the formulation of the regime's religious management policy. While the new regime was adamant in its opposition to autonomous religious parties, it lacked a coherent intellectual framework or policy approach to integrate religion until it faced opposition from some Muslim leaders (Ropi 2017, ch. 10). Eventually, the regime settled on a policy of de-politicizing religion, ensuring adherents to orthodoxy through the Ministry of Religious Affairs and at the same time mobilizing religion in support of the New Order's development plan and in opposition to anti-religious forces such as communism (Ropi 2017, ch. 11). These concrete actions rested on two underlying doctrinal premises. First, Indonesia was neither a secular nor a theocratic state but a religious one (Ropi 2017, ch. 10). Simply put, Indonesia would impose no specific religious ideology but would maintain public religiosity as a social good, permitting religious groups to ensure internal orthodoxy and receive state benefits so long as they supported the national consensus and worked toward national goals (Ropi 2017, ch. 10). The second premise was that, while religious freedom was recognized in the constitution of 1945, such freedom must be exercised responsibly by all parties (Ropi

2017, ch. 10). For the New Order, a "responsible" exercise of religious freedom did not produce "conflict that threatened the unity and oneness of the nation (*persatuan and kesatuan bangsa*)" (Ropi 2017, p. 130). Any exercise of religious freedom that created such conflict could, by this understanding, be subject to government action (Ropi 2017, ch. 10). Though many of these restrictions on religious freedom mirrored those Muslim nationalists themselves demanded after 1945, they became the most frequent victims of this policy in the first 20 years of the New Order.

Beginning in the late 1970s, systematic efforts were made to integrate Muslim organizations into the Pancasila corporatism of the New Order. Part of this initiative was new legislation requiring mass organizations to accept Pancasila. The corporatist logic behind this measure was of course impeccable, as it would only further enshrine the dominance of the Pancasila ideal and exclude notions such as liberalism, Marxism, and those strands of political Islam committed to a total vision of the Islamic state. Many Muslim activists saw the mass-organizations legislation as an attempt to "kill Islam with Pancasila" (Elson 2008, p. 260). Thus, within Islamic organizations, the process proved contentious.

By the early 1980s, NU was ready to seek a rapprochement with the regime (Ismail 1995, ch. 3). As will be discussed further, NU had seen the rise of a new generation of young, liberally oriented Muslim activists who decisively rejected the idea of an Islamic state. Finally, NU was always primarily interested in defending traditional Indonesian Islam against what it saw as puritan modernist Salafism of Middle Eastern origin. Hence, its ends were quite compatible with Indonesian nationalism based on Pancasila. As a result, NU announced its willingness to make Pancasila the sole basis of its organization, formally adopting this position at its 27th national congress in 1984 (Ismail 1995, ch. 3). At the same gathering, NU also announced its intention to forego direct political participation as an organization in the future and "return to the spirit of 1926," taking on a purely socio-religious role henceforward (Ismail 1995, ch. 3). As the subsequent history of Indonesia demonstrates, what was true of the organization as a whole did not necessarily also apply to the prominent leaders of that organization and, in particular, its longtime leader Abdurrahman Wahid.

For NU, Islam was formally de-politicized to a degree rarely seen elsewhere, a de-politicization allowed, from their perspective, due to the tolerant idea of public religion embedded in Pancasila. Since *ketuhanan yang maha esa* was, from the NU perspective, fully in accordance with Muslim doctrines, it was not necessary to pursue full Islamization of the state and not really even desirable. In fact, NU leader Achmad Siddiq even

> ...asserted that, for the Muslims, the establishment of the Pancasila-based state of Indonesia was the final goal of their political aspirations, not simply a transitional goal. This meant that any idea of establishing an Islamic state cannot be considered part of Muslim political aspirations, and any attempt to do so by any Muslim group would not represent the aspirations of the entire community. (Ismail 1995, ch. 3)

This declaration has governed the political participation of NU for at least 40 years and has turned the organization into one of Indonesia's chief bulwarks against any attempt at creating an Islamic state.

Even as the Suharto regime sought, with some modest success, to de-politicize Islam, the faith experienced an awakening and the strengthening of both pluralist and fundamentalist currents. Ironically, the combination of de-politicization, on one hand, and encouragement of religion in general, on the other, probably fostered this revival, as mosques and prayer meetings became some of the freest intellectual spaces under the New Order (Porter 2002, p. 247). On the fundamentalist side, the Dewan Dakwah Islamiyah Indonesia (DDII) served as a major source of support and organization (Solahudin 2013, p. 66). Founded in 1967 by Muhammad Natsir, a former Masyumi leader now disaffected with politics, the DDII served as a vehicle for the transmission of fundamentalist and pan-Islamist ideas from the Middle East to Indonesia (Solahudin 2013, pp. 66–67). DDII worked closely with the Wahhabi-influenced Muslim World League, headquartered in Saudi Arabia, as well as several international Muslim student organizations of similar inclination (Solahudin 2013, p. 66). Indeed, Muhammad Natsir eventually rose to the position of vice president within the Muslim World League (Van Bruinessen 2002, pp. 117–154). DDII followed in the long tradition of Islamic modernizers drawing on ideas from Mecca and Medina, and the somewhat shorter but still very real tradition of Wahhabi-influenced Islam born out of that movement's occupation of the two holy shrines in the nineteenth century (Van Bruinessen 1999, 2002; Laffan 2003). Unsurprisingly, these attitudes, combined with rising expectations of New Order support that were subsequently crushed, led to a radicalization of elements within modernist Indonesian Islam.

The radicals imbibed Middle Eastern Islamist notions about anti-Semitism and the international Zionist conspiracy and applied them to their own circumstances (Van Bruinessen 1999). Chinese Catholic business elites, in particular, were seen as part of this worldwide anti-Islamic movement (Van Bruinessen 1999). In part, this was opportunism, born of the ethnoreligious difference and real and perceived wealth of this community. In part, it was also a result of the connection between Indonesian intelligence services, led by Ali Murtopo, and the Center for Strategic and International Studies, a think tank started by Chinese Catholics (Porter 2002, ch. 5). Nevertheless, the framing of local Christians in the global Islamist discourse of anti-colonialism and anti-Zionism, notwithstanding the fact that most Indonesian Christians had as little connection to any international Zionist movement as their Hindu, Buddhist, or even abangan counterparts, would have serious implications for Indonesia in the late New Order period and beyond. Further, fundamentalists stepped up their attacks on Indonesian traditionalism, Islamic pluralism, and any practices smacking of localized Indonesian Islam (Van Bruinessen 2002). Nor did they back down in their call for an Islamic state by any means necessary (Solahudin 2013, ch. 1). Some of them even organized into a new Darul Islam movement, which would become the source of most of the radical Islamist terrorism Indonesia has experienced in subsequent decades (Solahudin 2013, ch. 1).

For all their growth in this time period, the fundamentalists did not have the Muslim sphere to themselves. A new generation of liberal and pluralist Muslim activists arose and spent a great deal of their time and energy countering this fundamentalist impulse. Like the fundamentalists, the pluralists grew, at least in part, out of the de-politicization of the Muslim sphere under the New Order. As Elson (2008, p. 261) explains: "The resistance of the old Muslim elite, ironically, assisted the emergence of a new set of more pragmatic Muslim leaders ... much less taken with old issues of the Islamic state ... [who] sought to develop a more pluralist vision of the place of Islam in the New Order scheme of things." Two leaders were particularly integral to this new pluralist elite: Nurcholish Madjid and Abdurrahman Wahid. The two men came from widely different backgrounds. Madjid's roots were in modernist Islam and, in particular, modernist student activism (Van Bruinessen 1999). Wahid, by contrast, was the scion of a prominent NU family, having two grandfathers who were founders of the organization (Porter 2002, ch. 6). Yet they both advanced conceptions of Islam characterized by pluralism, tolerance of religious minorities, pro-Pancasila, and openness to liberal thought and democratic values.

Nurcholish Madjid became the spokesman of the *pembaharuan* (renewal) movement, with its origins in the Muslim student association HMI (Van Bruinessen 1999). The underlying premise of Madjid's thought was that "Muslims had to seek the essence of God's message to the Prophet and not content themselves with a formal and literal reading of scripture. This inevitably necessitated sensitivity to context—the context of revelation as well as the context where the message had to be put into practice" (Van Bruinessen 1999, p. 56). If these ideas seem to resonate with liberal Christian theological notions, such resonance was no accident: Madjid was both American educated and influenced by liberal ideas that dominated religious studies and sociology of religion in the US at the time (Van Bruinessen 1999). He saw other religions, Christianity in particular, as valid paths to God and also quite openly embraced Pancasila and the quest for a truly Indonesian Islam (Van Bruinessen 1999).

Wahid's ideas, unsurprisingly, drew much more strongly on traditionalist sources and cannot be identified with Western liberal religious thought in the same way as Madjid's (Van Bruinessen 1999). Nevertheless, Van Bruinessen (1999, p. 56) asserts that Wahid "formulated even more daring ideas about equal rights for women and religious minorities, secularism, national integration and democratization than the pembaharuan group did." Educated at Al-Azhar University and in Baghdad, Wahid became a sharp critic of what he saw as the excessive reliance on formal memorization and shallow thinking in Islamic education (Stephens 2007). Yet he was equally critical of Western positivism, which, in his words, "relies too much on the idea of conquering knowledge and mastering scientific principles alone" (Abdurrahman Wahid quoted in Stephens 2007).

Both Madjid and Wahid were extremely firm in rejecting the notion of an Islamic state and in their embrace of Pancasila, positions that endeared both men to Suharto and the New Order in the 1970s and early 1980s (Van Bruinessen 1999). Yet, in an ironic reversal, this same commitment to pluralism and Pancasila would push Wahid into opposition in the 1990s, as the New Order sought an accommodation with the very forces of political Islam it previously sought to suppress.

PANCASILA AND DEMOCRATIZATION

Beginning in the late 1980s and accelerating throughout the 1990s, Suharto abruptly pivoted from opposition to any form of political Islam not circumscribed by Pancasila to active courting of Islamic modernist elites (Porter 2002, ch. 5). To a certain extent, the stage for this reorientation was set by the work of men like Minister of Religious Affairs Alamsjah Perwiranegara, who criticized the government's blanket hostility to Muslims as a group (Ismail 1995, ch. 2). Then too, Suharto had become suspicious of the military, which he feared was beginning to plan for a future without him (Porter 2002, ch. 6). The controversy swirled around a prominent Javanese Catholic general named Benny Murdani, who wished to preserve the military's role as the guardian of Pancasila corporate nationalism and so sought to constrain Suharto's choice of successor along lines deemed suitable to these goals (Porter 2002, ch. 7). Suharto, by contrast, demonstrated a preference for personalism above Pancasila, seeking to keep power concentrated in his hands and those of his family (Porter 2002, ch. 5 and 7). As Suharto became suspicious of the armed forces, he began to turn to the Islamic modernists and to cultivate those military officers and civilian officials with a more explicitly Islamist orientation. Foremost among this new Islamist faction within the corporatist elite was B.J. Habibie, the minister of technology and the man who would serve as vehicle for the hopes of Islamists in the 1990s. No event was more symbolic of Suharto's tilt toward the Islamists than his 1990 pilgrimage to Mecca. As Porter (2002, p. 88) explains: "The president was accompanied by a coterie of family members (including his brother-in-law Maj. Gen. Wismoyo Arismunandar, and his son-in-law Colonel Prabowo Subianto), his close business associate Bob Hasan, Armed Forces Chief Try Sutrisno, and cabinet ministers."

From a practical perspective, the tilt toward Islamists was represented in three ways. First, the number of Christians in high positions throughout the government and military was reduced (Porter 2002, ch. 6). Second, a new organization, Indonesian Association of Muslim Intellectuals (ICMI), was created to bring together and empower Muslim intellectuals supportive of Islamization (Ramage 1995, ch. 3). Through ICMI, Suharto gave advocates of political Islam the opportunity to participate in, and benefit from, the corporatist system (Porter 2002, ch. 5). Figures such as Habibie, ICMI luminary Amien Rais, and leaders of the Muslim student association HMI all increased their influence on Suharto and his government. Third,

Suharto passed new laws on religious education and religious courts, designed to strengthen political Islam institutionally (Ramage 1995, ch. 2).

The most effective opposition to this new movement toward Islamization came from one of Indonesia's most powerful and popular Muslim leaders: Abdurrahman Wahid. He saw ICMI, which represented the Islamic modernist stream within Indonesia, as a direct competitor to NU and was concerned about the impact the increasing prominence of ICMI might have on his organization (Porter 2002, ch. 6). Yet there was also a philosophical objection. As Porter (2002, ch. 6) explains, Wahid feared the mutual co-optation of Islamic modernists and the state, and feared that groups like ICMI, with their conception of an "Islamic society" imagined along the lines of Islamic modernist orthodoxy, was advocacy for an Islamic state by stealth that would necessitate the overthrow of both Pancasila and Indonesian nationalism. Wahid was very concerned about the potential role ICMI might play in Islamizing politics and society and viewed rhetoric about the need for an "Islamic society" with suspicion. In his own words:

> That's why I quarrel with Amien Rais, who would like to establish an Islamic society. For me an Islamic society in Indonesia is treason against the constitution because it will make non-Muslims second-class citizens. But an "Indonesian society" where the Muslims are strong—and strong means functioning well—then I think that is good. (Abdurrahman Wahid quoted in Ramage 1995, p. 64)

Indeed, Abdurrahman regularly and publicly expressed his concern about what he saw as an attempt by elements within ICMI to achieve Islamization by stealth and saw ICMI as a Trojan horse for disaffected and disappointed ex-Masyumi activists and their ideological heirs (Ramage 1995, ch. 2). Equally troubling, from Abdurrahman's perspective, was what he saw as the increasingly paranoid anti-Christian rhetoric emanating from elements within ICMI (Ramage 1995, ch. 2). All of this, he feared, might lead either to increased sectarian tension and conflict between Muslim activists and the army or to an increasing and, in his view, unwarranted relationship of mutual co-optation between Islam and the state (Ramage 1995, ch. 2).

In contrast, Abdurrahman:

> saw NU's vast constituency as a starting point for a pluralistic, civil society; one based on a tolerant society, democracy and respect for human rights. He

stressed the strategic role NU could play as an independent social force, a countervailing power to the state that would gain a better bargaining position in relation to state power. (Porter 2002, p. 110)

These views were controversial both within NU and even in his own family, with his uncle serving as one of Abdurrahman's chief internal antagonists (Ramage 1995, ch. 2). His ICMI antagonists often spoke of the need to "Islamize Abdurrahman" or accused him of showing undue favoritism to secular nationalists and religious minorities (Ramage 1995, ch. 2). One ICMI stalwart, after the formation of the organization, even went so far as to say that one of the organization's chief accomplishments would be to remove the perception that Abdurrahman Wahid spoke for Indonesian Islam (Ramage 1995, ch. 3). Yet a significant group of liberal-minded thinkers within NU fully agreed with the notion that their organization could be a force for pluralism, democratization, and civil society within Indonesian Islam (Porter 2002, ch. 6). In any event, even many of those who did not agree completely with Abdurrahman's liberalism saw him as a vital voice and a "bridge to the future" for both NU in particular and Indonesian Islam more broadly (Ramage 1995, ch. 2).

Practically, Abdurrahman Wahid's beliefs led to a number of concrete actions that both solidified his position as a leading opposition figure and seriously irritated Suharto. In 1992, as pressure mounted to endorse Suharto for a fifth term, Abdurrahman called for a mass rally (*Rapat Akbar*) to commemorate the anniversary of the formation of NU (Porter 2002, ch. 6). Rather than endorsing Suharto directly, he pledged his loyalty, and that of NU, to the Pancasila, an act to which Suharto could not object, but which stood as an implicit critique of the president's opening to Islamists (Ramage 1995, ch. 2). Even before the *Rapat Akbar*, Abdurrahman helped form the Forum for Democracy, a discussion group with a democratic and opposition flavor, in 1991 (Porter 2002, ch. 6). In 1995, he visited Israel and, on his return, stated his belief that Indonesia should recognize the Jewish state, an action that enraged pan-Islamists within ICMI (Porter 2002, ch. 2). Most of all, he continuously advocated both for democratization and against what he saw as the reconfessionalization of politics, and weakening of Pancasila, which ICMI represented. Suharto tried several times to remove Abdurrahman from the chairmanship of NU, in collusion with those forces within the organization hostile to him, but to no avail (Porter 2002, ch. 6). In the end, Abdurrahman Wahid, the chairman of Indonesia's largest Muslim organization, would also prove one of the fiercest and most persistent critics of the New Order's authoritarianism and Islamist opening, all in the name of the very Pancasila ideology on which Suharto's regime was premised.

In attempting to strengthen his regime by co-opting political Islam, President Suharto exacerbated ethnoreligious tensions, burned bridges with old allies, and hastened the fragmentation of Indonesian society. Yet what brought his regime down, in the end, had very little to do with Islam. A combination of increasingly blatant familial corruption and the disastrous 1998 financial crisis proved too much for the tottering New Order structure. Since its advent in 1967, the rule of Suharto and the New Order was based on two premises: economic development and stability within society. By 1998, it was clear that Suharto could no longer provide either. Thus, he resigned, leaving the government in the hands of his hand-picked successor, B.J. Habibie. For many Islamists, Habibie was seen as their champion in the byzantine world of New Order elite competition (Porter 2002, ch. 7). Others viewed him with more skepticism, even going so far as to question his commitment to Islam (Ramage 1995, ch. 3). In any case, the skills of an economic nationalist bureaucratic in-fighter with strong Islamist ties were not well suited to the chaotic politics of post-economic crisis and post-Suharto Indonesia. If Habibie represented the Islamist moment, it would prove a short one.

With respect to Islam's relationship with the state, the nearly 70-year period of democracy in Indonesia that has resulted from the fall of Suharto has been marked by contradictions. On one hand, explicitly Islamist parties in Indonesia have fared very badly in national elections. Typical, in this regard, was the first free presidential election, in which the various Islamist parties combined, if one excludes the explicitly non-sectarian political vehicles of Amien Rais and Abdurrahman Wahid, failed to reach 20 percent of the vote (Van Bruinessen 2002). Indeed, so dire was this finish that Rais, after uniting the various Islamist parties and finding insufficient support to re-elect Habibie, forged an alliance of convenience with Abdurrahman merely to stop Megawati Sukarno Putri, daughter of Sukarno, leader of the largest secular party and preferred candidate of many Christians, from becoming president. Thus, very briefly, Abdurrahman Wahid served as president of Indonesia. Yet on the other hand, Islamic populism has risen steadily throughout the period of democratization, backlit by a constant atmosphere of sectarian tension. All of this also ties in with complex issues of regionalism, decentralization, radical Islamic terrorism, economic development, and, particularly post-9/11, increasing attention to Indonesian Islam from Western observers in search of the magic formula for Muslim tolerance, liberalization, and modernization.

With respect to the regulation of religion and Islam's position in the state, post-New Order democracy represents, on the whole, continuity with the recent past. That is, attempts to make Indonesia an explicitly Islamic state have failed, but issues involving proselytization, houses of worship, and the government's role in policing the boundaries of Muslim orthodoxy remain. During the new constitutional consultative process that culminated in 2001, several Islamist parties, notable among them the Prosperous Justice Party or PKS, pushed for the reintroduction of the Jakarta Charter or, in some cases, the formal transformation of Indonesia into an Islamic state (Ropi 2017, ch. 13). Once again, these political Islamic activists were to be disappointed, as it was determined that the articles on religion should remain unchanged (Ropi 2017, ch. 13). Thus, both the Pancasila framework and the regulatory role of MORA remained as hallmarks of the Indonesian state. In that capacity, many of the religious tensions created or exacerbated by New Order-era policies remained. For example, an attempt in 2006 to clarify the New Order law restricting the building of new houses of worship clarified the process and made it easier in some ways while also increasing the bureaucratization of the permit process and limiting the growth of non-Muslim places of worship in Muslim-majority areas (Ropi 2017, ch. 14). Likewise, Ministry of Religious Affairs (MORA) was called upon to once again address the question of the Ahmadiyah, a Muslim community considered heretical by mainstream Muslim groups (Ropi 2017, ch. 14). During the New Order, Ahmadiyah faced legal exclusion and some harassment, but the government, perhaps motivated by a desire to placate Islamist sentiment, cracked down on the group in 2008 (Ropi 2017, ch. 14).

One new wrinkle in the balance between Islam and the state, about which some controversy remains and which might fairly be described as a live issue yet to be resolved, involves the implementation of sharia law at a regional and municipal level. After Suharto's resignation, Indonesia embarked on what Stepan and Künkler (2013, introduction) describe as one of the most rapid decentralization processes in history. While this process was remarkably successful in many ways, it also allowed for the proliferation of various sharia-based statutes in sub-regional municipalities (Künkler and Stepan 2013, introduction). Ismatu Ropi (2017, ch. 13) estimates some 75 of these municipalities have implemented sharia statutes, with regional concentrations in areas such as Aceh and West Java known for their strict Muslim orthodoxy. Once again, the tension between the religious freedom of the individual and the will of the group has proven controversial in Indonesia. Yet the sharia issue represents a very delicate question, given that some of these laws may contradict elements of the federal Indonesian legal code (Künkler and Stepan 2013, introduction). Not surprisingly, then, Indonesia's ongoing attempt to balance religion and the state remains a work in progress.

What is increasingly clear, however, is that NU is the pivot point on which the future of Indonesia's balance between religion and the state will turn. On one hand, NU has consistently eschewed any call for strident secularism; on the other, it has been equally firm, if not firmer, in rejecting an Islamic state. Thus, for example, NU sided firmly with secularists and religious minorities in the 2019 election to support the incumbent president, Jokowi, against his Islamist-leaning challenger, Suharto's son-in-law Prabowo. In return, Jokowi chose a vice president who is closely allied with NU and appointed the former head of Gerakan Pemuda (GP) Ansor (the NU youth wing) as his minister of religious affairs.

Given the important role it plays for Indonesia's future, then, it is significant that elements within NU have begun to expand on Abdurrahman Wahid's vision of Pancasila pluralism and Islamic reform, launching a truly audacious effort with potentially global implications. This program is succinctly summed up in a document called the Nusantara Manifesto, promulgated jointly by GP Ansor and Bayt-ar-Rahmah, a civil society organization closely associated with the newly elected general secretary of NU, K.H. Yahya Cholil Staquf; the Nusantara Manifesto clearly lays out this audacious program. Several critical elements from the manifesto stand out. First, the goal of the manifesto is to reform what it describes as "obsolete and problematic tenets of Islamic orthodoxy," in which they include "offensive jihad, slavery, the subordination of infidels, stoning adulterers, executing homosexuals and amputating the hands of thieves" (Ansor and ar-Rahmah 2018, Statement 109). As the manifesto explains: "Social groupings based on religious identity are a natural phenomenon. The problem with certain tenets of Islamic orthodoxy lies in the fact that these invariably incarnate as a form of political identity, with a marked tendency to embrace absolutism and a hidden or explicit agenda of dominating the existing political order, whatever that may happen to be. Whether this struggle to acquire political supremacy is waged blatantly or covertly is simply a matter of strategy and tactics" (Ansor and ar-Rahmah 2018,

Statement 23). This critique of Islamism has much in common with classical republican thought, particularly in its emphasis on non-domination. The manifesto sees this domination manifest both within Indonesia and globally. After analyzing the history of Indonesia's constitutional development discussed above, the Nusantara Manifesto concludes that "Islamism-especially as a political movement based on religious identity-is indeed a latent, enduring threat to the existence of the Unitary State of the Republic of Indonesia (NKRI) as a multi-religious and pluralistic (Pancasila) nation state" (Ansor and ar-Rahmah 2018, Statement 21). Yet the problem, as the manifesto makes explicit, is global:

> So long as obsolete, medieval tenets within Islamic orthodoxy remain the dominant source of religious authority throughout the Muslim world, Indonesian Islamists will continue to draw power and sustenance from developments in the world at large. This is especially true so long as key state actors—including Iran, Turkey, Saudi Arabia, Qatar, and Pakistan—continue to weaponize problematic tenets of Islamic orthodoxy in pursuit of their respective geopolitical agendas. (Ansor and ar-Rahmah 2018, Statement 36)

The response proposed in the manifesto is two-fold. First,

> Gerakan Pemuda Ansor and Bayt ar-Rahmah are moving systematically, and institutionally, to address those obsolete and historically-contingent (or *mutaghayyirat*) elements within Islamic jurisprudence that lend themselves to tyranny, by creating a theological framework for the recontextualization of Islamic teachings and the reform of problematic tenets within Islamic orthodoxy. (Ansor and ar-Rahmah 2018, Statement 97)

With the election of K.H. Yahya Cholil Staquf as general secretary of NU, it is reasonable to assume NU as a whole will also be committed to this project. The mechanism for this project is spelled out clearly:

> Islamic orthodoxy contains internal mechanisms, including the science of *uṣūl al-fiqh*—the methodology of independent legal reasoning employed to create Islamic law, or *fiqh* (often conflated with *shari'ah*)—that allow Muslim scholars to adjust the temporal elements of religious orthodoxy in response to the ever-changing circumstances of life. These internal mechanisms entail a process of independent legal reasoning known as ijtihad, which fell into

disuse among Sunni Muslim scholars approximately five centuries ago. (Ansor and ar-Rahmah 2018, Statement 106)

Here, the earlier discussion of collective *ijtihad* once again becomes relevant, since it creates an authoritative mechanism for new *fiqh* to be developed and accepted. Second, the manifesto calls for "a global strategy to develop a new Islamic orthodoxy that reflects the actual circumstances of the modern world in which Muslims must live and practice their faith" (Ansor and ar-Rahmah 2018, Statement 38). After listing out threats Muslims face in the global context, including the surveillance state of the Chinese Communist Party (CCP), the threat of Islamist violence, and the corresponding weaponization of polarization in many Western societies, the Nusantara Manifesto draws a connection between them all.

> Each is inextricably linked to the innate human tendency to dominate, or seek to dominate, others. And each illustrates the danger posed by welding dogma-whether secular or religious-to a political agenda backed by powerful economic interests and the use of technology to impose conformity (in effect, a "tribal identity") upon others, and crush the spirit of anyone who opposes this agenda. (Ansor and ar-Rahmah 2018, Statement 86)

Taken together, the Nusantara Manifesto points toward several realities of religion and state in contemporary Indonesia. First, as they have been since before independence, the traditional, largely Javanese Muslims NU represents remain a bulwark of both Pancasila pluralism and Indonesian nationalism. Second, this commitment is no longer just defensive. The Nusantara Manifesto uses Pancasila pluralism as an interpretive framework to recontextualize Indonesian Islam for the modern world. This builds off the sentiments expressed by Achmad Siddiq, in 1984, but instead of arguing that Islam is compatible with Pancasila, the manifesto implies that Pancasila is a more authentic expression of the true spirit of Islam than the "medieval Islamic orthodoxy" it finds "obsolete and problematic." This is a bold assertion—and one which, if it becomes widely accepted in Indonesia, would have huge implications. Third, NU sees this mission as not only national, but global, meaning that they envision Indonesia as playing a vital and specific role in twenty-first-century Islam. In effect, the manifesto argues that recontextualization for the modern context must be a global project and holds up Indonesia as a model and forerunner of that project. It is an assertion of a kind of Indonesian exceptionalism with a global mission that would redefine Indonesia's place in the global Islamic world. Fourth, the vision NU leadership holds for humanitarian Islam is self-consciously consistent with modernity, human rights, and a rules-based international order. Finally, given that the current head of MORA is the former leader of GP Ansor, and also brother to NU General Secretary K.H. Yahya Cholil Staquf, it is fair to say that the Indonesian state regulatory apparatus will likely support these efforts. The multi-interpretable Pancasila formula, then, may have taken on a form and mission with potentially global ramifications. If the hopes expressed in the Nusantara Manifesto indeed prove to be an enduring reality, then the impact of Indonesia's unique balance between religion and state may be felt around the world for years and decades to come.

References

Anderson, B. 2006. *Imagined Communities: Reflections on the Origin and Spread of Nationalism*. London: Verso books.

Ansor, G.P. and Bayt ar-Rahmah. 2018. *The Nusantara Manifesto*. Jakarta: Global Unity Forum. https://www.baytarrahmah.org/media/2018/Nusantara-Manifesto.pdf.

Asy'ari, H.S.H. 1926. *Introduction to the Fundamental Principles of Nahdlatul Ulama*. Transcript of speech delivered at inaugural meeting of Nahdlatul Ulama, Surabaya, Dutch East Indies, January 23. https://baytarrahmah.org/about-us/Introduction-to-the-Fundamental-Principles-of-Nahdlatul-Ulama.pdf.

Boland, B.J. 1982. The Political Struggle (1945–1955). In *The Struggle of Islam in Modern Indonesia* (pp. 7–84). Dordrecht: Springer.

Elson, R.E. 2008. *The Idea of Indonesia: A History*. Cambridge: Cambridge University Press.

Federspiel, H.M. 2001. *Islam and Ideology in the Emerging Indonesian State: The Persatuan Islam (Persis), 1923–1957*. Leiden: Brill.

Hosen, N. 2004. Nahdlatul ulama and Collective ijtihad. *New Zealand Journal of Asian Studies* 6: 5–26.

Ismail, F. 1995. *Islam, Politics and Ideology in Indonesia: A Study of the Process of Muslim Acceptance of the Pancasila*. PhD diss., McGill University. http://digitool.library.mcgill.ca/R/-?func=dbin-jumpfull&object_id=39924&silo_library=GEN01. Accessed 12 Oct 2017.

Künkler, M., and A. Stepan, eds. 2013. *Democracy and Islam in Indonesia*. Vol. 13. New York: Columbia University Press.

Laffan, M.F. 2003. *Islamic Nationhood and Colonial Indonesia: The Umma Below the Winds*. Abingdon-on-Thames: Routledge.

Menchik, J. 2016. *Islam and Democracy in Indonesia: Tolerance Without Liberalism.* Cambridge: Cambridge University Press.

Porter, D. 2002. *Managing Politics and Islam in Indonesia.* Abingdon-on-Thames: Routledge.

Ramage, D.E. 1995. *Politics in Indonesia: Democracy, Islam and the Ideology of Tolerance.* Abingdon-on-Thames: Routledge.

Ropi, I. 2017. *Religion and Regulation in Indonesia.* Singapore: Springer Nature.

Solahudin. 2013. *The Roots of Terrorism in Indonesia: From Darul Islam to Jema'ah Islamiyah.* Trans. Dave McRae. Ithaca: Cornell University Press.

Stephens, B. 2007. The Last King of Java. *The Wall Street Journal.* April 7. https://www.wsj.com/articles/SB117591182092262904.   Accessed 17 Oct 2017.

Van Bruinessen, M. 1999. Global and local in Indonesian Islam. *Southeast Asian Studies* 37 (2): 46–63.

———. 2002. Genealogies of Islamic Radicalism in Post-Suharto Indonesia. *South East Asia Research* 10 (2): 117–154.

CHAPTER 16

Relationship Between State and Religion in India: A Sphere of Indifference, Contradictions, or Engagement?

James Ponniah

TRAJECTORY OF STATE-RELIGION RELATIONSHIP IN PRE-BRITISH INDIA: A HISTORICAL OVERVIEW

Vedic Period

Ian Copland et al. in their work (2012) note that the Vedic period was quite a fluid lifeworld as people were still mobile with their herds and flocks, and it was only after the Vedic period that the idea of territorial kingdom began to emerge with the establishment of urban centres and little kingdoms ruled by a king with the help of "a retinue of dignitaries, *ratnins* (literally, 'bestowers of wealth')" (Copland et al. 2012, p. 35). Among them were the *purohits* and scholarly Brahmins who played a role in creating regular state apparatus (Copland) by accepting certain Kshatriyas as people of high status and endorsing their position as ruling

J. Ponniah (✉)
School of Philosophy and Religious Thought, University of Madras, Chennai, India

© The Author(s), under exclusive license to Springer Nature Switzerland AG 2023
S. Holzer (ed.), *The Palgrave Handbook of Religion and State Volume II*, https://doi.org/10.1007/978-3-031-35609-4_16

aristocrats. As years rolled on, just as the kingdom began to expand terri-
torially into the hinterlands, the body of Brahmins too began to grow in
big numbers in urban centres. In the context of expanding kingdoms, it is
no more city-based Brahmins but certain wandering mendicants known as
sramanas, that is, Buddhists, Jains, and Ajivikas at that time, who played a
'transitional role' in the making of the empires and in the state formation
during the late first millennium BC. "(T)he transitional period during
which urban-based Sanskrit culture galloped out from the thriving cities
into a hinterland populated mostly by unknown alien communities, and
before cultural homogenisation and consolidation brought them all into
its social net, the wandering monks were by far the best-equipped members of society to act as mediators between the metropolitan and local
cultures. This was their heyday" (Copland, p. 50).

The Sramanas, especially the Buddhist monks, who made frequent trips
between the forests to meditate and the remote villages in the hinterland
close to the forests to gather food, became mediators between the monarchs and the rural populace. While expanding their territory, just as the
king had to connect himself to the people in the hinterland and the rural
communities, the sramanas emerged as de facto mediators between the
state and its people. "The ruler needed the support of men of influence
and high reputation who could make cultural bonds between his metropolitan capital and the still-to-be assimilated minority cultures in the
countryside. Ideally, such men would have the capacity to impart, to these
unruly populations, a set of universal values, which could make sense to
any people from any culture. Such certainly was the Buddhist *dhamma*.
Their message was positive, reassuring and inclusive. This was precisely the
sort of inclusive programme that would allow a monarchical state to reach
out to its subjects in the absence of a common culture and language"
(Copland, p. 52).

In this regard, Ian Copland and his peers believe "the rulers in the early
stages of Buddhism's rise also took a practical interest in the dhamma as a
partner in the state-building project" (Copland et al. 2012, p. 53). As a
result, while great emperors like Ashoka (whose reign is usually dated
c.269–232 BC), the third ruler of the Mauryan dynasty, regarded the
Buddhist monks "politically valuable" (Copland), the latter acquired a
new status and visibility in the public sphere, as they "found themselves
incorporated, as paradigms of morality and respectability, within the state-
sanctioned social order" (Copland). Emperor Ashoka's inscriptions,
known as pillar edicts, duplicated at different sites throughout the empire

provide us with quite a deal of information about the religious policy of his empire. After the bloody Kalinga War which he won but at the cost of the lives of thousands of men and animals (Copland, p. 54), Ashoka converted to Buddhism and underwent a huge personal transformation. In particular, he was drawn towards the teachings of *dhamma*. Pillar Edict 6 clearly shows that he promulgated the practice of *dhamma* as a code of moral behaviour "for the welfare and happiness of the world" (as quoted in Copland, p. 54), thereby making Buddhism the dominant religion of his empire and providing royal patronage to it.

Some scholars tend to think that the *dhamma* Ashoka embraced cannot be exclusively confined to that of Buddhism alone as "the śramaṇas and the Brahmans are frequently twinned in the inscriptions as estimable groups of people worthy of equal respect" (Copland et al. 2012, p. 55). The central message of Ashoka's edicts was that "people should live in harmony and respect one another" (Copland). To ensure peace among the people Rock Edict 12 appeals to the members of the various sects and groups "to practise dhamma by restraint in speech, especially by moderation in praise of their own sect and criticism of others" (Copland). Though most of the royal edicts seem tolerant and humane, Rock Edict 9 is also judgemental and critical as it is contemptuous of ritualistic practices performed especially by women on occasions such as illness, marriages, births, and journeys (Copland). While some of the edicts found in Afghanistan were written in Greek and Aramaic, the equivalent Greek word chosen for *dhamma* were *eusebeia*, 'piety', and the Aramaic *qsyt*, 'truth'. Interestingly, a Greek inscription from Kandahar states that part of *dhamma* is devotion to the ruler because the king is seen as the guardian of *dhamma* and "the principles of a code of moral behaviour (are) to be supervised by the ruler" (Copland, p. 55). The later understanding in a way places the king as an overseer, Lord and Patron who not only will declare to the monks the key texts they should particularly study (Copland, p. 56) but also would mediate, arbitrate, and settle disputes that might otherwise give rise to schisms in Buddhism. For instance, the last line of Minor Rock Edict 3, the famous 'Bairat-Calcutta' inscription states, "This is written so that they [the monks and lay followers] shall know my intention (*abhipreta*)," which can be seen "as a warning to the Buddhist order that it should fall in line with the ruler's creed" (Copland, p. 55). In a similar vein, the Schism Edict found at Kausambi, Sanchi, and Sarnath reads, "Ashoka warns that whoever provokes schism in the sangha must wear white (like laymen) and live outside monastic accommodation" (Copland, p. 56). While such developments call into question the Dumontian view that "the political function in India was traditionally subordinated to the authority of organised religion" (Copland), the fact that Ashoka was "a sponsor of a great Buddhist Council" (Copland, p. 57) brings him closer to and makes him as a predecessor to Roman emperors like Constantine who convened the Council of Nicea to settled theological disputes between Christian churches during the early Christian era. Further, Ashoka created an institution called *dhammamahāmattas*, that is, commissioners of the *dhamma* whose function included establishing *dhamma*, "increasing the interest in dhamma, and attending to the welfare and happiness of those who are devoted to dhamma" (Copland) and "the supervision of prisoners and the poor, sick and old, and the administration of charitable organisations devoted to the dhamma" (Copland). All these policies, initiatives, and institutions that came into existence during this period clearly show that Ashoka transformed his empire into an agency of Buddhist *dhamma* whose outcome, he believed, would bring about peace and harmony to the whole of humanity and the cosmos.

Post-Vedic Gupta Period

The next Indian empire that is of relevance to our topic is the Gupta dynasty (320–540 CE). If the Mauryan Empire, especially under Ashoka, became a strong advocate of Buddhist *dhamma*, the Gupta dynasty projected itself as a staunch supporter of Brahmanic ideology. Copland et al. (2012) prefer to describe Gupta rule as the period of 'Brahmanical Revival' and 'Puranic Hinduism'. During this period, the urban state expanded into the hinterland with the help of Brahmins whom the kings sent out to colonise rural areas. "This process encapsulates the way of Brahmanism, during the centuries of the first millennium, evolved into a new synthesis. Local gods were recognised as special forms of Brahmanical deities, and localised rituals and stories were reinterpreted as expressions of the Vedic world view, which added to the corpus of Brahmanical legend and myth" (Copland, p. 64). While this attempt brought much diversity and plurality into the political system and Hindu religious universe, Brahmanic organising principles of the social order, namely Varnashrama dharma, offered a unified whole in the social realm and brought all social groups (castes) under one umbrella. To enforce compliance with the ideology of pyramidal social order wherein all caste groups were integrated and fitted on the ladder of social hierarchy, the kings did play a crucial role. Skandagupta, for instance, boasted in an inscription that no subject would dare deviate from his religious duty (*dharma*), which is at once a social duty that each one should discharge as his own duty (*svadharma*) as prescribed by his caste and mandated as a caste duty (*kula/jati dharma*). While Brahmins' advocacy of Varnashrama dharma ideology helped maintain and continue their position of supremacy as the top-most class in the social ladder, king's support for the same consolidated their position and role as the guardian of the state and its social order. Puranas written during this period produced cosmologies that furthered this process of integration and cohesion: "(T)he Puranas provided 'cosmological charters', certifying for each community, its unique place in the universe; in this way, people's loyalties to local gods and shrines became slowly linked to a wider explanatory framework, which was, at once, coherent and all-encompassing, and which bound them together to an extent well beyond the capacity of the political or 'national' institutions of those times" (Copland, p. 66).

Alongside upholding and advancing general Hindu ideas and ideals, the Guptas also favoured theistic Hinduism. They particularly favoured Vaishnavism, which received royal patronage. The Guptas made the sacred bird Garuda, a vehicle of Vishnu, as their royal emblem, used the boar (*Varaha*), one of Vishnu's incarnations (*avatar*) as a symbol of royal power, and inscribed on their coins as worshippers of Vishnu (Olson 2017, pp. 18–19). Theistic Hinduism, adopted as a state religion, witnessed phenomenal growth during the Gupta dynasty. The Crown's support for Hinduism not only included the construction of temples and pilgrimage sites, performance of pujas, continuation of Vedic rituals, and so on, but also was evident in the production of religious texts (such as Agamas and Puranas) and the promotion of art, architecture, and science such as the works of Aryabhatta (the first astronomer to calculate pie, to determine the length of the solar year, to argue for the spherical nature of the earth, and to explain the occurrences of eclipses), Bharata's Natyashastra (a treatise on dance, drama, and poetry), and Panchatantra (meant 'to educate young prince in the lessons of statecraft'). All of this speaks volumes for the Guptas and their rule that created a strong and unprecedented Hindu world and worldviews in the subcontinent. That explains why Hindu nationalists like Savarkar valorise this period as the golden age of Indian history.

Some writers point out that the Gupta state like that of Ashoka also followed a policy of religious tolerance. For instance, Samudragupta, though a strong follower of Brahmanic Hindu tradition in his personal life, displayed an attitude of openness and accommodation towards others. He permitted the Sri Lankan king to construct a *vihara* and a rest house near the Bodhi Tree at Gaya for the accommodation of the monks and visitors from the Island Kingdom (Darshini 2005–2006, pp. 167–172). The Chinese Buddhist traveller Faxian who visited India during the reign of Chandragupta II refers to the existence of two Buddhist monasteries in Pataliputra, one Hinayana and the other Mahayana with 600–700 monks (Darshini, p. 169). Based on the numismatic and epigraphic sources, Darshini is of the view that the religious policy of the Gupta kings is three-fold. "For legitimation of their authority they used the mystique of the Vedic rituals and symbolism on the one hand and appropriated some elements of divinity to their person on the other. But for their personal goals, they subscribed to one or the other of popular faiths, mostly of Brahmanic origin. In their public role, they assumed a liberal disposition, allowing freedom as well as, at times, promotion of religious beliefs and practices other than their own" (Darshini, p. 167).

Though inclusive religious policy remained in India as a common approach among most of the kings, pre-modern India was not totally devoid of religious conflict and the use of political force by the kings who disfavoured other religions and sought to destroy them in a few instances. To cite a few examples, Huna ruler Toramana in the fifth century CE is said to have destroyed a Buddhist monastery at Kausambi. More (in) famous than him is his successor Mihirakula (ruled between 515 and 550) who was described as a persecutor of the Buddhists. The Chinese traveller "Xuanzang describes Mihirakula as cruel and oppressive toward Buddhists" (Singh 2017, p. 272), while the Tibet traveller Taranatha also shares this view. While the coins of Mihirakula depict him as follower of Saivism and worshipper of Goddess Lakshmi, he is seen not only as anti-Buddhist as seen above but also as anti-Jaina as recorded in the ninth- and tenth-century Jaina texts which depict Mihirakula as oppressive, tyrannical, and anti-Jaina (Singh). Yet another king who earned a bad reputation for his anti-Buddhist policy was a Saivite king Shashanka in eastern India in the early seventh century. As noted by Xuanzang, he is said "to have destroyed monasteries, cut down the bodhi tree, and tried (unsuccessfully) to replace the image of the Buddha at Bodh Gaya with one of Shiva" (Singh 2017, pp. 273–274). Jha (2018) draws our attention to earlier instances of religious violence performed by kings like Jalauka, a Saivite king, who brought down Buddhist monasteries even during Mauryan emperor Ashoka's period. Similarly, Pushyamitra Shunga who toppled the Buddhist Mauryan dynasty has also destroyed the Ashokan pillared hall and the Kukutarama monastery in Pataliputra in 185 BCE and is believed to have vandalised the famous Sanchi Stupa, burned down the Ghositaram monastery in Kausambi, and murdered Buddhist monks. Thus, Indian historians in the likes of Singh and Jha debunk the popular idea of the "ancient period of Indian history as a golden age marked by social harmony devoid of any religious violence" (Ashraf).

Religious Policy of South Indian Kingdoms

1. Pallavas, Pandyas, and Cholas

Most of the kingdom that ruled different parts of India in the second half of the first millennium and in the first part of the second millennium, like their predecessors, offered patronage to both orthodox and heterodox religious traditions of India such as Jainism, Buddhism, Saivism, and Vaishnavism. For instance, Cheras, Cholas, Pandyas, Kalabhras, and Pallavas extended their support and patronage to both Vedic and non-Vedic Indian traditions (Sumesh 2021, p. 53). However, when kings converted from one religion to another, for instance, from Saivism to Jainism or Buddhism, they provided royal patronage to the newly embraced religion, making it a dominant religion. Thus, it is very common that a particular empire or dynasty provided patronage to different religious traditions during its period of reign. For example, the Pallava Dynasty which ruled South India from its capital Kanchi from the fourth to ninth century CE provided royal patronage to Jainism, Buddhism, and Hinduism. In its port city of Mamallapuram (known as Mahabalipuram today), from which they undertook maritime trade with South East Asia and beyond, we have famous cave and shore temples dedicated to Siva and Vishnu. One of its famous kings, Mahendravarman I, was converted to Saivism from Jainism into which he was born. While he was a great patron of art and architecture, creating a new Dravidian style known as Mahendra style, his exquisite monuments at Mamallapuram contain meticulously designed iconographies, rock-cuttings, and frescos that represented his religion and its myths and beliefs through art forms. Similarly, in the seventh century CE Pandya King Nedumaran (popularly known as *Koon* [hunchback] Pandiyan) converted from Jainism to Saivism and is said to have annihilated Jainism. The kings switching over from one religion to another often meant offering new patronage to a new religion which gained new push for growth. It also meant decline of the former religion which the king disowned. Whether or not such developments led to the physical destruction of the former religion is not clear in all cases. In the case of Nadumaran, he is commonly believed to be behind Sampanthar's (one of the most popular Saivite saints in the South) plan of impalement of 8000 Jaina monks living on eight hills around Madurai as found in the Saiva religious texts of the first seven Tirumurai(s). Scholars like Nilakantasastri (1975) and Champakalakshmi (2011) who have examined such texts and other sources of that period have questioned the historicity of this incident and are of the view that the narratives of impalement of Jaina monks in South India are only fictional and meant to produce and sustain the supremacy of Tamil Saivism in the popular imagination of the Tamil people.

It is to be noted that Sekkilar, a Saivite minister in the Cola court, was the author of *Periyapuranam*, the twelfth *Tirumurai* (the sacred scripture of Tamil Saivites). Similarly, Ottakkuttar, another Saivite, praised as Kaviccakkaravartti 'Emperor among poets', was the official poet to the three later Chola kings, namely, Vikrama Chola, Kulotunga II, and Rajaraja II. Ottakkuttar produced another Saiva text called *Takkaydkapparani*. The close affinity between the crown and religion is a universal phenomenon. Crown's support of a religious tradition was concretely materialised in the patronage extended to the production of religious texts in India too. For instance, the *Tevaram* hymns of Tirunavakkucarar, Sampanthar, and Sundramurthi were collected and codified as the first seven *Tirumurai* by Nambiyandar Nambi under the patronage of Rajaraja I at the beginning of the eleventh century CE (Veluppillai 1993, p. 338). Similarly, it is a well-known fact that three among five Tamil epics, namely, *Cīvaka Cintāmaṇi*, *Cilappatikāram*, and *Valayapathi*, were written by Tamil Jains, while the other two *Manimekalai* and *Kuṇṭalakēci* were authored by Buddhists. Such works may not have come into being between the first and tenth century CE without the patronage of the then ruling kings in Tamil Country. Besides, various attempts by scholars to evolve a periodisation of Tamil literature also indicate that the categories such as Jaina period, Buddhist period, Saiva and Vaishnava period, or Hindu Revival period are often repeated (Zvelebil 1992, pp. 12–16). Such scholarly views once again unpack the relationship between the empire and the history of local literatures, which are, more often than not, religious texts as we see in the case of Tamil Country.

Vijayanagar Empire

One of the important major kingdoms in pre-British India known for its active royal relationship with the religions of India is the Vijayanagar Empire. While many scholarly studies have depicted the Vijayanagar Empire as one of the largest Hindu kingdoms in South India, Stoker's recent work (2016) dwells deep into nuances of how the relationship between state and religion drove each other's growth, expansion, and consolidation. Vijayanagara patronage was consistently provided to the Brahmanic sectarian institutions, particularly *mathas*, with a Vedānta focus that shifted from the fourteenth-century Saṅgama dynasty's patronage to the Smārta Advaita community at Sringeri to Mādhva and Śrīvaiṣṇava institutions in the sixteenth century by Tuḷuva dynasty. Stoker (2016) shows how the royal court had to depend on these institutions to implement many features of its statecraft in that "*mathas* deployed royal patronage for economic and agrarian development" (p. 130), thereby integrating "recently conquered and rebellious territories more firmly into the empire" (Stoker). Vijayanagara royal patronage to different Brahmanic sects was context-specific and was offered to the one who would deliver political dividend. For instance, what drove court's support for Śrīvaiṣṇava institutions, on the one hand, was "concerns about heavily militarized chieftains and overlords (*nāyaka*s) in the regions of both southern Andhra and northern Tamilnadu, as well as by concerns about the Gajapati rulers' designs on prominent forts in the border zone between the two kingdoms" (Stoker, p. 132). On the other hand, the Śrīvaiṣṇavism was popular among the various sections of local population given its "mixed-caste devotionalism, together with their established tradition of Vedānta intellectualism" (Stoker), which "enabled this community to appeal simultaneously to different social groups" (Stoker). According to Stoker, this is what motivated the Tuḷuva court "to work with the Śrīvaiṣṇava leadership to forge relationships with a variety of constituents in regions of strategic significance to the empire" (Stoker). Through his case study of Vyāsatīrtha (1460–1539), one of the celebrated heads of Mādhva Matha during the rule of Kṛṣṇadevarāya (1509–1529), Stoker (2016) explores how a religious leader's (Vyāsatīrtha) success as a sectarian leader evolved by his relationships with both the court and other sectarian groups. His prominence in the court helped him to procure land from the Vijayanagar court to establish Mādhva institutions such as *matha*s and *agrahāra*s in new locations. Vyāsatīrtha also worked very closely with "alternative Vaiṣṇava groups to establish a transregional and trans-sectarian Vaishnavism that was of high political utility", in that the temple patronage helped to extend "military activities to a variety of publics" (Stoker, pp. 132–133).

Just as Vijayanagara patronage of various religious institutions encouraged intra-religious diversity, "Vijayanagara royals remained fairly non-committal when it came to personal religious affiliation" (Stoker, pp. 131–132). Nor did Vijayanagara rule endorse any particular religion as a state religion in the sense that the state did not impose any particular religion on its citizens. While it provided royal patronage to certain Brahmanic religious sects, it did not discourage or prohibit the practice of other religious traditions. The Vijayanagar Empire was emerging as a global economy in the sixteenth century as Kṛṣṇadevarāya's court's patronisation of religious institutions helped create a "distinctive Vijayanagar cosmopolitanism that integrated different regions and constituencies of the empire into a shared religious culture at certain strategically located temples" (Stoker, p. 137).

While the Saṅgama dynasty proclaimed itself as "sultans among Hindu kings" (Stoker, p. 7), as found in inscriptions as early as the fourteenth century, such self-referential identity markers "sought to establish a connection between the Vijayanagar Empire and the northern sultanates, which dominated much of the Indian subcontinent at that time" (Stoker), and "asserts the Vijayanagar court's distinctive identity in an increasingly Turkish, Persianized, and Islamic political environment" (Stoker). In this regard, Stoker goes on to observe "Vijayanagar court's increasing reliance on sectarian leaders of *mathas* to implement many features of its statecraft bore a close resemblance to the Deccan sultanates' use of Sufi shrines to similar ends" (Stoker, p. 138) and "was arguably a 'Hindu' version of this practice, inflected in ways that helped forge a distinctive imperial religious identity for the empire" (Stoker). Imperial religious policy did embrace "ecumenical tolerance of a diversity of religious institutions and its concurrent privileging of certain religious formations" (Stoker), which was in continuity with a long-practised tradition of 'favouritism and accommodation', that is, favouring of one tradition and the accommodation of all other traditions. Such a policy was in vogue way back from the third century BCE's Buddhist emperor Ashoka and was continued by various kings such as ninth-century Kashmir king Śaṅkaravarman, the Pandyas, the Cholas, and the Pallavas. However, we cannot ignore the fact that the sixteenth-century Vijayanagar Empire consciously constructed itself as a Hindu empire by articulating "a unified religious identity that was bound up with a specific cultural and economic way of life" (Stoker, p. 142). Through its patronage it "provided contexts within which shared religious identities were enacted, and it did so, not against, but in awareness of non-Hindu religious others" (Stoker). By promoting a "cosmopolitan, transregional form of temple worship" (Stoker), which "strove for a particular version of inclusivism, one that privileged specific religious articulations" (Stoker), Vijayanagara Empire evolved "particular form of transregional and trans-sectarian Hindu identity" and "distinguished itself from other religious and political formations of sixteenth-century South Asia" (Stoker).

MUSLIM RULERS

The religious policy of Muslim rulers in India is understood to be more nuanced by scholars today than before. Contrary to the colonial and the nationalist accounts of Muslim rule in India that depicted the latter's treatment of non-Muslims in a bad light (with the exception of Akbar), we learn today that Muslim kings, like their predecessors, were led by political expediency and pragmatism to construct and consolidate their territorial authority and political power. This meant rolling out at times favourable policies towards non-Muslim and offering support to them. For instance, just as they provided for the requisites of a dār-ul-Islām, proper Muslim society, such as mosques, *dargāhs* (tombs), madrasas, and the system of jurists in the *sharī*a, they also extended their patronage to non-Muslims too. "They financed the building of mosques and the funding of temples alike; and they were broadly non-discriminatory in their allocation of *madad-i ma'āsh* grants, which provided rights to land revenue" (Copland et al. 2012, p. 118) to different religious institutions. As a result, for instance, the Yogis (for instance, Gorakhnath Yogis of Jakhbar) just like the Sikhs came to possess extensive tracts of land in Punjab. Mughals were generally cordial towards Jains, because being rich merchants and bankers they supplied men, money, and resources to the Mughal state. They also made contributions to the construction and maintenance of the temples as we see in the case of famous Hindu pilgrimage sites such as Ayodhya, Mathura, and Vrindavan (Dogra). Even Aurangzeb, infamously known as a destroyer of temples, actually built more temples than what he destroyed (Copland et al. 2012, p. 119). Mughal rulers' policy of pragmatism meant providing concessions to non-Muslims. For instance, Akbar, in order to win the favour of Rajputs, abolished the *jizya* (the special tax on non-Muslims) and the pilgrim tax. He is also said to have practised religious inclusiveness by celebrating Hindu festivals such as Raksha-Bandhan and Diwali while avoiding meat on certain days of the week and appearing in public with a *tilak* mark on his forehead. In this context, it may be noted that the first Mughal emperor, Babur, advised his son Humayun on his deathbed not to "allow religious prejudices to influence ... his mind, and, in particular, to 'refrain from slaughter of cows'" (as quoted in Copland et al. 2012, p. 134) so that he could "obtain a hold on the hearts of the people" (Copland).

Pragmatism of the Muslim rulers, on the one hand, earned the wrath of non-Muslims in certain cases to please the Muslim *ulamā(s)* as we see in the case of Aurangzeb levying *jizya* (religious tax) on non-Muslims in 1679 (Copland et al. 2012, p. 115). It also meant on the other hand the antagonising of a certain section of the Muslim community to maintain the overall well-being of the kingdom and to maintain good law and order in the territory. For instance, Muslim rulers had to recognise and protect the liberties of non-Muslims living within the Islamic state such as giving freedom to worship in their own style, taking processions, undertaking pilgrimages, and performing Hindu rituals in places like Delhi, "sometimes within the shadow of the sultanate palace itself" (Copland et al. 2012, p. 99) much to the displeasure of orthodox Muslim critiques like Barani.

It is also true that Muslim rulers got involved in the religious matters that affected various religious traditions of the state. In the first place, Muslim rulers, as expected, intervened in the religious affairs of the Muslim community. For instance, 'The Infallibility Decree' of 1579, signed and declared by most of the state's leading *ulamā(s)*, openly raised Akbar to the status of ultimate authority over religious disputes and interpretations (Copland et al. 2012, p. 110), especially in the case of Shi'as and Sunnis, as *Tārīkh-i Alfī* (one of the incomplete Persian history texts commissioned by Akbar) observes. As with Muslims, the Mughals also intervened in the religious matters of non-Muslims too. Akbar is said to have successfully settled disputes between two warring sections of the Jains, resolved the issue of succession among the Sikhs, and functioned as an arbitrator between two rival groups of sannyasis and yogis at a shrine near Kurukshetra.

In this context of recounting Muslim ruler's perception, attitude, and treatment of non-Muslims in India, we may have to take into account how the Malaki and Hanafi schools in India during the Sultanate period framed the people of Indian religions such as Hindus, Buddhists, and Jains as 'Peoples of the Book' and Rama and Krishna as prophets. As 'inwardly' monotheists, Indians were labelled as *dhimmīs* and hence were required to pay a tax called the *jizya*, in place of *zakāt*, that is, the Islamic charitable levy (Copland et al. 2012, pp. 97–98). Such a view towards non-Muslims got formalised and institutionalised in Akbar's promulgation of *Din-i-llahi*, a syncretic religious vision drawn upon the ideas mainly from Islam and Hinduism and some from Christianity and Zoroastrianism. In this regard, reference also needs to be made to Akbar's project of the translation of the Hindu books such as the *Mahābhārata*, under the Persian title *Razmnāma* or The Book of War, the Rāmayāna, the Yoga *Vasishta*, and the *Harīvamsa*. Besides, some non-Muslims were also recruited into the administration of the Islamic states.

All these instances do not mean that there was no major hostility and conflict between Islamic rulers and non-Muslims. We have numerous examples of Muslim rulers' destruction of Hindu temples as we see not only in the case of sultans (Sultan Sikandar of Kashmir [1389–1413], known as the 'idol-breaker') and the emperors like Aurangzeb. Surprisingly, even Akbar, during the earlier years of his reign prior to the 1580s, described his rule in one of the victory proclamations as follows:

> As directed by the word of God, we, as far as it is within our power, remain busy in jihad and owing to the kindness of the supreme Lord, who is the promoter of our victories, we have succeeded in occupying a number of forts and towns belonging to the infidels and have established Islam there. With the help of our bloodthirsty sword we have erased the signs of infidelity from their minds and have destroyed temples in those places and also all over Hindustan. (as quoted in Copland et al. 2012, pp. 109–110)

Jahangir too executed the fifth Sikh Guru Arjun (1581–1606) as the latter was drawing closer to Prince Khusrau, who rebelled against the Mughal Empire. In a similar vein, the emperors felt themselves closer to certain Muslim groups and distanced themselves from other Muslim groups. For instance, the Mughal emperors' (like Akbar, Jahangir, and Shah Jahan) association with the Chishti Sufi order was stronger as they relied on Chishti's political support while they stayed away from the Central Asian Sufi order, Naqshbandiyya. Aurangzeb's failed struggle to win the favours of *ulamā* and the chief qāzī and to get legitimacy for his Muslim rule by making them read his name in the *Khuṭba*, or Friday sermon, also needs special mention here. Though Aurangzeb restored the non-Muslim tax to please the *ulamā (s)* and to enlist legitimacy for his rule, the emperor did face resistance from "some members of the ulamā—such as the qāzī who, in 1686, refused to declare that the war against the Deccani states of Bijapur and Golconda was a jihad" (Copland et al. 2012, p. 116). Even his famous project of *Fatāwāi Ālamgīrī*, a text of Hanafi jurisprudence, did not get the support from some of the Muslim theologians of that time. Thus, to sum up, it is not so much uniformity, homogeneity, and consistency, but diversity, heterogeneity, and context-specificity that characterise Muslim rulers' religious policy both towards Muslims and non-Muslims.

RELIGION AND STATE IN COLONIAL INDIA

During British Period

Though East India Company, the parent agency of the British rule in India, had enormous military power to conquer the subcontinent, it initially lacked knowledge about the local cultures, traditions, economic transactions, and social structures required to stay in control of the territory it occupied and to offer an efficient governance. As a result, the British in India made efforts to gain knowledge of the local situations and customs through their practice of Census of India conducted at the beginning of every decade and largely followed the policy of maintenance of status quo and non-interference in the domain of culture and religion which resulted in the East India Company Act of 1797, a policy of religious neutrality. As the British knowledge of India grew over a period of time during its long presence in India, it led to various administrative measures such as the enactment of the Religious Endowments Act of 1863 and the Madras Hindu Religious Endowments Act of 1927, which indicate that their idea of non-interference in the local culture and religion changed gradually on the ground, though the policy remained the same on paper. This self-denying administrative stance of the British rule was evident in the continuation of previous Hindu/Muslim kings' custom of the rulers being the patrons and custodians of the Hindu temples. It meant that British officials like district collectors and other local bureaucrats had to sponsor local festivities and receive first honours and so on. Such pursuit of local customary protocols by the British was not taken so well by the Christian missionaries and their cohorts in the Indian administrative service and produced reactions and debates far away in London.

British Raj's failure to adhere to its policy of religious neutrality can be further detected in their civilising mission of India enacting laws such as the abolition of Sati and human sacrifice and widow remarriage, often at the behest of Hindu reformers such as Raja Ram Mohan Roy and others. In response to one of the important political events of that time, the 1857 Sepoy Mutiny allegedly carried out by the Hindus and Muslims for religious reasons, the British wanted to revise their governance approaches in various domains including religion in India, while Christian missionaries distanced themselves from the British. A number of American and British missionaries also openly backed the idea of self-rule for Indians. "While all these meant that there was a growing separation between State and Church in India, the latter was no longer automatically seen by Indians as a proxy for imperialism, which made it easier for the missionaries to 'sell' Christianity as a liberal ideology" (Copland et al. 2012, p. 181). Interestingly, in post-mutiny India, the British Raj too, while disassociating itself from the Christianising project of the missionaries, did not stop considering itself as a 'Christian power'.

> If anything, the rebellion made the British even more conscious of themselves as Christians in a 'heathen' country; and this national identification was firmly embedded in the proclamation document itself, which defiantly asserted that future policy towards the Crown's new dominions in India would be guided by the 'truth of Christianity', a phrase apparently inserted into the government draft by the Queen at the suggestion of the Prince Consort. (Copland)

That explains why the Raj continued its reformist interventions in local traditions, at times favouring Christianity. The examples of the Age of Consent Act of 1891 raising the legal age of marriage to Hindu women to 12 (despite resistance from orthodox Hindus) and the Indian Succession Act of 1865 laying down fixed rules of governing inheritance of family property for the Hindu community serve as instances of the British selective interference in local practices of the Indian people even after 1856. But, the Christian Marriage Act of 1865–1872, which "facilitated conversion by enabling apostates from Hinduism (though not from Islam) to have their existing marriages legally voided" (Copland), was evidently pro-Christian as it was founded upon Pauline privilege in Christian canon law.

Further, while the 'Religious Endowments Act of 1863' sought to enable the British government to divest itself of the management of religious endowments, such policy of non-involvement was compromised in the case of the Golden Temple in Amritsar (Copland et al. 2012, p. 182). While the endowment act and its reforms brought somewhat a sigh of relief to the executive wing of the British Raj, it placed the judicial arm of the government under tremendous pressure. Tens and thousands of temple and religion-related disputes were brought to the court for settlement which not only made the government to "enforce(d) indigenous religious law, but helped to *shape* it" (Copland). Another instance where the British could not but handle the so-called religious customs of the Indian people were the occasions of religious festivals and processions which were to be monitored and interfered with at times as numerous studies have shown.

In this regard it also needs to be noted that the British government's adherence to Majesty's 1858 principle of neutrality across three British presidencies (i.e. the administrative units of the British Raj) was not at all uniform even with regard to the same Hindu religious practice. For instance, the Hindu practice of 'hook-swinging' was criminalised as per the Section144 of the Code of Criminal Procedure as the practice produced a 'demoralizing public spectacle'. However, Madras presidency allowed the practice to continue as it felt the banning of the ritual practice would amount to "contravention of ... Her Majesty's Proclamation of 1858, which expressly disclaims any intention of interference with the religious ... worship of any of Her subjects" (as quoted in Copland et al. 2012, p. 181).

Religion and Princely States in India

Princely states in India, which constituted two-fifths of British India, were paradoxical political entities in the sense they were relatively independent territories of governance under the control of the princes who in turn were controlled by and dependent on the British for foreign policies and military power. Mridu Rai (2004) in his work argues that it is the British and their political strategies that assigned a label of 'Hindu' or 'Muslim' to these states based on the religious tradition prevalent in that territory after Queen Victoria's November 1, 1858, proclamation. Among them, Mysore, Baroda, and Travancore were regarded as Hindu Kingdoms, while Hyderabad and Bhopal were projected as Muslim states. In this regard, Bhagavan observes, "While precolonial rulers tended to give some preferences to those of the same faith, they did not conflate their personal religious practice with the state. This practice gradually ceased, for the most part, over the late nineteenth century as the overarching British model kicked in" (Bhagavan 2008, p. 891). Just as "British administrators invented princely states as simplistic, religious backwaters" (Bhagavan), it not only served "as a contrast to Western progressivism" (Bhagavan), it also helped the Hindu nationalists to construct princely India as an ideal location for the Hindus. They valorised the Hindu rulers like Maharajas of Mysore who defeated the foreign enemies as they kept their kingdom intact in line with pure and ancient Hindu past. At the initiative of Dewan (Prime Minister) Sir Manubhai Mehta, one of the major architects of the princely state of Baroda's reforms, the princely states themselves showed interest to come together in the 1920s and formed the organ of the Chamber of Princes to bring about constitutional and democratic reforms throughout princely India. It later functioned as a "buttress against pan-Islamism" (Bhagavan 2008, p. 892), leading to a series of important meetings between the princely states of Gwalior, Bikaner, Kota, Jaipur, Alwar, and Dholpur and Hindu nationalist leaders like Savarkar, Moonje, and Shyama Prasad Mookherjee. It is to be noted that the Hindu Mahasabha adopted two strategies to construct its concept of 'Hindu Nation' in partnership with Hindu princely states. In the first place, it spread its ideology through its magazine, *Hindu Outlook* (an English magazine)—the Hindu nationalist mouthpiece that extolled the Hindu rulers of the princely states and their polices and reform measures and depicted them as the continuation of the Hindu kingdoms of the glorious past. Secondly, it held a number of conferences and regional meetings to rally the Hindu loyalists and unite the Hindus of India, especially the Hindus in princely states of India to enlist their support to build a Hindu India. The works of Bhagavan (2008), Ian Copland (2005), and others explore various aspects of princely states, their relationship with Hindutva ideology, and the role they played in the Hindu imagery to aspire for an ideal "Akhand Hindustan", that is, the one India of the Hindus (Bhagavan 2008, p. 881). In particular, they presented Hindu princely states as peaceful, unlike the British-controlled territories of India marked by conflict between religions. However, Verghese (2016) shows that in comparison to British-ruled India, religious conflicts in princely states were more frequent and religious restrictions were stronger. The first anti-conversion law was passed in pre-independent India's princely states of Raigarh, Patna, and Udaipur (Ponniah 2017, p. 82). Thus, the colonial narratives and post-colonial literatures about the princely states in India illustrate the fact that most of them were not only leaning towards one religion or the other (i.e. Hinduism or Islam) and lacked the state policy of religious neutrality, but some of the princely states also functioned as the epicentres of Hindu nationalism.

SECULARISM AS INDEPENDENT INDIA'S STATE POLICY TOWARDS RELIGION IN INDIA

No other concept is invoked, discussed, debated, and contested as much as the notion of secularism in our contemporary world when it comes to the relationship between the state and religion today. Semantics of the word 'secularism' has its own nuances and shades of relationship between state and religion that range from separation to indifference to involvement in different contexts of the world such as Europe, America, Africa, and Asia. Theorists on secularism[1] concur that India's secularism both in theory and in practice is a unique phenomenon. Since so much has been written about this topic, it is enough for the sake of the chapter to recall key data related to Indian secularism. The constituent assembly that discussed this matter at length decided to distance itself from the Western notion of 'strict separation and religion. Instead it "settled on the notions of *sarva dharma sambhava* (goodwill toward all faiths) and *dharma nirpekshata* (religious neutrality), to which duo a third, the Gandhian *vasudeva kudumbakam* (universal brotherhood), is frequently added"' (Acevedo 2013, p. 160). While these underlying ideas shaped the Indian constitution so as to contextualise the Western notion of secularism to address India's social reality of predominantly religious-minded population, the term 'secularism' itself was merely added in 1976, rather ornamentally, to the preamble of the constitution which was always secular since its inception as noted by the Supreme Court of India in the 1994 Bommai Case. Rajeev Bhargava well known for his works on Indian secularism has insightfully articulated sevenfold features of Indian secularism (Bhargava 2002). They are: (a) disestablishment of religion; (b) religious liberty to any one religious group; (c) religious liberty granted nonpreferentially to members of every religious group; (d) the liberty to embrace a religion other than the one into which a person is born and to reject all other religions; (e) no discrimination by the state on grounds of religion to entitlements provided by the state; (f) no discrimination in admission to educational institutions on grounds of religion; (g) equality of active citizenship and no discrimination on grounds of religion. The constitution of India embodies these features across its different articles. For instance, Article 27 and Article 28(1) embody the characteristics (a) namely 'disestablishment of religion', while Article 25 entitles Indian citizens to characteristic (c) in that it confers upon every citizen 'freedom of conscience and free profession, practice and propagation of religion' and Articles 26, 27, and 28 contain the feature (b) of secularism, namely, 'religious liberty to any one religious group'. Likewise Articles 15(1), 29(2), 16(1), and 325 embody different characteristics mentioned above. Analysing the articles mentioned above (2002) rightly demonstrates that Articles 15, 16, 25, 29(2), 325, 27, 28(1), and 60 support the 'Wall of Separation Thesis' found in Western nations. In this context, he also points to another set of articles, namely Articles 30(1), 30(2), 17, 25(2), and 25(2)(B) in the Indian constitution that militate against this stance of the state. For instance, Article 30(1) which provides the 'right of minorities to establish and administer educational institutions' and 30(2) which ensures that the state, in providing aid to educational institutions, does not discriminate against minority institutions are clear indications of the state privileging certain religious communities. On the other hand, the state does interfere in the domain of Hindu traditions as seen in Article 17 which criminalises the practice of untouchability which is essentially a Hindu social practice and in Article 25(2) which empowers the state to enact any law to reform religious institutions of a public character to make them accessible to all classes and sections of society. In particular, Article 25(2)(B) clearly singles out Hinduism and entitles, if not mandates, the state to interfere with Hindu religious traditions, customs, and practices and display the state's agency to regulate and reform the religion of Hinduism alone. In this regard, Mehta observes, "[T]he Indian state acquires authority over Hinduism, not because of its undoubtedly secular character, but because it has been authorized by Hindus to do so" (Mehta 2005, p. 57). Right from Raja Ram Mohan Roy, the father of Indian Renaissance who impressed upon the British Raj to criminalise the practice of Sati, to Ambedkar who wanted to reform Hindu personal code to the litigants of the Sabarimala temple case, it is the members of the Hindu community who approach the state and its agencies to bring about internal reformation in Hinduism.

In line with the internal voices then and now, the architects of Indian nation singling out Hinduism for constitutional reformation and legal supervision seems not unfair and unreasonable. The preamble of the Indian constitution espouses a new vision of India conceived as sovereign, democratic, republic, social, and secular. The preamble also encompasses constitutional guarantees such as justice, liberty, equality, and fraternity for all its citizens. While these constitutional guarantees embody the idea of India as a robust social, economic, and political democracy, the idea of social democracy and its attendant view of equal citizenship to all reigned supreme over all other views of India in the subsequent articles of the Indian constitution. If the *principle of secularism* is meant to treat all religions equally, the *principle of democracy* (especially social democracy) with its values of equality, justice, and fraternity promises not only to treat all citizens equally but also to secure equal rights for every citizen. As framers of the Indian constitution realised that Hinduism as a lived religious tradition with its traditional operative principle of *Varnashrama dharma* prohibited the vast majority of Indians (especially the people of Scheduled Caste or SC communities) from enjoying the democratic right of equal citizenship in India, they introduced articles such as 25(2)(B) to ensure every Hindu is entitled to rights and privileges of other citizens in the nation. In other words, the constitutional value of equality, in order to ensure equal treatment of all its citizens (social democracy), seeks to eliminate any discrimination in public spaces (as in Articles 15(2)(A) & (B) and 25(2)(B)) which also include Hindu temples. Hence what articles like 25(2)(B) are meant to do is that when there is a conflict between the practice of secularism (understood as 'religious neutrality') and that of democracy, especially social democracy, the latter would prevail over the former so as to remove inequality in the domain of religion, especially, Hinduism. But the architects of the constitution wanted to extend this to other religions too by trying to introduce common civil code, which is long overdue, but it unfortunately remains long overdue. Rajeev Bhargava prefers to name this variant of Indian secularism as principled distance, according to which "whether or not the state intervenes or refrains from action depends on what really strengthens religious liberty and equality of citizenship for all" (Bhargava 2002, p. 26). Principled distance then implies that "the state may not relate to every religion in exactly the same way, intervene to the same degree or in the same manner" (Bhargava). It does not predict a relationship of 'strict non-interference, mutual exclusion, or equidistance' between state and religion, but anticipates "a flexible approach on the question of intervention or abstention, combining both, dependent on the context, nature, or current state of relevant religions" (Bhargava).

Examining various views of India's secularism as Indian nation state's religious policy and Indian government's—primarily the judiciary's—internal regulation of religious traditions in India, Acevedo argues that "the Indian state neither is nor was meant to be secular" (Acevedo 2013, p. 138), as it is "the desire to separate religion and state rather than the fact or manner of separation" (Acevedo 2013, p. 162) that characterises the secular governance of the Indian nation state. In this regard, he detects at least two strong non-secular desires of the Indian state which has been in practice since its inception, that is, "the desire to support, protect, and encourage religion" (Acevedo 2013, p. 160) and the desire to internally regulate religions with a goal of reforming "Indian society, especially with regard to caste practices" (Acevedo). The downside of such a statist approach of "enshrining the state as the paramount agent of religious reform" (Acevedo 2013, p. 155) is that just as it assumes the moral responsibility of offering equal citizenship to all by creating an egalitarian social space, the state takes a high moral ground and places itself in a position of civilisational precedence and epistemological privilege. In these respects, the state believes that its measures are more progressive than the religion it seeks to reform and transform. Secondly, it believes that "no aspect of citizens' lives lies outside the rightful purview of the state" (Acevedo). Thirdly, it simply means that "citizen-believers are presumed incapable of functioning effectively as autonomous moral beings without the state's direction" (Acevedo). Jacobsohn calls this type of state's power to regulate as provisioned in the Indian constitution as "militant constitutionalism" in contrast to the "constitutional acquiescence" of the US constitution (Jacobsohn 2009). While the latter is founded upon an understanding of "not the direct source of major [social and political] revisions" (Jacobsohn 2009, p. 131), the latter such as the Indian constitution was conceived and constructed as a confrontational document that embodied "Nehruvian desire to oust dharma and introduce legal rationalism as the governing principle of Indian society" (Acevedo 2013, p. 163) and to create a new India. According to Acevedo, "the Indian Constitution encourages a dynamic equilibrium between these two visions of state–society relations" (Acevedo 2016, p. 558).

Places of Worship and State

No other venue offers better examples than the places of worship, especially the Hindu temples, when we want to examine how the elected governments in India contextualise the principle of secular state and play a role in regulating religion. At times, the way the provincial states administer, manage, and control the Hindu temples, especially in the southern states of India, namely, Tamil Nadu, Kerala, Karnataka, and Andhra Pradesh, the former constituents of Madras presidency during the British period, makes one wonder whether the principle of secularism, which is supposed to embody the state's policy of non-involvement in religious affairs, is conveniently suspended, if not violated, when it comes to Hindu temples. The inextricable relationship between the divinity and royalty, between the deity and the throne in India that began in pre-modern times which survived for different purposes through various forms of administrative apparatuses and bureaucratic regulations during the colonial era, seems to continue until today even in independent India. For instance, the existing department of HRCE or the Hindu Religious and Charitable Endowments (Administration) in the states of Tamil Nadu, Kerala, and Karnataka derives their legacy from colonial times. Various laws and regulations such as the Tamil Nadu Act of HRCE in 1951 (Venkataramanujam 2015, p. 258) are improvised versions and alternative forms of the colonial laws enacted in 1927 as the Madras Hindu Religious Endowments Act. The colonial policy of management of Hindu temples continued the previous kingdom's royal patronage of the temples, not so much to emulate the latter who did so to seek legitimacy and to expand and consolidate their temporal power, but to increase their revenue, to firm up social cohesion, and to maintain law and order. But the present state governments exercise their role of administering the temples with the secular understanding of 'temple as public trusts', which is distinguished from 'temple as religion' (Presler 1983). While the former understanding leads to the state's administration and regulation of the temporal, material, and financial aspects of the temple in the provincial states of India, the state governments do not remain entirely indifferent to the religious sphere of temples. The secular principle of non-interference in religious affairs simply failed when states and their courts had to intervene to support the demand for temple entry by many low caste groups and their movements in southern states. Such an involvement of the state in religious matters was out and open when the ruling Dravidian political parties in the state of Tamil Nadu boldly interfere in religious affairs of the temple by abolishing the heredity rights of temple priests, appointing non-Brahmin priests, and introducing the recitation of temple mantras in Tamil, instead of Sanskrit. It was also evident when the communist party's government in Kerala supported the legal petition in the court seeking all women's rights to enter into Sabarimala temple. The state policies and its schemes are often coloured and influenced by local contexts and existing socio-political situations. For instance, the present Tamil Nadu government is led by a supposedly atheist Dravidian party (DMK), which is conspicuously proactive in introducing new programmes and schemes for Hindu temples in Tamil Nadu. It includes a whole range of initiatives such as the renovation of thousands of Hindu temples all over the state at an estimated cost of 500 crores, free meals to 10,000 pilgrims to Palani for 20 days during 'Thai Poosam' and 'Panguni Uthiram' festival days, the establishment of new mega 'goshala' (cow shed) at a cost of Rs. 20 crore next to Sundararaja Perumal temple in Chennai, and a government-sponsored special spiritual tour for about 200 devotees to visit important Hindu temples from Ramanathaswamy temple, Rameswaram, to Sri Viswanathaswamy temple, Kasi, every year, and so on, all of which receive a good coverage in both print and electronic media. Political observers consider them an effective political strategy of the DMK to deprive the Hindutva BJP party of any opportunity to get a stronghold in Tamil Nadu by accusing the Dravidian and the atheist party of DMK of neglecting the interests of Hindus and ignoring their religion in the state. While DMK's support for the temple-related programmes and activities could offset the pro-Hindu political agenda of the BJP party which is in dire need of its political presence in the state of Tamil Nadu, such policies of the state government that allow only Hindu candidates to get teaching positions in the newly instituted colleges administered by HRCE seem to dent the secular credentials of Tamil Nadu state government.

The relationship between the state and temple management in the neighbouring state of Kerala is governed by two important systems, namely temples owned and managed by the state through statutory bodies like *Devaswom* and the system of temples directly regulated by the state in the Malabar region. While in the formerly princely states of Travancore and Cochin private temples are outside the ambit of state regulation in those areas, in the Malabar region all temples are managed by the state. In the formation of Kerala state in 1956, while many existing laws were changed by the democratically elected government, the laws related to temples were kept untouched. As a result, a monopoly of Brahmin priests and their customs continues to dominate in the former territories of Travancore and Cochin princely states through the *Devaswom* system. The Malabar region is governed by the laws and regulations of the Hindu Religious and Charitable Endowment Department, which owes its origin to the British, and such temples have less of monopoly by the Brahmins. This differential policy towards temples in the state was also followed by the democratically elected governments in Kerala like the communists in India and like the CPI-M (i.e. communist party of India-Marxist, heading the coalition known as LDF—Left Democratic Front), which are otherwise anti-religious. They have shown interest to reform Hinduism, as we see them consistently seeking to lift the ban on women's (aged between 10 and 50) entry into the famous temple of Ayyapa, a celibate male deity as articulated by one of CPI-M minister of *Devaswom*. (Devasia). Communists in Kerala as elsewhere display antipathy towards religion as evidenced in their government's decision to introduce in the school textbook a chapter entitled 'Mathamillathajeevan' (means 'Faithless Soul') and to change the school time inconveniencing the existing arrangements to accommodate the conduct of Madarasa classes outside school hours for the Muslim students. Such actions provoked strong protests from the Muslim Coordination Committee (MCC), formed in 2008 as a collective of Muslim organisations to mediate between the state government and the demands of the community and other faith communities (Raoof 2019). When the opposition of MCC and the Muslim league (which is part of LDF) to the communist attempts to devalue religion in Kerala grew stronger, the communists buckled under the pressure and changed the title of the chapter into 'Vishwasa Swathantryam' (means 'Freedom of Faith') and reverted to the original school timing as well. Thus, examples from Kerala just like from Tamil Nadu also go to confirm the thesis that a government's relationship with various religious traditions is context-dependent, fluid, and evolving and subject to factors such as historical precedence, party ideology, and political expediency.

Religion and State in the 'Second Republic'[2] of India

Mapping India's journey in democracy, Christophe Jaffrelot (2021), one of the prominent scholars on Hindutva politics in India, identifies three stages of democracy, namely "conservative democracy", "democratization of democracy", and "ethnic democracy". The first stage of India's democracy covering the period of Congress governments' rule under Nehru and Indira Gandhi is known for advancing democratic secular India in which the state's relationship with religions of India has been described as equal treatment of all religions. The thesis of universalist approach (Jaffrelot), variously described in India as *sarva-dharma-samabhava* (equal respect to all religions) and *vasudeva kudumbakam* (universal brotherhood), gave rise, even before the birth of Independent India, to its counter-thesis, albeit, communalist approach, spearheaded by two religio-political movements, one Muslim (Muslim League) and another Hindu (Hindu Mahasabha). While the former quickly achieved its goal with the birth of Pakistan as an Islamic nation, the latter has been working on making India a Hindu Raj for almost 100 years, deliberately targeting Muslims in the subcontinent as in-field Indians and loyal Pakistanis and Christians as putative "foreign" loyalists in alliance with Western Christians (Bauman and Ponniah 2016, p. 222). The phase of "conservative democracy", under the hegemony of upper caste Hindus, preferred to label itself as a secular country. While Nehru (the first prime minister of India) interpreted it as a state that "honours all faiths equally and gives them equal opportunities" (as quoted in Jaffrelot 2021, p. 8) and Radhakrishnan (the first president of India) understood it to be a nation "that will not identify itself with or be controlled by any particular religion" (Jaffrelot 2021). However, long debates that took place in the constituent assembly and the subsequent political development of a presidential order did display strong articulations of the newly born Indian Republic's inadvertent desire not only to make India a monolithic Hindu nation (the constituent assembly's heated debates regarding ban on cow slaughter and vegetarianism are very illustrative of this view) but also to maintain India as religiously Hindu (as seen in declaration of 1951 presidential order that denied the Dalits of India their freedom to opt of Hinduism for a religion of their choice by depriving the converted SCs of their right to access the state's affirmative action and its mechanisms of against untouchability and caste atrocities). While reaction to the hegemony of conservative democracy led to political consolidation and assertion of other backward classes (OBCs) described as 'democratisation of democracy', the political project of Mandalisation of India implemented by the second non-government in Delhi could also be seen as a political strategy of OBC groups to prevent the upper caste Sangh Parivar from vigorously pursuing their religio-political ideology. The demolition of Babri Masjid that took place at the connivance of the secular Congress rule in Delhi is seen as a failure of the state to safeguard the secular fabric of India. The governments that followed after this incident increasingly promoted the enactment of laws that placed minority in a precarious condition in the nation state of India and its public space. The next phase which Jaffrelot calls "ethnic democracy" draws our attention to India's political plight under Modi's government which is sliding into "an authoritarian Hindu Raj" (Jaffrelot 2021, p. 6). The idea of 'ethnic democracy' refers to a political system in which the putative majority group, defined by the criteria of ethnic, religious, or cultural characteristics (as in the case of Israel), makes a strong and singular claim to be the authentic inheritor of a nation wherein the minoritised outgroups are rather reduced to second-class status. According to Jaffrelot, the project of 'ethnic democracy' is implemented in two phases under Modi's government. The first phase from 2014 to 2019 witnessed the transformation of India's political order into a "de facto ethnic democracy" (Jaffrelot 2021, p. 157) which, without any big moves to change the foundational and legal arrangements of secular democracy, created a semblance of a Hindu state. The latter was materialised through a more insidious route and nefarious strategies to activate a "state of permanent mobilization" (Jaffrelot 2021, p. 248) by a range of vigilante groups that, backed by the state machinery, would systematically target the alleged 'enemies of the nation' such as minorities, secularists, liberals, and the NGOs. The second phase that started off after Modi's landslide victory in 2019 seeks to systemically lock this Hindutva claim to the nation into law (Nielsen and Nilsen 2021). The legislations that Modi's government passed in the parliament such as the Citizenship Amendment Act (CAA), criminalisation of triple talaq (instant divorce), and renewed debate about uniform civil code are meant to effectively marginalise religious minorities, especially Muslims, in particular and to relegate them to a status of second-class citizens. Given these political developments, India is quickly moving towards an official Hindu Raj, where religious majoritarianism is wedded to a visibly growing authoritarianism (Jaffrelot 2021, p. 440).

One of the key strategies of Hindu majoritarian polity is the marginalisation of the religious other and systemic deprivation of privileges and rights offered by the state to the minorities. One such move is the abrogation of Article 360 that cancelled the special status given to Jammu and Kashmir, which is predominantly a Muslim state. In doing so, Modi's government has not only divested the Muslims of Jammu and Kashmir (J&K) of their political autonomy, but also effectively brought the Muslims of J&K under the 'Hindu nation' of federal India. Thus, it has restored the political power equation to its pre-independent India, namely, it is a Muslim land with a majority Muslim population but ruled by a Hindu political dispensation. This current political reality of India is variously labelled as 'second republic' as mentioned earlier, a term that has unequivocally become a political trope and a singular political agenda, namely, the doctrine of Hindutva around which Modi's new Indian republic will be built (Kim 2017) by politically marginalising the minorities[3] and by systematically undermining the existing rights of two religious minorities, namely, Muslims and Christians, as provisioned in the constitution of India.

While this being the case of BJP's policy towards two religious minorities, namely, Muslims and Christians, the BJP government since 2014 has been pursuing a "new zone of consensus" (Kim 2017, pp. 360–364) with select religious minorities such as Sikhs, Buddhists, Parsi(s), and Jews in India. While pursuing the policy of selective "accommodation and recognition of cultural identity of religious minority" (Kim 2017, p. 361), the BJP government went a step further by granting minority status to the Jewish community in Maharashtra. The BJP government's strategy towards the religious minorities is variously described as a 'twin-track' approach, namely, promoting Hindutva ideology and pursuing cultural nationalism on one track and treading, rather cautiously and strategically, the path of constitutional framework on another track. The latter may require moderation of its ideological stance to accommodate minority interests "with a demonstrably Hindu bias rather than the dissolution of their distinctive identities" (Mitra 2005, p. 87). The twin tracking approach does come with dilemmas and ambivalent posturing of the BJP rulers towards religious minorities as seen in the rhetoric of Modi with his public statements such as his government is the "only Religion is India First" and its "Holy Book is Constitution" (Times of India 2015) and "my government will give equal respect to all religions and will not allow any form of violence against any religion....We consider the freedom to have, to retain, and to adopt, a religion or belief is a personal choice of a citizen" (The Hindu 2015). Even such a rhetoric from the prime minister is a rare occurrence as it comes only when the public outcry against his studied silence to the Hindu Right activists' inflammatory speeches and provocative acts of violence against minorities become too deafening to ignore. While analysing the present government's policies towards religious minorities, political observers consider that "the difference in approach toward religious minorities between the Congress and the BJP is not one of kind but of degree" (Kim 2017, p. 367) for various reasons: in the first place, as during BJP's rule, "the long period of post-independence governance under the Congress was also marked by peri-odic outbursts of high level communal violence against minorities" (Kim 2017). Secondly, the decline in the socio-economic status of the largest minority, namely, Muslims as shown in the Sachar committee report, points to the failure of successive Congress governments to help overcome the educational, social, and economic backwardness of Muslim minorities in India. This may be seen as a kind of antipathy extended to the Muslims in India during Congress rule in India, albeit, silently by Congress. What Congress has done quietly, BJP is doing more openly and loudly. Thirdly, the response of the federal state to the marginality of religious minorities has been inaction, rather deliberate negligence. Here too, as Kim argues, Congress' position has been very ambivalent, if not non-different from the BJP. For instance, Indira Gandhi's Congress government cancelled the National Commission for Minorities without any formal announcement. This was established by the first non-Congress government in 1978 led by Prime Minister Morarji Desai. Congress appointed Gopal Singh Panel to study the status of minorities in India but subsequently suppressed the Panel's report as it did not echo Congress government's stance on minori-ties. In this regard Kim writes: "Almost 24 years later this pattern was repeated by the Congress-led UPA government in its reluctance to release the report of the National Commission for Religious and Linguistic Minorities (2007)—which proposed reservations for Dalit Christians and Muslims—for fear of a political backlash" (Kim 2017, p. 369). The dis-tinction between caste and religion established at independence led to affirmative action in favour of the socio-economically disadvantaged caste groups especially for the Scheduled Caste Hindus. And, it was denied unjustly to the disadvantaged Scheduled Caste communities in other reli-gions in 1950 by a presidential order of Nehru's Congress government but extended subsequently to the SC communities of all other religions except to the disadvantaged religious minorities of Dalit Christians and Muslims. The presidential order of 1950 is a historical blunder and a gross violation of the very vision of independent India embodied in the pream-ble of its constitution because it singles out Dalit Christians and Dalit Muslims and nullifies their freedom of religion. This presidential order has taken away the freedom of religion from the Dalits of India, an erstwhile untouchability community which was deprived of almost all types of free-dom for about three millennia in Indian history, as this order subjects them to a new form of discrimination in the name of religion. Dalit Christians and Dalit Muslims have contested this order in the court as this religion-based discrimination is in violation of Article 15(1) (no discrimination on the basis of religion, race, or caste), excludes them from the ambit of the Protection of Civil Rights Act 1976 (POA 1996), and contravenes the provisions of Article 15(4) of the Constitution of India. (Nothing in this article shall prevent thesState from making any special provision for SC/STs.) To sum up, when we closely examine the policies during the long durée of previous Congress governments, they are very similar to those of BJP administrative policies on religious minorities except for "the ideological shift to the right", and it is rather evident that "there are more continuities in the policies with previous governments than radical discontinuities" (Kim).

Thus, when we analyse the way BJP and Congress have dealt with Muslims and Christians in India, we discover so much of continuities between them. From the intensity and the frequency with which BJP espouses Hindu nationalism in India and targets Muslims and Christians both rhetorically and in reality, it is clear that BJP practises 'Hyper Hindu Nationalism', as opposed to Congress which practises the same rather subtly and inadvertently, the variety of which can be labelled as 'Hibernate Hindu Nationalism'. To these two types, we can also add another variety, one that is practised by provisional governments like Dravidian parties in Tamil Nadu and the communists in Kerala, which is a calibrated version of treatment of 'Hindu interests' subject to the emerging needs and contexts of the state, be it political or ideological. This reformist and patronising approach with a special focus on Hindu traditions and temples in the states can be called a Dravidian version of Hindu nationalism (i.e. recognition of Dravidian parties' special treatment of 'Hindu interests' in Tamil Nadu) and a communist version of Hindu nationalism (i.e. recognition of the communist's special treatment of 'Hindu interests' in Kerala) and they can be grouped under the third category called 'Hyphenated Hindu Nationalisms'.

NOTES

1. There are at least three camps that view Indian secularism differently. They are anti-modernists (Ashis Nandy, T. N. Madan) who dismiss secularism as an imported Western concept which is ill-suited for India, contextualists

(Bhargava, Dhavan, Mehta, and Yildirim) who highlight the distinctiveness of Indian secularism that is dynamic, complex, and context-specific, and pseudo-secularists (basically Hindu nationalist camp in the likes of RSS) who call it bogus as it favours religious minorities and discriminates against the Hindu majority.

2. It refers to the end of the first phase of democracy under the Congress rule and the beginning of new phase of democracy with Modi's regime at Delhi. The latter may not mean much of constitutional changes in as much as it has inaugurated unprecedented political processes that would have lasting consequences for the future character of democracy in India.

   http://timesofindia.indiatimes.com/articleshow/39078542.cms?utm_source=contentofinterest&utm_medium=text&utm_campaign=cppst

3. This strategy of political marginalisation of minorities in India has got two sides: (1) reduction of the political power of minorities to legislate by systematically reducing the numerical strengths of minorities, especially Muslims in the Indian parliament (from 7% in 2004 to 3% of Muslims in 2014) and (2) reduction of minority's political power to rule independently as we see in the case of Christian minorities in North East India. Out of seven states in North East whose population is over 60% Christians, almost all states are ruled by BJP or its allies disenfranchising Christians off their autonomy to rule themselves independently of the BJP government in Delhi.

REFERENCES

Acevedo, Deepa Das. 2013. Secularism in the Indian Context. *Law & Social Inquiry* 38 (1): 138–167.

———. 2016. Temples, Courts, and Dynamic Equilibrium in the Indian Constitution. *The American Journal of Comparative Law* 64 (3): 555–582.

Ashraf, Ajaz. https://scroll.in/article/877050/religious-violence-in-ancient-india-a-lesson-for-those-who-write-history-textbooks-for-school.

Bauman, Chad, and James Ponniah. 2016. Christianity and Freedom in India: Colonialism, Communalism, Caste, and Violence. In *Christianity and Freedom*, ed. Allen Hertzke and Timothy Shah, vol. 2, 222–253. Cambridge: Cambridge University Press.

Bhagavan, Manu. 2008. Princely States And The Hindu Imaginary: Exploring The Cartography Of Hindu Nationalism In Colonial India. *The Journal of Asian Studies* 67 (3): 881–915. https://doi.org/10.1017/S0021911808001198.

Bhargava, Rajeev. 2002. What is Indian Secularism and What Is It For? *India Review* 1 (1): 1–32. https://doi.org/10.1080/146480208404618.

Champakalakshmi, R. 2011. Jainism in Tamil Nadu: A Historical Overview. In *Religion*, ed. R. Champakalakshmi, 356–410. Oxford: Tradition, and Ideology: Pre-colonial South India.

Copland, Ian. 2005. *State, Community and Neighbourhood in Princely North India, c.1900–1950*. New York: Palgrave Macmillan.

Copland, Ian, Ian Mabbett, Asim Roy, Kate Brittlebank, and Adam Bowles. 2012. *A History of State And Religion In India*. London and New York: Routledge.

Darshini, Priya. 2005–2006. Religion and Policy of Toleration in the Gupta Period: Numismatic and Epigraphical Facts. *Proceedings of the Indian History Congress, 66*, 167–172.

Devasia, T.K. 2015. https://scroll.in/article/771711/before-happytobleed-campaign-there-were-other-attempts-to-allow-women-into-sabarimala.

Dogra, Bharat. 2019. https://www.thenewleam.com/2019/01/recalling-the-muslim-rulers-who-built-temples/.

https://www.thenewsminute.com/article/tn-plans-renovation-1000-temples-new-cultural-centre-chennai-16361.

Jacobsohn, Gary Jeffrey. 2009. The Sounds of Silence: Militant and Acquiescent Constitutionalism. In *The Supreme Court and the Idea of Constitutionalism*, ed. Steven Kautz, Arthur Melzer, Jerry Weinberger, and M. Richard Zinman, 131–161. Philadelphia: University of Pennsylvania Press.

Jaffrelot, Christopher. 2021. *Modi's India: Hindu Nationalism and the Rise of Ethnic Democracy*, Trans. Cynthia Schoch. Princeton, NJ: Princeton University Press.

Jha, D.N. 2018. *Against the Grain: Notes on Identity, Intolerance and History*. New Delhi: Manohar.

Kim, Heewon. 2017. Understanding Modi and Minorities: The BJP-Led NDA Government in India and Religious Minorities. *India Review* 16 (4): 357–376. https://doi.org/10.1080/14736489.2017.1378482.

Mehta, Pratap Bhanu. 2005. Reason, Tradition, Authority, Religion and the Indian State. In *Men's Laws, Women's Lives: A Constitutional Perspective on Religion, Common Law and Culture in South Asia*, ed. Indira Jaising, 56–86. New Delhi: Women Unlimited.

Mitra, Subrata K. 2005. The NDA and the Politics of 'Minorities' in India. In *Coalition Politics and Hindu Nationalism*, ed. Katharine Adeney and Lawrence Sáez. London: Routledge.

Nielsen, K., and A. Nilsen. 2021. Love Jihad and the Governance of Gender and Intimacy in Hindu Nationalist Statecraft. *Religions* 12 (12): 1068. https://doi.org/10.3390/rel12121068.

Nilakantasastri, K.A. 1975. *A History of South India*. Madras: Oxford University Press.

Olson, Carl. 2017. *Many Colours of Hinduism: A Thematic-Historical Introduction*. New Brunswick, New Jersey, and London: Rutgers University Press.

Ponniah, James. 2017. Communal Violence in India: Exploring Strategies of its Nurture and Negation in Contemporary Times. *Journal of Religion and Violence* 5 (1): 79–102.

Presler, Franklin A. 1983. The Structure and Consequences of Temple Policy in Tamil Nadu, 1967–81. *Pacific Affairs, Summer* 56 (2): 232–246.

Rai, Mridu. 2004. *Hindu Rulers, Muslim Subjects: Islam, Rights, and the History of Kashmir*. Delhi: Permanent Black.

Raoof, Abdul. 2019. *State, Religion And Society: Changing Roles of Faith-Based Organisations In Kerala, Working Paper 458*. Bangalore: The Institute for Social and Economic Change.

Singh, Upinder. 2017. *Political Violence in Ancient India*. Cambridge, London: Harvard University Press.

Stoker, Valerie. 2016. *Polemics and Patronage in the City of Victory: Vyāsatīrtha, Hindu Sectarianism, and the Sixteenth-Century Vijayanagara Court*. Oakland: University of California Press.

Sumesh, R. 2021. Recasting the History of Jainism in Tamil Nadu. *Research Trends in Multidisciplinary Research* 31: 49–64.

The Hindu. 2015. To Retain or to Adopt Any Faith Is a Personal Choice: Modi. https://www.thehindu.com/news/national/Fanaticism-will-not-be-tolerated-says-Prime-Miinster-Narendra-Modi/article60118476.ece.

The Times of India. 2015. PM Modi: My Govt's Only Religion is 'India First'. *Holy Book is Constitution*, February 27.

Veluppillai, Alvappillai. 1993. The Hindu Confrontation with the Jaina and the Buddhist. Saint Tirunacampantar's Polemical Writings. *Scripta Instituti Donneriani Aboensis* 15 (January): 335–364. https://doi.org/10.30674/scripta.67219.

Venkataramanujam, R. 2015. Temple Administration in Tamil Nadu: A Colonial Legacy. In *Facet of Contemporary History*, ed. M. Thilakavathy and R.K. Maya. Chennai: MJP Publishers.

Verghese, Ajay. 2016. *The Colonial Origins of Ethnic Violence in India*. Stanford: Stanford University Press.

Zvelebil, Kamil V. 1992. *Companion Studies to The History of Tamil Literature*. Leiden, New York, Copenhagen & Koln: E.J. Brill.

PART IV

Religion and the State in the Middle East

Can Mosque and State Be Separated? Should They? The 'Divine Pattern,' Freedom, and Modernity

Karen Taliaferro

In Book VI of Plato's *Republic*, Socrates says to Adeimantus that it is 'sure…in the present state of society and government that if anything can be saved and turned to the good you will not be off the mark by attributing it to god's providence' (492e, Sterling and Scott 1985: 182). Due to the corruptive influence of bad education and sophistry—and the city's resultant opposition to philosophy—there can be 'no end of troubles for cities or for citizens' unless philosophers rule the city (501e, Sterling and Scott 1985: 191). Philosophers, however, cannot rule a city unless it is 'built by architects using measurements from the divine pattern' (500e, Sterling and Scott 1985: 190). Philosophers, in short, must become kings—but this cannot happen without 'divine intervention' (492e).

Socrates lived about a millennium prior to the dawn of Islam, and although medieval Islamic philosophers would borrow heavily from the

K. Taliaferro (✉)
Arizona State University, Tempe, AZ, USA
e-mail: Karen.Taliaferro@asu.edu

381

S. Holzer (ed.), *The Palgrave Handbook of Religion and State Volume II*, https://doi.org/10.1007/978-3-031-35609-4_17

Hellenistic tradition, Socrates' idea of 'god' was of course quite different from the monotheistic god of Islam, Allah. But the idea that the city must, if it is to be good—indeed, if it is to be characterized by anything but 'troubles' and degeneracy—be patterned after something divine was not new by the time the Prophet Mohammad established the first Islamic community in the Arabian peninsula. This idea does, however, lie at the heart of debates that have raged throughout the history of political and religious thoughts: To what extent can, or should, divine patterns be enforced through legislative and political means? This chapter examines this question in the Islamic context, from the religion's earliest days through medieval legal and educational developments and into the modern world, asking whether 'mosque' and 'state' can exist separately in the modern world—and if so, whether that is good. What is ultimately at stake, I argue, is the nature of freedom that modern Islamic societies seek: What does it mean to live in a free, religious society?

CAN MOSQUE AND STATE BE SEPARATED? A HISTORICAL OVERVIEW

Origins

Observers have perennially noted that Islam has always been a religion as well as a political community, creating a prima facie strike against the possibility of separating religion and state. There is strong evidence for this aspect of Islamic history, and while interpretation of the facts is hotly disputed, the facts themselves are largely agreed upon. Around 610 AD, a relatively unknown merchant named Mohammad began to receive revelations in a cave outside of Mecca, on the Arabian peninsula, revelations believed to be transmitted from God through the angel Gabriel (Jibrīl). Alarmed by these messages, Mohammad initially kept them to himself, but encouraged by his wife Khadijah, he eventually began to preach to other Meccans, who increasingly began to persecute Mohammad along with those few who believed his message. In 615 AD, therefore, Mohammad sent a group of his followers to Abyssinia (now Ethiopia); facing increasing opposition and having lost his wife, in 622 AD he and his followers migrated to Medina (then called Yathrib), where Islam became a political community (Lapidus 2014a: 35). Between 628 and 630 AD, Mohammad and his followers returned to Mecca, where they established the Kaʿaba, a pre-Islamic religious sanctuary believed originally to have been built by Abraham, as a site of pilgrimage. They also fought the Meccans at two separate points, eventually taking the city and thereby expanding their reign over the Arabian tribes (Lapidus 2014a: 31, 36). Mohammad died in 632.

This rudimentary historical narrative, however, masks some of the details on Islam's political origins. For one thing, it is notable that year 1 of the Muslim calendar[1] marks not the year of Mohammad's first revelations but of the migration (*hijra*) from Mecca to Medina, where the fledgling Islamic community first became a political unit. It was in Medina that Mohammad and his followers wrote what has become known as the Constitution of Medina (*al-ṣaḥīfa* or *dustūr al-Madīna*), a charter forged between the band of Muslims who had emigrated from Mecca and the Jews of Medina, as well as various other tribes. The specifics of the document are less salient here than the fact of its creation, for while the Constitution of Medina does not lay out timeless principles of law—it is perhaps more akin to a multinational treaty than to what would today be termed a 'constitution'—the fact that the Islamic community had standing to ratify, as it were, such a document reveals the political power this small band of religious believers had gained. The Constitution explicitly establishes Mohammad and his followers as an *umma*, a community—but a community in a specific sense, with particular legal obligations and rights based on the stipulations of the constitution. The first part of the constitution, for example, outlines the right and duties of the Muslim believers toward each other (e.g., 'A believer will not kill another believer for the sake of an unbeliever'[2]), as well as toward the two dominant tribes of Yathrib/Medina, with whom the constitution was forged. The second part of the constitution laid out a non-belligerence agreement with the Jews of Yathrib (Lecker 2012: 115; see also Guillaume 1955: 231–233). The upshot of this document—or rather, of the fact of its forging—is that the Islamic community was no longer only a group united by belief in Mohammad as a prophet and his message as divine; they were now bound in their political alliances (and, soon thereafter, attacks and battles; see, e.g., Lapidus 2014a: 35) by what is thought to be a proto-international legal document.

Origins are certainly not the whole of a people's or a religion's story. Still, the overall picture emerging from these early days of Islam is one in which its political and religious elements were never entirely distinguishable from each other. As Ira Lapidus notes, during Mohammad's time, there was likely no clear distinction between religious and political affiliation: 'acceptance of Islam was probably a gesture at once of political obeisance and of religious allegiance' (Lapidus 2014: 40). From at least the time that Mohammad and his followers migrated to Medina, then, Muslims have been constituted as both a religious and a political body, governed in their earthly lives both by a divine law for themselves and by political agreements in their relations with non-Muslims.

There is an important qualification to make here, however, for none of the foregoing should suggest that there was never a distinction between what was sacred and what was profane. Rushain Abbasi provides evidence that the *dīnī-dunyawī* (religious-worldly) distinction obtained quite clearly in the minds of medieval Muslims, arguing that this 'binary represented a conceptual separation of the world into distinct religious and non-religious spheres analogous to the modern religious–secular' separation. Nevertheless, even as that which was sacred and that which was not were distinguished from one another, the formal political and religious structures would have been intertwined; Abbasi agrees that it was 'not conceivable' to medieval Muslims that 'religion and state must remain separate' (Abbasi 2020a: 191–192).

This political-historical backdrop distinguishes Islam from the Christianity that is the focus of the majority of this volume, in which the founding figure of Jesus Christ explicitly distinguished 'what is Caesar's' from 'what is God's' (Mark 12:17). His followers, furthermore, far from establishing a sovereign political community in the earliest generations, rather lived as a religious minority under the rule of a pagan empire for the first centuries of the religion's existence. It is worth adding that Islam's origins are also distinguished from Judaism in an important sense. Islam has always been, like Judaism, both an immanent and transcendent religion, that is, it is always at once concretely political and this-worldly as well as other-worldly. Unlike Judaism, though, and like Christianity, Islam is a universalizing religion. Combined, these features mean that at its core, Islam cannot easily be privatized, for it is always political, nor does it exist easily as a minority religion, for it has a mandate to expand. It also means that the 'church and state' trope does not transfer neatly to 'mosque and state,' for the metaphorical mosque entails a great deal more concrete political power than does the church. This becomes clearer when we look at the role of sharī'a.

The Pull of Plurality and the Necessity of Oneness: Law and Politics in Islam

Sharīʿa is the body of laws regulating Muslim life as gathered and interpreted by scholars and religious leaders over the centuries. Sharīʿa is entirely central to the practice of Islam; it is not an exaggeration to say that there is no Islam without sharīʿa, for it is composed in large part of the very same words that are believed to have been revealed to Mohammad as recorded in the Qurʾān. (Wael Hallaq calls it an 'obvious fact' that the 'ethic of the Qurʾān not only pervaded the Sharīʿa but also constituted it' [Hallaq 2012a: 86].) Joseph Schacht, one of the twentieth century's leading interpreters of Islamic law, called Islamic law 'the epitome of Islamic thought, the most typical manifestation of the Islamic way of life, the core and kernel of Islam itself' (Schacht 1964: 1). Westerners often associate the term 'sharīʿa' with penal law or family law, but it has always encompassed far more than these; describing sharīʿa as both divine law and a way of life for a religious people perhaps paints a more accurate, if still somewhat vague, picture.

This centrality of sharīʿa further complicates our question of whether mosque and state can be separated. A religion that has always entailed not only ritual and belief but also a highly detailed, prescribed way of life in a divine body of law—especially given what we know from the Islamic community's origins in Medina—suggests that perhaps what the West would refer to as two separate entities, 'mosque' and 'state,' in fact belong in Islam to one overarching, binding Law, the sharīʿa. This makes what Westerners might think of as 'religious' practices and beliefs inseparable from the 'legal' aspects of Islam. And where there is law, there is usually political power. As Albert Hourani writes:

> Muslim theologians had always taught that, while some prophets were sent into the world to reveal a Book only, that is to say, to reveal a truth about God and the world, others were sent also to reveal a law, a system of morality derived from the Book, and to execute it; and that, while Jesus was a prophet of the first type, Muhammad was one of the second. To execute the law was an essential part of his mission; but this implies that he had political power, and that from the start the Islamic community was a political community. Moreover, since the Book and the law were given not for one generation only but for all time, there must always be someone who exercises political power in the *umma*. (Hourani 1983: 190)

In one sense, then, mosque and state cannot be separated because one entails the other—to have a mosque is to practice Islam, to practice Islam is to observe the sharīʿa, and the observance of sharīʿa requires enforcement by a political authority.

Legal Education in Medieval Islam

As usual, though, upon closer examination, the picture gets more complicated. One would imagine that, because of the centrality of oneness (*tawḥīd*), in Islam—as exemplified in doctrines of one God, one final Prophet (Mohammad), one book of divine revelation (the Qurʾān)—the sharīʿa would develop in a highly centralized, unified way. This was not the case. In the early years of Islam, legal education, and therefore the formation of legal doctrine, was conducted in *madhāhib*, or informal law schools. These were numerous, locally based, and diverse; given this, the sharīʿa was not interpreted in a wholly uniform way, at least in Sunni Islam.[3] However, within a few centuries, this *madhāhib* had consolidated into four principal schools of thought that survive to this day, the Ḥanafī, Shafiʿī, Ḥanbalī, and Malikī schools (named after their founders, who lived during the eighth and ninth centuries AD). This intellectual consolidation, however, did not immediately mean a geographical consolidation at this point in history (though such sorting would later occur[4]), which might have made the confluence of religious and political authority more natural. Although the schools had their origins in Medina, Basra, Baghdad, and Fustat, by means of the travel of students and teachers, Islamic legal education spread throughout the ʿAbbasid caliphate, which at its peak encompassed most of the modern Middle East and much of North Africa (Lapidus 2014a: 216). Colleges (*madāris*, plural of *madrasa*) were established especially by the tenth and eleventh centuries throughout the realm, with highly personalized—to the teacher's specialty and interests, that is—education based in homes or mosques (to which were added hostels for student residences). The mode of education was informal in that there were no official certificates or schedules to mark the completion of one's training (Lapidus 2014a: 217). The result of this personalization, as well as geographic and school-based variances, was a lack of uniformity of Islamic legal training.

Beyond the diversity of sharīʿa education, though, it is important to understand that although it is grounded in the Qurʾān, the sharīʿa itself is not a positive legal code divinely transmitted as such; rather, it has developed over time through *fiqh*, or Islamic jurisprudence. In the earliest years of Islam, this was an informal practice, consisting mainly of decisions and opinions handed down by Mohammad himself. Upon his death, the so-called Rightly Guided Caliphs, the four rulers who personally knew or were related to the Prophet himself, governed the *umma* from 632 to 661 and oversaw enormous territorial expansion through battles and large-scale conversions. But it was the second caliphate, the Umayyad dynasty (661–750), that allowed for the emergence of sharīʿa and *fiqh* in a politically formalized manner (Schacht 1964: 23). *Qāḍīs*, or judges of Islamic law, were appointed by Umayyad governors and began to hand down rulings on specific questions related to a number of aspects of public and private life, taking into account not only specific Qurʾānic guidance but also local custom (Schacht 1964: 23-24). This latter factor helps to explain why, in addition to the varied legal educations available in the medieval Islamic era, Islamic law could not be wholly unified—local customs varied and, though they were 'Islamized' by means of the same Qurʾān, juristic opinion (*raʾī*) was hardly guaranteed to converge on any standards of uniformity, especially given the widely divergent circumstances under which jurists were living by this—albeit still early—point in Islamic history. Even as the marriage between political power (or 'state,' though see below for more on that term) and religious authority was present from the beginning and only seemed to increase in the first centuries of Islam, then, it was widely variegated from place to place and school to school.

An Uneasy Marriage
One can draw two conflicting conclusions from all of this. In one sense, Islam's legal and political origins seem to suggest that an alliance between 'mosque and state' could work well within the Islamic framework; a state could simply adopt a school of legal thought and govern both politically and religiously from within that tradition. And indeed, this is largely descriptive of how contemporary Muslim-majority countries function. But such a neat alignment of mosque and state, even though commonly practiced, is not without its conceptual problems. As mentioned above, the idea of *tawḥīd*, or oneness (sometimes translated as 'unity'), is a vital one in Islamic theology, one that has implications for political structure. *Tawḥīd* is considered to be first and foremost a characteristic of God— God is one, 'there is no God but God.' But as Kenneth Cragg writes, *tawḥīd* as a concept often goes well beyond the mere idea of unity. It is 'aggressive...it means 'unity' intolerant of all pluralism'[5] (in ʿAbduh 1980: 12). The arrangement described above, then, though it may be the best

available modus vivendi given the modern international system in which each nation-state enjoys its own sovereignty, would in the eyes of many Muslims problematically identify the state, not Islam, as the origin of obligation.

Note that while the sovereignty of the modern nation-state may be fundamentally problematic for Islamic theology, this is not to claim that political authority *as such* is a problem. Muhammad ʿAbduh, a late eighteenth-century Egyptian Islamic scholar and reformer, was committed to the harmony of Islam and modernity. In his classic *Risālat al-Tawḥīd* (translated—fairly loosely—as *The Theology of Unity*), ʿAbduh wrote that nations are a part of God's divine plan, a plan that integrates 'their true well-being in this world here and now' with a view toward 'the other world' (ʿAbduh 1980: 137). The nations, then, are included in this *tawḥīd*, this oneness of God's character that encompasses human thought, action, and destiny. They promote God's '[d]ivine laws for the right ordering of thought and reflection, the discipline of desire and the curbing of ambition and lust' (ʿAbduh 1980: 138). As long as this is the case, according to ʿAbduh, 'God will never deprive a nation of His favor…Rather He will multiply their blessings in proportion…' (ʿAbduh 1980: 138). However, should a nation turn away from this holistic guidance toward the right way to live for this world and the next, 'happiness also takes its leave and peace with it. God then turns its strength into decline and its wealth to poverty. Well-being then gives way to wretchedness and peace to trouble. While they [i.e., such nations] slumber in neglect, they will be overpowered by others, either by tyrants or by just masters' (ʿAbduh 1980: 138). It is important, in such thinking, both that political authority exists and that it follows true Islam. This is true even given the modern world's fracturing into a nation-state system rather than a caliphate that would promote the unity of the Muslim *umma*. (According to Hourani, ʿAbduh accepted 'the institutions and ideas of the modern world; they had come to stay, and so much the worse for anyone who did not accept them.' Hourani 1983: 139.)

But to what does this tend? As Charles Butterworth points out, such an integralist approach to religion and politics, which perhaps strikes the modern Westerner as outdated or even scandalous in its fusion of the things of God and the things of man, should not be dismissed as 'benighted, backwards, and hopelessly illiberal' (Butterworth 1992: 27). At the heart of the dispute between the approach to governance that the West has taken since early modern times and that articulated by ʿAbduh (among others) is the question of whether the state should primarily promote freedom or virtue, including religious virtue. Needless to say, for a polity to function well and for humans to flourish, it needs some measure of both. The question then becomes, can an Islamic state promote freedom even at the risk of downplaying Islamic virtue?

Many modern thinkers believe that it can; in fact, recent decades have seen a rise in scholarship arguing that in order for Islamic virtue to survive and thrive, the state not only can but *must* prioritize freedom. This is the topic of the section below. However, there are two important variations of this argument, one that fundamentally accepts the modern world and one that sees in modernity a threat to Islam. I mentioned above that one could draw two conflicting lessons from the origins and legal framework of Islam, the first favoring an integralist approach, which runs contrary to the idea of mosque-state separation. But the second conclusion is that if the early years of Islam provide a normative model for the relationship between politics and religion, then the fracturing of the Islamic world that the modern nation-state system renders necessary means that Muslim societies face an impossible situation: How can they claim to be one *umma* if the political-religious authority in one state differs from that in another? In other words, according to this strain of thought, the state, in its modern form, is not and cannot be the equivalent of the Islamic *umma* and therefore must be kept separate from Islam; mosque and state must be separate.

Whose State? Which Sharīʿa? The Islamic Nation-State and the Modern Conundrum

The above discussion of the close relationship between mosque and state, however accurate, is nevertheless incomplete, for we have not yet dealt with the question of what we mean by 'state.' The story of the modern state that is the global norm of international relations and diplomacy is a European story, one in which centuries of religious war ended first with the Westphalian *cuius regio, eius religio*, making religion an internal state matter. As history carried the continent through the Enlightenment, experiments in empire and, not insignificantly, the birth of the United States as a nation that would take no state religion, modern citizens have come to expect religion to be a private, not state, matter. This being the case, to what can we look for guidance for those nations that were not central players in this story, the nations of mosques, most of which were until the twentieth century part of the international caliphate that was the Ottoman Empire?[6] Divine revelation provides little insight here; as Saïd

Amir Arjomand points out, 'the Qur'an...contains almost nothing that bears on state formation or public and constitutional law' (Arjomand 2009: 558). Nor does it make sense simply to transfer the church-state model into the Islamic world, given its history, the role of sharīʿa, and the importance of *tawhīd*. In short, Islam did not come about with the nation-state in mind, nor did the nation-state arise with Islam in mind. How, then, can—or should—Islamic states govern in modernity, vis-à-vis religious and political authority?

Unsurprisingly, opinions among scholars, not to mention politicians and activists, have varied widely on this question.[7] Islamic thinkers and activists advocating a separation of religion and state have proliferated during the twentieth and twenty-first centuries. These thinkers, political leaders, and activists advocate secularism to varied extents and in varied ways; Turkey's early twentieth-century turn to a fairly strict secularism under Ataturk is perhaps the most extreme example, but there are softer versions of secularizing movements, both political and intellectual: Tunisian *Ennahda* (Renaissance) party founder and eventual president Rachid Ghannouchi (b. 1941) comes to mind, as does the renowned Egyptian scholar (and eventual exile) Nasr Hamid Abu Zayd (1943–2010). Still, what all such figures have in common is some version of an embrace of modernity: the modern state, the progress of science and culture, and at least some level of interaction with the West can and sometimes should be integrated into the Islamic world. Many twentieth- and twenty-first-century Muslim reformists have called for Islam and the state to be separated, even as Islam and *politics* may, and even should, carry on a close relationship. Abu Zayd firmly advocated a secular state, going so far as to claim that '[s]ecularism in its essence is nothing but the true interpretation and rational understanding of religion' (Abu Zayd 2007: 11). Abdullahi An-Naim likewise writes, 'In order to be a Muslim by conviction and free choice...I need a secular state,' where 'secular' means that 'the state does not claim or pretend to enforce Sharīʿa' (An-Naim 2010: 1).

This is importantly distinguished from the idea of removing sharīʿa from society and politics; in fact, for An-Naim, the 'call for the state, and not society, to be secular is intended to enhance and promote genuine religious observance, to affirm, nurture and regulate the role of Islam in the public life of the community' (An-Naim 2010: 1). What An-Naim is suggesting is a situation similar to that of the United States, which has since its inception rejected the notion of a state religion (at the national level) but which has, at least until very recently, been one of the most religiously active societies in the West, including in its politics. Muhammad Shahrour, likewise, sees 'no incompatibility' between the layers of attachment a Muslim citizen would feel to her religion, ethnic group, and nation-state, suggesting that a divide between one's religious authority and one's political authority need not pose any difficulty. In fact, Shahrour states plainly that 'the less the state interferes with the religious and mundane choices of the people, the closer it is to God,' averring that this is what Mohammad effected in Medina (Shahrour 2018: 189, 192). In these visions of the relationship between mosque and state, the state must remain religiously neutral *so that* Muslims can practice their faith; otherwise, the predominant religious faith in any given society will enforce its views by means of the coercive power of the state (An-Naim 2010: 85).

This is not a uniformly held view, however, even among progressive Islamic thinkers. I mentioned above that among those scholars of Islamic thought calling for a separation between mosque and state are two different strains of thought, the second of which is characterized by thinkers who see in the modern nation-state a rejection of the norms of Islamic governance altogether. Wael B. Hallaq is perhaps most clear on this topic. While Hallaq writes in no uncertain terms concerning the imperative to separate mosque and state, for him, the separation is first *logically* necessary and only *therefore* normative. In other words, Hallaq does not advocate the separation between mosque and state on the same grounds as An-Naim (or Abu Zayd, or Ghannouchi), for whom the call for separation comes from a concern with the promotion of freedom. For Hallaq, on the other hand, the call for separation could perhaps better be described as a plea for protection *from* the modern state on the grounds that it is incompatible with true Islamic governance. 'The "Islamic state,"' he writes, 'judged by any standard definition of what the modern state represents, is both an impossibility and a contradiction in terms' (Hallaq 2012a: ix). It is important to note Hallaq's stress on the qualifier 'modern:' the modern state, which he sees as a creation of European nationalism and later colonialism, is non-Islamic; it does not and cannot reflect true sharīʿa, without which there could be no Islamic state. Nor should one be persuaded of its possibility by the vast number of Muslim-majority countries invoking sharīʿa as a (or the sole) basis for their laws: 'The Sharīʿa practices of the modern states in Islamic countries...*cannot—and thus must not—be invoked as a measure by which premodern paradigmatic Sharīʿa is understood, evaluated, or judged*' (Hallaq 2012a: 2, emphasis original). If by state we mean the modern state, so Hallaq's argument goes, then not only *can* mosque and state be separated, but they must.

Hallaq's claim needs some unpacking, however. His argument suggests that the 'premodern paradigmatic Sharīʿa' stands in a zero-sum competition with the bureaucratic logic of the modern state—a state, it should be added, which is a creation of European experience' (Hallaq 2012a: 25). In this case, one can have either the modern state—an amoral creation of the sovereign will that arrogates to itself the right to order human society—or the sharīʿa, which is both mosque and, if not exactly 'state' (for the state is by definition Western and human, not divine), then at least a way of ordering and living in society. This raises a question of the nature of law: Is law fundamentally human or divine? Hallaq's answer is worth consideration:

> Paradigmatic modern law is positive law, the command of the fiction of sovereign will. Islamic law is not positive law but substantive, principle-based atomistic rules that are…ultimately embedded in a cosmic moral imperative. For Muslims today to adopt the positive law of the state and its sovereignty means in no uncertain terms the acceptance of a law emanating from political will, a law made by men who change their ethical and moral standards as modern conditions require. It is to accept that we live in a cold universe that is ours to do with as we like. It is to accept that the ethical principles of the Qurʾān and of centuries-old morally based Sharīʿa be set aside in favor of changing manmade laws. (Hallaq 2012a: 88–89)

In Hallaq's analysis, then, one really must choose *either* mosque *or* the modern state, for the respective versions of law implicated in each are fundamentally opposed: sharīʿa is divine, but the state's law is human. There cannot be a Muslim state, at least not in the modern sense, nor can there exist a society in which mosque and state operate as independent, yet jointly authoritative, entities. One accepts either the sharīʿa or the state, not both.

It is important to take stock of the difference between Hallaq and An-Naim. Despite their agreement that mosque and the modern state must be separated, and despite the shared concern for the free practice of Islam that animates their calls for separation, An-Naim's and Hallaq's analyses represent pro-modern and anti-modern approaches, respectively. An-Naim enlists the aid of the state (and, importantly, constitutionalism; see Chap. 3 of An-Naim 2010) to carve out a sphere of free practice of the Islamic religion—a sanctuary for the *umma*, one might say (as well as a guarantee of the free practices of other religions). Hallaq, on the other hand, considers the modern state to be less a guarantee for the free practice of sharīʿa on the part of the *umma* than a potential obstacle to its realization. In this view, the separation of mosque and state is necessary but not sufficient; it eliminates a problem but does not necessarily guarantee that the sharīʿa will be properly sovereign, nor even understood in its proper terms. An-Naim accepts the form of the modern state as it has developed in recent centuries in the West, with its monopoly on the use of force, sovereignty in international relations, but also crucially as a reflection of the will of the people and usually a formally or at least de facto secular power. Hallaq sees within the sharīʿa a premodern logic that simply cannot be squared with the modern state.

SHOULD MOSQUE AND STATE BE SEPARATED? A SNAPSHOT FROM MOROCCO

The question of the separation of mosque and state is not only a theoretical but also deeply practical one, affecting the lives of hundreds of millions of Muslims across the globe, whether living in Muslim-majority countries or not. If politics is 'the art of the possible,' then even if Hallaq is correct and there can be no true sharīʿa in the modern state system, it is worth asking, what political and religious arrangements should contemporary Islamic societies promote?

This question cannot be settled by non-Muslim scholars such as myself. What we can do, though, is return to Socrates' contention that there can be no good city that is not 'built by architects using measurements from the divine pattern.' If God, going beyond the philosophers, reveals that divine pattern in the sharīʿa, what is the role of the state in promulgating and enforcing that sharīʿa on an institutional level?

This question preoccupied medieval Muslim philosophers, and their responses are worth lengthy consideration, from al-Farābī's *Virtuous City* to Ibn Rushd (Averroes 2008)'s *Decisive Treatise* and *Commentary on Plato's Republic*. But in examining the question in a modern context, Morocco's approach to mosque and state, *dīn wa dawlah*, illustrates well the complexities of translating a medieval pairing to a contemporary context.

Formally, Morocco stands squarely within what I referred to above as an integralist model of mosque-state relations. The King, believed to be a direct descendent of the Prophet Mohammad, carries the title of *Emir al-Muʾmanīn*, the leader of the faithful. Friday sermons for mosques throughout the country are written and distributed by the Ministry of Religious Affairs, and the 2011 constitution declares Islam to be the official religion of the state (Title 1, Article 3). At the same time, Morocco has poised itself as something of a leader for the continent of Africa as well as a bridge between Africa and the West. At the US-Moroccan Strategic Dialogue in 2014, for instance, Morocco was referred to as one of 'three pillars—Morocco, the United States, and Africa'—as well as a 'hub towards Europe and Africa.' More recently, the July 2019 edition of the French magazine *Le Point* had for its cover story 'Maroc: La Nouvelle Puissance' (Morocco: the New Power), which portrayed Morocco as an emergent global and continental leader due not only to its agile adaptation to a post-Arab Spring world but also its economically vital Port de Tanger Med as well as millions of foreign tourists each year (*Le Point* 2019: 40–42). In other words, Morocco has managed to maintain a close relationship between mosque and state while also participating in the modern international state system and earning the admiration of Western observers who might otherwise find state control over religion objectionable. How has it done so, and what, if anything, does this tell us about the relationship between mosque and state in the modern world?

While a complete answer to these questions far exceeds the scope of this chapter, one particular component in Morocco's *dīn wa dawlah* portfolio is worth a close examination. The Mohammed VI Institute for the Training of Imams, Morchidines, and Morchidates provides theological, spiritual, and practical formations for Moroccan as well as other African and even European imams (religious leaders who can preach in mosques) and informal religious leaders (*morchidines* for men and *morchidates* for women). The Institute has garnered significant attention within Western foreign policy and scholarly circles alike in recent years and is recognized not only for its internal role within Morocco's borders but also as a tool of soft power and diplomacy because of its outreach with other African nations, particularly West African nations (Hmimnat 2019, Wainscott 2018). Indeed, as Ann Marie Wainscott describes it—and as my own visit to the Institute and its Secretary General in the summer of 2019 affirmed—these efforts at cooperation have been strikingly successful, with increasing numbers of foreign states sending their own students to the Institute and thus actively seeking 'the involvement of a foreign country in domestic affairs' (Wainscott 2018: 2).

In a sense, the Institute resurrects the medieval *madrasa*, bringing students from across the Islamic world to study with religious leaders and scholars, housing them in situ, and providing them with a social, spiritual, and academic experience that they bring back to their home communities. At the same time, the Institute's curricular design seems tailored to twenty-first-century fears of radicalism along with a changing communications landscape: imams-in-training are educated not only in traditional theology but also in computer literacy so that they can combat radicalism online. *Morchidates* and *morchidines* are likewise trained to spot and intervene in signs of radicalism in their communities.

The Institute raises intriguing questions for mosque-state relations. Although it uses the state to regulate the mosque, it does so in such a way that aims to achieve the same moderation and tolerance that advocates of a separation of mosque and state seek. One of the major elements for which Western leaders have routinely praised Morocco is its 'moderate' Islam. At the Strategic Dialogue summit referenced above, for instance, the then-Secretary of State John Kerry praised Morocco for its 'commitment to fostering religious tolerance' (Kerry, 2014). *Le Point*'s coverage, likewise, included a rather ebullient article on the Institute's promotion of 'a "middle path" Islam [that is] open and tolerant' ('un islam du "juste milieu," ouvert et tolerant,' *Le Point* 2019: 52). Legally as well, the same Title 1, Article 3 provision of the Constitution that declares Islam to be the religion of the Moroccan state guarantees 'freedom of practice in religious matters' (*li kul wāḥid ḥurīyat mumārisa shuʾūnihi al-dīnīyah*).[8] And here we arrive at the difficulty, for it is the very mixing of mosque and state—so foreign to the modern West and so objectionable to many theorists and advocates of a separation—that would seem to contribute to the very moderation and tolerance that both Western observers and progressive Muslim thinkers seek, both within their own borders but also in international arena. Yet this peculiar blend of state intervention in religion and even 'religious diplomacy' that amounts to an exporting of Moroccan religious policy, a blend that seems in form so illiberal, also promotes liberal values of tolerance, moderation, and even interreligious understanding. (The curriculum, as shared with me by the Director General, includes texts on both Judaism and Christianity.)

Conclusion

I use the Institute and its role in both domestic and international religious affairs as an illustration of the complexity of the mosque-state question in countries that are at once historically part of the transnational Islamic *umma* yet are also fully integrated into the modern nation-state—characteristics that describe states from Indonesia to Bahrain to Mali. For discussions over whether religion and state should be kept apart are often characterized by assumptions that freedom, moderation, and tolerance fall on one side of the equation only. Advocates of the Moroccan model might respond that the Mohammed VI Institute aims precisely at freedom: by promoting religious tolerance, it opens up the public sphere for the coexistence of multiple ways of living faith and belief. Just as a state-sponsored American civics textbook might stress the underlying principles of the Declaration of Independence, this line of thinking would go, the Moroccan state has a duty to promote a Moroccan understanding of freedom using the resources of its own heritage.

Still, it must be admitted that on a more basic level, state control over mosques—and those who lead the faithful in them—does involve a surrender of at least individual freedoms. The Moroccan or Senegalese imam who passes through the door of the Mohammad VI Institute in some meaningful way gives up his right to determine for himself the interpretation and even application of sacred text and tradition. For at least some Muslims who believe Islam to be true and to be the path to true freedom, such a surrender may not be remotely troubling. To others, such as An-Naim, for whom faith needs to be kept separate from matters of the state, or others who share Hallaq's view that the square peg of the modern state cannot fit with the round hole of the sharīʿa, the idea of state control over religious education is anathema.

This, then, gets us to the overarching question of the nature of freedom in modern Muslim societies. Can a state actively promote freedom *through* its integration of mosque and state? In other words, can the divine pattern be instantiated in the state? Or, as Socrates' life seems to suggest, does the state tend to corrupt, or even destroy, those who promote the highest truths? This question clearly has empirical elements—one could easily point to the counterexample to Morocco that is Saudi Arabia, where a close (indeed, overlapping) relationship between mosque and state severely limits individual freedoms and fosters illiberalism—but at its heart, it is a question of the nature of human freedom itself. Must man, in Rousseau's famous words, be 'forced to be free'? If so, some measure of mosque-state integration seems inevitable, even good, for promoting freedom. If, on the other hand, the Qur'ān's declaration that 'there is no compulsion in religion' (2:256) forbids the modern state, with its Weberian monopoly on legitimate force, from interfering in matters of faith, then it would seem that the modern state must separate itself neatly from the mosque.

RELATED TOPICS

sharī'a, nahda movement, Constitution of Medina, liberal Islam

NOTES

1. That the year 622 AD is the same as Year 1 in the Islamic (Hijri) calendar should not lead the reader to conclude that the two calendars are simply 621 years apart, as the Hijri calendar is lunar. As I write this note in May 2020, for instance, the Hijri date is 9 Ramadan 1441.
2. وَلَا يَقْتُلْ مُؤْمِنٌ مُؤْمِنًا فِي كَافِرٍ in my translation; see https://site.eastlaws.com/Dostor/DostorElmadina/Dostor_Elmadian_Show for Arabic text of Constitution of Medina.
3. The minority Shiī Muslims, who broke away from the sect that would come to be called Sunni Islam not long after the death of the Prophet Mohammad, differed from the latter on the question of who rightly succeeded the Prophet as imam, or leader of the Islamic community. Due to the fact that the vast majority (around 80%) of global Muslims are Sunnī, and because the treatment of 'mosque and state' in a Shiī context would require a separate treatment, this chapter does not, regrettably, address the Shiī case. It is worth pointing out, however, that the Shiʿa practice their faith with a more centralized religious authority; what this portends for the possibility of the separation of mosque and state is a fascinating question that must be set aside for a later inquiry.
4. The four legal schools did eventually sort themselves geographically; what is now Saudi Arabia, for instance, was historically a Ḥanbalī region, though in more recent centuries it has adopted the jurisprudence of Ibn Wahhab, whereas North African (not counting Egyptian), West African, and some Sub-Saharan African countries use Malikī legal theory. Turkey, the Levant, most of Egypt and central Asian countries are Ḥanafī, and northeast African and southeast Asian countries are among the predominantly Shafiī countries.
5. For the Arabic grammarian, it is worth noting that *tawḥīd* is a 2nd *wazan* verbal noun (*maṣdar*).

6. Whether the Ottoman Empire constituted a true caliphate is in dispute but is not terribly important here; the essential point is that its breakup did not lead naturally into a Westphalian nation-state system.

7. While they are not included in my account, it is important to note that one strain of responses has been marked by a radical rejection of the Western version of modernity altogether. Early twentieth-century Islamists, including Sayed Qutb (1906–1966), Hasan al-Banna (1906–1949), and Abul Ala Maududi (1903–1979), responding to a combination of imperialism, Western influence on society and government, and the concomitant secularism, advocated a radical rejection of the separation of mosque and state and sought a return to premodern Islam, sometimes, as in the case of Qutb, advocating violence in order to do so. See, for example, Butterworth 1992.

8. This is my translation of the Arabic constitution's provision, which suggests the broadest protection. The French version guarantees 'le libre exercice du culte,' the free exercise of *worship*. These two should be taken as authoritative over English translations, as the Moroccan Constitutional Court's website (https://www.cour-constitutionnelle.ma/ar/دستور-المملكة-المغربية).

offers only the Arabic version, while the Moroccan government's website (http://www.maroc.ma/en/system/files/documents_page/bo_5964 bis_fr_3.pdf) offers the French. None offer an authorized English translation.

References

Abduh, M. 1980. *The Theology of Unity.* Trans. Isḥaq Musaʿad and Kenneth Cragg. New York: Arno Press.

Abbasi, R. 2020a. Did Premodern Muslims Distinguish the Religious and Secular? The Dīn–Dunyā Binary in Medieval Islamic Thought. *Journal of Islamic Studies* 31 (2): 185–225.

Abu Zayd, N.H. 2007. *Naqd al-Khiṭāb al-Dīnī (Critique of Religious Discourse).* Casablanca, Morocco: al-Markaz al-Thaqāfī al-ʿarabī.

An-Naim, A. 2010. *Islam and the Secular State: Negotiating the Future of Sharia.* Cambridge, MA: Harvard University Press.

Arjomand, S.A. 2009. The Constitution of Medina: A Sociological Interpretation of Muhammad's Acts of Foundation of the Umma. *International Journal of Middle East Studies* 41: 555–575.

Butterworth, C. 1992. Political Islam: The Origins. *Annals of the American Academy of Political and Social Science* 524: 26–37.

Guillaume, A. 1955. *The Life of Muhammad: A Translation of Ishaq's Sīrat Rasūl Allāh.* Oxford, UK: Oxford University Press. Excerpted at https://www.constitution.org/cons/medina/con_medina.htm. Accessed 15 May 2020.

Hallaq, W.B. 2012a. *The Impossible State: Islam, Politics, and Modernity's Moral Predicament.* New York: Columbia University Press. Kindle edition.

Hmimnat, S. 2019. *Training Malian Imams in Morocco: Challenges and Prospects.* Moroccan Institute for Policy Analysis. https://mipa.institute/6639.

Hourani, A. 1983. *Arab Thought in the Liberal Age, 1798-1939,* 1983. Cambridge, UK and New York: Cambridge University Press.

Kerry, J. 2014. Remarks at Opening Plenary of the U.S.-Morocco Strategic Dialogue. April 14, 2014. https://2009-2017.state.gov/secretary/remarks/2014/04/224411.htm

Le Matin. 2019. La Fondation Mohammed VI des oulémas africains lance son site web et le projet de magazine des oulémas africains. https://lematin.ma/journal/2019/fondation-mohammed-vi-oulemas-africains-lance-site-web-projet-magazine-oulemas-africains/316272.html. Accessed 24/07/2019

Lapidus, I. 2014a. *A History of Islamic Societies.* New York: Cambridge University Press.

Lecker, M. 2012. Constitution of Medina. In *The Princeton Encyclopedia of Islamic Political Thought.* Princeton, NJ: Princeton University Press.

Schacht, J. 1964. *An Introduction to Islamic Law.* Oxford, UK: Clarendon Press.

Shahrour, M. 2018. *Islam and Humanity: Consequences of a Contemporary Reading.* Trans. George Stergios. Berlin, Germany: Gerlach Press.

Wainscott, A.M. 2018. Religious Regulation as Foreign Policy: Morocco's Islamic Diplomacy in West Africa. *Politics and Religion* 11: 1–26.

Further Reading

Abbasi, Rushain. 2020b. Did Premodern Muslims Distinguish the Religious and the Secular? The Dīn-Dunyā Binary in Medieval Islamic Thought. *Journal of Islamic Studies* 31 (2): 185–220.

Review and critique of literature purporting to show a collapse of the distinction between religious and worldly categories in early Islam. At once defends the notion of a lack of separation between religion and state while showing that early Muslims did distinguish between what was strictly religious and what was not. Good for understanding Islamic thought on its own terms rather than either through or opposed to Western categories of religious and secular.

Averroes. 2008. Decisive Treatise and Epistle Dedicatory. Translated, with introduction and notes, by Charles E. Butterworth. Provo, UT: Brigham University Press.

A careful translation, with parallel Arabic, of one of the most important medieval texts on the harmony of religious law and philosophy.

Hallaq, Wael B. 2012b. *The Impossible State: Islam, Politics, and Modernity's Moral Predicament,* 2012. New York: Columbia University Press.

A leading scholar of Islamic law takes a critical view of the modern state and concludes that it is fundamentally incompatible with sharīʿa.

Lapidus, Ira. 2014b. *A History of Islamic Societies*. New York: Cambridge University Press.

A comprehensive history of Islam as both a religion and polity from its inception till contemporary times. Widely considered a classic, Lapidus' history is an excellent reference for students and scholars alike.

CHAPTER 18

Islamic Reform Movements and Mosque-State Relations: Prospects and Realities

Charles McDaniel

Even before the horror of 9/11, conversations about the need for a Protestant-like reformation of Islam had become amplified among scholars both within and outside the Muslim world. The not-so-implicit reasoning behind these debates was the hope that such a movement might moderate radical elements and quell tensions that, at the time, threatened conflicts on many fronts, like the one in Afghanistan that drew the United States into what has become the most protracted war in the nation's history. This chapter revisits the debates of that period as well as developments in Islamic conceptions of social order that are reshaping the relationship of mosque and state in predominantly Muslim countries.

One notable scholar of Islam who suggested that an Islamic reformation has been underway for some time is Dale F. Eickelman, whose 1998 article in the *Wilson Quarterly* speculated that the latter half of the twentieth century eventually will be seen 'as a time of change as profound for

C. McDaniel (✉)
Baylor University, Waco, TX, USA
e-mail: Charles_McDaniel@Baylor.edu

S. Holzer (ed.), *The Palgrave Handbook of Religion and State
Volume II*, https://doi.org/10.1007/978-3-031-35609-4_18

401

the Muslim world as the Protestant Reformation was for Christendom' (Eickelman 1998, p. 80). Eickelman, now emeritus professor of anthropology and human relations at Dartmouth, believed that the proliferation of technology, especially in the form of mass communications, would lead to a more literate and educated Muslim public and break down barriers that had kept Muslim culture from participating in the myriad benefits to modernization. According to Eickelman (1998, p. 80), Western values were making inroads into Islamic society such that 'in unprecedentedly large numbers, the faithful—whether in the vast cosmopolitan city of Istanbul or in Oman's tiny, remote al-Hamra oasis—are examining and debating the fundamentals of Muslim belief and practice in ways that their less self-conscious predecessors would never have imagined. This highly deliberate examination of the faith is what constitutes the Islamic Reformation.' Eickelman suggests that such reflective deliberation constitutes what he calls the 'Islamic Reformation.'

In 2004, I noted how establishing the standard of sixteenth-century Christianity for evaluation of contemporary events in Islam is seemingly paternalistic; yet, many scholars, both Muslim and non-Muslim, have found the temptation irresistible. The comparison is justified to an extent in observing common tensions within the respective religions. Both have witnessed controversy and often conflict over the influences of rationalism and mysticism, the mediating role of the clergy, the importance of orthodoxy vis-à-vis orthopraxy, and the right/obligation of the believer to access the sources of faith and apply independent judgment in determination of religious meaning. Thus, to the extent that Islam is now experiencing theological and institutional changes like those of Christianity in the sixteenth century, it may be that Islamic conceptions of governance and of the relationship between mosque and state are changing as well.

Evidence of an Islamic Reformation

The impact of the printing press in projecting the reform ideas of Martin Luther, John Calvin, Huldrych Zwingli, and others to a progressively literate European population in the sixteenth century was essential to the Protestantization of Christianity. Today, the Internet and social media carry the challenges of self-styled imams to Islamic tradition to the remotest reaches of the Muslim world. The imprint of modern communications on the Muslim faith is unmistakable. It has contributed to the rise of a class of 'micro-intellectuals' with broad access to the global community, resulting in what Eickelman, along with anthropologist Jon W. Anderson (2003, pp. 12–13), have characterized as a 'reintellectualization' of Islam. Interestingly, French scholar Olivier Roy (1998, p. 75) sees something different in the rise of what he calls 'neofundamentalism,' a bottom-up Islamization movement that is often anti-intellectual and less politically ambitious. Regardless of the exact nature of this phenomenon, its influence on Islamic culture is clear. Lay Muslims, such as the Syrian engineer Muhammad Shahrur, proffer new conceptions of the faith that challenge the monopoly over interpretation of the Qur'an and Shariah held by *ulama* (religious scholars) since the time of the medieval jurists. Shahrur's book is unique, blending images from the Qur'an and civil engineering, as well as various linguistic forms in an eclecticism demonstrating that 'Islamic discourse and practice is rapidly shifting from the boundary-minded forms it assumed after the advent of European imperial expansion into Muslim lands to a more confident and differentiated internal and external dialogue' (Eickelman and Anderson 2003, pp. 12–13).

The popularity of Shahrur's book and others like it by lay Muslims also reflects that growth in Muslim literacy worldwide has created demand for religious works beyond the ability of the Islamic establishment to respond to it, not unlike the impact of Luther's writings on a newly literate German population five centuries ago. According to Eickelman (2003, p. 42), 'through fragmenting authority and discourse, the new technologies of communication, combined with the multiplication of agency facilitated by rising education levels, contribute significantly to re-imagining Middle Eastern politics and religion.' Eickelman's statement suggests regional boundaries to this phenomenon that somewhat misrepresent his position. In reality, he discerns similar changes occurring in diasporas throughout Europe and the Americas, in Asia and Africa, and in the far reaches of Islam where 'increasingly vocal debates on what it means to be a Muslim and how to live a Muslim life' are being played out in myriad cultural contexts (Eickelman and Anderson 2003, p. 7). Debates in those diverse contexts also are inspiring reimagination of the relationship between mosque and state.

Prominent Muslim scholars have engaged in the debate about whether Islam needs reform or whether it is experiencing one now. Eight years before Eickelman's assessment, Abdullahi An-Na'im's *Toward an Islamic Reformation* conceived the need for a kind of reform that denotes a key difference between contemporary events in Islam and those of Europe in the sixteenth century: *many Islamic activists seek the reform of their faith while retaining society's foundation on Islamic law (Shariah)*. An-Na'im's (1990, pp. 1–2) desire is 'to evolve an alternative and modern conception of Islamic public law that can resolve those problems and hardships created by more rigid applications of what he terms 'historical Shariah.' In the same way, the Shiite scholar Abdulaziz Sachedina (2001, pp. 43–44, pp. 99–101) and his Sunni contemporary Khaled Abou El Fadl (2004, pp. 30–36) believe that significant reform *within* the context of a Shariah-based society is not only possible but essential. Thus, scholars from diverse Islamic perspectives suggest that secularization may not be *assumed* as critical to the reform Eickelman and others believe is occurring on a global scale.

While most Muslim reformers stop short of calling for the secularization of Islamic society, they commonly employ the language and even the doctrinal rationale of the Protestant Reformation. Iranian dissident Hashem Aghajari was sentenced to death in 2002 for giving a speech on 'Islamic Protestantism,' a sentence later commuted to five years in prison. He criticized Shiite clerics who stand between God and believers and who block access to the Qur'an. Aghajari (Savyon 2002) condemns the corruption of 'core Islam' by 'traditional Islam,' which includes layers of clerics supported by the Iranian regime. In a remarkably Lutheran characterization, Aghajari states: 'The Protestant movement wanted to rescue Christianity from the clergy and the Church hierarchy... We [Muslims] do not need mediators between us and God. We do not need mediators to understand God's holy books... We don't need to go to the clergy; each person is his own clergy.' Aghajari's belief in each person as 'his own clergy' shares notable similarities with Luther's 'priesthood of the believer.' Additionally, his statement calling for the separation of 'core Islam' from 'traditional Islam' that he believes has been distorted by the layering of laws and traditions specific to distinct cultures sounds remarkably like the reform ideas of Ali Shariati (d. 1977), the Iranian revolutionary and academic whose work focused on the sociology of religion. As Aghajari (Savyon 2002) notes, just as the religious scholars of previous generations 'had the right to interpret the Koran [in their way], we have the same right. Their interpretation of Islam is not an article of faith for us.'

However, Aghajari's belief that each Muslim generation has its own right to interpretation is controversial. An obstacle to reform in Islam is found in the potential privatization of faith that is seen to have resulted from the Protestant Reformation and the possibility for a similar transformation in Islamic society. As Allawi (2009, p. 136) notes: 'The privatization of Islam may be the ardent wish of both God-intoxicated individuals and secular modernisers, but it does not appeal to the broad sweep of Muslims, who still expect to see a public manifestation of Islam in their daily lives.' For Allawi, as for others who might see need for reform, there is inherent difficulty dividing the public and private spheres of Islamic society in ways 'that makes the task of 'reforming' Islam so fraught with difficulty and unpredictability.'

Muslim reformers often are divided in their respective conceptions of human and divine justice, with divisions commonly centering on Western norms of human rights and political governance. Among contemporary reformers, faith is rarely divorced from those institutions necessary to determinations of justice and the unity of the Muslim *umma*. Sachedina (2001, pp. 43–44) believes this confluence of faith and law is as necessary to the individual's justification before God as it is to maintain a kind of harmony unattainable in societies where the two are estranged:

> Islamic law as an expression of the human endeavor to carry out the divine will on earth is actually identical to the belief that faith is an instrument of justice. When law and faith merge in an individual's life, they create a sense of security and integrity about the great responsibility of pursuing justice for its own sake. And when this sense of security and integrity is projected to the collective life of the community, it conduces to social harmony... The separation of law and faith, on the other hand, results in the lack of commitment to justice that leads to chaos, violence, and even war.

What often divides Muslim reformers is the extent to which they perceive the potential for human fallibility in the discernment and application of Islamic law. For some, like El Fadl (2004, p. 34), the flaws are significant to the point that a 'religious state law is a contradiction in terms.' Thus, maintenance of an integral connection between individual faith and law is essential to the existence of Islam. Diminishment of either results in dualism and dissolution, not unlike that which many perceive to have resulted from the Protestant Reformation.

Abdel-Hakim Ourghi (2019, p. 15), the Algerian scholar at the University of Education, Freiburg, insists that not only an Islamic reformation but also an Islamic enlightenment is well past due. Such movements necessitate 'taking the canonical sources of Islam...and subjecting them to a more rational discussion, more nuanced perception, and fuller understanding.' Ourghi opposes conservatives like Muhammad Sameer

Murtaza who, in his 2016 book *The failed reformation*, only 'pretends' to engage in true Islamic reform while noting the failed attempts of the past and argues, in essence, that Islam needs no reform. In particular, Ourghi (2019, p. 14) notes the resistance of so-called imported imams in Europe who 'have institutionalized a kind of ban on inquiry in the Muslim communities of Europe' and who 'impose their teachings on the members of their communities with prefabricated answers, relying on outdated viewpoints that are supposed to be valid for all times and places.' Ourghi (2019, p. 15) promotes a reconciliation of Islam with reason such that it is capable of bringing out the faith's deep spirituality and humanistic values that support both religious inclusion and a spirit of freedom.

Ayaan Hirsi Ali (2015), a Somali-born Dutch academic who is now a fellow at Stanford's Hoover Institution, is among those who contend that because of the Reformation and Enlightenment in Western culture, most Jews and Christians do not heed those elements of scripture that advocate violence and encourage intolerance of other faiths. But it is arguable whether Islam requires the decisive break inspired by Luther and others to lessen its own radicalism and bring it into the community of nations. And many question the results today of past attempts to 'Protestantize' the faith. Mohammed al-Abbasi (n.d.) states: 'Predictably enough, our own Islamic Protestantism, like that of Calvin, Luther and Cromwell, has in practice yielded division rather than unity, and mental and cultural poverty rather than a new brilliance. Not only are the Muslim Protestants (*salafis*, as they inaccurately call themselves) at loggerheads with traditional orthodox ulema, but they find it notoriously hard to agree among themselves.'[1]

One may question whether an equivalent to the dramatic fracture in Europe that was the Protestant Reformation is necessary in the Islamic context. While it is likely that reformation and enlightenment in the West laid the groundwork for the advance of tolerance and attenuation of religious violence (certainly, the Reformation in its 'immediate context' *inspired* violence), perhaps a better question is whether Islam may 'skip past' such a tumultuous event and avoid similarly tragic consequences to those that resulted from the European wars of religion in the sixteenth and seventeenth centuries. And that assumes a similar instance of religious reform is even feasible. Ali Allawi (2009, p. 113) offers a concise argument for why a Protestant-like reformation of Islam is a virtual impossibility: Islam 'does not have a church with a fossilized hierarchy at whose apex rests a supreme religious authority.' Lacking an equivalent to the hierarchal and authoritarian structure of the Catholic Church in Christendom, it may be that the nature of Islamic reform must differ in kind as well as degree. Allawi (2009, p. 113) goes on to note that viewing the Iranian revolution as a reform movement loses any sense of commonality with the Protestant Reformation of the sixteenth century because, rather than disseminating religious authority and individualizing faith, 'a religious hierarchy was imposed on the state when none existed before.' Thus, the goals and structure of Islamic reforms, in the Iranian case and others, diverge significantly from the reforms of Luther, Calvin, Zwingli, and other notable Protestant reformers.

Some Muslim reformers have recognized what they see as flaws in Islamic reform efforts of the past, including the Iranian Revolution. Allawi notes particularly the role of Abdolkarim Soroush (Allawi 2009, p. 126), who has emerged as a vigorous opponent of Iran's system of *wilayat-al-faqih* (rule by jurists) and its 'quasi-infallible status.' He touts the virtues of freedom and democracy while challenging the rather unbounded claims to authority of Iran's *ulama*. According to Allawi, Soroush's platform for reform repositions Islam as reconcilable with democratic values while not avowedly accepting them:

> Modern notions of freedoms, rights and democracy are reconciled with religious knowledge rather than tested against some invariant standard of reference drawn from traditional theology or jurisprudence. Soroush's ideal is not a secular, not even a democratic, society but a religious community where the sense of the sacred hovers over humanity. Knowledge of the sacred, however, is derived from the collective human experience in all the sciences and disciplines. (Allawi 2009, p. 126)

In this way, Soroush offers a platform that can help inspire reform in both Islamic and liberal-democratic societies, calling attention to the oppression imposed by austere forms of religious law on the one side and the loss of a sense of the sacred on the other.

The potential for disagreements among Muslim reformers has been amplified by the greater accessibility of sacred texts via the Internet and other forms of mass communication and the development of electronic forums for *lay interpretation* that are beyond the control of the Islamic establishment. That this 'establishment' is institutionally diverse and lacks a formal hierarchy may mean that the dissemination of the exegetical function that is occurring may be accomplished with less conflict than was the case in the Protestant era of Christianity. Regardless, evidence demonstrating an attenuation of clerical command over the Qur'an's interpretation offers the most substantial evidence for Eickelman's thesis. 'Contextualist' approaches to Qur'anic interpretation such as that proposed by Abdullah Saeed (2006, p. 1) oppose the legalistic-literalistic approach that has dominated interpretive forms for much of Islam's history.

Perhaps the greatest obstacle to genuine deliberation concerning the need for reform in Islam and a rethinking of the relation between mosque and state is perception, not only that of Islamists and their understanding of divinely revealed *Shariah* that must be the basis for any rightly guided social order, but also the perceptions of Muslim secularists and Western Christians who believe that Islamists speak for all of Islam. Gudrun Krämer (2009, p. 109) notes how many factions to the mosque-state discussion believe that application of *Shariah* 'presupposes an Islamic state authority.' That presumption leads to an equally distorting assumption: 'Islam is not only…"religion and world" (*al-islam din wa-dunya*). It is also "religion and state" (*al-islam din wa-daula*)' (Krämer 2009, p. 109). It is these assumptions, ultimately leading to the conclusion that Islam cannot exist peacefully in conditions where other religions are allowed equal status, that incite the most extreme elements among both Muslim and non-Muslim. Yet Krämer (2009, p. 121) has shown how such assumptions do not arise 'naturally from Islam' but rather are 'contemporary interpretations, which in many ways express political experiences and expectations.' He believes that religion and state have no closer association in the Islamic historical context that they do in the European experience, extending from the Middle Ages right up through the modern period.

For Krämer (2009, p. 121), the key to understanding Islamic societies is focusing on 'the importance of Islamic law and ethics'; hence, 'the crucial issue is not the separation of church [mosque] and state but the relationship between Sharia and public order.' Muslims can and do live in liberal, secular orders, and even in quite unique political contexts in predominantly Muslim countries such as that in Indonesia where the nation is, by population, the largest Muslim state in the world; yet, where 'in the name of the state ideology of Pancasila, Islam represents just one of several recognized religions.' Yet, recently, *Shariah* and its hardline enforcement have become entrenched in Aceh Province. That it has occurred in a country constitutionally committed to religious pluralism suggests there is 'play in the joints' in adapting to federalist and other systems of governance, and efforts should continue in determining the appropriate relationship between *Shariah* law and democratic institutions.

ISLAMIC REFORM AND THE IMPACT ON MOSQUE AND STATE

If we have learned anything, it is that the desire of some to reform Islam as religion and the desire to achieve more liberal and democratic governments in Muslim nations are different issues. Many groups are active in these efforts and espouse different objectives. Islamist groups that advocate reform often conceive of 'purer' Islamic societies minus the contradictions that they see as resulting from Western influences. Islamic modernists are divided between those who believe Islam can thrive within a secular state founded on a religionless or religiously neutral constitution, and those who see *Shariah* as adaptable, capable of serving as the foundation for modern forms of governance.

Some critics have been alarmed that new constitutions in Iraq and Afghanistan contain language to the effect that Islam is the 'official' religion of the respective countries and, in the case of Iraq, a 'fundamental source' of legislation. Such language commonly is found in the constitutions of predominantly Muslim countries. The United States has charted its own course for advancing constitutional democracy in predominantly Muslim countries; yet, initial efforts have enabled considerable ambiguity in defining the degree of separation between mosque and state that should exist in Iraq and Afghanistan. Harvard University law professor Noah Feldman (U.S. Department of State 2004, p. 35), an adviser to the State Department in the development of the Afghan constitution, notes the Afghan court system is drawn from a mix of secular and Islamic judges and 'presumably has the power to adjudicate whether a given law violates the values of Islam.' Importantly, in those areas such as personal status law where is applicable, the 'particular school of Shariah that a given person belongs to will be respected, so no one will be obligated to follow a branch of Shariah that is not their own branch.' Feldman's belief that such 'experiments' in Islamic constitutionalism have the 'possibility' of success also suggests the possibility of failure. American sponsorship of what Fareed Zakaria (1997) famously described as 'illiberal democracy' concedes the complexities involved in planting constitutional government in nation-states where the role of religious law is long-established. It also demonstrates the U.S. government's desperation to 'tame' the Muslim world in the aftermath of 9/11 that, ironically, may produce unintended and illiberal consequences.[2]

Despite the sensationalist expressions of those fearing that *Shariah* law will somehow take hold in Oklahoma and other traditionally non-Muslim regions, Sadik al-Azm (2019, p. 19) offers an important level-setting perspective: 'with the exception of Saudi Arabia and Iran, Shariah law is nowhere significantly and/or seriously applied in the contemporary Muslim world, save in the sphere of family and personal status law.' Al-Azm's observation implies two important principles: first, that with few exceptions, *Shariah* rule is not the austere, freedom-denying, and all-encompassing sociopolitical structure portrayed by many non-Muslim critics; and, second, that Islam as culture, like Judeo-Christian culture, is being reformed in significant ways in the context of a modern, global society that acts on all religions simultaneously. Al-Azm (emphasis Al-Azm's 2019, p. 20) quotes the frustrations of an Islamist activist to reinforce his point: '*the modern and nominally Muslim nation-states, though having never declared a separation of mosque and state, nonetheless subvert as a way of life, as an all-encompassing spiritual and moral order and as a normative integrative force by practicing a more sinister de facto form of secularism and a functional form of the separation of state and mosque.*'[3]

Intense focus on Qur'anic-inspired fatwas issued by religious leaders who, while being influential in their circles, remain largely on the fringe of mainstream Islamic culture, has fueled anger among non-Muslim critics who insist that changing Islam at its theological core is the only way forward. Yet, both Judaism and Christianity have holy war (*haram*) written into their sacred canon. Christian nations do not call for the total annihilation of conquered peoples; nor is the Catholic just war tradition a prevailing source for how Western democracies that are 'culturally Christian' comport themselves in wartime. Muslim nation-states are, to a significant extent, similarly dependent on and independent of their religious foundations. So, regarding any reforms required, it appears at least one major reform must take place in the thought of non-Muslims who believe the very existence of *Shariah* is a fundamental block to predominantly Muslim countries joining the community of nations. That notion is unproven and, based on the status of Islamic law expressed by many Muslims, wrongheaded. Yet as Sayej (2018, p. 171) observes, 'the notion that sharia is immutable black-letter law appears over and over in debates among non-Muslims about Islam and democracy, often yielding absurd or extremist conclusions.'

Islamist groups do often step in and actively compete with state governments in the provision of social services and by offering spiritual and moral guidance, and those governments have not always taken kindly to these perceived intrusions. Following the lead of the Muslim Brotherhood in Egypt and Hezbollah in Lebanon, the grand ayatollahs of the Hawza in Iraq filled what many believe was a critical role in the post-Saddam transition to a more democratic government in that country. They largely rejected any direct role as political actors, preferring instead to moderate their interventions according to principles of *irshad wa tawjih* (guidance and direction) in looking out for the overall good of the Iraqi people (Sayej 2018, p. 175). There was no insistence of a strict imposition of Islamic law but rather that state-crafted law should not violate *Shariah*. Grand Ayatollah Ali al-Sistani took an increasing role in Iraqi politics in order to counter Iran's growing influence in the country. Such a turn was significant for a man who, as a member of the 'quietist tradition of Najaf,' traditionally avoided political activism (Arango 2015).

This transition of the government in Iraq provides additional evidence that institutional reform of mosque and state can happen without significant theological reform to guide their development. Rather than the grand program of reconstruction sought by members of the Western coalition in the post-Saddam era, Iraq has emerged at the center of a contest between Iranian-inspired Islamists seeking a form of *velayat-e faqih* (rule by jurists) and those promoting Islam as a religion compatible with a secular state, or at least with some hybrid form where secular and *Shariah* law exist side by side. To claim that religious reform is a prerequisite to political stability is an exaggeration that may, in fact, instill disquiet in the consciousness of Iraqis and others in the region. The resulting condition may make a truly stable and sustainable order unobtainable.

There is enough flexibility among *madhabs* (schools of Islamic jurisprudence) and configurations of mosque and state in the Islamic world to enable continued experimentation respecting the compatibility of *Shariah* with modern, liberal forms of governance. For all the media attention drawn to the Islamic State of Iraq and Syria (ISIS) and the Taliban, attempts to establish hardline Islamist regimes have failed more often than they have succeeded. The case of Tunisia is particularly interesting in this regard. Secular and Islamist parties have vied for power in that country for decades. Tunisia in general has been liberalizing over time, most notably under the leadership of Habib Bourguiba, who was president from 1957 to 1987. Advancement of women's rights was a major part of his presidency, with Bourguiba seeing both the economic benefits and social justice in such a movement (Masri 2017, p. 226). According to Safwan Masri (2017, p. 226), Bourguiba insisted that these reforms be accomplished within an Islamic framework, 'arguing that he had used *ijtihad* [application of independent reasoning in interpreting Islamic law for particular issues] and his own critical thinking skills to arrive at the proper reinterpretation of Islam.' While not a traditional theologian, Bourguiba appealed to an Islamic theological principle in expanding rights for women in Tunisian society.

In other ways, Bourguiba undermined traditional religious authority in Tunisia by constructing a common judiciary and disbanding both Qur'anic and rabbinical courts. He also implemented a uniquely Tunisian form of *laïcité* that placed limits on religion's role in public life while largely avoiding the secularism charge often levied against Ataturk's reforms in Turkey (Masri 2017, pp. 235–236).

Other institutional 'innovations' are observed in Tunisian mosque-state relations. Whereas in the Jordanian constitution, as in many Islamic countries in the Middle East, Islam retains its status as the 'religion of the state' and in some cases even non-Muslims are subject to *Shariah* personal status law, Tunisia has established a 'ministry of religious affairs' to support the nation's commitment to pluralism. This contrasts with many Islamic countries where ministries of 'waqfs' (state endowments targeting expressly Islamic goals) are common (Masri 2017, p. 61).

In recent times, reforms in Tunisia have proceeded *with the active participation of Islamist groups.* After a people's revolt against the autocrat Ben Ali in January 2011, the Islamist Ennahda party came to power by gaining the largest number of seats in the October parliamentary elections that followed. A turbulent period ensued in which political parties of varying stripes from secularist to Islamist vied for power. Violence was common, but the assassinations of two leaders of the political left, Chokri Belaid and Mohamed Brahmi, constituted a watershed for Tunisian politics and for Ennahda particularly in the realization that efforts to enforce a strict Islamic regime were likely to fail (Masri 2017, pp. 65–66). Ennahda found its own political ambitions were being undermined by violence perpetrated by more extremist elements in the Islamist movement, including the Salafist group *Ansar al-Shari'a* (Masri 2017, p. 65).

Following the continuation of violence, the ruling coalition headed by Ennahda was dissolved, and the group moderated its positions respecting the development of a constitutional government, including radically lowering demands for the criminalization of blasphemy, the allowance for polygamy, and the insistence that the constitution specifies *Shariah* as *the* source of legislation (Ruthven 2016, p. 145). Malise Ruthven quotes an official from the Ennahda party that the Ennahda membership gained considerable knowledge by observing the Egyptian experience with the Muslim Brotherhood: 'they [the Ennahda membership base] saw how the Brotherhood's insistence on unilateral acts might benefit you in the short term, but you lose in the long run. Your existence in the political scene is tied to the guarantee of democracy' (Ruthven 2016, p. 145).

The Tunisian experience makes an 'institutional' case that Islam needs no theological reformation to support transition to a more inclusive society embracing democratic principles. There is adequate room for experimentation with hybrid systems of *Shariah*/secular law to enable greater human rights and peaceful coexistence with non-Muslim countries. And non-Muslims should remind themselves that for the great majority of the world's population for more than 15 centuries, peaceful coexistence between Muslims and non-Muslims has been the norm.

That said, Islam's theological structure incorporates legal and political elements in ways that are likely to cause future confrontations. The dependency of Islam on *Shariah* will continue to pose challenges (and, in some cases, promote conflict) for democratic governments in countries where Islam is the dominant religion. However, even in the strictest regimes, where attempts to establish theocracy often employ violence, such efforts are failing. Religious zealotry, even in countries perceived to be the most radical, commonly is overstated. A report from the Iranian Ministry of Culture and Islamic Guidance in 2011, for example, noted that in the three decades following the Iranian Revolution, attendance at Friday prayers in the country dropped from nearly 50 percent of the population to only around 3 percent (Ruthven 2016, p. 148). Thus, at least based on formal measures of religiosity, Iran seems to have declined in religious devotion from the time of the Shah to the present.

The question is whether something on the order of a true separation between mosque and state, similar to that between church and state in the American context, is achievable or even necessary for enabling peaceful relations between Islam and the West. Alexander Benard (2008) believes that a model for Muslim countries might be found in American history, beginning with the colonial experience. Americans commonly forget that Puritan groups, products of the continuation of Protestant 'reformations,' formed the Massachusetts Bay Colony in the 1630s and, in many ways, replicated the established church-state structure of the system they were attempting to escape. The Massachusetts Bay General Assembly viewed its responsibilities as extending to the religious uniformity of the colony and installed oppressive laws for dealing with dissidents. Religious freedom was achieved only through an evolutionary process that required a 'Great Awakening,' which promoted both religious and political liberty. The American Constitution with its First Amendment, protecting religious freedom and establishing an effective 'firewall' between church and state, was implemented to maintain not only the independence but also the vigor of American religion, as James Madison famously noted in *Memorial and Remonstrance* (Madison 1785). Benard (2008) notes that 'public opinion on church-state separation in the colonies bore an uncanny resemblance to current views in the Islamic world,' and he believes that American historical experience should be promoted to Muslim countries along with statistics showing the 'high levels of American religious observance,' and polls reporting that 'over 90 percent of Americans believe in God, and 65 percent affirm "strong religiosity."' Benard (2008) notes how a large contingent of Muslim 'conservatives' falls between supporters and opponents of mosque-state separation; they 'believe that God must play an important role in their lives, but do not have very strong opinions about mosque-state separation.' Thus, for purposes of 'advancing mosque-state separation, moderates must present themselves to conservatives as potential allies, not enemies.' With support of historical evidence, conservatives may be convinced that degrees of separation can be 'good' for religion, just as Ennahda appears to have been so influenced in the Tunisian context.

There is another analogy to be drawn between Islam's current challenges in defining the appropriate relationship between mosque and state and the American experience. While the great divide of Muslim opinion on the subject, from Islamist to secularist, might be seen as a hindrance, American history demonstrates quite similar conditions at the time of the nation's founding. During the American Revolution and extending to development of the American constitution, conservative Puritans, traditional Anglicans, freethinkers, and members of emerging evangelical denominations came together in common cause to establish independence and forge a document allowing individual Americans to determine their level of religious observance. Despite the 'danger' some Muslims may perceive to such a system, the numbers do not lie. The United States remains one of the most intensely religious nations in the world. If nothing else, Benard's work and that of other scholars remind us that respecting religion and state, the historical experiences of Islamic countries and Western liberal democracies are not as disparate as we often assume.

CONCLUSION

Despite the insistence of both Muslim and non-Muslim critics, Islam refuses to be the monolith that many assume it, or wish it, to be. That was the case when calls for an Islamic reformation reached a fever pitch in the aftermath of 9/11, and it remains the sticking point for those who insist that such reform is essential to the world's future security. Theological diversity has persisted in Islam, extending to the very first century of Islam's existence, when conflict among Sunni, Shia, and Kharijis led to a splintering of belief about the true nature of Islam as religion. Within Shiism alone, there is an amazing diversity of believers who adhere to their own distinct ranking orders of imams, despite Qur'anic injunctions that would seem to preclude elevation of the Prophet's successors to such status. Farhad Daftary (n.d.) observes the extension of 'lively discourses' in the tradition beyond the religious to the political order, 'which remained closely linked to religious perspectives and theological considerations, the diversity in early Islam ranged widely from the viewpoints of those (later designated as Sunnis) who endorsed the historical caliphate to the various oppositional groups (notably the Shi'a and the Khawarij) who aspired toward the establishment of new orders.' Yet that has not been the predominant perception among non-Muslims. Even Alexis de Tocqueville, in his remarkable *Democracy in America*, wrote that because the Qur'an contains not only religious doctrine but also elements of politics, law, and even scientific theory, Islam 'will never predominate in a cultivated and democratic age, while [Christianity] is destined to retain its sway at these as at all other periods' (de Tocqueville 1988, p. 445).

Luther did not espouse the secularization of German society in the sixteenth century but only uncomfortably reshaped his theological reforms in a 'magisterial' direction out of sheer necessity. The survival of those reforms depended on it. The Lutheran Reformation, especially viewed in light of Philipp Melanchthon's civic and educational reforms, was as much institutional as theological, and quite specific to the German context in which it took place. European principalities were exerting their authority against not only the papacy but also the wider Holy Roman Empire, which culminated in the Peace of Westphalia in 1648. Other national reformations followed much the same design. Roman Loimeier (2005, p. 226) notes the most obvious of these in the English Reformation, which 'was an Act of State, not rooted in theological or religious but in pragmatic political considerations.' Thus, what sometimes began as attempts at theological reform often were rechanneled for pragmatic purposes and reshaped the societies in which they began.

The broad institutional nature of reform in Islam is perhaps even more pronounced than for European nations in the sixteenth century. In a sense, it must be. There is no equivalent to the papacy in Islam; even traditional seats of authority like al-Azhar in Egypt have waned in influence over the last century. And, while the majority of Muslim believers are in no way 'evangelical,' there are many examples, particularly from Africa, where Islamic reformers characterize evangelical-styled relationships 'between the individual believer ('abd/mu'min) and his Lord (rabbihi)' (Loimeier 2005, p. 217). Those will likely continue, but the more impactful Islamic reforms, especially for the relationship of mosque and state, will be those negotiated by figures like al-Sistani, who navigate a rocky passage between Islamism and secularism in different and changing cultural contexts.

For those who believe the secularization of Islamic society is an impossibility, Turkey stands as an obvious counterpoint, an extension of the Ottoman Empire that exhibited rather distinct spheres of religious and political authority. Indonesia's system of Pancasila, the 'five principles,' which read as if they could have been written by America's founding fathers, has enabled at least the vision of true religious pluralism in the world's most populous Muslim country. And it may be that seeds of secularization already have been sown, at least in some regions. Observing the intense rivalry between groups like the Taliban in Afghanistan and the ayatollahs of Iran, Roy (1998, p. 202; quoted in Ansari 2019, p. 16) claims that 'the crisis of religious legitimacy is leading to the supremacy of politics, and subsequently to a *de facto* secularization.' Thus, it could be in some cases that religious conflict, rather than hardening theocratic ambitions, inspires structures capable of taming those ambitions and promoting democratic values.

Ansari (2019, p. 13) offers cautious optimism that may portend good things for political participation and the future stability of Iran. He notes the development of a robust civil society extending to 'Iran's first revolution in 1906' and 'centered upon a myth of political emancipation.' The result has been development of a 'political consciousness' among the people that has positioned a traditional society for its encounter with modernity (Ansari 2019, p. 13). The dynamism of this creative force can have good and bad consequences; it was responsible for overthrowing the oppressive regime of the Shah but also gave legitimacy to the reign of Ayatollah Khomeini, and then later helped support construction of Ali Akbar Hashemi Rafsanjani's 'bourgeois republic' (Ansari 2019, pp. 24–25). The point, however, is that a society so often perceived in the West as fundamentalist and authoritarian is, in fact, far more 'democratic' in terms of those forces that shape its development than is often given credit. The Iranian experience also points to another similarity with the American colonial period: both were greatly shaped by civil society and the development of a collective political consciousness. That point alone suggests that, with respect to liberty and human rights, as well as the relationship of mosque and state, Islamic societies develop with trajectories that are in no way dictated by their theological foundations.

RELATED TOPICS

Islam, The Reformation, Politics

NOTES

1. Salafism is one of many Islamic movements that idealizes a golden age and desires to return the faith to its more pristine state under the Prophet Muhammad. According to UCLA law professor Khaled Abou El Fadl (2003, p. 55), 'the founders of Salafism maintained that on all issues Muslims ought to return to the original textural sources of the Qur'an and the *Sunnah* (precedent) of the Prophet. In doing so, Muslims ought to reinterpret the original sources in light of modern needs and demands without being slavishly bound to the interpretive precedents of earlier Muslim generations.'

2. Ray Takeyh (2001, p. 70) has stated that 'the integration of an Islamic democracy into global democratic society would depend on the willingness of the West to accept an Islamic variant on liberal democracy.' He goes on to speculate on what an Islamic democracy would look like: 'Undoubtedly, Islamic democracy will differ in important ways from the model that evolved in post-Reformation Europe. Western systems elevated the primacy of the individual above the community and thus changed the role of religion from that of the public conveyor of community values to a private guide for individual conscience. In contrast, an Islamic democracy's attempt to balance its

emphasis on reverence with the popular desire for self-expression will impose certain limits on individual choice. An Islamic polity will support fundamental tenets of democracy--namely, regular elections, separation of powers, an independent judiciary, and institutional opposition--but it is unlikely to be a libertarian paradise.'

3. The quotation was taken from Sivan (1985, no page given).

REFERENCES

Al-Abbasi, M. n.d. Protestant Islam [online]. *Cambridge Mosque Project.* Accessed 10 March 2020. http://www.masud.co.uk/ISLAM/misc/pislam.htm.

Al-Azm, S. 2019. *Occidentalism, Conspiracy, and Taboo: Collected Essays on Islam and Politics.* Berlin: Gerlach Press.

Ali, A.H. 2015. Why Islam Needs a Reformation. *Wall Street Journal* (Print edition), March 20. Accessed 4 April 2020. https://www.wsj.com/articles/a-reformation-for-islam-1426859626.

Allawi, A. 2009. *The Crisis of Islamic Civilization.* New Haven, CT: Yale University Press.

An-Na'im, A. 1990. *Toward an Islamic Reformation: Civil Liberties, Human Rights, and International Law.* Syracuse, NY: Syracuse University Press.

Ansari, A. 2019. *Iran, Islam and Democracy: The Politics of Managing Change.* Berkeley, CA: Gingko Press.

Arango, T. 2015. In Bid to Counter Iran, Ayatollah in Iraq May end up Emulating It. *New York Times,* November 1. Accessed 4 October 2020. https://www.nytimes.com/2015/11/02/world/middleeast/iraq-iran-ayatollah-sistani.html.

Benard, A. 2008. The Advantage to Islam of Mosque-state Separation. *Hoover Institution Policy Review,* January 29. Accessed 22 March 2020. https://www.hoover.org/research/advantage-islam-mosque-state-separation.

Daftary, F. n.d. Diversity in Islam: Communities of Interpretation, the Institute of Ismaili Studies. *The Institute of Ismaili Studies.* Accessed 10 April 2020. https://iis.ac.uk/ru/academic-article/diversity-islam-communities-interpretation.

Eickelman, D. 1998. Inside the Islamic Reformation. *Wilson Quarterly* 22 (Winter): 80–89.

———. 2003. Communication and Control in the Middle East: Publication and its Discontents. In *New Media in the Muslim World,* ed. D. Eickelman and J. Anderson, 33–43. Bloomington, IN: Indiana University Press.

Eickelman, D., and J. Anderson. 2003. Redefining Muslim Publics. In *New Media in the Muslim World,* ed. D. Eickelman and J. Anderson, 1–18. Bloomington, IN: Indiana University Press.

El Fadl, K.A. 2003. The Ugly Modern and the Modern Ugly: Reclaiming the Beautiful in Islam. In *Progressive Muslims: On Justice, Gender and Pluralism,* ed. O. Safi. Oxford, UK: Oneworld Publications.

El Fadl, K. 2004. *Islam and the Challenge of Democracy.* Edited by J. Cohen and D. Chasman. Princeton, NJ: Princeton University Press.

Krämer, Gudrun. 2009. Islam and Secularization. In *Secularization and the World Religions.* Eds. Hans Joas and Klaus Wiegandt. Trans. Alex Skinner. Liverpool, UK: Liverpool University Press.

Loimeier, R. 2005. Is There Something Like "Protestant Islam"? *Die Welt des Islams* 45 (2): 216–254.

Madison, J. 1785. Memorial and Remonstrance Against Religious Assessments. *The American Yawp Reader.* Accessed 12 April 2020. http://www.american-yawp.com/reader/a-new-nation/james-madison-memorial-and-remonstrance-against-religious-assessments-1785/.

Masri, Safwan. 2017. *Tunisia: An Arab Anomaly.* New York: Columbia University Press.

Ourghi, A. 2019. *Reform of Islam: Forty Theses for an Islamic Ethics in the 21st Century.* Berlin: Gerlach Press.

Roy, O. 1998. *The Failure of Political Islam.* Translated by C. Volk. Cambridge, MA: Harvard University Press.

Ruthven, Malise. 2016. Mosque and State: The Future of Political Islam. *Foreign Affairs* 95 (5): 142–148.

Sachedina, A. 2001. *The Islamic Roots of Democratic Pluralism.* Oxford, UK: Oxford University Press.

Saeed, A. 2006. *Interpreting the Qur'an: Towards a Contemporary Approach.* New York: Routledge.

Savyon, A. 2002. *The Call for Islamic Protestantism: Dr. Hashem Aghajari's Speech and Subsequent Death Sentence. MEMRI,* special dispatch no. 445. Accessed 11 March 2020. https://www.memri.org/reports/call-islamic-protestantism-dr-hashem-aghajaris-speech-and-subsequent-death-sentence.

Sayej, C. 2018. *Patriotic Ayatollahs: Nationalism in Post-Saddam Iraq.* Ithaca, NY: Cornell University Press.

Sivan, E. 1985. *Radical Islam: Medieval Theology and Modern Politics.* New Haven, CT: Yale University Press.

Takeyh, R. 2001. Faith-based Initiatives: Can Islam bring Democracy to the Middle East. *Foreign Policy* 127 (November/December): 68–70.

de Tocqueville, Alexis. 1988. *Democracy in America.* Ed. J. P. Mayer. Trans. George Lawrence. New York: Harper & Row.

U.S. Department of State. 2004. Constitutionalism in the Muslim world: A Conversation with Noah Feldman. *Electronic Journals* 9 (1). Accessed 4 March 2020. https://china.usembassy-china.org.cn/wp-content/uploads/sites/252/2016/12/issues_of_democracy.pdf.

Zakaria, F. 1997. The Rise of Illiberal Democracy. *Foreign Affairs* 76 (November/December): 22–43.

CHAPTER 19

Religion and the State in Afghanistan

Charles Ramsey and Eric Patterson

INTRODUCTION

For a country whose population is almost entirely Muslim and whose government aspires to be Islamic, tracing the role of religion in Afghanistan is far more complex than one might assume. The transition to a constitutional monarchy in 1964 and the gradually developing economy of the 1970s gave no immediate sign of the decades of war that would follow, or of the extremist Islamist ideologies now associated with the country's Taliban leadership, but old regional rivalries and dramatic ideological divisions have precipitated the transition of this country's return to the status of a failed state at the heart of Central Asia. The decisions facing this precarious regime are raising difficult questions about what it means to be a nation founded upon religious values.[1]

It was only in 1921 that Afghans became independent of British protectorate rule. King Ghazi Amanullah Khan (b.1892–d.1960), who ruled Afghanistan for 10 years from 1919 to 1929, inaugurated a

C. Ramsey
Baylor University, Waco, TX, USA

E. Patterson (✉)
Religious Freedom Institute, Washington, DC, USA
e-mail: eric.patterson@rfi.org

© The Author(s), under exclusive license to Springer Nature
Switzerland AG 2023
S. Holzer (ed.), *The Palgrave Handbook of Religion and State
Volume II*, https://doi.org/10.1007/978-3-031-35609-4_19

421

comprehensive series of political reforms reminiscent of those of Ataturk in Turkey and Reza Shah in Iran (Dalrymple 2021; Emadi 2005; Ahmed 2017). However, he was deposed soon thereafter, and a new constitution that was passed in 1931 and amended in 1946 introduced free elections, a free press, and a parliamentary system. Amid this rapid modernization led by Prime Minister Daud Khan who became the first President of Afghanistan, there were also rising Cold War tensions, and in 1952 a coalition with strong support from traditional religious and tribal leadership came to power and established the government system as a constitutional monarchy with a bicameral legislature, which was ratified in a new constitution in 1964 (Crews and Tarzi 2008).[2] It was in reference to this constitution that the Taliban regime in 2021 announced their role as a "caretaker government" (Rashid 2010; Deutsche Welle 2021).

The turmoil continued, however, and in 1973 Daud Khan staged a coup and reshaped the government as a republic with noted American-style characteristics, only to be ousted in the 1978 Saur Revolution by the leftist People's Democratic Party. This instigated an uprising across the country resulting in a Soviet invasion to support the formation of a communist regime. The highly diverse and decentralized guerrillas came to be known as the mujahidin, a resistance force united by their opposition to the Soviet invasion and those enforcing a communist ideology. Though the Soviets withdrew in 1989, civil war continued among these factions giving rise to a fledgling group calling themselves 'the Taliban,' which managed to take control over much of the country prior to the U.S.-led coalition's invasion in 2001. The celebrated liberation of Afghanistan by the U.S. and international forces fueled a concerted effort to delineate a broad-based dialogue on the best form of governance for the war-torn nation. One consequence of this was the ratification of a new constitution in 2004, which established a republican form of government, defined as one in which sovereignty belongs "to the nation, manifested directly and through its elected representatives. The nation of Afghanistan is composed of all individuals who possess the citizenship of Afghanistan" (The Constitution of Afghanistan, 2018, ch. I, art. 4). All of Afghanistan's citizens in this paradigm were entrusted with the power and responsibility to select their representatives to govern, as similarly stated in Article 1 of the 1964 constitution, which indicated that the elected representatives were accountable to the people.

The Soviet invasion in 1978 marked the beginning of more than 40 years of continuous war even after the Soviet withdrawal in 1989, which has resulted in a country marred by violence, rife with ethnic conflict, a collapsed economy, and a constant string of humanitarian crises. Lying deep beneath the conflict there are tectonic plates of culture and tradition that undergird competing visions for the structure and authority of its government (Green 2016). This chapter considers Afghanistan in context, describes factors in the rise of the Taliban, and sketches some indicators for the trajectory of the present regime. We also explore the competing ideas and actors leading up to the current iteration of the Taliban regime and consider the current concerns and future possibilities for this nation that finds itself again at a crossroads.

SOVEREIGNTY: POPULAR OR DIVINE?

The West macabrely parses every word distributed by Afghanistan's newly installed Taliban regime. What we hear, first and foremost, is that Afghanistan's institutions will operate only on sharia law.

> "There will be no democratic system at all ...," Taliban commander Waheedullah Hashimi said in an interview with Reuters. "We will not discuss what type of political system should we apply in Afghanistan because it is clear. It is sharia law and that is it." (Gopalakrishnan 2021)

In her book, *The Mighty and the Almighty,* former U.S. Secretary of State Madeline Albright wrote about the clash of two competing conceptions of politics: "The resulting turbulence [in the Muslim world] is the product of a momentous and inherently complex encounter between two profound ideas: that all power comes from God, and that legitimate authority on Earth comes from the people" (2006, p. 216). Albright's "resulting turbulence" is a philosophical clash between "two profound ideas" and two contrasting notions of sovereignty. In short, the West's *political* concept of popular sovereignty is viewed by many as being incompatible with the Taliban and other Islamists' religious conceptions of Divine sovereignty. Contending with these differences has opened the possibility for Muslim societies to adopt liberal democratic ideas inherent in modern national states and to embrace political equality, representative government, religious tolerance, and social pluralism, as have highly religious societies from other faith traditions, such as the United States, Poland, Israel, Thailand, and Hungary, to name but a few. A rising challenge for Muslim societies, however, in grappling with the legacy of Western colonialism and the emergence of new Islamic political structures, has been to formulate a system of government that authentically reflects the religious and cultural norms of their particular nation.

Popular Sovereignty in Western Democratic Theory

Popular "sovereignty" is a key presupposition of democratic theory, particularly in the American tradition. Individuals willingly assign some of their rights to the state in exchange for protection. In democracies, however, this exchange is assumed to be willing, and hence in theory the creation and sustenance of the state is predicated on the decision of the sovereign populace. The American revolutionaries argued that their break with the English Crown was on just such lines: London had lost its claim to govern because it had abused its power—the sovereign people were asserting themselves in forming a new association. The "consent of the governed" assumes a sovereignty of the citizenry when it comes to governance. That sovereignty is not a religious concept *per se*. The Declaration of Independence, for example, makes no claim that the sovereign people are the ultimate repository of truth or morality, indeed, the opening of the Declaration refers to the "Laws of Nature and of Nature's God." This suggests that an ultimate moral code does exist outside of the whims of the consenting governed (Younte 2022).

Consequently, the idea of sovereignty in American democratic theory is a political idea for how governments should be established and operate—in ways that are consonant with morality and based on as well as limited by the sovereignty of the citizenry. That sovereignty only extends to the political realm, both to check unrestrained government power and to underscore the opportunity and responsibility of citizens to constructively advance "life, liberty, and the pursuit of happiness." Over time, the definition of a sovereign citizenry has expanded, evolving from the male land owner (including proprietorship of human chattel) to include men and women regardless of race, religion, or wealth. That expansion has coincided, particularly in the past half century, with a dramatic opening in the mores and moral strictures of American life—from the existentialism and postmodernism of academic theory which questions any universal ethical code to profound challenges to old patterns of society: declines in religious practice, the sexual revolution, a new pluralism in religious affiliation (due in part to immigration and the presence of large non-Christian and non-Jewish diasporas), changes in family structure and alternative claims of family and marriage (e.g. same-sex unions), and the like. It is not necessarily the case that the founders' claims of a sovereign people directly caused this "dramatic opening" in American life, but a fundamental argument of its varied proponents is that the people have the right to define "the pursuit of happiness." This, of course, is a key basis for the "culture wars" in American society of the past two generations, as competing claims of morality, law, and experience are ferociously debated and protested against by partisans, religious actors, intellectuals, and average citizens. These competing ideas from the American and European experience have been—often but not always inadvertently—carried into the constitutional processes in countries like Afghanistan and have often felt imposed. Many have argued that democratic principles have a legitimate place in Muslim intellectual history, but that these follow their own logical trajectories (Barfield 2010; Iqtidar 2021). Afghanistan was in a process of cultural and generational negotiation prior to the last four decades of war, and Afghans were making strides toward developing a form of government consistent with their own values—one that presents its own unique calibration of divine and popular sovereignty.

Muslim Views of Sovereignty

In the extreme, Islamists like the Taliban, al-Qaeda (AQ), ISIS, and Boko Haram appeal to the Divine sovereignty explicated in scripture as the justification for rejecting the Western "separation of church and state" system and for promoting government-sponsored prosecution and persecution for individual cases of blasphemy and apostasy. This confrontation was popularized with Sayyid Qutb's *Milestones* and monumental *In the Shade of the Qur'an* a half-century ago. Qutb argued that the West, and the authoritarian governments then in power in many Muslim countries, rejected divine sovereignty over mankind. More specifically, humankind rebelled and chose not to listen to the interventions found in prophetic revelation. For Qutb, there is not only a universal moral order but a sociopolitical order clearly specified in the Qur'an (Rahman 2020). God has provided man "divine guidance concerning everything... including faith, morals, values, standards, systems, and laws" (Qutb 2015, p. 207).

Half a century later the debates still rage in many quarters of the Muslim world about these issues, both in theory and in the practice of democratic governments in Turkey, Indonesia, and elsewhere. What is important, however, is that for many Islamists this view makes democracy at best problematic and at worst heretical because of the notions of radical individual freedom as well as the notion that political institutions and the moral order are defined by popular sovereignty, both of which violate divine sovereignty (Bahlul 2000). Moreover, for the Taliban, who believe that the Qur'an and Hadith clearly specify an enduring Muslim political order, democratic mechanisms such as parties and elections make no sense. As the Taliban spokesman said: "there will be no democratic system at all" (Gopalakrishnan 2021).

This is a debate playing itself out across the greater Muslim world. Several years ago, for example, radical Islamist Abu Bakr Ba'shir, leader of Al-Gama'a Al-Islamiyya in Indonesia, argued:

> The path taken by many political parties in their effort to establish an Islamic regime is not the right path, because these parties adopt democracy. Democracy is not an Islamic means. Democracy runs counter to Islam, because it emphasizes the sovereignty of the people, whereas Islam emphasizes the sovereignty of Allah. Thus, if we are to submit to the law of Allah, Muslims have no choice but to say: 'We hear and obey.' In democracy, Allah's commands may be open to discussion, and if we agree with them, we accept them, but if we do not agree with them, we reject them. Herein lies the flaw. Therefore, as long as the Islamic political parties endeavor to adhere to Islam by means of democracy, they will not achieve their goal. (Patterson 2021)

In short, an area where religion and democracy intersect, or better 'collide,' is the fundamental conceptualization of sovereignty and its expression in matters of faith, government, and society. The political philosophy associated with Western classical liberalism, desired by billions of people suffering under authoritarian regimes the world over, seems to be in direct conflict with Muslim voices, like the Taliban's, who not only demand divine, spiritual, and moral sovereignty over the affairs of humanity but also narrowly expressed guidance on sociopolitical systems, which contravenes any form of political popular sovereignty.

One question confronting the present regime in Afghanistan is whether there is an authentically Muslim and culturally acceptable form of representative, pluralistic, rights-protecting political system that reflects their particular view of the interrelation of popular and divine sovereignty. Will the practices of representative government (e.g. elections, political parties, constitutions, laws, and minority rights) be understood as incompatible with their practice of Islam, or will they develop a political system that provides these for their highly diverse populace? Indeed, the Qur'an and Hadith have a great deal to say about protecting minorities, honoring women and the vulnerable, and promoting justice for all. This was the basis for various more pluralistic forms of Muslim-majority government in Persia, Spain, the Ottoman Empire, and today in places like Pakistan, Indonesia, and Jordan. Many of these societies saw tremendous social flourishing as people were true to their faith without the need for the radical violence of the Taliban as seen in 1996–2001. Whether the present regime returns to a constitutional monarchy according to the 1964 constitution, or adopts another form of non-hereditary leadership, as exemplified by the first four caliphs (*rashidun*) in the seventh century, they are sure to meet the similar challenges of sustaining popular support even as they appeal to divine sovereignty to legitimize their rule. Keeping this paradigm of divine and popular sovereignty in mind, we now turn to consider some of the unique features of the Afghan context.

The Lay of the Land

Afghanistan has a significantly diverse population and the country's land-mass covers over 250,000 square miles of mountains and deserts bridging and bordering six countries: Turkmenistan, Uzbekistan, Tajikistan, and China on the north and northeast, Pakistan on the south and southeast, and Iran on the west. But this large and deceptively open space is inhabited by a mélange of ethnicities and tribes with a deep sense of history and an intricate system of competition and collaboration.

Central Asia, with Afghanistan at its heart, is characterized by ethnic, cultural, and religious diversity: Uzbeks, Tajiks, Persians, Arabs, Pashtuns, Hazaras, and others. Statistics from 2001, however rough, demonstrate this diversity. The population at that time was estimated at just under 22 million inhabitants, of which 38% were Pashtun, 25% Tajik, 19% Hazara, and 16% Uzbek. From a religious standpoint, this means that the country was roughly 80% Sunni and 20% Shia, with rare pockets of Hindus, Sikhs, and Christians.

There were significant changes in the period following the foreign military intervention in 2001. The population of Afghanistan exploded to nearly 40 million, among which some were refugees who had returned to Afghanistan after the wars of the 1980s and 1990s (Macrotrends 2022). The population makeup also shifted during this time, with one estimate suggesting that the Hazara percentage dropped by half of its earlier estimate. As of 2021, the population is estimated to be 42% Pashtun, 27% Tajik, 9% Hazara, 9% Uzbek, 4% Aimak, 3% Turkmen, and 2% Baloch. Less than 1% of the population is made up of other religious and ethnic groups (World Population 2022).

The growing power and influence of the Taliban in the mid-1990s caused the traditionally diverse and relatively harmonious religious landscape to take a violent and brutal cast. The Taliban was comprised mainly of ethnic Pashtuns, and as their control expanded into other regions, they increasingly sought to demand conformity to their particular norms of religious allegiance and comportment. The most different group, and the one that experienced the brunt of Taliban persecution, was the Hazara, an ethnically Turkish group that is largely Shia.[3] The diminution of the Hazara population and the marginalization of non-Sunni groups is a reminder that despite 20 years of foreign assistance Afghanistan remains one of the most religiously repressive places in the world. Many attacks have targeted places of worship and religious leaders. In 2020 alone, there were 19 attacks, leading to over 115 fatalities, against the Hazara community alone. Violence against religious and ethnic minorities and the enforcement of social mores, including the conduct and dress requirements, continue in Afghanistan and this is not likely to change within the near future.

Despite such a dismal record, it is important to guard against a tendency to dismiss Afghanistan as simply a land of war. For too long it has been regarded as a "graveyard of empires" as recorded in colonial "Great Game" literature. The region has fostered great civilizations that included leading scientists and philosophers. Afghans established far-reaching empires and ruled the crossroads, where pathways converged to and from India, China, and the Middle East, carrying the world's knowledge and commercial riches.[4] As historian Phillip Jenkins has cautioned, we should guard against assuming there is something innately wrong with these people in comparison to other regions of the world. "Out-of-control clergy, religious demagogues, religious parties usurping the functions of the state...It all sounds like the worst stereotypes of contemporary radical Islam," as Jenkins noted in describing a turbulent phase in Mediterranean Christianity, "but the problem lay not in any characteristics of the religion itself, of its doctrines or Scriptures, but in the state's inability to control private violence" (2010, p. 30). Afghanistan is in the throes of a difficult season in its history, one that began before the Taliban and will likely continue in the foreseeable future. Strenuous efforts were made over the past 20 years with great support from the international community to develop a sustainable political framework for moving forward. There were significant strides forward after the devastation of the 1990s, and yet now again the country's governance has been seized by the Taliban.

ENTER THE TALIBAN

The Taliban first emerged in the 1990s in the wake of a devastating civil war. After the 1989 Soviet withdrawal and the subsequent collapse of the Soviet-supported Afghan government in 1992, there was a power vacuum, and a civil war broke out among the former anti-Soviet fighters known as mujahidin.[5] Many of these fighters became disillusioned with the chaos and lack of security and basic services. This was not a well-planned and coordinated Islamist uprising, as Ahmed Rashid has convincingly argued, but rather more like a haphazard act of desperation to curtail what had become a devastatingly bad situation. Many in this coalescing movement shared the experience of studying in the madrassas of neighboring Pakistan, seminaries which prepare graduates for employment in mosques, but that also double as orphanages and sanctuaries for poor children. The sprawling and extensive network of madrasas and mosques along the border regions of Pakistan and Afghanistan became staging points in the early days, and it was quickly realized that this sense of religious affiliation—following decades of fighting the godless communist— provided a broad tent under which to gather. It was for this reason that they began to refer to themselves as the Taliban (plural of *talib*, a student, in this case, of Islam) to distinguish themselves from the pre-existing mujahidin in 1993. Theirs was a localized Islam informed as much by Pashtun culture as an adequate understanding of the Qur'an and Hadith (Ahmed 2013).

Taliban beliefs and practices were consonant with, and derived in part from, the conservative tribal traditions of Pashtuns, who represent a significant portion, though not a majority, of Afghanistan's complex ethnic composition, and who have traditionally ruled the region. These share a cultural and linguistic heritage with those inhabiting the long stretch of borderlands between these two countries. The Taliban gradually took control of a significant region ruled by the *Loy Kandahar*, and this has remained their center of power. In April 1996, a leadership confederacy (*shura*) of 1000 community leaders appointed Mullah Omar as the *de facto* ruler of the land the *amir-ul mominin* (Commander of the Faithful) and declared war against President Burhanuddin Rabbani's government in Kabul. Only two years after their meager emergence, the force had captured Kabul and executed the ethnic Pashtun and former socialist President Mohammad Najibullah, bringing an end to the wave of socialist and secularist leadership in Afghanistan.

Following the August 1998 al-Qaeda bombings of U.S. embassies in Africa, the U.S. attacked multiple targets in Afghanistan. The United Nations, however, was unable to persuade the Taliban leadership to expel Bin Laden, and this proved costly for the Taliban in the wake of the 9/11 attacks in 2001. The Taliban was unable to mount an immediate resistance to the invasion and many of the senior leaders took sanctuary across the mountainous border in Pakistan. However, by 2005 they had regrouped and by 2006 were clashing regularly with U.S. forces as they sought to hinder the progress of the U.S.-backed government in Kabul. Despite the presence of over 100,000 U.S. troops, and billions of dollars in development funds, there were unmet expectations that fueled the Taliban resistance. Following the departure of the international forces, and the collapse of the elected government, a new regime has been formed. Let us now seek a more nuanced understanding of the Taliban and particularly what distinguishes them from competing Islamist forces who continue to vie for control of Afghanistan.

ANALYSIS OF THE TALIBAN'S RISE

It is important to consider the war from the Taliban perspective. In the months following the U.S. invasion, as Craig Whitlock has argued, there were ample signals provided by Mullah Omar and the Taliban leadership that they were willing to compromise and to become part of a ruling coalition (2022). The working assumption, however, was that these could not be trusted because of their history as enemy combatants and due to their extreme Islamist ideology (Marsden 2002). There was also a functioning narrative among policymakers that the Taliban was defeated and would dissipate. It is possible that had more intentional engagement and inclusion been achieved, then former members of the Taliban could have simply joined the ranks of many other former militants in competing and collaborating to rebuild the nation (Gutman 2008, p. 233). Their exclusion, however, created a cadre who were excluded from the new system and courted by external elements pursuing their own agendas to undermine the new nation state (Goodson 2011).

The Taliban leadership structure, however, remained viable. During their rule in the 1990s, Mullah Omar's deputies eliminated the bureaucracy, whether royalist or communist, as well as opponents from competing mujahidin factions (Siddique n.d., p. 52). Religious networks of mosques and madrasas opened the way for the Taliban to penetrate villages and tribal clans and to consolidate power throughout the Pashtun south through interpersonal bonds. Positions of power and influence were given to cronies, and this preferential treatment undercut pre-existing government systems, leading to even greater confusion and inefficiency.

Though never completed, a constitution (*dastur*) prepared in 1998 prescribed a basic view of government outlined from the Hanafi tradition of jurisprudence (Kakar and Schiwal 2021). The emir, Mullah Omar, was given sweeping powers. State jobs, as listed in Article 7, were given to be assigned according to religious merit and propriety (*taqwa*), not social indebtedness (*andiwali*). Like the Saudi model, a department was created for the "Promotion of Virtue and the Prevention of Vice (*munkirat*)" that served as the morality police with sweeping powers to enforce strict Qur'anic ordinances (*hudood*) such as stoning and amputation. Official Gazette No. 77, added later by the Ministry of Justice in 2001, listed hundreds of strict moral laws found in the Hadith but that had seldom if ever been applied literally (Siddique n.d., p. 54). Yet Article 99 of the 1998 *dastur* stated that the regime ascribed to the Universal Declaration of Human Rights and backed the charters of UN, Organization of Islamic Cooperation (OIC), and the Non-Aligned Movement, along with others not in contradiction to Islamic principles and national interests (Siddique n.d., p. 55). More a work in progress than a final draft, the 1998 *dastur* provided an initial draft for a constitution that outlined some of the working ideas for the leaders of the emirate.

The exclusion and enmity experienced by the Taliban from the new government being formed with American support were such that their credibility would be at stake among competing Islamist factions if they were to accede to the 2004 constitution. Although the constitution commences by invoking the sacred name of Allah, the clauses contained within the document are clearly indicative of a high regard for popular sovereignty. Like more progressive Islamic republics, this constitution protected the rights of women and minorities, and opened the way for a meager form of pluralism. One problem for the Taliban, however, is the severe shortage of other options. Even in the 1999 *dastur*, the regime ascribed to the Universal Declaration of Human Rights and the charters of the UN and OIC. Though such details were overshadowed by the draconian laws and their violent enforcement, these overtures signaled a desire to engage with the global community, not as a means of capitulation but as part of a larger vision to have a government consistent with the idealized values of their faith tradition. There is a paucity, however, of functioning governmental systems in the world today derived from traditional Islamic law and so Afghans, like many others in predominantly Muslim nations, are striving to craft a system with its own checks and balances and that accords with their own sense of agency. Formed in the Hanafi school of law, Taliban jurists draw from different sources than the monarchical Gulf Emirates or Saudi Arabia, or from modernist systems of Turkey, Iran, Pakistan, or Indonesia. They see each of these as having fallen short. The Taliban, like many Islamists today, desire to establish a system reconstructed according to the primary sources, the Hadith and Qur'an, inspired by the earliest Muslim communities in Medina, Kufa, and Basra. This is an exercise in historical imagination, where the Hanafi legal code is reconstituted not according to medieval Central and South Asian examples, but rather in ways analogous to the founding years of the community under the direct guidance of the Prophet. This quest is not unique to the Taliban or to militant Islamists. There are many nations, including many of those listed above, that are actively attempting to evaluate and remove accretions from Western legal structures and to replace these with ones in more direct accordance with an Islamic ideal. This requires a disciplined bracketing of the present order and an experimentation grounded largely in historiographical assumptions and religious imagination. Though inspired by the past, the key architects of an imagined Islamic state are themselves cognizant that this is a thoroughly modern venture and that they operate within political and epistemological frameworks that would be virtually unimaginable to their predecessors (Lawrence 2000). In their minds, a lasting peace and stability will not come until this process of rolling back colonial structures and replacing these with better ones is accomplished.

HANAFI TRADITIONALISM, NOT SALAFI GLOBALISM

If the Taliban is to develop the sinews needed for a new emirate, then where will it look for authoritative guidance? Are there models that shape this understanding? In addressing such questions, it is essential to recall that there are significant historical, cultural, and theological differences between many of the Islamist parties functioning in diverse global contexts (Mansurnoor 2002). The Taliban and its rising opponent ISK (Islamic State Khorasan 2018), for example, have considerable differences that are ideological in nature and that go beyond competition for power and scarce resources, differences significant enough for the fighting to persist.

One way to discuss these differences is to juxtapose the Taliban's Hanafi traditionalism with that of the Salafi globalism promoted by ISK and al-Qaeda (AQ). From the outset of the war in 2001, Islamists such as Osama bin Laden, AQ, and ISK have exploited the situation to further ends greater than the welfare of Afghanistan. It is a vision for a new caliphate that links like-minded regional emirates who pledge loyalty to the caliph or the Ruler of the Faithful (*emir ul-mumineen*) (Kennedy 2016). Khorasan is the name used in classical Arabic writings for a region in Central Asia that includes present-day Afghanistan. The notion of establishing ligaments to the caliphate has evolved into what is now known as the Islamic State, with affiliates in the Levant, Syria, India, Africa, or Khorasan. The political vision is undergirded by Salafi theological propositions that gained currency in the eighteenth century in the Hijaz, or what is now Saudi Arabia (Peters 1980). This approach, as Jane McAuliffe succinctly noted, marked a shift away from the traditional method (*taqlid*) of the schools of jurisprudence like the Hanafi, as still held today by the Taliban leadership (Hassan 2009, p. 182).[6] The traditional approach was tethered to the assumption that the founder of the legal tradition proceeded under divine and somewhat infallible (*maʿṣūm*) protection (Peters, n.d.). In other words, divine sovereignty in sharia was assured by the protected status of these legal thinkers and their juridical decisions. For the Salafi, however, the four historic schools of law had proven equally inadequate in guiding the community, and this was the reason for the loss of sovereignty experienced by Muslim rulers and the dissolution of the caliphate (Jalal 2016). They argued that reliance upon a particular school has splintered the community, and the way forward was to consolidate these fractured under one central religious authority. ISK advocates allegiance to a standardized faith and practice and to a central global authoritarian caliphate. The Taliban, however, are concerned with the local and national issues and desire to form a government in keeping with a traditional path with deep roots in South Asia.

Though the differences may seem overly granular, these fault lines have crystallized over centuries and are not easily abandoned. The differences between the Taliban and ISK are laden with historical symbolism that continues to hold currency in the region. This dates back to the early nineteenth century when Sayyid Ahmad Barelvi and the so-called Indian Wahhabis established one of the first modern attempts to re-imagine a political entity upon the example of the earliest Muslims in Medina in the borderlands between Pakistan and Afghanistan. Their respective followers seek to carry this mantle and mission to establish a state truly based solely on sharia (Ingram 2009).

The Taliban movement, as the name implies, was incubated in traditional Hanafi madrasas. More specifically, they are part of a large network of madrassas called the Deobandi, which began as a grassroots movement to sustain religious education in the wake of the 1857 Sepoy Rebellion in India. British reprisals following the war targeted Muslims and decimated the traditional structures of patronage for their centers of learning. The Deoband scholars (*ulama*), as Muhammad Qasim Zaman cogently explained, have regarded themselves as "custodians of change" who must steward and regulate the influence not only of the liberal progressives but also of Salafi conservatives, known in the region as the Ahl-e Hadith (Ramsey 2016; Zaman 2004).

It is important to note that nearly one-third (over 484 million) of the world's 1.57 billion Muslims live in South Asia, and of the four historical schools of jurisprudence (*madhab*), the Hanafi, named after the founder Abū Ḥanīfah, or Nuʿmān ibn Thābit ibn Zūṭā ibn Marzubān (d. 772 in Baghdad), is by far the largest. Though accurate statistics are lacking, according to Tariq Rahman's study, enrollment in Deoband madrasas experienced exponential growth from 1979 to over 2000, and these show no signs of abatement (Jaffrelot 2015, pp. 544–46). It is vital to note that this trend indicates that this form of education and the inherent socialized worldview continues to expand in the region. In other words, the group discussed here, the Deobandi, is one of the largest and most dynamic groupings within Sunni Islam in the world.

NATIONALISM, NOT PAN-ISLAMISM

Some have argued that the Taliban's rank and file is far less driven by jihad and Islamic fundamentalism than we may have assumed. In a recent analysis of poems reproduced widely as Taliban propaganda, "the expected themes of war and suffering, of opposition to cruel invaders, revenge, and the innocence of the noble villager are all here. But what is striking is how lightly the poetry rests on religious oppositional themes. Instead, Taliban poetry is infused with a nostalgic, even romantic ethos" (Strick van Linschoten and Kuehn 2012). Among the Pashtun there have been monarchists, communists, and nationalists, and there are also Islamists such as those in the Taliban. It is important to recall that the Taliban rule was imposed. In the 1990s and again in 2021, the Taliban's draconian policies have not been welcomed by any segment of Afghan society (Siddique n.d., p. 56). While the Taliban has been perceived by outsiders to be adhering to the cultural mores of *pashtunwali*, they have frequently contradicted central aspects of these customary expectations, even murdering tribal leaders to create a vacuum they themselves could fill.[7] But for such force to be imposed, there must have been extraordinary support. If the support did not come from the Afghan people, as many question, then where else could it have come?

Underneath their ideological fervor, as Selig Harrison observed, there is also a simmering movement of Pashtun nationalism (2008). This is Afghanistan's largest ethnic group, comprising some 41 million people who inhabit both sides of the Durand Line separating Pakistan and Afghanistan (Jones 2009; Khan 2014). Many Pashtuns feel that their people have been some of the most misunderstood and maligned of the twenty-first century because their land has become a staging ground for a global conflict (Siddique 2014, n.d. p. 11). Many Afghans, as historian Rasul Amin observed, saw the Taliban as an "effort by Pakistan to colonize Afghanistan in the name of Islam" (Siddique n.d., p. 57). As has been argued extensively, Pakistan has sought to consolidate its own considerable ethnic diversity under the overarching banner of Islamic nationalism. According to this logic, Islamic identity rather than ethnolinguistic identity is what unites the people of Pakistan. Similarly, it has been argued that Pakistan supported the Afghan Taliban to de-emphasize Afghan national identity and to replace this with a shared transnational Islamic identity. For Pakistan, a unity of Afghan and Pakistani Pashtuns could seed a new nation state, a so-called Pashtunistan, resulting in a further truncated Pakistan similar to that experienced with the loss of East Pakistan in 1971, which became Bangladesh. Pakistan's entanglement with the Taliban—however this may have happened—needs not to be seen as wholly vile and nefarious. Pakistan was deeply involved in supporting the mujahidin fighting the Soviets, and it makes sense that they would do everything possible to support the formation of a stable and amicable regime at their doorstep. Collaboration, however, does not entail subordination. Pakistan may have worked closely with elements of the Afghan Taliban, but that does not mean they control them and can guarantee that they will follow orders. Thus far, the Taliban has sought an independent and self-determined Afghan state over any form of pan-Islamism, whether shaped by Saudi Arabia, Pakistan, or the so-called Islamic State.

A nationalist narrative presents a different account of the Taliban's trajectory. Consider the breakdown in negotiations in 2014. The refusal of the Taliban to engage with the elected Afghan government and the Afghan government's opposition to U.S. negotiations with the Taliban constrained and eventually led to the dissolution of talks. At that point, the possibility of Taliban participation in a shared government under the 2004 constitution remained plausible. This opportunity was further stymied, however, by a contentious change in Taliban leadership in 2015. The new leader, Mansour, was killed in a U.S. drone strike in Pakistan in May 2016 and was succeeded by Haibatullah Akhundzada, the current emir. By 2018, a U.S. withdrawal was increasingly evident and the Taliban controlled almost 40% of the country. Further talks led to the February 2020 U.S.-Taliban compromise whereby the United States agreed to withdraw all U.S. and international forces by May 2021 and the Taliban agreed to prevent other groups (such as al-Qaeda) from using Afghan soil to threaten the United States and its allies. The U.S. withdrawal was not explicitly conditioned on the Taliban reducing violence against the Afghan government, making concessions in prospective intra-Afghan talks, or taking other actions. The near absence of Afghan resistance to the Taliban takeover in 2021 is open to interpretation, but many regard this as a pragmatic recognition that a new national process would be required to constitute a nation independent from foreign intervention and the return to a "protectorate" system similar to that imposed by British colonial forces. There were adequate military resources to fight the Taliban, but that was not the will of the people.

EMIRATE VERSUS REPUBLIC

At this stage in 2022, only broad strokes can be discerned for how the government will function as it transitions from republic to emirate. The country is currently ruled by a leadership council (*rahbari shura*) that is led by the emir, his deputies, and some 20 other individuals. The council claims to be a "caretaker" government in accordance with the 1964 constitution until there is sufficient stability and direction to establish a more delineated forward process. Spokesmen for the current regime have stated that they do not seek to establish an "Islamic Republic," like that in Pakistan or Iran nor to follow a democratic process, but they also show no signs of reinstating the monarchy or to follow the Saudi or United Arab Emirates models either (Banuazizi and Weiner 1988). Indeed, the silence and secrecy of the regime has made it difficult for the Afghan people and for the international community to understand or collaborate toward a more positive direction. At this stage silence prevailed and the regime remained isolated, even while the pressing and most basic needs of the people continued to escalate.

One of the points of contention that stalled negotiations between the elected Afghan government and the Taliban was the demand to uphold the integrity of the republic according to the 2004 constitution (Zalmay 2016; Thier 2010). This provided legal guarantees for universal suffrage, a system of checks and balances, and a delineated roadmap for political participation. The Taliban, however, expressed a clear desire for a more "Islamic" system of government and have continued to apply the emirate nomenclature. The emirate and republic models at first glance appear to have irreconcilable differences as they originate from the different ends of the divine/popular sovereignty spectrum. There are, however, more nuanced possibilities along this spectrum that should not be overlooked or lost in translation. One must recall that even policy experts struggle to juxtapose with any degree of precision the distinguishing features of a republic and an emirate. Negotiators identified several overlapping and mutually beneficial goals, not the least of these being a peaceful and inclusive state that respects Islamic values. When principles and necessary outcomes are emphasized rather than labels, new possibilities emerge that may open the way toward renewed negotiations.

The key attributes of a republic, as seen in the 2004 constitution, call for a high value of public participation. All citizens of age, male and female, select their leaders through elections. In this model no one is above the law, and laws are passed through an elected legislature. The legislature is one of three independent branches of government, each to check the other's power. Finally, all citizens have basic rights which cannot be infringed upon. This framework has been in place for almost 20 years, giving a broad exposure and experience of agency in participation and leadership for females and ethnic and religious minorities. These significant strides have marked a generation, and these freedoms once given will not easily be relinquished. The framework applied in the constitution is similar to that which has been accepted by many of the majority Muslim states around the world, including Pakistan and Iran, two neighboring countries functioning as Islamic republics.

The Taliban ruled briefly from 1996 to 2001 as a self-described emirate. According to a draft constitution from 1998, and more expressly in practice and rhetoric, this conception sought to function according to divine sovereignty as manifested in the implementation of sharia. This is not sharia drawn from a bound and codified book, but rather through a dynamic oral tradition derived from the interpretative treatises of the Hanafi tradition. In this sense the Hadith functions as an authoritative canon, but it is an open canon to be studied in the light of precedent and reason. It is important to recall, however, the transitory nature of a "caretaker government" and of this tendentious document. The draft, which is all that is presently available, cites the Qur'an for authority (Surah al-anʿām, The Cattle, Q6:57), "The command (decision) rests with none but Allah," but as with most juridical works, an appeal to scripture is to be expected. Such a citation, in the juristic literature, is traditionally followed with references to pertinent Hadith and exegetical commentaries that clarify the rationale and line of thinking. The absence of further discussion in the *dastur* underscores its draft nature and that the document is still in process (Semple 2014). The document states that the nation is ruled by an emir, who, though chosen by a limited group of leaders, has final authority and responsibility. The emir is chosen by a select *shura*, or council, and the emir in turn oversees the constituency of the council. All branches of government are subject to the authority of the emir, and the basic rights are defined by sharia as interpreted by the council (Semple 2014). Though some may read this as equivalent to a dictatorship, it is more likely a reference to guardianship, a concept which has deep roots in juristic scholarship and which became a central feature of the Iranian constitution. Whether the emir will have the near absolute authority or whether this is a more symbolic position, as has been exercised by some of the Taliban emirs since 2001, is yet to be seen. In due course, however, as has been the experience of Iran, scriptural evidence will be required to legitimate and sustain this council and the role and qualifications of its members and of the emir. A cabal of strongmen can seize power, but it is only by extremely draconian means that they could sustain such a grip apart from some degree of public support.

The question of an ideal and authentically Muslim form of governance has been a central line of inquiry among Hanafi scholars in Pakistan since the school's inception, and the experience of these jurists may offer some additional perspective.[8] Many South Asian jurists were not satisfied with adopting a framework that was derived from British sources for this new nation carved out as a homeland for Muslims. A full examination of these discussions is beyond the scope of this chapter, but some of the ideas that crystallized in the 1970s continue to hold traction in Islamist thinking. One of these ideas concerns the definition and functions of citizenship. Citizenship, for many of these religious and political thinkers, did not provide the right to direct political participation. The state they argued, whether emirate or republic, should have representative democracy rather than universal suffrage in order to prevent the manipulation of communities as vote banks. As to representation, rather than a parliamentary system, they proposed the formation of a council, or *shura,* composed of persons of demonstrated moral character (Islahi 1976, pp. 16–17, 39). They called for an established standard to delineate the selection of suitable candidates. Those in leadership, particularly at a senior level, should be honest and of honorable character, rather than those with a dubious or criminal record. This line of Hanafi jurists allowed for full female participation at all levels of national leadership. This school of thought also opposed the establishment of political parties (Islahi 1976, p. 26). The partiers are regarded as the primary problem in the current system in Pakistan because they foment division and ultimately exist for their own ends rather than that of the government and community. Finally, they did not support the idea of a set term for an elected official. If the person is in error, then he or she needs to be forced out promptly rather than allowed to complete a predetermined time in office. Similarly, if the leader is succeeding toward the vision, then let him remain in power. In each of the points addressed, theorists blend a profound knowledge of religious sources and history and a candid assessment of human nature.

Is this a vision for an emirate or of a republic? There is voting and a form of representative democracy, perhaps akin to the original vision of a republic in Athens. It is not universal suffrage and clearly falls short of the free-enterprise system of competing political parties in the West, but even Pakistan's experience with democracy has been fraught with inconsistencies and corruption. The system is not working: elected officials seldom complete their term in office without a military coup or some ouster due to corruption allegations. Still, pressure continues to mount from the West to fabricate a democracy with results that are obviously fraudulent. If this system is not working in Pakistan, or in any of the neighboring countries, then why should one expect it to work in war-ravaged Afghanistan?

It is notable that these two systems, the emirate and the republic, not only differ in their basic attributes, but seem diametrically opposed or at least mutually exclusive. That said, there are several important principles that appear to be broadly agreed between the parties. Some of these, as Alex Thier has cogently argued, are that Afghanistan needs to be governed by a written constitution that reflects Afghan values and traditions and that as a sovereign state the governance must be inclusive of its ethnic, sectarian, and geographic diversity. Thier notes that this also includes a shared vision for the nation to have positive and peaceful relations with its neighbors and that the territory not be used as a haven for terrorist groups (Thier 2020, pp. 1–7). Beyond these broad commonalities, it is difficult to discern a trajectory for the evolving Afghan state. Confusion and instability remain as do the pressing needs of the population.

CONCLUSION

This chapter began by attempting to slow the Western reader down and discuss the differing presuppositions between the West and traditional Afghan leaders, including the Taliban, about political legitimacy and sources of authority. The West is used to looking to law-based and rights-based forms of authority, expressed best in Western concepts such as the "rule of [secular] law," popular sovereignty, representative government, and human rights. In contrast, an entirely different framework animates many Afghans, particularly those associated with the current Taliban regime. They are more likely to emphasize the sovereignty of Allah, submission to an understanding of Islam taken from the first centuries of the expanding, militaristic Islam and traditional forms of government (e.g. emirate). Moreover, authentic, local expressions of the Pashtun honor code, emphasizing both hospitality and revenge, create an entirely different dynamic that is contrary to Western expectations.

We have also shown some of the formative experiences that have shaped the Taliban's intransigence and militancy. Although there are important roots in the victorious mujahidin of the 1980s, particularly in the senior ranks of the Taliban, nonetheless, the experience of asserting rule in the 1990s, as well as watching the vicissitudes of other forms of Islamic government (e.g. from Gulf emirates to Pakistan, Turkey, Iran), and education in Deobandi madrassas in Pakistan have all shaped how the Taliban understands the responsibility for ruling Afghanistan.

Over time, it appears that there are at least two main factors that will be paramount for the Taliban's success or failure in power beyond 2022. The first is whether or not the Taliban can adjust itself, in contrast to its 1990s self, to the increased diversity of the country. Not only is Afghanistan ethnically diverse with its Pashtuns, Uzbeks, Tajiks, and Hazaras, but the populace's engagement with the outside world makes today's Afghans a different, more diverse, and a more worldly wise citizenry. Will the Taliban resort only to using force to cow its population, or will the Taliban be more open to diversity? The second critical factor is regime performance. Will the Taliban find a way to stabilize the economy and ensure a basic livelihood for the populace? Even in poor countries, citizens do expect a level of security. If the Taliban, with all its self-declared righteousness, cannot ensure food and security for the population, it will become increasingly isolated and illegitimate.

NOTES

1. The authors would like to thank the following research assistants for their invaluable help on this essay: Religious Freedom Institute interns Sage Yassa (Baylor University), Piper Levine (Baylor University), Andrew Davenport (Regent and Pepperdine Universities), and Jackson Reinhart (Vanderbilt and Northwestern Universities).
2. For greater detail, see Edward Girardet, *Afghanistan: The Soviet War* (London: Croom Helm, 1985); M. Hasan Kakar, *Afghanistan: The Soviet Invasion and the Afghan Response, 1979–1982* (Berkeley, CA: University of California Press, 1995).
3. This oppression is well known today due to its documentation by journalists and in popular media, including the famous *Kite Runner* book and film.
4. See, for example, Nile Green, "A History of Afghan Historiography," in *Afghan History Through Afghan Eyes* (Oxford, England: Oxford University Press, 2016); and S. Frederick Starr, *Lost Enlightenment: Central Asia's*

Golden Age from the Arab Conquest to Tamerlane (Princeton, New Jersey: Princeton University Press, 2015).

5. See Anthony Davis, "How the Taliban Became a Military Force," in *Fundamentalism Reborn? Afghanistan and the Taliban*, ed. William Malay (London: Hurst & Co, 1998); and Ahmed Rashid, *Taliban: Militant Islam, Oil and Fundamentalism in Central Asia* (New Haven, Connecticut: Yale University Press, 2000).

6. For a fuller description, see Jane Dammen McAuliffe, "The Tasks and Traditions of Interpretation," in *The Cambridge Companion to the Quran*, ed. Jane Dammen McAuliffe (Cambridge: Cambridge University Press, 2007), 181–210; Wael B. Hallaq, "Was the Gate of Ijtihād Closed?," *International Journal of Middle East Studies* 16, no. 1 (March 1984): 30.

7. *Pashtunwali* is the honor code of the Pashtun nation and is replicated among many of their neighbors. To simplify, this Central Asian code is often explained as having three foundational principles: hospitality, refuge, and justice (revenge). These are nested in other cultural values such as courage, honor, and the obligations of patriarchy. It is noteworthy that Pashtunwali is justified on cultural rather than Islamic (Qur'anic) grounds. See Amato, Jonathan N, *Tribes, Pashtunwali and How They Impact Reconciliation and Reintegration Efforts in Afghanistan* (Charleston, South Carolina: BiblioBazaar, 2012). *ISBN 978-1-248-98954-8*. The three primary pillars of Pashtunwali are *badal*, or revenge, *melamstia*, or hospitality, and *nanawatia*, or refuge.

8. The Jama'at-i-Islami continues to be highly regarded in the seats of learning attended by the present Taliban leadership. Among these, Amind Ahsan Islahi (1904–1997) is regarded as one of the greatest jurists of the past century. He was appointed to the Council of Islamic Ideology in 1979, by General Zia ul-Haq who sought to reify the Islamic character of the republic through the *Nizam-e-Mustafa* (Rule of the Prophet). Islahi attempted to chart an "Islamic state" for the modern world (Islahi 1976, pp. 16, 39).

Works Cited

Ahmed, Akbar. 2013. *Thistle and the Drone: How America's War on Terror Became a War on Tribal Islam*. Washington, DC: Brookings Institute Press.

Ahmed, Faiz. 2017. *Afghanistan Rising: Islamic Law and Statecraft Between the Ottoman and British Empires*, 207–235. Cambridge, MA: Harvard University Press.

Afghanistan Population. World Population. Accessed 25 April 2022. https://worldpopulationreview.com/countries/afghanistan-population.

Afghanistan Population 1950–2022. 2022. Macrotrends. https://www.macrotrends.net/countries/AFG/afghanistan/population.

Deutsche Welle. 2021, September 7. Afghanistan: Taliban Announce New Caretaker Government. https://www.dw.com/en/afghanistan-taliban-announce-new-caretaker-government/a-59113329.

Albright, Madeline. 2006. *The Mighty and the Almighty: Reflections on America, God, and World Affairs,* 216. New York: Harper.

Bahlul, Raja. 2000. People vs God: The Logic of 'divine sovereignty' in Islamic Democratic Discourse. *Islam and Muslim-Christian Relations* 11 (3): 287–297.

Banuazizi, Ali, and Myron Weiner, eds. 1988. *The State, Religion, and Ethnic Politics: Afghanistan, Iran, and Pakistan.* Syracuse, New York: Syracuse University Press.

Barfield, Thomas. 2010. *Afghanistan: A Cultural and Political History.* 1st ed. Princeton, New Jersey: Princeton University Press.

Crews, Robert D., and Amin Tarzi. 2008. *The Taliban and the Crisis in Afghanistan.* 1st ed. Cambridge, Massachusetts: Harvard University Press.

Dalrymple, William. 2021. *Return of a King: The Battle for Afghanistan.* London, England: Bloomsbury.

Emadi, Hafizullah. 2005. *Culture and Customs of Afghanistan.* 1st ed. Westport, Connecticut: Greenwood Publishing Group.

Goodson, Larry P. 2011. *Afghanistan's Endless War: State Failure, Regional Politics, and the Rise of the Taliban.* University of Washington Press.

Gopalakrishnan, Raju. 2021. Exclusive: Council May Rule Afghanistan, Taliban to Reach out to Soldiers, Pilots. Edited by M. Collett-White. *Thomson Reuters,* August 18. https://www.reuters.com/world/asia-pacific/exclusive-council-may-rule-afghanistan-taliban-reach-out-soldiers-pilots-senior-2021-08-18/.

Green, Nile. 2016. *Afghan History Through Afghan Eyes.* Oxford, England: Oxford University Press.

Gutman, Roy. 2008. *How We Missed the Story: Osama bin Laden, the Taliban, and the Hijacking of Afghanistan,* 233. Washington, D.C.: United States Institute of Peace.

Harrison, Selig S. 2008. 'Pashtunistan': The Challenge to Pakistan and Afghanistan. *Real Instituto Elcano.* https://media.realinstitutoelcano.org/wp-content/uploads/2021/12/ari37-2008-harrison-pashtunistan-afghanistan-pakistan.pdf.

Hassan, Riffat. 2009. Islamic Modernist and Reformist Discourse in South Asia. In *Reformist Voices of Islam: Mediating Islam and Modernity,* ed. Shireen Hunter, 182. New York, NY: Routledge.

Ingram, Brannon. 2009. Sufis, Scholars and Scapegoats: Rashid Ahmad Gangohi and the Deobandi Critique of Sufism. *The Muslim World* 99: 478–501.

Iqtidar, Humeira. 2021. Is Tolerance Liberal? Javed Ahmad Ghamidi and the Non-Muslim Minority. *Political Theory* 49 (3): 457–482.

Islahi, Amind Ahsan. 1976. *The Islamic State (Islāmī Riyāsat)*. Translated by Tariq Mahmood Hashmi. Lahore: Al-Mawrid. 16–17, 39.

Islamic State Khorasan (IS-K). 2018. Center for Strategic and International Studies. https://www.csis.org/programs/transnational-threats-project/past-projects/terrorism-backgrounders/islamic-state-khorasan.

Jaffrelot, Christophe. 2015. *Pakistan Paradox: Instability and Resilience*, 544–46. Oxford, England: Oxford University Press.

Jalal, Ayesha. 2016. *Self and Sovereignty: Individual and Community in South Asian Islam since 1850*, 386–460. New York: Routledge.

Jenkins, Phillip. 2010. *Jesus Wars: How Four Patriarchs, Three Queens, and Two Emperors Decided What Christians Would Believe for the Next 1,500 Years*, 30. New York, NY: HarperCollins.

Jones, Seth G. 2009. *In the Graveyard of Empires: America's War in Afghanistan*. 1st ed. New York, NY: W.W. Norton & Company.

Kakar, Palwasha R., and Julia Schiwal. March 2021. As Children of Adam: (Re) Discovering a History of Covenantal Pluralism in Afghan Constitutionalism. *The Review of Faith & International Affairs* 19 (1): 56–68.

Kennedy, Hugh. 2016. *Caliphate: The History of an Idea*. London, England, Basic.

Khan, Feroz Hassan. 2014. The Durand Line: Tribal Politics and Pakistan-Afghanistan Relations. In *Culture, Conflict, and Counterinsurgency*, 148–175. Redwood City, CA: Stanford University Press.

Lawrence, Bruce. 2000. *Shattering the Myth: Islam Beyond Violence*, 51–106. Princeton: Princeton University Press.

Mansurnoor, Iik Arifin. 2002. Islam in Brunei Darussalam and Global Islam: An Analysis of Their Interaction. In *Islam in the Era of Globalization: Muslim Attitudes Towards Modernity and Identity*, ed. Johan Meuleman, 71–98. New York: Routledge.

Marsden, Peter. 2002. *The Taliban: War and Religion in Afghanistan*. New York: Zed Books.

Patterson, Eric. 2021. The Taliban and "Sovereignty": Popular vs. Divine. *Religious Freedom Institute*, September 8. https://www.religiousfreedominstitute.org/blog/the-taliban-and-sovereignty-popular-vs-divine.

Peters, Rudolph. 1980. Idjtihād and Taqlid in 18th and 19th Century Islam. *Die Welt des Islam* 10: 131–145.

Qutb, Sayyid. 2015. *In the Shade of the Qur'an*. Translated and edited by Adil Salahi. Vol. 5, 207. The Islamic Foundation.

Rahman, Tariq. 2020. *Interpretations of Jihad in South Asia: An Intellectual History*. 2nd ed, 193–210. Berlin, Germany: DeGruyter.

Rashid, Ahmed. 2010. *Taliban: Militant Islam, Oil, and Fundamentalism in Central Asia*. New Haven, Connecticut: Yale University Press.

Ramsey, Charles. 2016. Anti-Saint or Anti-Shrine? Tracing Deobandi Disdain for Sufism in Pakistan. In *Sufism, Pluralism, and Democracy*, ed. Clinton Bennett and Sarwar Alam, 103–120. Sheffield: Equinox.

Semple, Michael. 2014. *Rhetoric, Ideology, and Organizational Structure of The Taliban Movement*. United States Institute of Peace. https://www.usip.org/sites/default/files/PW102-Rhetoric-Ideology-and-Organizational-Structure-of-the-Taliban-Movement.pdf.

Siddique. n.d. *The Pashtun Question*, pp. 11, 52–6.

Siddique, Abubakar. 2014. *The Pashtun Question: The Unresolved Key to the Future of Pakistan and Afghanistan*. 1st ed. London, England: Hurst.

Strick van Linschoten, Alex, and Felix Kuehn, eds. 2012. *Poetry of the Taliban*. London, England: Hurst & Co. https://www.e-ir.info/2012/08/21/review-poetry-of-the-taliban.

The Constitution of Afghanistan. 2018. *Afghanistan Online*, April 3. https://www.afghan-web.com/government-politics/constitution/.

Thier, J. Alexander. 2010. Big Tent, Small Tent: The Making of a Constitution in Afghanistan. In *Framing the State in Times of Transition: Case Studies in Constitution Making*, ed. Laurel E. Miller. Washington, DC: U.S. Institute of Peace Press.

———. 2020. The Nature of the Afghan State: Republic vs. Emirate. *Afghan Peace Process Issues Paper*, United States Institute of Peace, November, 1–7.

U.S. Library of Congress. Congressional Research Service. 2021. Taliban Government in Afghanistan: Background and Issues for Congress, by Clayton Thomas. R46955. https://crsreports.congress.gov/product/pdf/R/R46955.

Whitlock, Craig. 2022. *The Afghanistan Papers: A Secret History of the War*. New York: Simon & Schuster.

Younte, An. 2022. The Myth of the Secular Revolutionary: On Fanon's Religion. *Contending Minorities*, April 7. https://contendingmodernities.nd.edu/decoloniality/the-myth-of-the-secular-revolutionary-on-fanons-religion/?utm_source=feedburner&;utm_medium=email#_ftnref1.

Zaman, Muhammad Qasim. 2004. *The Ulama in Contemporary Islam: Custodians of Change*. Oxford: Karachi.

Zalmay, Khalilzad. 2016. *The Envoy: From Kabul to the White House, My Journey Through a Turbulent World*. St. Martin's Press.

CHAPTER 20

Religion and the State: Iraq—Tracing the Final Decades in the History of Iraq's Jewish Community

Michael Brill

On March 15, 2021, Dhafer Fouad Eliyahu, nicknamed the "doctor of the poor," died at the age of 61 after suffering a stroke. Eliyahu had worked as an orthopedic surgeon at Baghdad's Wasiti Hospital, where he even treated those who could not afford medical care. During the early days of the 2003 U.S.-led invasion of Iraq and throughout the worst years of sectarian violence that soon followed, Eliyahu continued to see and treat patients. His death reduced Iraq's dwindling Jewish community to no more than three individuals. Iraq's "last Jewish doctor," as Eliyahu was memorialized, came from a prominent family of medical clinicians. His mother was one of Iraq's first female doctors, operating her own private clinic in Baghdad during the 1950s (Julius 2021). Eliyahu's sister, Khalida, was Iraq's last Jewish dentist, although out of security concerns, ceased practicing dentistry in favor of working at an orphanage. Over the years, with no Jewish women remaining in Iraq to marry, Khalida had attempted

M. Brill (✉)
Princeton University, Princeton, NJ, USA
e-mail: mbrill@princeton.edu

447

S. Holzer (ed.), *The Palgrave Handbook of Religion and State Volume II*, https://doi.org/10.1007/978-3-031-35609-4_20

on several occasions to find a wife for her brother, but he always refused. One of his colleagues described him as "an example of humanity and humility" (Joffre 2021).

Eliyahu's death occurred shortly after and during the same month as Pope Francis's historic visit to Iraq, the first ever by a Pontifex. The trip included a highly symbolic interfaith ceremony at the Plain of Ur, where religious tradition holds was both the birthplace of the prophet Abraham and the site of god's revelation to him. Media coverage of the papal event noted the absence of a Jewish delegation, despite previous statements that Jews would be included. During the week prior to the visit, a Vatican spokesperson said that while he did not know if Jewish rabbis would participate in the ceremony, he was sure some Jews would attend. Later, Albert Hisham, the coordinator of the event for Iraq's Catholic Church, said that planners had contacted all the Iraqi Jews they could identify. "We invited them, but there are so few of them—maybe ten or twelve people," he explained (Horowitz and Santora 2021). However, Iraq's Jewish community was even smaller than he appeared to realize and did not include any rabbis. The man who had served as the community's last rabbi and slaughterer, along with being its youngest member in his mid-40s, Emad Levy, migrated to Israel in 2010 (Pohoryles 2018). Iraq's Jews had not been able to form a minyan, the quorum of ten adult males required for traditional public worship, for many years.

This chapter will illustrate how and why Dhafer Fouad Eliyahu and his sister Khalida became two of Iraq's last Jews. Their history and that of the final decades of Iraq's Jewish community, even between 1951 and 1973, but especially from the 1970s to the present day, is one that largely remains to be written (Smith 2019, p. 26). While a smaller chapter of a much longer and larger history, the story of Iraq's last Jews has import for the preservation of Jewish heritage sites, Iraqis interested in the historical diversity of their country's population and religious groups, along with the Jewish communal property, including documents and religious texts, still held by the Iraqi state, much of which was looted by prior ruling regimes (Fischbach 2008). Similarly, the history of Iraq's last Jews over the previous several decades has implications for the potential repatriation of the Iraqi Jewish Archive to Iraq from the United States, where it was moved for preservation and safekeeping as a consequence of the 2003 War (Ledger 2005; Montgomery 2013; Selchaif 2022). On a very human level, the story of Iraq's last Jews is a compelling one in that it features a decreasing number of individuals who were either unable or unwilling to leave the place of their birth and ancestral homeland. After presenting an overview of the history of Iraqi Jewry, this chapter will draw on news articles, documents from Western governments, and records of the formerly ruling Ba'th Party while attempting to piece together and trace the history of Iraq's last Jews. These events transpired against the backdrop of the consolidation of the Ba'th Party and Saddam Hussein's dictatorship, multiple wars, and regime change in 2003.

BACKGROUND

The history of Iraqi Jewry dates back more than 2600 years. As one of the world's oldest and most storied Jewish communities, Jews came to territory now constituting the Iraqi state after 586 BCE in the Babylonian captivity or exile. The army of Neo-Babylonian King Nebuchadnezzar II had defeated the Kingdom of Judah, destroyed Solomon's Temple, and forcibly resettled many Judeans in the land of Mesopotamia, which subsequent Jewish sources would refer to as Babylon. Over the next millennium, the area became a center for Jewish learning and culture in exile. Jewish sages produced the Babylonian Talmud during the sixth century CE. Beginning in the seventh century and during the subsequent five centuries, Babylon's Jews lived at the center of Islamic civilization, a period only disrupted by the Mongol invasion. Then, between the mid-sixteenth and early twentieth centuries, the land of Iraq was ruled by the Ottoman Empire. Iraq's Jews, as a protected minority community but still second-class citizens, were sometimes persecuted, impacted by political instability, and caught in power struggles between imperial officials in Istanbul and local ones in Baghdad. However, following the Tanzimat reforms of the nineteenth century, Jews in Iraq increasingly became part of the empire's economic, social, and political life (Sassoon 2022, pp. 5–8; Rejwan 1985, pp. 177–184). World War I and the occupation of Iraq by the British ended Ottoman rule. The subsequent British mandate made the Jews, like Iraq's other inhabitants, subjects of the Hashemite Kingdom under King Faisal I.

Nearly a century ago, Baghdad's Jews were roughly a third of the city's population and dominated its commercial life. Having adapted many features of Arab culture, even developing their own Baghdadi Judeo-Arabic dialect that used Hebrew script with the Arabic language, Jews were active participants in the public sphere under the monarchy. Jewish intellectuals engaged in political debates and articulated a pluralistic vision for Iraqi national identity (Bashkin 2009, pp. 185–190; Schlaepfer 2016, pp. 99–178). Given the long history of Jews in the lands constituting the modern Iraqi state, it likely would have been inconceivable for someone alive then to imagine that a century into the future, the number of Jews in both Baghdad and the entirety of Iraq could be counted on one hand. Yet with the independence of the Kingdom of Iraq in 1932, the political currents of Arab nationalism resulted in a growing number of legal restrictions imposed on Iraq's Jews by the state. In 1941, in the aftermath of the suppression of a pro-Nazi coup in Baghdad by the British, anti-Jewish sentiments precipitated a pogrom, known as the Farhud, or "violent dispossession," resulting in the killing of over 180 Jews and injuring of more than 1000 (Bashkin 2012, pp. 100–140). Although order was restored, the pogrom was an ominous foreshadowing of official persecution by the state later in the decade.

The attitudes of Iraqi officials toward developments in Palestine at the end of the British mandate had major implications for the future of Iraq's Jews. Following the decisive defeat of the Arab armies and volunteer forces, which included Iraqi troops and volunteers, by Israeli forces in the 1948 Arab-Israeli War, the Iraqi state targeted its Jewish population in revenge, accusing them of being communists, Zionists, spies, and a disloyal fifth column. Like other politically marginalized population groups, Jews were drawn to the Iraqi Communist Party, which Iraqi state authorities viewed as a political threat due to its central role in protests that occurred during the 1940s and 1950s. Still, the number of Jews in the party likely never rose above the low hundreds. With respect to Zionism, however, even at the height of its appeal in Iraq between 1948 and 1949, some 2000 among upwards of 130,000 Jews could be counted as members of the political movement (Bashkin 2012, pp. 144–146, 226).

Irrespective of reality, the brutal dynamic of Arab states targeting their domestic Jewish populations following military defeats against Israel occurred elsewhere and would be employed by successive governments in Iraq as well. The legal persecution of Iraq's Jews resulted in their effective denaturalization by the state and alienation from it. Between 1949 and 1952, facing an uncertain future regardless of which choice they made, some 123,000 Jews fled Iraq. The majority of them were airlifted to Israel between 1951 and 1952 in Operation Ezra and Nehemiah (Ben-Porat 1998). This exodus also included more or less all of the Jewish population in northern Iraq, some 25,000 people who were culturally distinct and generally poorer than their Jewish counterparts in central and southern

Iraq. Jews in northern Iraq spoke Neo-Aramaic, along with the languages of their neighbors, which included Arabic, Kurdish, Turkish, and Farsi. The majority lived in the rural villages of Iraq's Kurdistan region and worked in agriculture or as craftsmen. While Jews from the region were some of the first to migrate to Palestine from Iraq, even as early as the sixteenth century, their collective migration as a community was a result of the policies enacted by the Iraqi state. Northern Iraq's Jews first left for Baghdad, where they joined the rest of Iraq's departing Jews (Zaken 2007, pp. 195–196). In exchange for being permitted to leave Iraq by the state, Jews were stripped of their citizenship, property, and assets, except for the equivalent of $140 and the personal property they could carry in a single bag that did not exceed 66 pounds. Roughly 6000 Jews remained in Iraq after the completion of the airlift, at which point further Jewish migration was made illegal (Bashkin 2012, pp. 189–192, 220).

During the 1950s, the Jews who decided to remain in Iraq generally had the means to withstand or circumvent the state's punitive and confiscatory measures or had businesses and commercial interests too complicated to unwind. Iraqi officials had even been surprised by the large number of Jews who had chosen to depart Iraq, reducing the community to a small fraction of what it had been just a few short years prior. Politically, the monarchy had more pressing concerns, such as the Middle East's geopolitical rivalries and the machinations of its own officer corps. On July 14, 1958, Iraq's Free Officers, Arab nationalists who styled themselves like Egyptian President Gamal Abd al-Nasr and his colleagues, overthrew the monarchy in a violent military coup that killed King Faisal II, several members of the royal family, and Prime Minister Nuri al-Said. Brigadier Abd al-Karim Qasim proclaimed the Republic of Iraq and was installed as prime minister. The son of a Sunni Muslim Arab father and a Shiʿite Muslim Fayli Kurd mother, Qasim was a nationalist, yet reversed the policies of the monarchy targeting Iraq's Jewish community (Batatu 2004, pp. 764–860).

Qasim's tenure in power seemed to usher in a new liberal age for Iraq's remaining Jews. He was seen attending Jewish communal functions and even pictured shaking hands with the chief rabbi (Haim 1976, p. 207). His 1961 decision to expropriate and demolish part of Baghdad's Jewish cemetery in order to make room for a tower imitating that of Nasr's in Cairo was an affront to the community, but on balance, his policies were tolerant, especially compared to his predecessors and eventual successors. Under Qasim's rule, Iraq's Jews were granted full freedom and equal rights (Moreh 2008, pp. 7–8). Saeed Herdoon recalled, "I remember fondly the period from 1958 to 1963 during the regime of Abd Al-Karim Qassem—it was a very good time for the Jews... It was the real golden age of Iraqi Jews. In fact, I never had any problems with ordinary Iraqi Muslims throughout my life" (Herdoon 2008, p. 129). Some took advantage of Qasim's easing of restrictions on Jewish migration to leave Iraq, but at the time, many with family members in Israel were aware of the hardships they had faced upon arrival at transit camps, which not only were economic but included discrimination from Ashkenazi-dominated society. In addition to Iraqi Jews being viewed with suspicion as reluctant immigrants to Israel instead of committed Zionists, their Arab culture had been perceived as backward (Bashkin 2017, p. 6).

The violent overthrow and killing of Qasim in 1963 had nearly immediate deleterious effects on Iraq's Jewish community. The coup, led by a coalition of Arab nationalist officers, brought the Arab Socialist Baʿth Party to power for ten months, before being sidelined by its rivals. The subsequent tenure of Abd al-Salam Aref in power was accompanied by new measures targeting Iraq's Jews, which included denying them passports, exclusion from colleges, and revocation of citizenship for any Jew outside of Iraq for more than three months. Aref also reinforced the ban on Jewish migration. After Aref's death in 1966, his brother Abd al-Rahman Aref assumed power, yet with little change in the policies toward Iraq's Jews (Moreh 2008, pp. 8–9). The next watershed moment was the Six-Day War of June 1967, which resulted in an even more decisive victory for Israel than that of the 1948 Arab-Israeli War. The political fallout from the defeat in the Arab world intensified the scapegoating of indigenous Jewish populations and destabilized the existing political order. In this environment, the Baʿth Party under the leadership of Ahmed Hassan al-Bakr, who was assisted by his cousin Saddam Hussein, returned to power in 1968 by way of a bloodless coup. At the end of the Six-Day War the previous year, about 3350 Jews remained in Iraq. By the early 1970s, just a few years into the Baʿth Party's rule, this figure would be reduced to only a few hundred Jews still living in the country (Bashkin 2012, p. 230).

Escalation of Persecution After the Defeat

Iraq's remaining Jews again became scapegoats following Israel's victory in the Six-Day War. Jews were fired from government jobs, confined to house arrest, had their phonelines cut, bank accounts frozen, and property confiscated. Over the next two years, some 300 people were arrested and imprisoned, a substantial percentage of Iraq's remaining Jews. Those seized were subjected to harsh conditions and torture. The return of the Baʿth Party to power in July 1968 expedited the process of vilifying Iraq's Jewish community. When Israeli aircraft struck Iraqi military forces stationed in Jordan in December 1968, the Baʿth announced a hunt for Zionist spies. On January 27, 1969, the Baʿth hanged and publicly displayed in Baghdad the bodies of 14 alleged spies, including 9 Jews, inviting the Iraqi public to view the spectacle (Sawdayee 1974). As gruesome as the event was, the hangings were still in the beginning of the ordeal suffered by Iraq's Jews under the Baʿth Party over the course of the next few years. In 1969 alone, forty Jews were executed or tortured to death. The son of Grand Rabbi Sassoon Khedouri was imprisoned and tortured, which compelled his father to make public statements in support of the Baʿth. Following international condemnation of the hangings and persecution of Iraq's Jews, the Baʿth published an English language book titled *Iraqi Jews Speak for Themselves*, which featured statements by the grand rabbi and other Jews, allegedly made on their own volition. Explaining that Khedouri "made a number of important statements following the campaigns let loose on Iraq by Zionism and Israel at the time of the execution of the traitorous spies," the book quotes him as saying, "I hereby proclaim that the Jews of Iraq are enjoying their religious freedom in full and are exercising their rites and religious ceremonies in absolute freedom as is the case with the rest of the countrymen" (Iraqi Jews Speak for Themselves 1969, pp. 3–4). Making matters worse, Jewish emigration was still illegal according to Iraqi law.

As part of Israel's "doctrine of the periphery," which sought to cultivate ties with rebel groups and regional states that were similarly at odds with the Arab states at the forefront of the Arab-Israeli conflict, the Mossad and Israeli Defense Forces established contacts with Iraq's Kurds beginning in 1961 (Abramson 2018, pp. 396–398). These efforts focused on the Kurdistan Democratic Party (KDP) under Mustafa Barzani, who had initiated a revolt against Baghdad's rule in northern Iraq. The Baʿth Party inherited this conflict and when a ceasefire agreement was signed in 1970, it created an escape route for Iraq's remaining Jews, traversing Iraqi Kurdistan to reach Iran, before traveling onward to Israel and sometimes beyond to England, the United States, or elsewhere. Although relations between the KDP and the Baʿth began deteriorating in 1972, this brief window nevertheless permitted the majority of Iraq's remaining Jews to flee the country, although many required multiple escape attempts before succeeding.

Between 1970 and 1973, facing condemnation in international public opinion and pressure from the U.S., Canadian, British, Israeli, and other European governments, the Iraqi Ba'th continued to persecute the country's remaining Jews, enforced the ban on Jewish emigration, while in some instances, appeared to facilitate emigration. British diplomatic records from 1971 contain lists of Jews arrested over the previous year, along with those who were detained while attempting to flee Iraq. They also contain reports of Jews being extorted for large sums of money in exchange for passports (NEQ 18/11971: 17–19, 60–62). U.S. diplomatic cables from early 1973 report that Israel had asked the U.S. government to have Yugoslavian President Josip Broz Tito lean on the Iraqi government to release Jews who were still imprisoned and permit their emigration (1973STATE056698_b 1973). U.S. officials were also alerted to the murder of Reuven Kashkush's family in April, along with that another 16 Iraqi Jews had disappeared since February (1973STATE080551_b 1973). Due to diplomatic relations between the United States and Iraq being suspended after the Six-Day War, U.S. officials were heavily reliant on the Italian embassy in Baghdad for information. While Italian officials confirmed that Kashkush's family had been murdered by the secret police, they also reported that the "Iraqi government appears to be facilitating emigration of Jews," warning that further appeals from Western governments on the subject could be counterproductive. They made note of the fact that European embassies in Baghdad had issued 30 visas in recent weeks (1973ROME03615_b 1973). In the end, at least 2500 of Iraq's remaining Jews fled the country during the Ba'th Party's first half-decade in power (Marcus 1996). Of those who remained, a figure now under a thousand individuals, many were elderly or physically incapable of attempting the trip. By going to great lengths in vilifying a Jewish minority that was already a shadow of its pre-1951 self, the Ba'th drove a majority of those left out of Iraq.

Apparent Moderation

On November 26, 1975, the Iraqi Ba'th's Revolutionary Command Council adopted a resolution signed by President Ahmed Hassan al-Bakr inviting "all Iraqi Jews who left Iraq since 1948 to return home and enjoy equal rights with all Iraqi citizens." The Ba'th took out English language advertisements in the *New York Times* and other Western newspapers, which reminded readers, "It should be known that the Iraqi Jews who left the country after 1948 left on their own. *No one was expelled.*" Underscoring the propaganda value of the ad, it concluded with, "Given the economic crisis gripping the Jews in the Zionist entity, it goes without saying that Iraqi Jews returning home are assured of a much better standard of life." While the discrimination and prejudice facing Iraqi and other Mizrahi Jews in Israeli society were real, the Iraqi Baʿth found very few interested in accepting their invitation. Of the few who did, some then returned to Israel only to be imprisoned for aiding an enemy state (Roby 2022, pp. 260–261, 273, 278–280; Lippman 1976; Washington Post 1979). The overwhelming majority of Iraqi Jews living in Israel or elsewhere had no illusions about the nature of the Baʿth's rule or their experiences being driven out of Iraq over the previous quarter-century. Since the Jewish community in Iraq had been reduced to roughly 500 people, many of whom were elderly, it held less potential value for future vilification in the context of the Arab-Israeli conflict on the part of the Baʿth.

After Saddam Hussein's formal takeover of the presidency in 1979, Iraq was soon engulfed in war with the Islamic Republic of Iran between 1980 and 1988. This conflict, along with growing U.S. and Western support for Iraq against Iran, facilitated greater access to Iraq by Western media. A number of journalists visited Baghdad's Jewish community, generally under close supervision by government minders. In early 1983, Nick Themmesch, writing for *New York Jewish Week*, visited Meir Tweg Synagogue, the last active one, where he met Rabbi Reuben Naji Elias, president of Iraq's Jewish community. In the presence of accompanying Iraqi officials, Elias told Themmesch in English that "Conditions have improved since Hussein took over the Baath Party," going on to explain, "Hussein is good for us. The previous regime wouldn't let Jews sell their businesses when they wanted to leave, and was very hard on us. There were bad feelings toward Jews before Hussein. Everything is better now" (Themmesch 1983). Similar sentiments were encountered by Milton Viorst, when he visited Baghdad's Jewish community while working on a two-part article for the *New Yorker* in 1987. As he reported on the approximately 300 remaining Jews, "The situation improved as Saddam Hussein assumed more power, they said, and today Jews are treated like other Iraqis. They have their old businesses back, mainly in the import-export trade." Viorst added, "In truth, with the congregation too small and too old to be viable, Iraq's Jews are almost all certain to leave Iraq after the war" (Viorst 1987, pp. 113–114). While the situation for Iraq's remaining Jews was better relative to the reign of terror that accompanied the Baʿth's early years in power, the official narrative repeated by community leaders to foreign media conveniently excised the fact that Saddam played a prominent role in the party, and the security services in particular, during the Baʿth's prior persecution of the community. The expectation that the Iraqi Jewish community was rapidly approaching its end, on the other hand, would prove premature, even throughout two additional wars.

Iraq's Jews Between the Gulf Wars

In the few years immediately after the 1990–1991 Gulf War, 80 more Jews fled Iraq, many of whom were granted British and Dutch visas (Tsur 1994). By 1998, only 76 Jews were still living in Iraq (Barkho 1998). On October 4, 1998, a Palestinian Gunman killed two Jews and two Muslims in an attack against Baghdad's Jewish community. Saddam's regime made a notably conspicuous effort to track down the attacker before executing him in 1999. News coverage observed that Iraq's last Jews "realize they are on the verge of extinction," a recurring theme and finality they would stave off for the next quarter-century, perhaps longer than most expected or even realized. Community elder Ibrahim Yusef Saleh echoed the sentiments of his predecessor Elias from the 1980s, stating to a Western journalist, "Since 1968, when this government came to power, the situation was different. We have full liberty. We have open trade and business" (LoLordo 1998). While Saddam and the Baʿth may have seen no further point in persecuting Iraq's Jewish community, instead showcasing them as a protected and loyal minority, in contrast to the Zionist Jews in Israel, their internal records would reveal that the remaining Jews were still closely monitored.

In June 2001, the secretary of Iraq's National Security Council, which acted as a coordinating body between the various branches of the Baʿth Party's security services, ordered them to gather information on the "number of Jews or the families from the Jewish faith originally who converted to Islam or Christianity, along with their locations inside in Iraq, in order to place them under surveillance and monitor their movements" (JPIDS 001_0032 2001). The resulting investigation produced detailed information on Iraq's 39 remaining Jews; 36 resided in Baghdad, whereas Basra, Wasit, and Duhok each had one (JPIDS 001_0015–0016 2001).

The documentation included information about not only the remaining Jews, but also people who the regime defined as being of "Jewish origin," including those who ostensibly converted during earlier periods of persecution (Sassoon and Brill forthcoming). The documents reveal that the trigger for the study was not anything pertaining to Iraq's 39 remaining Jews, but rather reports that converts in northern Iraq, much of which achieved de facto autonomy from Baghdad following the 1990–1991 Gulf War, were "apostatizing from their current faith and returning to the Jewish faith" (JPIDS 002_0050 2001). Iraq's security services had detected the movement of people between northern Iraq and Israel, which they viewed as cover for Mossad operations. During prior years, the security services reported that Mossad agents had arrived in Erbil to facilitate the travel of individuals of "Jewish origin" to Israel (BRCC 01_3608_0004_0105 1994). Read together, the Baʿth's documents draw attention to an episode that received little attention at the time or since: between the early 1990s and 2001, the Mossad working with the Jewish Agency brought over 1000 people claiming to be Jews or possessing Jewish heritage from northern Iraq to Israel. Fewer than 100 ultimately stayed, with most traveling onward to Europe or returning to Iraq. The fallout from the episode, especially in Israel, made organizations there considerably more cautious when contacting Iraq's remaining Jews in the wake of the 2003 War (Brill forthcoming).

CONCLUSIONS: FROM 2003 TO THE PRESENT

The 2003 U.S.-led invasion and occupation of Iraq resulted in a wave of news articles about Iraq's remaining Jews. One of them, whose family fled in 2001, left Iraq in March 2003, just prior to the war (Raddler 2003). Of the 34 remaining Jews, 6 elderly persons between the ages of 70 and 99 left for Israel in July on a charter flight organized by the Jewish Agency and the Hebrew Immigrant Aid Society. Among the six was Ezra Levy, father of Emad, who would ultimately follow in his father's footsteps by making the journey to Israel in 2010. The remaining 28 Jews were all contacted by the Jewish Agency, but said they were reluctant to leave Iraq or needed more time. Half of them were over the age of 70. Sassoon Saleh Abd al-Nabi, age 90, required three days of efforts to convince him. "In Iraq I was all alone and I didn't have much fun, but I didn't want to come to Israel; I thought it was too late," he explained (Tait 2003). Salima

Moshe Nissim of Basra, age 79, lost her last relative in Iraq when her mother died in 1967. In Israel, she was reunited with her sister Marcel Madar, who was among those who fled Iraq in 1951. Nissim said, "I was all alone in Basra and I was never happy because I could not see my family" (Myre 2003).

After additional migration to Israel and elsewhere, only 13 Jews remained in Iraq by February 2004 (Filkins 2004). By July 2007, the number had dropped to nine, when Reverend Andrew White, the Anglican chaplain to Iraq, attempted to draw attention to Iraq's remaining Jews, saying their situation was "more than desperate" and that they wanted to leave Iraq (Van Biema 2007). Although Israeli and Dutch officials disputed White's claims, the several remaining Jews were not immune from the sectarian violence ravaging much of Baghdad. In 2006, one Jew had been kidnapped and killed by gunmen believed to be members of Al-Qaeda (Max 2007; Farrell 2008). The community suffered a major scare in 2011, when diplomatic cables obtained and published by *Wikileaks* contained the names of and detailed information about each remaining individual (Gutman 2011). Despite fears for the worst, the disclosure did not lead to any attacks. Five years later, news coverage noted that while they were still "living in fear," Iraq's Jews were largely concealing their identities and surviving similarly to how they had before, thanks in no small part to help from Muslim and Christian neighbors, along with one member of the Iraqi parliament (Rosenberg 2016).

By 2017, the community reportedly counted only five members (Shute 2017). The death of elderly community matriarch Marcel Menahim Daniel in 2020 reduced its ranks to four, making Khalida Fouad Eliyahu Moualim the new acting community leader. Her brother Dhafer's death the following year brought its number of members down to three. In one of the 2008 diplomatic cables leaked by *Wikileaks* that is still relevant to the subject today, U.S. Ambassador to Iraq Ryan Crocker summarized the current status of and apparent future for Iraq's remaining Jews, writing, "As things stand, the Jews of Baghdad currently form a 'community' in name only… They remain in Iraq, but not of it, hiding at the center of a country whose majority may, one day, welcome them again, but does not accept them at present." He concluded, "It seems unlikely that this fact of Baghdad life will change soon, and so these nine individuals may author the last chapter to the story of an ancient people in an ancient land" (08BAGHDAD1454_a 2008).

REFERENCES

Abramson, Scott. 2018. A Historical Inquiry Into Early Kurdish-Israeli Contacts: The Antecedents of an Alliance. *Journal of the Middle East and Africa* 9 (4): 379–399.

Barkho, Leon. 1998. Last 76 Jews in Iraq Realize That They Are on Verge of Extinction. *Chicago Tribune*, March 27.

Bashkin, Orit. 2009. *The Other Iraq: Pluralism and Culture in Hashemite Iraq.* Stanford: Stanford University Press.

———. 2012. *New Babylonians: A History of Jews in Modern Iraq.* Stanford: Stanford University Press.

———. 2017. *Impossible Exodus: Iraqi Jews in Israel.* Stanford: Stanford University Press.

Batatu, Hanna. 2004. *The Old Social Classes and Revolutionary Movements of Iraq: A Study of Iraq's Old Landed and Commercial Classes and of its Communists, Ba'thists, and Free Officers.* London: Saqi Books.

Ben-Porat, Mordechai. 1998. *To Baghdad and Back: The Miraculous 2,000 Year Homecoming of the Iraqi Jews.* Jerusalem: Gefen Publishing House, Ltd.

Brill, Michael. forthcoming. The History of Northern Iraq's Jews and the Forgotten 1990s "Aliyah" from Iraqi Kurdistan.

Farrell, Stephen. 2008. Baghdad Jews Have Become a Fearful Few. *New York Times.* June 1.

Filkins, Dexter. 2004. Iraqi Council Weighs Return of Jews, Rejecting It So Far. *New York Times.* February 28.

Fischbach, Michael R. 2008. Claiming Jewish Communal Property in Iraq. *Middle East Research and Information Project* 248: 5–7.

Gutman, Roy. 2011. Wikileaks shakes security of Iraq's tiny Jewish community. *McClatchy.* October 7.

Haim, Sylvia. 1976. Aspects of Jewish Life in Baghdad Under the Monarchy. *Middle Eastern Studies* 12 (2): 188–208.

Herdoon, Saeed. 2008. Section Three: Our Country No More. In *Iraq's Last Jews: Stories of Daily Life, Upheaval, and Escape from Modern Babylon,* ed. Tamar Morad, Dennis Shasha, and Robert Shasha, 128–131. New York: Palgrave Macmillan.

Horowitz, Jason, and Marc Santora. 2021. Absent from an event highlighting the bonds of Judaism, Christianity and Islam: A Jewish presence. *New York Times.* March 6.

Iraqi Jews Speak for Themselves. 1969. Baghdad: Dar al-Jumhuriyah Press.

Israeli Who Returned From Iraq is Jailed. 1979. *Washington Post.* April 21.

Joffre, Tzvi. Dr. Dhafer Fuad Eliyahu, One of the Last Jews in Iraq, Passes Away. *Jerusalem Post.* 18 Mar. 2021.

Julius, Lyn. 2021. Jews vanish from Iraq, but still have no closure. *Jewish News Syndicate*. March 21

Ledger, Dana. 2005. Remembrance of Things Past: The Iraqi Jewish Archive and Legacy of the Iraqi Jewish Community. *The George Washington International Law Review* 37 (3): 795–830.

Lippman, Thomas W. 1976. Iraq Displays a Jew Who Returned. *Washington Post*. July 26.

Lolordo, Ann. 1998. In Iraq, Respect for the Jews Baghdad: A Tiny Minority That has Seen Good Days and Bad is Treated Well Under Saddam Hussein. *Baltimore Sun*. November 13.

Marcus, Raine. 1996. Jews Who Escaped Iraq in 1970s Hold Reunion Tonight. *Jerusalem Post*. August 1.

Max, Arthur. 2007. Conditions Worsen for Iraq's Last Jews, But do They Want to Leave? *Jerusalem Post*. August 8.

Montgomery, Bruce P. 2013. Rescue or Return: The Fate of the Iraqi Jewish Archive. *International Journal of Cultural Property* 20: 175–200.

Moreh, Shmuel. 2008. Introduction: The Historical Context. In *Iraq's Last Jews: Stories of Daily Life, Upheaval, and Escape from Modern Babylon*, ed. Tamar Morad, Dennis Shasha, and Robert Shasha, 3–10. New York: Palgrave Macmillan.

Myre, Greg. 2003. After the War: Reunion: 52-Year Separation Ends as Iraqi Jews Arrive in Israel. *New York Times*. August 28.

Pohoryles, Yaniv. 2018. The last Jew Who Made Aliyah from Iraq. *Ynetnews*. April 19.

Raddler, Melissa. 2003. Last Jew to leave Iraq? *Jerusalem Post*. April 10.

Rejwan, Nissim. 1985. *The Jews of Iraq: 3,000 Years of History and Culture*. London: Weidenfeld and Nicolson.

Roby, Bryan K. 2022. Not All Who Ascend Remain: Afro-Asian Returnees from Israel. *International Journal of Middle Eastern Studies* 54: 260–281.

Rosenberg, David. 2016. Living in fear: Iraq's last Jews. *Arutz Sheva*. March 13.

Sassoon, Joseph. 2022. *The Global Merchants: The Enterprise and Extravagance of the Sassoon Dynasty*. London: Penguin Random House.

Sassoon, Joseph, and Michael Brill. forthcoming. After the Exodus: The History of Iraq's Last Jews.

Sawdayee, Max. 1974. *All Waiting to Be Hanged: Iraq Post-Six-Day War Diary*. Tel Aviv: Levanda Press Ltd.

Schlaepfer, Aline. 2016. *Les intellectuals juifs de Bagdad: Dscours et allegeances (1908–1951)*. Boston: Brill.

Selchaif, Leila. 2022. The Iraqi Jewish Archive in Exile: A Legal Argument for Equitable Return Practice. *Northeastern University Law Review* 14 (1): 275–317.

Shute, Joe. 2017. Remembering the last Jews of Iraq. *Telegraph*. November 22.

Smith, Marcus Edward. 2019. *Those Who Remained: The Jews of Iraq Since 1951.* Doctoral Dissertation: Purdue University.

Tait, Robert. 2003. Israel takes Iraqi Jews Back to the Promised Land. *The Times.* August 1.

Themmesch, Nick. 1983. *A Rare Visit to Iraq's Capital Affords a Look at its Last Synagogue and 400 Surviving Jews.* Mar: New York Jewish Week.

Tsur, Batsheva. 1994. 80 Jews left Iraq over last 3 years. *Jerusalem Post.* December 15.

Van Biema, David. 2007. The Last Jews of Baghdad. *Time.* July 27.

Viorst, Milton. 1987. A Reporter at Large: The View from the Mustansiriyah—I. *New Yorker.* October 12, 93–113.

Zaken, Mordechai. 2007. *Jewish Subjects and Their Tribal Chieftains in Kurdistan: A Study in Survival.* Boston: Brill.

Archival Sources

Jewish Presence in Iraq Dataset (JPIDS), Iraq Memory Foundation, Hoover Institution Library and Archives. Stanford, California.

Ba'th Regional Command Collection (BRCC), Iraq Memory Foundation, Hoover Institution Library and Archives. Stanford, California.

Treatment of Jews in Iraq, Part A. Near Eastern Department. NEQ 18/1. 1971. London.

Wikileaks

PART V

Religion and the State in Africa

CHAPTER 21

Formations of the Secular: Religion and State in Ethiopia

Jörg Haustein

Political religion has been a resurgent topic in Ethiopia in recent years. In particular, PM Abiy Ahmed, who came to power in 2018, has puzzled and fascinated journalists and political observers (DeCort 2022; The Economist 2018, 2022; Galindo 2022; Rémy 2021; Schaap 2021). Here was an avowed Pentecostal who, at least initially, was given an enthusiastic reception in this traditionally Orthodox and Muslim country with its 50 years of secularism in socialist and post-socialist garb. In sharp distinction to his predecessors, Abiy embraced a sermonizing rhetoric of hope, love, and forgiveness, yet his regular appeals to Ethiopia's multi-religious heritage and its prosperous future "under God" rang increasingly hollow against a string of inter-ethnic and inter-religious riots that tore apart communities and led to record numbers of internally displaced people. Abiy earned the Nobel Peace Prize for his reconciliation with Eritrea and only one year later led his country into a brutal civil war, with religious symbology featured in both his Prize acceptance speech and his framing of the war.

J. Haustein (✉)
University of Cambridge, Cambridge, UK
e-mail: jh2227@cam.ac.uk

© The Author(s), under exclusive license to Springer Nature
Switzerland AG 2023
S. Holzer (ed.), *The Palgrave Handbook of Religion and State
Volume II*, https://doi.org/10.1007/978-3-031-35609-4_21

465

The allure of Abiy's religio-political platform and its contradictions is understandable, in particular among secular commentators. Yet it has often produced unhelpful fixations on Abiy's personal convictions, Pentecostal prosperity promises, or transatlantic evangelical politics.[1] While all these factors play *some* role in Abiy's politics, the more salient question is how his religious identity and rhetoric could find support among an Ethiopian public that is overwhelmingly neither Pentecostal nor Evangelical and, moreover, how Abiy could sustain his religious platform even as he lost large constituencies across the country, including some Evangelicals. The task, therefore, is to elucidate the deeper structure of religion and state in Ethiopia that allowed Abiy's invocations of God to resonate.

This requires a careful historical analysis of nexus between religion and politics in the formation of the modern Ethiopian nation state from the late nineteenth century onward. We will pay particular attention to how the various regimes regulated religious institutions and co-opted them for legitimating particular formations of nationhood and governance. From this, a long history of faith and power in Ethiopia will emerge, which provides the fertile soil for Abiy's political program. This history will also enable us to trace the rise of Protestantism from a marginal identity to a significant political power, despite being the youngest and only third-largest religious constituency in Ethiopia. Finally, the historical overview will also show that modernizing demands of state neutrality and secularity have shaped Ethiopia's religious politics since the early twentieth century, which, as the conclusion will argue with Talal Asad, necessitates a re-framing of political secularity as a regime of practice that is not premised on an increasing absence of religion.

NATION-BUILDING AND RELIGIOUS PLURALITY: THE IMPERIAL RECORD

Ethiopian historiography has largely subscribed to the notion that freedom of religion and state neutrality in religious matters took hold in the country in the process of modernization and nation-building. A widespread expression of this sentiment is the often-cited phrase "Faith is private, the country is collective" (*haymanot yägəll näw, agär yägara näw*), variously attributed to the two emperors most often commemorated as founders of the Ethiopian modern nation state: Menelik II (r. 1889–1913) and Haile Selassie I (r. 1930–1974) (Archbishop Yesehaq 2005, p. 82; Makki 2011, p. 278; Abbink 2011, p. 259). This quote should not be mistaken for an expression of Imperial policy (Tibebe Eshete 2009, 410n40), however, even as such sentiments were held among the intellectual reformers of the era (Bahru Zewde 2002, 136f.). Instead, where the political system accommodated religious plurality and established the foundations for a secular state, this was driven by a variety of political constellations rather than the ideological pursuit of a modern nation state.

Modern Ethiopia was no stranger to religious plurality and its political consequences. The tensions between the Orthodox Emperors and vassal Muslim states came to a head in the Abyssinia-Adal War of 1529–1543. With Christian Ethiopia saved from collapse by Portuguese intervention, this conflict would define inter-religious relations in Ethiopia for centuries to come. The continued Portuguese presence at first earned Susenyos' (r. 1606–1632) conversion to Catholicism in an alliance with Western Christendom, which, however, ended in disaster when Jesuit priests attempted to impose European rites (Marcus 1994, pp. 39–40). During the subsequent restoration of the Orthodox state in the Gondar era (1632–1706), Catholics were reconverted or expelled while the emperors moved to end Christological conflict within the Ethiopian church (Henze 2001, pp. 100–107; Marcus 1994, pp. 43–44). Muslims and Jews were segregated from Christians (Ahmad 2000) and substantial efforts were made to integrate the immigrating Oromo into imperial rule through assimilation and conversion. Protestant missions commenced toward the end of the subsequent "era of the princes" (1755–1855), which was marked by a collapse of central authority, but they immediately ran into political difficulties when Emperor Tewodros II (r. 1855–1868) sought to harness the missionaries' technological abilities for his project of restoring the Empire and finally held them hostage to press for weapons from Queen Victoria (Arén 1978, pp. 45–104).

After Tewodros fell by his own hand in the British expedition to rescue the hostages, a new project of imperial restoration ensued under Yohannes IV (r. 1871–1889) premised on the enforcement of religious uniformity. Re-emerging Christological conflicts in the Orthodox Church were settled through political pressure, and Christianity was made the religion of all citizens. Apart from Yohannes' own piety, there were two political reasons for this. Firstly, Yohannes' reign was marked by conflict with his Muslim neighbors, from the encroachment of Egypt in the 1870s to his battles with the Mahdists in the 1880s, which in the end cost his life. In this environment, the claim to defend Christianity helped to rally large armies while Muslims were forced to convert (Marcus 1975, p. 40, 58, 11). The second reason for Yohannes' program of religious unification was that his political base lay in the predominantly Orthodox highlands of Tigray, Gondar, and Gojjam, whereas the Shewan kingdom of his foremost rival and ultimate successor, Menelik II (r. 1889–1913), drew its strength from expanding into the Muslim and "pagan" areas of the east and south (Marcus 1975, p. 27). Compelling Menelik to enforce religious uniformity in his domains was a way to weaken his appeal and blunt the insurgent potency of the multi-religious periphery (Marcus 1975, p. 58).

When Menelik inherited the empire upon Yohannes' death, Ethiopia's religious politics shifted once again. With the north weakened by warfare, disease, and famine, Menelik continued the expansion of Ethiopia into the south, east, and west. This shift in the geographic orientation of the country necessitated the integration of religious diversity, even as the subsequent installation of settler-landlords reinforced notions of Amhara-Orthodox dominance (Marcus 1975, 193f.; Erlich 1994, pp. 74–82). In foreign politics the calculation changed as well. Menelik's main worries were no longer Egypt nor Sudan, but the encroaching European colonialism, particularly in Italy's fraudulent claim to a protectorate over Ethiopia. It was now a Christian nation that, according to Menelik, sought to "ruin the country and to change our religion" (Marcus 1975, p. 160), until it was repulsed to Eritrea in the battle of Adwa (1896) for more than a generation. Seeking to balance out French and British interests in Sudan, Menelik even established cordial relations with the Mahdist caliphate (Marcus 1975, p. 178).

The tactical embrace of Islam had its limits for Christian Ethiopia, however, as Menelik's never-crowned heir, his grandson Lij Iyasu, was to find out. Iyasu's father, a Muslim leader and close ally of Menelik in Wollo, converted to Christianity under Yohannes' edict of religious uniformity. When named as heir to the throne, Iyasu was only 13 years old. His inexperience and impulsiveness created many enemies as he tried to step out of the shadow of his appointed regents in Menelik's dying years. The most apparent challenger to his rule was Tafari Makonnen, the later Emperor Haile Selassie I, then-governor of Harar. For all his failings, Iyasu sought to establish his power in his popular appeal away from the machinations of the palace, which included a vision of religious and ethnic equality (Marcus 1975, p. 252, 258). It was from this position that he began to integrate Muslim politicians into Ethiopian rule, again in a combination of domestic and international calculations. On the domestic front, this embrace of Islam would strengthen his base in the east of the country and prevent his Orthodox rival Tafari from building a political movement there. Internationally, his embrace of Islam aligned Ethiopia with Germany and the Ottoman Empire in the First World War in the hope of containing the foremost colonial powers in the region (Marcus 1975, pp. 266–68). Though it remains disputable whether Iyasu actually did convert to Islam himself (cf. Marcus 1975, pp. 267–176; Erlich 1994, pp. 84–90; Bahru Zewde 2001, pp. 124–28), this was the accusation that led to his downfall and the installation of Menelik's daughter Zewditu (r. 1916–1930) as empress, with Tafari appointed as her regent and heir.

During his regency, Tafari became "the natural ally of the progressives" (Bahru Zewde 2001, p. 110) as he struggled against the conservative establishment and their figurehead, the devout and traditionally minded Zewditu. Yet with his ascent to the throne in 1930, it became clear that the primary drive behind Haile Selassie's reforms in education, administration, and the military was the consolidation of imperial absolutism while still improving the image of Ethiopia abroad. One of his first acts as newly proclaimed emperor was to task the reformist intellectual Tekle-Hawariat Tekle-Mariyam with drafting an Ethiopian constitution. This constitution, promulgated in 1931, was modeled on the Japanese Meiji era constitution, which in turn had been based on the Prussian model of an imperial monarchy (Bahru Zewde 2002, p. 62; Clarke 2004). Yet the Ethiopian constitution took even further the absolutist tendencies of its templates, foregoing an independent parliament and eliding civil rights, including the freedom of religion. The Ethiopian state, instead, rested solely on the "imperial dignity" of Haile Selassie (Arts. 3, 5), who sovereignly "instituted" legislative chambers (Art. 7) and "recognized" a very basic set of individual rights and duties (Arts. 18–27).

The 1931 constitution made no reference to the Ethiopian Orthodox Church, which had crowned Ethiopian monarchs for centuries, nor to religion in general. This was a sharp departure from the traditional, thirteenth-century constitution of Ethiopia based on the national myth of the *Kəbrä Nägäśt* and the legal code of the *Fətḥa Nägäśt*. This is not to argue that Haile Selassie saw himself as a secular monarch or abandoned the Orthodox faith. In fact, he crystallized the religio-political myth of the *Kəbrä Nägäśt* in the constitutional persona of the Emperor, "whose line descends without interruption from the dynasty of Menelik I, son of King Solomon of Jerusalem and the Queen of Ethiopia, known as the Queen of

Sheba" (Art. 3). Yet this constitutional enshrinement of the *Kəbrä Nägäśt* as national myth also entailed its secularization in two regards. Firstly, the inherited promise of divinely sanctioned, eternal rule was now translated into the legal persona of the Emperor and his family, in compliance with the requirements of modern constitutionality. And secondly, the Abyssinian-Orthodox exceptionalism upheld by the *Kəbrä Nägäśt* was replaced by the construct of the nation state, which at least in theory entailed the recognition of multiple religions and ethnic groups, even if in practice it often meant little more than the forceful imposition of regulation upon them.

The secularizing consequence of the constitutional nation state can be seen in subsequent legislation that set up the state as the regulator of religious rights and arbiter of religious conflict. Already before the Italian occupation from 1936 to 1941, the Emperor issued a set of laws to reform the Orthodox church, especially in areas of land ownership and finances (see Shenk 1972, pp. 71–29). After Haile Selassie had returned from exile, this was followed by extensive "Regulations for the Administration of the Church" of 1942 (Shenk 1972, pp. 221–27), subjecting ecclesial rights, institutions, and finances to imperial supervision (Clapham 1969, p. 82). This coincided with Haile Selassie's efforts to secure the Church's autocephaly from its traditional dependency on the Coptic Church, thereby making it a fully national church.

The Emperor also worked toward the integration of foreign missions in order to harness their developmental capacity. The "Regulations Governing the Activities of Missions" in 1944 provided a first legal recognition for foreign missions and set up the state as regulator of multi-religious coexistence (for a copy of the decree, see Aymro Wondmagegnehu and Motovu 1970, pp. 170–74). The regulations foresaw the division of the country into areas that were open for missionary proselytization because they consisted predominantly of non-Orthodox inhabitants and "Ethiopian Church areas," where missionary labors were to be limited strictly to development work. The areas were not delimited by the decree itself, but left to subsequent committee regulation. While for the first time giving a legal footing to missions beyond political toleration, the decree in practice gave Orthodox opposition a powerful lever against foreign missions where they could be construed to have violated its religious or linguistic stipulations (Hege 1998, pp. 128–31; Etana Habte Dinka 2018, 297f.).

After the Emperor had consolidated his constitutional power and his prerogative in religious matters, the relationship between nation and religion was re-calibrated again in the 1955 revision of the constitution, promulgated on the 25th anniversary of Haile Selassie's coronation. On the one hand, the traditional alignment between the state and the Orthodox Church was now enshrined in the constitution itself, making it the established church of the Ethiopian Empire (esp. arts. 10, 16, 20, 21, and 126). On the other hand, the constitution provided a more robust list of civil rights, including the first formal guarantee of non-interference in the exercise of "any religion or creed," albeit governed by broadly defined political constraints (Haustein 2011, p. 5). The emergence of these civil rights was due to the influence of Haile Selassie's American adviser John Spencer, who drafted the original English text on the basis of the US Constitution (Spencer 1984, p. 258). Yet, as subsequent developments would show, religious liberty remained a right in theory only as neither the political system nor the courts upheld it in practice.

The Civil Code of 1960 also ruled out discrimination on the basis of religion, but at the same time awarded a privileged legal position to the Orthodox Church as the only religious institution formally established by law. Other associations, including religious ones, could apply for registration with the Ministry of the Interior under regulations published in 1966 (Tsahafe Taezaz Aklilu Habte Wold 1966). For Ethiopian Muslims, treated by Haile Selassie from the start of his tenure with the gesture of a "patronizing Christian king" (Erlich 2019, p. 55), the Civil Code and registration procedure were a retrograde development. Though Islamic jurisdiction and institutions had been enshrined into law during the Italian occupation (Østebø 2012, pp. 125–29), they were now deliberately excluded from Haile Selassie's modernizing legal framework. A draft chapter for the 1960 Civil Code making special provisions for Muslims was excluded from the final version, and qāḍī courts were not even mentioned in Ethiopian procedural law (Hussein Ahmed 2006, pp. 9–10). Thus, while Muslim courts and some Islamic institutions, such as schools, continued to be recognized in practice, they were offered no suitable legal footing, other than those for the registration of associations. This hardly amounted to a recognition of the long-standing presence of Muslims in the country, nor did it fit their mode of organization.

The Protestant mission churches, for the time being, continued operating under the grants of the 1944 Missions' Decree. This left the first test of the registration provisions to a small, but ambitious religious fringe:

Ethiopian Pentecostals. Pentecostalism had entered Ethiopia in the 1960s through the work of Finnish and Swedish Pentecostal missions, yet after a short time an independent group broke away from the missions to form the first national Pentecostal assembly, the Ethiopian Full Gospel Believers' Church (Haustein 2011, pp. 37–136). This church was led by university students, whose modernizing aspirations and educational mobility quickly galvanized a young movement for reviving Ethiopian Christianity. Such a mission-independent variant of Protestantism did not fit the tolerated paradigm of "foreign" missionary Christianity and quickly encountered opposition. The registration request was turned down, entailing the closure of the church.

At first, the young Pentecostals complied with this ruling, resorting to small meetings and missionary shelter while seeking to negotiate with the authorities (Haustein 2011, pp. 137–51). When this led nowhere, the students continued to insist on their constitutional right to freedom of religious practice, and conflict mounted. A government circular of 1971 attacked Pentecostals alongside Jehova's witnesses as one anti-social and dangerous movement and encouraged authorities in Addis Ababa to silence their meetings (Haustein 2011, pp. 155–60). The Pentecostal youths, in turn, decided to defy the government closure openly by hosting a large public service in the summer of 1972. This was shut down by the police and about 250 worshipers were arrested. The youths now sought to argue their case in front of the High Court, where the verdicts against them were upheld (Haustein 2011, pp. 172–75). Efforts to ramp up international pressure on Ethiopia through the press and the World Council of Churches also failed (Haustein 2011, pp. 176–87), but they showed to what extent Pentecostals and their allies embodied a modernizing agenda that the old regime could no longer contain, much like the communist student movements that precipitated Haile Selassie's fall.

This, then, was the inheritance of imperial religious politics at the eve of the Ethiopian revolution. The integration and management of religious plurality had been a long-standing issue that only grew as the country expanded to incorporate large Muslim areas to the east as well as traditional religionist and increasingly Protestant areas to the south and the west. Yet as the center of gravity for the ruling elites remained in the Orthodox highlands of the country, Ethiopian Christianity remained the de-facto ruling religion of the country. This is not to argue that Ethiopia was a theocracy. Rather, the state emerged as an institution vis-a-vis the church as emperors made substantial efforts to align the Orthodox Church with the requirements of imperial rule. The fate of religious minorities ranged between suppression and benevolent toleration, the latter in particular if a political benefit was to be gained from embracing the non-Orthodox periphery. Yet their firm integration into Ethiopian statehood was ruled out as Iyasu's experiment showed.

Under Haile Selassie this framework of religious toleration in a de-facto Orthodox state found its constitutional embodiment. This tacit legal framework for a multi-religious Ethiopia centered on the centralizing prerogative of the Emperor himself, who after bringing the church under his control was defined as an Orthodox persona. Provisions of religious liberty remained mostly modernist virtue signaling toward secular statecraft, which stood in stark contrast to discriminatory practices toward non-Orthodox communities. Yet the constitutional foundationalism of Haile Selassie's reforms should not be underestimated, because it set up the state as guarantor of religious rights and arbiter of inter-religious coexistence, even if as a not yet realized promise.

'THE REVOLUTION ABOVE ALL!': RELIGION AND THE DERG

The Ethiopian Revolution was the culmination of several popular demands, one of which was equal rights for all religions. Wide-scale protests and strikes erupted from February 1974, beginning with taxi drivers, students, and teachers as well as mutiny within the army (Scholler and Brietzke 1976, 4f.). In April 1974, Muslims held a large demonstration in Addis Ababa with about 100,000 participants forwarding 13 demands, including a separation of religion and politics as well as the right to form a national organization of Islam (Hussein Ahmed 2006, p. 10; Østebø 2012, p. 198). This led to protests by the Orthodox establishment (Hussein Ahmed 2006, p. 11), though it is worth noting that the demonstration received some support from Christians as well.

A new constitution was drafted to accommodate the various grievances and relieve political tensions (Scholler and Brietzke 1976, pp. 154–83). With respect to matters of faith, this draft for the first time forwarded a constitutional right to form religious associations for the propagation of any faith as long as it is "not used for political purposes or its presence prejudicial to public order or morality" (Art. 24). The wide remit of this safeguarding clause would have meant little change in practice because it still gave the state all the power to intervene and regulate. On the whole, the constitution fell far short of a separation of church and state, since it continued to mandate that the Emperor belong to "the Monophysite Ethiopian Orthodox Church" and that prayers for him were offered in all religious services (Art. 9). Still, Patriarch Theophilos condemned the constitution for failing to define a special legal persona for the Orthodox Church, which he feared was a first step to the disestablishment of the church (Shenk 1994, p. 208).

These discussions mattered little in the end as the draft was made redundant by the revolution. A coordinating committee within the army, commonly known by the Amharic term *derg* (committee), had already begun its reach for power by placing mass media institutions under its control. As the Derg consolidated power and stepped up its attacks on the emperor, even the patriarch fell into line. In his traditional broadcast on Ethiopian New Year (11 September 1974), he omitted the constitutionally demanded prayer for the emperor and his family but blessed the revolutionaries instead, casting their cause as a "holy movement" (Haile Larebo 1986, p. 150). Haile Selassie was deposed and arrested by the Derg the very next day, never to be seen in public again.[2]

The revolution soon took a violent turn with a shoot-out between different factions of the Derg and the murder of political prisoners. As Mengistu Hailemariam emerged from the shadows and began his rise to the top, the Derg published a declaration of socialism as its governing philosophy. This was coined as a special Ethiopian variant of communalism arising from the cultural and religious traditions of the country:

> The political philosophy which *emanates from our great religions* which teach the equality of man, and from our tradition of living and sharing together, as well as from our history so replete with national sacrifice is Hibrettesebsawinet (Ethiopian Socialism). (Provisional Military Government of Ethiopia n.d., p. 7, emphasis added)

This was flanked by a declaration of religious, ethnic, and gender equality, alongside an invocation of the unity of Ethiopia as "the sacred faith of all our people" (Provisional Military Government of Ethiopia n.d., p. 7). This declaration of socialism found much support within various religious constituencies. Some Orthodox clergy pointed to the similarity between Jesus' teachings and the ideals of socialism (Teferra Haile Selassie 1997, p. 154). Muslims for the first time enjoyed the national recognition of three Islamic holidays (Hussein Ahmed 2006, p. 11), and the General Secretary of the Lutheran Ethiopian Evangelical Church Mekane Yesus

(EECMY), Gudina Tumsa, issued a pastoral letter in support of socialism, promising to hand over the church's charitable institutions to the state, now that the government had committed to take care of the people's needs (Haustein 2009, p. 126). Likewise, members of the Derg and official newspapers emphasized the common ground between religions and Ethiopian socialism (Tibebe Eshete 2009, 212f.)

It is important to take note of this initial amicable embrace between religious communities and the Derg's proclamation of socialism because subsequent repressive measures against religions have led opponents and supporters of the revolution alike to contend that the regime pursued sinister plans for the destruction of Ethiopian religions from the start (Teferra Haile Selassie 1997, p. 154; Schwab 1985, 92f.; Bonacci 2000, pp. 593–605).[3] However, such a simple juxtaposition of socialism and religion obfuscates the much more complicated formation of religion and politics under the Derg. What the revolutionary regime had inherited from Haile Selassie was a highly centralist state ruling over an ethnically and religiously fractured country. While the imperial tie between the Orthodox Church and the state was quickly severed, the Derg in essence took the same constitutional position as Haile Selassie: the state arrogated the power to govern all religious affairs for the good of the country. As with Haile Selassie, this entailed a mix of co-optation, regulation, and repression.

The powerful Orthodox Church was aligned most swiftly, beginning with the land reform of 1975, which deprived the church of its economic foundation and made it dependent on state subsidies (Haustein 2009, p. 152). For a while, the clerical hierarchy resisted reform efforts, and Patriarch Theophilos finally fell out with the Derg when he defied government orders not to ordain new bishops. He was deposed in early 1976, arrested after escaping house arrest, and finally murdered in prison three years later. The patriarch's deposition was not merely an authoritarian act by the revolutionaries but supported by political conflict within the church, with Theophilos' opponents gaining the upper hand and inviting government intervention (Wudu Tafete Kassu 2006, pp. 310–23). Under the eyes of the Derg, the church now elected a replacement in the inward-looking monk Abunä Takla Haymanot, who would not contest the authority of the state. That the state used the Church's internal turmoil for its alignment rather than destruction shows how much the institution was needed by the government. Mengistu Hailemariam, who hailed from the ethnic minority of the Konso in south-western Ethiopia, may have originally intended to rebuild the nation from the socio-religious margins of the country, but in the light of violent infighting of the Red Terror, the ongoing Eritrean war of independence, and the Ogaden War, he soon needed a centralized church and Abyssinian nationalism as political rallying base (Haile Larebo 1986, pp. 152–53). This political arrangement of church and state held throughout the Derg, and despite some infringements on Orthodox practice, the church managed to grow significantly (Wudu Tafete Kassu 2006, pp. 296–305).

Islam was also co-opted by the state, serving as a counterweight to the continuation of Orthodox privileges. In 1976, the Derg agreed to the formation of the Ethiopian Islamic Affairs Supreme Council (EIASC). This seemed like the fulfillment of a long-standing demand, but it also gave the government a central handle by which to co-opt Islam. Moreover, a certain ambiguity remained. A series of two conferences on "Religion Does not Divide Us" around the Ogaden conflict betrayed the nervousness of the government about the mobilizing potential of Islam and other religious groups (Tibebe Eshete 2009, pp. 213–14). The EIASC was never granted full legal recognition, and its first chairman suffered a brutal attack on his family (Østebø 2012, pp. 199–200). The *hajj* and the import of religious literature remained restricted, as were Sufi practices and prayers in official settings. With a marked increase in government schools, the state also attempted to replace traditional Islamic institutions of learning, but thereby also fueled Islamic Reform movements through promoting educational modernism (Østebø 2012, pp. 226–35). Altogether, Ethiopian Muslims tend to remember the Derg's policies as mainly a symbolic recognition of Islam: despite official recognition, a sense of Amhara-Christian dominance remained.

On the Protestant side, the Derg's record was incongruent (cf. Tibebe Eshete 2009, pp. 209–72). Larger churches were forcibly aligned, beginning in 1979 with murder of Gudina Tumsa, whose sustained attempts to engage constructively with socialism were seen as a threat while his brother, Baro Tumsa, had become a leading Oromo nationalist and guerrilla fighter against the Derg. With the arrest and murder of Gudina, the government began to confiscate assets and close scores of local parishes in various mainline denominations, but despite these oppressive measures most mainline denominations managed to attain official recognition by the mid-1980s. Alongside the Orthodox Church and the EIASC, Protestants were consulted in the drafting of the 1984 constitution, secured the reopening of churches, and obtained a seat in parliament (Eide 2000;

Haustein 2009, pp. 124–30). Marginal churches, like Mennonites and Pentecostals, on the other hand, were not an interesting target for co-optation, and from 1978 onward they suffered near-universal closures, as well as intimidation, interrogation, and incarceration of members and leaders.

Pentecostals, in particular, were seen as a disruptive presence that made them vulnerable to attacks (for a full account, see Haustein 2011, pp. 188–247). While not politically oriented, they would clash with authorities when prioritizing their faith over the requirements of the state, such as absenting themselves from socialist youth gatherings or refusing to shout slogans they deemed blasphemous, like "the revolution above all!" Abstention from alcohol, effervescent religious practices, and a proselytizing zeal also exposed them in local communities, so that Protestant leaders in mainline churches occasionally collaborated with the Derg in ousting Charismatic groups (Haustein 2011, pp. 239–47). Pentecostals and Charismatics quickly reestablished resilient underground networks, which further set them up as the epitome of "illegal" religion and arguably increased their attractiveness to ordinary Ethiopians as the failures and brutality of the Derg mounted. In its campaigns against these groups, the Derg began to vernacularize the derogatory epithet "Pente," which now came to be applied to mainline Protestants as well, some of whom had never even heard of the term or Pentecostalism (Donham 1999, pp. 144–45).

Therefore, the secular formation of Socialist Ethiopia was not so much an ideological onslaught on religion as it was a radical continuation of Haile Selassie's centralist nation-building project. There surely were Marxist ideologues, who advanced "scientific socialism" in opposition to religion (see Østebø 2012, p. 199), but the primary political energy was directed toward making religions subservient to a Leninist state apparatus through aligning hierarchies, suppressing "insurgent" religion, and disturbing religious practice where it clashed with the requirements of collective organizations. Constitutionally secular, and ideologically atheist, the socialist state thus retained and perhaps even increased the political significance of religions by the centralizing controls it imposed. Aligned religious leaders lent the state political legitimacy, while alienated religious groups formed alternative political communities, be it through Pentecostal underground churches, Protestant missionary support for Oromo liberation movements (Haustein 2009, 128f.), or the rise of Islamic reformism as a response to the co-optation of ʿulamā (Østebø 2012, pp. 220–35).

Liberation and Control: Religion and Ethnic Federalism

In 1991, the Derg was ousted by a coalition of rebel armies, led by the Tigrayan People's Liberation Front (TPLF). The TPLF, which would go on to dominate the next three decades of Ethiopian politics, came from a similar ideological background as the regime it fought. Its leader, Meles Zenawi, had only renounced Marxism-Leninism in 1990, at about the same time as Mengistu Hailemariam (Andargachew Tiruneh 1993, p. 362). Yet like the Derg, its former ideological leanings never prevented the TPLF from recruiting and co-opting religion during its insurgency. The TPLF leadership refrained from attacks on monastic and ecclesial privileges, Orthodox priests were recruited as combatants or for practical support, and Muslim support for the TPLF rose as the Derg failed to deliver on religious equality (Young 1997, pp. 174–78). At the same time, the TPLF also stepped into the established political role of regulating the church from the start by organizing church conferences, pushing for a separate secretariat of the church in the "liberated territories," and seeking structural reforms.

Once the TPLF had ousted Mengistu, it sought to establish a new governing formula for Ethiopia in the political construct of ethnic or "multinational" federalism. This staked the Ethiopian nation state no longer on the integrity of the center, but envisioned a constitutional contract between the "nations, nationalities and peoples of Ethiopia" ("The Constitution of the Federal Democratic Republic of Ethiopia" 1995a, preamble). Politically, this entailed the formation of a governing coalition made up of ethnic parties, the Ethiopian People's Revolutionary Democratic Front (EPRDF). The administration of the country was organized into ethnically defined states or regions, which were allowed to adopt their own languages and scripts, and even given the right to secede. Earlier notions of Abyssinian cultural supremacy were replaced by an official valorization of cultural and ethnic diversity, visualized in seemingly ubiquitous depictions of "cultural" dances on state television.

This project of ethnic federalism was a radical and promising attempt to solve the age-old tensions between Ethiopia's fragmentary and centrist tendencies, but it was fraught with significant tensions. The recognized main ethnic groups were very different entities in terms of their geographic distributions, cultural configurations, and internal plurality (Merera Gudina 2006; Assefa Fisseha 2006). In addition, the political dynamic of centralization continued unabated. In the edifice of the EPRDF, the TPLF established an undisputed hegemony over the army, the political process, and economic assets (Vaughan 2015). In 1998–2000, it took the country into a bloody war with Eritrea, which substantially weakened both countries. Elections were riddled with fraud and the systematic discrimination of opposition parties. There was no freedom of the press, and where protest movements arose, the state reacted with brutality. Even the regime's ambitious and remarkably successful development policy was marked by centralization and bureaucratization.

The EPRDF's stance toward religions was characterized by a similar ambivalence of freedom and hegemony. The official policy was one of a strictly secular state. For the first time, the Ethiopian constitution provided a robust formula for freedom of religion and the non-discrimination of religious minorities. In accordance with the old 1966 regulations, all religious groups could now attain legal status through registration as a voluntary association, even as the Ethiopian Orthodox Church remained the only officially established religious body. Yet on the other hand, the promise of state neutrality was not adhered to when political considerations got in the way (Haustein and Østebø 2013). Soon after the TPLF had taken over Addis Ababa, the Derg-aligned Orthodox Patriarch Abunä Merkorios (installed in 1988) was forced to abdicate and replaced by a former protege of the Patriarch Theophilos, whom the Derg had murdered. Once again, this was a mix of political pressure on the church and internal disputes within it, but this time, the uncanonical deposition of a patriarch resulted in a long schism between the Ethiopian Orthodox Church and an exile synod based in North America. Yet it also gave the EPRDF a Tigrayan Patriarch who toed the line and made constant political intervention unnecessary.

Muslims, on the other hand, saw sustained government interference, most vividly in the co-optation of the EIASC and the introduction of restrictions on Muslim piety in public schools and universities. Much of this was framed as protecting Ethiopia from "religious extremism," typically in connection with events that fueled concerns about Islamic terrorism in the country: the 1995 assassination attempt on Mubarak in Addis Ababa, 9/11 and the subsequent "war on terror," as well as Ethiopia's invasion of Somalia in 2006 (Haustein and Østebø 2013, 166f.; Mohammed Dejen Assen 2016). As with the Derg, the state interventions tended to produce the opposite of what was intended. The government's sponsorship of the Sufi movement (al-Ahbash) is an especially instructive example of how EPRDF interference eroded the legitimacy of the EIASC and thereby the very "Ethiopian Islam" they sought to promote through this conduit (Østebø 2013).

Protestants appear to have benefited the most from the EPRDF regime. For the first time, they were placed on a more or less equal footing with Orthodoxy and Islam, including the right to register churches and gain access to land for church buildings and burial grounds. Having already grown substantially in the underground, Protestant numbers now soared. Their population share increased from just over five percent in the mid-1980s to well over 25 percent in recent statistics.[4] This growth and proliferation all over the country was marked by a substantial fragmentation of the Protestant church landscape and fueled to a large degree by Pentecostal movements. Charismatic beliefs and practices became deeply embedded in most mainline Protestant denominations as the earlier derogatory epithet "Pente" became a widely accepted self-designation for all evangelicals (Haustein and Fantini 2013).

Pentecostals largely understood their success as the "fruit" of the endured persecution and as a vindication of their political strategy: Liberty and growth did not come through investment in "worldly" politics but through spiritual resilience and defiance in the face of oppression. For much of the EPRDF era, this legacy of persecution entailed a widespread disengagement from formal politics in favor of "healing the country" through personal conversions. This coalesced with the now-popularized dictum of "religion is private" as well as with the developmental aspirations of the state: Pentecostal entrepreneurship and emphasis on good Christian character made them model citizens of the new Ethiopia (Freeman 2013; Fantini 2015). Accordingly, converted ex-politicians like Tramrat Layne, PM of the transitional government, were held in higher regard than Pentecostal politicians who had risen through the party ranks. Even Meles' successor, the Pentecostal PM Hailemariam Desalegn, did not earn a full Protestant embrace. Arguably, this was not only because of the churches' reticence to embrace the political system, but also because Hailemariam belonged to the widely ostracized anti-trinitarian sect of Oneness Pentecostalism (Haustein 2013).

Beyond its direct engagement with religious groups, the EPRDF intervened in two areas that influenced all religions. Firstly, in seeking to cut off political influence from outside the country, the government changed the regulations for civil society organizations in 2009, enforcing a strict separation between advocacy organizations and development work, with outside funding severely curtailed for the former. In practice this meant that charitable work by religious organizations had to be split off into separate entities, with partially detrimental effects in development areas of religious concern, such as efforts to curb FGM/C (Haustein and Tomalin 2019, p. 12). Secondly, in 2010 the government pushed for the establishment of Inter-Religious Councils at national and local levels. This would provide an official representation of all major religious groups, which the government could draw upon for political support in various circumstances. This fit with the EPRDF's political aesthetics of an inclusive and peaceful management of Ethiopia's diversity, but it also made religious leaders vulnerable to political co-optation. Among Protestants the question of representation even resulted in a split in the long-standing Evangelical Churches Fellowship of Ethiopia (established in the early days of the Derg) when the two largest Protestant churches secured a direct seat in the Inter-Religious Council rather than be represented by the Fellowship along with most other Protestants.

The official secularism and pluralizing logic of the EPRDF regime, therefore, came with a certain systemic affinity for Protestantism and promoted its growth. The mostly Pentecostalized proliferation of Protestant churches through fragmentation and voluntary associations matched the *divide et impera* strategy of the state and its administrative bureaucracy, while the movement's internal differences and its largely apolitical vision of a spiritual transformation of the country presented no direct challenge to those in power. Yet the substantial growth of Protestantism represented a rising political capital that prepared the re-emergence of religious narratives at the center of Ethiopian nationhood.

EMPIRE RESURGENT? ABIY AHMED'S GOD TALK AND ETHIOPIAN NATIONALISM

In February 2018, Hailemariam Desalegn announced his resignation as PM and Chairman of the EPRDF. This was precipitated by three years of protest and unrest, led by the Oromo, the largest ethnic group of Ethiopia with a long history of political marginalization. Hailemariam's resignation sparked a political crisis with the various ethnic parties within the EPRDF vying for power. In the end, Abiy Ahmed from the Oromo Democratic Party managed to gain the crucial support of the Amhara National Democratic Movement and was elected as Chairman of the EPRDF and sworn in as PM. It soon became apparent that this was more than a swing of political power toward the Oromo within the governing coalition. Instead, Abiy moved to abolish the ERDF's ethnic rendering of politics altogether and reverted instead a one-nation ideal of Ethiopia, albeit qualified by a philosophy of unity from diversity as articulated in his governing philosophy of "Medemer" (synergy) (Abiy Ahmed 2019a).

Politically, this made sense. The system of ethno-regional federalism was controversial, in particular among urban elites and certain parts of the formerly predominant Ethiopian highlands that felt disowned by the TPLF's erasure of the old imperial symbols of nationhood. Aligning with these forces was the most straightforward way for Abiy to broaden his Oromo power base into a national coalition that could displace the hegemony of the TPLF and circumvent the fragility of ethnic coalitions with their long history of tactical maneuvering. Therefore, Abiy quickly built a broad popular platform through a series of liberating reforms and weakened the TPLF by making peace with its old archenemy in the north: the Eritrean President Isayas Afewerki. He then set about transforming the EPRDF from an ethnic coalition into a programmatic party, the Prosperity Party.

The audaciousness and pace of these reforms can only be understood properly if one takes religion into account, which, in a sharp departure from his predecessors, has risen to the forefront of Abiy's political rhetoric (Haustein and Dereje Feyissa 2022, 486f.). There are a number of reasons for this. The most obvious one is Abiy's personal faith as a Pentecostal Christian who seems to be driven by a strong sense of divine purpose and calling. Among Pentecostals, stories abound of his reign forecast by prophecy, and a well-established pastor and historian of Abiy's denomination, the Full Gospel Believers' Church, even recounted how Abiy himself claimed about 20 years ago that he would be PM one day (Etalem Mesgana 2020). In his acceptance speech after he was elected to this office, Abiy himself took up the mantle of destiny by recounting how his mother whispered into his ear as a young boy that one day he would serve his nation from the palace. On multiple occasions since, he has reiterated the notion that his rule was ordained and upheld by God (Haustein and Dereje Feyissa 2022, p. 486).

Abiy's Pentecostal faith has attracted much attention from supporters and critics alike, but it is important not to reduce his emphasis on religion to the biographic domain. Rather, there are two, equally important, *political* factors for why religion plays such a prominent role in the PM's governing platform. Firstly, his biographical background and political career impressed upon him the political potency of religious identities in Ethiopia. Hailing from a Muslim father and an Orthodox mother, Abiy converted to Pentecostalism sometime in his youth.[5] This personal acquaintance with all three faiths alike soon became an important resource as he transitioned from his military to his political career. Posted in his hometown of Beshasha in the Jima zone, he was engaged in Christian-Muslim peacebuilding and conflict resolution initiatives that followed violent inter-religious clashes in 2006. Subsequently, as parliamentarian and Deputy President of Oromia Region, he intensified these efforts in his support for the Religious Forum for Peace (Abiy Ahmed 2017). This led to his PhD thesis on "Social Capital and Its Role in Traditional Conflict Resolution in Ethiopia: The Case of Inter-Religious Conflict in Jimma Zone State," which he defended at Addis Ababa University in 2017 (Abiy Ahmed Ali 2016). Brokering inter-religious peace and emphasizing the multi-religious character of Ethiopia thus became part of Abiy's own political capital as he ascended into power.

Accordingly, Abiy quickly involved himself in religious policy when he became PM. He inserted himself into the already advanced negotiations to mend the schism between the Ethiopian Orthodox Church and the exile synod, and to much acclaim he brought them to a successful end. In addition, Abiy also helped reconcile a faction among Muslims between some of the Oromo protest leaders and the EIASC, whose leadership had been installed by the previous government. In addition to these reconciliation efforts, Abiy sharply departed from the usual evangelical exclusivism in embracing all religions: he paid tribute to the role of the Orthodox Church in Ethiopian history, became the first PM to attend *iftār* celebrations in *Ramaḍān* 2019, and signaled his support for the celebration of Oromo traditional religion (Haustein and Dereje Feyissa 2022, p. 489). More fundamentally, he established Islam and Protestantism as fully institutionalized religions in Ethiopian law, giving them the same status as the Orthodox Church. On the Muslim side this amounted to the recognition of the EIASC as legal representative of the Islamic community while on the Protestant side a new entity had to be formed in the Evangelical Council, which unites (almost) all major Protestant denominations and gives them legal status.[6]

A second political reason for Abiy's foregrounding of religion in his governing platform is the link between Ethiopian national identity and religious exceptionalism. The idea that Ethiopia is a nation especially blessed by God has a long-standing expression in the ancient myth of the

Kəbrä Nägäśt, which claims that the Ethiopian emperors are descendants of Solomon and locates the Ark of the Covenant in Axum. Protestants, and in particular Pentecostals, have tended to embrace these myths as part of their story as well while seeking to connect their own history to Orthodox religious renewal movements. For Muslims, Ethiopia is loaded with similar historical significance as the country of the first *hijra*, where most of Mohammed's companions found refuge even before the Prophet's exodus to Medina, and as the place from which the first *mu'azzin* originated, as well as Mohammed's nurse. As these myths entail powerful religious affirmations of Ethiopian national identity, it is no wonder that Abiy's political project of emphasizing Ethiopia's unity over ethnic diversity would seek to capitalize on religion. This can be seen in Abiy's regular invocations of God's favor on Ethiopia and in his newly installed tradition to end political speeches with the phrase "May God bless Ethiopian and all its peoples." Even in his Nobel Peace Prize acceptance speech he argued that the "thousands of years" of Ethiopia's independence were linked to the peaceful coexistence between Islam and Christianity (Abiy Ahmed 2019b).

Abiy's religious governing platform therefore presents much more than narrow evangelical politics. In essence, it is a nod to the old imperial/Orthodox vision of "one Ethiopia under God," now broadened into a multi-religious proposal, delivered in Pentecostal style. Yet the limits of Abiy's governing pitch also emerged early on. From September 2018 onward, the country has been afflicted by numerous violent inter-ethnic and inter-religious clashes that left behind hundreds of casualties and millions of internally displaced people (for an overview and detailed analysis, see Østebø et al. 2021). As the authorities struggled to prevent, contain, and reconcile such conflicts Abiy's lofty rhetoric of synergy and Ethiopian unity proved vacuous against grievances that had been boiling under the surface for decades. People increasingly resorted to the safety of kinship communities defined by ethnic or religious boundaries, with each clash deepening antagonisms and sowing expectations of further conflict (Østebø et al. 2021, p. 31).

This failure of governance left Abiy vulnerable to criticisms of being driven by religious zeal rather than political realism. Most prominent among is critics were leading members of the TPLF, who as early as August 2019 contrasted their secular "realism" with Abiy's "Great Ethiopia mantra" of a country prospering as it stretched its hands to God (Haustein and Dereje Feyissa 2022, 490f.). This contrast only increased as Abiy failed to forge a political compromise with the TPLF and pushed ahead with his reform agenda. When during the first wave of the COVID pandemic he postponed federal elections beyond the parliamentary mandate, he set up the country for a constitutional crisis, with the TPLF holding the scheduled elections in Tigray anyway. By November 2020 this erupted into a bloody civil war between the TPLF and the central government, which also saw the involvement of Eritrean soldiers on the side of Abiy—a sinister consequence of the peace deal he had received the Nobel Peace Prize for.

The war has exacerbated both the ethnic divides of the country and the dispute about its political direction. Other ethnically based rebellions have joined the fray, most importantly a resurgence of Oromo liberation fighters in the West, pursuing, for a time, a loose and largely ineffectual alliance with the TPLF. The government's brutal suppression of this insurgency further eroded Abiy's already waning support among his own ethnic group. His project became beholden to centrist forces only, ranging from urban elites to Amhara nationalists. For his enemies, this was proof that Abiy's project in the end was one of Empire *redivivus*, given the near-universal hold the Amhara have had on the Ethiopian throne. Orthodox inflammatory preachers, like the controversial deacon and government advisor Daniel Kibret, who compared the TPLF to Satan and called for their eradication, only added to this impression, though similar rhetoric could be heard among Pentecostals as well. The peace deal with the TPLF resulted in further political turns, with Amhara nationalists turning against Abiy.

Religious communities, meanwhile, are left divided. The war has resulted in a schism in the Ethiopian Orthodox Church between a Tigray and Ethiopia branch. Within the EIASC the fight between a Sufi faction and a reformist wing has re-erupted while a serious (and now institutional) division between founding members of the Evangelical Council has rendered futile Abiy's attempt to foster Protestant unity. Evangelicals no longer support Abiy universally and the Tigray War has prompted the first among them to call for his resignation (Naol Befkadu 2021; for an Evangelical counter-piece, see Getachew Tamiru 2021). Abiy's promise to rebuild Ethiopia around intra- and inter-religious peace has clearly fallen short, and yet it lingers on.

Conclusion: Religion and Secularity in the Ethiopian Nation State

In his *Formations of the Secular* Talal Asad (Asad 2003, p. 25) argued that the epistemic regime of "the secular" emerged alongside "the religious," rather than against it, in a complex history of "changes in the grammar of concepts." As such, "the secular" is "neither continuous with the religious that supposedly preceded it (that is, it is not the latest phase of a sacred origin) nor a simple break from it (that is, it is not the opposite, an essence that excludes the sacred)." Rather, Asad understood the secular as a concept that combines "certain behaviours, knowledges, and sensibilities in modern life" in a genealogy that only "in certain respects [...] overlaps with 'the religious.'" Thus,

> A secular state is not one characterized by religious indifference or rational ethics–or political toleration. It is a complex arrangement of legal reasoning, moral practice, and political authority. This arrangement is not the simple outcome of the struggle of secular reason against the despotism of religious authority. We do not understand the arrangements I have tried to describe if we begin with the common assumption that the essence of secularism is the protection of civil freedoms from the tyranny of religious discourse, that religious discourse seeks always to end discussion and secularism to create the conditions for its flourishing. (Asad 2003, p. 255)

This clears important conceptual space for the study of religion and the state in Ethiopia. Once we part with the zero-sum-game notion that modern political regimes move from religiosity to secularity (or "back" to religiosity in post-secular "regression"), then previously "ambiguous" historical constellations become decipherable. A constitution that simultaneously declares freedom of religious practice and mandates the head of state to be Orthodox, or a Marxist government that introduces Muslim holidays are no longer deficient or "not yet complete" regimes of secularism, but fully partake in the global regime of the secular from a context where religion has a different political significance compared to North America or Europe, which typically serve as templates for "proper" secular states.

From this vantage point it becomes clear why Abiy's invocation of God in his political rhetoric is not a case of "post-secular regression," in strange contrast to the fact that he went further than all his predecessors in securing religious equality before the law. Instead, Abiy's prominent inclusion of religion in his political platform merely represents the latest turn in the long history of the *Ethiopian* secular episteme: a polity in which the state seeks to incorporate religious diversity while harnessing its political power.

In this long history, three particular dynamics stand out. Firstly, as has become clear, religions retained significant political capital in the modern Ethiopian nation state, even as it complied with the secular requirements of constitutionally enshrined religious liberty or Marxist progressivism. This does not make Ethiopia a theocratic polity or one that is governed by religious interests. Instead, in all its dealings with religion, the state asserted its independence as an arbiter of religious plurality and manager of religious affairs. Religions, meanwhile, retained their insurgent potential against overarching state power, prompting the repression of religious movements deemed against "national interest." In his rise to power, Abiy sought to recruit this insurgent potency of religious idealism for his rapid reform agenda but clearly underestimated its particularizing force that came to light in numerous inter-religious clashes.

Secondly, the only other political capital with similar if not more purchasing power in Ethiopia is ethnicity, typically as an expression of marginalized political interests against a centralist state. Religion and ethnicity have an extremely complex and multi-layered relationship in Ethiopia (Østebø et al. 2021), but in much of the Ethiopian state narrative, ethnicity has been framed as a disintegrative force while ("properly managed") religion was drawn into representations of national unity. The only exception to this was EPRDF rule, where national unity was premised on the administration of ethnic diversity while religion, at least in official rhetoric, was relegated to the private sphere. Consequently, Abiy's radical dismantling of TPLF hegemony coincided with a revival of religious rhetoric in proclaiming a state that acknowledges but was no longer defined by ethnic differences. The historical depth of divine exceptionalism in the Ethiopian nation state ideal also explains why Abiy's political platform so far was able to survive its many harsh encounters with reality and still finds much support among certain constituencies. Yet as a Protestant Oromo, Abiy's only path to inherit this religious exceptionalism of the Abyssinian-Orthodox empire was what Robert Bellah (1970) called "civil religion". Accordingly, the Solomonic myth was extended into a pan-ethnic and multi-religious promise of "one nation under God."

Finally, this is linked to the ongoing religious pluralization of Ethiopia, of which Abiy (and in fact his predecessor Hailemariam Desalegn) is the latest political culmination. Politically, the privileged position of Orthodoxy was dismantled in a slow but so far unrelenting process from Haile Selassie's legal gestures at religious liberty, to the socialist parity in religious oppression and co-optation, and finally the post-Marxist instrumentalist secularity. Culturally, the Orthodox monopoly was diminished by the pluralization of Christianity in the rise of Pentecostalized Protestantism, as well as by an increased visibility and assertiveness of Islam. Yet contrary to classical secularization theories (e.g., Berger 1980), this pluralism has not made religion less relevant or less contested. Religion has retained its importance for community and identity formation and the resulting strains of religious pluralization are visible in contemporary Ethiopia. The political place of Islam in Ethiopia remains precarious despite Abiy's unprecedented overtures to Muslims. Likewise, the current Orthodox-"Pente" truce might well prove to be a fleeting effect of the current power constellation. With Neo-Orthodox movements prospering, the Church's ancient claim to cultural and political hegemony is never far. Whatever the future holds, Ethiopia's religious diversity will remain key to its promise of a nation state.

NOTES

1. For example, much has been made of Abiy's connections with American evangelicals and his attendance at Prayer Breakfasts, a central hub of evangelical lobbying in Washington (see, e.g., Verhoeven and Michael Woldemariam 2022, p. 14). Yet it was actually the Orthodox emperor Haile Selassie who brought the first Prayer Breakfast to Ethiopia in 1971 (New York Times 1971).
2. He was kept under house arrest and murdered by the Derg in August 1975 (Erlich 2019, pp. 182–5).
3. In particular, in 1981 an alleged secret Derg memorandum was published in various outlets that appeared to show a detailed plan for eradicating religion in Ethiopia. Its authenticity was denied by the government and later scholarship has concluded that the document was likely forged (Haile Larebo 1986, p. 156; Eide 2000, p. 163).
4. The last census (2007) has Protestants at 18.6%, but the latest Ethiopian Demographic and Health Survey (2016) suggests that this has grown to 23.4% among 15–49 year olds (Central Statistical Agency 2017). The (repeatedly postponed) next census would have to confirm these numbers,

although in the past the EDHS projections have been in line with the Protestant growth trajectory in the census figures. (For a more differentiated breakdown of Protestant growth, see Haustein 2014, p. 121.)

5. According to the above-mentioned story, he would have been a Pentecostal already in the autumn of 2000.
6. The Council gave itself a basic trinitarian formula, which by default excludes Oneness Pentecostals, a large group in Ethiopia (see Haustein 2013).

REFERENCES

"The Constitution of the Federal Democratic Republic of Ethiopia." 1995a. *Federal Negarit Gazeta of the Federal Democratic Republic of Ethiopia*, p. 1.

Abbink, Jon. 2011. Religion in Public Spaces: Emerging Muslim-Christian Polemics in Ethiopia. *African Affairs* 110: 253–274.

Abiy Ahmed. 2017. Countering Violent Extremism Through Social Capital: Anecdote from Jimma, Ethiopia. *Horn of Africa Bulletin* 29: 12–17.

———. 2019a. *[Synergy]*. Addis Ababa.

———. 2019b. *Lecture, Nobel Peace Prize 2019.* https://www.youtube.com/watch?v=jESA8MLAuCw.

Abiy Ahmed Ali. 2016. Social Capital and Its Role in Traditional Conflict Resolution: The Case of Inter-Religious Conflict in Jimma Zone of the Oromia Regional State in Ethiopia. PhD thesis, Addis Ababa University, Addis Ababa.

Ahmad, Abdussamad H. 2000. Muslims of Gondar 1864–1941. *Annales d'Éthiopie* 16: 161–172.

Andargachew Tiruneh. 1993. *The Ethiopian Revolution 1974–1987: A Transformation from an Aristocratic to a Totalitarian Autocracy*. Cambridge: Cambridge University Press.

Archbishop Yesehaq. 2005. *The Ethiopian Tewahedo Church: An Integrally African Church*. Nashville, Tennessee: Winston-Derek Publishers.

Arén, Gustav. 1978. *Evangelical Pioneers in Ethiopia: Origins of the Evangelical Church Mekane Yesus*, Studia Missionalia Upsaliensia; 32. Stockholm: EFS Förlaget.

Asad, Talal. 2003. *Formations of the Secular: Christianity, Islam, Modernity.* Stanford, CA: Stanford University Press.

Assefa Fisseha. 2006. Theory Versus Practice in the Implementation of Ethiopia's Ethnic Federalism. In *Ethnic Federalism: The Ethiopian Experience in Comparative Perspective*, ed. David Turton, 131–164. Oxford: James Currey.

Aymro Wondmagegnehu, and Joachim Motovu. 1970. *The Ethiopian Orthodox Church*. Addis Ababa: Ethiopian Orthodox Mission.

Bahru Zewde. 2001. *A History of Modern Ethiopia 1855–1991*. Addis Ababa: Addis Ababa University Press.

————. 2002. *Pioneers of Change in Ethiopia: The Reformist Intellectuals of the Early Twentieth Century*. Oxford: James Currey.

Bellah, Robert N. 1970. *Beyond Belief: Essays on Religion in a Post-Traditional World*. New York: Harper & Row.

Berger, Peter L. 1980. *The Heretical Imperative: Contemporary Possibilities of Religious Affirmation*. London: Collins.

Bonacci, Giulia. 2000. Ethiopia 1974–1991: Religious Policy of the State and Its Consequences on the Orthodox Church. In *Ethiopian Studies at the End of the Second Millennium: Proceedings of the XIVth International Conference of Ethiopian Studies November 6–11, 2000, Addis Ababa*, ed. Baye Yimam, Richard Pankhurst, David Chapple, Yonas Admassu, Alula Pankhurst, and Teferra Birhanu, 593–605. Addis Ababa: Institute of Ethiopian Studies, Addis Ababa University.

Central Statistical Agency. 2017. *Ethiopia Demographic and Health Survey 2016*. Rockville, MD: The DHS Programme.

Clapham, Christopher. 1969. *Haile-Selassie's Government*. London: Longmans.

Clarke, J. Calvitt. 2004. Seeking a Model for Modernization: Ethiopia's Japanizers. *Selected Annual Proceedings of the Florida Conference of Historians* 11: 35–51.

DeCort, Andrew. 2022. Christian Nationalism Is Tearing Ethiopia Apart. *Foreign Policy*, June 18. https://foreignpolicy.com/2022/06/18/ethiopia-pentecostal-evangelical-abiy-ahmed-christian-nationalism/.

Donham, Donald L. 1999. *Marxist Modern: An Ethnographic History of the Ethiopian Revolution*. Berkely, California: University of California Press.

Eide, Øyvind M. 2000. *Revolution and Religion in Ethiopia: Growth and Persecution of the Mekane Yesus Church, 1974–85*. Oxford: Currey.

Erlich, Haggai. 1994. Ethiopia and the Middle East: Rethinking History. In *New Trends in Ethiopian Studies. Papers of the 12th International Conference of Ethiopian Studies. Michigan State University 5–10 September 1994. Volume I: Humanities and Human Resources*, ed. Grover Hudson and Harold G. Marcus, 631–641. Lawrenceville, New Jersey: Red Sea Press.

Erlich, Haggai. 2019. *Haile Selassie: His Rise, His Fall*. London: Lynne Rienne Publishers, 2019.

Etalem Mesgana. 2020. *Amazing Miracle in Ethiopia Interview with Pastor Bekele Woldekidan Part II*. https://www.youtube.com/watch?v=ywTGtO8vEE4.

Etana Habte Dinka. 2018. Resistance and Integration in the Ethiopian Empire: The Case of the Macca Oromo of Qellem (1880s–1974). PhD thesis, SOAS, London.

Fantini, Emanuele. 2015. Go Pente! The Charismatic Renewal of the Evangelical Movement in Ethiopia. In *Understanding Contemporary Ethiopia: Monarchy, Revolution and the Legacy of Meles Zenawi*, ed. Gérard Prunier and Éloi Ficquet, 123–146. London: Hurst.

Freeman, Dena. 2013. Pentecostalism in a Rural Context: Dynamics of Religion and Development in Southwest Ethiopia. *PentecoStudies* 12: 231–249.

Galindo, Antoine. 2022. Religion and Politics Prove a Heady Mix for Abiy. *Africa Intelligence*, March 21.

Getachew Tamiru. 2021. Abiy Deserves Our Respect, Not Calls for Resignation. *Ethiopia Insight*, October 28.

Larebo, Haile. 1986. The Orthodox Church and the State in the Ethiopian Revolution, 1974–84. *Religion in Communist Lands* 14: 148–159.

Haustein, Jörg. 2009. Navigating Political Revolutions: Ethiopia's Churches During and After the Mengistu Regime. In *Falling Walls: The Year 1989/90 as a Turning Point in the History of World Christianity*, Studien Zur Außereuropäischen Christentumsgeschichte (Asien, Afrika, Lateinamerika); 15, ed. Klaus Koschorke, 117–136. Wiesbaden: Harrassowitz.

———. 2011. *Writing Religious History: The Historiography of Ethiopian Pentecostalism*, Studien Zur Außereuropäischen Christentumsgeschichte (Asien, Afrika, Lateinamerika); 17. Wiesbaden: Harrassowitz.

———. 2013. The New Prime Minister's Faith: A Look at Oneness Pentecostalism in Ethiopia. *PentecoStudies* 12: 183–204.

———. 2014. Pentecostal and Charismatic Christianity in Ethiopia: A Historical Introduction to a Largely Unexplored Movement. In *Multidisciplinary Views on the Horn of Africa*, Studien Zum Horn von Afrika; 2, ed. Hatem Eliese, 109–127. Köln: Rüdiger Köppe Verlag.

Haustein, Jörg, and Emanuele Fantini. 2013. Introduction: The Ethiopian Pentecostal Movement – History, Identity and Current Socio-Political Dynamics. *PentecoStudies* 12: 150–161.

Haustein, Jörg and Dereje Feyissa. 2022. The Strains of 'Pente' Politics: Evangelicals and the Post-Orthodox State in Ethiopia. In *Routledge Handbook on the Horn of Africa*, ed. Jean-Nicolas Bach, 481–494. London: Routledge.

Haustein, Jörg, and Terje Østebø. 2013. EPRDF's Revolutionary Democracy and Religious Plurality: Islam and Christianity in Post-Derg Ethiopia. In *Reconfiguring Ethiopia: The Politics of Authoritarian Reforms*, ed. Jon Abbink and Tobias Hagmann, 159–176. Abingdon: Routledge.

Haustein, Jörg, and Emma Tomalin. 2019. *Keeping Faith in 2030: Religions and the Sustainable Development Goals: Findings and Recommendations*. https://www.religions-and-development.leeds.ac.uk/research-network.

Hege, Nathan B. 1998. *Beyond Our Prayers: Anabaptist Church Growth in Ethiopia, 1948–1998*. Scottsdale, Pennsylvania: Herald Press.

Henze, Paul. 2001. *Layers of Time: A History of Ethiopia*. London: Hurst and Company.

Hussein Ahmed. 2006. Coexistence and/Or Confrontation? Towards a Reappraisal of Christian-Muslim Encounter in Contemporary Ethiopia. *Journal of Religion in Africa* 36: 4–22.

Makki, Fouad. 2011. Empire and Modernity: Dynastic Centralization and Official Nationalism in Late Imperial Ethiopia. *Cambridge Review of International Affairs* 24: 265–286.

Marcus, Harold G. 1975. *The Life and Times of Menelik II: Ethiopia 1844–1913.* Oxford: Clarendon Press.

———. 1994. *A History of Ethiopia.* Berkeley, California: University of California Press.

Merera Gudina. 2006. Contradictory Interpretations of Ethiopian History: The Need for a New Consensus. In *Ethnic Federalism: The Ethiopian Experience in Comparative Perspective,* ed. David Turton, 119–130. Oxford: James Currey.

Mohammed Dejen Assen. 2016. Contested Secularism in Ethiopia: The Contention Between Muslims and the Government. PhD thesis, Addis Ababa: Addis Ababa University.

Naol Befkadu. 2021. Dear Abiy, Please Resign: A Plea from a Fellow Ethiopian Evangelical. *Ethiopia Insight,* October 4.

New York Times. 1971. Prayer Breakfast Introduced in Ethiopia, January 17.

Østebø, Terje. 2012. *Localising Salafism: Religious Change Among Oromo Muslims in Bale, Ethiopia.* In *Islam in Africa; 12.* Leiden: Brill.

———. 2013. Islam and State Relations in Ethiopia: From Containment to the Production of a 'Governmental Islam'. *Journal of the American Academy of Religion* 81: 1029–1060.

Østebø, Terje, Jörg Haustein, Fasika Gedif, Kedir Jemal Kadir, Muhammed Jemal, and Yihenew Alemu Tesfaye. 2021. *Religion, Ethnicity, and Charges of Extremism: The Dynamics of Inter-Communal Violence in Ethiopia.* Brussels: European Institute of Peace. https://www.eip.org/wp-content/uploads/2021/03/Ostebo-et-al-2021-Religion-ethnicity-and-charges-of-Extremism-in-Ethiopia-final.pdf.

Provisional Military Government of Ethiopia. n.d. *Declaration of the Provisional Military Government of Ethiopia.* Addis Ababa. https://invenio.unidep.org/invenio//record/23120/files/ETH_A4039_9.pdf.

Rémy, Jean-Philippe. 2021. Abiy Ahmed, chef de guerre avec un prix Nobel de la paix. *Le Monde,* February 4. https://www.lemonde.fr/afrique/article/2021/02/04/abiy-ahmed-premier-ministre-d-une-ethiopie-entre-guerre-et-paix_6068696_3212.html.

Schaap, Fritz. 2021. Ethiopia's Chosen One: A Brutal War Waged By a Nobel Peace Prize Laureate. *Spiegel International,* October 28. https://www.spiegel.de/international/world/ethiopia-s-chosen-one-a-brutal-war-waged-by-a-nobel-peace-prize-laureate-a-d2f4d03e-90e4-49a4-918b-96d4543f722b.

Scholler, Heinrich, and Paul Brietzke. 1976. *Ethiopia: Revolution, Law and Politics,* Afrika-Studien; 92. München: Weltforum Verlag.

Schwab, Peter. 1985. *Ethiopia: Politics, Economics and Society.* London: Frances Pinter.

Shenk, Calvin E. 1972. *The Development of the Ethiopian Orthodox Church and Its Relationship with the Ethiopian Government from 1930 to 1970.* New York: New York University. PhD thesis.

———. 1994. Church and State in Ethiopia: From Monarchy to Marxism. *Mission Studies* 11: 203–226.

Spencer, John H. 1984. *Ethiopia at Bay: A Personal Account of the Haile Sellassie Years.* Algonac, Michigan: Reference Publications.

Teferra Haile-Selassie. 1997. *The Ethiopian Revolution 1974–1991: From a Monarchical Autocracy to a Military Oligarchy.* London: Kegan Paul International.

"The Constitution of the Federal Democratic Republic of Ethiopia." 1995b. *Federal Negarit Gazeta of the Federal Democratic Republic of Ethiopia*, p. 1.

The Economist. 2018. God Will Make You Prosper: Charismatic Christianity Is Transforming Ethiopia, November 24.

———. 2022. Make Me a City: Power and Planning in Ethiopia, June 18.

Tibebe Eshete. 2009. *The Evangelical Movement in Ethiopia: Resistance and Resilience.* Waco, Texas: Baylor University Press.

Tsahafe Taezaz Aklilu Habte Wold. 1966. Legal Notice No: 321 of 1966. Regulations Issued Pursuant to the Control of Associations Provision of the Civil Code of 1960. *Negarit Gazeta* 26: 1–10.

Vaughan, Sarah. 2015. Federalism, Revolutionary Democracy and the Developmental State, 1991–2012. In *Understanding Contemporary Ethiopia: Monarchy, Revolution and the Legacy of Meles Zenawi*, ed. Gérard Prunier and Éloi Ficquet, 283–311. London: Hurst & Company.

Verhoeven, Harry, and Michael Woldemariam. 2022. Who Lost Ethiopia? The Unmaking of an African Anchor State and U.S. Foreign Policy. *Contemporary Security Policy*, Online.

Wudu Tafete Kassu. 2006. The Ethiopian Orthodox Church, the Ethiopian State, and the Alexandrian See: Indigenizing the Episcopacy and Forging National Identity, 1926–1991. PhD thesis, University of Illinois, Urbana, IL.

Young, John. 1997. *Peasant Revolution in Ethiopia: The Tigray People's Liberation Front, 1975–1991.* Cambridge: Cambridge University Press.

CHAPTER 22

Christianity and Politics in a Polarized State: The Case of Nigeria

Bulus Galadima

INTRODUCTION

Nigeria has been in the news in recent times over the destructive and deadly religious *cum* ethnic violence perpetrated by the activities of the extremist Islamic group Boko Haram, Fulani Herdsmen, and other fundamentalist Muslim sects during the presidency of a Fulani Muslim. Despite all efforts, neither the Nigerian government nor the religious leaders have been able to respond effectively to stop these attacks. The promotion of interreligious dialogues has not been highly successful either. This chapter seeks to explain what factors contributed to the current situation. It posits that such understanding is vital and valuable for illuminating the reasons behind the presence and activities of fundamentalist Islamic groups for the rest of Africa. In Nigeria, not only do the religious relationships shape the politics and ethnic identity, but the politics has in turn also influenced the religious and ethnic understanding and actions within this political milieu. The West played a pivotal role in the creation of the current situation. Lamin Sanneh, for instance, has argued that the modern West created the

B. Galadima (✉)
Biola University, La Mirada, CA, USA

© The Author(s), under exclusive license to Springer Nature Switzerland AG 2023
S. Holzer (ed.), *The Palgrave Handbook of Religion and State Volume II*, https://doi.org/10.1007/978-3-031-35609-4_22

political and religious institutions and prescribed separation as the nature of the relationship between politics and religion. However, Africans (especially Muslims in Africa) did not subscribe to this assumption (Sanneh 1996, p. 87).

The 200 million person population of Nigeria, the most populous in Africa, is almost evenly split between Christianity and Islam, the two major religions. There have been several approaches to studying and understanding the contentious relationship between Christians and Muslims in Nigeria. Interreligious dialogue has been the oldest and most dominant. Nimi Wariboko has suggested that the current approach of interreligious dialogue is overused. He called for new approaches to study the religious interrelationship in the Nigerian geopolitical space. This study employs other lenses and approaches to contribute to the dialogue of the relationship between Christianity and Islam within the Nigerian political space (Reisacher 2017, pp. 57–59).

There has been a lot of religious violence in Nigeria and it is still ongoing. There are several efforts to catalog the atrocities committed against Christians. The evidence suggests a systematic targeting of Christians and minority ethnic groups, especially in the Middle-Belt region of Nigeria. The International Organisation for Peace Building and Social Justice through its subsidiary International Committee on Nigeria (ICON) in 2020 compiled a report of the activities of the terrorist group *Boko Haram* and of the Fulani Herdsmen, noting that they are two of the world's top five deadliest groups and they operate with impunity in Nigeria and the Lake Chad region. These groups have killed over 27,000 civilians and have displaced 2–3 million internally and externally (ICON 2020, pp. 13–17). Over 700 villages have been sacked and the likelihood of return is very slim (Akote et al. 2021). These atrocities have been going on for over twenty years. ICON classifies it as a silent genocide that has implications for the international community (ICON 2020, p. 119). These killings are daily occurrences with only a few making the headline news. Two notable ones were the murder of over forty people during worship in a Catholic church in Owo, Ondo state, on Sunday, June 5, 2022 (Babajide 2022), and the stoning and burning to death of a twenty-one-year-old female student, Deborah Samuel, for blasphemy by Muslims in Sokoto on Thursday, May 12, 2022 (The Guardian, May 23, 2022).

While such dastardly acts are often construed to be purely religious, I will argue that the activities of Islamic religious extreme groups in Nigeria have deeply rooted political and ethnic undertones. In other words, religion, ethnicity, and politics are inextricably linked among many Nigerians to the extent that they can easily be conflated. The way forward is neither a conflation nor a separation of religion and politics, but a form of dialogue that is rooted on the idea of human dignity and worth which are part and parcel of the traditional African value system that both Christians and Muslims and indeed African Traditional Religionist in Nigeria share.

Religion and Politics in Nigeria: A Complicated Relationship

The current Nigerian political system goes back to the colonial period. Andrew Walls explained that the Great European Migration "had religious as well as economic and political effects" (Walls and Ross 2008, p. 193). The colonial administrators and missionaries brought these systems into Africa. One cannot understand fully the current Nigerian situation without understanding these two Western groups. Vaughan opines that the nineteenth- and twentieth-century state of Nigeria was built on the structures of Christianity and Islam (Vaughan 2016). Wariboko builds on this by linking "the intricate dynamics of Christian-Muslim interactions to the political structure and ethos of state formation" (Reisacher 2017, p. 59). According to him, "[T]he two religions and the state are mutually shaping one another, and the trio together shape society's configuration of power" (Reisacher 2017, p. 60). Thus in order to adequately explain the Nigerian political milieu, one must address the complex interactions of Christianity, Islam, the colonial administration, and, to a large degree, the African Traditional Religion and culture because it has enduring qualities and features which have shaped and are still shaping Christianity and Islam.

Suffice it to say that the colonial administration cannot be equated with the missionaries. However, it must be admitted that they are "cut from the same cloth." Though their missions in Africa were different, they shared a similar worldview and there were times their activities and mission converged. There is no doubt that Christianity and colonization had profound and varied impact on African societies. On the eve of Nigeria's independence in 1960, "political competition between individual Nigerians and between ethnic and religious groups intensified." Niels Kastfelt has noted that the roots of the radicalization of religion which is threatening the existence of Nigeria as a nation that started in the 1980s can be partly traced to the politics of the 1950s before independence (Kastfelt 1994, pp. x & 1). But one can argue that it goes even earlier than that to the time of the early missionaries.

Copious historical evidence exists to show that the British Colonial Administration aided and abetted the emergent Muslim Hausa-Fulani political class in their bid to dominate the ethnic minorities in Northern Nigeria. This led the ethnic groups to unite and form their own political parties to resist the apparent, socio-political domineering posture of the Muslim Hausa-Fulani class. In order to fully comprehend what is happening, one has to consider the interactions by actors and factors at the local, regional, and national levels. This is because each of these levels adds a level of complexity to the political discourse and how the local and regional actors and/or factors related to the national and accessed the resources. Kastfelt summarizes it thus: "[A]t the national level the power of the new political class was mostly bureaucratically defined, whereas at the local level it was also based on ethnic and religious affiliation" (Kastfelt 1994, p. 4). The colonial administration created a political class that was an important link between the local and the regional and national, but this class did not align with the indigenous political structures. This caused a lot of disruption in African communities and society. For instance, "The British support of the Fulani led them to set up sharp physical boundaries for the work of the missionaries who were prohibited from operating in Muslim areas" (Kastfelt 1994, p. 18).

The missionaries created a new political elite whom they trained in the mission schools; consequently, "[t]he political impact of the mission schools in the 1940s and 1950s was not only due to its actual political influence, but also to the fact that the colonial administrators often held the view that the mission schools were clandestine centers of Nigerian political activities" (Kastfelt 1994, p. 22; cf. Ajayi 1965). For the most part, this political function of mission schools was not intentional but accidental (Sanneh 2009, p. 141, 146). In fact, this did not happen before the Second World War. Between the 1920 and 1930s, "newly converted Christians were occupied with religious not political matters" (Kastfelt 1994, p. 23). Kastfelt has demonstrated that the missionaries who came before the war were unprepared and unconcerned about political matters. Those who came after the Second World War, even if they were interested in political matters, were ill-equipped and generally apathetic. He noted that "not all missionaries were equally concerned with these wider problems of church development. Many of them were not particularly interested at all in general societal problems and did not clearly perceive the immediate consequences of the political changes for the churches" (Kastfelt 1994, p. 44). Though this was about the church in Adamawa Province, but the same could be said of the mission churches in general. Some Nigerian Christians began to complain that the missionaries did not treat them properly, portraying themselves like the colonial administrators. This led to clashes between some members of the church and the missionaries. This sometimes led to situations where anti-European slogans were directed toward the missionaries in the church (Kastfelt 1994, p. 45).

From the time of its founding as a homogeneous nation—the Lugard amalgamation of the Southern and Northern protectorates in 1914—Nigeria's history has been fraught with many social problems, the salient factors being ethnic, religious, and political. What was passed down by the colonial administration was the product of hapless and arbitrary political arrangements which was bound to ignite political, ethnic, and religious conflicts. Barely half a decade after Nigeria's independence from the British colonial administration, on October 1, 1960, the nation experienced political tumult followed by a Civil War precipitated by ethno-religious and political permutations. Matthew Kukah explained:

> After the project of the Nigerian state had been put in place by British colonialism, the British then logically … initiated the process of the subsequent modernization of the new state and its incorporation into the new economy. Even on a theological front, the systematic destruction, distortion and, in some cases, the outright elimination of the African religious universe by such universal religions as Islam and Christianity, all meant that today, the African religious worldview remains a severely fractured, disoriented and, some would say, a fractured macrocosm. As such, even in exercising its salvific role in the lives of African citizens, both Islam and Christianity became very serious sources of severe strains and disruptions on African polities as the new identities created by them would later have explosive consequences. (Kukah 1999, p. 39)

The contemporary civil process is full of many paradoxes. On the one hand, Nigerians gloat about their freedom from the colonial masters and rejoice in the fact that they are governed by their own laws and leaders, and on the other hand, they are constantly plagued by ethno-religious conflicts that threaten the unity of the nation. On the one hand, there is a phenomenal increase of religious awareness which is unprecedented in the history of the country with churches and mosques dotting the landscape, and, on the other hand, there is an alarming increase in religious intolerance, extremism, wanton corrupting influences, and contrivances noticeable among Christians and Muslims alike. These paradoxes are noticeably rooted in a shallow view of government and society that conflates religion and politics. Christianity and Islam—the two dominant religions—have inadvertently (and sometimes consciously) contributed in divergent ways in heightening tensions in the nation's socio-political order.

The question "Why are Nigerian Christians and Muslims opposed to one another?" is a complex one. Simplistic answers that many Nigerians have imbibed tend to point to the disparate religious creeds and the conflicting views of jihadist and pacifist traditions in Islam and Christianity, respectively. For instance, in Christianity the idea of separation of church and state could be traced back to Jesus' two statements: "Give to Caesar what belongs to Caesar and give to God what belongs God" (Matt. 22:20–22) and "[You] are not of the world just as I am not of the world" (John 17:16). While not advocating a separatist or dualist view, Jesus was later to be understood as setting the agenda for the distinction between the sacred and the temporal realms. In contrast to Jesus, Muhammad, the founder of Islam, did not make the distinction between what is sacred and what is secular. In a famous quote attributed to him in the Hadith, Muhammad enjoined his followers: "Work for this world as if you would live forever. Work for the world to come as if you would die tomorrow" (Brown 2000, p. 46). In the light of this injunction, the early Muslims saw their engagement in the political affairs of the society as that of a "religious imperative of implementing God's plan in this world" (Brown 2000, p. 47). While the messianic (political) expectations of the early followers of Jesus were dashed by what they might have perceived as Jesus' inability to overthrow the Roman government and establish a new kingdom on earth that would ameliorate their political and social plights, Muhammad was considered by his early followers to be not "only a prophet and a teacher, like the founders of other religions; he was also the head of a polity and of a community, a ruler and a soldier" (Lewis 1990, p. 266, 49).

In their attempt to persuade the indigenous peoples to throw away their traditional religions, the Islamist jihadists and Christian missionaries were radical in their insistence that their followers must dissociate themselves from members of other religions. In Christianity, the emphasis was on the need to separate oneself from unconscionable pagan influence of Islam and Traditional religions. Sanneh elucidated thus:

From the first century of its encounter with West Africa, missionary Christianity has encouraged the view that the overtaking of Islam is an over-riding consideration. Thus, whatever the real history of relations with Muslims, and however genuine the attempts to arrive at a sympathetic understanding of Islam, the myth has been perpetuated that Christianity is locked in a bitter rivalry with it, with Africa serving as the arena and the prize. Western colonialism merely bolstered this competitive myth and invested it with greater potency. (Sanneh 1983, p. 210)

In Islam, the emphasis was on dissociating from what was conceived as the underhanded nature of the Bible and the "unprincipled" doctrine of the Trinity. The jihadists adopted a militant non-conformist approach in their proselytization in Northern Nigeria while the Christian missionaries saw themselves as being saddled with the responsibility of liberating the natives from the scourge of animism and Islam. The colonial administration saw the *White Man's Burden* as that of civilizing *savage and dark* Africa among other things.

Not only did the Islamist jihadists and Western missionaries use radical and aggressive methods in their proselytizing agendas, but they also emphasized the need to completely throw away one's cultural norms, tra-ditions, belief system, and values. The Hausa-Fulani natives who embraced Islam through the activities of the jihadists saw themselves as having the mandate to convert other people to Islam using every available means. Equally, some of the Christian missionaries insisted that to be a Christian means to totally dissociate oneself from the indigenous African social, cul-tural, and political entanglements.

Consequently, most indigenous people began to throw away their rich cultural values of tolerance, unity, communal living, deference, honesty, and accountability to satisfy the demands of their newly found religions. Muslims and Christians gradually began to embrace the culture of the jihadists and the Western missionaries, respectively. The culture of the indigenous people was soon to be viewed as archaic, primitive, barbaric, and uncivilized. The Muslim jihadists and the Christian missionaries imposed their cultural, political, and social values as though they were part and parcel of the central messages of those religions. Nigerians subse-quently began to lose their unique cultural identity. Religion, therefore, gradually began to divide the people rather than unite them. Inevitably, a chasm of religious suspicion emerged. Christians became leery of Muslims and traditional religious adherents, and Muslims on their part became disgruntled and disenfranchised toward Christians and the African Traditionalists. The resultant consequences were enormous. Brothers and sisters became enemies on religious grounds.

Subsequently, therefore, Muslims and Christians began to see themselves as rivals with each camp fighting hard to conquer as many territories as possible. The consequent results were mutual suspicion, intolerance, and a constant struggle by both Muslims and Christians to gain territorial control. Missions in both religions became a matter of religious rhetoric and aggression. The Muslim clerics taught their followers to deride and be suspicious of Christians, and the Christians made every effort to propagate the sentiment that Islam is not a religion of peace but of the sword. The situation could rightly be described as that of "active aggressive suspicion." Active aggressive suspicion by Muslims and Christians soon became not only a matter of exerting control but also of religious violence as a means to prove, assert, and maintain that control. Religion gradually became politicized, and politics became religionized. Entire geographical landscapes were soon to be described in ethno-religious terms. To belong to a particular ethnic or tribal group meant to belong to a particular religion. Failure to identify with the religion of your ethnic or tribal group was considered perfidious—the oddity rather than the norm. Religion suddenly became a matter of territoriality.

The Nigerian Christians were taught by the missionaries that this world is not their home, hence the need to shun worldly affairs and the concomitant subtle entanglements. Politics was said to be a dirty game and Christians who got involved in the political affairs of their society were deprived of the sacraments of baptism and communion. Politics was for the unregenerate members of the society, or backslidden Christians not for committed Christians. Because of this, until fairly few decades ago, Nigerian Christians did not consider themselves as having a stake in the political process and governance of the nation. Because they had for a long time held to the Western idea of the separation of church and state, Nigerian Christians tended to downplay the political at the expense of and in preference of the religious.

Most present-day Nigerian Christians, like their Muslim counterparts, do not assume a separatist or dualistic outlook that forswears political participation. As a matter of fact, majority of contemporary Christians encourage active participation in politics. But this phenomenon is fairly a recent development. Nigerian Christians, it can be argued, have evolved in their theological thought about politics. About four decades ago, the popular form of Christianity in Nigeria was orthodox Protestantism, hence its emphasis on non-participation in politics. But with the popularization of African Pentecostalism, Christians gradually began to grasp the need for political involvement and participation, emphasizing that it is the only panacea for curbing the Islamization of the nation. For the missionaries and Nigeria Christians, the view that Islam is the challenge has not changed. While the missionaries adopted the separation of church and state and personal faith, the Nigerian Christians have evolved over time to adopt a more public faith and integration of church and state.

For Nigerian Muslims, religion has always been part of politics and politics is often depicted as a vehicle for religious promulgation and propagation. The Muslims believe that the state exists to promote Islam and the rule of Allah on earth. To be ruled by non-Muslims (infidels) was against the Islamic tenet. This is because of the understanding that Muslims are not "meant to be alien-ruled" (Cragg 1986, p. 6). Bernard Lewis noted that in Islam, "For true believers to rule misbelievers is proper and natural, since this provides for the maintenance of the holy law, and gives the misbelievers both the opportunity and the incentive to embrace the true faith. But for misbelievers to rule over believers is blasphemous and unnatural, since it leads to the corruption of religion and morality in society, and to the flouting or even the abrogation of God's law" (Lewis 1990, pp. 53–54). This explains why Nigerian Muslims have always deemed themselves as having the legitimate right of authority and civil governance. They therefore would not, either theoretically or practically, consider as equal those who belong to another religious tradition; and neither would they ever willingly cede political authority to non-Muslims. Sanneh was right in observing that "Islam takes command of prominent centers of public life, and from there proceeds to extend its sway over the rest of society. However, the trail by which Islam arrives has been blazed by traditional religions" (Sanneh 1996, p. 13).

While Nigerian Christians and Muslims share certain cultural norms and values, they are very much divided on religious and political grounds. The reason for this is not far-fetched: religion and politics are indissolubly linked. The truism often shows off its ugly head during political campaigns and elections. With the 2023 Nigerian presidential, national assembly, and governorship elections campaigns already on, the religious atmosphere of the country is already charged, and politicians, for better or worse, will use this to their advantage. Nigerian politics can rightly be described as the politics of religion in which one cannot but notice the politicization of religion and the religionization of politics.

The politics of religion in which religious sentiments, not socio-economic ideologies, take precedence is mostly seen during national elections. Politicians and some elite members of the Nigerian society understand the volatile nature of politics in terms of its religious connotations, and sadly most of them appeal to religion as a means to their political end. It is common for politicians to use religious rhetoric and misbegotten ruses during political campaigns with the sole purpose of deceiving the populace to vote for them on religious grounds. Matthew Kukah upbraids such unwanted conflation of religion and politics saying:

> Right before our eyes, what we call religious crises are often crises over unresolved antagonisms within the cleavages of the political classes. In their pursuit of their personal exploitations for accumulation, they are blind to the boundaries of religion and ethnicity. But in real life, our people are being held hostage by the darker forces of politics as politicians generate and deploy hostile narratives to divide the poor and the weak. (Kukah 2015)

Moreover, the Nigerian political atmosphere influenced the relationship between the missionaries and Nigerian Christians in the North. For example, the teachers in Christian Schools in Adamawa region in the Northeastern Nigeria, where Boko Haram is very active today, once unionized against the missionaries and asked for higher pay. Teachers and medical workers went on a ten-day strike in 1949. There were other issues like racism and hypocrisy of missionaries, that is, preventing Nigerian Christians from drinking while Christians in Denmark drank privately and publicly. These and more combined to energize this attitude of resisting the missionaries (Kastfelt 1994, p. 58).

Subsequently, when political parties were formed, the colonial administration sided with the Northern People's Congress (NPC) which was embraced by the majority of the Muslims. As Kastfelt explains, "The dominating position of the NPC can be explained, of course, by its intimate connection with the Islamic aristocracy and the local administrations in Northern Nigeria. … NPC dominance in the North was further strengthened by the support it received from most of the chiefs and emirs of the North, and most British colonial administrators in the North were generally known to sympathize with the party" (Kastfelt 1994, p. 72). However, as it turned out, the NPC was strongly opposed to the idea of minority demands for greater local self-determination.

This issue of minority self-determination has been a vexing issue in Nigeria from the time of its independence until now. Before independence, in 1957 the British Government established a commission (named after its chairman, Sir Henry Willink Commission, also referred to as the Minorities Commission) to study this matter. Christians made sure to let the commission know during their visit to Nigeria that "[t]he Christians felt that the British colonial administration constantly favoured the Muslim Fulani and Hausa" (Kastfelt 1994, p. 75). In fact, during their fact-finding mission in 1957, the *Sarkin Hong*, Chief of Kilba, imprisoned four Christians. Among the charges against them was talking about politics, preaching without the chief's permission, and claiming Christianity was better than Islam. This last charge was because one of them preached from St. John 14:6 which says, "[N]o man cometh to the Father, but by me." This matter was brought to the attention of the commission. Nothing was done about it. The colonial administration justified the imprisonment. The Christians of Northern Nigeria vehemently disputed this position. The report of the commission sided with the interest of the Colonial Administration. It said that "within the Northern System Muslim, Christian and pagan could live happily side by side and that there was a growing sense of loyalty to a Northern Region which was united by history and tradition" (Kastfelt 1994, p. 76).

This is still the case across huge swaths of Northern Nigeria, where inherent practices of blatant marginalization of the Christian viewpoint in the civic space almost unapologetically hold sway. Worse still, the evidence suggests this has been elevated to the level of impunity. Muslims in Nigeria feel at liberty to execute anyone they allege has committed acts of blasphemy. A most recent example is that of Deborah Samuel who was recently murdered in cold blood in Sokoto, Nigeria. The news of her gruesome murder made several headlines both nationally and internationally.

The state in West Africa is not only a strategic site for conflicts and collaborations between Christianity and Islam, but also co-opts them to steadily attack its citizens. The significant roles of Christianity and Islam in the function and dysfunction of the state, which is antagonistic to its citizenry, provide a veritable lens to ethically examine the political theology of state and society that conditions Christian-Muslim relations in postcolonial West Africa. Thus, the basic question this chapter asks and answers is this: how do the Christian-Muslim relations in West Africa shape state formation and statecraft and in turn feed from the same? These consider-ations will be directed toward unpacking the missiological implications of the logics of both religions intersecting and intertwining in state formation.

Wariboko is right that most of the conversation about politics and reli-gion in Nigeria has focused on interreligious dialogue between Christianity and Islam. He therefore proposes that moving the study of Christian-Muslim relations beyond the interpersonal relations level and setting it within *longue duree* of history makes it more robust. He says that the relationship between Christianity and Islam has affected state formation and that these two religions have in turn been and are being shaped by this interaction and by the state. He follows Vaughan who states that "Muslim and Christian structures set the foundation on which the state was grafted in the nineteenth and twentieth centuries. ... The state itself also acts to set the stage on which the structures of Christianity and Islam are interact-ing and developing; the two religions and state are mutually shaping one another, and the trio together shape society's configuration of power." He adds that "[t]he intersections and competitions of Islam and Christianity, which are decisive and integral for state formation, are important for understanding how interactions of Christianity with the state have shaped the philosophy of mission and patterned the evolution of Christian mis-sionary praxis in West Africa" (Reisacher 2017, p. 60). Wariboko's posi-tion aligns with Levtzion and Randall's observation of mutual influence between foreign religion and politics within the African context, observ-ing that,

> [i]n Africa, diversity has produced rich traditions of widely varied religious meanings, beliefs, and practices. Islam energized, enlivened, and animated life in African communities, and at the same time Islam has been molded by its African settings. As a result of the interaction between Muslim and African civilizations, the advance of Islam has profoundly influenced reli-gious beliefs and practices of African societies, while local traditions have "Africanized" Islam. The ways Islam has thrived in the rich panoply of continent-wide historical circumstances have fostered discord at least as often as these ways of Islam have helped realize unity and agreement. (Levtzion and Pouwels 2000, p. ix)

Statecraft is not new to West Africa. Prior to the coming of Islam, Christianity, and the colonial powers to West Africa, there were numerous kingdoms in this region going back several millennia succeeding each other. The Nok culture of Northern Nigeria, for example, dates back to c. 1000 BC and disappeared c. 300 AD. They engaged in iron smelting by 550 BC (Diamond 1997, p. 294). West Africa is a deeply religious sphere and thus a fertile ground for the reception of spirituality and religions of all kinds. But given the scope of this analysis, we will limit our remarks to Northern Nigeria. There is no doubt that British colonial administration had a profound impact on the nature, structure, and practice of both Christianity and Islam in Nigeria. One example of this is the current deli- cate attempt to balance power between all parties at the national level. If the presidential candidate is a Muslim, his deputy must be Christian, and the chairman of the party cannot be from the same religion as the presi- dent. These unwritten rules guide the selection of leaders into these posi- tions to ensure a balance of power and that no religion is dominating the other. It must be noted that the African Traditional Religionists are not included in this rotation.

Sanneh has suggested that the problem of Christian-Muslim relations facing Africa is also a challenge confronting the West not only because of the new face of Western societies but also because it gives secular political power primacy over religion and also because many Muslims are migrating to the West. These current issues in Africa will soon become Western issues as well (Sanneh 1996, pp. 111–145). Muslims, because of their holistic worldview, find it difficult to reconcile themselves/their religion/their practices to this Western ideology of confidence in the primacy of politics over religion.

Two Preachers, Different Legacies

To analogize the legacy of Islam and Christianity in modern Nigerian poli- tics, let's now turn to briefly compare two contemporary figures of Christianity and Islam in Northern Nigeria—Paul Gindiri and Abubakar Gumi—and how their lives buttressed the religious traditions of their time.

Sheikh Abubakar Mahmud Gumi (1922–1992)

No doubt, Sheikh Abubakar Mahmud Gumi was a central figure in Islam in Nigeria and had contributed immensely to its development and advo- cacy especially during the 1950s and 1960s. His influence continued into the twenty-first century particularly because of two important Islamic organizations associated with him: the Jama'atu Nasil Islam and Yan Izala.

The death of Ahmadu Bello in 1966 brought Gumi into the limelight of Islamic leadership in Northern Nigeria and indeed Nigeria. Karl Meier noted, "Although he rarely addressed a press conference, he was a favourite source for Western and Nigerian journalists wishing to gauge the political temperature of northern Nigeria" (Meier 1992).

Gumi was born in 1922 in Gummi near Sokoto. He excelled in both Qur'anic and Western education and was quickly noticed by Ahmadu Bello, the Premier of Northern Nigeria from 1954 to 1966. He studied law and trained to be a qadi at the Kano Law School (aka Northern Provinces Law School/School of Arabic Studies) (Aliyu and Sifawa 2018, pp. 66–87) from 1943 to 1947. He later studied in Sudan. Gumi met Bello in Mecca during a pilgrimage in 1955 (Hill 2010, pp. 20–21). Impressed by the young scholar from Sokoto, Bello made Gumi his interpreter in Saudi Arabia during his visit to North Africa. Gumi cherished his relationship with the late Premier, Ahmadu Bello. About his relationship with Ahmadu Bello, later in a 1987 interview, Gumi said, "I was the man behind him" (Loimeier 1997, p. 112). Gumi was also given several influential roles such as liaison in affairs concerning the condition of Nigerian Muslims in Saudi Arabia, deputy Grand Khadi (and later Grand Khadi) of Northern Nigeria, and member of the Supreme Council of the University in Medina, Saudi Arabia.

At that time, Nigeria was a British colony and there was a suspension of the diplomatic relationship between Britain and Saudi Arabia over the British attack on Egypt in 1956. In an effort to forestall the deportation of Nigerians living in Saudi Arabia, Bello, Tafawa Balewa, and Gumi sent a Nigerian envoy to replace the British Consulate in Jedda to protect the Nigerian pilgrims in 1958. All these diplomatic arrangements were secured two years before Nigeria became independent. Unsurprisingly, Gumi is quoted to have once said in Hausa, "*Siyasa tafi muhimmanci da sallah*" (Politics is more important than prayer.)

Gumi cared about the Nigerian Muslim masses and gave them a voice. Under the advice of Ahmadu Bello, he was a key contributor to the founding of an Islamic organization called *Jama'atu Nasril Islam* (Society for the Support of Islam) in 1962. Over a decade later, along with one of his students, Sheikh Ismaila Idris (1930–2000), he founded a new Islamic organization called *Jama'at Izalat al-Bid'a wa-Iqamat as-Sunna* (The Association for the Eradication of the Innovation and the Establishment of the *Sunna* or Tradition) in 1978. This group, which is now a strong movement, is known in Hausa as *Yan Izala* (children of Izala). Gumi "stressed the importance of education for the Muslim masses in order to cleanse the religion of all bid'a [heresy]" (Loimeier 1997, p. 16 & 327). Jonathan Hill describes it as an organization that promotes Islamic juris-prudence and literal interpretation and observance of the Qur'an (Hill 2010, p. 18). Gumi was the first religious leader in Nigeria to charge Sufism with heresy and innovation. This resulted in a severe fracture within Islam in Northern Nigeria.

Over the years Gumi consolidated his power and influence and became more radicalized. He exploited the dissatisfaction of the masses with the leadership and domination of the Hausa-Fulani elites who were not as devout as they desired. He promised the masses a pure Islamic State. A utopia where all Islamic laws would be implemented including the *zakat* tax on the wealthy to redistribute to the poor.

Among Gumi's accomplishments was the empowerment of Muslim women and their integration into various facets of life. Loimeier explained, "The push for better Islamic education has increased considerably, and since the 1970s the Muslim women have been gradually integrated into the social and political life of the country. Abubakar Gumi and the '*Yan Izala* also stressed the importance of better education for women. ... At the same time Gumi supported the stronger participation of women in the political process, at least since 1982, even if this strategy in the beginning grew primarily out of tactical considerations in regard to the 1983 federal elections for which the Muslim women had to be mobilized as voters" (Loimeier 1997, p. 17). Gumi's opponents had to follow suit to empower women. Thus, Gumi led in strengthening of religious issues, but also in politicization of Islam in Nigeria. This is another illustration of how the context was shaping religion. Loimeier has observed that "Gumi was much more concerned with the conversation of the political power of the Muslims and not so much with the criticism of certain un-Islamic aspects of the Shagari administration. ... Gumi supported the political mobiliza-tion of Muslim women" (Loimeier 1997, p. 166).

Nigerian Muslim women in 1985 founded Federation of Muslim Women's Association of Nigeria (FOMWAN) with the support of Gumi and *Yan Izala*. These women felt it was their duty not only to vote but also to run for and occupy political office so that they are not dominated by non-Muslims. In one interview over political leadership, Gumi said the polarization in Nigeria is not between the North and the South, but between Christianity and Islam. He did not believe a Muslim should join a party where a non-Muslim is the leader. Over this issue, he was willing to divide Nigeria (Loimeier 1997, pp. 170–171). There is no question that *Yan Izala* imitated some of the strategies of the Christian Evangelistic Group known as New Life for All. Following the example of their Christian counterparts, 'Yan Izala travel from town to town in Northern Nigeria holding large gathering of Muslims, preaching and teaching in public squares. They mount large loudspeakers on vehicles playing Islamic music or messages.

Gumi accepted General Gowon as the Nigerian Military Head of State as long as there was a Muslim who could help codetermine the policy of the regime. His position changed when a Northern Nigerian Muslim chief of army staff was replaced by a Christian from the Middle-Belt region. Again, Gumi was cordial with the government during General Obasanjo's regime when there was a Muslim in the Head of the State's Cabinet (Loimeier 1997, pp. 163–165). Clearly, the founding of an Islamic organization called Jama't Nasir Islam (JNI) in 1962 with the support of Gumi further entrenched the politicization of Islam in Northern Nigeria. This likely became the most significant alliance of Muslims in Northern Nigeria. "This organization was to take on the task of improving Islamic education of the Muslims in the North and to serve as a platform for the promotion of the political and religious aims of Muslims in Nigeria" (Loimeier 1997, p. 113).

Moreover, Gumi was not only a religious leader. He also held prominent positions in the government. He was appointed advisor to the Federal Government by General Murtala Mohammed in 1975 and was appointed the Grand Mufti of Nigeria in 1976. In this capacity, he was to oversee the Federal Shari'a Court of Appeal in Nigeria, the highest position in the Nigerian Islamic judicial system. The second part of this appointment did not fully materialize because Murtala Mohammed was assassinated in a coup. His successor, General Olusegun Obasanjo's regime, did not follow through to create a Federal Shari'a Court of Appeal with this appointment. However, Gumi continued to draw salary for this post until 1986 when he retired (Loimeier 1997, pp. 164–165).

Gumi was a pragmatist. He sought to use political means to accomplish his goals because that was both effective and efficient. At the height of his popularity among Muslims in Northern Nigeria (1978–1979), Gumi made two critical decisions that also marked the beginning of his decline. First, he openly supported the militant anti-Sufi posture of *Yan Izala*. Second, he supported the election of Shehu Shagari, his classmate in grade school, and could not bring himself to criticize Shagari's government when leaders in his administration were openly accused of corruption. These two acts alienated a lot of Northern Muslims. Gumi lost his hegemony over the Muslim *Umma* in Northern Nigeria. He even supported the re-election of Shagari in 1983 by mobilizing women (Loimeier 1997, p. 166).

Gumi who is recognized in the Islamic world as a scholar of repute died in London on September 11, 1992. He translated the Koran into Hausa, a language spoken by millions of people in Northern Nigeria and other countries in Africa. For this he was awarded the King Faisal International Award considered to be the highest service honor in Islam. Over the years, he forged friendships with the leaders of many Islamic countries in the Middle East. He procured millions of dollars for Islamic causes in Nigeria. These countries and groups sought his counsel when they were considering making donations to Islamic groups in Nigeria (Loimeier 1997, pp. 154–157). Gumi has influenced Islam and politics in Nigeria and his legacy is being carried on by his son, Sheikh Ahmad Gumi, who also commands some degree of national prominence in religion and politics.

Evangelist Paul Gofo Gunen Gindiri (1935–1996)

Paul Gindiri was born in 1935 in Pumbush Gindiri, Plateau State, Nigeria, to non-Christian parents, but became a Christian to the consternation of his father (Dung 2002, p. 5). He attended a mission in junior primary school but could not continue because his father refused to pay for his education. Although he had never left his village, Gindiri dreamt of going to the city of Jos, Nigeria, in search of a better life. He shared this dream with his parents, and they had conflicting views. His father opposed the idea because he would lose his son's help on the farm. But his mother supported it and gave Paul more money to add to what he had saved. This made it possible for him to go to the city (Dung 2002, p. 8).

Paul Gindiri became a very successful truck driver traveling to different towns in the Northeastern part of Nigeria. During his many travels, he encountered Muslims and learned the Hausa language and a great deal about Islam (Dung 2002, pp. 17–20). After a spell of profligacy, he rededicated his life to Christianity and began outreach to Muslims. He engaged in public preaching and debating with Muslims in the city of Jos. He was a polemicist and a fearless evangelist, modeling his life and preaching after the Apostle Paul (Gaiya 2004). While Gindiri preached in the streets, he experienced hostility from some of the Muslims. On one occasion people threw sand at him and in another a man tried to whip him. Later in life regular death threats became common phenomena for him (Dung 2002, pp. 37–41).

With the formation of an evangelistic outreach group called *New Life For All* (*Sabon Rai Don Kowa*), Paul Gindiri found like-minded believers with whom he went deeper into the heart of Hausa land, many of which places the colonial administration had prevented missionaries from penetrating. During this period the new chief of Jos converted to Christianity. Ahmadu Bello mounted pressure on the chief to convert to Islam, but he refused and supported mission work in Jos (Dung 2002, p. 32). Gindiri revitalized and personally funded the New Life For All (NLFA) forming Gospel teams to go out on evangelistic outreaches. He continued these ventures from the late 1960s into the 1980s. He went into Muslim areas and emirates where the gospel had not been preached before. His usual practice was to make a courtesy call on the Emir of the town he was entering to greet him and inform him of his intentions. He would get permission from the chief or Emir to preach on the palace grounds (Gaiya 2004). On many occasions Gindiri and his team were arrested and prosecuted before Muslim judges and later released.

Gindiri began a transportation business using his personal trucks to support outreaches to different parts of the North. "Since he had the resources, he felt nothing could deter him from preaching the gospel in the emirates" (Dung 2002, p. 87). As a firebrand evangelist in the 1970s in the middle belt, Gindiri was one of the greatest Christian revivalists of all times in Northern Nigeria. Many Christians in Northern Nigeria credit him for the spiritual revival in their lives (Gaiya 2004). He mobilized a lot of Christians in Northern Nigeria and they suffered greatly for it. Several acts of atrocities were committed against Christians. Churches were, and are still, often denied land certificates in Muslim states. They were maltreated, denied their basic rights, or even killed (Dung 2002, p. 88). Though many Muslims disliked or even hated him for his message, they respected him for his candor, courage, honesty, and high moral integrity in his business dealings. Gaiya credits him with proposing Christian response to Muslim violent attacks and calls him "the architect of the theology of Christian self-defense in Nigeria" (Gaiya 2004). This position became widely adopted by Christians in Northern Nigeria and by the Christian Association of Nigeria (CAN). Gindiri had several encounters with the government. He was a critic of the government corruption and the unfair treatment of Christians.

Paul Gindiri's influence on Nigerian Christianity and politics is only limited to Northern Nigeria. His is only remembered by the generation who knew him. He died on April 8, 1996. He is succeeded by his son, Musa Paul Gindiri, who is an evangelist. However, he does not have the type of influence his father had.

Notice that the contrast between these two religious leaders is stark. Let's turn to briefly examine some similarities and differences between Sheikh Abubakar Gumi and Evangelist Paul Gindiri who are emblematic of the state of Christian and Muslim political engagement in Nigeria.

First, let's consider some similarities. There is no doubt that both men were respected by the followers of their religions and had great following among the masses of their respective religions in Nigeria (and beyond). They were very passionate about their religion and promoted the purity of their religion. Both men were fearless and spoke boldly against political leadership when they deemed fit, making them strong critics of the government. They both influenced the formation of grassroots movements in their respective religions. Both supported the use of force where necessary to defend their religion.

In contrast, however, they differed in how they engaged in politics. Gumi held political offices throughout his career and was deeply involved in politics, holding regional and national positions. Right from his youth, Gumi was in the corridors of power. He was always involved in politics in one way or the other. He held several positions and even represented Nigeria in Saudi Arabia. However, his involvement has always been connected with the promotion of Islam. But Gindiri, on the other hand, never engaged in partisan politics as an official or hold a position in Government. He prided himself as not being a politician even though he spoke strongly about political issues. While Gindiri did not organize beyond his evangelistic outreaches in Northern Nigeria, Gumi had influence nationally and internationally. Gindiri neither took political office nor held one. Though both men had significant influence on their various constituents, Gumi was more intellectual and adept at using the political sphere than Paul Gindiri. While Gindiri's influence was in the lives that he touched and interacted with, he did not have direct legacy in the political realm. But Gumi's influence was on individuals and on the political stage nationally.

NIGERIAN CHRISTIANS IN POLITICS

As previously noted, the missionaries did not encourage Christian participation in politics in Nigeria. If anything, they seemed to dissuade Christians from such involvement. But as time went by, Nigerian Christians began to see the need for political engagements. The idea of cultural self-perception coupled with the existential realities with which they were confronted in the new order helped in fostering the need for political participation. Kastfelt identified four paths into political activism. First, obtaining mission education and serving in the military. Second, obtaining mission education and then doing theological training through church and secular leadership. Third, going to a mission school and then proceeding to earn higher degrees in other fields of study in Western education. Fourth, obtaining mission education and getting into business and becoming financially independent. "These were paths to the local, regional and national political centres, where the distribution of bureaucratic resources was controlled, and from where it could be channeled to the local communities" (Kastfelt 1994, pp. 128–129).

The missionaries, at best, were ambivalent about the idea of Christians in politics and their relationship with political power. As a result, most Nigerian Christians held similar views. They held a dichotomized instrumentalist view of the world that separated secular and sacred realms of life. If a Christian engaged in politics, it was because of what politics could do for the church, not as a career for self-promotion and aggrandizement. Thus, no politician was supported or promoted by any church or denomination during the independence struggle. Christians who were involved in politics were conflicted about it. Because of the misguided hermeneutics of the missionaries, Christians who engaged in politics felt like they were doing something that was not ideal for a Christian. They struggled with their conscience on whether they could participate in politics and still be faithful Christians. The prominent Scripture passages they used to justify their position were Matthew 22:21 where Jesus encouraged His followers to render to Caesar what is Caesar's and render to God what is God's, and Joshua's declaration to the Israelites that they must choose whom they would serve (Joshua 24:15). Politics was seen as Caesar's realm, not God's. To engage in politics was to serve the world rather than God.

When Nigerian Christians began to engage in politics, they justified their activism by saying it was to protect the church from being overrun by Muslims. They also argued that since Christians were saddled with the responsibility of being the light of the world, active political engagement was one of the ways to bring that mandate to fulfillment. Some also referred to Moses and David as models of people who engaged in leadership and politics. The goal was to save the church from misrule and injustice (Kastfelt 1994, p. 137).

For the most part Christian participation in politics was instrumental. It was to protect and benefit the church, not necessarily as an advocacy for good governance for all. The thought of good governance often emerged when people engaged in politics for the survival of their ethnic group. The missionaries and Nigerian Christians at this time viewed power and politics as corrupt or impure. Even today politics and power are still suspect among Nigeria Christians. At best, they are perceived as a necessary evil we must live with rather than as neutral concepts and a realm which can be used for good or evil. The Nigerian Christian agency and self-determination on participating in politics are even more notable because the same scriptures that were used by the missionaries to justify separation of church and state were also used by Nigerian Christian politicians to engage in politics.

It would appear that Nigerian Christian political activism in contemporary times is motivated primarily by ethnic determination and secondarily by Christian preservation. The evidence of this is seen in the manner in which Nigerian Christians respond to news of attacks on Christians in the far North. Christians are only outraged enough by the attacks to take action when it happened to a person they know or if the victim is from their ethnic group. However, things are changing slowly, probably because Christians in the South, in particular, are sensing that they are also in imminent danger. This is probably good because there is no biblical mandate to "defend Christianity" through the use of force. Ethnic preservation is conflated with Christian preservation in the communities facing attacks because these two groups are often coterminous.

Nigerian Christians were ill-equipped to engage in politics. They had to figure this out on their own because the missionary Christianity bequeathed to them did not address the issues of their socio-political and economic existence. Western presence in Nigeria through the duo of the British Colonial administration (directly) and the missionaries (indirectly) combined, though unwittingly, and emasculated the indigenous non-Muslim groups and Christians from any meaningful political activism. The British colonial administration wanted the missionaries to curtail the political activism of the Christians. They penalized some missionaries for the political activity of some Christians.

THE QUESTION OF COLONIAL LEGACY
AND CONTEMPORARY REALITIES

As Jared Diamond has observed, "Africa's past has stamped itself deeply on Africa's present" (Diamond 1997, p. 137). After the abolition of the slave trade in all British territories, it was suggested that trading in natural resources would be more profitable than trading in human beings. Thus, the African interior attracted European missionaries and philanthropists who brought the Bible and the plough. Europeans formed companies to explore natural resources for the industries of Europe (1841). The Landers Brothers combined religious, commercial, and scientific interests in their exploration. They supported the Anglican Christian Missionary Society's (CMS) work of evangelizing the interior and had missionaries like Rev. J.F. Schon a German CMS missionary and Samuel Ajayi Crowther on their team (Dung 2002, p. 93). At the Berlin Conference in 1884, Africa was eventually partitioned among the European countries. However, less than half a century later in the 1880s the Royal Niger Company, under the leadership of George Goldie, separated the mercantile and religious interests in order to ensure greater profit margins. "Goldie's work resulted in the reduction of other European commercial competition in Nigeria. He also went into the interior of the North of Nigeria and made treaties with Chiefs and with the Northern Emirs" (Dung 2002, p. 95). In some cases, Goldie was hostile toward Christian missionary work.

By 1900 when Northern Nigeria was declared a British Protectorate by Frederick Lugard, the colonial administration decided to follow the separationist path charted by the Royal Niger Company and to keep missionary work from interfering with political administration "because he believed that they were more of a hindrance than a help. He also felt they created problems in dealing with Muslims" (Dung 2002, p. 96). There appeared to be some flexibility on this issue with Lugard himself, but with time, the position of his successors on this issue calcified.

The British colonial presence in Nigeria was clearly a capitalist venture with little if any Christian religious or humanitarian interest. Thus, the colonial administration made treaties with the existing Islamic leadership to ensure it got access to the natural resources (Dung 2002, p. 96). By so doing, it further strengthened the political grip and influence of the Muslim leaders over territories that they previously had not conquered. In a bid to ease their administration, the British colonial rulers placed non-Muslim groups in the Middle-Belt region, under the rulership of titular

Muslim leaders. These non-Muslim groups were majorly composed of people who had never been previously conquered by the Muslims or ever historically under Islamic rule or emirates (Dung 2002). Turaki said, "Many of the NMG [Non-Muslim Group] were forcefully placed under the Hausa-Fulani rulers, against their wishes. Thus, under colonialism, the hegemony of the Hausa-Fulani over the NMG was consolidated and the continuation of the dominance of Sokoto Caliphate. ... It was for this reason that the Muslim groups had a social and historical advantage over the NMG" (Turaki 2017, pp. 132–133).

Missionaries were allowed to go anywhere, but they were barred from Muslim territories without the permission of the Emirs. Thus, the British Colonial administration basically legitimized and entrenched the Islamic political leadership in Northern Nigeria. This system of indirect rule gave the Muslim Emirs a strong and privileged position in the colonial admin-istration. Although the British implemented numerous changes in the areas of finance and taxation, the judicial system, and territorial law, "they did not question the existing social system in the North, but modernized it along existing lines" (Loimeier 1997, p. 5). The British colonial policies "institutionalized" the conflict between Christianity and Islam giving the latter "superior status and socio-political roles" (Turaki 2017: p 131).

The policy of favoring Muslims continued until all the missionary orga-nizations in the Middle-Belt region held a meeting in Miango, near Jos, Nigeria, in the early 1900s. They reached a unanimous decision to go against the colonial government's restriction of access to Muslim areas to preach the gospel. In his speech, Bingham, one of the founders of SIM (Sudan Interior Mission), said,

We never sought government aid when we went into these provinces before the British occupation. We claim that since that occupation, the British gov-ernment has no right to bar our entrance. While acknowledging our debt to many friendly residents who have sought to aid us, we refuse any longer to leave the question of religion to be decided by residents or governors, many of whom have no interest in the religious. We ask for our Muslim fellow-subjects of the British crown the same religious liberty that we ask for our-selves. ... With our final appeal to government, therefore, we should serve notice that now we ask for rights. We are not supplicating for favors, and if these rights cannot be assured to us, then we must take the only course left open: We are going into the northern territories as ambassadors of Jesus Christ, who, sitting upon the Throne of power says, 'All authority is given to me in heaven and on earth. Go ye therefore and make disciples of all the nations.' (Dung 2002, pp. 101–102)

With this resolution, Christian missionaries declared their "independence" from the colonial administration and asserted their freedom to enter all territories and to preach unrestricted and undeterred. However, they were mindful to stay clear of political entanglements. Still, they did not consider it expedient to equip the (especially, Northern) Nigerian Christians to participate in politics.

I contend that during the colonial era just before independence, Ahmadu Bello, a grandson of the nineteenth-century Jihadist Shehu Usman Dan Fodio and the premier of Northern Nigeria at independence, sought to modernize the North through administrative reforms in the bureaucracy, the judiciary, educational systems, and religion. He made strenuous efforts to overcome apparent religious divisions and contradictions among the Muslims, desiring to and strengthening their unity (Loimeier 1997, p. 325). Ahmadu Bello strongly promoted further integration of Islam and politics. Loimeier observed, "Since the 1950s the religious scholars together with their supporters have taken active part in politics and become sought-after partners for the political parties" (Loimeier 1997, p. 326). He had earlier explained,

> Promotions to the top posts in the regional civil service were given to those who were prepared to convert to Islam …. at the same time pursued the Northernization policy by which southerners were removed from the northern Nigerian civil service. … He went on mass islamization campaigns, promising lots of political and material advantages to prospective converts …. many non-Muslims in Nigeria began to harbour the fear that he was using his political position as a weapon to give a new face to the jihadic islamization process. Thus, the minorities of the Middle Belt who had successfully resisted the jihadists' [sic] in its military aspects now feared that they would be subjected to political pressure and discrimination to force them to become Muslims. (Loimeier 1997, p. 59)

IMPLICATIONS FOR CHRISTIANITY AND POLITICAL ENGAGEMENT IN AFRICA

One of the ways the state demonstrated its control over ecclesiastical matters was through the seizing of church and school buildings in many countries in Africa. In Ethiopia in 1955, the revision of the constitution said that the Ethiopian Orthodox Church was an established Church with state backing. Symbolizing the state approval, the Emperor's and Patriarch's thrones were beside each other in the Cathedral in Addis. The church gave the Emperor the right to attend the synod. He was also given veto power over decisions. During this period, the elected Archbishop swore an oath of allegiance to the Emperor (Sanneh 1996, p. 93).

In the 1970s, the churches in Ethiopia, Angola, and Mozambique faced difficult times because of the socialist or Marxist regimes. Elsewhere on the continent things were difficult for Christians. In 1977 in Uganda under General Idi Amin, Archbishop Lanani Luwum was murdered. In the 1980s there were political tensions that affected the church in Liberia, Zaire, Nigeria, the Sudan, Zambia, and Kenya (Sanneh 1996, p. 93). As Sanneh explained, "When the church entered confidently and uncritically upon the heritage of its secular captors, it gave up its autonomy as the price for being included in the affairs of state. This created a peculiar situation: the church appropriated the national cultural enterprise as a devout vocation, fitting into Locke's idea of 'the reasonableness of Christianity,' though the ideal vocation, with intrinsic religious merit was abandoned" (Sanneh 1996, pp. 132–133).

It is important to note that the form of Christianity that came to Africa was too Western and out of step with "the African experience to enable people to decide what religious foundations to put in place for constructing a new society in new times" (Sanneh 1996, p. 134). While Christians were at a loss on how to engage issues of state and society, the Muslims knew exactly what to do and how to use the colonial administration to their advantage. Sanneh says, "[I]f it is the case that Christians are mere rookies at the game of politics and state building, then it is hard to see how they could be charged with public responsibility for the policies of colonial regimes in Africa and for the enduring effects of those policies in postcolonial Africa" (Sanneh 1996, p. 134).

Muslims, on the other hand, who knew how to engage the colonial administration, were "masters of their own affairs, even where they are only a tiny fraction of the population" (Sanneh 1996, p. 134). In Northern

Nigeria, they got the British colonial administration to ban Christians from offering catechetical instruction in areas where Muslims resided. One ruler who converted to Christianity from Islam was deposed and Christian places of worship were torn down by the British Colonial Administration. And "[w]hen the Chief of Kabwir became sufficiently interested in the Gospel to neglect some of the rights associated with his office, he was replaced by the government. A Sura Chief with similar sympathies was replaced because he discontinued the practice of compulsory Sunday farming" (Dung 2002, p. 101). The consequences were enormous. "Thus colonialism became the Muslim shield and the guarantor of Islam as the public alternative to Christianity for Africans" (Sanneh 1996, pp. 134–135).

Unfortunately, the colonial legacy that created the conditions for which many Nigerian Muslims think and act as if they are the only candidates with an inherent right to rule Nigeria perpetually continues to be venerated by some Muslim fundamentalists. As Sanneh clarified, "Muslims are not reassured by the doctrinal minimalism of Christians and others who are willing to accept humanly constructed national constitutions for a secular state, but refuse the role of revealed law in public affairs. Or, equally inconsistently, Christians plead for ethnic or cultural priority over any claim for religious primacy, and yet insist that they speak also as religious people. Yet, how can religion count for anything when thus reduced to an ethnic decoy or a cultural filter?" (Sanneh 1996, p. 132). In Northern Nigeria, the colonial administration through its indirect rule policy promoted Islamic interest in governance and denied the African Indigenous Religionists and African Christian participation. "Thus, colonialism, while strengthening Muslim territoriality, reinforced the privatization of Christianity" (Sanneh 1996, p. 135).

Even in contemporary times, there are still some Nigerian Christians who are suspicious of political engagements. While the African Pentecostal and the Charismatic movements have promulgated the idea of Christian socio-political engagements in the past four decades, some Christians still think that politics is purely a secular realm thereby widening the gap between the sacred and the secular. As Sanneh put it, "A notion has grown that politics impinge on religion in a superior way: that the state as the superior and ultimate representation of human reality will survive the demise of religion and, meanwhile, must actively work toward that end. The state has seized on its instrumental capacity to press its right to limitless power" (Sanneh 1996, pp. 96–97). Contrary to the Nigerian Christian proclivity to dichotomize the secular from the sacred realms, however, an Islamic communiqué states:

> Muslim demand for the full and uninhibited application of the Shari'a remains, not only a priority, but a lifetime objective of the Council of 'Ulama, and of every Muslim in the country; so also has the demand for Islamic education, a just and equitable economic system, and an appropriate political dispensation. Muslim total opposition to secularism remains firm and unshakeable; the idea of separation of religion and state is universally acknowledged as a Christian concept and is absolutely alien to Islam. Muslims want to live entirely under the guidance of Islam, in obedience to Allah and his messenger and have nothing whatsoever to do with secularism! (Loimeier 1997, pp. 378–379)

The first observation about this statement is the attack on secularism, which is foreign not only to Islam but also to the African worldview, which is otherwise holistic. However, secularism is wrongly labeled as Christian. The next observation is that the demand for Islamic education and life under Shari'a is curiously parallel to the demand by the radical group in Nigeria called *Boko Haram*. It should be noted that the communiqué was issued by the Council of 'Ulama—the learned Islamic scholars, not the radicals. What was in the view of a few scholars three decades ago has now become a mainstream and extremist position. The last paragraph of the communiqué is quite revealing. It says,

> Finally, the Muslims all over the country are hereby called upon to do all in their power to defend the cause of Allah and to take all necessary steps to defend themselves as they can no longer rely on the state and its security agencies. For the Muslims have every reason to believe that the army, the police, and state security services are not willing to protect the life, honor, and property of Muslims. The Muslims are also called upon to take it a duty to pray to Allah for Islam to prevail and for the continued strength of the Muslim umma. Allah's message is sufficient as an assurance and a consolation: "Turn unto Allah for aid, and have patience in adversity. Verily, all the earth belongs to God: he gives a heritage to us as He Wills of His servants; and the future belongs to the God-conscious. ... It may well be that your Sustainer will destroy your foe and make you inherit the earth: and thereupon He will behold how you act" (Qur'an: 7:128–29). (Loimeier 1997, pp. 378–379)

This is a very chilling way to end an address to the nation. Instead of speaking to the nation, they were addressing Muslims. Unambiguously, it incites Muslims to use violence. If this is the way to peace and harmony, it is essentially saying those who are enemies of Muslims will be destroyed. Earlier the statement called Muslims all over the country "to do all in their power to defend the cause of Allah and to take all necessary steps to defend themselves."

In December 2011, the then CAN (Christian Association of Nigeria) President, Rev. Ayodele Joseph Oritsejafor, issued a statement on the issue of attacks being meted out against Christians. Oritsejafor urged followers to take revenge, but said they should defend themselves, their property, and their places of worship "in any way they can." "The consensus is that the Christian community nationwide will be left with no other option than to respond appropriately if there are any further attacks on our members, churches and property," Oritsejafor said (Agence France-Presse 2011).

CONCLUSION

Religion cannot be excluded from politics in Nigeria. Neither is it possible nor desirable. Wariboko is right that there is the need to create a distinct kind of theopolitical practice that seeks to suture the public and private spheres of life in West Africa. In fact, Sanneh argues strongly in favor of a kind of theopolitics for West Africa rather than the secular Western state that puts a wedge between state and religion. West Africans like other Africans are supremely religious. I believe that approaching the Muslims with a theopolitical ideology rather than a secular ideology gives Christians grounds to engage in dialogue. This dialogue can possibly lead to a common definition and understanding. As Sanneh says, "However we view religion, we cannot be content with one side talking to itself about the other" (Sanneh 1996, p. 88).

In Nigeria, the colonial administration was responsible for not only protecting and promising the Muslims non-interference by the missionaries, but they also went further to place the Muslims as rulers over tribal groups that the Muslims had never conquered. This created the situation where the Muslims consider it their right to be in power. With every passing year, their audacity continues to grow. There has been an understanding that appointments into public offices should be balanced between the two major religions. For example, if the president was a Muslim, then the vice president will be a Christian and the president of the Senate who is next in line will be a Christian. Even the Chairperson of the ruling party will not be of the same religion as the president in order to ensure a balance of power. However, in the upcoming 2023 presidential election, the ruling party All Progressives Congress (APC) has put forth Muslim presidential and Muslim vice presidential candidates. This has led to a lot of outcry in the nation. *The Vanguard* said, "The choice of a Muslim/Muslim ticket by the presidential candidate of the All Progressives Congress, Asiwaju Bola Tinubu, has generated controversies in Nigerian politics and exacerbated religious sentiments" (Ecoma 2022). This shows that many people understand this unwritten rule and think of its violation as unfair.

The missionaries as noted earlier did not prepare Christians for life in the political arena. Nigerian Christians are still figuring it out on their own. But Christians need to be wary of using Christianity in politics the way Muslims do it to serve their religion. If Christians thus employ religion, the situation will never change because another Muslim leader will revert to their former ways and further entrench their position exacerbating the religious animosity. This challenge is one that needs to be resolved not only for Nigeria or Africa but for the world in an increasingly pluralistic global context. Nigerians need to find a way of coexisting in an increasingly religiously pluralistic society. One of the implications of this is that Christians in Nigeria need to avoid the danger of replacing their religious metaphysics with a political metaphysics and political messianism—a type of creed in which people place their hope and trust (Sanneh 1996, p. 91).

The great medieval African Muslim scholar Ibn Khaldún notes that religion has two purposes in politics: "It is either a social ornament or a ruling ideology, useful or necessary." He says that "effective leadership is a matter not of revealed truth but of pragmatic competence. Good leaders are determined by the quality of their rule as seen by their subjects rather than by the purity of the ideals to which they subscribe." He added, "If such rulership is good and beneficial, it will serve the interests of the subjects. If it is bad and unfair, it will be harmful to them and cause their destruction" (Sanneh 1996, pp. 102–103). God has shown us the good that he requires of us. These mandates are found in the minor prophets Micah, Hosea, and Amos. It is to act justly and love mercy and to walk humbly with our God [Micah 6:8] and to let justice and righteousness characterize our dealings [Amos 5:24]. The Christian calling is to a life of obedience to God not the building an earthly kingdom. We have transcended the era of Christendom. If Christians suffer loss or harm in the process of obedience to the Word of God, they need to remain faithful to the end knowing that this world is not their ultimate goal. However, they can organize around the goal of defending their ethnic territory. In that regard they have a right to self-determination without invoking defending Christianity as the basis of their defense. "Politics as religion redeems no more than religion as politics" (Sanneh 1996, p. 93).

Christians must desist from using politics to bolster their religion or vice versa because of the danger of running both aground. Khaldún's advice to Muslims is apt for Christians. He says we ought not try to "patch our worldly affairs by tearing our religion to pieces. Thus, neither our religion lasts nor (the worldly affairs) we have been patching" (Sanneh 1996, p. 93). While Christians have a right to be suspicious of Muslim political leaders using political power as an instrument of their religion, they should also be suspicious of Christian leaders who use political power as an instrument of Christianity. They are no different from the Muslim politicians they are resisting. Instead, such leaders need advocate and support the creation of structures and laws that would make it difficult for the political system to be abused by a leader of any religious persuasion. Religious leaders need to distance themselves enough from corridors of political power so that they can confidently and credibly perform their pastoral and prophetic roles in the political sphere.[1]

NOTE

1. I am grateful to Seth Kajang, Haroun Audu, and Tyifhouh Emmanuel for their helpful comments to an earlier version of this chapter.

REFERENCES

Agence France-Presse. 2011. Nigeria's Christians Vow to Defend Themselves in Wake of Attacks. *The National News*, December. https://www.thenationalnews.com/world/asia/nigeria-s-christians-vow-to-defend-themselves-in-wake-of-attacks-1.575819.

Ajayi, J.F.A. 1965. *Christian Missions in Nigeria 1841–1891: The Making of a New Élite*. London: Longmans.

Akote, Abubakar, et al. 2021. *Nigeria: Inside Northern Communities Sacked By Bandits, Ethno-Religious Conflicts*. https://allafrica.com/stories/202203120223.html. Accessed 27 September 2022.

Aliyu, Nura, and Attahiru Ahmad Sifawa. 2018. Islamic Intellectual Transformation and Revivalism in Northern Nigeria in the 20th Century: A Study of the Factor of the Kano Law School (aka Northern Provinces Law School/School of Arabic Studies). *RIJHIS* 2 (1): 66–87.

Babajide, Abdul. 2022. Owo Church Attack: How Four Gunmen Attacked Worshippers, Killed Women, Children – Eyewitnesses. *Daily Post Nigeria*, June 5. https://dailypost.ng/2022/08/05/owo-church-attack-how-four-gunmen-attacked-worshuppers-killed-women-children-eyewitnesses/.

Brown, Carl L. 2000. *Religion and State: The Muslim Approach to Politics.* New York: Columbia Press.

Cragg, Kenneth. 1986. *The Call of the Minaret.* London: Collins.

Diamond, Jared. 1997. *Guns, Germs, and Steel: The Fates of Human Societies.* New York: W.W. Norton & Company.

Dung, Gyang Luke. 2002. *Paul G. Gindiri: The Firebrand Evangelist.* Jos: New Life For All.

Ecoma, Victor. 2022. The Muslim/Muslim Ticket and Nationhood. *Vanguard News,* August 8. https://www.vanguardngr.com/2022/08/the-muslim-muslim-ticket-and-nationhood/.

Gaiya, Musa. 2004. Paul Gofo Gunen Gindiri. *Dictionary of African Biography.* https://dacb.org/stories/nigeria/gindiri-paul/. Accessed 20 October 2020.

Hill, Jonathan N.C. 2010. *Sufism in Northern Nigeria: A Force Or Counter-Radicalization?* Carlisle, Pennsylvania: United States War College Press.

International Committee on Nigeria. 2020. *Nigeria's Silent Slaughter: Genocide in Nigeria and the Implications for the International Community.* Virginia: Falls Church.

Kastfelt, Niels. 1994. *Religion and Politics in Nigeria: A Study in Middle Belt Christianity.* London: British Academic Press.

Kukah, Matthew H. 1993. *Religion, Politics and Power in Northern Nigeria.* Ibadan, Nigeria: Spectrum Book.

Kukah, Matthew H. 1999. *Democracy and Civil Society in Nigeria.* Ibadan, Nigeria: Spectrum Books.

———. 2015. *Future of Religion in Nigeria's Politics.* http://www.vanguardngr.com/2015/11/future-of-religion-in-nigerias-politics-by-matthew-kukah/. Accessed October 22 2018.

Levtzion, Nehemia, and Randall L. Pouwels. 2000. *The History of Islam in Africa.* Athens, OH: Ohio University Press.

Lewis, Bernard. 1990, September. The Roots of Muslim Rage. *The Atlantic,* p. 266.

Loimeier, Roman. 1997. *Islamic Reform and Political Change in Northern Nigeria.* Evanston, IL: Northwestern University Press.

Meier, Karl. 1992, September 15. *Obituary: Sheikh Abubakar Mahmud Gumi.* Independent. DOA 23 November 2016. http://www.independent.co.uk/news/people/obituary-sheikh-abubakar-mahmud-gumi-1551628.html.

Reisacher, Evelyne A., ed. 2017. *Dynamics of Muslim Worlds: Regional, Theological, and Missiological Perspectives*. Downers Grove, IL: IVP Academic.

Sanneh, Lamin. 1983. *West African Christianity: The Religious Impact*. Maryknoll, NY: Orbis.

———. 1996. *Piety and Power: Muslims and Christians in West Africa*. Maryknoll, NY: Orbis Books.

———. 2009. *Translating the Message: The Missionary Impact on Culture* (Revised and Expanded Edition). Maryknoll, NY: Orbis Books.

The Guardian Nigeria. 2022, May 23. Despicable Murder of Deborah Samuel in Sokoto.   https://guardian.ng/opinion/despicable-murder-of-deborah-samuel-in-sokoto/.

Turaki, Yusufu. 2017. *The British Colonial Legacy in Northern Nigeria: A Social Ethical Analysis of the Colonial and Post-Colonial Society and Politics in Nigeria*. Jos, Plateau: ECWA Productions.

Vaughan, Olufemi. 2016. *Religion and the Making of Nigeria*. Durham, NC: Duke University Press.

Walls, Andrew, and Cathy Ross, eds. 2008. *Mission in the Twenty-first Century: Exploring the Five Marks of Global Mission*. Maryknoll, NY: Orbis Books.

CHAPTER 23

Religious Liberty in South Africa

Radley Henrico

INTRODUCTION

Western societies have become increasingly modern, globalized, multicultural, secular, and pluralistic.[1] This begs the question of the extent to which religious freedoms in such societies are protected. South Africa has an estimated population of **606** million (Stats. South Africa 2022).[2] Statistics of religions and religious affiliations in the 2015 census[3]—population at 54.4 million—reveals a plethora of religions.[4] Account must also be had of traditional African healers (*Sangomas*) who form part of African religious practices (Truter 2007: 56)[5] and the role played by African indigenous[6] religions.[7] Moreover, the increase of religious diversity raises various concerns, one of which is the vexed question of whether non-mainstream religions are as deserving of protection as mainstream religions. Not all religions enjoy equal protection enjoyed by mainstream religions.[8] In particular, the protection afforded to religious freedom in the workplace may best be understood by coming to grips with the dynamics of unfair discrimination (Seiffert 2017: 124).

R. Henrico (✉)
University of Western Cape, Cape Town, South Africa
e-mail: rhenrico@uwc.ac.za

S. Holzer (ed.), *The Palgrave Handbook of Religion and State Volume II*, https://doi.org/10.1007/978-3-031-35609-4_23

Entrenchment of the right to religious freedoms[9] and equality rights in a multicultural society bring to the fore the contestation often arising when such rights clash with secular values. Nowhere is this contestation more apparent than the workplace. I have elsewhere alluded to the contention by Benecke that religious discrimination tends to manifest itself more in the workplace than "in the process of buying an apple" (Henrico 2019b: 120). Support for this proposition is to be found in the number of cases reported in South Africa pertaining to unfair discrimination on religious grounds in the workplace,[10] as opposed to greater society. I refer to this as the "proximity phenomenon" since the workplace is essentially a micro-image of our macrocosmic society and, for all intents and purposes, "showcases" the conflict arising from religious liberties expressed in the secular employment relationship (Henrico 2019b: 121). The inherent requirement of a job (IROJ) or the operational requirements of the employer may be such as to impose a reasonable and justifiable limitation on religious liberties in the workplace.

This chapter aims to reflect broadly on the constitutional and legislative regimes governing religious liberty in South Africa. The aforesaid discussion is contextualized with reference to the conceptual meaning of "religion" and religious liberty in the South African secular democratic order. The importance of celebrating religious diversity as opposed to mere toleration is discussed. The chapter proceeds to focus on manifestation of religious liberties with reference to religious observances, and symbols and problems arising from conflicts with the IROJ. This necessitates a discussion on why reasonable accommodation fulfills a better purpose if used more expansively in terms of mutual accommodation. The latter imposes duties on employees and employers alike to seek a resolution to conflicts. The aforesaid is discussed as a prelude to an analysis of relevant case law in South Africa. Case law reveals the extent to which our courts appear to adopt a "nuanced context-sensitive approach" when balancing competing interests arising from the expression of religious liberties in a secular society.

THE SOUTH AFRICAN LEGAL FRAMEWORK GOVERNING RELIGIOUS LIBERTY

Constitutional Perspective

Specific Constitutional Provisions

Section 1(a) of the Constitution of the Republic of South Africa, 1996 (the Constitution),[11] declares the Republic of South Africa a sovereign and democratic state founded on the value of human dignity, achievement of equality, and the advancement of human rights and freedoms (Henrico 2015: 275). Express acknowledgment is made of the supremacy of the Constitution and the rule of law.[12] The right to equality is a self-contained right embodied in section 9 as follows:

(1) Everyone is equal before the law and has the right to equal protection and benefit of the law.
(2) Equality includes the full and equal enjoyment of all rights and freedoms. To promote the achievement of equality, legislative and other measures designed to protect or advance persons, or categories of persons disadvantaged by unfair discrimination.
(3) The state may not unfairly discriminate directly or indirectly against anyone on one or more of the following grounds, including race, gender, sex, pregnancy, marital status, ethnic or social origin, colour, sexual orientation, age, disability, religion, conscience, belief, culture, language and birth.
(4) No person may unfairly discriminate directly or indirectly against anyone on one or more grounds in terms of subsection (3). National legislation must be enacted to prevent or prohibit unfair discrimination.
(5) Discrimination on one or more of the grounds listed in subsection (3) is unfair unless it is established that the discrimination is fair.[13]

Section 15 (1) of the Constitution guarantees that "[e]veryone has the right to freedom of conscience, *religion*, thought, belief and opinion."[14] The above concepts are all associated with innately held views by an individual human being. Although not all instances of being steeped in a particular state of mind, such as the belief in veganism, is related to religion, everyone who is a follower of a particular religion has a "belief" or state of mind influenced and informed by religious beliefs.[15] All beliefs are not grounded in religion; however, all religions are based on beliefs. Section 31(1) and (2) of the Constitution caters for cultural, religious, and linguistic communities as follows:

(1) Persons belonging to a cultural, religious or linguistic community may not be denied the right, with other members of that community—

  (a) To enjoy their culture, practise their religion and use their language; and
  (b) To form, join and maintain cultural, religious and linguistic associations and other organs of civil society.

(2) The rights in subsection (1) may not be exercised in a manner inconsistent with any provision of the Bill of Rights.

Thus, communities or associations are given the right to practice religious beliefs in a manner that is not contrary to any provision of the Bill of Rights (the BOR). Essentially, communities, associations, and individuals are prohibited from exercising their religious rights in a manner that would cause harm to anyone (Du Plessis 2016: 350).[16] The associational rights under section 31(1) provide the necessary protection to an organization, group, or community wishing to be identified in terms of a particular religion with the constitutional right to self-determination to realize their religious goal as a collective whole or movement subject to the condition that such an objective does not undermine other fundamental rights in the Bill of Rights. Sections 15(1) and 31(1) must be read against the backdrop of the constitutional protection afforded to everyone from equal treatment by not being unfairly discriminated against, directly or indirectly, on the grounds of religion in terms of section 9 of the Bill of Rights.

Equality and Dignity

Our law recognizes that equality must be conceived of in a substantive, as opposed to a formal, notion. As such, account is taken of the differences of individuals and the need to include or accommodate diversity of differences.[17] Individuals must be recognized for their uniqueness as individuals in a pluralistic society. Support for this recognition is found in the Constitutional Court case of *President of the Republic of South Africa v. Hugo*, in which Goldstone J stated:

> We need therefore to develop a concept of unfair discrimination which recognizes that although a society which affords each human being equal treatment on the basis of equal worth ... we cannot achieve that goal by insisting upon identical treatment in all circumstances before that goal is achieved.[18]

Human dignity is an inexorable part of the right to equality.[19] The value of dignity was highlighted by the Constitutional Court as a significant aspect of the impact unfair discrimination had on an individual in the case of *Hoffman v. South African Airways*. As to whether the airline's policy had discriminated against the applicant on the basis of his HIV-positive status, Ncgobo J observed as follows:

> At the heart of the prohibition of unfair discrimination is the recognition that under our Constitution all human beings, regardless of their position in society, must be accorded equal dignity.[20]

Locating human dignity as an inseparable component of our equality jurisprudence[21] has best been described by Sachs J—concurring—in *National Coalition for Gay and Lesbian Equality* as thus:

> [T]he equality principle and the dignity principle should not be seen as competitive but rather as complementary. Inequality is established not simply through group-based differential treatment, but through differentiation which perpetuates disadvantage. ... Such focus is in fact the guarantor of substantive as opposed to formal equality.[22]

The inner worth of individuals in society holds the promise that all are deserving of treatment in accordance with the values and principles of the Constitution. Dignity is also seen as the imperative in terms of which the autonomy of the individual is respected insofar as he or she can make self-informed choices and decisions, thus denoting freedom (Boethius 2009). More notably, within the South African context of a history steeped in entrenched racial discrimination and a constitutional dispensation promising a better life for all (as discussed later), thus playing a crucial role in the protection of religious freedoms (Henrico 2016a: 81–83).

The Point About "Unfair Discrimination"

Differentiation *per se* does not constitute discrimination in the legal sense (Henrico 2019b: 122). It is important to conceive of the distinction between "discrimination" in the pejorative (hurtful) (*Brink v. Kitshoff* 1996) and non-pejorative (non-hurtful) sense. Differentiation in the pejorative sense translates into "unfair discrimination" (Lenta 2009: 835; Henrico 2015: 288; Henrico 2019b: 122). The South Africa's history of inequality due to apartheid remains an ever-present concern. Our experience of apartheid racial discrimination culminated in "discrimination" being referred to as "unfair discrimination" (Henrico 2019b: 122).

Consequently, discrimination in South African labor law (and equality jurisprudence) evolved into the concept of unfair discrimination (Henrico 2016a: 71). Conceptually, "unfair discrimination" was also due to legislative influence (see Labour Relations Act 28 of 1956) which sought to codify "unfair labour practices." The concept came to be interpreted as "the unfair discrimination by any employer against any employee" (Du Toit et al. 2015: 571). Under the constitutional dispensation, this approach was to continue, and a three-pronged test was set out by the Constitutional Court in *Harksen v. Lane NO & Others* (1998):

(a) Does the provision differentiate between people or categories of people? If so …
(b) Does the differentiation amount to unfair discrimination? This requires a two-stage analysis:

    (i) Firstly, does the differentiation amount to "discrimination"? If it is on a specific ground, the discrimination will have been established. If it is not on a specific ground, then whether or not there is discrimination will depend upon various considerations such as impairment of human dignity ….
    (ii) If the differentiation amounts to "discrimination," does it amount to "unfair discrimination"? If it has been found to have been on a specific ground then unfairness will be presumed. If on an unspecific ground, unfairness will have to be established by the complainant.

If, at the end of the enquiry, the differentiation is found not to be unfair, then there will be no violation. (Strydom 2015: 35)

Our courts—while continuing to recognize the term "unfair discrimination"—do not follow the *Harksen* test slavishly (Henrico 2016a: 129). Instead, a more holistic approach is taken of a host of factors. Rationality has been emphasized as a means to test whether the basis of the differentiation can be said to be permissible as was stated in *Prinsloo v. Van der Linde* (1997):

In regard to differentiation the constitutional state is expected to act in a rational manner.[23]

The importance of rationality, as a means determining the fairness of the differentiation, was further emphasized in *Minister of Finance v. Van Heerden* (2004) by Ngcobo J:

> The proper approach to the question whether the impugned rules violates the equality clause involves three basic enquiries: first, whether the impugned rules make a differentiation that bears a rational connection to a legitimate government purpose; and if so, second, whether the differentiation amounts to unfair discrimination; and if so, third, whether the impugned rules can be justified under the limitations provision. If the differentiation bears no such rational connection, there is a violation of section 9(1) and the second enquiry does not arise. Similarly, if the differentiation does not amount to unfair discrimination, the third enquiry does not arise.[24]

By looking at whether unfair discrimination has taken place albeit on what appears to be neutral or *prima facie* non-discriminatory grounds, the rationale of indirect discrimination underscores what has been previously stated about the importance of addressing substantive equality (Henrico 2016a: 135). This much appears from *City Council of Pretoria v. Walker* (1998), where the following is stated:

> The fact that the differential treatment was made applicable to geographical areas rather than to persons of a particular race may mean that the discrimination was not direct, but it does not in my view alter the fact that … it constituted discrimination, albeit indirect, on the grounds of race. (see Henrico 2016a: 135)

Direct and Indirect Unfair Discrimination

Prohibiting unfair discrimination, either "directly" or "indirectly," in section 9 must be read with the injunction contained in subsection (5) (Henrico 2016a: 133). Discrimination on a listed ground is presumed to be unfair unless established to have been fair. Reported cases indicate that in most instances discrimination manifests itself in subtle ways in which the discrimination may *prima facie* be non-discriminatory or neutral, but the consequence is aimed at specific categories of persons. An example would be an employer who advertises a position in the company but only for employees with specific qualifications,[25] which qualifications are not required for the performance of the job, or where the corporate culture of an employer imposes certain "requirements" on an employee or applicant for employment, the effect of which is discriminatory in nature (Du Toit and Potgieter 2014: 27).

Indirect (disparate) discrimination[26] is a less obvious form of differentiation, yet still unfair.[27] The Constitutional Court has interpreted it to mean neutral criterion or action which "has a disproportionate impact upon a particular group of employees" and "cannot be justified in terms of objective employment-related requirements" (Du Toit et al. 2015: 666). Whether discrimination takes place on a direct or indirect basis, the onus is on the applicant to prove, on a balance of probabilities, that differentiation took place on a listed ground.[28] The evidential onus of proving—on a balance of probabilities—the fairness of the discrimination rests on the respondent.

I have elsewhere asserted that most reported cases pertaining to unfair discrimination have been adjudicated on the basis of indirect discrimination (Henrico 2016a: 135).[29] Discrimination, whether it is direct or indirect, will be unfair if it is a conduct that affects or impairs the fundamental human right and dignity of another human being.[30] We have been sensitized to the notion that we are all subjects of a diverse pluralistic society with a heritage of past injustices based on intolerance of differences and that we must now embrace our differences. It is understandable that general expressions of intolerance toward others on the grounds listed in subsection (3) are unacceptable. These grounds can also be referred to as explicit or obvious grounds upon which a person has been discriminated against (Du Toit et al. 2015: 665). To expect such person to discharge an onus of proving that the discrimination is unfair would be inequitable.

Transformative Constitutionalism and Ubuntu

The aforesaid constitutional provisions are subject to purposive interpretations by our courts. They strive to animate the values underlying an open and democratic society based on human dignity, equality, and freedom with reference to the Bill of Rights.[31] According to Klare (1998: 150), this approach is conducive to a "democratic, participatory and egalitarian" South Africa brought about by means of transformative constitutionalism.[32] The latter has been interpreted to mean a changed socio-economic order.[33] Intrinsic to transformative constitutionalism is the notion that South Africa has moved from a "culture of authoritarianism" under apartheid to "a culture of justification" (Mureinik 1994: 31;

Henrico and Fick 2019: 81) in terms of which the exercise of all public power must be justified (Burns and Henrico 2020: 10–11; 15–20).

Indigenous law is an elemental aspect of the Constitution, confirmed in *Bhe & Others v. Khayelitsha Magistrate & Others* (2005). *Umuntu ngumuntu ngabantu* that "a person is a person because of people" (*ubuntu*)[34] (a Zulu proverb) which encapsulates a "sense of community."[35] An obligation to care for family members (community responsibility) is "[a] vital and fundamental value in [the] African social system" and recognized in the African Charter on Human and Peoples' Rights (the Charter).[36]

Inexorably linked to *ubuntu* are notions of respect for life and human dignity. *Ubuntu* was earmarked in *S v. Makwanyane* as "permeating the Constitution … and specifically fundamental human rights." Madala J observed that "in contrast to the apartheid legal order … the post-apartheid order of constitutionalism requires courts to develop and interpret entrenched rights in terms of a cohesive set of values, ideal to an open and democratic society" (Henrico 2016b: 824).

Limitations of Equality Rights

All rights in the BOR are subject to the limitation clause—section 36. Equality rights, as read with the right to religious freedom,[37] may be reasonably and justifiably limited in terms of section 9(5) (Henrico 2016a: 124). This exercise is a proportionality analysis entailing the balancing of conflicting rights and interests (Dworkin 2013: 139). Religious freedoms conflicting with secular values, whether in open society or in the workplace, need to be adjudicated upon. Proportionality is also recognized as a material "ingredient of reasonableness" (see Sachs J in *Minister of Health v. New Clicks South Africa (Pty) Ltd* (2006)). Fairness is also a factor considered reference to the aforesaid (Pretorius 2010: 553–554; Henrico 2016a: 118–133), as is the concept of reasonable accommodation with reference to the expression of religious liberties in the workplace that conflict with either the IROJ or the operational requirements of the employer (OPER).[38] The principle of legality (which has been interpreted by courts as an incident of the rule of law) is a further factor to be considered, namely that everyone (government, individual, and juristic persons) is subject to the rule of law (Henrico 2021: 528).

From specific legislative provisions (discussed later), the aforementioned concepts inform the resolution of conflicts arising between the intersection of religious liberties and secular norms or values in general and specifically the workplace.

Constitutional Interpretation of Religious Liberties

When adjudicating religious freedom disputes, our courts are called upon to balance conflicting rights and interests. No precise constitutional methods of interpretation have been laid down (Du Plessis 1996: 226). Du Plessis argues that there has been a lack of consistency of reasons advanced in this regard. Klaaren also points to a lack of consistency in terms of interpretive approaches (Klaaren 1997: 5).

Case authority on equality jurisprudence reveals that our courts attempt to give expression to the values infusing the Constitution, particularly those resonating with freedom, equality, and human dignity. This also means our courts essentially give effect to transformative constitutionalism in that the judgments are testimony to the imperative for the necessary change (transformation) of our society in its aspiration toward the achievement of social justice (Henrico 2016a: 144).

Legislative Perspective

Importance of Legislative Framework

Legislation must be enacted to prevent and prohibit unfair discrimination in terms of section 9(4) of the Constitution. Although the basis upon which unfair discrimination is highlighted—in terms of section 9(3)—it is subject to a defense that differentiation is fair in terms of section 9(5). A legislative framework is necessary to give effect to the normative constitutional rights. By-passing such legislation would violate the principle of subsidiarity (avoidance).[39]

Interpretation of Legislative Provisions

As for the interpretation of legislative provisions, the Constitutional Court has endorsed the following interpretative approach in *NUMSA v. Intervalve (Pty) Ltd* (2015), where Nkabinde J stated:

> While grammar and dictionary meanings are the primary tools for statutory interpretation, as opposed to being determinative tyrants, context bears great importance. […]. (Henrico 2016a: 149–150)

Imperatives of social justice, inclusivity of diversity, religious freedoms, labor peace in the workplace (as a microcosm of society) will also be used to address religious discrimination in the workplace.[40]

The interpretation of legislation must give effect to the spirit, purport, and objects of the Bill of Rights together with any obligations imposed upon the Republic of South Africa as a member state of the ILO in addition to concerns of transformative constitutionalism as previously mentioned (Henrico 2016a: 151). Equality jurisprudence in South Africa is "legislatively showcased" first and foremost by labor legislation. It is for this reason that this chapter deals first therewith before discussing legislation applicable to the public (non-workplace) regulation of religious liberty.

The Employment Equity Act

Section 6(1) of the Employment Equity Act 4 of 2000 (the EEA) proscribes unfair discrimination, directly or indirectly, based on religion. However, discrimination on the basis of an IROJ will not constitute unfair discrimination (see section 6(11)(1)(b) of the EEA). The need for unfair discrimination on either a direct or an indirect (disparate) basis as reflected in section 9(3) of the Constitution is maintained in the provision of section 6(1) of the EEA. A burden of proof rests on the employer to "disprove the factual basis of the complainant's claim" or "to justify the measure concerned on grounds including but not limited to rationality and fairness."

Differential treatment which cannot be justified and impacts adversely upon a person's human dignity is objectionable because of the harm caused. It is also objectionable on grounds that it is "simply arbitrary." A burden of proof is placed on the employer, facing an unfair discrimination allegation on a listed ground, such as religion, of proving the discrimination did not take place, or is rational and not unfair, or is otherwise justified. Hence, we see the onus of proof dealing with notions of rationality and justifiability. As our courts are called upon to assess claims brought under the EEA, it will be necessary that the scope of the claimant's claim or the employer's defense is adjudicated with reference to considerations of rationality and justifiability. Religion is one of the grounds listed in section 6(1) as a result of which an employee would merely have to prove the existence of a distinction, preference, or exclusion, namely that he or she was differentiated against based on religion. After this has been established, the evidential onus is on the employer as pointed out earlier.

Amendments to the EEA in 2013 which introduced notions of "arbitrary" differentiation and placed the onus of proving discrimination on the plaintiff have been the subject of academic criticism. However, the fact that emphasis is placed on notions of rebutting an unfair discrimination claim by proving that the conduct can be justified lends credence to the fact that tensions arising from conflicting fundamental rights are best determined with reference to principles based on rationality, reasonableness, proportionality, and fairness. An employer faced with a claim of religious discrimination may escape liability with reference to the IROJ or OPER. The defenses contained in section 6(2) of the EEA have been adopted from article 1(2) of the ILO Convention 111. Case authority, as discussed later, provides guidance as to what constitutes fair discrimination with reference to the IROJ or OPER.

The Labour Relations Act

In terms of the Labour Relations Act 66 of 1995 (the LRA), unfair discrimination on the basis of religion that results in a dismissal constitutes an automatic unfair dismissal in terms of section 187(1)(f), which provides that:

> the employer unfairly discriminated against the employee, directly or indirectly, on any *arbitrary ground*, including, but not limited to, … *religion*.[41]

An employee is thus protected against religious unfair discrimination in terms of the LRA and the EEA. However, in terms of the LRA, a dismissal will not be unfair if it is based on the IROJ (section 187(1)(f)(a)). Both the EEA and LRA provide the employer with a defense to a claim of unfair discrimination on the grounds of religion. The precise difference in terminology between the two Acts is that whereas the EEA merely refers to "a job," the LRA refers to "the particular job." This difference in semantics is not crucial. Unlike the LRA, where a ceiling is set on compensation and the form of remedy, namely compensation or reinstatement, in terms of the EEA, the Labour Court may in addition to awarding compensation also award damages. Unfair discrimination on religious grounds during the course of employment, but which does not result in dismissal, is dealt with under the EEA. An employee is protected against religious unfair discrimination in terms of both the LRA and the EEA.

The Promotion of Equality and Prevention of Unfair Discrimination Act

The Promotion of Equality and Prevention of Unfair Discrimination Act 4 of 2000 (PEPUDA), does not apply to the workplace. It seeks to give effect to section 9 of the Constitution. The significance of PEPUDA lies in the factors to be taken into account in determining whether discrimination is unfair. If the complainant proves discrimination took place on one of the prohibited grounds, then unfairness is presumed unless the respondent can prove otherwise. Of the factors to be taken into account (in determining fairness), the most significant is the reference to steps taken to "accommodate diversity" (section 14 (1)(3)(*i*)(i)). This relates to the concept of reasonable accommodation discussed in section "Reasonable Accommodation of Religious Liberties".

Common to the LRA, EEA, and PEPUDA is the prohibition against "unfair discrimination" on the grounds of religion. The non-self-executing provisions of subsection 4 of the Constitution have resulted in the enactment of the LRA, EEA, and PEPUDA.[42] Section 5(1) of PEPUDA specifically binds the state and all persons. The EEA is binding on an organ of state as defined in section 239 of the Constitution and all other employers. The same designation is attributed to employers in terms of section 1(a)–(e) of the LRA. The provisions of the aforesaid legislation when dealing with unfair discrimination prohibit "any person" from unfairly discriminating against another person (in the case of PEPUDA) or an employee (in the case of the EEA and LRA) on the grounds of religion. No special dispensation or exception is given to cases where the state is an employer. From this, it is clear that the legislative framework gives impetus to subsections (3) and (4) of section 9 equality proviso in the Constitution in that neither the state nor any person may unfairly discriminate against another person. Conceptually, this feature underscores the fact that South Africa is a secular society premised on state neutrality. The state does not play an active role in determining the extent to which right to freedom of religion can or cannot be pursued, save to the extent that it has sought to legitimately address a potential conflict of fundamental rights through the general limitation of rights clause as discussed earlier. National legislation and international instruments[43] regulating unfair discrimination on the grounds of religion do so without providing any explanation or definition as to the concept or term "religion." The same holds true for the Constitution. Consequently, protection of religious freedom calls for closer examination of what is meant by the term "religion."

UNDERSTANDING THE TERM "RELIGION" IN THE CONTEXT OF THE SOUTH AFRICAN SECULAR DEMOCRATIC ORDER

The Term "Religion"

An analogy is often drawn between religion and medicine. It has been said that just as in medicine, where it is sometimes easier to identify illness than health, so with religious freedom, in that it is easier to define unfair discrimination on the basis of religion than to define religion itself (Marshall 2013: 11–16). It is useful to examine how "religion" as a concept has been addressed in terms of case law to gain some understanding of the term (Henrico 2015: 784). These cases show there is no universal definition of the concept "religion." Whether this is as a result of the fact that "religion" has been couched together with other fundamental rights contained in section 15(1) of the Constitution or due to the fact that "religion" *per se* is incapable of a precise definition by reason of it being a personally held belief phenomenon remains unanswered. In *Publications Control Board v. Gallo (Africa) Ltd* (1975), Rumpff CJ relied on various dictionary meanings of "religion" and concluded that "[r]eligious *beliefs* are highly subjective and are founded on *faith*. It is not a sphere in which objective concepts of reason are particularly apposite" (Henrico 2016a: 26–17).

This association between "religion," "belief," and "faith" came to be relied on in our constitutional dispensation in *S v. Lawrence, Negal, Solberg v. The State* (1997), where the Constitutional Court per Chaskalson P referred to the observation made by Dickson CJC in *R v. Big Drug Mart Ltd* (1985) namely that "[t]he essence of the concept of religion is the right to entertain such religious *beliefs* as a person chooses."[44]

The appellant—a voluntary association representing 14,500 pupils from almost 200 Christian schools in South Africa "to promote evangelical Christian education"—in *Christian Education South Africa v. Minister of Education* (2000) challenged the constitutionality of legislation prohibiting corporal punishment in schools contending that corporal punishment was central to their Christian ethos. Sachs J pointed to the importance of a "nuanced and context-sensitive form of balancing" required when applying the limitation test in terms of section 36 of the Constitution. Heeding the definition accorded to freedom of religion by Chaskalson P in *Lawrence*, Sachs J held:

[R]eligion is not always merely a matter of private individual conscience or communal *sectarian* practice. ... Religion is not just a question of belief or doctrine. It is part of a way of life, of a people's temper and *culture* (emphasis added). (Henrico 2016a: 28)

In *Prince v. President of the Law Society of the Cape of Good Hope* (2002) the court was called upon to decide the constitutionality of prohibiting the use or possession of cannabis when its use or possession was employed for religious purposes by the Rastafari religion. While the court also relied on the aforesaid *dictum* of Dickson CJC in *R v. Big M Drug Mart Ltd*, Sachs J stated:

The *beliefs* that believers hold sacred and thus central to their religious faith may strike non-believers as bizarre, illogical or irrational. (Henrico 2016a: 30)

Parallels can be drawn between the description given by Rumpff CJ in the *Publications Control Board* of religion transcending the boundaries of rationality and Sachs J in the *Prince* case observing that religion can be anathema to rationality. In *MEC for Education: Kwazulu Natal v. Pillay* (2008), the court was called upon to consider the validity of a school's decision prohibiting one of its Hindu/Indian pupils from wearing a gold nose stud for religious reasons. Langa CJ stated: "[w]ithout attempting to provide any form of definition, religion is ordinarily concerned with personal *faith* and *belief*."[45]

While no universal definition exists for "religion", the debate concerning the definition is, however, universal (Watson 2009: 494). Account must also be had of the fact that "religion" is more case than text specific. It would be uncommon for our courts to impose a literal definition or universal term to serve as a *panacea* of understanding freedom of religion. In giving effect to the right to freedom of religion, conceptually "religion" has been interpreted alongside clusters of other rights such as "belief," "conscience," and "culture." Moreover, human dignity has come to play an important role in informing the interpretation of "religion" as a concept in the context of religious freedom. Our courts have teased out interpretations of "religion" consonant with the values and principles underlying the Constitution. Imposing a formal interpretation upon the term could also spell stultification for future cases, in terms of the context in which the term is adjudicated (Dworkin 2013: 119). The competing values and interests arising from the text of the Constitution impose an interpretive duty upon our courts which transcend viewing the concept of "religion" through the confines of a mere strict definition (Currie and De Waal 2015: 147–148).

Our case law shows religion is not confined to a mere belief or doctrine or even conscience. For many individuals, religion is what defines the way and manner in which they live their lives. In other words, religion lends shape and form to individuals' lifestyles (requiring protection where necessary) in our democratic order.

Secularism in South Africa

With the array of religions in South Africa, against the backdrop of the constitutional protection afforded to religious liberty—in terms of both individual (section 15) and associational (section 31)—the question arises as to the nature of secularism in South Africa. As seen by the definition of "secularism" later, this would refer strictly to a non-religious society. Realistically and practically, it would be misplaced to describe South Africa as non-religious. The fact is that our current society evidences both a variety of religious faiths and effectively leaves the choice of a particular religion, or even choosing not to be religious, up to every individual. More significantly, government does not play an official role in the affairs of religion. There is no official or formal policy in terms of which religion is enforced on the citizens of South Africa.[46] This state of neutrality on the part of government is underscored by the National Policy on Religion and Education (hereafter the Policy) which expressly provides as follows:

> Under the constitutional guarantee of freedom of religion, the state, neither advancing nor inhibiting religion, must assume a position of *fairness*, informed by parity of esteem for *all religions*, and worldviews.[47]

Section 7 of the South African Schools Act 84 of 1996 gives effect to the aforesaid neutrality the following words:

> Subject to the Constitution and any applicable provincial law, religious observances may be conducted at a public school under rules issued by the governing body if such observances are conducted on an equitable basis.[48]

A similarity can be drawn with the US. As far as protecting the right to freedom of religion is concerned, the US relies on the "establishment clause." In terms of the above model, there is no involvement between the state or government and any religious affiliation and/or the practice thereof. Rawls advocates that this form of government is to be encouraged since the state refuses to use any particular form of religious ideology which it imposes on its citizens (Rawls 1993: 29–33; Henrico 2016a: 62). Religion and the freedom to practice one's beliefs is a matter left to the conscience and personal subjective belief of each and every person—it is not and should not be a realm into which the government intends venturing. This has attracted some criticism on the grounds that it is not sufficient for a government to simply distance itself from notions of religious freedom as demonstrated by the "establishment clause." The reasoning behind the criticism is that government should not be so passive in relation to issues impacting on liberal democracies.

However, when government has become more proactive in legislating laws, for example, those which call for the banning of religious symbols in forcing women of the Muslim faith to remove the *hijab*, *niqab*, or *burqa* for air travel or for driver's license purposes, which laws are upheld and enforced through the judiciary,[49] its conduct has not escaped scrutiny and will undoubtedly be the matter of ongoing criticism and debate. The state, even in what may conceivably be considered to be highly liberal democracies, will always have an overriding interest in the name of public policy to limit basic and fundamental religious freedoms.[50] "Secularism" is derived from Latin *saecularum*, meaning "from time to time" or "for all eternity" (Benson 2013: 16). It is associated with being non-religious (Benson 2000: 520). The point is that it must be understood in the context of a society not regulated as a theocracy,[51] but one in which allowance is made for pursuit of individual and collective freedoms subject to the rule of law (Campos 1994: 1814). Iran, Syria, and Afghanistan can be regarded as theocratic states, where Islam is adopted not only as the official religion but as the absolute rule of God as the law. This system is criticized by virtue of its totalitarianism and dictatorship (Ahmed and Ginsburg 2014: 12). The nexus between these regimes and religious fundamentalism with the extant problem of the Islamic State of Iraq and Syria (ISIS) and terrorism stem from trenchant religiously held views which express hostility in respect of any non-fundamentalist religion (Rausch 2015: 29–31).

Irrespective of the "secularism" label, ultimately what matters is the extent to which citizens are at liberty to practice freely their religious beliefs without fear of reprisal. The practice of such beliefs may, however, be limited by conduct that is harmful to others, alternatively adversely impacts upon their human dignity.[52] The ever-present specter of modern-day terror attacks and ongoing potential attacks on the lives of innocent people by religious fundamentalists underscores the heightened relevance of religion in secular and non-secular societies. Such terror attacks, while capable of being construed and interpreted through the prism of various political ideologies and views, are premised on the fundamental notion of intolerance. This is the most extreme manifestation of intolerance. However, it can also be defined as intolerant where the other view is summarily dismissed merely because it is different and for reasons pertaining to rationality or grounds that are justified. To the extent that a believer holds such views with reference to his or her own religious convictions and does not express them in a manner that poses harm to any person or living being, it cannot be deemed objectionable.

This collision of individual interests can take place in the public realm, for examples where women are forced to clothe their bodies in a certain manner, and the enforcement of women having to wear the *hijab* in a theocracy. Some individual females may feel that the enforcement of such a dress code infringes their individual freedom of choice. On the other hand, the banning of women wearing face coverings (commonly referred to as the *burqa* or *niqab*) in public in France and Brussels since 2010 and 2011, respectively, has been met with criticism that it is an undue limitation on their right to religious freedom. The above instances are in some or other way all demonstrative of a lack of tolerance to permit others to express their religious freedom in a particular manner (Henrico 2017: 229–241).

The Importance of "Celebrating" Religious Diversity

South Africa has been described as a "rainbow nation," a term coined by Archbishop Desmond Tutu during South Africa's transition to a democratic dispensation (Buqa 2015: 1–8). Divergent views and ideologies especially in so far as religious beliefs are concerned and the expression of such beliefs in a democratic order that seeks also the protection of secular rights can lead to various complexities. This problem must be considered in the context of a call for unity in our diverseness. In addition, the commitment to a tolerance of differences—or even the celebration thereof—is quintessential to our constitutional order (Sachs 2013: 147–160; Henrico 2017: 229, 574). The celebration of diversity resonates with a commitment for change, namely transformative constitutionalism to a society as envisaged by Karl Klare[53] to mean:

> a long-term project of constitutional enactment, interpretation, and enforcement committed (not in isolation, of course, but in a historical context of conducive political developments) to *transforming* a country's political and social institutions and *power relationships* in a democratic, *participatory* and *egalitarian* direction. (Klare 1998: 150)

What is envisaged is a change initiated by a process of participation by role-players in our society[54] in a peaceful manner, activating social change through legal means in a spirit of equality and care (Meyerson 2011: 139–141; Ackermann 2014: 24; Henrico 2015: 784–803; Henrico 2014: 742; Henrico 2019a: 17–20). Express recognition of this diverseness of South African society is found in the Preamble of the Constitution which provides that "South Africa belongs to all who live in it, *united* in our diversity." We have also previously discussed the importance of substantive equality. Through recognition (and celebration) (Chaskalson 2000: 200) of differences (even where such differences require reasonable accommodation), inclusivity is provided for in our constitutional dispensation.[55]

Secularism, multicultural diversity, and the necessity of having to live together as South Africans were referred to by Sachs J in *Minister of Home Affairs v. Fourie* (2006). Similar sentiments were expressed by Tlaletsi J in *Kievits Kroon Country Estate (Pty) Ltd v. Mmoledi* (2012) to the effect that:

> [i]t will be disingenuous of anybody to deny that our society is characterized by a diversity of culture, traditions and beliefs. That being the case, there will always be instances where these diverse cultural and traditional beliefs and practices create challenges within our society. … What is required is reasonable accommodation of each other to ensure harmony and to achieve a united society.[56]

Hence, there is mutual respect between fellow citizens. Irrespective of the degree to which someone holds a particular view, whether religious or secular, the purpose of the Constitution is to permit such views, however varied, to be held in a non-destructive manner without any sense or notion of mutual destructiveness. Express reference to the capacity to manage and accommodate different views at once, some would argue, brings to mind the notion of having to tolerate. Both cases emphasize the need to accommodate differences. The former emphasizes that this must be done in manner that is non-destructive. The latter emphasizes the notion of harmony as a result of accommodation that may result in a united society.[57]

I criticize the term "tolerance" in that it brings to mind more negative than positive connotations. Having to "put up with something" may imply no alternative short of enduring a penalty or regime of displeasure. It is notionally associated with a state of affairs that will endure as long as it has to be withstood. An employee who describes his or her working conditions as tolerable essentially describes a lackluster situation. Notionally, the term has strong associations with being compelled to do something rather than acting of one's own volition. Thus, in the context of accommodating differences in a multicultural society, mere "tolerance" is unhelpful. Celebrating our multicultural diversity has a closer fit with the "rainbow nation" metaphor. Reasonable accommodation is required to ensure harmony. By substituting tolerance with celebration, the differences required to be accommodated essentially no longer are experienced as a burden. In this sense, effect is also given to the concept of *ubuntu* in that we care for others not due to a sense of forbearance and tolerance but in a spirit of celebration of who and what we are as people and citizens capable of transforming South African society into a culture demonstrative of harmony, care, giving, and concern for others.

The Constitutional Court in *City of Tshwane Metropolitan Municipality v. Afriforum* (2016) highlights the importance of *ubuntu*, and also has consequences for the celebration of diversity. In delivering judgment for the majority of the court, Mogoeng CJ observed:

> All peace- and reconciliation-loving South Africans whose world-view is inspired by our constitutional vision must embrace the African philosophy of "ubuntu." The African world-outlook that one only becomes complete when others are appreciated, accommodated and respected, must also enjoy prominence in our approach and attitudes to all matters of importance in this country.[58]

City of Tshwane had to do with matters relating to the renaming of street names in Pretoria, earmarked as the administrative capital of South Africa. In *City of Tshwane* the court highlighted issues important to the success of transformative constitutionalism. Apart from *ubuntu*, they are tolerance, substantive equality, unity in diversity, protection of cultural identities, and the need to transform society. The most interesting aspect of the judgment lies in the dissenting view regarding the protection to be afforded to minority cultures.[59] The judgment points out that just because "we disagree so profoundly with [their] view of history," those views must still be provided a place in our constitutional dispensation. This is captured in the following *dictum*:

> There are many cultural, religious or associational organisations that have roots in our divided and oppressive past. Are they all now constitutional outcasts, merely because of a history tainted by bloodshed or racism? If that is what the Constitution demands, we would wish to see a longer, gentler and more accommodating debate than happened here.[60]

Accommodation in a "rainbow nation" must require recognition of both "mainstream" *and* "minority" views. Democracy should not be tested only in terms of the extent to which we can boast the diverseness of our society, but rather the extent to which even the most marginalized in our society are included. In this sense, if emphasis is placed more on celebrating rather than tolerating differences, greater impetus is given to the conceptual notion of a "rainbow nation." Hence, a conceptual celebration of differences, as opposed to mere tolerance thereof, may add more value to the sense of unification through *ubuntu* and thereby contribute more valuably to our transformative constitutional mandate that seeks to establish a more equal society.

Having discussed the importance of celebrating diversity of religious differences in a secular society, it is important to consider the phenomenon of complexities arising from the expression of religious freedoms in a secular society.

Manifestation of Religious Liberties

Expression of religious freedom is most often manifested in terms of the display of particular religious signs and symbols.[61] Religious observances by religious associations such as churches may require their employees to be of a certain faith. In this way, employees may be treated preferentially. In and of themselves, such observances and symbols are merely demonstrative of a particular religious belief. The manifestation and expression thereof in the workplace is considered later.

Religious Observances and Symbols in the Workplace

An individual of a particular religious faith or belief may abide by the tenets of such religion through certain observances[62] or symbols[63] or dress[64] associated with a religion. Doing so in the privacy of their home or their church poses no problem. Problems arise where, for example, an on-board flight assistant is made to wear a uniform associated with the airline and the airline carrier services a predominantly Muslim clientele. The latter may express complaints when served by a flight assistant visibly displaying a crucifix as a sign of the Christian faith (Henrico 2016a: 66).

Another example is someone applying to be a marriage licensing officer. What if their religious beliefs conflict with marriages between same-sex couples? The IROJ is that a marriage licensing officer is required to perform the necessary formalities—as required by the relevant applicable legislation, namely the Civil Union Act 17 of 2006—and comply with the law to formalize the ceremony, irrespective of the sexual orientation of the persons getting married. Does the IROJ outweigh the licensing officer's religious freedom?[65] If the marriage officer is in the service of the State then section 31 "refusal to solemnize" is not applicable. Although same-sex unions can now be solemnized under the Civil Union Act, a marriage officer, other than one referred to in the Act, may object on the grounds of religion to solemnize the union. Here we see protection of religious freedom over the right outweighing the competing right.

A further example is a nurse in the private or public sector insisting on displaying a crucifix around their neck. Health and safety requirements of the job impose obligations on employers and employees to ensure the general safety and hygiene of patients which interests outweigh the religious liberty in question. Male employees of the Sikh faith cover their heads with a turban and may find the wearing of a helmet objectionable.

Religious observances in the workplace also impact upon religious holidays. As businesses become reflective of diversified cultures, so too does this reflect in the religious make-up of staff. Employees insisting on practicing religious observances, namely celebration of "holydays," could potentially have a devastating impact on an employer's business.[66]

The workplace requires a balance of interests to be addressed, maintaining the viability of the employment relationship in advancing the commercial interests of the employer and protecting the rights of an employee. Such competing interests inform the question of the optimal balance to be struck. The right to religious liberty, expressed by way of religious observances or dress codes or symbols, must be assessed against limiting such freedoms, where reasonable and justified, in terms of section 36 of the Constitution on account of the IROJ (Henrico 2016a: 68–69).

Observances, Symbols, and the IROJ

An IROJ may be the performance of abortions at a medical clinic, which an employee finds objectionable on the grounds of religion. Alternatively, the dress code which the employer requires the employee to follow may be at odds with religious beliefs of the employee such as a prohibition on wearing any jewelry or a headscarf. Moreover, an applicant for employment wearing a *hijab*, *niqab*, or *burka* on account of their Islamic faith might find themselves not being considered for the position since the IROJ—as advertised—is that a specific uniform is worn while performing duties of a particular appointment.[67]

A further example is where an employee is a Rastafarian and in keeping with their religious belief considers it necessary to wear their hair in a Tam. An IROJ, as a security officer, is that in keeping with a uniform appearance and the "concept of discipline and order" all males and females, regardless of their religion, must cut their hair very short and wear a tight-fitting cap. The mere fact that it is an IROJ does not mean that the limitation on the employee's right to express his religious freedom is reasonable, rational, or even justifiable. This is said on account of the fact that in a multicultural plural society suitable measures must be taken to tolerate (or *celebrate*) a diversity of traditions, cultures, and views. However, the overarching *caveat* to this must always be that it causes no harm to others in that it does not impair their fundamental right to human dignity (Ackermann 2014: 76–77).

The aforesaid examples serve as possible instances of the confluence of competing rights and interests creating potential for conflict. In the employment relationship, various fundamental and constitutionally and legislatively enshrined rights are accorded both the employee and the employer. None of these rights are absolute; they are to be balanced. Complexities arising from the competing aforesaid rights and interests are vexed by the inherent imbalance of power characterizing the employment relationship—and perhaps this is just a microcosmic exemplar of the greater social inequality divide that currently exists (Du Toit 2014: 2623–2625). Put differently, one cannot ignore the fact that in most employment relationships the balance of power is pitted in favor of the employer, placing the employee by default in a disadvantageous and more vulnerable position (Kahn-Freund 1972; Davidov and Langile 2011).

The presence of potential conflict *per se* does not necessarily transpose into the need for concern. It is where the rights and interests of the respective parties to the employment relationship are potentially compromised in general, or where the dynamic of the trust imperative of such relationship, in particular, is impacted on, that the need to address these concerns arises. A particularly useful method of addressing such conflict of rights is to take account of the extent to which differences can be reasonably accommodated. The latter notion has attracted the concern of our courts when adjudicating religious freedoms that clash with secular rights and interests. It is for this reason that such concept requires some consideration.

Reasonable Accommodation of Religious Liberties
Reasonable accommodation is dealt with, albeit obliquely, in section 1 of the EEA. The provision obliges employers to take suitable measures to modify or adjust the job or work environment to accommodate designated group, namely disabled employees. The LRA has no similar provision or any provision relating to reasonable accommodation. Significantly, South African Charter of Religious Rights and Freedoms makes provision for the following: "Every person has the right to have their religious beliefs reasonably accommodated." We need to also recall the reference in PEPUDA to "accommodate diversity" as discussed in section "The Promotion of Equality and Prevention of Unfair Discrimination Act". Although accommodation referred to in the EEA is employed with reference to disabled persons and PEPUDA does not apply to the workplace, it is important that a generous meaning be attached to the notion of reasonable accommodation. It is a concept that essentially addresses the disparity that may arise between a disabled employee and an employer who is required to take reasonable measures, short of undue hardship. The rationale for reasonable accommodation is the achievement of substantive equality, conversely the elimination of unfair discrimination (Henrard 2001: 61–62; Henrico 2016a: 174–175).

To "accommodate diversity," alternatively "reasonable accommodation" gives impetus to our equality jurisprudence and the advancement of transformative constitutionalism in the realization of social justice

(Henrico 2016a: 175). Reasonable accommodation in the context of unfair discrimination in the workplace is of particular importance for reasons relating to tolerance and what is reasonable and justified (Henrico 2016a: 176).

Reasonable accommodation is sufficiently flexible to be used as a method of analysis of the steps taken not only by the employer but also by the employee. Thus, conceived of in the light of *mutual* accommodation, the method considers both the employee's and the employer's actions in addressing ways of resolving religious liberties conflicting with secular values in the workplace (Henrico 2012: 503; Henrico 2016a: 177). Mutual reasonable accommodation is premised on the following:

- both employee and employer are entitled to fair labor practices in terms of Constitution;
- in misconduct cases, it is important to consider the competing interests of both employee and employer;
- the IROJ will play a material role in determining the extent to which religious liberties of an employee should be limited. Even OPER has a role to play in assessing the extent to which expression of religious liberties should be restricted. Moreover, in OPER disputes, both parties are duty bound to seek alternatives to a dismissal.[68]
- constructive dialogue on the part of both parties translates into both parties assuming initiatives as role-players in the workplace seeking a win-win situation, obviating the need to resort to formal adjudication.
- In a society striving toward fulfilling an egalitarian mandate, taking into account a plurality of interests means there should be a means of "levelling the playing fields."

Our courts have not been hesitant to employ the reasonable accommodation test in striking a balance between the expression of religious liberties and the IROJ or OPER. Clearly, the test facilitates a more equitable approach to adjudication (Henrico 2016b: 847). An examination of South African case law on the exercise of religious liberties reveals how our courts deal with fundamentally conflicting constitutionally protected rights and how the reasonable accommodation test has been employed in workplace disputes with a view to protecting religious liberties in a secular society.

CASE LAW ON THE EXERCISE OF RELIGIOUS FREEDOM

Balancing Competing Rights: Religious Liberties in a Secular Society

In *Zabala v. Gold Reef City Casino* (2009), the applicant alleged that her dismissal was automatically unfair in terms of section 187(1)(f) of the LRA for reasons relating to her belief, conscience, and culture. Pillay J dismissed the claim finding there had been a failure to prove differentiation. Although discrimination on the basis of religion did not feature in the case, it is worth noting given the close association of the grounds as discussed in section "The Term "Religion"". Moreover, the case highlights the recognition given to the three-pronged test in *Harksen* (see section "The Point About "Unfair Discrimination"") and the status of *Harksen* in our equality jurisprudence. There is no evidence that the *Harksen* test has continued to be adopted consistently as a patina by our courts in determining discrimination disputes. Although *Harksen* has not been set aside, due account must be taken of the fact that our courts have not been consistent in following the application of the so-called *Harksen* test. Instead, there has been a greater tendency to adjudicate matters in a "nuanced context-sensitive" manner as was mentioned by the Constitutional Court in *Christian Education South Africa*. The *MEC for Education: KwaZulu Natal v. Pillay* (2008) entails a non-workplace-related dispute that provides impetus to our equality jurisprudence in its reasoning that "religion" must be understood in the context of strong associational ties not only with "faith" and "belief" of an individual but also with "traditions" and "cultures" of the community associated with the identity of the individual. The case recognizes that a cultural belief is as deserving of protection as a religious belief. This is important for certain persons since expression of religious liberties extends beyond spiritual beliefs. As such, religious freedom must be understood to include both cultural and spiritual beliefs.

In *Strydom v. NG Gemeente Moreleta Park* (2009) the applicant was an independent contractor in the position of organist and music teacher at a church. The governing body terminated the contract upon learning that the applicant was in a same-sex relationship. Since the applicant was not an employee, he claimed unfair discrimination in terms of PEPUDA. As a defense, the church argued that an IROJ was that the applicant could not be in a homosexual relationship since this was out of kilter with the church's doctrine and its constitutional right to religious liberty. The termination of the contract adversely impacted upon Strydom's dignity in that it caused him to suffer depression. Strydom's claim against the church was upheld and the case highlights the right to equality and human dignity in a pluralistic society in which diversity should be celebrated (Henrico 2016a: 318).

In *FAWU v. Rainbow Chicken Farms* (2001) the applicants alleged having been automatically dismissed in terms of section 187(1)(f) of the LRA for reasons relating to their religious belief. They were employed as butchers by the respondent who slaughtered chickens in accordance with Halaal standards. The applicants refused to work on *Eid ul Fitr*, a Muslim holiday, but not an official public holiday. A collective agreement (CA) provided that all employees were only entitled to government-gazetted holidays which did not include the Muslim holiday. They failed to report for work on the Muslim holiday pursuant to which they were found guilty of refusing to work in terms of the CA. On review before the Labour Court, and in dismissing their claim, Revelas J observed:

> The individual applicants *were specifically employed because they are Muslims.* It is an *operational requirement.* Consequently, I do not believe that the respondent's conduct, by not consenting to giving the butchers the day off on Eid, amounts to unfair discrimination as envisaged by section 187(1)(f) of the Act.[69]

FAWU alerts one to the important role played by rationality when determining reasonableness and justifiability in the adjudication of competing fundamental rights. Gauging whether a distinction has taken place on the grounds of religion and determining the unfairness thereof can only properly be assessed with regard to adopting the reasoning consistent with a "nuanced context-sensitive" approach. An important aspect of this assessment is also to take due account of the knowledge on the part of the employer (Henrico 2016a: 322).

Dlamini v. Green Four Security (2006) dealt with the dismissal of security guards who refused to shave their beards. The applicants urged a beard was essential to their religious beliefs. They alleged their dismissals were automatically unfair under section 187(1)(f). In dismissing their claim, Pillay J considered whether the shaving of beards as demanded by the employer was an IROJ which would not be deemed to be discrimination in terms of the provisions of article 1(2) of ILO Convention 111. The manner in which Pillay J adjudicated the dispute points to some significant aspects. First, the applicants failed to demonstrate a strict adherence to their faith (the evidence showed they were selective in the religious practices they followed); the court pointed out that minority religious groups were as deserving of protection as larger groups. Second, the court noted that the IROJ applied to all employees and not just the applicants. In establishing justification, Pillay J referred to the so-called strict scrutiny test applied by the US Courts and duly took account of the extent to which, when applied, the test requires proof that a measure which restricts religious freedom must serve a "compelling State interest" which was rejected by the Court in *Christian Education* in favor of a "nuanced context-sensitive" balanced approach.[70]

Third, the court examined the limitation of religious rights in terms of article 1(2) of ILO Convention 111 as well as the beneficial occupational requirement as referred to in Canadian in this regard; it looked at the reasonable accommodation test in the Canadian case of *Bhinder* (1985). Pillay J's rationale for placing so much emphasis on the *Bhinder* decision can be critiqued as being misplaced, given that Bhinder was overruled by the Supreme Court in *Central Alberta Dairy Pool* (1990) which decision was confirmed in the *Meiorin* (1999) case; however, due credit must be given for recognition of the reasonable accommodation test.

Pillay J must be lauded for the compelling manner in which she sought to strike a balance between the competing interests. Due account was thus taken of reasonableness and rationality to the extent that both interests could be tolerated and accommodated. In this respect Pillay J drew on the authority of the *Lawrence* case and stated:

> Society in general and workforces in particular can cohere if everyone accepts that certain basic norms and standards are binding. Workers are not automatically exempted from by their beliefs from complying with workplace rules [Christian Education para 35]. If they wish to practise their religion in the workplace, an exemption or accommodation must be sought.[71]

Pillay J found the IROJ requiring employees to be clean-shaven was justified. It must be acknowledged that Pillay J adjudicated the matter in a "nuanced context-sensitive" approach. This much appears from the fact that a mere reading of the wording of section 187(2)(a) gives no indication as to how to establish fairness in relation to the IROJ. However, Pillay J's analysis of the law, both national and international, she in substance, gave effect to the purpose of the LRA which was to give effect to the rights in the Constitution and the ILO obligations, respectively. Without accounting for the concept of reasonable accommodation articulated in terms of PEPUDA, Pillay J nevertheless incorporated it as a necessary means of assessing the extent to which the limits on the religious liberties could be justified with reference to the IROJ (Henrico 2016a: 324).

The issue of reasonable accommodation was never called into question since it was never alleged that the respondent failed to reasonably accommodate. Moreover, *Harksen* was never used as a means by which the court established the existence (or extent) of unfair discrimination. Pillay J's regard to ILO Convention 111 is to be welcomed since same is consistent with section 39(2) of the Constitution (Henrico 2016a: 325).

In *Lewis v. Media24 Ltd* (2010) the applicant sued for damages basing his claim on alleged unfair discrimination based on section 50(2)(a) of the EEA. The applicant claimed that the publication business and policies of the respondent discriminated against his religious and political views. He also alleged the respondent forced him to work on Shabbat knowing he was Jewish and that his employment was terminated when he refused to work. The applicant's credibility was questioned as was the general poor impression he made on the court. The applicant was neither able to establish the respondent had knowledge of the applicant's religious affiliations nor that requiring him to work on a Friday night was in breach of the applicant's religious beliefs and practices. The court (per Cheadle AJ) dismissed the application observing the following in respect of accommodation:

> [W]ithout deciding whether an employer is obliged to accommodate an employee's observance of a religious practice even if the employee does not himself observe it in a manner contemplated by the religion, an employer may surely raise the question over whether a commitment to observe a religious practice is genuine. ... Accommodation of religious minorities may require operational changes. ... Such changes are only justifiable if the employee's observance of his religion is genuine and in line with religious practice. Accordingly, doubt expressed as to the employee's religious commitment may be hurtful but does not on that ground alone constitute discrimination.[72]

Although the court gave effect to the *Harksen* test, this was only to the extent of enquiring whether the applicant had established a case of direct discrimination that would give rise to the onus of proof shifting to the respondent to show that the discrimination was justified. The judgment contributes to religious discrimination jurisprudence in the way it contextualizes reasonable accommodation. Reference to "accommodation of religious minorities [requiring] operational changes" implies a duty in both parties to seek a viable resolution, hence the need for mutual accommodation as opposed to mere reasonable accommodation. Cheadle AJ also recognized the need to embrace all forms of religious freedoms, even minority ones, as was articulated by Pillay J in *Dlamini*. However, the extent to which accommodation of such beliefs is seen as reasonable will be determined by the sincerity of those beliefs. It must be recalled that in *Dlamini*, the applicants were selective as to what tenets of their religion they observed. While they insisted on growing their beards—contrary to the IROJ—they were not as insistent when it came to attending church services. Similarly, in *Media24*, one cannot help but reflect on what the outcome would have been had evidence shown the applicant to have been more consistent with their religious observances (Henrico 2016a: 327).

In *Kievits Kroon Country Estate (Pty) Ltd v. Mmoledi* (2014),[73] the employee was dismissed for being absent without permission. The employer's defense to a claim of unfair discrimination on cultural and religious grounds was that the employee willfully absented herself from work thereby disobeying a lawful instruction. The employee urged she had no option but to attend a traditional course to be trained as a *sangoma* in response to a calling from her ancestors. Initially, the employer granted the employee paid leave to accommodate her but the request to attend further sessions was denied since the employer was very busy, short-staffed, and needed the services of the employee. The labor tribunals upheld the employee's claim. In the Supreme Court of Appeal, Cachalia JA took account of the fact that the employer initially accommodated the cultural and religious beliefs, but that at the internal disciplinary hearing, neither the employer nor the chairperson was willing to accept that such beliefs were sufficient to induce a form of illness on the part of the respondent and neither did a letter from a *sangoma* to this effect suffice (Henrico 2016a: 329).

In addition, Cachalia JA took into account that traditional belief systems common to the employee relating to culture, customs, and ideas of our country could not be disputed. These religious beliefs form part of "customs, ideas and social behaviour" that could not be evaluated according to "the acceptability, logic consistency or comprehensibility of the belief." In dismissing the appeal of the employer, Cachalia JA held:

[T]he appellant could have explored with the respondent alternatives to her taking leave at the time, such as her attending the course when it was convenient to accommodate her request if possible.[74]

As we saw in the *Dlamini* case, the religion in question—though a minority practice in comparison to mainstream religions—was deserving of respect and protection. However, had the applicants in the case demonstrated a more consistent observance to their tenets of belief, it may and could have led to the employer being required to take further measures to accommodate their religious beliefs (Henrico 2016a: 330). What clearly emerges is the assessment of conflicting rights through a "nuanced and context-sensitive" lens as suggested by the court in *Christian Education*. The adjudication of religious disputes is not a simple matter. This is borne out by the dictum of Sachs J in *Christian Education*:

> [R]eligious and secular activities are, for purposes of balancing, frequently as difficult to disentangle from a conceptual point of view as they are to separate in day to day practice. … certain aspects may clearly … belong to the citizen's Caesar and others to the believer's God, there is a vast area of overlap and interpenetration between the two. It is in this area that balancing becomes doubly difficult.[75]

Irrespective of the "irrationality" or "bizarreness" thereof, the religion is not disqualified from protection (Henrico 2016a: 331). Whether additional steps to accommodate would have imposed undue hardship does not appear from the judgment. The SCA made no mention of any duty upon the employee also to seek ways of accommodating the conflict. The Labour Appeal Court (LAC), in finding the dismissal to have been unfair, also endorsed the finding of the tribunal that the employer should at the very least have granted the employee unpaid leave to complete the "traditional healer's course," and without expressly engaging the accommodation test as set out under section 14 of PEPUDA, held:

> [T]here will always be instances where these diverse cultural and traditional beliefs and practices create challenges within our society, the workplace being no exception. The Constitution of the country itself recognizes these rights and practices. … What is required is *reasonable accommodation of each other to ensure harmony and to achieve a united society.*[76]

This reasoning is encouraging since it rightly extends the reasonable accommodation to mutual accommodation. *Department of Correctional Services v. POPCRU* (2013) was an appeal to the SCA from the LAC which upheld the finding of the Labour Court (LC) that the dismissal of the employees was automatically unfair in terms of section 187(1)(f) of the LRA for reasons relating to unfair discrimination on gender, religion, and cultural grounds. The employees worked as prison warders and were dismissed for refusing to cut their dreadlocks in accordance with the dress code. They claimed their hairstyles were consistent with their Rastafarian beliefs. They also advanced cultural reasons. In dismissing the appeal, Maya JA, with reference to the *Harksen* test, held:

> Relevant considerations … include the position of the victim of the discrimination in society, the purpose sought to be achieved by the discrimination, the extent to which the rights or interests of the victim of the discrimination have been affected, whether the discrimination has impaired the human dignity of the victim, and whether less restrictive means are available to achieve the purpose of the discrimination.[77]

Maya JA went on to observe that:

> a policy that effectively punishes the practice of religion and culture degrades and devalues the followers of that religion and culture in society; it is palpable invasion of their human dignity which says their religion or culture is not worthy of protection and the impact of the limitation is profound.[78]

Different approaches were adopted by the courts in determining discrimination. The SCA relied fully on *Harksen* as authority for proving discrimination, while the LAC adopted a "nuanced context-sensitive" approach. Essentially, the SCA found that the employer's policy penalized the employees for exercising their rights to practice a religion or culture. This violated their human dignity. The emphasis placed by the LAC and the SCA on principles of equality and human dignity is welcome since these fundamental rights inform the conceptual framework of religious discrimination; however, there was no need for the SCA to employ the *Harksen* test as it did. The more expansive approach adopted by the LAC was commendable. After considering whether there had been direct discrimination and having found that to be the case, it also consider indirect discrimination which was found to be the case. The LAC found that due to the laxity in enforcement of the dress code, the employer was unable to prove the fairness of the discrimination (Henrico 2016a: 336). What is most informative is the list of factors set out by the LAC that give substance to the "nuanced context-sensitive" approach. These factors are as follows:

- an ostensibly neutral policy of the employer which applies to all employees can still be discriminatory if it offends an individual employee's religious beliefs;
- the employee must show that the policy interfered with their ability to practice their belief;
- the principle involved must be a central tenet of the faith;
- the employer must be aware of the employee's religious convictions;[79]
- once the above has been established, the employee would prove a case of *prima facie* unfair discrimination. The employer must show that the rule is an IROJ or that the discrimination was fair;[80]
- the employer must establish that it has taken reasonable steps to accommodate the employee;
- the principle of proportionality must be applied, meaning an employer may not insist upon obedience to a workplace rule where that refusal would have little or no consequence to the business. (Henrico 2016a: 333)

The *Dlamini* and *POPCRU* cases raise interesting aspects noteworthy of comparison.[81] Both cases imposed certain IROJ on the applicant employees. In *Dlamini*, a requirement of being a security guard was to have a shaved or trim beard. The dress code (the code) of the Correctional Services Department in *POPCRU* prohibited males from wearing dreadlocks.[82] The respondents in *POPCRU* were unable to successfully prove the rationale for discriminating against the applicants. No nexus could be established between the need for males wearing their hair short and the need to maintain discipline and ensure security. The belief of the applicants was related to both culture and religion in *POPCRU*. In *Dlamini* the belief of the applicants was based solely on religion. Essentially, in neither *POPCRU* nor *Dlamini* were the employers able to establish that the IROJ were of such a nature as to outweigh the religious practices of the employees. However, the difference in findings by the courts in *Dlamini* and *POPCRU*[83] is attributable to the extent to which the employees chose to practice and observe their respective religions. In

POPCRU, no question was raised as to the manner in which the employees practiced their religion. The applicants in *Dlamini*, however, were shown to selectively practice their religious belief.

In *TDF Network Africa (Pty) Ltd v. Faris* (2019), the LAC had to decide whether discrimination on the grounds of religious belief was fair and rationally connected to a legitimate imperative that did not unduly impair the dignity of the employee. Faris was employed by TDF in 2011 as part of its graduate training program. Her dismissal arose from refusing to do stock-taking on Saturdays on account of her being a Seventh Day Adventist (Adventist). Faris testified that during her telephonic interview she informed TDF that her religious beliefs prevented her from working on Saturdays. According to TDF, it was during the interview that the employee was alerted to the fact that she would be required to work on weekends. Faris did not object. Moreover, had TDF been informed she could not work weekends, they would not have employed her since Saturday stock-taking was an IROJ. When presented with her employment contract, Faris informed HR she could not work on weekends. HR and management denied the above allegations.

It is common cause that Faris signed her written contract of employment in terms of which a provision is made for her to work reasonable overtime from time to time. Faris was repeatedly requested, as a manager, to attend stock take over weekends to which she retorted she was unable to on account of her religious beliefs. Faris was dismissed pursuant to incapacity proceedings and the LAC (relying on the factors set out in *POPCRU*) found the dismissal to have been automatically unfair on the grounds of religious discrimination. The court held that the employer failed to prove it was impossible to accommodate Faris without incurring undue hardship.

What Must Be Distilled from the Above Case Analysis?

It remains settled law that our courts will not question the sincerity of the religious belief which an employee holds.[84] However, as in *Dlamini*, a court cannot simply ignore the manner in which an employee exercises their religious belief. In this sense, the religious belief on the part of the individual enables a more holistic assessment of what measures can and should be adopted to address the IROJ. In this regard, Govindjee (2016: 121) refers to a judgment of the Labour Court (LC) in *Carlin Hambury v. African Trading Corporation* in which an employee claimed an automatic unfair dismissal on the grounds of refusing to work overtime on Saturdays on the basis of being a Seventh Day Adventist. The LC dismissed the claim, finding that the IROJ took precedence over the applicant's constitutional rights. In particular, the court found that an IROJ was that the applicant be available on Saturdays. There is no indication from the *Carlin* case of the extent to which the applicant selectively practiced his religious faith. What *Carlin* does indicate is that if our courts can find that IROJ takes preference over an employee's religious freedom, such authority can effectively strengthen an employer's argument that where an employee has been selective as to their religious practices, there is no rational or justifiable basis for the religious practice taking precedence over the IROJ.

This also influences the reasonable accommodation test. It makes sense to view it through the lens of "mutual accommodation" by questioning the extent to which an employee is selective about their religious practices. Where selectivity is present (as in *Dlamini*), more should be expected of an employee in terms of demonstrating ways in which to accommodate a workable solution to the inherent tension arising from a conflict of rights. If the mutual accommodation test is not employed, then it is only fair that an employee who professes to have a sincerely held religious belief but is selective as to the manner in which they practice such belief, then they stand to be treated in a manner that is less accommodating than an employee who is fastidious and notionally less adaptable to changes in terms of the IROJ.

Case law referred to in this chapter indicates a tendency on the part of our courts to call on the employer to be proactive in relation to religious liberties or allegations of religious discrimination. In defending a claim of discrimination on the grounds of religion, the employer is required to prove it was fair. In most instances, the defense is based on the IROJ. To address the situation where the employer is often required to refrain from continuing a course of action. One case in point is *POPCRU* in which the employer was admonished to refrain from a strict adherence thereto in favor of the religious beliefs of the claimant employees. These imposed obligations should in a sense be regarded notionally as negative obligations. This must be understood in the context that all claims of religious discrimination in the workplace that have been analyzed are instances in which the employer has been required to "react." Negative obligations are equally applicable to the reasonable accommodation test and duties imposed on employers. Whether an employer is able to demonstrate that religious discrimination is fair on the basis of the IROJ or that reasonable accommodation of the employee's religious freedom has taken place translates into what can only be described as the employer "reacting" to an allegation of unfair discrimination rather than taking proactive steps and measures in the workplace that would actually eliminate religious discrimination in the workplace.

These so-called negative obligations must be distinguished from the positive obligations imposed on an employer in respect of a claim of religious discrimination. Positive obligations notionally go much further in addressing the issue of whether an employer has acted fairly in all circumstances. To begin with, the issue of reasonable accommodation urges an employer to take steps to accommodate the religious beliefs of the employee, as was apparent in the cases of *Dlamini*, *Media24 Ltd*, *Kieviets Kroon*, *POPCRU*, and *TDF Network*. Moreover, if one is to give more effect to the spirit of the EEC which seeks to eliminate discriminatory practices in the workplace, then imposing duties upon an employer akin to what is imposed on employers under the various extant codes to be found in the EEA (e.g., Code of Practice on Sexual Harassment) is a step in the direction of raising general awareness in the workplace about the sensitivity of religious liberties.[85] This general awareness translates into a broader education about rights in the workplace with a view to fostering constructive dialogue between employees and employers in the workplace.

This means that one must, in considering religious discrimination in the workplace, also take into account the broader dimension of equality jurisprudence. In this respect, equality and human dignity are central role-players as evidenced in various decisions handed down by our courts in equality jurisprudence in general as well as in non-workplace-related religious discrimination disputes. The rationale for focusing on this aspect is not only to edify our understanding of the role played by substantive equality and human rights but to also look at the development of the common law as an organic area of our law which, in a notional sense, contributes significantly to transformative constitutionalism through judgments addressing equality disputes which in turn translate into social justice. Judgments handed down in non-workplace-related religious discrimination disputes—such as *Fourie*, *Lawrence*, *Christian Education*, *Prince*, and *Pillay*—and workplace-related judgments analyzed herein are useful for purposes of establishing whether there is a uniform test invoked in the adjudication of religious liberty disputes. It would appear that the rationale for the "nuanced context-sensitive" approach as articulated by Sachs J in *Christian Education* is a shift from the strict formula set out in

Harksen. The former approach on all accounts is more appropriate due to the following reasons:

1. Every dispute is decided with reference to the uniqueness of its own facts and circumstances.
2. Courts must assess disputes in terms of how they are pleaded by the parties.
3. Parties must rely on national legislation and not directly on the Constitution.
4. Definitions ascribed to unfair discrimination ought to be ascertained with reference to the ILO III Convention as given effect to by the EEA and LRA.
5. Failure on the part of the Convention to provide a means of determining the unfairness of the discrimination entitles the court to consider *relevant* jurisprudence concerning the right to equality and human dignity.[86]
6. Assessment of limiting religious liberties in the workplace must be considered taking into account any IROJ. To properly consider this, due account must be had to factors such as reasonableness, rationality, as well as proportionality; regard being had to the interests of both parties.
7. An expansive extension of reasonable accommodation to mutual accommodation requires both employee and employer to seek a workable solution to the problem at hand.

Concluding Remarks

The expression of religious freedoms on the part of individuals when conflicting with secular rights of individuals or organizations in society and particularly the workplace can be problematic. The limitation placed on the expression of religious freedom must be judged against the reasonableness and rationality of any IROJ. In addition, issues of reasonable accommodation on the part of the parties also require analysis. It is in this sense that religious discrimination in the South African workplace context requires consideration and analysis. Under the constitutional dispensation in South Africa, provision is made for the protection of fundamental rights and freedoms. These are, however, all subject to general limitation, should such limitation be reasonable and justifiable in an open and democratic society based on freedom, equality, and human dignity.

There can be no doubt that the right to religious freedom is protected. The right not to be religious is equally protected, inasmuch as the Constitution recognizes the right to have any opinion or belief. What this means is that individuals are at liberty to believe and form views in relation to specific ideas, concerns, and issues as they wish, free from interference either by other individuals or by the state. The state does not profess to proclaim any religious or non-religious point of view and, in fact, plays no role in the opinion or belief an individual holds, whether it be religious or non-religious. To this extent, notionally, it is argued that South Africa is a neutral society in relation to the expression of religious freedom on account of a non-interventionist role on the part of the government. The expression of freedom of religion aligns itself with the normative concept of tolerance. The ushering in of the democratic dispensation did not translate into a sudden awareness of "religiousness." At the bare minimum, however, there is awareness of the fact that freedom of religion extends not only to mainstream religious groups, but must include the lesser-known religions.

If we conceive of secularism in the context of tolerance and pluralism, we must make allowance for the expression of individual (majority and minority) religious liberties as we must for religious freedoms on the part of associations and organizations. However, these freedoms are not absolute. Any limitation on the religious liberty of an employee by the employer must be determined in the context of whether there is a reasonable and justifiable basis. How fundamental rights which clash with each other are to be balanced in a fair manner is not always a simple assessment. Although the notion of reasonable accommodation referred (as gleaned from the EEA) is employed with reference to persons from a designated group (disabled persons), this notion has come to be employed in equality jurisprudence, particularly in religious discrimination disputes, with reference to measures that are appropriate and suitable to make allowance for the individual's particular make-up. The duty to reasonably accommodate forms an essential ingredient of the enquiry into the justification of the limitation. There can be little to no doubt that reasonable accommodation has played and will continue to play a significant role in the determination of religious discrimination disputes in the workplace. The impetus reasonable accommodation gives to equality jurisprudence is noteworthy, not least on account of the fact that it is a means of assessing what measures have been taken to embrace an individual who is different.

Reasonable accommodation, as defined currently in terms of the EEA, is restrictively defined and more closely aligned to address instances of accommodating disabled persons. On the other hand, the notion of reasonable accommodation employed by PEPUDA has a broader and less restrictive meaning. Although PEPUDA is applicable to non-workplace discrimination disputes, until such time as the definition of reasonable accommodation in the EEA has been amended so that instances of religious workplace discrimination can also fall within its ambit, our courts will have no option but to follow the guidelines offered by PEPUDA. It would benefit both parties to the employment relationship, as role-players in our constitutional dispensation to take up the challenge of addressing the issue of unfair discrimination on the basis of religion by having regard to the above factors in seeking constructive ways and measures in dealing with such disputes. However, the disparity in the bargaining power and the inherent imbalance in the employment relationship are significant factors that impede constructive dialogue. The result is that religious discrimination in the workplace is currently addressed more in the form of the legislative and constitutional framework as an occurrence after an incident has taken place. All reported cases analyzed in this chapter are evidence of this fact.

Proving fairness of a distinction in the basis of religion with reference to reasonable accommodation is a recognized basis of defense by our courts. Unfortunately, the statutory provision of reasonable accommodation in terms of religious discrimination in particular is not given expression to in either the EEA or the LRA. For this, we turn to PEPUDA which, although applicable to non-workplace discrimination disputes, must be acknowledged in terms of the requirements set out in section 14 of determining (un)fairness, as being considerably more far-reaching. In terms of the factors listed under section 14, PEPUDA offers greater guidance on what should be regarded as fair. Both the constitutional and legislative regime impose duties upon our courts to interpret the text giving expression to religious freedoms and their limitations, in a particular context. As such, it is imperative that this legislative framework is amended, as previously stated, in a manner that permits our courts when adjudicating upon a dispute to have regard to as many factors as possible. In this way, it facilitates and gives impetus to the "nuanced context-sensitive approach" required in the adjudication of religious discrimination disputes.

NOTES

1. In the sense that a society is representative of people from diverse cultural, ethnic, racial, and religious backgrounds (see Coertzen 2012: 178; Henrico 2016a: 3).
2. For statistical data on religious groups in South Africa as in 2007, see Coertzen (2014: 127) and Henrico (2016a: 4).
3. What is meant by "observation" appears from Statistics South Africa (2015) (hereafter the Survey) to be gauged in terms of the frequency with which a member of a particular religious belief attends church or religious services. While "affiliation" is not defined, it could arguably be gauged in terms of membership fee records and or fees paid (see Henrico 2016a: 15). The aforesaid figures can be taken as being presently appreciably higher due to the fact that they refer to the 2015 Stats Survey. Such information was not included in the Community Survey dated 2016 conducted by Stats SA between Census 2001 and 2021.
4. The so-called mainstream religions are Christianity, Judaism, Islam, and Hinduism. Non-mainstream include Baha'ism, Jainism, Shintoism, Sikhism, Taoism, Zoroastrianism, Syncretism, Rastafarianism, and African (or indigenous) religions.
5. Though *Sangomas* are traditionally associated with medicinal healing, they form part of a religious dimension in certain African beliefs.
6. Described as consisting of some "one thousand African peoples (tribes) … each [having] its own religious system" (Awolalu 1976: 2; referring to Mpiti 1969: 1).
7. A study conducted in 2010 revealed that approximately one-third or more of the South African population possessed traditional African sacred objects such as shrines to ancestors, feathers, skins, skulls, skeletons, powder, carved figurines, or animal objects (see Pew Forum on Religion & Public Life 2010: 33–35). About 12 percent of the total number of followers of African traditional religion in 2007 were in South Africa (see Coertzen 2014: 127). Coertzen (2014: 129) also points out that signatories to the SACRRF included representatives of the African traditional religions. Whether witchcraft can be considered a religion in terms of African traditional beliefs is a vexed issue (see Van der Vyver and Green 2008: 339–343).
8. These are the so-called popular religions: Christianity, Judaism, Islam, and Hinduism.
9. For purposes of this chapter, the terms "freedom" and "liberty" are used interchangeably.
10. See, for instance, the cases of *Hoffman v. South African Airways* 2000 1 SA 1 (CC) paras 34–38; *Zabala v. Gold Reef City Casino* 2009 1 BLLR 94 (LC) para 21; *Motaung v. Department of Education* 2013 34 ILJ 1199

(LC) para 12; *FAWU v. Rainbow Chicken Farms* 2000 1 BLLR 70 (LC) paras 30–34; *Dlamini v. Green Four Security* 2006 11 BLLR 1074 (LC) paras 14–18; *Lewis v. Media24 Ltd* 2010 31 ILJ 2416 LC paras 32–45; *Kievits Kroon Country Estate (Pty) Ltd v. Mmoledi* 2014 35 ILJ 209 (SCA) paras 23–32; *SACTWU v. Berg River Textiles, a division of Seardel Group Trading (Pty) Ltd* 2012 33 ILJ 972 (LC) paras 38–48; and *Department of Correctional Services v. POPCRU* 2013 JOL 30347 (SCA) paras 10–25. For non-workplace unfair discrimination cases, see *Christian Education South Africa v. Minister of Education* 2000 4 SA 757 (CC) paras 19–27; *De Lange v. Presiding Bishop of the Methodist Church* 2016 1 SA 1 (CC) paras 38–43; *Prinsloo v. Van der Linde* 1997 6 BCLR 759 (CC) paras 15–22; *President of the RSA v. Hugo* 1997 4 SA 1 (CC) paras 39–43; *Harksen v. Lane* 1998 1 SA 300 (CC) paras 40–53; *S v. Lawrence S v. Negal S v. Solberg* 1997 4 SA 1176 (CC) paras 100–107; *Prince v. President of the Law Society of the Cape of Good Hope* 2002 2 SA 792 (CC) paras 33–50; *MEC for Education: Kwazulu-Natal v. Pillay* 2008 1 SA 474 (CC) paras 36–52; and *Strydom v. NG Gemeente Moretela Park* 2009 30 ILJ 868 (EqC) paras 25–47 (see Henrico 2019b: 119).

11. Which came into operation on 04 February 1997, replacing the Constitution of the Republic of South Africa, Act 108 of 1996 (the Interim Constitution).

12. Section 1(c). Sections 1–6 (Chap. 1) form part of the founding provisions of the Constitution, whereas sections 7–39 (Chap. 2) constitute the Bill of Rights component of the Constitution.

13. It must be pointed out that in terms of section 8(2) of the Constitution, the Bill of Rights applies vertically and horizontally.

14. Emphasis italicized.

15. The degree of adherence to a particular religion and its tenets of faith to the extent that one can be described as adhering thereto in an ardent (orthodox) or informal and casual manner would vary from person to person and religion to religion.

16. Referred to as the "harm principle" espoused by John Stuart Mill, namely that persons may conduct themselves as they please provided they do no harm to others (see Du Plessis 2016: 349–356).

17. See *Minister of Home Affairs v. Fourie* 2006 1 SA 524 (CC) para 60.

18. For other cases in which a substantive equality approach was endorsed, see *National Coalition for Gay and Lesbian Equality v. Minister of Justice* 1999 1 SA 6 (CC); *Minister of Finance v. Van Heerden* 2004 6 SA 121 (CC); and *Bato Star Fishing (Pty) Ltd v. Minister of Environmental Affairs* 2004 7 BCLR 687 (CC).

19. In terms of section 10 of the Constitution, "Everyone has inherent dignity and the right to have their dignity respected and protected."

20. See para 27 of *Hoffman v. South African Airways* (2001).
21. See comments by Mahomed DP in *AZAPO v. President of the Republic of South Africa* 1996 4 SA 671 (CC) para 1. See also Moseneke (2015: 5-6); Lenta (2012: 241); and Henrico (2016a: 81–82).
22. See para 125 of *National Coalition for Gay and Lesbian Equality* (2004).
23. See para 25 of *Prinsloo v. Van der Linde* (1997).
24. See para 111 of *Minister of Finance v. Van Heerden* (2004).
25. See the US case of *Griggs v. Duke Power Co* 401 US 424 (1971). See Currie and De Waal 2015: 238 and Henrico 2016a: 133–138.
26. It is commonly associated with American jurisprudence given its first usage in the US Supreme Court matter of *International Brotherhood of Teamsters v. United States* 431 US 324 (1977) 335. See Thompson and Benjamin *South African Labour Law* Vol II CC 1–32.
27. A further example of disparate discrimination is where prima facie the employer treats all workers equally by providing a food canteen at the workplace. However, insofar as the canteen fails to cater for halaal food to accommodate Muslim workers, the end result is that such failure has the potential to indirectly discriminate against such workers. See *Mvumvu v. Minister of Transport* 2011 2 SA 473 (CC) paras 30–33.
28. See *Pillay v. Krishna* 1946 AD 946 at 951–952; *Leonard Dingler Employee Representative Council v. Leonard Dingler (Pty) Ltd* 1997 11 BLLR 1438 (LC) 289 G-H 292, 293 A; and *Lukie v. Rural Alliance CC t/a Rural Development Specialist* 2004 8 BLLR 769 (LC).
29. See, for example, *Democratic Party v. Minister of Home Affairs* 1999 3 SA 254 (CC); *S v. Jordan* 2002 6 SA 642 (CC); *Association of Professional Teachers v. Minister of Education* 1995 16 ILJ 1048 (LC) 1048 at 1083; *Leonard Dingler Employee Representative Council v. Leonard Dingler (Pty) Ltd* 1997 11 BLLR 1438 (LC) 292; *Kadiaka v. Amalgamated Beverage Industries* 1999 20 ILJ 373 (LC) para 32; *Louw v. Golden Arrow Bus Services (Pty) Ltd* 2000 21 ILJ 188 (LC) para 29; *POPCRU v. Department of Correctional Services* 2010 10 BLLR 1067 (LC); and *Department of Correctional Services v. POPCRU* 2011 32 ILJ 2629 (LAC), Henrico (2016a: 135).
30. See *National Coalition for Gay and Lesbian Equality v. Minister of Justice* 1999 1 SA 6 (CC) paras 19–27, 28, 117–121; *Satchwell v. President of the Republic of South Africa and Another* 2002 6 SA 1 (CC) paras 25–27. See Henrico (2016a: 136).
31. See section 39(1) & (2) of the Constitution which imposes this duty of interpretation on a court, tribunal, or forum when interpreting the Bill of Rights. Also see *S v. Makwanyane* 1995 (3) SA 391 (CC) par 10. See Henrico (2016b: 822).

32. The term "transformative constitutionalism" was coined by Karl Klare. For further reading, see Van der Walt (2006: 1); Van Marle (2009: 194); Le Roux (2007: 59) and Henrico (2016b: 822); and the authorities cited at ft 26.

33. Currie and De Waal (2015: 150); Meyerson (2011: 139–141); Ackermann (2014: 24); Du Plessis (2011: 94); O'Regan (2012); Klare (1998: 146); Mureinik (1994: 31); Bilchitz and Williams (2012: 159); Bishop and Brickhill (2012: 711); Henrico (2015: 784); and Henrico (2014: 742). See Henrico (2016b: 822).

34. As referred to by Langa J in *MEC for Education: KwaZulu Natal & Other v. Pillay* 2008 (1) SA 474 (CC) para 53 who, it is submitted by necessary inference, aligned the concept "we are not islands unto ourselves" with the more familiar notion coined by John Donne's famous words that "No man is an island" as appears in his 1624 poem *Devotions Upon Emergent Occasions and Several Steps in My Sickness Meditation XVII*, see Henrico (2016b: 823) and esp ft 31.

35. Per Ngcobo J in *Bhe* para 163. See Henrico (2016b: 823).

36. Per Ngcobo J in *Bhe* para 166. The Charter, also known as the Banjul Charter was adopted in Nairobi on 27 June 1981 which came into effect on 21 October 1986, is an international human rights instrument that was duly signed and ratified by South Africa on 09 July 1996; see Henrico (2016b: 823).

37. Either as an individual right under s15(1) or an associational right under s31(1) of the Constitution.

38. A further example is where a Catholic diocese who appoints staff at specific church locations to give Sunday school lessons to children would conceivably have as an IROJ that the person who is appointed is a member of the Catholic faith as opposed to a person who is an atheist, agnostic, or member of the Hindu faith believing in a religion that is out of kilter with the Catholic tenets of faith and doctrines (see Henrico 2016a: 125).

39. *S v. Mhlungu* 1995 3 SA 867 (CC) para 95; *Mazibuko v. City of Johannesburg* 2010 4 SA 1 (CC) para 73; *Sidumo v. Rustenburg Platinum Mines Ltd* 2008 2 SA 24 (CC) para 248; *SANDU v. Minister of Defence* 2007 5 SA 400 (CC) para 51; and *Minister of Health v. New Clicks SA (Pty) Ltd* 2006 2 SA 311 (CC) para 437. An exception would be where the statute in question is constitutionally challenged; see Henrico (2018: 288–307).

40. In terms of sections 39(2) and 173. See Fagan (2004: 117); *S v. Makwanyane* 1995 3 SA 391 (CC) para 451; *Glenister v. President of the RSA* 2011 3 SA 347 (CC) paras 189–190; and *Carmichele v. Minister of Safety and Security* 2001 4 SA 938 (CC) paras 38, 39.

41. Emphasis added. Three grounds of unfair discrimination which are listed herein and which are not contained in section 9(3) of the Constitution are

arbitrary grounds, political opinion, and family responsibility. Family responsibility, political opinion, and arbitrary grounds are also contained in s 6(1) of the EEA. HIV status, on the other hand, although included in s 6(1) of the EEA, is not listed as a ground under s 187(1)(f) of the LRA (see Henrico 2016a: 181).

42. This is not to the exclusion of a private dispute relating to religious discrimination in the workplace that may arise as between co-workers which would either be dealt with in terms of a disciplinary hearing, alternatively more formally in terms of the provisions of PEPUDA, the latter of which will not fall within the scope of this research.

43. For example, Articles 2 and 18 of the Universal Declaration of Human Rights; Article 1 of the International Covenant on Economic, Social and Cultural Rights; Articles 1 and 3 of the International Covenant on Civil and Political Rights; Articles 2 and 3 of the ILO Declaration on the Elimination of All Forms of Intolerance Based on Religion or Belief; and Article 1 of the ILO Discrimination (Employment and Occupation) Convention 111.

44. See para 92 of *Publications Control Board v. Gallo (Africa) Ltd* (1975).

45. See para 47 of *MEC for Education: Kwazulu Natal v. Pillay* (2008).

46. See Leatt (2007: 29); Ismail (2001: 563–586). Also see *S v. Lawrence, S v. Negal; S v. Solberg* in which the Constitutional Court had to consider the validity of the Liquor Act 27 of 1989 under the interim Constitution. See Henrico (2016a: 65).

47. See paragraph 5 in page 5 of the National Policy on Religion and Education (the Policy) available at https://www.gov.za/sites/default/files/gcisdocument/201409/religion0.pdf (accessed on 15 January 2022).

48. The South African Schools Act is available online at https://www.gov.za/sites/default/files/gcis_document/201409/act84of1996.pdf (accessed 15 January 2022).

49. In *Muhammad v. Paruk* 553 F. Supp.2d.893. (E.D. Mich 2008), a Muslim woman's claim against a car rental company who insisted she remove her veil was dismissed. The decision was upheld by the Supreme Court.

50. See the report by Kader Asmal, Minister of Education on the National Policy on Religion and Education (*GG.* 25459 of 2003-09-12) 3–5, in which reference is made to various models of secularity in modern democracies. See Henrico (2016a: 63).

51. In terms of imposing religious law like *Sharia* which is used interchangeably with Islamic law. See Oraegbunam (2011: 99–102).

52. Take, for example, the incident in South African where a church pastor sprayed insecticide on congregants claiming that by doing so he could heal them. The Human Rights Commission of South Africa, it is submitted,

would have had the necessary authority and jurisdiction to address and investigate the matter.

53. See Klare (1998: 146); Van Marle (2009: 288–289); Davis and Klare (2010: 408–412); Henrico (2016a: 91).

54. Various role-players in our society include persons such as government, business, labor, educators, and civic organizations. See Van der Westhuizen (2008: 251); See Henrico (2019a: 20).

55. See *President of the RSA v. Hugo*; *National Coalition for Gay and Lesbian Equality v. Minister of Justice*; and *Minister of Finance v. Van Heerden*; *Bato Star Fishing (Pty) Ltd v. Minister of Environmental Affairs*.

56. See para 26 of the *Kievits Kroon Country Estate (Pty) Ltd v. Mmoledi* (2012).

57. For other judgments emphasizing the need for accommodation of differences in a pluralistic society, see *Christian Education South Africa v. Minister of Education* para 23; *President of the RSA v. Hugo* para 41, 112; *National Coalition for Gay and Lesbian Equality* para 125–126; *Bato Star Fishing v. Minister of Environmental Affairs and Tourism* para 76; *MEC for Education: KwaZulu Natal v. Pillay*; *Strydom v. NG Gemeente Moreleta Park* para 25; *Dlamini v. Green Four Security* par 10; *Lewis v. Media24 Ltd* (2010) para 127–128; *SACTWU v. Berg River Textiles, a division of Seardel Group Trading (Pty) Ltd* (2012) para 38; and *Department of Correctional Services v. POPCRU* (2013) para 21–23.

58. See para 11 *City of Tshwane Metropolitan Municipality v. Afriforum* (2016).

59. In *City of Tshwane Metropolitan Municipality v. Afriforum*, Afriforum relied partly on section 31 of the Constitution as a cultural community of Afrikaans people who depended for their sense of being and belonging on the old names of the streets in Pretoria as a historical treasure and heritage being preserved (see paras 25–28 and 50).

60. See para 134 of *City of Tshwane Metropolitan Municipality v. Afriforum and Another* (2016).

61. Such as, for example, the wearing of a crucifix in terms of the Christian faith, wearing a Tam in terms of the Rastafarian faith, a *niqab* in terms of the Islamic faith, or a *kippa* (yamaka) in terms of the Jewish faith.

62. For example, a Seventh Day Adventist who refuses to work on a Saturday alternatively believes it to be a sin to submit to or be a recipient of a blood transfusion.

63. The crucifix is worn by many Christians as a manifestation of their Christian beliefs. Male members of the Jewish faith commonly wear the yarmulke (*kippah* or skullcap) on their heads. Females of the Muslim faith traditionally wear veils covering their head and/or faces. These are but three instances of only the most mainstream religions. In traditional African religious beliefs, symbols can range from anything between the visible wearing of beads, amulets, or animal skins to the painting of one's face out of respect

for the ancestors and spirits. See Chawane (2014: 220); Henrico (2016a: 66).

64. For example, a Sikh employee who insists on wearing a *Kara* bracelet or Muslim women who insist on wearing the *hijab*, *burqa*, or *niqab*. For further reading, see Squelch (2013: 38–57); Henrico (2016a: 66).

65. Section 31 of the Marriage Act 25 of 1961 provides as follows: "Nothing in this Act shall be construed so as to compel a marriage officer who is a minister of religion or a person holding a responsible position in a religious denomination or organisation to solemnize a marriage which would not conform to the rites, formularies, tenets, doctrines or disciplines of his religious denomination or organization."

66. Whether or not this would in fact be the case would be context-specific in that it would naturally depend on the nature of the business, whether it is capital or human resource intensive, and obviously the total number of employees seeking to take leave in respect of a religious holiday. See Cook (2013: 444–445). For further reading on accommodating religious holidays in the workplace, see Henrico (2016a: 68).

67. This is most often evident in posts where uniformity of dress code is an IROJ such as, for example, a flight attendant. Recently, the media has focused on the case of Major Isaacs in the SANDF who insists on wearing a headscarf in accordance with her Islamic faith.

68. Under section 23. See *NEHAWU v. University of Cape Town* 2003 3 SA 1 (CC) paras 40, 52–54; Olivier (2016: 160) and Henrico (2016a: 177).

69. See para 21. Emphasis added. It is important to note the basis upon which the employer took the applicants into his employ. It was because they were Muslim. This case emphasizes the fact that in certain instances, due to the nature of the job in question, the employer is acutely aware of the nature of the employee's religion. Given the employer's knowledge of the faith of the applicants in *FAWU* it is unlikely that this was used as a basis upon which to discriminate against the employees. See Henrico (2016a: 319–320).

70. Para 30 referring to paras 29–30 of *Christian Education*. The rejection of such test is also consistent with Canadian jurisprudence which does not suggest any support for a "compelling state interest" or similar based standard.

71. See para 32 of *S v. Lawrence S v. Negal S v. Solberg* 1997.

72. See para 128 of *Lewis v. Media24 Ltd* (2010).

73. The case is relevant to South African equity jurisprudence and specifically religious discrimination on the basis that the employee's "perminitions" to undergo training as a traditional healer was a personally held cultural belief which our courts have acknowledged are constitutionally protected, see paras 22 and 25–28. Also see *Lawrence* para 35; *MEC for Education:*

KwaZulu Natal v. Pillay para 47; *Christian Education* paras 33–34; and Stone (2009: 219–235); Henrico (2016a: 328).

74. See para 30 of *Kievits Kroon Country Estate (Pty) Ltd v. Mmoledi* (2014).

75. See para 34 of *Christian Education South Africa v. Minister of Education* 2000.

76. See para 26 of *Christian Education South Africa v. Minister of Education* 2000.

77. See para 21 of *Department of Correctional Services v. POPCRU* (2013).

78. See para 22 of *Department of Correctional Services v. POPCRU* (2013).

79. This is an interesting and significant aspect. Some may argue that it is self-explanatory; however, arguably it should be a requirement in discrimination disputes. Awareness on the part of the employer of the employee's religious beliefs offers more benefits than disadvantages. Awareness can act as a necessary catalyst to for dialogue between employee and employer which, if used to address any potential conflict, can act as a means of effective dispute resolution. Furthermore, it also imposes a duty upon the employer to take steps to address the IROJ. Moreover, it enables reasonable and necessary measures to be addressed that seek to accommodate the religious beliefs of the employee. Lack of knowledge on the part of the employer played a significant role in the judgment of Cheadle AJ in *Media24* para 126.

80. This requirement is almost prescient of the amendment that would appear in s 11(1)(b) of the EEA, as amended by s 6 of Act 47 of 2013, which in essence provides that if unfair discrimination is alleged on a listed ground, the employer against whom the allegation is made must prove that the discrimination is not unfair.

81. Also see case note discussion in Govindjee (2007: 360–368). In this insightful article the learned author compares the reasoning adopted by the different courts in the *Pillay* and *Dlamini* cases. While correctly pointing out that each case essentially dealt with criteria, the consequences of which impacted upon the applicants by way of indirect discrimination, certain factors are highlighted in an attempt to reconcile the different outcomes of the cases (371). One is that culture (as a more expansive term) was the dominating theme in *Pillay* as opposed to religion in the *Dlamini* case. Another is the fact that in *Pillay*, PEPUDA was applied whereas the EEA was applied in *Dlamini* (372).

82. A similar requirement was not imposed on female employees. On the contrary, female employees could wear their hair long which would then be in apparent breach of the code.

83. Namely that in *Dlamini* the applicant employee's unfair discrimination claim on the basis of religion was rejected and in *POPCRU* the claim of

unfair discrimination on the basis of religious and cultural discrimination was upheld.

84. See *Lawrence* para 33; *Christian Education* para 6; MEC *for Education: Kwazulu Natal v. Pillay* para 146; *Prince v. President of the Law Society of the Cape of Good Hope* para 97; and *Dlamini* para 16.

85. The existence of a Code of Good Practice on Religion is no guarantee or assurance against religious discrimination in the workplace. However, at the very least it creates a mechanism in terms of which parties to a possible dispute and/or co-employee can at an early stage identify any potential conflict of fundamental rights and seek to engage in constructive measures of appropriate dispute resolution.

86. Emphasis added. Conceivably a case which is not employment related may still be relevant to an employment-related dispute where the nexus between the two cases in question is based on unfair discrimination. A case in point is *Mangena v. Fila South Africa (Pty) Ltd* 2009 (12) BLLR 1224 (LC) which concerned itself with an application based on s 6(1) of the EEA wherein the applicant alleged unfair discrimination on the basis of race or color (para 2) and in which Van Niekerk J referred to *Harksen* as authority for establishing unfair discrimination (para 5).

References

Literature

Ackermann, L. 2014. *Human Dignity: Lodestar for Equality in South Africa*. Cape Town: Juta.

Ahmed, D., and R. Ginsburg 2014. *Constitutional Islamization and Human Rights: The Surprising Origin and Spread of Islamic Supremacy in Constitutions*. University of Chicago Public Law & Legal Theory Working Paper No. 477, pp. 12–15.

Awolalu, J. 1976. What is African Traditional Religion? *Studies in Comparative Religion* 10 (2): 1–28.

Benson, I. 2000. Notes Towards (Re)defining of the Secular. *University of British Columbia Law Review* 33: 520–549.

———. 2013. Seeing Through the Secular Illusion. *Supplementum* 12: 12–29.

Bilchitz, D., and Williams, A. 2012. Religion and the Public Sphere: Towards a Model that Positively Recognises Diversity. *SAJHR* 146–175.

Bishop, M., and Brickhill, J. 2012. In the Beginning was the Word: The Role of the Text in the Interpretation of Statutes. *SALJ* 681–716.

Boethius, A. 2009. *The Consolation of Philosophy* (Trans. W. Cooper).

Buqa, W. 2015. Storying Ubuntu as a Rainbow Nation. *Verbum et Ecclesia* 36 (2): 1–8.

Burns, Y., and R. Henrico. 2020. *Administrative Law*. LexisNexis.

Campos, P. 1994. Secular Fundamentalism. *Columbia Law Review*. https://scholar.law.colorado.edu/faculty-articles/763/.

Chaskalson, A. 2000. Human Dignity as a Foundational Value of Our Constitutional Order. *SAJHR* 193–205.

Chawane, M. 2014. The Rastafarian Movement in South Africa: A Religion or Way of Life? *Journal for the Study of Religion* 27: 214–237.

Coertzen, P. 2012. Religion and the Search for the Common Good in a Pluralistic Society—Reformed Theological Perspectives. *Supplementum* 53: 175–190.

———. 2014. Constitution, Charter and Religious in South Africa. *African Human Rights Law Journal* 14 (1): 126–141.

Cook, A. (2013). God talk in a secular world. *Yale Journal of Law and Humanities*: 444–445.

Currie, I., and J. De Waal. 2015. *The Bill of Rights Handbook*. Cape Town: Juta.

Davidov, G., and B. Langile. 2011. *The Idea of Labour Law*. Oxford: Oxfrod University Press.

Davis, D., and Klare, K. 2010. Transformative Constitutionalism and the Common and Customary Law. *SAJHR* 403–509.

Du Plessis, G. 2016. The Legitimacy of Using the Harm Principle in Cases of Religious Freedom Within Education. *Human Rights Revision* 349.

Du Plessis, L. 1996. Legal Academics and the Open Community of Constitutional Interpreters. *SAJHR* 226.

———. 2011. The Status and Role of Legislation in South Africa as a Constitutional Democracy: Some Explanatory Observations. *Potchefstroom Electronic Law Journal* 14.

Du Toit, D. 2014. Protection Against Unfair Discrimination: Cleaning Up the Act? *Industrial Law Journal* 2623–2636.

Du Toit, D., and M. Potgieter. 2014. *Unfair Discrimination in the Workplace*. Cape Town: Juta.

Du Toit, D., et al., eds. 2015. *Labour Relations Law: A Comprehensive Guide*. 6th ed. LexisNexis.

Dworkin, R. 2013. *Religion Without God*. Harvard University Press.

Fagan, A. 2004. Section 39(2) and Political Integrity. *AJur* 117.

Govindjee, A. 2007. Of Nose Studs, Beards and Issues of Determination. *Obiter* 28 (2): 357–373.

———. 2016. Freedom of Religion, Belief and Opinion. In *Introduction to Human Rights*, ed. A. Govindjee, 121. LexisNexis.

Henrard, K. 2001. Diversity in South Africa Against the Background of the Centrality of the New Equality Principle in the New Constitutional Dispensation. *Journal of African Law* 51–72.

Henrico, R. 2012. Mutual Accommodation of Religious Differences in the Workplace – A Jostling of Rights. *Obiter* 3: 503–525.

———. 2014. Revisiting the Rule of Law and Principle of Legality: Judicial Nuisance or Licence? *Journal of South African Law* 4: 742–759.

———. 2015. South African Constitutional and Legislative Framework on Equality: How Effective is it in Addressing Religious Discrimination in the Workplace? *Obiter* 36: 275–287.

———. 2016a. *Religious Discrimination in the South African Workplace.* LLD thesis, North-West University.

———. 2016b. Educating South African Legal Practitioners: Combining Transformative Legal Education with Ubuntu. *US-China Law Review*: 817–823.

———. 2017. Revisiting a Culture of Tolerance Relating to Religious Unfair Discrimination in South Africa (Part 1). *Obiter* 2: 229–241.

———. 2019a. The Proselytization of Religious Bodies in South Africa: The Suppression of Religious Freedom? *Potchefstroom Electronic Law Journal* 22 (1): 1–27.

———. 2019b. Beyond Mere Rules and Regulatory Frameworks: A Reply to M Beneke 'Discrimination in Working Life and Anti-Discrimination Law— Experiments and Experiences in Germany and Europe. In *Legality and Limitation of Powers: Values, Principles and Regulations in Civil Law, Criminal Law, and Public Law*, ed. C. Hugo and M. Möllers, 119–134. Nomos.

———. 2021. Administrative Law and Voluntary Religious Associations. *Journal of South African Law* 521–537.

Henrico, R., and S. Fick. 2019. The State of Emergency Under the South African Apartheid System of Government: Reflections and Criticisms. *Zeitschrift für menschenrechte (Journal for Human Rights)* 71.

Ismail, J. 2001. South Africa's Sunday Law: Finding a Compromise. *Indiana International & Comparative Law Review* 1–23.

Kahn-Freund, O. 1972. *Labour and the Law.* Stevens & Sons.

Klaaren, J. 1997. Structures of Government in the 1996 Constitution: Putting Democracy Back into Human Rights. *Sought African Journal on Human Rights* 3.

Klare, K. 1998. Legal Culture and Transformative Constitutionalism. *South African Journal on Human Rights* 14: 146–188.

Le Roux, W. 2007. Bridges, Clearings and Labyrinths: The Architectural Framing of Post-Apartheid Constitutionalism. In *Post-Apartheid Fragments: Law, Politics and Critique*, eds. W. Le Roux and K. Van Marle, 61. Pretoria: Pretoria University Law Press.

Leatt, A. 2007. Faithfully Secular: Secularism and South African Political Life. *Journal for the Study of Religion* 29–44.

Lenta, P. 2009. Taking Rights Seriously: Religious Associations and Work-Related Discrimination. *South African Law Journal* 126: 827–860.

————. 2012. The Right of Religious Associations to Discriminate. *South African Journal of Human Rights* 231–257.

Marshall, P. 2013. Conceptual Issues in Contemporary Religious Freedom Research. *International Journal of Religious Freedom* 6: 7–16.

Meyerson, D. 2011. *Jurisprudence.* Oxford: Oxford University Press.

Moseneke, D. 2015. Personal Tribute to Former Chief Justice Pius Langa. *Acta Juridica* 3–9.

Mpiti, J.S. 1969. *African Religions and Philosophy.* 2nd ed., Heinemann.

Mureinik, E. 1994. A Bridge to Where?: Introducing the Interim Bill of Rights. *South African Journal on Human Rights* 10 (1): 31–48.

Olivier, M. 2016. Labour Rights. In *Introduction to Human Rights Law*, ed. A. Govindjee, 157–170. Cape Town: LexisNexis.

Oraegbunam, I. 2011. Jurisprudential Review of the Controversies on the Nature of Islamic Law. *American Journal of Comparative Law* 95: 99–102.

O'Regan, K. 2012. Text matters: some reflections on the forging of a constitutional jurisprudence in South Africa. *Modern Law Review* 1–72.

Pretorius, J. 2010. Fairness in Transformation: A Critique of the Constitutional Court's Affirmative Action Jurisprudence. *SAJHR* 536–570.

Rausch, C. 2015. Fundamentalism and Terrorism. *Journal of Terrorism Research* 6.

Rawls, J. 1993. *Political Liberalism.* Columbia University Press.

Sachs, F. 2013. The Sacred and the Secular: South Africa's Constitutional Court Rules on Same-Sex Marriages. *Kentucky Law Journal* 102: 147–158.

Seiffert, A. 2017. Religious Expression in the Workplace: The Case of the Federal Republic of Germany. In *The Significance of Religion in Today's Labour and Social Legislation*, eds. U. Becker, S. Krebber, and A. Seiffert, 121–163. Germany: Mohr Siebeck Tübingen.

Squelch, J. 2013. *Religious Symbols and Clothing in the Workplace: Balancing the Respective Rights of Employees and Employers*, 38–57. *Murdoch University Law Review.*

Stone, C. 2009. 'Speaking with our spirits': The Representation of Religion in Marlene van Niekerk's *Agaat*. In *Religion and Spirituality in South Africa: New Perspectives*, ed. D. Brown, 219–235. University of KwaZulu-Natal Press.

Strydom, E.M.L., ed. 2015. *Essential Employment Discrimination Law.* Cape Town: Juta.

Truter, I. 2007. African Traditional Healers: Cultural and Religious Beliefs Intertwined in a Holistic Way. *South African Pharmaceutical Journal* 74 (8): 56–60.

Van der Vyver, J.D., and M.C. Green. 2008. Law, Religion and Human Rights in Africa: An Introduction. *African Human Rights Law Journal* 8 (2): 337–356.

Van der Walt, J. 2006. Legal History, Legal Culture and Transformation in a Constitutional Democracy. *Fundamina* 1: 1–47.

Van der Westhuizen, J. 2008. A Few Reflections on the Role of Courts, Government, the Legal Profession, Universities, the Media and Civil Society in a Constitutional Democracy. *SAHRJ* 251–272.

Van Marle, K. 2009. Transformative Constitutionalism as/and Critique. *Stellenbosch Law Review* 20 (2): 286–289.

Watson, P. 2009. *EU Social and Employment Law Policy and Practice in an Enlarged Europe.* Oxford University Press.

Case Law

AAA Investments v. Micro Finance Regulatory Council 2006 BCLR 1255 (CC).

Association of Professional Teachers v. Minister of Education 1995 16 ILJ 1048 (LC) 1048.

AZAPO v. President of the Republic of South Africa 1996 4 SA 671 (CC).

Bato Star Fishing (Pty) Ltd v. Minister of Environmental Affairs 2004 7 BCLR 687 (CC).

Bhe and Others v. Khayelitsha Magistrate and Others 2005 (1) SA 580 (CC).

Brink v. Kitshoff 1996 4 SA (CC).

Carmichele v. Minister Safety and Security 2001 4 SA 938 (CC).

Christian Education South Africa v. Minister of Education 2000 4 SA 757 (CC).

City Council of Pretoria v. Walker (CCT8/97) [1998] ZACC 1; 1998 (2) SA 363.

City of Tshwane Metropolitan Municipality v. Afriforum and Another 2016 (9) BCLR 1133 (CC).

De Lange v. Presiding Bishop of the Methodist Church 2016 1 SA 1 (CC).

Democratic Party v. Minister of Home Affairs 1999 3 SA 254 (CC).

Department of Correctional Services v. POPCRU 2013 JOL 30347 (SCA).

Dlamini v. Green Four Security 2006 11 BLLR 1074 (LC).

Du Plessis v. De Klerk 1996 3 SA 850 (CC).

FAWU v. Rainbow Chicken Farms 2000 1 BLLR 70 (LC).

Glenister v. President of RSA 2011 3 SA 347 (CC).

Griggs v. Duke Power Co 401 US 424 (1971).

Harksen v. Lane 1998 1 SA 300 (CC).

Hoffman v. South African Airways 2000 1 SA 1 (CC).

International Brotherhood of Teamsters v. United States 431 US 324 (1977).

Kadiaka v. Amalgamated Beverage Industries 1999 20 ILJ 373 (LC).

Khumalo and Governing Body of the Juma Musjid Primary School & Others v. Essay NO & Others 2011 (8) 761 (CC).

Kievits Kroon Country Estate (Pty) Ltd v. Mmoledi (2012) 33 ILJ 2812 (LAC).

Kievits Kroon Country Estate (Pty) Ltd v. Mmoledi 2014 35 ILJ 209 (SCA).

Leonard Dingler Employee Representative Council v. Leonard Dingler (Pty) Ltd 1997 11 BLLR 1438 (LC) 289 G-H 292, 293 A.

Lewis v. Media24 Ltd (2010) 31 ILJ 2416 LC.

Louw v. Golden Arrow Bus Service (Pty) Ltd 2000 21 ILJ 373 (LC).

Lukie v. Rural Alliance CC t/a Rural Development Specialist 2004 8 BLLR 769 (LC).

Mangena v. Fila South Africa (Pty) Ltd 2009 (12) BLLR 1224 (LC).

MEC for Education: Kwazulu-Natal v. Pillay 2008 1 SA 474 (CC).

Minister of Finance v. Van Heerden 2004 6 SA 121 (CC).

Minister of Health v. New Clicks South Africa (Pty) Ltd (2006).

Minister of Home Affairs v. Fourie 2006 1 SA 524 (CC).

Motaung v. Department of Education 2013 34 ILJ 1199 (LC).

Mvumvu v. Minister of Transport 2011 2 SA 473 (CC).

National Coalition for Gay and Lesbian Equality v. Minister of Justice 1999 1 SA 6 (CC); *Minister of Finance v. Van Heerden* 2004 6 SA 121 (CC).

NUMSA v. Intervalve (Pty) Ltd and Other CCT72/14: [2014] ZACC 35.

Pillay v. Krishna 1946 AD 946.

POPCRU v. Department of Correctional Services 2010 10 BLLR1067 (LC).

President of the RSA v. Hugo 1997 4 SA 1 (CC).

Prince v. President of the Law Society of the Cape of Good Hope 2002 2 SA 792 (CC).

Prinsloo v. Van der Linde 1997 6 BCLR 759 (CC).

Publications Control Board v. Gallo (Africa) Ltd 1975 (3) SA 665(A) 671H).

R v. Big Drug Mart Ltd (1985).

S v. Jordan 2002 6 SA 642 (CC).

S v. Lawrence S v. Negal S v. Solberg 1997 4 SA 1176 (CC).

SACTWU v. Berg River Textiles, a Division of Seardel Group Trading (Pty) Ltd 2012 33 ILJ 972 (LC).

Satchwell v. President of the Republic of South Africa and Another 2002 6 SA 1 (CC).

South African Revenue Services v. CCMA 2016 ZACC.

Strydom v. NG Gemeente Moreleta Park 2009 30 ILJ 868 (EqC).

Zabala v. Gold Reef City Casino (2009) 1 BLLR 94 (LC).

INTERNET SOURCES

Pew Forum on Religious Life, Tolerance and Tension: Islam and Christianity in Sub-Saharan Africa. 2010. Available at https://www.pewresearch.org/religion/2010/04/15/executive-summary-islam-and-christianity-in-sub-saharan-africa/ (Accessed in 20 June 2023).

Statssa.gov.za. Available at https://www.statssa.gov.za/publications/P0302/MidYear2022.pdf (Accessed on 20 June 2023).

CHAPTER 24

The Relationship Between the Church and State in Zimbabwe

Joachim Kwaramba

INTRODUCTION

This chapter explores the relationship between the church and the state in the country of Zimbabwe. Efforts to establish a relationship between the two institutions are arguably traceable to the era of the disintegration of the Roman Empire around AD400 and to the ascendancy of Christianity as the official religion of that Empire in 310 (Boucher and Kelly 2009). This is the position that has been advanced by a number of church leaders in Zimbabwe who always argue for a peaceful environment. Based on ideas drawn from this history, it is evident that the behavior of churches significantly draws from the above intellectual foundation. Therefore, the gist of this study is to explore the relationship between the church and the state in the context of Zimbabwe.

J. Kwaramba (✉)
University of Zimbabwe, Harare, Zimbabwe

© The Author(s), under exclusive license to Springer Nature
Switzerland AG 2023
S. Holzer (ed.), *The Palgrave Handbook of Religion and State
Volume II*, https://doi.org/10.1007/978-3-031-35609-4_24

THE CATHOLIC BISHOPS AND THE STATE

Catholic bishops all over the world communicate their opinions on the prevailing situation through letters. Thus, in the context of political and economic injustice, it was not expected that Catholic bishops in Zimbabwe would remain silent in the face of human rights abuses. In fact, as argued by Jere and Magezi (2018), pastoral letters have been pivotal in disseminating important messages from church leadership to congregants, and to government as a whole, thereby reflecting the ideology of the Catholic Church in the political, societal, and economic affairs of people. The Zimbabwe Catholic Bishops is a group of bishops representing ten Zimbabwean provinces and each province has a bishop, who then forms part of the Zimbabwe Catholic Bishops. These groups have many mandates, of which one is the prophetic duty to give voice to the cries from the parched throats of the poor, dying, and miserable of society (Wiryadinata 2018). Informed by the foregoing, this paper briefly highlights the contents of the letter and its possible implications.

The first concern the bishops raise in relation to the Zimbabwean situation is that dissenting voices are being suppressed, especially those in opposition to Zimbabwe African National Union Patriotic Front (ZANU-PF), and those aligned to the Movement of Democratic Change Alliance (MDC-A). In explaining this problem, the Catholic bishops write that "the suppression of people's anger can only serve to deepen the crisis and take the nation into deeper crisis" (ZCBC 2020, online). They add that "the crackdown on dissent is unprecedented." They ask, "Is this the Zimbabwe we want? To have a different opinion does not mean be an enemy" (ZCBC 2020). It is clear that the Catholic bishops are not happy with the persecution of opposition to ZANU-PF, since the government's actions do not reflect the Zimbabwe envisaged by the second republic of President Emmerson Mnangagwa. Through this point, the bishops evoke the need for a non-violent society, which listens to different voices and does not crack down on them, as multiple voices are a cornerstone of a democratic society. The second aspect raised by the Catholic bishops is the extreme level of corruption present at all levels of society, including government. The Catholic bishops argue that "the corruption in the country has reached alarming levels, there hasn't been equally a serious demonstration by government to rid the country of this scourge" (ZCBC 2020). When the second republic came into being, one of the promises by

President Emmerson Mnangagwa to the people of Zimbabwe was an end to corruption, which had brought the country to its knees.

However, this was easier said than done and, unfortunately, government officials, who were supposed to be the harbingers of the end of corruption, only became more corrupt. For instance, Obadiah Moyo was dismissed as the minister of Health after being involved in corruption deals that cost the government over US $60 million (BBC News 2020; News24 2020). However, since he is aligned to the regime, he is a free man and immune to the law, despite evidence of misuse of public funds meant for the health ministry. Corruption cases that involve government officials die a natural death in the courts, while those who expose corruption are subjected to humiliation and imprisonment without trail, as illustrated by the cases of Hopewell Chinono and Job Sikala (Chikowere 2021; Mafata 2021). In summary, the law in Zimbabwe seems to favor corrupt individuals and persecutes those who expose corruption. This suggests a captured judiciary, which makes the rhetoric of fighting corruption a political gimmick that promotes the agenda of the rich and blocks the general populace, including poor people, from having direct contact with the responsible authorities within the government structures regarding the value of human life. A society cannot be considered truly human when it neglects poor and marginalized people, especially within the political, legislative, and religious space. Furthermore, silencing voices in society only leads to greater frustration of the people and exacerbates the situation (Mares 2020). Cognizant of the foregoing, the Catholic bishops allude to the need for a united people, who are not divided along political lines. They argue, "[W]e want our politics to build a united nation and not to divide us, turning the military who ought to continue the memory of the late heroes against the people who fed and clothed them. Some of our vocal political leaders are busy re-creating the war situation of us and them" (ZCBC 2020). In addition, the Catholic bishops note, "It feels the poor have no one to defend them. They do not seem to feature on the national agenda. Their cry for an improved health system goes unheeded." In this regard the Catholic bishops ask, "In the face of growing numbers of COVID-19 infections where does the nation turn to?" In addition, the bishops report that "we notice with wounded hearts that government officials seem to have more personal protective equipment (PPE) than our nurses and doctors."

Unfortunately, the plea for health and an effective "transport system that meets their transport blues are met with promises and more promises and no action" (ZCBC 2020, online). Another point raised by the Catholic bishops is the government's failure to take responsibility for the deteriorating economic and political environment. In fact, rather than taking responsibility, the government points the finger to stakeholders. The Catholic bishops note, "All we hear from them is the blame of our woes on foreigners, colonialism, white settlers and the so-called internal detractors. When are you going to take responsibility for your own affairs? When are we going to submit to the requirements for national accountability?" (ZCBC 2020, online). According to the Catholic bishops, taking responsibility is key for national development and, to date, the Zimbabwean government is far from recognizing itself as the enemy of the people and the international community. With this in mind, the solution to the Zimbabwean problem is far from being found; thus, the Bishops felt obligated to remind politicians of their accountability, as a way to redress the trajectories faced by the Zimbabwean people.

RESPONSES TO THE LETTER BY GOVERNMENT AND ITS PROXIES

The points raised above by the Catholic bishops were not well received by the government of Zimbabwe and its proxies, though it resonated with the general population, who are facing daily struggles. While some scholars may argue that Catholic Church is a colonial project, it does not take away their ability to contribute to the reconstruction of the African space in terms of democracy and good governance. In this, the letter has positive contribution to the Zimbabwean political landscape even though it was seen as a direct attack on the regime and as a mouthpiece of opposition to political parties and regime change elements that work to undermine the sovereignty of Zimbabwe. Thus, according to politicians, the letter represents an example of a "third force" (third force is a term used by ZANU-PF in reference to its enemies who, they claim, want to displace them) that seeks to dismantle the democratically elected government (Dube 2020a).

The letter of the Catholic bishops was seen as a direct attack on the government, thus warranting a sharp response by the Minister of Information and Publicity, Monica Mutsvangwa. In her response, she accuses the Catholic bishops of being misguided people who are being used by individuals to push a political agenda. One of the bishops was singled out as the force behind the letter, namely Archbishop Charles

Ndlovu, the leader of the Zimbabwe Catholic Bishops' Conference (ZCBC). She describes Bishop Ndlovu as a "righteous Ndebele minority," who is promoting a regime change agenda and "fanning the psychosis of tribal victimization" (Ndebele 2020). She levels this accusation even though the letter does not make reference to tribal issues. This response was not only an attack on Bishop Ndlovu, but on the Ndebele people, who have suffered under ZANU policies, some going back several decades. For instance, in Gukurahundi, more than 20,000 Ndebele were killed in the early 1980s. The response is a reminder of unresolved social challenges, and the minister indirectly reopened the wounds suffered by the Ndebele people. The minister's response suggests that ethnic issues in Zimbabwe, when not addressed, tend to be bought back into the fold during struggle and disagreement.

According to the minister, the bishops' letter was a script by "evil minded" people, who are fanning the flames of ethnic division; she made comparisons to the role of the church in the 1994 Rwandan genocide (BBC News 2020). However, looking at the letter shows no suggestion that Catholics wanted to incite people to engage in violence or suggests a link to the Rwandan genocide. However, since the Rwandan genocide was based on ethnicity, the minister suggests that another genocide was possible if Catholic leaders write such things, especially under the leadership of minority Ndebele Bishop Ndlovu. In my own assessment, nothing warranted the minister referring to the genocide or to castigate Bishop Ndlovu alone, since the letter was a representation of the experiences of the people of Zimbabwe and represents the views of all the bishops who signed the letter. The response by the ministry indicates that there is background information on the relationship of the state and Bishop Ndlovu that people are not privy to and which needs to be explored further.

Another figure in the ministry is the permanent secretary, Nick Mangwana, who responded to the letter by noting that "it is most unfortunate when men of the cloth begin to use the pulpit to advance a nefarious agenda for detractors of our country" (Guardian 2020). In addition, the Ministry of Information saw the letter as an attempt "to manufacture crises" (BBC News 2020). Such accusations by ministry officials are "psychologically damaging, religion-culturally disengaging and destructive to successful social, political and economic development and human progress" (Kaunda 2015). The ministry's response ignores the realities suffered by the people of Zimbabwe and shows that politicians are detached from the realities faced by the Zimbabwean people. Furthermore, the response indicates a lack of commitment by the Zimbabwean government to address the lived realities of the people and that speaking truth to power is dangerous, despite claims that freedom of speech exists. It is not only politicians who responded to the letter negatively, but religious leaders aligned with the regime did too. A regime enabler is an individual or group that helps politicians gain power and then helps them to maintain power (Magaisa 2019). The role of the religious enablers in relation to the Catholic bishops' letter was to discredit the alternative religious voice in the Zimbabwean political space. In this case, religion is used as a counter-revolutionary strategy to silence emerging voices with a different view to ZANU-PF. Mutendi, as a regime enabler, inherited church leadership from his father in 1976. Because his church is one of the biggest in Zimbabwe, it is a rich hunting ground for politicians to capture the religious constituency (Dube 2020b).

Politicians have strategically positioned people like Mutendi for political mileage. Magaisa (2019) reports that "the perfect facade of normalcy of some religious leaders is designed to cover the sordid reality of the regime." In response to the Catholic bishops, Mutendi, as regime enabler associated with the ruling elite, argues that the letter is irrelevant and dug up old graves. He notes that, instead of opening old wounds, like the Gukurahundi issue, churches should divert their energies toward preaching messages of hope to a nation burdened by drought and sanctions-induced economic hardships (New Zimbabwe 2020). He argued that church leaders should not speak out about past wrongdoings, but should focus on giving hope to their flock. There is no need to remind people of the past, because everyone has a dark past (New Zimbabwe 2020). Thus, instead of engaging with the contents of the letter, Mutendi considered the Catholic bishops' letter as "inappropriately prescriptive and grossly disrespectful" (Guardian 2020). On that note, it is clear from their response that religious leaders, like Mutendi, legitimize a regime through blindness to wrongdoing, as a way to remain politically relevant and ensure reciprocal benefits. Another influential religious leader who responded to the bishops' letter is Apostle AndrewWutawunashe, who represents the Zimbabwe Indigenous Inter-Denominational Council of Churches (ZIICC). Wutawunashe states that, as a religious movement, it categorically dissociates itself from calls by certain religious leaders to march against the government and to reignite conflicts and wounds for the sake of healing (Pindula News 2020). It is not surprising that Wutawunashe would want to distance himself from this letter and the political issues it refers to, as he has been involved in various political issues in Zimbabwe in the past and sided with the regime. He is a known political activist who champions the regime agenda, has officiated at ZANU-PF functions, and has castigated those with a different political agenda. His view on the letter is centered around the notion that the religious regime should please the political masters.

Therefore, Wutawunashe finds it impossible to speak up against the regime, especially when he benefits from the regime. In this regard, the paper agrees with Matthews (2019) that democracy itself is undermined when the needs of the majority of its population are ignored, and preference given to that of the political and economic elite, which implies a skewed nationalism favoring a few who are aligned to the regime. In short, the responses of regime-enabling religious leaders, which negate issues of justice and disregard poor people, religious pluralism, and democracy, dilute the prophetic role of the church in critical affairs related to nation building. Hence the analysis of this paper indicates that the responses by the government and its proxies can be summed up as "to hell with the bishops." The responses indicate that the "majority of Africans remain mentally colonised" (Kaunda 2015). In light of the foregoing, "unfortunately, a section of religion is being used to legitimatise, sustain and even promote political tyranny and oppression" (Zimunya and Gwara 2013). The responses illustrate that religion tends to be relegated to the exclusive realm of ideology or belief, especially if religion does not advance the political ideology of the day doing so obscures its overwhelming impact on social institutions (Johnson 2015).

The responses of government and religious leaders to the bishops' letter call us to rethink the foundations of our knowledge on and the role of religion in society and politics (Tarusarira 2020). It is clear that the political space in Zimbabwe is not prepared to hear alternative voices that promote democracy through fair representation, which manifest in allowing multiple voices to engage in matters that affect humanity. So, the relationship of the state and the church is fluid, and it is influenced by what the regime's opinion is on the church's teaching. But what stands out with the Zimbabwean context is that the adherents of the indigenous church are given preferential treatment over the followers of all other religious faiths, which are perceived as foreign to the nation (Ferrari 1997).

THE CHURCH AND THE CONSTITUTION-MAKING PROCESS

It has been underscored that the church has contributed to the contentious issues in the constitutional-making exercise. The Evangelical Fellowship of Zimbabwe (EFZ) through its leader Goodwill Shana has indicated that it does not condone homosexual activities. Renowned radio preacher and Apostolic Faith Mission in Zimbabwe pastor, Reverend Happymore Gotora, has also condemned the act as unbiblical. Churches like Zimbabwe Assemblies of God Africa (ZAOGA) have also utilized the media to condemn the activity. The issue of homosexual acts has been used by Kunonga as leverage against the Gandiya-led Church of the Province of Africa mainly because of the church's links with the Church of England, which has some bishops who have defended homosexuality as a fundamental right. This is, albeit, of the fact that no one from the Gandiya-led congregants has openly supported the activity. The dominance of Kunonga in Harare Province can best be explained in the way constitutional issues are handled by seemingly "orthodox" or conservative followers of the bishop who usually do not question the cleric. Due to the incessant opposition from the church, the first published draft of the new constitution excluded the right. This demonstrates the importance of the church in society as the custodians of moral values without whom the politicians could have been swayed by public opinion to entrench the unnatural right in the supreme law.

THE CHURCH AND RULE OF LAW

The church has also been accused of interfering with the separation of powers in Zimbabwe. The Chief Justice of the Supreme Court of Zimbabwe warned Anglicans whose matters were before the courts to stop engaging the executive leadership on the matter. Nemukuyu (2012, p. 1) notes that the Chief Justice ordered that "all the matters relating to the above parties will be determined by the same court." Although the court is expected to determine the rightful owner of the Anglican property, the wrangle was an acid test on the church's role in politics within the Government of National Unity (GNU) context. The Anglican Archbishop of Canterbury, Rowen Williams, is believed to have engaged President Mugabe during his visit to Zimbabwe in 2011. This did not deter the Church of the Province of Africa bishops from coming up with positions regarding sticky issues such as selective application of the law in the GNU environment. Bishops Cleopas Lunga (Matabeleland), Dr. Julius Makoni (Manicaland), Dr. Chad Gandiya (Harare), Godfrey Tawonezvi (Masvingo), and Ishmael Mukuwanda (Central Zimbabwe) came up with a position paper wherein they indicated that they are "disturbed that the police have taken sides." Undeterred by the red line issued by the Supreme Court of Zimbabwe, the bishops registered their wish therein that "we are therefore appealing to President of the Republic of Zimbabwe, His Excellency President R. G Mugabe, members of the Government of National Unity, the co-ministers of Home Affairs and the Police Commissioner General to intervene in this matter where innocent and peace loving worshippers are being driven out of their church buildings for no legitimate reason" (Lunga et al. 2012, p. 1). The sentiments of the bishops hold since the police were driving people in Chivhu which falls out of the jurisdiction of Harare Province where the property wrangle spilled into the courts. The church continued to fight for recognition in the GNU as it appears that the visit by the Anglican Leader Archbishop, Williams, yielded nothing in terms of uniting the divided church in Zimbabwe.

The Church and the Elections

The indigenous churches like the white garment churches have been accused of supporting Zimbabwe African National Union Patriotic Front (ZANU-PF). The churches that have courted controversy include Johanne Masowe and Johanne Marange. The ZANU-PF leadership has frequently fellowshipped with the two indigenous churches whose membership is scattered around the country. The ZANU-PF politburo members have also been part of the religious visits and this has been seen as a step toward winning the votes from the usually conservative sect members. The Johanne Masowe Echishanu in particular has openly supported ZANU-PF, particularly during the last days of the late Madzibaba Nzira. Even opposition leaders like Mr. Tsvangirai, who is also the prime minister in the GNU, removed their shoes to join the Marange followers in worship. This may have been a deliberate ploy by the two dominant political parties to infiltrate or manipulate the populous worshippers into supporting them. Some indigenous church leaders like Paul Mwazha of African Apostolic Faith Church have maintained a low profile in the GNU. Mwazha condemned sanctions just like other church leaders like Kunonga and Makandiwa. Prophet Makandiwa signed the Anti-Sanction Petition that was the brainchild of ZANU-PF. The petition saw the European Union (EU) removing some of the individuals like Senator Georgias. The EU also engaged Zimbabwe through representatives of the political parties and the role of the church in this regard cannot be underestimated.

Ex-communicated Bishop Dr. Nolbert Kunonga "openly stated that he was a proud recipient of land through the government Land Reform Program and openly supported ZANU (PF)" (Muchechetere 2009, p. 14). Other mainline church bishops who have brazenly shown their partisanship include "Bishop Levy Kadenge a former Methodist Church in Zimbabwe Bishop who was also chided by his church leadership for openly supporting the opposition" (Muchechetere 2009, p. 14). Bishop Dube "former head of the United Baptist Church and former governor of Manicaland under ZANU (PF) was also partisan and a fierce critic of opposition politics" (Muchechetere 2009, p. 14). The family of God Church led by Prophet Andrew Wutawunashe has been accused of form-ing "Faith For the Nation" that "articulated the policies of ZANU (PF) and openly opposed, even in the media any church leadership that sought to sanction the ruling party and government as in the June 2008 elec-tions" (Muchechetere, 2009, p. 14).

The church has been used as a platform for political glorification. *The Herald* of 3 October (2012, p. 2) carried a story where ZANU-PF polit-buro member Tendai Savanhu donated groceries to 51 households made up of the elderly, people living with HIV and AIDS, orphans, and the vulnerable living at Matapi Hostels in Mbare. Laudable as this move might be, the politician was in the company of Pastor Alwyn Bizure of Adonai Ministries as he moved into each household. The man of the robe com-mended "Cde Savanhu and ZANU-PF leadership in Mbare for putting God's word into practice by assisting the disadvantaged groups in soci-ety." The man of the cloth went on to say that "this gesture by Cde Savanhu shows ZANU PF has God-fearing leadership that are obedient and visionary" (Herald 2012, p. 2). It can be argued that since the church leaders wield influence over their followers the politicians find it easy to exploit this comparative advantage for cheap political scores; hence, the recipients can be easily swayed by the remarks from the man of the cloth and can be influenced in their choices in the constitutional referendum and most importantly the elections that were held in March 2013. Religious leaders may be more social savvy than their flocks or those who look up to them as men of God. The glorification of one party by a man of the cloth may send wrong signals to the other parties in the GNU and augurs well with the sentiments of opposition functionaries referred to above that churches should not claim to be apolitical when they are not. It is easy for religious leaders to be used as pawns in the much bigger chess game.

A CHURCH DIVIDED ECHOES OF COUNTER-MESSAGING

In post-independent Zimbabwe, especially beyond the year 2000, the government has responded to the criticism of historical ecumenical bodies by influencing the formation of pro-government church groups. During the Mugabe era, the Apostolic Christian Council of Zimbabwe (ACCZ) was formed to counter the messages of church bodies that were critical of government. In the post-Mugabe era, Zimbabwe witnessed the formation of the Zimbabwe Indigenous Inter-Denominational Council of Churches (ZIICC) for the same purpose. The "second republic" may have felt that the ACCZ was pro-Mugabe; hence, it would not serve its best interests. Thus, despite the bishop's letter galvanizing massive support from groups mentioned above, the ZIICC moved in to counter these and show support for the government.

The ZIICC through its patron, Nehemiah Mutendi, and spokesperson, Andrew Wutawunashe, reacted to the bishops' letter. Wutawunashe spoke against the bishop's pastoral letter as one that sought to revive old grudges or wounds. He argued, "We take strong exception to and categorically dissociate ourselves from calls by certain religious leaders to march against the government and to reignite conflicts and wounds of the past to heal us, from which God answered our prayers by bringing political leaders to the negotiating table whose reconciliation was achieved" (The Herald 19 August 2020). He rejected the bishops' pastoral letter's narrative that the government was intolerant, corrupt, violating human rights, and does not have any regard for the rule of law. Instead, Wutawunashe blamed targeted sanctions for the continued suffering of citizens. On the other hand, Mutendi chastised the bishops for placing judgment on the government rather than advocating for positive and constructive discourse. It is clear from the above that the ZIICC spoke out in favor of government. As a result, Dube (2021) called its leading members "regime enablers." The issue of sanctions has provided cover for the failures of the Zimbabwean government to a point that it does not account for anything without blaming sanctions. However, what is clear is that the church in Zimbabwe continues to have a divided voice when it comes to issues that concern the government. This continues to be the weakness of the church as it seeks relevance within the Zimbabwean political space. This proves Tarusarira's observation correct when he argues that Christian actors in both colonial and post-colonial Zimbabwe have played dynamic roles, with some working in collaboration with the perpetrators of violence and fanning conflict, while others resisted and/or intervened to resolve the conflict (Tarusarira 2016).

The March Is Not Ended: The Pastoral Letter that Provided a Rallying Point for the Nation

The government's political response to the Zimbabwe Catholic Bishops' Conference (ZCBC)'s pastoral letter was perceived as a direct attack on the church in general. The ecumenical bodies in Zimbabwe and beyond released their statements of solidarity with the bishops. It was a rare show of unity, which I argue can provide faith communities with an avenue of speaking with one voice as a way of dealing with conflict in their different contexts. Internationally, solidarity statements were received from the World Council of Churches, Methodist World Council, the Lutheran World Federation, World Communion of Reformed Churches, Catholic Bishops of Southern Africa, and Catholic Bishops of Zambia, among others. In Zimbabwe, the Evangelical Fellowship of Zimbabwe, the Zimbabwe Council of Churches, The Anglican Council of Zimbabwe, as well as the Zimbabwe Conference of Major Religious Superiors, stood in support of the ZCBC's pastoral letter. As this article is focused on the response within Zimbabwe, I will present the responses of some of its ecumenical bodies. The EFZ released its own pastoral statement in support of the ZCBC's pastoral letter. In the statement, the EFZ affirmed the correctness of the content of the bishop's letter. It argued, "True democracy is not built on threatening and criticising those who speak up or speak out; it is not in denying inconvenient and unpalatable truth, it is not in demonising those we disagree with. Democracy welcomes truth" (EFZ 2020, p. 8). Democracy is built on the search for truth.

The EFZ charged that while the government had managed to stop the demonstrations of 31 July 2020, it had not managed to contain the truth. From their perspective, despite the criticism leveled upon the church, for them the truth could not be stopped. They said, "[H]arsh criticism may be levelled against the Church but the truth continues to march on" (EFZ statement, Evangelical Fellowship of Zimbabwe 2020). Turning to cases of abductions and victimizations of political activists and journalists, the EFZ said "abductions, torture and incarcerations may be unleashed on journalists and every voice of dissent but the truth will still march on like it did during the struggle for independence against more sophisticated and superior force of arms, and a state machinery that made every aspirant of freedom a hunted terrorist" (Evangelical Fellowship of Zimbabwe 2020). In a direct attack on those in power, the EFZ further charged, "Truth may be on the cross today, and wrong may be on the throne but on the third day, it will rise again because the truth still marches on" (Evangelical Fellowship of Zimbabwe 2020). This was an indictment on the political leadership whom the EFZ perceive as irrelevant to the needs of Zimbabweans. In concluding its statement, the EFZ called for inclusive engagement, dialogue, and transformation. Referencing a pastoral letter which it had released on 4 August 2020, the EFZ reiterated that Zimbabwe had multi-layered crises which had given rise to discontent and protest movements such as the hashtag Zimbabwean Lives Matter.

From the EFZ's standpoint, the government needed to prioritize dialogue to "address the underlying causes of the crisis that exists in Zimbabwe in order to create a Zimbabwe that all citizens yearn for." In the same vein, the ZCC also released a statement titled "Echoing 'The March is not ended.'" It affirmed its support of the bishops' pastoral letter, which it described as "honest communication." In its statement, the ZCC refuted the government's blame of the economic crisis on natural disasters such as Cyclone Idai and the COVID-19 pandemic as well as international isolation. It called on the government to also put into cognizance some of the serious causes of the economic crisis such as corruption, policy inconsistencies, and the government's failure to unite the nation toward a common vision. It noted that it has always shifted blame and labeled critical voices as "regime change agents" or terrorists. Yet, many conclude that the government is not willing or able to engage with its citizens on the level of ideas. From the ZCC's analysis, this robs the citizens of any hope that things could improve.

The ZCC further described the government's response as "overtly too emotional and disrespectful for formal communication" (Zimbabwe Council of Churches 2020). It condemned the personalized attacks on Archbishop Ndlovu. It argued that the singling out of Archbishop Ndlovu was meant to destroy the unity of the church by isolating an individual from the collective discernment process.

The aim was seen as that of diluting the collective voice of the churches. As a result, the ZCC condemned the government for misusing public resources to slander the person of Archbishop Ndlovu. The ZCC argued that this was an inappropriate deployment of state resources by the government. It called on government through its public officials to instill positivity on the basis of ideas rather than to use public media to reinforce negativity. The ZCC further noted that the government's response to the bishops' pastoral letter had missed an opportunity to unite the nation. Furthermore, the ZCC rejected the government's comparison of the pastoral letter with the Rwandan genocide. Such comparison was seen as frivolous and insensitive, while at the same time giving the impression that the government was paying lip-service to national healing and reconciliation. The government was then reminded of the historical critical role that the churches have always played in relation to the state, arguing that the church in its ecumenical form has always fought for justice, peace, and unity.

Other solidarity messages came from individual denominations. For example, the Anglican Council of Zimbabwe released its statement on 24 August 2020. Affirming the church's prophetic role in society, it cited Ezekiel 3:17, which states, "Son of Man, I have made you watchman to the House of Israel. Therefore, hear the word at my mouth and give them warning from me." The government disregarded the bishops' pastoral letter, which seemed to "dismiss the fact that the church is called to exercise its prophetic role, which can mean challenging political leaders on their conduct of affairs, particularly if this affects the people of God" (Anglican Council of Zimbabwe 2020). The Council reiterated that indeed "the march is not ended" until and unless the issues raised by the people of Zimbabwe (through the bishops) are attended to and resolved holistically. The Council saw the response of the government as unproductive to the efforts being made by key stakeholders including the church to unite the nation. It, therefore, called on the government to engage all stakeholders in dialogue, to respect the constitution, and to respect all section 12 of the constitution. The Council reiterated that the mandate of the church is to speak to government which believes that "the voice of the people is the voice of God" without fear or favor.

Apart from ecumenical bodies supporting the bishops, some civil society organizations released statements of solidarity. The Human Rights NGO Forum affirmed its support for the bishops' pastoral letter. It noted that the response of the government showed that it was in denial of issues raised by the bishops, yet these were already in the public domain, particularly the fact that the letter called for peace, constitutionalism, and respect for human rights. It further encouraged the Information Ministry to pay attention to Zimbabwe's Bill of Rights, specifically to section 60, which deals with issues pertaining to freedom of conscience, and section 61, which focuses on freedom of expression. From its analysis, the response of the government infringed on these two constitutionally protected rights. It reminded the government of the critical role of the church in advocating for social justice. Therefore, silencing the church to speak up against injustices "is deplorable, unwarranted and a betrayal of the people's revolution against autocracy and mass human rights violation which started during the liberation struggle" (Human Rights NGO Forum 2020). In this regard, the Human Rights NGO Forum called on the government to respect freedom of expression and human rights, show tolerance of divergent views and accept constructive criticism, accept that Zimbabwe is in a crisis, and work toward genuine concerns raised by the ZCBC rather than distorting history calculated specifically to discredit the ZCBC.

Need to End Corruption

It has been noted that the church plays a critical role in ending corruption through letters. The letter speaks of corruption, a critical element for political-economic development of any society to address poverty which is rife, but it is ignored by the regime and its proxies. When the second republic emerged in 2017, people had high hopes that the new regime would fight corruption at all levels of government. In an attempt to keep its promises, a new anti-corruption commission was set up by the new government and a few people were arrested, such as former minister of Local Government, Ignatius Chombo, and former minister of Tourism, Prisca Mupfumira. These arrests were welcomed; however, it became clear early on that while these two officials had been corrupt during their tenure, the real reason for their arrest was that they belonged to a ZANU-PF splinter group, commonly known as G40.

In the new republic, imprisonment is not a consequence of corruption, as is claimed, but is used to settle political scores (Machakaire 2020). To this end, corrupt people continue being rewarded by the system, and the law seems to be incapacitated to evoke justice, which suggests that the judiciary has been captured and serves to punish political foes. Against this background, the bishops' letter sought to sensitize the government to the

596   J. KWARAMBA

fact that corruption does not benefit anyone not even corrupt officials themselves. This claim was exposed by the COVID-19 pandemic, during which money meant for Personal Protective Equipment (PPE) was stolen. This left health workers without the equipment needed to execute their jobs, which further lead to shortages of medication in hospitals and an increase in the mortality rate. If money had been used where needed, these challenges could have been mitigated.

Thus, according to decoloniality thinking, there is a need to continuously expose and challenge corruption in all spheres of life, as one of the ways to reinvent a better Zimbabwe. To ordinary Zimbabweans, a letter by the bishops, emphasizing that corruption had to end, should have been welcomed by all hands; instead, it was refuted and classified as a letter that manufactured crises. This rejection of criticism is "an impediment to economic advancement, irrelevant for modern societies and something that would fade away in time" (Lunn 2009, p. 29). In conclusion, if Zimbabwean politicians and government's proxies are sincere about ending corruption, the letter by the bishops could have stimulated engagement and introspection, and should have ensured that corrupt officials are subjected to fair and just prosecution, rather than being used to silence political foes and whistle blowers. Taking note of the need to end corruption especially coming from the church perspective is very important since it ignites the commitment of religious communities in mitigating social ills. By so doing religion contributes to sustainable development and an accountable society.

Thinking anew about poor people providing care and protection for poor people is at the heart of the Christian message. Consequently, the Catholic bishops refer to the need for politicians to take care of poor citizens, in particular, providing for their health and meeting their transportation needs, especially at the dire time of COVID-19. One wonders why politicians reacted with anger when the Catholic bishops sided with poor citizens. It probably reveals that in their wealth the cries of poor people disturb their comfort and privacy. In fact, over the years, churches have played a key role in speaking out against abuses of human rights, social injustice, and poverty. Advocacy on behalf of poor, marginalized, and oppressed people has been and remains a major contribution by churches to civil society (Gibbs and Ajulu 1999, p. 57). Thus, the bishops' emphasis on the need to take care of poor people is not out of the ordinary, but it is a moral obligation for politicians and religious leaders. Thus, any government or religious group that does not have poor people at the center of its narrative is irrelevant and creates an angry society that will be hard to govern. In short, a rereading of the letter suggests that we should rethink how religious and political discourses in Zimbabwe relate to poor people. Thus, a letter becomes a reminder of the basic tenets of religion which taking care of the poor, oppressed, and disadvantaged members of society and seemingly the Catholic Church maintains the ideology of the poor as the center of religion and politicians are not exempted from this divine mandate.

How Social Distancing and Lockdown Affect the Way the Church Operates

It has been noted that the church activities were directly affected in many ways. The church's role and how it operates are generally used to involve face-to-face human fellowship and interaction of people, and this resonates with Biri (2012) who noted that some of the characteristics of church fellowshipping in Pentecostal churches include face-to-face interaction and spiritualism manifested in glossolalia and other manifested gifts of the Holy Spirit. The social aspect where people came together just to sit down and interact at a human level defined a typical church service in all the churches. The lockdown and social distancing affected directly the human-level face-to-face interaction that involved people sitting down in the presence of a clergy to receive Biblical teaching, to pray, to be prayed for, to minister, and to be ministered to. As a result of the COVID-19 regulations, the free exercise of religion became impossible. Scholars allude to the fact that the church by its very nature is supposed to be an organization that caters to its own financial issues, and for the members of the community as noted by Biri (2012). The lockdown restrictions affected the financial position of the church because the absence of face-to-face meetings made it difficult for the collection of offerings and tithes in the normal way that churches operated before lockdown. This was despite the digital platforms that people can use to send their money to the church. It was said that there are some people who feel that for them to get blessed properly the money should be thrown into the offering basket; hence, they tend to slacken in their giving. It was also established that the lockdown had affected the church sacraments. After all, one cannot receive a sacrament from the church if one is not allowed to be there.

Maranatha, Briefing (2012) posits that Pentecostal churches in Zimbabwe interpret church fellowshipping as involving a sharing of friendship among believers, mutual love and trust, and also as involving the members being brothers and sisters in the same family. The church has therefore been characterized as a big family, which is usually made strong by coming together of its members. Many perceived the requirement to socially distance as a violation of the brotherhood of the church. Doing so violated the scriptural teaching which reads: "[N]ot giving up meeting together, as some are in the habit of doing, but encouraging one another—and all the more as you see the Day approaching" (Heb. 10:25 NIV). Biri argues that the requirement to socially distance weakens the church. His argument likens the church to a human body, which is made up of hands, head, fingers, heart, and lungs (Biri 2012). Any removal of any part was feared to incapacitate the function of the body. The same effect was explained in the context of social distancing, which was believed to be weakening the church, the body of Christ.

OPINION OF CHURCH TOWARD SOCIAL DISTANCING AND LOCKDOWN POLICY POSITIONS

The enforcement of lockdown regulations in Zimbabwe like all the countries was done regardless of any objections from the people. Churches like any other institution found themselves obliged to comply. Sentiments from the church, however, showed that not everyone fully agreed with the policy position. The church generally agreed with health experts on the need to socially distance taking into consideration how the virus is transmitted. However, it was also argued that this policy position conflicted with people's faith in the sense that Christians believe the church is an essential organization just like hospitals where all the sick would come to be healed. Christians view shutting down the churches in the same way as shutting down hospitals and other essential agencies. The church's role, though different, is no less important than that of the hospital.

THE VACCINATION CALL AND THE REACTION
OF THE CHURCH

It is apparent that the call for mandatory vaccination has proven to be one of the most contentious issues surrounding COVID-19. This is not only true in Zimbabwe, but it is true the world over. States across the globe have vigorously pushed for the citizens to get vaccinated with the hope to shorten the pandemic's life cycle. However, respective states are not only dealing with vaccine availability and the associated logistical issues, but there are also the mounting reservations that some people have against the vaccines. These include adverse reactions to the vaccines as well as moral problems with the use of fetal remains to develop them. Divergent political opinions have also divided people over their attitude toward vaccination with countries. For example, in the USA political lines are drawn over the issue of whether or not COVID-19 was born naturally or created in a Chinese laboratory. In Zimbabwe, the state has struggled with religious viewpoints which raise skepticism over the drive for mass vaccination. It is notable that the state has used policy positions to encourage and almost coerce people into embracing vaccination. The Zimbabwean government actually used its coercive power when it pronounced that all its civil service employees were expected to be fully vaccinated or risked their employment terminated. This was also followed by lockdown reviews that were subsequently made allowing those who were fully vaccinated to attend church services. Even though such policies targeted as many eligible people as possible to get vaccinated, there have been some mitigating variables including access to the actual vaccines across the parts of the country.

The exploratory engagements with church principals (such as fasting, prayer, etc.) showed that the government had not managed to fully enforce its policy pronouncements to ensure total compliance. This meant that church-goers saw the unenforceability as weakness and continued to attend church services even though they were not vaccinated. It has been also noted that the decline in COVID-19 infections especially during mid-year 2021 created complacency among citizens who believed that COVID-19 was coming to an end. It was only after the resurgence of infections by the Omicron variant that the people became aware the pandemic was far from over. The role of religion was critical in shaping how people made decisions about health matters during the pandemic, especially in Pentecostal churches.

Relevance of the Church in the Context of COVID-19 Lockdown

Against the many ramifications of the COVID-19 lockdown on the church, it emerged that there were many measures that the church had adopted to remain relevant as well as to fulfill its mandate in society. Churches went digital to some extent. By this they sought to deal with the limitation over face-to-face interaction and running of the church. The most common platforms used for interaction were WhatsApp, Facebook, and Zoom, which gave churches some level of continuity in terms of dissemination of information, preaching of the word, and praying. Face-to-face interaction among the church members had therefore migrated to digital, in a way confirm the assertion by Biri (2013) that ICT has enabled churches to defeat geographical barriers and reach their audience. Churches are no longer meeting in terms of the church buildings as was the case before the lockdown. The practice of delegating people to visit church members had also ceased in compliance with the prevailing regulations. Yet, even with the digital platforms, much is missing. Anointing with oil, the laying on of hands, embracing one another, and being in corporate worship cannot be done via the internet.

The lockdown put a great deal of pressure on pastors who relied on fulltime ministry to support their families. Such pastors were sustained by ministry work that they had been doing through the offerings and the tithes from the church. These church offerings had significantly diminished during the lockdown period. This meant that pastors had to look for alternative ways of putting food on the table. This divided the pastors' attention and took away from ministering to their congregants. This has created divided attention on the part of pastors who now have to assume the role of feeding their families to supplement whatever they are getting from the church. There is no doubt that the church landscape has been transformed by the regulations inspired by COVID-19 in Zimbabwe. The church believed that they had a much higher role in the society that included the governance of the country and the attendant decisions that affected people in their daily activities.

Adequacy of the Available Platforms to Sustain Church Activities

Just like many other institutions in Zimbabwe, churches devised ways to remain afloat under the COVID-19 lockdown. The adoption of digital platforms as a medium of communication enabled church activities to continue. This has been supported by the Apostolic Faith Church member, who aptly said,

> [T]he digital platforms are very exclusionary in nature because there is an assumption that a lot of things are actually in existence, so from the administration of the church side we can organize and say we are going to have our service over the platform but we don't know whether our people have enough smart phones, we don't know whether the people have digital data, we don't know if the network in the area is also good enough to allow uninterrupted service, so I am very clear that people are excluded, it's not adequate. The quality of digital platforms we are using to broadcast sermons is not the best because there is poor lighting, there is poor cameras, poor technology, so the quality of the word is compromised the hearers cannot participate. Some of the platforms like Facebook are not a two-way communication, it is a one-way communication so even the preacher does not know how the audience is reacting and if somebody wants to be prayed for you can't have physical proximity to pray because of the inadequacy of the technology. (Mrs. Maidei)

This finding confirms Magezi (2015)'s finding that the use of ICT to spread the gospel in Zimbabwe has not been without its own challenges.

Socio-effects of COVID-19 Lockdown on the Church

In trying to solve the problem caused by COVID-19, the government shut down the churches. By disconnecting people from church, the government created a slew of new problems. Along with the effects of the lockdown on the operations of the church, respondents also observed social effects among church congregants. It was mentioned that new problems such as loneliness and depression emanating from social isolation were on the rise. This was mainly due to the new social order that government created. It was established that people have found themselves disconnected from the usual social networks that gave them support on many life issues. The immediate contacts that many people had access to, become close family members, of which it was indicated to be inadequate to deal with the many social challenges that people face. The governmental lockdown had created a cocktail of challenges for people. The lockdown affected their spiritual lives and their livelihoods. This in turn ended up hurting their marriages as people unusually spent more time together due to lockdown. Not only did these couples struggle financially due to COVID-19, but they also did not have the marital support from the church. It therefore followed that the chances for conflict increased significantly, yet the mandate diminished the church's social support network.

On top of that, some people suffered severe loneliness because they live alone. Cases of loneliness were also available from congregants who increasingly found the burden of losing livelihoods and missing their relatives too high to manage. In this vein, Manyawu (2008) comments that "Pentecostal adherents rely on mutual relationships for support and assistance in times of need; hence, isolation has shattered the lives of many." It was also observed that people generally have social challenges, but the lockdown had compromised or eliminated the communication channels people use to get help. The church's social network system in Zimbabwe and Africa at large plays a huge role in the wellbeing of families and people in particular. Such networks have relatives, friends, church mates, workmates, schoolmates, neighbors, as well as other unmentioned relations. Such networks rely on frequent interactions which are primarily face to face. People then rely on these networks for help. The lockdown significantly compromised the effectiveness of the church's network.

Conclusion

The chapter has attempted to establish the relationship between the church and the state in Zimbabwe. The evidence suggests that religion and politics are interwoven and have been so since the medieval era when political thinkers such as St. Augustine and St. Aquinas attempted to theorize on the subject. The church is an instrumental unit in influencing government policy, albeit in some instances its influence suffers from the culture of political exclusion. This is hardly surprising since the church is part of the civil society organizations which have had a bumpy relationship with the government whenever they attempt to query its decisions or actions.

The chapter has also demonstrated how the government's reaction to COVID-19 has affected the operations of churches in Zimbabwe. Key policy pronunciations of social distancing and staying at home had direct and indirect implications on church members as well the administration of the church. The chapter has shown that the mobilization of resources required to run a voluntary organization such as a church from its members has been significantly affected. Although the chapter showed that adoption of digital platforms to communicate emerged as the most obvious option. This chapter also highlighted the many challenges the government mandates created. The church's mission was negatively affected by the lockdown and the shot mandate. This chapter also concludes that the church regrets the way it was "sidelined" in the promulgation of the policy position on COVID-19. There is a strong sentiment that the state could have engaged the church more as they also had the capacity to provide solutions to the problem. It also concludes that the church was ill-prepared to deal with the aftermath of the lockdown at many levels.

References

Anglican Council of Zimbabwe. 2020. Anglican Council of Zimbabwe Joins Human Rights Struggle, August.

BBC News. 2020. Zimbabwe Rejects Catholic Bishops' Criticism of Corruption and Abuse. *BBC News*, August 16. https://www.bbc.com/news/world-africa-53798787.

Biri, K. 2012. The Silent Echoing Voice: Aspects of Zimbabwean Pentecostalism and the Quest for Power, Healing and Miracles. *Studia Historiae Ecclesiasticae* 38: 37–55.

Biri, K. 2013. African Pentecostalism and Politics in Post-colonial Zimbabwe: A Comparative Critique of the Leadership Styles of Ezekiel Guti and Robert Mugabe. In *Prayers and Players: Religion and Politics in Zimbabwe*. Harare: Sapes Books.

Boucher, D., and P. Kelly, eds. 2009. *Political Thinkers: From Socrates to the Present*. Oxford University Press.

Chikowere, Frank. 2021. Another Zimbabwean Activist Arrested, While Journalist Hopewell Chin'ono and His Lawyer Appear in Court. *Daily Maverick*, January 11. Accessed 14 February 2021. https://www.dailymaverick.co.za/article/2021-01-11-another-zimbabweanactivist-arrested-while-journalist-hopewell-chinono-and-his-lawyer-appear-in-court/

Dube, Bekithemba. 2020a. Religious Leaders as Regime Enablers: The Need for Decolonial Family and Religious Studies in Postcolonial Zimbabwe. *British Journal of Religious Education* 43: 46–57.

———. 2020b. Covid-19 and #Zimbabwelivesmatter: Rethinking the Need for Social Justice and Respect for Human Rights in Zimbabwe. *Gender & Behaviour* 18: 326–335.

Dube, Bekithemba. 2021. Covid-19 and #Zimbabwelivesmatter: Rethinking the Need for Social Justice and Respect for Human Rights in Zimbabwe. *Gender & Behaviour* 18: 326–335.

Evangelical Fellowship of Zimbabwe. 2020. Solidarity Statement with the Zimbabwe Catholic Bishops Conference's Pastoral Letter on the Current Situation in Zimbabwe of 14 August 2020—We Stand with Truth as Articulated by the Bishops. Harare: EFZ.

Ferrari, Silvio. 1997. The New Wine and the Old Cask. Tolerance, Religion and the Law in Contemporary Europe. *Ratio Juris* 10: 75–89.

Gibbs, Sara, and Deborah Ajulu. 1999. The Role of the Church in Advocacy: Case Studies from Southern and Eastern Africa. INTRAC Occasional Paper. Accessed 12 January 2021. https://www.intrac.org/wpcms/wp-content/uploads/2018/11/OPS-31-The-Role-of-the-Church-in-Advocacy.pdf.

Guardian. 2020. Catholic Bishops in Zimbabwe Speak Out for First Time on Human Rights Abuses. https://www.theguardian.com/global-development/2020/aug/24/catholic-bishops-in-zimbabwe-speak-out-for-first-time-on-human-rights-abuses-mnangagwa.

Herald Reporter. 2012. Savanhu Donates to the Elderly. *The Herald*, October 3, Harare.

Human Rights NGO Forum. 2020. Zimbabwe Human Rights NGO Forum Statement Calling for Respect for Human Rights and Observance of the Law During COVID-19 Lock Down.

Jere, Qeki, and Vhumani Magezi. 2018. Pastoral Letters and the Church in the Public Square: An Assessment of the Role of Pastoral Letters in Influencing Democratic Processes in Malawi. *Verbum et Ecclesia* 39: 1–9.

Johnson, Sylvester. 2015. *African American Religions, 1500–2000: Coloniality, Democracy, and Freedom.* Cambridge: Cambridge University Press.

Kaunda, Chammah. 2015. The Denial of African Agency: A Decolonial Theological Turn. *Black Theology* 13: 73–92.

Lunga, C. et al. 2012. *Continued Harassment of Anglican Church Members in the Anglican Diocese of Masvingo in the Church of the Province of Central Africa.* Harare.

Lunn, Jenny. 2009. The Role of Religion, Spirituality and Faith in Development: A Critical Theory Approach. *Third World Quarterly* 30: 937–951.

Machakaire, Tarisai. 2020. Mupfumira, Chombo Further Remanded. *Daily News,* March 4. Accessed 12 January 2021. https://dailynews.co.zw/mupfumira-chombo-further-remanded/.

Mafata, Masego. 2021. Court Upholds New Charge Against Zimbabwean Journalist. *GroundUp,* January 13. Accessed 12 February 2021. https://www.groundup.org.za/article/court-upholds-charge-against-zimbabwean-journalist/.

Magezi, V. 2015. God-image of Servant King as Powerful But Vulnerable and Serving: Towards Transforming African church Leadership at an Intersection of African Kingship and Biblical Kingship to Servant Leadership. *HTS Theological Studies* 71 (2): 01–09.

Magaisa, Alex. 2019. The Regime and Its Enablers. *Saturday Big Read,* December 14. Accessed 18 December 2019. https://www.bigsr.co.uk/single-post/2019/12/14/Big-Saturday-Read-The-regime-and-its-enablers

Manyawu, A.T. 2008. Modern African Pentecostal Discourse: A Textual Analysis of Prayer Texts of a Word of Life Church Senior Pastor. *Review of Southern African Studies* 12: 1–29.

Mares, Courtney. 2020. Nuncio Meets Zimbabwe Government Minister after Clash Over Catholic Bishops' Letter. *Catholic News Agency,* August 20. Accessed 12 January 2021. https://www.catholicnewsagency.com/news/nuncio-meets-zimbabwe-government-minister-afterclash-over-catholic-bishops-letter-76302.

Matthews, Thandiwe. 2019. To Be Equal and Free: The Nexus between Human Rights and Democracy. In *A Companion to Democracy #1.* E-Paper. Sarajevo: Heinrich Böll Stiftung. Accessed 1 February 2021. https://www.boell.de/sites/default/files/202001/200128_Human%20Rights%20and%20Democracy%20Paper%20%28UPDATEv004%29.pdf.

Mbiti, J.S. 1998. African Theology. In *Initiation into Theology: The Rich Variety of Theology and Hermeneutics,* ed. S. Maimela and A. König, 141–158. Pretoria: JL van Schaik.

Muchechetere, A. A. 2009. A Historical Analysis of the Role of the Church in Advocating foe Good Governance in Zimbabwe: Heads of Christian Denominations (HOCD) Advocating in Zimbabwe's Political, Social and Economic Impasse from 2003 to 2008. ALMA, Harare Unpublished Dissertation.

Murithi, T. October 2012. Briefing: The African Union at Ten: An Appraisal. *African Affairs* 111 (445): 662–669. https://doi.org/10.1093/afraf/ads058

Ndebele, L. 2020. Government and Catholic Church Clash over Criticism on Human Rights. *TimesLive,* July 17. Accessed 7 January 2021. https://www.timeslive.co.za/news/africa/2020-08-17-government-and-catholic-church-clash-over-criticismon-human-rights/.

Nemukuyu, D. 2012. Supreme Court to Decide On Anglican Row This Month. *The Herald I*, 2012, Harare.

New Zimbabwe. 2020. Mutendi Chides Catholic Bishops For 'Digging Dark Past', 'Lie'. *New Zimbabwe*, August 19. https://www.newzimbabwe.com/mutendi-chides-catholic-bishops-for-digging-dark-past-lies.

News24. 2020. Zimbabwe Health Minister Arrested Over Coronavirus Supplies Scandal. *News24*, June 19. https://www.news24.com/news24/africa/news/zimbabwe-health-minister-arrested-over-coronavirus-supplies-scandal-20200619.

Pindula News. 2020. Wutawunashe and the Indigenous Churches Join the Govt in Calling the Catholic Bishops' Letter to the Govt Genocidal. *Pindula News*, August 19. https://news.pindula.co.zw/2020/08/19/wutawunashe-andthe-indigenous-churches-join-the-govt-in-calling-the-catholic-bishops-letter-to-the-govt-genocidal/.

Tarusarira, Joram. 2016. Religion and Coloniality in Diplomacy. *The Review of Faith & International Affairs* 18: 87–96.

Tarusarira, J. 2020. The Zimbabwe Council of Churches and 'Crisis' Ecumenical Groups. In *The Zimbabwe Council of Churches and Development in Zimbabwe*, 65–78. Palgrave Macmillan.

The Herald. 2020. Indigenous Churches Preach Peace. August 19. https://www.herald.co.zw/indigenous-churches-preach-peace/.

The Legal Monitor. 2012. Zim's sad Peace Day, GPA Anniversary: Clock Turning Back to 2008 Era. Edition 162, Zimbabwe Lawyers for Human Rights: Harare.

Tibaijuka, A.K. 2005. Report of the Fact-Finding Mission to Zimbabwe to Assess the Scope and Impact of Operation Murambatsvina. UN Special Envoy of Human Settlement Issues in Zimbabwe, New York.

United States Institute of Peace. 2003. Zimbabwe`s Torturous Road to a New Constitution and Elections, Special Report, Washington DC, I09. Accessed 12

Wiryadinata, H. 2018. An Understanding the Pauline Christology Significance of Firstborn (Prototokos) In The Light of Paschal Theology: Critical Evaluation on Colossian 1: 15–20. *KURIOS (Jurnal Teologi dan Pendidikan Agama Kristen)* 4 (1): 14–25.

Zimbabwe Catholic Bishops Conference (ZCBC). 2020. The March is Not Ended: Pastoral Letter of the Zimbabwe Catholic Bishops Conference on the Current Situation in Zimbabwe. Accessed 12 February 2021. http://kubatana.net/2020/08/14/the-march-isnot-ended-pastoral-letter-of-the-zimbabwe-catholic-bishops-conference-on-the-current-situation-in-zimbabwe/.

Zimunya, Clive Tendai, and Joyline Gwara. 2013. Pentecostalism, Prophets and the Distressing Zimbabwean Milieu. In *Prophets, Profits and the Bible in Zimbabwe*, ed. Ezra Chitando, Masiiwa Ragies Gunda, and Joachim Kügler, 87–202. Bamberg: University of Bamberg Press.

CHAPTER 25

Arranging Religion in Egypt: New Alignments Between the Egyptian State, al-Azhar, and the Coptic Orthodox Church

Rachel M. Scott

INTRODUCTION

In 2013, just over two years after the Egyptian Revolution in which President Hosni Mubarak was removed, a military coup took place. On July 3, the Egyptian military ousted President Muhammad Mursi and the majority Muslim Brotherhood parliament. 'Abd al-Fattah al-Sisi announced that President Mursi had failed to fulfill the wishes of the Egyptian people and that new presidential and Shura Council elections would occur.

When Sisi made his announcement, both the shaykh of al-Azhar, Ahmed al-Tayyib, and the Coptic Orthodox Pope, Tawadros II, were at his side. It was a powerful visual moment of exchange between the military, which had re-captured the state, and the shaykh of al-Azhar and the Coptic Orthodox Pope. All parties gave something and gained something in return. The new

R. M. Scott (✉)
Virginia Tech, Blacksburg, VA, USA
e-mail: rmscott@vt.edu

607

S. Holzer (ed.), *The Palgrave Handbook of Religion and State*
Volume II, https://doi.org/10.1007/978-3-031-35609-4_25

regime received religious legitimacy from the two institutions that represented Islam and Christianity, respectively. In turn, the shaykh of al-Azhar, long threatened by the Muslim Brotherhood's invocation of Islam, regained its role as the institution that would be the authoritative representative of Islamic law. The Coptic Orthodox Pope gained greater assurance that the new regime would be more supportive of the rights of Coptic citizens, since the Coptic Orthodox Church had long feared the Muslim Brotherhood's call for the application of the sharia. This moment of exchange became reflected in the beginning of the new constitution, which was promulgated after the coup in 2013. It reads, "The army of the people defended the people's wishes with the blessing (*mubarak*) of the noble al-Azhar and the national church" (Dustur jumhuriyyat misr al-'arabiyya 2014)

So, what did it mean for al-Azhar and the Coptic Orthodox Church to give the takeover of the Egyptian state by the Egyptian military its blessing? Why was such a blessing needed? What does this tell us about religion and its relationship with the state in Egypt?

It is customary to frame religion and its relationship with the state in Egypt in religious or secular terms. During the Egyptian Revolution and counter-revolution (2011–2013), those who took part in the debates about how to mold the post-revolutionary political order consistently framed the choice as one between a religious state and a secular state. Yet, this chapter argues that we should consider religion and its relationship with the Egyptian state not through the religious-secular binary but through the state's relationship with what might be termed state-related religious organizations, in this case al-Azhar and the Coptic Orthodox Church. Looking at how religion is invoked and negotiated between the state and al-Azhar and between the state and the Coptic Orthodox Church illustrates both the capabilities and limits of the state's control over religion. It also illustrates the capabilities and limits of these two religious organizations.

When thinking about the role of religion in Egypt, it is often assumed that this means the role of Islam. However, religion in Egypt operates in various forms and at various levels. First, there is Islamic law, which, according to the constitution, is the major source of legislation in Egypt. Second, there is Islamic identity more broadly in the sense that Islam is the religion of the state and Egypt is perceived as an Islamic society. Lastly, there is the sense that Egypt is a country that respects religion and is broadly supportive of Judaism, Christianity, and Islam.

When thinking about the relationship between the state and the organizations of al-Azhar and the Coptic Orthodox Church one also has to consider what the state is and what state-related or state-linked organizations are. There is no consensus on what the state actually is and where its boundaries begin and end. Akhil Gupta has argued that there is no reliable starting point from which we can see the state (Mitchell and Owen 1991, p. 28). Noah Salomon contends that it is difficult to pinpoint what exists outside the purview of the state, since the state is indeterminate and can be found in unexpected places (Salomon 2016, p. 4).

Certainly, one should avoid reference to the state as something that is separate from society and acts upon it (Mitchell and Owen 1990, p. 180). Likewise, distinguishing between the state and the government, by which the state is maintained, is not always easy. This is particularly so in the Middle East, although Egypt is the Middle Eastern state in which the distinction is most apparent (Owen 2000, p. 5). In the case at hand, it is not possible to say that al-Azhar and the Coptic Orthodox Church exist outside the state. Neither are they fully part of it. In fact, it is the ambiguity of their interconnected yet differentiated relationship with the state that is key to understanding how religion operates in Egypt.

For Joel Migdal, the state is "an organisation, composed of numerous agencies led and coordinated by the state's leadership (executive authority) that has the ability or authority to make and implement the binding rules for all the people" (Owen 2000, p. 5). Migdal argues that while modern states seek to control and regulate relations between citizens, there are many arenas, or social organizations, where it cannot do this or where its attempt to do so is contested. State officials, he argues, either "seek predominance over those myriad other organizations" or seek "to authorize particular other organizations to make those rules in certain realms" (Migdal 1987, p. 396). Migdal maintains that "the most subtle and fascinating patterns of political change *and* political inertia come in accommodations between states and other powerful organizations in society" and that these accommodations cannot be "predicted simply by assuming the autonomy of the state" (Migdal 1987, p. 398).

This chapter addresses the interaction between the state and al-Azhar and between the state and the Coptic Orthodox Church in the realm of religion, and it explicates the extent to which the state seeks to define the parameters within which these organizations can direct religious affairs. In looking at such relationships, it elucidates the limits that the Egyptian state encounters in its direction of religion in the face of both al-Azhar and the Coptic Orthodox Church. Migdal argues that in every country there are "unanticipated accommodations" between social organizations and state officials (Migdal 1987, p. 404). The goal of this chapter is to explore such patterns of political change by looking at the kinds of accommodation and forms of tension that have occurred between the state and al-Azhar and between the state and the Coptic Orthodox Church.

Al-Azhar and the Coptic Orthodox Church both have an institutional history that predates the development of the modern Egyptian state. The institutional life that both al-Azhar and the Coptic Orthodox Church had before the modern Egyptian state has influenced the perception held by those within both organizations that the organization should be independent from the state. Of course, both institutions have been impacted by the state and are subject to its regulations in different ways.

While al-Azhar and the Coptic Orthodox Church have some level of independence from the state, one cannot say that either—particularly al-Azhar—is separate from the state. This is where drawing a line between the regime and the state and between the state and society becomes difficult. Writing about Egypt's constitutional order prior to 2013, Nathan J. Brown has argued that in the past century, the Egyptian state has attempted "to subsume religious institutions and authority within its own structures" (Brown 2013, p. 233). Thus, he contends, the Egyptian state has nationalized religion and tried to "incorporate Islam within the Egyptian state" (Brown 2013, p. 234).

Yet, al-Azhar and the Coptic Orthodox Church have pushed back against the state in various ways. Al-Azhar, in particular, occupies a more ambiguous position than its absorption by the state allows for. This has been particularly so since the revolution, but it has long been linked to the state yet separate from it, even though the extent of such separation has varied. Indeed, it is the role of al-Azhar and the Coptic Orthodox Church as connected to—but historically independent from—the state that provides insight into both the state's attempts to direct religion and into the limits of its capacity to direct religion. Understanding al-Azhar and the Coptic Orthodox Church as state-connected or state-dependent organizations can help focus on moments of contention and accommodation that take place between these organizations and the Egyptian state.

This chapter illustrates the ways in which al-Azhar and the Coptic Orthodox Church exist in a relationship of mutual support and tension with the Egyptian state. It illustrates how the state has been trying to limit the power and independence of al-Azhar. It also shows how the state has been allowing the Coptic Orthodox Church to expand its authority. This chapter therefore looks at how—and the extent to which—the state authorizes these two religious organizations to make rules that the population must abide by and mold norms which the population is directed to follow. The post-revolutionary period has been characterized by increased tension between al-Azhar and the state as both are pushing back against one another to dominate the discourse on what constitutes Islam. Central to such conflict between al-Azhar and the state is the increasing support that the state has shown for Christianity and the Coptic Orthodox Church, which has been able to consolidate its control. In fact, the state's current good relationship with the Coptic Orthodox Church has given it increased leverage over al-Azhar. Therefore, not only are the relationships that the state has with al-Azhar and with the Coptic Orthodox Church subject to change, but the nature of one relationship impacts the other.

Given how pervasive and entrenched the Egyptian state is, it is tempting either to look at the Egyptian state and its direction of religion from the perspective of the all-pervasiveness of the state or to look at religious movements that set themselves up in opposition to the state. Many discussions about the association between religion and state in Egypt have focused on Islamist movements and their attempts to take over the state and mold it in its image. Less consideration has been given to the institutional dynamics between the center of state power and religious organizations that are enmeshed with the state yet are also in some way distinct from it. While Nathan Brown and Michele Dunne have done good work on the relationship between the various institutions of Egypt's religious establishment, namely al-Azhar, the Ministry of Fatwas (*Dar al-ifta*), and the Ministry of Endowments (*Wazirat al-Awqaf*), this chapter looks at the aspects of those relationships that shed light on the ways in which such organizations are independent of the state and thus able to push back against it and limit the state's control over religion.

THE ISLAMIC HERITAGE (*TURATH*)

Here it is important to briefly venture into the Islamic conceptual heritage to think about the state's relationship with both al-Azhar and the Coptic Orthodox Church. This is not to claim that a continuous Islamic norm is the key to understanding contemporary Egypt. Yet, understanding the Islamic conceptual inheritance can be useful for understanding some of the attitudes and assumptions that inform contemporary debates about the state's relationship with such institutions in Egypt.

Ira Lapidus questions the prevailing view that classical Islamic society did not distinguish between religion and politics. Lapidus argues that in the Abbasid period there "was the emergence of religious activity independent of the actual authority of the Caliphs" so that there was "a differentiation of political and religious life into organized and partly autonomous entities" (Lapidus 1975, p. 368, p. 384). It is well known that Islamic law was developed outside the purview of the state. The interpretation of the sharia was undertaken by scholars who were not government employees. These scholars endeavored to make sure that the rulers did not encroach upon their role by trying to interpret Islamic law. In addition, Islamic jurisprudence was formulated within the framework of the four Sunni schools of law, which allowed for the fact that there was more than one answer to a legal question. This multivalence meant that, in many respects, Islamic jurisprudence could not easily be subsumed into centralized state law. This separation between jurists and the state was compromised in the post-classical period (Kuru 2019, p. 4). While the closer association between jurists and the state maximized state power, it was seen as a departure from the optimal situation. Such separation was seen as necessary for religious scholars to expound on Islamic legal questions in an unbiased way. This sense of separation is key to understanding how the religious scholars within the institution of al-Azhar understand the institution's role.

Ira Lapidus refers to the above relationship between religious scholars and the state as a differentiation between political and religious life. This was indeed true, but such a differentiation, I argue, is influenced by a secular perspective that separates the religious from the political. While the state did not control the interpretation of Islamic law, its role was not separated from what might be understood as the religious sphere since it was obliged to enable Muslims to live according to the sharia. The ruler's mission was thus to protect Islam even if that mission did not extend to the interpretation of Islamic law.

The other force that existed to limit the judicial power and reach of the Islamic state was the system of the legal self-determination of non-Muslims. One of the central features of the sharia was its granting of a level of legal independence for non-Muslims. Non-Muslims were allowed to petition their own communal courts for legal adjudication in cases that did not involve members of another religion and did not involve the death penalty. The scope of such independence varied considerably as did the frequency with which Muslims interacted with non-Muslims in the courts. The schools of law debated about the specific details, but the underlying assumption was that non-Muslims, in a number of circumstances, were able to pass judgment according to their own laws and in their own courts (Fattal 1958, pp. 353–55).

THE CONSTITUTION

The historical legacy of the ulama (religious scholars) in al-Azhar and that of the judicial self-determination of non-Muslim communities have continued to impact the way that the modern Egyptian state has directed religion. While the modern Egyptian state has partially subsumed both al-Azhar and the Coptic Orthodox Church into its structure, both organizations have a certain amount of independence. Such independence has influenced their ability to negotiate with the state in the shaping of religion.

Some key constitutional texts can illustrate how the parameters within which the state, al-Azhar, and the Coptic Orthodox Church can direct religion are defined. Article 1 of the Egyptian Constitution declares that Egypt is based on the concept of citizenship and Article 2 promises that "Islam is the religion of the state, Arabic is the official language, and the principles of the Islamic sharia are the main source of legislation." Article 74 prohibits parties that are based on religion (Dustur jumhuriyyat misr al-ʿarabiyya 2014).

One of the striking features of the 2014 Constitution is its support for the unity of Muslims, Christians, and Jews (although the latter's numbers are very small indeed). The constitution's preamble describes the historical and religious connections between Judaism, Christianity, and Islam. Article 3 officially acknowledges that there is a legal sphere over which non-Muslims have self-determination outside of the direct control of the state by assuring that "the principles of the religious laws of Christian and Jewish Egyptians are the main source for the legal regulation of their personal status affairs, their religious affairs, and for the nomination of their religious leaders" (Dustur jumhuriyyat misr al-ʿarabiyya 2014). Further articles, listed under transitional provisions, signify the state's support for Coptic Christians. Article 235 undertook to support the building and repair of churches, and, in Article 244, the state endeavored to "to ensure appropriate representation for Christians" in the next parliament (Dustur jumhuriyyat misr al-ʿarabiyya 2014).

Returning to Article 2, which declares the "principles of Islamic sharia are the major source of legislation," previous constitutions had never mentioned who was to be in charge of interpreting the sharia. This, according to Jakob Skovgaard-Petersen, points to the fact that, previously, the sharia was considered important whereas the religious scholars were not (Skovgaard-Petersen 2013, p. 279). After the Revolution of 2011, however, the Constitution of 2012 gave al-Azhar a greater—but ambiguous—role in the interpretation of the sharia. To resolve such ambiguity, the preamble to the Constitution of 2014 affirmed that the rulings of the Supreme Constitutional Court are the source for the interpretation of the principles of the sharia and not al-Azhar. However, Article 7 of the Constitution of 2014 also gave al-Azhar two important things: a claim to being the main authority for the religious sciences and assurance that it is independent and has control over its own affairs (Dustur jumhuriyyat misr al-ʿarabiyya 2014).

The Constitution of 2014, along with the short-lived Constitution of 2012, were the first constitutions in Egypt to define a formal position for the religious scholars. While the 2014 Constitution clawed back some of the authority that al-Azhar had been given under the 2012 Constitution, the Constitution of 2014 is notable in that it fulfills the expectation, long held in Islamic thought, that to fulfill its mission of expounding on matters related to Islamic law, al-Azhar should have a level of independence from the state.

AL-AZHAR

Al-Azhar is shaped—and, to a certain extent, controlled—by the Egyptian state. Yet, in its position as standing for the authoritative interpretation of Islamic law in a state that declares Islam as its official religion, it has the capacity to limit the power of the state. The 2011–2013 revolutionary period led to the increased power and independence of al-Azhar. Al-Azhar's endorsement of the military coup of 2013 illustrated the importance of its supportive role of the state and the need for it to provide the state with religious legitimacy. However, more recently, its relationship with the regime has become strained as the latter has tried to usurp the organization's capacity to authoritatively stand for Islamic law. At the same time, due to the level of independence that al-Azhar gained in 2012, al-Azhar has been able to resist such attempts to displace it, although its legitimacy has been harmed by its support for the 2013 coup.

Founded in 972, al-Azhar is made up of a number of organizations. Al-Azhar represents the foremost center of Sunni Muslim scholarship worldwide and its university is considered one of the most prominent Islamic educational institutions. Al-Azhar is made up of the following institutions: al-Azhar's High Council; al-Azhar's Senior Scholars' Council, which issues authoritative interpretations; the Islamic Research Academy, which is the institution's supreme body for Islamic research; the University of al-Azhar; and al-Azhar's educational section (al-Majlis al-'ala li-l-quwat al-musallaha 2012). The latter includes primary and secondary schools which contain approximately 2 million students. Al-Azhar is also able to censor material deemed contrary to Islamic law.

Al-Azhar has a strong sense of the importance of its supportive role of the state and the nation. Throughout Islamic history, the ulama have tended—with important exceptions—to be politically conservative and have emphasized that supporting the political status quo is better than civil strife (Jad al-Haq 1983, p. 3742). Al-Azhar has a strong sense that such a supportive role is best performed while being independent from the state. Despite the historical reality, such separation from the state was seen as necessary to protect the ulama's ability to be political in the broader sense of protecting society by transcending particular political differences. Being too close to the workings of government, the arena in which those political differences are worked out on a day-to-day basis, was seen as having the potential to undermine the scholars' role (al-Ghazali 2006, p. 103).

Central to al-Azhar's identity are the four schools of law and the differences of opinion between them. Similarly, the al-Azhar Senior Scholars' Council and the al-Azhar Islamic Research Academy are able to issue *fatwas*, and the issuance of *fatwas* is central to how the institution sees itself. It is often emphasized that *fatwas* are non-compulsory and courts are under no obligation to follow them (al-Awwa 2003, p. 22, pp. 29–30). However, the shaykh of al-Azhar, Ahmed al-Tayyib, once insisted that the Egyptian parliament always follows the opinion of al-Azhar (Ahmed al-Tayyib, interviewed by the author 2008).

The plurality of Islamic jurisprudence with its four Sunni schools of law sometimes provided a challenge for the Islamic polity which wanted to make one interpretation of law the law of the land. In the post-classical period, the Ottoman Empire tried to assert the Hanafi school of law as the official school of law. It is no surprise that the modern Egyptian state's project of extending its control over law also involved attempts to bring al-Azhar under its influence. In 1956, President Gamal 'Abd al-Nasser

(1918–1970) incorporated the sharia courts, which the ulama had, until then, controlled, into the national court system (Moustafa 2000, p. 5). Al-Azhar was thereby no longer privately funded but rather financially supported by the state.

Critiques of al-Azhar have often focused on how its financial support by the state has compromised its ability to expound on Islamic law in an unbiased manner. This is partly why the Muslim Brotherhood was able to garner so much support in the second half of the twentieth century and in the first two decades of the twenty-first century. Under President Mubarak (r. 1981–2011), the reputation of al-Azhar declined as Islamists called the al-Azhar scholars "the Sheikhs of the Sultan" (Ziada 2022).

Up until the Revolution of 2011, al-Azhar had no formal constitutional role. Yet, after the Revolution of 2011, how to delineate the position of al-Azhar and of the Supreme Constitutional Court became a topic of debate. Al-Azhar issued a formal document in which it petitioned for the organization to have independence from the Egyptian state. While the document did not reflect any intent for al-Azhar to take on a legislative role, it claimed that al-Azhar has the right to authoritatively give opinions on Islamic law on the basis of its knowledge of the Islamic sciences and its expertise in Islamic heritage, Islamic thought (*al-fikr al-Islami*), and *ijtihad*. It solicited a "plan for the independence of the organization of al-Azhar" and petitioned for the return of the Senior Scholars' Council, which had been abolished in the 1960s. It also called for conferring upon the latter the right to nominate and elect the shaykh of al-Azhar (al-Tayyib 2011).

In 2012, the Supreme Council of Armed Forces (SCAF) issued a decree responding to these requests by referring to al-Azhar as a "*haya mustaqila*" (an independent organization) and by pledging that the "state guarantees the independence of al-Azhar." The decree recreated the Senior Scholars' Council and made it the body that elects the shaykh of al-Azhar. This was important, since, as a result, the shaykh of al-Azhar was no longer elected by the president (al-Majlis al-'ala li-l-quwat al-musallaha 2012). The 2012 SCAF decree also ensured that al-Azhar is the institution that stands for the authoritative interpretation of Islam, stating that "al-Azhar is the final recourse (*marji' niha'i*)" in all Islamic issues (al-Majlis al-'ala l-il-quwat al-musallaha 2012).

The SCAF decree of 2012 also made al-Azhar's Senior Scholars' Council responsible for nominating Egypt's Grand Mufti (al-Majlis al-'ala l-il-quwat al-musallaha 2012). Previously, the mufti had been appointed by the president. The *Dar al-Ifta* (the Ministry of *Fatwas*) was first established in 1895 and came under the control of the Egyptian Ministry of Justice until 2012. It gives an official interpretation of Islamic law when asked to do so by other state bodies. Sentences that involve the death penalty must be reviewed by the Grand Mufti, although the Mufti's opinion does not have to be taken. Brown argues that "the office has grown up alongside the modern Egyptian state, advising its officials (and members of the public who seek its guidance) on religious matters" (Brown and Dunne 2021, p. 4).

As was related above, the Constitution of 2014 did not give al-Azhar the authority to decide whether legislation is compatible with the sharia. However, it did formally sanction al-Azhar as the institution that should be consulted in Islamic affairs. It thus gave al-Azhar some kind of influence in the legislative process in instances where legislation intersects with the sharia.

Any discussion of al-Azhar vis-à-vis its role in the production of authoritative Islamic discourse must consider the impact that the removal of the Muslim Brotherhood from the public sphere has had. The removal of the Muslim Brotherhood has significantly reduced the influence of Islamist intellectual voices. The removal of such voices has opened up the space for al-Azhar to assert itself. Ahmed al-Tayyib had long disliked the Muslim Brotherhood and felt that the organization wished to undermine the position of al-Azhar.

However, the removal of the Muslim Brotherhood came at a cost. As Masooda Bano points out, al-Azhar's "alliance with General 'Abd al-Fattah al-Sisi's government" has "seriously compromised its moral authority" (Bano 2018, p. 715). 'Ali Guma'a, former Mufti and member of the al-Azhar's Senior Scholars' Council at the time, famously made a speech to the Egyptian Security Forces during the coup of 2013, arguing that it is religiously permitted to depose a president if he threatens national stability. He argued that the Armed Forces always side with the truth and act on behalf of the weak and on behalf of victims of aggression. The Security Forces, 'Ali Guma'a claimed, have never acted in "self-interest." Using an oft-used comparison, he likened the conflict between the military and the Muslim Brotherhood to the seventh-century conflict between the Caliph 'Ali and the Kharijites, arguing that those who supported the Muslim Brotherhood were inciting civil strife (*fitna*), had lost their minds, were inverting the truth, and were using words such as democracy and legitimacy in which they did not believe (Guma'a 2014). Given that his speech was seen as an endorsement of the massacre of hundreds of protesters that followed in August 2013, 'Ali Guma'a words are a painful reminder of the ugliness of what can happen when religious scholars ally themselves too closely to those in power.

With the Muslim Brotherhood gone from the public sphere, al-Azhar has played a more assertive role in policing Egypt's moral and cultural spheres. Having what one newspaper refers to "detoxif[ied] the university from the affiliates of the Muslim Brotherhood," al-Azhar has tried to replace the Muslim Brotherhood in a number of areas (Ziada 2022). For example, it has established medical convoys in Egypt and abroad. These convoys, made up of Azhari doctors and imams, have traveled to poor rural areas to provide free-of-charge medical and social services. This is the kind of grassroots social work that had made the Muslim Brotherhood so popular. Al-Azhar has also established *fatwa* booths in metro stations in Cairo so that the Egyptian public can easily access religious scholars for guidance ('Adil 2017).

However, Ahmed al-Tayyib might wonder whether he should have been more careful what he wished for. The removal of the Muslim Brotherhood from the public sphere has not resulted in al-Azhar's unquestioned dominance over Islamic discourse. After the coup of 2013, Sisi claimed that Islamic discourse and extremism were problems that needed to be solved in part as a way of justifying the crackdown on the Muslim Brotherhood. Yet, Sisi did not allow al-Azhar to monopolize interpretations of Islamic law. In fact, he claimed that al-Azhar is part of the problem. President Sisi, the Egyptian parliament, and other state officials have become involved in the debate about Islamic discourse, and such involvements have included strong critiques of al-Azhar and of the jurisprudential heritage, with its emphasis on conformity to the four schools of law, that it represents. Brown and Dunne describe it as "a political tug of war over control of the religious establishment," whereby "parliamentarians feel free to weigh in; prominent intellectuals go beyond the president's direct but very general rebuke to specific attacks on al-Azhar" (Brown and Dunne 2021, p. 2, 10).

The above can be seen in the discussions that have taken place about atheism since the Revolution of 2011–2013. In 2014, Egypt's Ministry of Youth and Sports and the Endowment Ministry's mosques management unit were working with a group of psychiatrists as a part of national strategy to eradicate atheism (Jawhari 2014). In 2015, the Egyptian Ministry of Youth, in cooperation with the al-Azhar Foundation, launched an initiative to confront "extremism and atheism" stating that "atheism is a national security issue ... if atheists rebel against religion, they will rebel against everything else" (Sahih Misr 2021). In 2019, the al-Azhar Center for Electronic Fatwas established a unit entitled "*barnamij bayan muwajahat al-ilhad* (Program for the Declaration to Combat Atheism)." Its activities have included posting thousands of comments intended to promote Islam and refute atheist opinions. In 2018, the Deputy Sheikh of al-Azhar, Mahmoud Ashour, appeared on television to debate with an atheist, Muhammad Hashim. Both Mahmoud Ashour and the host of the program humiliated Hashim by claiming that he needed psychiatric help (al-Hadath al-yawm 2018). In a further example, in 2019, the blogger Anas Hasan was arrested for publishing his support for atheism and for criticizing religion, and the following year he was sentenced to three years in jail for directing "The Egyptian Atheist's Facebook page" (Egyptian Initiative for Personal Rights 2020).

President Sisi has entered into the debate and, in so doing, has publicly distanced himself from al-Azhar. In July 2015, he announced that he understood that some youth had become atheist because "they could not bear," referring to the Muslim Brotherhood, "the religious strife and abuse of Islam that had occurred in recent years." He stated that he was "not worried [about atheists], not because I am not earnestly concerned with God, but because I know that this matter will end, God willing" (Nada 2015). In 2018, Sisi stated that every citizen has the right to choose his own faith. In fact, he argued, he has the right to choose to have no faith (Ibrahim 2018), and, during a session of the World Youth Forum in the same year, he claimed: "If we had religions in Egypt other than Christianity, such as Judaism, or any other religion, we would build houses of worship for them, even if these were not divinely-revealed religions, because the citizen has the right to worship or not worship as he wishes" (al-Sawi 2018). Finally, in 2021, President Sisi announced: "I respect those who have no religious faith. If someone were to say to me 'I am not a Muslim, or a Christian, or a Jew, or of any religion at all,' I would say to them you are free and I respect your wishes" (Sahih Misr 2021).

Such divergence of perspectives between al-Azhar and the regime is striking. In speaking about matters related to religion, Sisi has encroached upon al-Azhar's domain. Such encroachment can also be seen in the debate over divorce. In 2017, President Sisi demanded that only written—and not verbal—divorces would be valid, pointing to the social harm that verbal divorces cause to Egyptian women and society as a whole. At the annual celebration of police day, Sisi turned to al-Tayyib, who was also in attendance, and accused the latter of "exhausting him" on the issue. Nevertheless, the Senior Scholars' Council pushed back against Sisi and issued a ruling unanimously rejecting the ban on verbal divorce, arguing that Muslims have practiced verbal divorce since the time of the Prophet and therefore it is against the sharia to ban it (France 24, 2017).

Other important public figures have jumped in to critique al-Azhar. For example, the Egyptian sociologist and author Saad Eddin Ibrahim berated al-Azhar for its resistance to any change claiming that al-Azhar will not, in fact, be the institution that will provide the needed renewal of religious discourse. Ibrahim criticized al-Azhar for its rigid conservatism and for its persecution of those, including 'Ali 'Abd al-Raziq and Nasr Hamid Abu Zayd, who have tried to bring about religious reform. He compared al-Azhar unfavorably with the institution of al-Zaytuna in Tunisia, which has taken important steps to reform issues such as inheritance and women's rights (Ibrahim 2018). Such a climate is a far cry from the time leading up to the coup in 2013 when liberals and secularists set up "The Battlefront for the Defense of al-Azhar," calling al-Azhar their refuge and Egypt's "religious frame of reference (*murja'iyya*)" ('Abd al-Wahid 2013). As Rafiq Habib, a prominent Christian intellectual with previous Islamist sympathies, rightly concluded at the time, such anti-Islamist parties were using al-Azhar to counteract the strength of the Islamic movement (Habib 2013, p. 7).

Yet, al-Azhar is not without friends, as the applause that Ahmed al-Tayyib received during a recent clash with Muhammad 'Uthman al-Khasht, Professor of Philosophy of Religion at Cairo University, indicates. At the International Conference on the Renovation of Islamic Discourse in 2020, al-Khasht argued that current Islamic scholarship is static and out of date. He argued that it is necessary to return to the Qur'an and only what is true of the Sunna as the standard for every place and time. He called for by-passing the Islamic heritage (*turath*) and critiqued Islamic discourse's lack of critical thought, its emphasis upon copying and repeating, and its lack of engagement with modern humanities, social sciences, and scientific methods, arguing that "nobody owns the absolute truth." Al-Khasht called for the updating of religious studies and not for its revival contending that "reviving Islamic religious studies includes reviving all the old religious understandings." In response, Ahmed al-Tayyib argued that al-Khasht was advocating the "abandonment of Islamic teachings rather than a renewal of Islamic discourse." Al-Tayyib said that al-Khasht sought not a renewal but a negligent rejection of the *turath*. Al-Tayyib expressed shock at all the current disparagement of the *turath* in Egypt and referred to the constant calls by people to criticize the *turath* and ignore it as escalated, overbid, and exaggerated. Al-Tayyib affirmed that the Islamic intellectual heritage, the *turath*, was central for the ability of a group of Arab tribes, "who did not know left from right," to enter Andalusia within 80 years (al-Tayyib 2020).

The Sisi regime has gone further than debating with al-Azhar over the renewal of Islamic discourse and has tried, unsuccessfully, to nullify the independence that al-Azhar gained after the revolution. In 2017, a draft law was proposed, Article 2 of which would have limited the term of the shaykh of al-Azhar to six years with the possibility of one re-election. This contravened Article 7 of the Egyptian Constitution, which states that the shaykh of al-Azhar is chosen by members of the Senior Scholars' Council and cannot be dismissed (Dustur jumhuriyyat misr al-'arabiyya 2014). Additionally, in what could only be read as a snub to the current shaykh, Article 5 of the law set up an investigation committee consisting of the seven oldest members of the Senior Scholar's Council in the event that the shaykh of al-Azhar fails to fulfill his duties (al-Ashwal 2017).

While this draft law did not progress any further, in 2020, the Egyptian parliament approved a draft bill to make the Ministry of Fatwas and the Grand Mufti independent of al-Azhar. The aim of the bill was for the Egyptian government and not al-Azhar to control the Ministry of Fatwas. The bill included giving the president increased control over the beginning and end of the appointment of the Grand Mufti (Hejazi, 2020). In effect, the Ministry of Fatwas would have "become a competing religious body" reporting directly to the Egyptian government thereby "overshadowing the authority of al-Azhar" (Bar'el 2020). In response, al-Tayyib sent a strongly worded letter to the House of Representatives containing the opinion of the Senior Scholars' Council that the draft law violates the constitution, claiming that Article 7 makes "al-Azhar the main reference in all issues that relate to the issuance of *fatwas* and the decision maker in all that is related to the sharia" (Hejazi 2020). The law, the Senior Scholars' Council claims, would turn *Dar al-Ifta'* into an entity that is parallel to al-Azhar, thereby robbing the latter of one of its most important competencies, that is, the issuance of *fatwas*. In an attempt to separate the Ministry of Fatwas from the state and join it with al-Azhar, al-Tayyib's letter referred to the Ottoman Empire when the headquarters of the mufti were based in the mosque of al-Azhar and not the Sublime Porte. Al-Azhar accused the draft law of thereby constituting an "aggression against the competence and independence of the Senior Scholars' Council" (Hejazi 2020). The proposal, it argued, would result in the subordination of the issuance of *fatwas* to the government (Hejazi 2020). This draft law did not progress any further, since al-Azhar was able to use Article 7 of the Constitution of 2014 to push back against attempts by the state to encroach on its autonomy.

Al-Azhar emerged from the revolution in a stronger position than it had been, having had its role constitutionally defined and protected. While the state has attempted to bring al-Azhar to heel and subvert its independence, al-Azhar has used such constitutional protections to limit the state's interference. Thus, on account of the way that its role had been defined by the Constitutions of 2012 and 2014, al-Azhar was able to resist encroachment by the state and protect itself. Yet, the president's constant attempts to undermine al-Azhar and the damage that al-Azhar's support of the coup of 2013 has done, illustrate the limits of the position it claims for itself as the authoritative representative of Islamic law. The next section will discuss another component of these new alignments, and that is the relationship between the Coptic Orthodox Church and the state. About 6–8% of the population of Egypt are Coptic Christians, but their importance to how Egypt understands itself and to the relationship between the state and al-Azhar is far greater than such numbers would indicate.

THE COPTIC ORTHODOX CHURCH

The Coptic Orthodox Church dates back to the first century CE in Alexandria. Pope Tawadros II is the 118th Coptic Patriarch. The Coptic Orthodox Church has autonomy from the state, yet legally some of its structures are dependent upon state oversight (Brown et al. 2021, p. 127). For example, the People's Assembly has to give its assent to any new laws that the Coptic Community Council adopts before they are valid in the national courts. In addition, while the Pope is chosen by divine lot, his appointment has to be recognized by presidential decree.

The Coptic Orthodox Church has never had any formal role as defined by the constitution. While Article 3 made no specific statement about the Coptic Orthodox Church, it granted Christian Egyptians the right to use their own religious law for their personal status affairs. Throughout the twentieth century, the Coptic Orthodox Church, amid a growing sense of Coptic religious and ethnic separateness, emerged as the institution that would politically speak for Coptic Egyptians. This resulted in the marginalization of lay Copts, who had dominated the communal council in the first half of the twentieth century. Nasser's policy of land redistribution in the 1960s further weakened the Coptic elite. According to S.S. Hasan, President Nasser "emasculated" the lay Coptic Communal Council and made it "easy for Pope Cyril VI to make short shrift of it with government connivance. He abolished the longtime rival for control of the church and its properties altogether" (Hasan 2003, p. 104). As a result, a particular kind of relationship between Cyril VI and subsequent popes on the one hand and President Nasser and subsequent presidents on the other emerged, a relationship that has been described in the words of Fiona McCallum as "a modern variation of the historical millet system" (McCallum 2012, p. 109). Pope Cyril VI (1959–1971) would go before President Nasser and speak of the challenges facing the Coptic community while calling on the community to be loyal to the Nasserist regime. In return, Cyril VI could expect that the state would consider him the formal spokesperson of the Coptic community and seek to protect the community. This model of church-state relations has continued to this day since it serves both the church and the Egyptian regime.

Relations between Pope Shenouda III, Cyril VI's successor, and Anwar Sadat were less amicable. The church opposed Article 2 of the 1971 Constitution which was amended in 1980. This resulted in a standoff between the Pope and President Sadat, and in 1981 President Sadat canceled the presidential decree that had appointed Pope Shenouda. While relations between the Mubarak regime and the Coptic Orthodox Church were less contentious, the Mubarak regime remained intransigent on—and unresponsive to—a number of issues of concern to Copts. One of those issues was the building and repair of churches. The other issue was a unified personal status law for Christians. This is notwithstanding the fact that there were frequent incidents of violence against Copts, to which the state was often unresponsive. At times, it appeared that the state condoned such violence. In addition, there were frequent claims that Copts were marginalized and discriminated against, particularly in the political and administrative spheres.

The coup that resulted in the end of Muhammad Mursi's presidency and the onset of the presidency of 'Abd al-Fattah al-Sisi resulted in important shifts in the relationship between the Coptic Orthodox Church and the state. Support for Christianity and for the rights of Christians as a community in the constitutional debates that unfolded after the 2011 Revolution was a means by which the forces which supported the coup outdid the Islamists (Scott 2021, pp. 117–147). In so doing, the concept of Egypt as an Islamic state has been reconfigured to be more supportive of Christianity. Supreme Court justice Adel Omar Sherif states that, in the court's view, "a constitution does not simply reflect norms of a mandatory character, but rather it substantiates advanced concepts which in their entirety and together are expected to establish new patterns of behavior" (Sherif 2012, p. 129). We can see this in relation to Article 3, which has established a new pattern in the relationship between the state and the Coptic Orthodox Church. Support for Coptic Christianity bolsters the regime and gives it religious legitimacy as it claims to speak for a more religiously inclusive type of Islam. This has strengthened the position of the president in its bid to assert control over al-Azhar.

Article 3 of the 2014 Constitution, with its official recognition and endorsement of Christianity, enabled the Coptic Orthodox Church to consolidate its control over Coptic Egyptians and, in turn, limit the state's control over Coptic citizens. This can be seen in the area of personal status law. Since 1970s, the church had asked the state to recognize a papal decree from 1971 forbidding the remarriage of any Coptic Christian who obtained a divorce under any other circumstance other than having been the victim of the adultery of their spouse (Kamal 2006, pp. 18–19). The Egyptian courts refused, insisting that the more lenient Coptic bylaws of 1938, which had been passed by the Egyptian parliament, were binding (Supreme Constitutional Court 2000). In 2008–2010, a conflict erupted between the regime and the church when the Supreme Administrative Court ordered Pope Shenouda to issue remarriage licenses and argued that the church only exercises its legal competence subject to state law and the Egyptian judiciary (Supreme Administrative Court 2010).

Pope Shenouda then made changes to the Orthodox Church's regulations of 1938, which the Coptic Community Council then adopted (Patriarchate of the Coptic Communal Council 2008). These amendments were then sent to the administrative courts, and the courts started enforcing them. This was followed by the Supreme Constitutional Court's suspension of the decision of the Supreme Administrative Court. This represented the expansion of the Coptic Orthodox Church's control over the religion of Christians and the limitation of that of the state. The state had capitulated to the Coptic Orthodox Church's demands to decide what constitutes and what does not constitute the personal status law for Christians as applied by the national courts.

Article 3 of the 2014 Constitution served to consolidate the parameters within which the Coptic Orthodox Church could direct religion. It also allowed the church to widen these parameters. Subsequently, the Orthodox Church drafted new bylaws in 2016, which have yet to be approved by the People's Assembly. These draft bylaws assert that it is the Clerical Council and not the state judiciary that is able to give a Copt permission to remarry. They also assert that no Coptic Christian can appeal in front of any state judicial body against a religious decision made by the church (Article 134). The bylaws also emphasize the church's judicial independence by asserting that the Clerical Council is legally bound by Biblical teachings and the traditions of the Coptic Orthodox Church, with the implication that these stand above state law as far as the legal affairs of Coptic Christians are concerned (al-Nass al-kamil 2016).

The Coptic Orthodox Church's position on divorce is one important way in which the state has accommodated the Coptic Orthodox Church and, in turn, limited the reach of laws issued by the state that are applicable to all Egyptian citizens. Other actions indicate an important trend toward the state's affirmation of Coptic Christians and a more inclusive Egyptian religious identity. In the process, the type of Islamic state Egypt is is being rearticulated to be more religiously open. Some of President Sisi's doctrinal interventions have concerned Christians and the divinely revealed religions. Sisi's language is a far cry from that of Sadat who told Pope Shenouda III that he was a Muslim ruler of an Islamic country. This does not deny that incidents of discrimination and violence against Christians occur. However, there has been an important shift in the language of the state, although that is not to say that such language necessarily translates into less discrimination more broadly. The continued expression of support for Christianity has been bolstered by tensions between al-Azhar and the state. While the Muslim Brotherhood, long disliked by Ahmed al-Tayyib, has been marginalized, the presidency, emboldened by political discourse toward Christians, is using its voice to reduce the power of al-Azhar.

For example, the building and renovation of churches are much easier than they had been under President Mubarak, although Christians still encounter a number of challenges (Ibrahim, 2019). The Hatti Humayun decree, which was issued by the Ottoman Sublime Porte in 1856, contained limitations on the building of churches. This decree was inherited by the modern Egyptian legal system in 1915. As a result, throughout the twentieth century, securing licenses to build new churches and repair existing ones was extremely difficult and bureaucratically cumbersome. In the

1970s, Copts sought a halt to restrictions on the building of churches, although extremist Islamist sentiments, which argue that no Muslim state—or individual—should finance or contribute to church building, were influential at the time ('Abd al-Qudus 1980). Toward the end of the Mubarak era, church building and renovations became easier and more church building permits were granted. However, the fact that the Constitution of 2014 mentioned the building and renovation of churches in its transitional provisions illustrates the shift in sentiments that has taken place on the subject since the 1970s.

Al-Azhar is broadly supportive of the building and repair of churches, although in 2014, al-Azhar maintained that "as long as this does not harm national security" (Isa 2016). Once again, President Sisi struck a different tone to that of al-Azhar. In January 2015, Sisi attended Christmas Mass and is the first Egyptian president to have attended Mass every year (Masrawy 2021). In 2016, Sisi apologized, while standing next to Pope Tawadros in a church service, for the delays that had taken place in repairing churches that had been damaged in sectarian attacks (CGTN Africa 2015). A new Church Construction Law was passed in 2016. Since then, the Coptic Orthodox Church and the Coptic media have welcomed the extent to which churches have been registered and constructed (U.S. Embassy in Egypt 2022). In 2018, the Egyptian Minister of Religious Endowments stated that "defending mosques and churches is a religious and a national duty" (Hashish 2018). The new Cathedral of the Nativity of Christ was commissioned by 'Abd al-Fattah al-Sisi and inaugurated by him and Pope Tawadros in early 2019. The new cathedral has enabled the state to portray itself as the defender of Coptic Christians. Additionally, Sisi announced that the state will bear the cost of establishing churches for Christian communities, in addition to mosques, schools, and nurseries in the new cities that are being proposed for development in Egypt (Masrawy 2021).

The state has also advocated for greater interreligious tolerance and respect in the Egyptian school system. In 2021, the Ministry of Education instituted a new training program for school principals and developed a new curriculum that included religious tolerance. In March 2021, the Ministry of Education approved the study of values and verses that have the same meaning in Judaism, Christianity, and Islam as part of the curriculum. Such a move now enables, for the first time, Egyptian students to study Jewish scripture (Mikhail 2021). Kamal Amer, member of the Egyptian parliament, argued that the three religions all have shared values and that President Sisi wants students to be instructed in such values in order to confront religious fanaticism (Jerusalem Post 2021).

A further sign of the shift that has taken place in the Egyptian public sphere toward the affirmation of Christian-Muslim unity can be seen in Sisi's nomination, early in 2022, of Boulos Fahmy Iskander as head of the Supreme Constitutional Court. Fahmy is the first Coptic Christian judge to serve as head of the court. The nomination of a Christian as the head of the court was invoked as "historic" and an indication of the state's adherence to the concept of citizenship as stated in the constitution (Ayyad 2022).

In response to Fahmy's nomination, al-Azhar could not but say the right thing and support such a move. Yet, one wonders if al-Azhar has been boxed in. There has long been unease in Islamist circles regarding the ability of the Supreme Constitutional Court justices to decide on Article 2 cases since they have no expertise in the Islamic sciences. Such unease can only be compounded by the nomination of a Christian as head of the court. Moderate Islamist thinking does not preclude the possibility of a Christian head of the Supreme Constitutional Court, given the kind of institutional diffusion of roles and responsibilities that exist in a modern nation state (al-Bishri 1988, p. 682, 685; Abu al-Futuh 2005, pp. 117–127). At the same time, al-Azhar has often taken a position that is more conservative than that of reformist Islamist perspectives. It is not easy to imagine that al-Tayyib would have had no legal qualms about a Christian head of the court. Nevertheless, in a Facebook post, Ahmed al-Tayyib hoped that Fahmy would have success in his new position (al-Tayyib 2022). Likewise, the Grand Mufti of Egypt, Shawqi Ibrahim 'Abd al-Karim 'Allam, supported the move arguing Egypt "is a model for achieving the principle of citizenship for all without any religious or racial discrimination" ('Allam 2022). Sisi's appointment of Fahmy as head of the court marks a further attempt to embrace Christianity. In so doing, Sisi is trying to curtail al-Azhar by seizing the moral high-ground.

CONCLUSION

The congratulations on the nomination of a Christian as head of the Supreme Constitutional Court are illustrative of the important shifts that have occurred in the connections between religion and state in Egypt since the Egyptian Revolution. The Muslim Brotherhood has effectively been removed from the public sphere and al-Azhar has gained a level of independence that has been constitutionally sanctioned. One might have anticipated al-Azhar to have emerged from the revolutionary period as the supreme institution that would give expert opinions on Islamic law. Yet realignments never occur in linear ways. The metaphorical death of the Muslim Brotherhood in Egypt has, in fact, resulted in important and perhaps unforeseen reconfigurations in existing political relationships. Supporting Sisi in his move against the Muslim Brotherhood and the violence that ensued came at a cost. Al-Azhar now has to contend with an increasingly strident and vocal president and parliament which are not content to let al-Azhar's claim to represent Islam go unchallenged. President Sisi is trying to define Egypt as a different kind of Islamic state and, in so doing, present a different religious vision of Egypt that is not solely defined by al-Azhar.

Thus, the tensions between al-Azhar and the president have been connected to—and enabled by—the president's assertion that Egypt is an Islamic state that is religiously supportive of Christianity and distant from extremist and more traditional approaches. The state has been increasingly supportive of the Coptic Orthodox Church in terms of both its rhetoric and other initiatives. The state's good relationship with the Coptic Orthodox Church is therefore facilitating its ability to undermine the power of al-Azhar. This shows that not only are the relationships that the state has with al-Azhar and with the Coptic Orthodox Church negotiated, but the nature of one relationship impacts the other.

The state is currently using the Coptic Orthodox Church to limit the power of al-Azhar, and, in so doing, establish itself as religious mediator in chief. In fact, if there is anything that Egyptian politics of late has taught us it is that the pendulum constantly shifts. One possible shift relates to Sisi's employment of broad religious language beyond the divinely revealed religions. Such language in support of atheists and of people who are religious but not Muslim, Jewish, or Christian may well have important consequences for the Egyptian religious landscape. Sisi may, for example, encounter pressure from many Coptic Christians who want to conduct their personal status affairs without the supervision of the Coptic Orthodox Church and seek to appeal to the constitutional principle of equal citizenship. This might well put pressure on the president to translate his rhetoric into action, bringing it into conflict with the Coptic Orthodox Church.

Returning to Migdal, who maintains that political change comes "in accommodations between states and other powerful organizations in society" (Migdal 1987, p. 398), this chapter has moved away from seeing opposition groups as key to the relationship that religion has with the state in Egypt to look at the subtle shifts in power relations between the state and two state-related organizations, al-Azhar and the Coptic Orthodox Church. By focusing on where the state and state-related organizations meet one can see how each party—the state on the one hand and the two religious organizations on the other—pushes the other in its attempt to control and shape religion.

REFERENCES

'Adil, Basil. 2017. Fatwa 'ala al-Mahata (Fatwa at the Station). *al-Masri al-yawm*, July 27.

'Abd al-Qudus, Muhammad. 1980. 'Limatha nu'arid fikr majmu'at al-adyan (Why Do We Oppose the Idea of the Alliance of Religions). *al-Da'wa*, January.

'Abd al-Wahid, Maher. 2013. 'Jibhat al-difa' 'an al-Azhar taltaqi bi-'al-Tayyib' al-yawm (The Front for the Defense of al-Azhar Meets with al-Tayyib Today). *al-Yawm*, January 16.

Abu al-Futuh, 'Abd al-Mun'im. 2005. *Mujaddidun la Mubaddidun (Renewers not Dissipators)*. Cairo: tatwir li-l-nashr wa l-tawzi.'

Allam, Shawqi. 2022. *Facebook*, February 10. https://ar-ar.facebook.com/EgyptDarAlIftaMedia/posts/3065514870333233

al-Ashwal, Ismail. 2017. 'Infirad: mashru' ta'dil qanun al-Azhar yatadamman muhasabat al-imam al-akbar (Alone: The Proposal to Amend the Law of al-Azhar Includes Accountability for the Grand Imam). *al-Shuruq*, April 24.

al-'Awwa, Muhammad Salim. 2003. *'Azmat al-mu'assasa al-diniyya (The Crisis of the Religious Establishment)*. Cairo: dar al-shuruq.

Ayyad, Ibrahim. 2022. Historic Decision to appoint Christian Judge as head of Egypt's Supreme Court. *al-Monitor*, February 15.

Bano, Masooda. 2018. At the Tipping Point? Al-Azhar's Growing Crisis of Moral Authority. *International Journal of Middle East Studies* 50 (4): 715–734.

Bar'el, Zivi. 2020. Sissi Sets His Sights on al-Azhar: The Beating Heart of Egypt's Life. *Haaretz*, July 27.

al-Bishri, Tariq. 1988. *al-Muslimun wa l-Aqbat fi Itar al-Jama'a al-Wataniyya (Muslims and Copts in the Framework of the National Community)*. Cairo: dar al-shuruq.

Brown, Nathan J. 2013. Islam in Egypt's Cacophonous Constitutional Order. In *The Rule of Law, Islam, and Constitutional Politics in Egypt and Iran*, ed. Saïd Arjomand and Nathan J. Brown, 233–248. Albany: State University of New York Press.

Brown, Nathan J., Shimaa Hatab, and Amr Adly. 2021. *Lumbering State, Restless Society: Egypt in the Modern Era*. New York: Columbia University Press.

Brown, Nathan J., and Michele Dunne. 7 June 2021. Who Will Speak for Islam in Egypt—And Who Will Listen? In *Islamic Institutions in Arab States: Mapping the Dynamics of Control, Co-option, and Contention*, ed. Frederic Wehry. Carnegie Endowment for International Peace.

al-Ghazali, Muhammad. 2006. *Min huna na'lam …! (From Here We Learn)*. Cairo: nahdat misr.

Egyptian Initiative for Personal Rights. 2020. Economic Misdemeanour Appeals Court Upholds Verdict Against Blogger, with 3 Years' Imprisonment and a 300,000 EGP Fine for Managing the 'Egyptian Atheists' Facebook page. June 23.

Fattal, Antoine. 1958. *Le Statut Légal des non-Musulmans en Pays d'Islam (The Legal Status of Non-Muslims in Islamic Lands)*. Beirut: Imprimerie Catholique.

Guma'a, 'Ali. 2014. Ali Gomaa's Message to Egyptian Security Forces Delivered Prior the 2013 Rabaa Massacre Part 1 of 2. *YouTube*, September 14. https://www.youtube.com/watch?v=LCQqrryBy1E

Habib, Rafiq. 2013. Al-Azhar wa l-ikhwan: al-sira'a al-muftarad 'ala al-murja'iyya (al-Azhar and the Brotherhood: The Assumed Struggle over the Frame of Reference. *Tahawwulat al-dawla wa l-mujtama'a ba'ad al-rabi'a al-'arabi (Transformations of the State and Society after the Arab Spring)*, April.

Hashish, Sana. 2018. 'Wazir al-Awqaf: al-difa'a 'an al-masajid wa l-kana'is wajib shar'i wa-watani (The Minister of Endowments: Defending Mosques and Churches is a National Duty). *al-Wafd*, January 22.

Hasan. 2003. *Christians versus Muslims in Modern Egypt: The Century-Long Struggle for Coptic Equality*. Oxford: Oxford University Press.

Hejazi, Sa'id. 2020. Nass khitab rafd al-Azhar li-qanun tanzim dar al-ifta' qabl munaqashatihi bi-l-barlaman (Text of al-Azhar's Refusal of the Law for the Organization of the Ministry of Fatwas Before its Discussion in Parliament). *al-Watan*, July 19.

Ibrahim, Ishak. 2019. The Reality of Church Construction in Egypt, *Egyptian Initiative for Personal Rights*, https://eipr.org/en/blog/ishak-ibrahim/2019/07/reality-church-construction-egypt

Ibrahim, Saad Edin. 2018. al-Mu'asasa al-azhariyya lan tujaddid al-khitab al-dini (The Institution of al-Azhar Will not Renew Religious Discourse). *al-Masri al-yawm*, December 21.

Isa, Sherif. 2016. al-Mawqif al-rasmi li-l-Azhar min bina al-kana'is (The Official Position of al-Azhar on Building Churches). *al-Mal*, September 8.

Jad al-Haq, 'Ali Jad al-Haq. 1983. *'Kutay'ib al-farida al-gha'iba wa l-rad 'alayhi (The Booklet of the Missing Duty and the Response to it)*. In *al-Fatawa al-islamiyya*, 10/31, *Dar al-ifta al-misriyya*; Cairo, 3726–3761.

Jawhari, Muhammad. 2014. 'Bi-l-ta'awun ma'a awqaf wa asatidha al-tibb al-nafsi (Cooperation with (the Ministry of) Awqaf and Professors of Psychiatry), *al-Ahram*, June 18.

Kamal, Karima. 2006. *Talaq al-aqbat (Divorce of the Copts)*. Cairo: dar al-mirit.

Kuru, Ahmet T. 2019. *Islam, Authoritarianism, and Underdevelopment: A Global and Historical Comparison*. Cambridge: Cambridge University Press.

Lapidus, Ira M. 1975. The Separation of State and Religion in the Development of Early Islamic Society. *International Journal of Middle Eastern Studies* 6 (4): 363–385.

al-Majlis al-'ala li-l-quwat al-musallaha. 2012. al-Majlis al-'ala li-l-quwat al-musallaha marsum bi-qanun raqm 13 li-sanat 2012 (The Supreme Council of Armed Forces Decree no. 13 of the year 2012). *al-Jarida al-rasmiyya*, 3, January 19.

McCallum, Fiona. 2012. Religious Institutions and Authoritarian States: Church–state Relations in the Middle East. *Third World Quarterly* 33 (1): 109–124.

Migdal, Joel S. 1987. Strong States, Weak States: Power and Accommodation. In *Understanding Political Development*, ed. Myron Weiner and Samuel Huntingdon, 391–434. Boston: Little Brown.

Mikhail, George. 2021. Egypt to Introduce Judaism in Schools. *al-Monitor*, March 2.

Mitchell, Timothy, and Roger Owen. 1990. Defining the State in the Middle East: A Report on the First of Three Workshops Organized by The Social Science Research Council's Joint Committee on the Near and Middle East. *MESA Bulletin* 24: 179–183.

———. 1991. Defining the State in the Middle East: A Report on the Second of Three Workshops Organized by The Social Science Research Council's Joint Committee on the Near and Middle East. *MESA Bulletin* 25: 25–29.

Moustafa, Tamir. 2000. Conflict and Cooperation between the State and Religious Institutions In Contemporary Egypt. *International Journal of Middle East Studies* 32 (1): 3–22.

Nada, Mustafa. 2015. Mulhidun li-l-Shuruq: khitab al-Sisi 'anna ijabi (Atheists to al-Shuruq: Sisi's Speech About us is Positive). *al-Shuruq*, July 16.

Owen, Roger. 2000. *State, Power and Politics in the Making of the Middle East*. London: Routledge.

Patriarchate of the Coptic Orthodox Communal Council. 2008. Qirar ta'dil la'ihat al-ahwal al-shakhsiyya li-l-aqbat al-urthuduks. *al-Waqa'i al-misriyya*, 126, Year 181, June 2.

Salomon, Noah. 2016. *For the Love of the Prophet: An Ethnography of Sudan's Islamic State*. Princeton: Princeton University Press.

al-Sawi, Fadi. 2018. Ba'ad hadith al-Sisi 'an huriyyat al-'ibada … kayfa mahhadat al-dawla li-bina' kana'is bi-misr (After Sisi's Talk about Freedom of Worship, How Has the State Facilitated the Building of Churches in Egypt)? *Misr al-'arabiyya*, November 8.

Scott, Rachel M. 2021. *Recasting Islamic Law: Religion and the Nation State in Egyptian Constitution Making*. Ithaca: Cornell University Press.

Sherif, Adel Omar. 2012. The Relationship between the Constitution and the Sharī'ah in Egypt. In *Constitutionalism in Islamic Countries: Between Upheaval and Continuity*, ed. Rainer Grote and Tilman J. Röder, 121–133. Oxford: Oxford University Press.

Skovgaard-Petersen, Jakob. 2013. Egypt's *Ulama* in the State, in Politics, and in the Islamist Vision. In *The Rule of Law, Islam, and Constitutional Politics in Egypt and Iran*, ed. Saïd Arjomand and Nathan J. Brown, 279–302. Albany: State University of New York Press.

Supreme Administrative Court, May 29, 2010, no. 12244/55.

Supreme Constitutional Court, June 3, 2000, no. 151/20.

al-Tayyib, Ahmed. 2011. Nass wathiqat al-Azhar hawl mustaqbal misr (The Document of al-Azhar concerning the Future of Egypt).

———. 2020. Sheikh Al-Azhar: NO to Renovation of ISLAM! *YouTube*, February 5. https://www.youtube.com/watch?v=4WT_oLPH4QU

———. 2022. *Facebook*, February 9. https://www.facebook.com/Official AzharEg/posts/498019538349232

U.S. Embassy in Egypt. 2022. 2021 Report on International Religious Freedom: Egypt. June 6.

Ziada, Dalia. 2022. The Untold Story of al-Azhar and the Egyptian Revolution. *al-Majalla*, January 7.

No author

'Ana ahtaram 'adam al-i'tiqad (I Respect Those Who Have No Religious Belief).' 2021. *Sahih Misr*, September 12.

Taqnin al-awda' wa tha'r: kayf taghayyar wad' al-aqbat khilal 7 sanawat hukm al-sisi (Legislating Rules and Revenge: How has the Situation of Copts Changed during the Seven Years of Sisi's Rule?). 2021. *Masrawy*, June 9

Egypt's Education Ministry to Teach Judaism in Schools for First Time Ever. 2021. *Jerusalem Post*, March 9.

Fmr Deputy Sheikh of al-Azhar Mahmud Ashour and Egyptian Atheist Mohammad Hashem. 2018. *al-Hadath al-yawm, MEMRI TV*, February 11. https://www.facebook.com/memri.org/videos/10156224522094717/

Misr: al-Azhar yu'arid al-sisi bi-sha'n hazr al-talaq al-shafawi (Egypt: al-Azhar Opposes al-Sisi on the Issue of Forbidding Oral Divorce). 2017. *France 24*, February 5.

al-Nass al-kamil li-mashru' qanun al-ahwal al-shakhsiyya li-l-aqbat 2016 wa l-la'iha al-dakhiliyya li-l-majlis al-iklirki (The Complete Text of the Proposed Coptic Personal Status Law of 2016 and the Internal Bylaws of the Clerical Council). 2016. *Faith Protectors Association*-Rabitat Hamlat al-'Iman, Cairo.

Egypt's President Sisi Attends Christmas Mass. 2015. *CGTN Africa*, January 7. https://www.youtube.com/watch?v=y7IC-MiHzbA

Dustur jumhuriyyat misr al-'arabiyya (Constitution of the Arab Republic). 2014.

PART VI

Religion and the State in the United States, Canada, Mexico, South America, and Cuba

CHAPTER 26

Why Do We Think the Framers Wanted to Separate Church and State?

Donald L. Drakeman

The phrase 'separation of church and state' has become a part of our constitutional vocabulary. In judicial opinions and scholarly articles, along with countless political speeches and blog postings, church-state arguments have typically revolved around whether some familiar practice—the National Day of Prayer, municipal Christmas displays, legislative chaplains, funding for religious schools, and so on—has breached the wall of separation between church and state that the Framers erected in the First Amendment. Since the word 'separation' does not appear in the Constitution itself, and as far as we know, it was never even uttered during the constitutional debates, we should ask why we think the Framers meant to separate church and state.

Our search for the answer to that question begins not at the time when the Bill of Rights was written in 1789, but when the Supreme Court first interpreted the First Amendment's religion clauses 75 years later. It was then, in the aftermath of the Civil War, and as a result of a fascinating

D. L. Drakeman (✉)
University of Notre Dame, Notre Dame, IN, USA
e-mail: ddrakema@nd.edu

S. Holzer (ed.), *The Palgrave Handbook of Religion and State
Volume II*, https://doi.org/10.1007/978-3-031-35609-4_26

collection of historical contingencies, that separation became the theme of modern church-state constitutional jurisprudence. By starting the story of separation in the nineteenth century, we can see why many people currently think that separation is what the Framers had in mind. Then, by looking back to the Founding Era, we can discover what they actually set out to accomplish, which is quite different from our modern notion of the separation of church and state. That historical analysis will show that the Constitution's Framers were concerned only with the narrow question of whether there would be a 'Church of the United States,' much as there was a 'Church of England' at the time. In addressing that specific issue, they were not trying to make a fundamental commitment to the principle of church-state separation, or to any broad principle relating to religion and government.

THE JUDICIAL ORIGINS OF SEPARATIONISM

It all started with a wedding (Reynolds v. United States 1878). On 3 August 1874, 32-year-old George Reynolds married Amelia Jane Schofield. This was a first marriage for Amelia Jane, but it was George's second, and that was the problem. He had just violated a new federal law against polygamy. Reynolds was convicted, and he appealed to the Supreme Court. One of his claims was that, since his Mormon faith required him to be polygamous, he was merely exercising his constitutionally protected religious rights. This case, which did not arise until 90 years after the First Amendment was adopted, provided the opportunity for the Supreme Court to interpret the religion clauses for essentially the first time. The main reason for the absence of prior cases involving church-state issues was that the Supreme Court had decided early in the nineteenth century that the First Amendment only applied to actions of the federal government, whereas most cases that raised church-state issues involved state, not federal, laws, and state court judges considered those cases in light of their own state constitutions. In this case, however, Reynolds lived in Utah, which, at that time, was not yet a state: it was a US territory, and thus governed directly by federal law.

Chief Justice Morrison Waite was not sure what to do in this case of first impression. He had little experience in constitutional law. Before he was appointed Chief Justice by President Ulysses S. Grant, he had been a little-known railroad lawyer from Toledo, Ohio. He was what we would now call a stealth nominee from a swing state during a tight presidential election. Some of his more prominent colleagues on the Supreme Court bench referred to him as 'His Accidency.' Nevertheless, the Chief Justice appears to have felt a special responsibility for important constitutional cases, and so, according to his biographer, he changed his initial vote so that he would be in the majority, which would allow him to write the Court's opinion in the *Reynolds* case (Magrath 1963, p. 524).

With no previous Supreme Court opinions interpreting the religion clauses, Chief Justice Waite turned instead to his next-door neighbor. The neighbor was historian George Bancroft, perhaps the preeminent American historian of the era, who happened to be in the middle of writing a history of the Constitution. Bancroft pointed to one of his personal heroes, Thomas Jefferson, saying that Jefferson's Virginia Statute on Religious Freedom 'shows the opinion of the leading American statesmen' at the time of the Constitution. The fact that Jefferson was out of the country as Minister to France when the First Amendment was adopted never came up (Drakeman 2009, p. 31).

As far as we can tell, the Chief Justice then went to the library and skimmed through the index to Jefferson's collected works. There, he discovered an otherwise obscure 1802 letter written to a group of Baptists in Danbury, Connecticut, in which Jefferson said that the First Amendment had built a 'wall of separation between church and state.' This letter had essentially been buried in the archives for nearly 80 years until Chief Justice Waite came across it. According to Waite, '[c]oming as this does from an acknowledged leader of the advocates of the measure, it may be accepted almost as an authoritative declaration of the scope and effect of the amendment.' Bancroft soon received a thank-you note from the Chief Justice: 'As you gave me the information on which the judgment in the Utah polygamy case rests, I send you a copy of the opinion that you may see what use has been made of your facts' (quoted in Drakeman 2009, pp. 1–2).

Interestingly, Jefferson's language about the wall provided no comfort for Reynolds, who might have hoped that it would have prevented the federal government from adopting a traditional Christian approach to monogamous marriage. Rather, the Chief Justice noted that the State of Virginia had banned polygamy even after enacting Jefferson's religious freedom statute, and he invoked James Kent's well-known legal commentary to the effect that 'it is within the legitimate scope of power of every civil government to determine whether polygamy or monogamy shall be the law' (Reynolds v. United States 1878, p. 166). Although the

Jeffersonian metaphor of a wall of separation did not affect the outcome in the *Reynolds* case, the evocative language would return in many future cases, including the next major church-state case: *Everson v. Board of Education*, which reached the Court half a century later in 1947.

Between these two cases, the Supreme Court decided that the First Amendment's religion clauses had been 'incorporated' by the Fourteenth Amendment's 'due process' clause. As a result of this 'incorporation doctrine,' those provisions had become applicable to actions of state and local governments, and not just to 'Congress,' as the language specified (Cantwell v. Connecticut 1940). Until that time, each state's approach to church-state issues was governed by its own constitution and statutes. From that point, the Court's church-state decisions would require that all of the states would be subject to the same national rules.

Everson involved a state law providing bus fares for children attending religious schools. Justice Hugo Black was the author of the Court's majority opinion, and he embraced Chief Justice Waite's 'wall of separation' approach to the religion clauses but nevertheless upheld the bus fare reimbursement program. Justice Black began the majority opinion by noting that many of the 'early settlers' came to America 'from Europe to escape the bondage of laws which compelled them to support and attend government favored churches.' In particular, by the time of the American Revolution, the people Black described as America's 'freedom-loving colonials' had won a hard-fought political battle to eliminate Virginia's established Anglican Church. This dramatic and catalytic event in Virginia, according to Black, later culminated in the religion clauses of the First Amendment to the US Constitution, 'the drafting and adoption of which Madison and Jefferson played such leading roles' (Everson v. Board of Education 1947, pp. 15–16).

Black thus followed the historical analysis in *Reynolds* and concluded that the religion clauses of the First Amendment 'had the same objective' as Jefferson's Virginia Statute for Religious Freedom and his 1802 letter about a 'wall of separation between church and state.' Black's opinion in *Everson* ultimately followed this separationist theme to reach a broad conclusion that one scholar has labeled 'the most famous *dictum* in any Supreme Court opinion on the Establishment Clause' (Howard 1985, p. 88). Black's opinion stated that neither the state nor the federal government 'can pass laws which aid one religion, aid all religions, or prefer one religion over another' (Everson v. Board of Education 1947, pp. 16–17). This interpretation, which prohibits even nondenominational, or 'nonpreferential,' aid for religion, has become the extended play version of the wall of separation metaphor in many modern constitutional debates. The four dissenting justices shared Black's commitment to the wall of separation but thought the bus fares violated its strict requirements and thus argued for an even stricter version of separation.

The Metaphor of Separation and Constitutional Law

These two cases show how the wall metaphor created the foundation for the Supreme Court's 'separationist' approach to the establishment clause, which prevailed during much of the twentieth century. It led to Supreme Court's decisions of striking down prayer and Bible reading in the public schools, barring state funding for religious schools, and censoring what the justices' thought were unduly religious Christmas displays on public property. For our purposes, the question is: was that legal legacy simply a jurisprudential accident attributable to His Accidency, a quirk of constitutional history resulting from the fact that the Chief Justice happened to live next door to a historian with a fondness for Thomas Jefferson?

That is certainly a possible historical conclusion. Had Waite not lived next to Bancroft, the Chief Justice might well have turned instead to the leading constitutional commentary of the day—former Supreme Court Justice Joseph Story's *Commentaries on the Constitution of the United States*, first published in 1833. Doing so would have launched the Supreme Court's Establishment Clause jurisprudence in a very different direction than Jefferson's metaphor of a wall separating church and state. Story wrote that, at the time of the adoption of the First Amendment, 'the general if not the universal sentiment in America was, that Christianity ought to receive encouragement from the State so far as was not incompatible with the private rights of conscience and the freedom of religious worship' (Story 1833, vol. 3, p. 726). If Chief Justice Waite had followed the views of his Supreme Court predecessor instead of his next-door neighbor, the meaning of the Establishment Clause would have emerged from the nineteenth century with a much different interpretive gloss, and Jefferson's now-famous letter about the wall might be just another document in the archives.

Even more broadly, we can ask whether, absent the Chief Justice's neighborly chat, the separation of church and state would never have been seen as a fundamental constitutional principle. Some justices and numerous other commentators have argued that Story's version is the correct understanding, and that the Court's reliance on Jefferson's concept of a wall of separation is simply wrong. As Justice William Rehnquist said in his dissenting opinion in Wallace v. Jaffree (1984), where he cited Story's *Commentaries on the Constitution* favorably: 'It is impossible to build sound constitutional doctrine upon a mistaken understanding of constitutional history, but unfortunately the Establishment Clause has been expressly freighted with Jefferson's misleading metaphor.' Perhaps, as Justice Rehnquist argues in that case, nonpreferential aid to religion should always have been seen by the Court as entirely consistent with the Constitution.

THE CULTURAL BACK STORY OF SEPARATION

Although the Supreme Court's debut of the 'wall of separation' interpretation did not occur until the *Reynolds* case, the notion of church-state separation had become increasingly common during nineteenth century, well before Chief Justice Waite had his conversation with George Bancroft. Four years before the *Reynolds* case, President Grant had declared, in a widely publicized 1875 speech, that it is essential to 'keep the church and the state forever separate' (quoted in Green 1992, pp. 47–48). For Grant and many others in that era, however, the concept of separation did not necessarily apply to all church-state issues. It had a special focus: it was a principle that related directly to the divisive, and sometimes violent, political controversies over state funding for Roman Catholic schools.

Many Roman Catholic immigrants to America in the nineteenth century were distressed by the fact that the public schools typically included Protestant prayers and readings from a Protestant version of the Bible. When the schools were unwilling to excuse the Catholic children from those religious activities, Catholic churches set out to establish separate schools. In communities where Catholics had a considerable degree of political power, they were often able to obtain state funding for those religious schools. After battles between Protestants and Catholics over Catholic school funding became a national political issue, Grant's Republican Party sought to pass 'a constitutional amendment separating church from state—particularly the Catholic Church from the American states' (Hamburger 2002, p. 322). Congressman James G. Blaine proposed such an amendment in 1875. It started by copying the First Amendment's language but applied it directly to the states: 'No state shall make any law respecting an establishment of religion or prohibiting the free exercise thereof.' Then it specifically addressed the school issue: 'no money raised by taxation in any State for the support of public schools ... shall ever be under the control of any religious sect' (United States Congress 1876, vol. 4, p. 5245).

It was in the context of these 'school wars' that the notion of church-state separation became increasingly common. The nineteenth-century theme of separation related directly to parochial school funding, and, ironically, it was more often employed to defend rather than attack the 'nondenominational' Protestant prayers and Bible reading in the public schools. Nor did it prevent President Grant from handing over the management of the federal 'Indian agencies' to religious groups with the expectation that they would, as Grant reported to Congress, 'Christianize and civilize the Indian' (Grant 1905, p. 110). As one historian has observed, by '1872 the churches effectively controlled some nine hundred government employees' (Keller 1983, p. 168). For Grant and his many supporters, keeping 'Church and State forever separate' did not mean either the removal of religious activities from the public schools or putting a stop to efforts to convert Native Americans to Christianity. Instead, it had a very specific focus: excluding the influence of Catholicism from publicly funded education. The president described his goal as preventing the states 'from giving public funds to any schools that taught 'sectarian tenets,' so that Americans would not 'sink into acquiescence to the will of intelligence, whether directed by the demagogue or priestcraft'" (quoted in Hamburger 2002, p. 323).

Congressman Blaine's proposed amendment was never adopted, but President Grant's rhetoric caught on to such a great extent that many people began simply to assume that the separation of church and state was guaranteed by both state and federal constitutions (Hamburger 2002, pp. 322–326). Numerous states even adopted versions of Blaine's language as amendments to their own constitutions. Over time, the Supreme Court would not only identify separation as the political principle represented by the Establishment Clause, but it would also expand its definition of separation so much further that, by the middle of the twentieth century, the justices would strike down even the nondenominational prayers and Bible reading that had been a part of the public-school day for much of the nation's history. The concept of keeping church and state 'forever separate,' which had originally been employed primarily to protect the public-school system's distinctly Protestant character, would ultimately exclude any and all religious activities in the schools. Twentieth-century separation was thus a very different concept than the prevailing nineteenth-century version, and, as the following section will show, both were striking departures from the simple question the Framers thought they were answering in the Bill of Rights.

The Eighteenth-Century Background to the Establishment Clause

Throughout nearly all of the Supreme Court's religion decisions, from Chief Justice Waite's 1878 opinion in *Reynolds* to several twenty-first-century cases, the justices have routinely looked back to the time of the Establishment Clause's adoption for guidance about its meaning. Essentially all of the justices—from both the liberal and the conservative sides of the Court—have turned to history to find the meaning of this part of the Constitution. If we do the same, it becomes clear that, although many of our church-state debates today had close counterparts over 200 years ago, the Framers and the ratifiers were not in fact seeking to settle any of those contentious church-state topics via the Establishment Clause. Had they tried, they surely would have failed to reach any common understanding, since these issues were at least as controversial then as they are now (Drakeman 2020).

America has had church-state disputes throughout virtually all of its history, starting well before the time of the Constitution. Church-state issues in the various states continued to be controversial between the Revolutionary War and the time when the First Amendment was ratified in 1791, especially since the new American states were no longer British colonies and needed to adopt constitutions to replace their royal charters (Muñoz 2015). Whenever these church-state issues arose, they invariably ignited public debate and political conflict, as we can see in the battles in Massachusetts and Virginia over religious taxes (Drakeman 2020).

About one-quarter of the American population lived in either Massachusetts or Virginia when the Bill of Rights was adopted. Both states had recently experienced sustained political debates over whether there should be a very clear financial link between church and state in the form of ecclesiastical taxes—that is, taxes payable by all citizens that would be collected by the government, with the money allocated either to a church selected by the town in which the taxpayers lived (Massachusetts) or to the church they attended, or, if none, to other religious purposes (Virginia).

The primary rationale for the taxes was that many people believed that religion is necessary to support a well-functioning civil society. In the words of the 1784 Virginia tax bill, 'Christian knowledge hath a rational tendency to correct the morals of men, restrain their vices, and preserve the peace of society; which cannot be effected without a competent provision for learned teachers' (quoted in Buckley 1997, pp. 188–189). Similarly, the proposed 1780 Massachusetts Constitution declared that 'the happiness of a people, and the good order and preservation of civil government, essentially depend upon piety, religion and morality,' which require 'the public worship of God' and 'the support and maintenance of public Protestant teachers of piety religion and morality' (Dreisbach and Hall 2009, 246). The word 'teachers' in this context meant ordained clergy, that is, the minister of the local church.

Distinguished political leaders spoke up for one side or the other in both states. James Madison and Thomas Jefferson, with the vocal support of Virginia's growing number of Baptists, led the opposition to the Virginia bill that called for a general assessment for 'Teachers of the Christian Religion.' However, it had a very popular sponsor, the patriot leader Patrick Henry, and it was supported by future Chief Justice of the United States John Marshall and other distinguished Virginians. Meanwhile, in Massachusetts, the religious tax was promoted by that state's future Chief Justice, Theophilus Parsons, and it faced vocal opposition from many Baptists, including prominent religious liberty spokesman, Isaac Backus.

Backroom political scheming accompanied the speeches, petitions, and editorials in both states. In Virginia, Madison maneuvered Patrick Henry into the governorship and out of the legislature, where Henry had previously convinced a majority to support the tax. With Henry gone, the tax bill died in committee without a formal vote. Meanwhile, in Massachusetts, Theophilus Parsons' committee was responsible for counting the ratification votes, and it declared that the tax provision had been ratified even though it had not garnered the super-majority vote required for adopting a constitutional provision. Taken together, the political battles that led to the bill's failure in Virginia, as well those responsible for its success in Massachusetts, where tax support for churches continued for another 50 years, demonstrate that there was no national consensus on any broad church-state principles at the time of the Constitution. Quite to the contrary, church-state issues were hotly disputed whenever they arose.

THE ESTABLISHMENT CLAUSE AND THE BILL OF RIGHTS

If members of the public in two very populous states were so sharply divided on such a basic church-state issue as religious taxes, we need to ask how a nationwide decision about church-state relations could have been included in the Bill of Rights virtually without comment or controversy. The answer is that the original goal of that provision was not to settle any fundamental church-state policies; rather, it was limited to confirming the one thing everyone *did* agree on: Congress would not have the power to establish a national church along the lines of the Church of England. Accordingly, when the Framers adopted the Establishment Clause, they were simply answering a non-controversial, yes-or-no question about a national 'Church of the United States' without having to deal with their— and their fellow citizens—fundamental differences of opinion about church-state issues. Those issues would continue to generate political battles in all of the various states, where they would often be resolved differently from one state to another. That diversity of outcomes would continue until the Supreme Court adopted the incorporation doctrine in the twentieth century and set itself up to establish nationwide church-state standards.

The original meaning and limited scope of the Establishment Clause can be seen in the history of its adoption. It came about as a result of amendments proposed by a few of the state conventions that ratified the Constitution, although it is worth noting that most of the states did not propose any amendments on church-state issues. All together, the various states recommended a total of 210 amendments on a wide range of political issues; of these many diverse proposals, only 4 dealt with the issue of religious establishments. Three states proposed an anti-establishment amendment in almost identical language that was based on a proposal from Virginia, 'no particular religious sect or society ought to be favored or established by law in preference to others' (Kurland and Lerner 1987, vol. 5, p. 16), and New Hampshire submitted an amendment reading, 'Congress shall make no laws touching religion' (Elliot 1996/1836, pp. 325–336).

The First Congress had the task of creating the new federal government, and adopting constitutional amendments was not a high priority. Nevertheless, to appease the Antifederalists, amendments would need to be considered, and James Madison, who had originally thought amendments unnecessary, offered an initial set of proposals. Madison had won a closely contested race for one of Virginia's seats in the House of Representatives, and he had promised his Baptist constituents, many of whom had supported his efforts to defeat Virginia's ecclesiastical tax, that he would address their concerns about church-state issues. Accordingly, when Madison assembled a draft Bill of Rights, he included a national non-establishment clause. In introducing it, he said, 'whether the words are necessary or not, he did not mean to say, but they had been required by some of the State Conventions, who seemed to [think that Congress might have the power to] establish a national religion.' His draft amendment read, 'nor shall any national religion be established' (Cogan 1997, p. 60).

When the House had its brief debate on Madison's proposal, there was impressively little interest. Daniel Carroll, a Roman Catholic from Maryland, was the only one who spoke in favor of it. He said, '[M]any sects have concurred ... that they are not well secured under the present constitution.' He said he would not 'comment ... about phraseology' since he just wanted to satisfy the community's wishes (Cogan 1997, p. 59).

Roger Sherman of Connecticut, a strong supporter of the tax-supported Protestant churches in his state, said the language was unnecessary because 'Congress had no authority ... to make religious establishments,' an argument Madison himself had made in Virginia's ratifying convention. In response, Madison said again what it meant: 'that congress should not establish a religion and enforce the legal observation of it by law' (Cogan 1997, p. 60).

A committee removed the politically charged word 'national,' which was a term the Antifederalists vigorously opposed, so it read, 'nor shall any religion be established.' This led Connecticut's Samuel Huntington to worry that the federal courts might read it in a way that would prevent them from enforcing financial pledges for the support of local churches. Madison then proposed to put 'national' back in, so that it would be clear that it was only a 'national religion' being discussed (Cogan 1997, pp. 60–61).

Samuel Livermore from New Hampshire, which, like Massachusetts, also had ecclesiastical taxes, introduced his state's 'no touching' proposal: 'Congress shall make no law touching religion,' saying that 'the sense of both provisions was the same' (Cogan 1997, p. 57). His language passed 31–20. A few days later, it was replaced by language from Fisher Ames of Massachusetts that read, 'Congress shall make no law establishing religion' (Cogan 1997, p. 57). That was the final House version, and it had been introduced by a representative from a state that had, in 1780, adopted a constitutional mandate in favor of religious taxes. It then moved to the Senate, where there are no records of the debates. The Senate approved a different language than the version submitted by the House: 'Congress shall make no law establishing articles of faith or a mode of worship' (Cogan 1997, p. 6). In the end, after further revisions by a House-Senate conference committee, the final version read: 'Congress shall make no law respecting an establishment of religion' (Cogan 1997, p. 11).

All of the records available to us indicate that the Establishment Clause was understood by the members of the First Congress as relating solely to the question of whether Congress had the power to set up a national church. Because of the amendment's narrow purpose, members of Congress who held diametrically opposing views on whether states should have tax-supported churches—such as conference committee members James Madison from Virginia, on the one side, and Connecticut's Roger Sherman, on the other—could both find the amendment acceptable. The Establishment Clause had nothing to do with their own states' activities. Nor did it stand for any broad, national principle about the best way for governments and religion to interact. Rather, it simply answered the question of whether there would be an American counterpart to the Church of England, which is why it was enacted without any apparent controversy.

That the amendment was designed by its Framers to answer such a specific question seems clear from the records, but does that, in fact, represent the original meaning of the Establishment Clause? Lawyers and judges have sometimes argued about whether our understanding of a provision's original meaning should be determined by looking at what the members of Congress said when they were drafting the language or by what the ratifiers or the general public would have understood the provision to mean. In this case, it is not necessary to decide between these two approaches because they both point in the same direction. Our records of the Framers' statements come from published newspaper reports; accordingly, it is very likely that the general public—including those who would vote on ratifying the First Amendment—understood it in the same way that the Congress did.

It took the nineteenth-century Protestant-Catholic 'school wars,' Chief Justice Waite's discovery of Jefferson's letter, and, ultimately, the incorporation doctrine—that is, the twentieth-century Supreme Court decision that the Establishment Clause would apply to every state, town, and local school board as well as to Congress—to transform a narrow provision about an official national church into a broad judicial doctrine for resolving all sorts of church-state questions wherever they appear. In other words, politicians and Supreme Court justices in the nineteenth and twentieth centuries created a constitutional principle of church-state separation that they grafted onto a clause that was created for an entirely different purpose. Beyond clarifying that there would be no national church, the First Amendment left all of the inevitably difficult church-state issues to the states, where they would be resolved locally until the twentieth century, when the Supreme Court would essentially assume national jurisdiction over church-state questions.

HISTORY AND INTERPRETATION

The Supreme Court has regularly been criticized for misreading the history of the Establishment Clause. In one very negative commentary on the Court's opinion in the *Everson* case, for example, Edward Corwin argued that 'the Court has the right to make history ... but it has no right to make it up' (Corwin 1951, p. 116). Although there is no sign that the justices have actually fabricated historical events in their 'wall of separation' opinions, they have certainly emphasized only one side of the story by focusing on Virginia, where religion taxes were defeated, rather than Massachusetts, where they became a constitutional requirement. Justice Wiley Rutledge provides a clear insight into how at least one justice viewed this version of history as a convenient story that allowed him to reach an outcome that he sought primarily for other reasons.

Justice Rutledge was the author of the dissenting opinion in *Everson* that faulted the majority for not being sufficiently true to its Jeffersonian principles. But he was not, in the first instance, motivated by a desire to stick closely to an originalist approach to constitutional interpretation. Well before he considered any historical issues, he voted that the parochial school busing program was unconstitutional, writing in a confidential memorandum to the other justices: 'We all know that this [case is about] a fight by the Catholic schools to secure ... money from the public treasury. It is aggressive and on a wide scale' (Rutledge 1946, p. 5).

By the time the Court announced its decision, Justice Rutledge discovered an approach to church-state history that would allow him to write an opinion that did not rail against an 'aggressive' fight by the Catholic schools. Instead, it read like a treatise on religion and government in eighteenth-century Virginia. He later explained his originalist rationale to a likeminded friend by saying, 'I felt pretty strongly about the ... case but tried to keep the tone of what I had to say moderate and also to avoid pointing ... in the direction of any specific sect. The Virginia history was admirable for [that] purpose' (Rutledge 1947).

WHY *DO* WE THINK THE FRAMERS WANTED TO SEPARATE CHURCH AND STATE?

To answer the question posed by this chapter, we think the Constitution's Framers wanted to separate church and state because Supreme Court justices have devised a memorable constitutional creation myth about the origins of the Establishment Clause. That creation myth resonated with an approach to church-state issues that became broadly—but not universally—popular only a century later. The story has been so convincing that our national church-state vocabulary has come to be dominated by the language of separation to such an extent that an *Oxford Encyclopedia* notes, 'Separation of church and state [became] viewed as a cornerstone of American democracy' (Green 2014). As that has occurred, the First Amendment's historical context has been all but completely lost. A complex eighteenth-century environment, featuring a diverse range of approaches to the relationship of church and state in thirteen different colonies, has been replaced with a simple, straightforward narrative in which the views of Madison and Jefferson, which only barely prevailed in Virginia, and lost in New England, have been held out as the true American approach to church and state. That separationist story has been told so often, over more than a century, that it is not hard to see why judges, the public, and even some historians have come to think that the Framers wanted to separate church and state—even if that is not what actually happened.

REFERENCES

Buckley, T. 1997. *Church and State in Revolutionary Virginia, 1776–1787.* Charlottesville: University Press of Virginia.
Cantwell v. Connecticut [1940] 310 (Supreme Court of the United States); 296.
Cogan, N., ed. 1997. *The Complete Bill of Rights.* New York: Oxford University Press.
Corwin, E. 1951. *A Constitution of Powers in a Secular State.* Charlottesville, VA: Michie.

Drakeman, D. 2009. *Church, State, and Original Intent*. New York: Cambridge University Press.

———. 2020. Which Original Meaning of the Establishment Clause is the Right One? In *The Cambridge Companion to the First Amendment and Religious Liberty*, ed. M. Breidenbach and O. Anderson. Cambridge: Cambridge University Press.

Dreisbach, D., and M. Hall, eds. 2009. *The Sacred Rights of Conscience: Selected Readings on Religious Liberty and Church-State Relations in the American Founding*. Indianapolis, IN: Liberty Fund.

Elliot, J. 1996/1836. *The Debates in the Several State Conventions, on the Adoption of the Federal Constitution, as Recommended by the General Convention at Philadelphia in 1787*. 2nd ed. Buffalo, NY: William S. Hein & Co.

Everson v. Board of Education [1947] 330 (Supreme Court of the United States); 1.

Grant, U. 1905. Second Annual Address. In *A Compilation of the Messages and Papers of the Presidents, 1789–1902*, ed. James Daniel Richardson. New York: Bureau of National Literature and Art.

Green, S. 1992. The Blaine Amendment Reconsidered. *The American Journal of Legal History* 36 (1): 38–69.

———. 2014. The Separation of Church and State in the United States [Online]. *Oxford Research Encyclopedia of American History*. https://oxfordre.com/americanhistory/view/10.1093/acrefore/9780199329175.001.0001/acrefore-9780199329175-e-29. Accessed 26 May 2019.

Hamburger, P. 2002. *Separation of Church and State*. Cambridge, MA: Harvard University Press.

Howard, A. 1985. The Wall of Separation: The Supreme Court as Uncertain Stonemason. In *Religion and the State: Essays in Honor of Leo Pfeffer*, ed. J. Wood Jr. Waco, TX: Baylor University Press.

Keller, R. 1983. *American Protestantism and United States Indian Policy, 1869–82*, 1983. Lincoln: University of Nebraska Press.

Kurland, P., and R. Lerner, eds. 1987. *The Founders' Constitution*. Chicago: University of Chicago Press.

Magrath, C. 1963. *Morrison R. Waite: The Triumph of Character*. New York: Macmillan.

Muñoz, V. 2015. Church and State in the Founding-Era State Constitutions. *American Political Thought* 4 (1): 1–38.

Reynolds v. United States [1878] 98 (Supreme Court of the United States); 145.

Rutledge, W. 1946. *Memo After Conference* [Memo]. Library of Congress, Wiley B. Rutledge Papers, *Everson* File, Box 143. Washington, DC.

———. 1947. *Letter to Ernest Kirschten* [Letter]. Library of Congress, Wiley B. Rutledge Papers, *Everson* File, Box 143. Washington, DC.

Story, J. 1833. *Commentaries on the Constitution of the United States*. Boston: Hilliard, Gray, and Company.

United States Congress. 1876. *Congressional Record*. 44th Congress, 1st Session. Washington, DC: Government Printing Office.

Wallace v. Jaffree [1984] 472 (Supreme Court of the United States); 92.

FURTHER READINGS

Hamburger, P. 2002. *Separation of Church and State*. Cambridge, MA: Harvard University Press.

This is a highly influential book describing the how the concept of separation became embedded in our understanding of the First Amendment's religion clauses.

Muñoz, V. 2009. *God and the Founders: Madison, Washington, and Jefferson*. New York, NY: Cambridge University Press.

Named the best book in religion and politics in 2009–2010, this book compares and contrasts the views of three important founders on church-state issues.

Smith, S. 2014. *The Rise and Decline of American Religious Freedom*. Cambridge, MA: Harvard University Press.

This author shows how the modern Supreme Court's approach to church-state issues misreads the Founders' understanding of the role of religion and religious institutions in America.

Wilson, J., and D. Drakeman, eds. 2020. *Church and State in American History: Key Documents, Decisions, and Commentary from Five Centuries*. New York, NY: Routledge.

This widely used text contains many key documents, including the records of the adoption of religion clauses, and traces church-state issues in America from 1610 to 2018.

CHAPTER 27

American Church—State Relations: Jefferson's Conception of Religious Freedom

Garrett Ward Sheldon

The United States of America is the world's premier experiment in religious freedom, and Thomas Jefferson is the philosopher behind that experiment. His ideas were codified initially at the state level with the Statue for Establishing Religious Freedom and then at the national level through the religious clauses of the United States Constitution.

The American conception of religious liberty is based on the premise that the full and free expression of religious beliefs, without government control over, or coercion of, religious faith, both respects the God-given freedom of the human mind and will, and ultimately produces the most knowledgeable, happy, virtuous citizens, and just, orderly republic. It is seen as a natural right, given by God and our nature, not granted (or taken away) by the government. A just government respects the liberty of conscience and free exchange of ideas. A fair country is not afraid of open, tolerant debate over religious beliefs (as long as it doesn't lead to violence) and, in fact, such reasoned debate leads to a more rational citizenry and just state.

G. W. Sheldon (✉)
University of Virginia Wise, Wise, VA, USA
e-mail: gws@uvawise.edu

651
S. Holzer (ed.), *The Palgrave Handbook of Religion and State Volume II*, https://doi.org/10.1007/978-3-031-35609-4_27

Jefferson was born into a colonial Virginia dominated by the established, state-controlled Church of England. This official Anglican Church required, by law, all citizens to financially support this religious institution, attend its church services regularly, observe major life events (baptism, marriage, funerals) within its confines and practices, and believe in its doctrines, to be able to enjoy full personal, political, and civil rights. Other Christian denominations (e.g. Presbyterian, Catholic, Baptist) and faiths (Jewish) may enjoy 'toleration' of their beliefs, but their practices and privileges were restricted and limited. For example, 'dissenting' sects had to secure state and church permission to hold worship services, and Baptist ministers were often imprisoned for simply preaching the Gospel in unapproved areas (such as open fields or houses within the diocese).

Jefferson and others (notably his colleague James Madison, the 'Father of the Constitution') regarded such a state-sponsored church and its restrictions on the investigation, discussion, and personal decisions on matters of religious faith as violative of natural law and the individual liberty of conscious, discovery of divine truth, and prevention of both church and state corruptions. As Jefferson wrote in his Statue for Religious Freedom in Virginia (which later became the model for the religious clauses of the First Amendment of the United States Constitution): 'Almighty God hath created the mind free ... any attempts to influence it by temporal punishments ... are a departure from the plan of the Holy Author of our religion' (Jefferson 1902, vol. 8, p. 455). So, state restrictions on religious belief and practice are usually motivated by pride and a desire to maintain worldly power and control, and prevent independent inquiry (and, possibly, criticism of government policy and officials).

For Jefferson, true religious belief must be voluntary, freely chosen, not coerced or forced; derived from free exploration of religious ideas, discussion, debates, thought, prayer. God respects and encourages the lively intellectual and spiritual inquiry using the human reason. He imparted in human nature, reflecting the divine reason (Logos): order, contemplation, wisdom, truth. The biblical characters Abraham, Moses, and Job often questioned and even argued with God, and the Lord engaged such expressions, not pleased with ignorant, blind, compelled 'belief.' He wants the faithful to come to Him freely, gladly, voluntary, or it does not mean anything, is not really 'faith' unless understood and freely embraced—not imposed by force, fear, or manipulation. 'The life and essence of religion,' Jefferson wrote, 'consist in the internal persuasion or belief of the mind' (Jefferson 1902, vol. 2, p. 101). Jesus himself often taught through questions and stories, attempting to make others think and learn on their own.

Human reason, intelligence, and thought 'will ultimately decide, as it is the only oracle which God has given us to determine between what really comes from Him and the phantasms' (Jefferson 1902, vol. 6, p. 387). Adults *should* be encouraged to investigate spiritual matters and have the confidence to think and question. Jefferson might be considered naïve for believing that everyone was as intellectual as he was and not emotional and irrational, but he thought such a free, reasonable environment might lift people out of their ignorance and violence. For him, such free, open respect and tolerance of others' search for religious truth would actually discourage hatred and prejudice. 'Bigotry is the disease of ignorance ... enthusiasm of the free and buoyant. Education and free discussion are the antidotes of both' (Jefferson 1905, vol. 7, p. 27). Truth emerges from the exchange of different views. As Jefferson famously said in the Statute for Religious Freedom, combining freedom of thought and speech with religious liberty: 'Truth is the proper and sufficient antagonist to error, and has nothing to fear from the conflict, unless, by human interposition, disarmed of his natural weapons, free argument and debate, errors ceasing to be dangerous when it is permitted freely to confront them' (Jefferson 1902, vol. 8, p. 455). So, ideally, if conflict and disagreement are occurring at the *intellectual* and *verbal* levels, they will less likely turn into violence and social upheaval. The most disciplined, free environment should also be the most peaceful.

This Jeffersonian argument for liberty of religious belief and expression through full, free, confident discussion and learning is prescient of his case for academic freedom at the founding of the University of Virginia, where he famously declared, 'Here we are not afraid to follow the truth wherever it may lead, nor to tolerate any error, so long as reason is left free to combat it' (Jefferson 1905, vol. 7, p. 196).

Applied to religious truth, this leads Jefferson to advocate, 'leaving everyone to profess freely and openly those principles of religion which are the inductions of his own reason, and the serious convictions of his own inquiries' (Jefferson 1902, vol. 8, p. 189). The state should not coerce certain religious beliefs, nor suppress others (so long as they do not violate the natural rights of life, liberty, and property).

Thus, as in all of Jefferson's defense of intellectual liberty, the proper response to bad ideas is not censorship or repression (by fallible humans with their own prejudice, interests, and errors) but responding to them with good ideas—correcting incomplete views with a more complete perspective; refuting error with truth. With this confidence, truth will triumph over error in a 'free marketplace of ideas.' This also sharpens the mind, teaching it to think critically, fully, confidently, and creatively. Such freedom of thought, speech, and belief was, for Jefferson, 'among the most inestimable of our blessings ... liberty to worship our Creator in the way we think most agreeable to His will' (Jefferson 1902, vol. 8, p. 119). It is designed to develop the highest intellectual and spiritual faculties, making individuals happier and the society more productive and just.

This is why he was against a state church and 'against all maneuvers to bring out a legal ascendency of one sect over another' (Jefferson 1902, vol. 6, p. 268). Not only was it unjust; it literally could not be done, given human independence, and would just result in stunted, ignorant and miserable people. If thinking and questioning were part of human nature, then for the government to suppress that was to violate humanity. But diversity of religious belief and expression was to be encouraged in society, including at the public university, and this would produce more contented individuals and a more pleasant, civilized society.

So, for example, Jefferson's opposition to a chair (professorship) of Divinity at the University of Virginia was often misunderstood as a hostility to religion in public higher education when, in fact, it was his commitment to a more complete, lively, and effective religious presence at the university. He proposed to have all church denominations present at UVA, albeit unofficially, and as an integral part of higher learning, religious education, and public morality. 'A remedy' for encouraging religious liberty within the halls of the public university, Jefferson wrote,

> has been suggested of promising aspect, which, while it excludes the public authority from the domain of religious freedom, will give the sectarian schools of divinity the full benefit the public provisions made for instruction in the other branches of science ... suggested by some pious individuals, who perceive the advantages of associating other studies with those of religion, to establish their religious schools on the confines of their University, so as to give their students ready and convenient access and attendance on the scientific lectures of the University. Such establishments would offer further and greater advantage of enabling students of the University to attend religious exercises with the professor at their particular sect, either in the rooms of the building still to be erected ... or in the lecturing room of such professor. ... Such an arrangement would complete the circle of useful sciences embraced by this institution, and would fill the chasm now existing,

on principles which would keep inviolate the constitutional freedom of religion. (Jefferson 1905, vol. 15, p. 404)

This perfectly shows the positive, inclusive nature of Jefferson's idea of religious freedom: to include all faiths freely, voluntarily, tolerantly, even in the public square. His was not a 'negative' view that wishes to forbid and exclude all religion from public life. This positive view of religious liberty is further expressed in Jefferson's description of his hometown of Charlottesville, where, initially, no church buildings existed and all denominations shared the public courthouse.

> In our village of Charlottesville there is a good deal of religion, with only a small spice of fanaticism. We have four sects, but without either church or meeting house. The courthouse is the common temple, one Sunday a month to each. Here Episcopalian and Presbyterian, Methodist and Baptist, meet together, join in hymning their Maker, listen with attentions and devotion to each other's preachers and all mix in society with perfect harmony. (Jefferson 1905, vol. 15, p. 404)

Such peaceful, confident, intelligent, free, and tolerant expression of belief and faith was what Jefferson hoped for in religious liberty in America. And it would produce, he believed, the essential Christian ethics and morality necessary to a virtuous, law-abiding, prosperous and happy republic.

The 'free marketplace of ideas' with respect to religious views, for Jefferson, would distill what was, for him, common to all denominations—the 'ethics of Jesus': love, respect, charity, forbearance, forgiveness and sacrifice. As he wrote to John Adams:

> If by religion, we are to understand sectarian dogmas, in which no two of them agree, then your exclamation ... is just, that this would be the best of all possible worlds, if there were no religion in it; but, if the moral precepts innate in man ... as necessary of a social being, if the sublime doctrines ... taught us by Jesus of Nazareth in which we all agree, constitute true religion, then, without it, this would be ... 'something not fit to be named, even indeed a Hell'. (Jefferson 1959, vol. 2 p. 512)

So, religious liberty, for Jefferson, was not merely to avoid the tyranny and corruption of a state church, but to inculcate and advance a 'mere Christianity' as C. S. Lewis called it, a basic Christian morality, internal to individual citizens, of decency, charity, self-restraint, and lawfulness, which is necessary to a democracy. For Jefferson, the ethics of Jesus is a necessary moral foundation of a free society:

> His moral doctrines, relating to kindred and friends, were more pure and perfect than those of the most correct philosophers in inculcating universal philanthropy not only to kindred and friends, to neighbors and country-men, but to all mankind, gathering all into one family, under the bonds of love, charity, peace, common wants and common aids. (Jefferson 1943, p. 949)

Such basic Christian morality, advanced by the lively exchange of religious views, was needed for an American republic of such diversity, freedom, and individual rights. Without such an underpinning of social ethics, a democracy, as he had learned from Plato, could easily degenerate into selfishness, anarchy, depravity, and lawlessness. So, as he wrote to Judge Augustus Woodward: 'Ethics, as well as religion are supplements to law in the government of men' (Jefferson 1905, vol. 16, p. 19); and to William Johnson, 'the state's moral rule of their citizens' is enhanced by 'enforcing moral duties and retraining vice' (Jefferson 1943, p. 322). The more liberty of religion inculcates morality into citizens and they become self-controlled, law-abiding, and charitable, the less the state will have to impose rules and punishments externally. So, freedom of religion for Jefferson will advance a more orderly, decent, productive, and contented American republic.

This Jeffersonian conception of church and state, religion and politics, remains a curiosity in much of the world, and yet, its American creed seems to produce one of the most spiritually active societies and a lively, yet stable, democracy.

FURTHER READING

Sheldon, Garrett Ward, ed. 1990. *Religions and Politics: Major Thinkers on the Relation of Church and State.* New York and Berne: Peter Lang Publishing.
    A collection of major theologians (St. Augustine, Aquinas, Luther, Calvin, etc.) on politics, as well as American documents on Supreme Court cases on church and state.
Sheldon, Garrett Ward, and Daniel Driesbach, eds. 2000. *Religion and Political Culture in Jefferson's Virginia.* New York: Rowman and Littlefield.
    A collection of essays by scholars on politics, culture, and religion in colonial and early republican Virginia.

Sheldon, Garrett Ward. 1991. *The Political Philosophy of Thomas Jefferson*. Baltimore: The Johns Hopkins University Press.

A survey of the philosophical sources of Jefferson's political theory including views on religious liberty.

REFERENCES

Jefferson, Thomas. 1902. *Writings*. Vol. 1–8. Ed. Paul Leicester Ford. New York: G.P. Putnam's Sons.

———. 1905. *The Writings of Thomas Jefferson*. Vol. 1–17. Ed. Albert Ellery Bergh. Washington, DC: Thomas Jefferson Memorial Association.

———. 1943. *The Complete Jefferson*. Ed. Saul Padover. New York.

———. 1959. *The Adams-Jefferson Letters*, Vol 2. Ed. Lester J. Cappon. Chapel Hill: University of North Carolina Press.

CHAPTER 28

An Uneasy Relationship: Religion and Politics in Canada

Janet Epp Buckingham

Ed. Shannon Holzer, *Routledge Companion to Church and State*

From the early beginnings of Canada as a colonized nation, politics and religion have been deeply intertwined. Early settlers to Canada brought the Bible and Roman Catholicism and attempted to evangelize the Indigenous Peoples of Canada. Soon after England gained control of the colonies in British North America in 1763, it was politically expedient to grant religious rights to Quebec's Roman Catholic population to keep them from joining with the American colonies in rebellion against Britain. This established Canada as a country with a French Roman Catholic population and an English Protestant population. There was much conflict between Catholics and Protestants in Canada up until the 1960s when secularization began to take hold. As Joel Thiessen surmises, "Until the 1960s religious leaders and organizations played a major role in providing education, health care and social services, and frequently lobbying

J. E. Buckingham (✉)
Trinity Western University, Langley Twp, BC, Canada
e-mail: Janet.Epp-Buckingham@twu.ca

S. Holzer (ed.), *The Palgrave Handbook of Religion and State Volume II*, https://doi.org/10.1007/978-3-031-35609-4_28

political leaders on issues of interest to religious groups" (Thiessen 2015, p. 9).

Religious minorities have been present in Canada from its early days. Jews immigrated from Europe. Hindus, Muslims and Sikhs immigrated from India. Buddhists and Confucianists immigrated from East Asia. As well, many Christian minority religious groups have found a home in Canada: including Mennonites, Doukhobors, Hutterian Brethren, Coptic Christians, Seventh Day Adventists, and adherents of the Church of Jesus Christ of Latter-day Saints.

Despite the challenges and conflicts religious adherents face in Canada, they continue to have robust engagement in the public square. In 2021, one national political party was led by a Sikh and another by a Jew. Christians and Muslims are also politicians. Many religious organizations regularly engage in consultations with politicians on a wide variety of policy issues, including but not limited to religious freedom. When Parliament is sitting, there is a regular Wednesday morning prayer group of Christians from across party lines. An annual National Prayer Breakfast brings together politicians, diplomats and Christian leaders in Ottawa.

This chapter will look at the early days of Catholic/Protestant conflict and how that played out politically. It will then examine the treatment of religious minorities. It will assess the impact of secularism and the Charter on religion and religious freedom. Finally, it will examine the current role of religion in politics in Canada, focusing mainly on federal, or national, politics.

BASICS OF POLITICS AND RELIGION IN CANADA

The Canadian Political System

Canada is a federal country with a national government, ten provincial governments and three territories, which are sparsely populated, in the north. The nation was founded with four initial provinces in 1867 by an Act of the British Parliament. The British North America Act, now the Constitution Act, 1867, established the governmental system "similar in Principle to that of the United Kingdom" (Constitution Act, 1867, Preamble). Six additional provinces were added between 1870 and 1949, each by an Act of the British Parliament. The national legislature, Parliament, is bicameral, comprised of an elected House of Commons and an appointed Senate. The House of Commons is constituency based with a first-past-the-post elector system. In 2021, there are 338 Members of Parliament and 105 Senators. Provincial governments are unicameral.

Canada is a constitutional monarchy with King Charles III the reigning monarch. He is represented in Canada by his regent, the Governor General, who exercises the powers of the monarch on his behalf. The King appoints the Governor General for a five-year term on the advice of the Prime Minister. The Governor General then appoints a Lieutenant Governor for each province, who exercises similar functions.

Religious Demographics—What an Evolution!

In the most recent census, 2021, 53.3% of Canadians identified as Christian.[1] Approximately 30% of Canadians identify as Roman Catholic and 23.5% as Protestant. In 201, approximately 11.2% of Canadians identified with a minority religion: Muslim, Hindu, Sikh, Buddhist or Jewish. Muslims are the largest of these with 4.9% of Canadians identifying as Muslim. Approximately 34.6% of Canadians respond that they have "no religion" on the census.

These statistics show a massive change since 1871, the first census after nationhood. In that census, 98% of the population identified as either Roman Catholic or Protestant (Statistics Canada 2001, p. 3). In 1961, 93.3% of the population identified as Christians (Ferguson 2005, p. 359). Only .5% identified as no religion.

Even now, statistics indicating religious affiliation can be misleading as many who identify as Christian on the census are what is referred to as "census Christians" as religion does not play any meaningful role in their lives. Church attendance is a more relevant indicator, and it is low; in 2013, only 13% of Canadian said that they attended a religious service on a weekly basis (Hiemstra and Stiller 2016). This is in contrast to just after the Second World War when weekly attendance at a religious service was 67% (Noll 2006, p. 249).

The Catholic/Protestant Conflict in its Political Context

La Nouvelle France

French explorers were the first Europeans to arrive on the eastern shore of what is now Canada. They brought with them Jesuit missionaries, the famous Black Robes. Their objective was to convert the Indigenous Peoples to Catholicism (Crowley 1996, p. 37). Priests, brothers and nuns from other orders also established missions and schools. In 1674, the Pope appointed the first Bishop in Quebec (Crowley 1996, p. 20). In this region, Protestants were prohibited from making public professions of faith and were denied government appointments (Crowley 1996, p. 48).

After the 1759–1763 conflict between the France and England, the Treaty of Paris transferred Quebec to British control in 1763. Article IV guaranteed freedom of religion in the colony "as far as the laws of Great Britain permit." British governors found that acceptance of the Catholic clergy assisted them in maintaining the loyalty of the people of Quebec. Catholic clergy became the natural leaders after French political leaders returned to France. These French Catholic leaders ensured the continuation of both French culture and Catholic education. In 1774, unrest in the American colonies led the British government to make a commitment to the people of Quebec that they could maintain their language, religion and civil law. The Catholic religion became synonymous with French culture, whether inside or outside of Quebec. This also had a significant impact on politics as Catholic clergy often weighed in on politics during elections. This was so pronounced that in 1877, the election of the Hon. L.H. Langevin was overturned as a result of undue influence of the clergy (*Brassard v. Langevin*, 1877).

The "New" Canada

For their part, the British brought the Church of England to others of the North American colonies. However, there was an influx of Loyalists after the American War of Independence, bringing with them a variety of other Protestant religions.[2] This effectively prevented the British from having an established church. Schools and hospitals in English Canada were established by Protestant clergy and denominations. Because no one Protestant denomination was dominant, there was not the same kind of church influence on culture and politics as existed in Quebec. Christians and Christianity had significant influence on public life, however.

In 1867, a fledgling nation of Canada comprised of four provinces formed north of the United States of America. Canada was formed as a federal country with a strong central government and weak provincial governments. At the time the Constitution Act, 1867 was negotiated, education was provided by church bodies, both Roman Catholic and Protestant. In Quebec, the majority was Roman Catholic, and the minority was Protestant. In other parts of the country, the reverse was true. For this reason, s. 93 of the Act guaranteed denominational education.

As suggested above, the French Catholic population did not limit itself to Quebec. In fact, they settled across what is now Ontario and even set up settlements in what is now the Prairie provinces. Where there were schools, they were usually run by Catholic clergy or orders. One of the first political crises to rock the new nation of Canada was over denominational school rights in the newest province of Manitoba, which joined as a province in 1870. By 1890, English immigrants were the majority so the provincial government eliminated funding for Roman Catholic schools.

This crisis, dubbed "The Manitoba School Question," was part of a larger political battle between Catholics bishops in Quebec and the anti-Catholic Orange Order in Ontario. Historian O.D. Skelton surmises, "The school was merely the arena where religious gladiators displayed their powers, an occasion for stirring the religious convictions and religious prejudices of thousands and of demonstrating how little either their education or their religion had done to make them tolerant citizens" (Skelton 1921, p. 440).

It was often the courts that were called in to settle political questions arising from religious disputes. No less than two legal challenges were decided by the highest court, then the Judicial Committee of the Privy Council in London (*City of Winnipeg v. Barrett*, 1892; *Brophy v. A-G Manitoba*, 1895). The Prime Ministers over a six-year period were beseeched to intervene. One Prime Minister was forced to resign when half his Cabinet Ministers turned on him over his introduction of remedial legislation to reinstate Catholic school rights (Weir 1917, ch. II). It did not help that Prime Minister Mackenzie Bowell had once been Grand Master of the Orange Order! In the end, it became an election issue; Wilfrid Laurier won the 1896 election with his promise to resolve the issue by negotiation (Robertson 1971, pp. 78–81).

Laurier negotiated with the Manitoba Premier, Thomas Greenway, an agreement whereby religious instruction could be offered after the normal school day as requested by a certain number of parents. Laurier wisely obtained the Pope's support for the compromise to assuage criticism from the Catholic hierarchy (Schull 1965, pp. 330–334). The agreement required that the Manitoba legislature pass legislation to affect the terms of the agreement.

For the first century of Canada's history as a country, political leaders assumed that Canada was a Christian country. Church representations were considered when policies were made on a wide variety of subjects from divorce law to education policy (Buckingham 2014, p. 163). When several of the largest Protestant denominations joined together to form the United Church of Canada in 1925, the union was affected by legislation in all provinces (Mason 1956). This highlights the cooperation between state and church in Canada. That cooperation, however, was limited to the Christian church. Religious minorities tended to be ignored or marginalized.

Much of the conflict between Roman Catholics and Protestants in Canada came to an end in the 1960s with rapid secularization. This trend was most dramatic in the province of Quebec. Prior to the 1960s, everything in Quebec was run by the Roman Catholic Church: labor unions, hospitals, schools and social services. During the 1960s, however, Quebecers rejected the church's control over their lives. This decade in Quebec is called the Quiet Revolution as the state took on roles previously held by the church.

POLITICS, RELIGION AND MINORITIES

Marginalization of Religious Minorities

With Roman Catholics and Protestants forming the dominant culture in a maturing Canada, there was little room for religious minorities, even though they were part of Canada from its early days. As noted above, missionaries came to Canada to convert the Indigenous Peoples even before settlement began. This Christianization became coercive in 1884 when the Indian Act was amended to ban the potlach and again in 1895, when several additional Indigenous religious practices were outlawed (Henderson n.d.). In 1888, the federal government began to financially support church-run residential schools, which prohibited students from following their traditional religious practices (Milloy 1999). These coercive laws were not changed until at least the middle of the twentieth century. Indigenous Peoples in Canada did not have the right to vote until 1960, so they had no representation in political life.

The Canadian government gave priority to immigrants from Europe, who were mostly Christian. The most established minority religious group in Canada is Jewish. There were Jews in Canada prior to Confederation. They began arriving in larger numbers when they faced hostility in Europe between 1880 and 1914. The largest populations of Jewish people in Canada are in Toronto and Montreal.

The Canadian government recruited Chinese workers to build the national railway in the latter part of the nineteenth century. Some of these Chinese workers were Buddhist, Muslim or Taoist. While they were encouraged to return to China after they stopped working on the railway, some stayed and settled in western Canada. After 1900, despite strict immigration rules, Sikhs, Hindus and Muslims started immigrating to Canada. None of these religious minorities found a warm welcome, nor were they represented in the political system.

Up until the 1950s, there was no Minister of Education in Quebec; schools were run by a Catholic school board and a Protestant school board. This obviously left religious minorities a difficult choice. The majority of Jewish students were educated in Protestant schools. However, the parents' taxes were not necessarily directed to the Protestant school board. In 1903, the Jewish community in Montreal and the Protestant School Board came to an agreement, enshrined in legislation, that for the purposes of education, Jewish students would be treated as Protestants (Act to amend the law concerning education with respect to persons professing the Jewish religion, 1903). Jewish parents then requested that Jews be able to sit on the school board and that Jewish teachers be hired.

The "Jewish School Question" erupted in the early 1920s with conflict within the Jewish community as well as controversy in both the Protestant and Catholic communities in Quebec. Premier Taschereau established a Royal Commission comprised of representatives of each of the religious communities. He further referred the 1903 legislation to the Quebec Court of Appeal to determine its constitutionality. The decision was ultimately appealed to the Judicial Committee of the Privy Council (then the highest court of appeal for Canada), which ruled that this was *ultra vires* but left it open to the Quebec government to form a new school board (*Hirsh v. Protestant Board of School Commissioners of Montreal* 1928).

Proposed legislation was defeated, leaving the Jewish community to negotiate even to retain the status quo. It was not until the 1960s that Jews got government funding for their own schools. Finally, in 1997, Quebec obtained a constitutional amendment to allow school boards to be established as linguistic, rather than religious, school boards (Constitutional Amendment 1997).

Another religious minority that faced marginalization in Canada is the Jehovah's Witnesses. In their early days in Canada, the Jehovah's Witnesses used very strong language in their proselytism efforts. This was one of the main reasons why radio licenses were revoked for five stations run by Jehovah's Witnesses (then known as the International Bible Students Association) (Penton 1976, p. 97). There had been an outcry against radio broadcasts by Jehovah's Witnesses that denounced Roman Catholics and the Pope.

In the province of Quebec, which was strongly Roman Catholic before 1960, the vitriol against Catholicism made the Jehovah's Witnesses a target for reprisals. As with Jews, Jehovah's Witnesses did not easily adapt to the schooling system, which was divided into Roman Catholics and Protestants. In some rural areas, only Roman Catholic schools were available. These schools did not want Jehovah's Witness children to attend their schools. This issue resulted in a court battle. The court ruled that the Roman Catholic school must accept Jehovah's Witness children and that the children could not be forced to follow Roman Catholic religious practices (*Chabot v. Commissioners of Lamorandiere* 1957).

Between 1920 and 1960, Jehovah's Witnesses faced limitations on proselytism, a core tenant of the Jehovah's Witness faith, in many parts of Canada (Buckingham 2014, pp. 107–110). Municipalities passed laws to restrict street preaching and distribution of literature. Only in Quebec, however, did the government wage an all-out campaign against Jehovah's Witnesses. Quebec officials prosecuted Jehovah's Witnesses under little-used Criminal Code provisions that prohibited blasphemous libel (*R. v. Kinler*, 1925) and then seditious libel (*Duval v. R.* 1938). Thousands of charges were laid against Jehovah's Witnesses. A Montreal restauranteur, Frank Roncarelli, furnished bail for some of those accused. When Quebec Premier Maurice Duplessis determined his identity, he ordered that Roncarelli's liquor license be revoked. This effectively put Roncarelli's restaurant out of business. Roncarelli sued the premier personally and won a decisive victory at the Supreme Court of Canada (*Roncarelli v. Duplessis* 1959). The court ruled that government officials do not have discretion to revoke a liquor license for reasons completely unconnected with the business.

The most egregious violation of the rights of Jehovah's Witnesses, however, came during the Second World War, when the organization was banned (Botting 1993, p. 197). Until 9/11, the Jehovah's Witnesses were the only religious organization ever banned by the Canadian government (Penton 1976, p. 34).[3] Even more extraordinary is that it was at the behest of Roman Catholic bishops in Quebec, who accused the Jehovah's Witnesses of undermining the war effort. In 1940, the Canadian government made it illegal to be a Jehovah's Witness and to possess their literature. The ban was not lifted until 1943.

Victories for Religious Minorities

The repression of Jehovah's Witnesses in Quebec, and the outright banning in the rest of Canada during the war years, resulted in this religious minority campaigning for a Bill of Rights to be enacted in Canada. Jehovah's Witnesses went door to door and collected over 500,000 signatures in favor of a Bill of Rights (Penton 1976, p. 197; Berger 1982, p. 174). The Jehovah's Witnesses found a ready ear for their plea for a Bill of Rights in John Diefenbaker, a Member of Parliament from Prince Albert, Saskatchewan. Other religious minorities, most notably the Jewish community, also lobbied for protection for human rights (Lambertson 2005). Diefenbaker promoted the establishment of a federal Bill of Rights from his political office (Diefenbaker 1985, p. 38). It was not until he became Prime Minister in 1959 that he was able to bring this to fruition. Diefenbaker considered the enactment of Canadian Bill of Rights in 1960 as one of his greatest accomplishments.

The repression of Jehovah's Witnesses in Quebec also inspired a passion for human rights in another politician who would later become Prime Minister (Trudeau 1968, pp. 11, 171, 210). Pierre Elliott Trudeau lived in Quebec during that time period and later developed the Canadian Charter of Rights and Freedoms, which was enacted in 1982 (Canadian Charter of Rights and Freedoms 1982). The advantage of the Charter over the previous Bill of Rights is that the Charter is a constitutional document and applies to provincial governments as well as the federal government. Canadian courts have given the Charter a transformational interpretation.

During public consultations leading up to the adoption of the Charter of Rights, religious groups made many submissions. Their most significant contribution was the recommendation for a preamble that would recognize the "supremacy of God." Leading evangelical Christian organizations, such as the Evangelical Fellowship of Canada and the televangelist David Mainse, mobilized petitions and letter-writing to federal politicians (Egerton 2000, p. 90). Canadian Christians were concerned that having constitutional protection for human rights would lead courts to adopt the American anti-establishment approach to religious liberty. Deputy House Leader David Smith, a Baptist, urged the Prime Minister to include such a preamble. Prime Minister Trudeau finally agreed and included the following as the Preamble to the Charter of Rights, "Whereas Canada is founded upon principles that recognize the supremacy of God and the rule of law." George Egerton comments that the evangelical Christians who believed that such a preamble would prevent courts from removing "all public functions and privileges of religion in the construction of a completely secular state" were disappointed (Egerton 2000, p. 107). The preamble did not provide a "sacred canopy" to protect the place of religion in society.

The Charter requires all levels of government to respect the human rights it guarantees. Section 2(a) of the Charter protects "freedom of conscience and religion" as a fundamental freedom. In addition, section 15 guarantees equality without discrimination on the basis of religion, among other enumerated grounds. These provisions should have provided strong protection for freedom of religion in Canada. Instead, however, they accelerated processes of secularization (Brown 2000).[4]

SECULARIZATION—PUSHING RELIGIONS ASIDE

Push #1: Restricting the Public Expression of Religion

One of the first cases under the Charter to reach the Supreme Court of Canada addressed religious freedom. That case was decided in 1985, only three years after the adoption of the Charter. The case was *R v. Big Drug Mart* (1985) and was a test case to challenge the law prohibiting shop opening on Sundays. Big M Drug Mart deliberately opened on Sunday so that it would face a criminal charge and could raise the Charter protection for religious freedom as a defense.

Of course, there is a back story to this case. Back in the early 1900s, Christians lobbied both federal and provincial governments to establish laws prohibiting shop opening on Sundays. It was not clear which level of government had jurisdiction over this issue. It was ultimately decided by the courts that the federal government had jurisdiction under its power over criminal law given that the purpose of Sunday closing was to protect religion (*A.G. Ontario v. Hamilton Street Railway*, 1903; *In re Legislation Respecting Abstention From Labour on Sunday*, 1905). It was this aspect of the legislation that doomed it in the *Big M Drug Mart* case. The court referred to previous decisions on this matter and decided that a law with the purposes of protecting religion automatically violates religious freedom. This legal case was a forewarning that, as religious organizations had feared, the Charter was being interpreted in a way that advanced secularism in Canada.

In the province of Quebec, secularism has now been fully realized in Bill 21, *Act respecting the laicity of the state*. This legislation, passed in June 2019, bans all government employees who deal with the public from wearing religious symbols: including teachers, police and judges. The province of Quebec, as noted above, has a unique history and culture in Canada, being French and Roman Catholic. During the Quiet Revolution in the 1960s, however, Quebec transformed from being the most religious to the least religious province in Canada. Mark Noll quotes a priest from a Denys Arcand film, "In 1966 all the churches emptied out in a few weeks. No one can figure out why."[5] In the 1950s, weekly attendance at mass was 90% of the population. That has dropped to 4% recently (Jenkins 2021). This shows the secularization of Quebec.

A number of high-profile incidents occurred in 2007 involving accommodation of religious minorities. This culminated in the Quebec government appointing a high-level commission to address "reasonable accommodation." The Bouchard-Taylor Commission hearings were characterized by high levels of religious intolerance to minorities in Quebec. Participants "massively espoused the concept of secularism" and affirmed that religion should be kept in the private realm (Bouchard and Taylor 2008, p. 43). While the Bouchard-Taylor Commission recommended that the state work toward building an intercultural identity among Quebecers as a foundation for accommodation, the state instead opted to exclude and marginalize minority religions. The government has argued that it is necessary to protect the neutrality of the state and that Quebecers have a right not to have religion imposed on them.

The ruling Parti Quebecois proposed a Charter of Quebec Values in 2013 to restrict public employees from wearing religious symbols and requiring any person receiving government services not to wear a face covering. This did not pass and became an election issue in the subsequent election; the government was defeated. It was an election issue again in the 2018 election, which the relatively new Coalition Avenir Québec (CAQ) won, partly on the campaign promise of reviving the legislation. The provisions of Bill 21 are substantially similar to the original proposed Charter.

It is very telling that the Quebec government invoked the notwithstanding clause to avoid a legal challenge (Canadian Charter of Rights and Freedoms, 1982, s. 33). This clause allows a government to pass a law violating certain rights if it invokes the clause. It effectively admits that the legislation violates fundamental rights and freedoms protected in the Charter, in this case section 2(a), which guarantees religious freedom. The use of the notwithstanding clause must be renewed every five years so this will come up again in 2024. Until that time, the imposition of secularism remains the law in Quebec.

Push #2: Restricting Religions in Schools

Legal challenges under the Charter continued, challenging the Christian underpinnings of Canadian society. The education system was a particular target. Two legal challenges in Ontario resulted in the removal of the Lord's Prayer as part of opening exercises in public schools (*Zylberberg v. Sudbury Board of Education* 1988) and periods of religious instruction during the school week (*Canadian Civil Liberties Assn. v. Ontario (Minister of Education)* 1990). Christian parents strongly objected to this secularization of public schools, which had historically been based on Protestantism. Some parents chose to remove their children from the public school system and instead have them educated in Christian private schools. Christian parents joined with parents of minority religions in Canada to urge the Ontario government to provide funding for these private, faith-based schools. The government refused and the parents brought a legal challenge, which they lost (*Adler v. Ontario* 1996). One of the parents pursued a legal challenge internationally to the United Nations Human Rights Committee. Ultimately this international tribunal ruled that the Ontario government violated international human rights standards because it funded Roman Catholic schools but not those of other minority religions (*Waldman v. Canada*, 1996). The Ontario government responded by providing a tax credit for tuition for all private schools in the province, not just those based on religion. Even this small concession was revoked when the government changed.

The trend toward secularization in education has continued. Both the provinces of Quebec and Newfoundland obtained constitutional amendments in the late 1990s to deconfessionalize their education systems. Each of these processes took more than a decade with numerous government consultations and commission reports to effect the change. Each also involved legal challenges from religious communities that were not happy with significant policy changes.

The province of Newfoundland joined Canada in 1949 with a constitutional guarantee of denominational school rights. While much of the rest of Canada had a Roman Catholic system and a Protestant system, Newfoundland had a multi-denominational system with guaranteed constitutional rights for several denominations. Because many communities are small in that province, it resulted in a multiplicity small schools with few resources (Newfoundland and Labrador 1986). The province held two referenda and the majority of the population voted in favor of a constitutional amendment to amalgamate all of the schools under one Ministry of Education (*Constitutional Amendment* 1988).

Despite the expense and inefficiency of having many small denominational schools, many parents wanted their children to receive religious instruction in school. When schools were secularized, given the experience of Ontario, it seemed likely that religious instruction would be removed altogether. For Newfoundland, Premier Clyde Wells ultimately resolved the conflict using the following wording for the constitutional amendment:

> (2) In and for the province of Newfoundland, the legislature shall have exclusive authority to make laws in relation to education, but shall provide for courses in religion that are not specific to any religious denomination (3) Religious observances shall be permitted in a school where requested by the parents (*Constitutional Amendment* 1988).

Because it was in the constitutional provision, this guaranteed that it could not be challenged under the Charter. The wording implies, however, that religious instruction will continue to be Christian, which does not leave room for religious minorities.

The province of Quebec was equally complex. As noted above, the province of Quebec had a dual denominational system with publicly funded Roman Catholic and Protestant school boards. While the Roman Catholic education system was mainly French, the Protestant system was mainly English. It took the Quebec government from 1982 to 1997 to succeed in deconfessionalizing the schools and reorganizing them along linguistic lines. During these years, there were several legal challenges. Even when the constitutional amendment was secured in 1997 to deconfessionalize the schools, at the behest of the Roman Catholic Church the provincial government passed a law to maintain religious instruction, invoking the notwithstanding clause to protect it from constitutional review.[6] The church feared that someone would bring a court challenge under the Charter and the courts would strike down religious instruction based on Ontario court ruling.

Following the constitutional amendment deconfessionalizing the schools, the Minister of Education, François Legault, appointed a Task Force on the Place of Religion in the Schools in Quebec. In 1999, the task force recommended that the government establish a required course on religion taught from a cultural perspective (Quebec, Task Force on the Place of Religion in Schools in Québec 1999). Religious instruction could be taught outside school hours. The Quebec government ultimately established a new Ethics and Religious Culture course in 2008 and made it mandatory across all schools. Loyola High School in Montreal, a private Roman Catholic school, sought an exemption on the basis that the course must be taught from a religiously neutral perspective. The Minister of Education would not grant exceptions even for faith-based schools. Loyola High School challenged this and won a minor victory when the Supreme Court of Canada ruled that it was not required to teach the portion of the course about Catholicism from a neutral perspective (*Loyola High School v. Quebec (Attorney General)* 2015). The remainder of the course continued to be mandatory.

Push #3: Restricting the Scope of Religious Universities

While many Canadian universities were founded by Christian denominations, most have become secular, state-funded institutions. A new cadre of private Christian universities has been established by evangelical Protestant denominations. These universities have faced a variety of challenges, from accreditation of new programs to censure for requiring faculty to adhere to statements of faith or codes of conduct (Canadian Association of University Teachers n.d.).

Trinity Western University, located in British Columbia, is the oldest of these private universities, having been established in 1962 as a junior college and receiving full university accreditation in 1984. It is also the largest. In 1987, Trinity Western applied to have a program in teacher education accredited. The British Columbia College of Teachers, the accrediting body, denied accreditation on the basis of the university's code of conduct, which condemned homosexual behavior. The university challenged this in court and won a decisive victory at the Supreme Court of Canada in 2001 (*Trinity Western University v. British Columbia College of Teachers* 2001).

When Trinity Western University applied in 2014 for accreditation of a legal education program, it was approved by the Federation of Law Societies of Canada, the national accrediting body. However, three provincial law societies, which approve students to practice law in their respective provinces, refused to approve the university, meaning that graduates of the Trinity Western law school could not be called to the bar in those provinces. Again, Trinity Western challenged this in court, but this time lost at the Supreme Court of Canada in 2018 (*Law Society of British Columbia v. Trinity Western University* 2018; *Trinity Western University v. Law Society of Ontario* 2018). The court ruled, in a split decision, that the university could not impose a faith-based code of conduct on non-Christian law students at the university. While Trinity Western decided not to start a law school, it was pushed to rescind its mandatory code of conduct or face review by other professional accrediting agencies.

Interestingly, Trinity Western was required to obtain approval for its professional programs both from the British Columbia government and from the professional accreditation body. In both the above situations, the government accreditation process would have approved the program. The professional accreditation bodies which are the governing bodies of the professions, denied approval. This shows that these bodies are also highly politicized.

Push #4: Restricting Religious Views on Abortion

It was a crime to induce an abortion in the first Criminal Code passed in Canada in 1892. It is indicative of the change in values during the 1960s that the law was amended in 1969 to allow doctors to induce abortions if the pregnancy threatened the life or health of the mother (Criminal Law Amendment Act 1968-69). These legal abortions were required to take place in a hospital. A therapeutic abortion committee, comprised of three doctors, had to certify that the abortion was necessary. This amendment was part of a large package of amendments to the Criminal Code, which also legalized homosexual acts, legalized and regulated gambling and legalized contraceptives. It is an understatement to say that the bill was controversial. The Minister of Justice who introduced this package into Parliament was Pierre Elliott Trudeau, who later became the Prime Minister who introduced the Charter of Rights and Freedoms.

Churches, particularly the Canadian Conference of Catholic Bishops, opposed allowing abortion under any circumstances. Abortion physician Dr. Henry Morgentaler immediately established a private abortion clinic in Montreal, performing abortions without regard for the requirements of a therapeutic abortion committee or a hospital. The 1969 omnibus bill had clearly opened a path for continued battles over its extension.

Morgentaler set out to challenge the law. He had three successive jury trials, each time being acquitted of violating the Criminal Code. He then established a similar clinic in Toronto. Following the adoption of the Charter in 1982, he and his colleagues made public statements about abortion, hoping to incite criminal charges against them. They succeeded. They then challenged the constitutionality of the Criminal Code provision as violating section 7 of the Charter, which protects the life, liberty and security of the person, in defending the charges. In 1988, the Supreme Court of Canada struck down the Criminal Code prohibition on procuring abortions (*R. v. Morgentaler* 1988).

In its ruling, the Supreme Court of Canada gave some advice on how the legislature could pass a law on abortion that would be constitutional. The Minister of Health at the time was Jake Epp, a known evangelical Christian. Epp introduced Bill C-43 in 1990. The bill set out a trimester system: abortion on demand in the first trimester; if the life or health of the mother was threatened in the second trimester and very narrow exemptions in the third trimester. The bill was very controversial and was opposed by both pro-choice advocates and Roman Catholic pro-life advocates. It passed in the House of Commons but when the vote was tied in the Senate, by tradition, it was deemed defeated. Epp was personally targeted by conservative Christians who opposed any legalization of abortion.

Since Bill C-43 was defeated in 1991, there has been no law governing abortion in Canada, making it one of only three countries in the world with no restrictions on abortion. Christian Members of Parliament have continued to introduce Private Members Bills related to abortion, but none have passed. The most recent attempt prohibits sex-selective abortion, which is widely practiced in certain ethnic communities in Canada.[7]

Each year on May 13, the March for Life brings together pro-life advocates for a protest march and demonstration at Parliament Hill in Ottawa. It is the largest annual protest on the Hill. It has a strong Christian theme, playing Christian music and characterized by prayers. It is strongly supported by Roman Catholics, who bus in high school students from the region. Many Christian, pro-life Members of Parliament participate as speakers at this demonstration.

Push #5: Separating Marriage and Divorce from Religion

Religious communities have deep interests in issues relating to regulation of marriage and divorce. Many religious communities have rituals for marriages. Many also have rules around the dissolution of marriages, including the Jewish and Muslim communities. Religious officials have lobbied governments for changes to marriage or divorce law. They have also fully participated in consultations when changes are proposed. While it is a shared interest between religions and governments, governments have not necessarily made the civil institution of marriage consistent with the religious institution of marriage.

At the time of Confederation in 1867, one of the divisive issues was which clergy could solemnize marriages. For this reason, in the constitution, the federal government has jurisdiction over "marriage and divorce" (Constitution Act, 1867, s. 91(26)) and the provinces have responsibility for "solemnization of marriage" (Constitution Act, 1867, s. 92(12)). Without understanding that Quebec representatives were adamant about retaining control over marriage for the Roman Catholic Church, the division is nonsensical.

Following Confederation, the Quebec government proceeded to pass laws that required Roman Catholics to be married by Roman Catholic clergy, else their marriages would not be recognized. This law made it impossible for Roman Catholics to marry someone from another faith. Couples would go to another province to have their marriages solemnized but then when they returned to Quebec, their marriages were not recognized. By 1912, this was enough of an issue that the federal government proposed legislation to ensure that a marriage solemnized in one province would be recognized in other provinces. Given the division of powers over marriage, the federal government sent a reference case to the Supreme Court of Canada to determine its constitutionality. On appeal to the Judicial Committee of the Privy Council, the court ruled that this legislation was beyond the jurisdiction of the federal government (*Re the Marriage Law of Canada* 1912).

Similar to marriage, many religions have rules related to divorce. The Roman Catholic Church does not recognize divorce, even civil divorce granted by the state. Jews and Muslims have fairly simple divorce laws and religious courts that apply religious law to child custody. Until 1968 the federal government had no law regulating divorce. Nova Scotia, New Brunswick and British Columbia had legislation setting out a procedure for divorce. Any couple not living in one of those provinces was required to seek private legislation in the Senate of Canada to obtain a divorce.

Significant social change between 1900 and the 1960s relating to families and divorce was also reflected in church attitudes toward divorce. James Snell states, "every major Christian denomination in Canada at the turn of the century spoke out against divorce" (Snell 1991, p. 32). When Parliament held a Special Joint Committee on Divorce in 1966, seven religious organizations testified in support of the federal government legislating a procedure for divorce (Canada 1966). The federal Parliament passed the first Divorce Act in 1968. It has since been amended to allow for no-fault divorce. After lobbying from the Jewish community, the Divorce Act was further amended in 1990 to allow civil courts to require that a religious divorce be a requirement for a civil divorce (Divorce Act 1990, s. 2).

Most religious communities in Canada were deeply opposed to changing the definition of marriage to include same-sex couples. Several same-sex couples started legal actions against the federal government in 2000 challenging the heterosexual definition of marriage. The federal government had no legislated definition of marriage, so the courts were considering the common law definition, which rested on a case from 1866 from Britain (*Hyde v. Hyde and Woodmansee* 1866). In province after province, courts changed the definition of marriage from "between one man and one woman" to "between two persons." The federal government did not appeal any of the appeal court decisions to Supreme Court of Canada, so there was no decision from the highest court of appeal on the definition of marriage.

There was significant pressure on the federal government to pass legislation to have a single definition of marriage for the whole of the country. In 2004, the Governor General sent a reference case to the Supreme Court of Canada to determine the constitutionality of proposed legislation redefining marriage. Many religious institutions intervened at the court hearing, arguing that religious adherents and institutions that did not recognize same-sex marriage for religious reasons would be marginalized and face discrimination. The Supreme Court ruled that these concerns were hypothetical and assured the religious communities represented that their rights would be protected (*Reference Re Same-sex Marriage* 2004, para. 52).

The federal government proceeded to introduce the proposed legislation into Parliament. There were rancorous committee hearings in both chambers. Many religious leaders were deeply opposed to redefining marriage despite that it had already been redefined by the courts. Many also raised concerns about losing the legal privileges churches and religious institutions enjoyed from the government. These included special tax treatment for the institution, its donors and clergy. A Roman Catholic Member of Parliament, Richard Marceau, proposed including an additional clause in the legislation that would prohibit loss of federal government benefits on the basis of religious practices relating to marriage (Civil Marriage Act 2005, s. 3.1). With this amendment, the Civil Marriage Act passed.

While the Civil Marriage Act had a clause that purported to protect religious officials from being required to solemnize same-sex marriages, the solemnization of marriage is a provincial jurisdiction. Some provincial governments proceeded to amend their legislation to allow religious officials not to participate in same-sex weddings.[8] Some provincial governments, however, made it clear that civil marriage officiants would be required to solemnize same-sex marriages, despite any religious objections.[9]

Between 1867 and the present day, there has been a massive change in the relationship between religions and the state in Canada with respect to marriage and divorce. In 1867, the state followed the lead of the major Christian religious institutions in Canada and had very little regulation of marriage and divorce. By 2021, the state controlled marriage and divorce, which were in many ways quite different than religious practices. Religious officials were struggling to be accommodated in following their various religious practices in relation to marriage and divorce.

The Current State of Religion and Politics in Canada—Where Are We Going?

Religion and Political Parties

In examining the roles religious communities have made to have an impact on public policy, it raises questions about whether religious adherents engage directly as politicians and if religious constituencies vote based on political policies. Religious adherents do run for office and have been elected as politicians. At the time of writing in Canada, there are five parties represented in the House of Commons. One of these is led by a Jew, a second by a Sikh and the Prime Minister is a self-identified, but non-practicing, Catholic. Many Members of Parliament identify as Christian, Jewish, Muslim, Sikh or Buddhist.

While Canada has seen the rise and fall of many political parties, the Conservative Party and the Liberal Party have been the two dominant parties that have existed since the founding of the country. Only these two parties have formed the government. Religious historian Mark Noll notes, "[T]he Liberals and Progressive Conservatives always cultivated their ties to leaders of Canada's main churches..." (Noll 2006, pp. 259-260). Of the 23 Prime Ministers since 1867, at least eight can be identified as having a strong personal faith: three being Roman Catholic and five Protestant.

Neither the Liberal Party nor the Conservative Party has religious foundations. However, the Reform Party was founded in 1987 led by Preston Manning, an evangelical Christian. While the party's focus was on Western Canadian issues, it gained strong support from evangelical Christians across the country. When the party merged into the Conservative Party in 2003, it retained the support of this religious community. By way of contrast, however, when Justin Trudeau became leader of the Liberal Party in 2013, he announced that the Party was pro-choice and all Liberal candidates to run in the next election would be expected to support that position. That excluded Christians who support pro-life.

The New Democratic Party (NDP) was founded in 1932 as a socialist party (See Lexier et al. 2018). It has formed the official opposition once but more often has held the balance of power when there has been a minority Parliament. Its founding leader, J.S. Woodsworth, was a former Presbyterian preacher and a founder of the Social Gospel movement in Canada. When the party reinvented itself in 1958 to be a social democratic party, its leader was Tommy Douglas, a former Baptist pastor. Douglas had been Premier in his home province of Saskatchewan and inaugurated the first universal health care program in Canada. Since the 1960s, the United Church of Canada, the largest Protestant denomination, has been referred to as "the NDP at prayer." This shows a close affiliation between this social gospel denomination and the political party. As recently as the 2011 election, the leader of the party, Jack Layton, launched his campaign at a United Church. The current leader of the NDP, Jagmeet Singh, is Sikh.

The Green Party is still a fledgling party despite its almost 35-year history as a national political party in Canada.[10] Like the NDP, the Green Party attracts religious adherents that focus on social justice. Elizabeth May served as leader of the party from 2006 to 2019 and is a deacon in the Anglican Church. She raised a storm of controversy during the 2019 election by stating in an interview that her hero was Jesus Christ. She then apologized for bringing her religion into politics. The next leader, Annamie Paul, was Jewish.

The Bloc Quebecois was founded in 1991 to represent the interests of the province of Quebec. It has formed the official opposition. In keeping with Quebec demographics, most members would identify as Roman Catholic or no religion.

In many countries, there are strong correlations between religious affiliation and voting patterns. These patterns exist in Canada but are not strong. There was a significant correlation between Roman Catholics and the Liberal Party into the 2000s (Mendelson and Nadeau 1997; Bélanger and Eagles 2006). Conservative Protestants have historically been inclined to vote for the Conservative Party.[11] Those who claimed no religious affiliation were more inclined to vote for the New Democratic Party (Wilkins-LaFlamme 2016, p. 502). An interesting change has taken place more recently, however. By the 2011 election, those who are highly committed to their religious faith tend to vote Conservative. Those who identify as non-religious tend to vote for the NDP outside of Quebec and for the Bloc Quebecois in Quebec (Wilkins-LaFlamme 2016, p. 502).

This indicates that religious adherents do not vote as blocs. They often do not vote based on policies. Even though many Roman Catholics generally adhere to the church's teaching opposing abortion, they support the Liberal Party which requires candidates to agree to vote pro-abortion. This means that religious lobby groups have less sway with politicians as they cannot bring their constituency to vote a particular way.

Religious Advocacy Groups and the Public Square

The era when church leaders regularly interacted with politicians about policy is long gone in Canada but that does not mean that there is no religious influence. Rather, the role of advocating to government has been taken up by organizations that have developed specializations in government advocacy.

The Canadian Conference of Catholic Bishops was founded in 1943 as the national assembly of the Bishops of Canada (Canadian Conference of Catholic Bishops n.d.). Its office is located in Ottawa. While its primary function is not government relations, it speaks on behalf of the Bishops on matters of faith and morals to politicians and government agencies. This is the body that speaks with the most authority on behalf of the Catholic population of Canada, which has the largest number of adherents of all religious groups in the country.

Many Protestant organizations have offices in Ottawa. The Evangelical Fellowship of Canada (EFC) established an office in Ottawa in 1996, specifically to advocate to the federal government on matters of importance to the evangelical Christian population (Evangelical Fellowship of Canada n.d.). The EFC represents at least 40 denominations and Christian organizations across Canada. The Mennonite Central Committee Canada, a relief, development and peace agency representing 15 Anabaptist denominations, has had an office in Ottawa since 1975 (Mennonite Central Committee n.d.). It recently renamed this office the Peace & Justice Office, which is reflective of its Anabaptist focus on peace issues. World Vision, the largest international development agency in Canada, is a Christian organization which has had an Ottawa presence for many years. Its current office has numerous staff who advocate on a variety of issues related to the work of World Vision, such as children's rights to education, maternal health and child labor (World Vision n.d.).

Two Christian organizations focus on the spiritual well-being of politicians. Evangelistic organization, Power to Change, established The Christian Embassy in Ottawa in 1984 to network politicians and ambassadors for the purpose of evangelism in the Christian faith (Christian Embassy n.d.). The National House of Prayer was established in 2005 to have a prayer focus for government and to "restore godliness in our land" (National House of Prayer n.d.). People from this organization regularly pray with and for Members of Parliament and Senators and for specific policy issues.

A final group of Christian organizations have roots in the Christian Reformed church, although they do not advocate on the same issues or from the same perspective. Cardus is the only Christian think tank in Canada and has an office close to Parliament Hill (Cardus n.d.). Cardus produces high-quality research and seeks to disseminate it to policymakers. It has both Christian Reformed and Roman Catholic roots. Citizens for Public Justice was founded by Christian Reformed adherents but is now broader in its focus. It relocated from Toronto to Ottawa in 2007 and advocates against poverty, for environmental stewardship and for refugees. The Centre for Public Dialogue is an office of the Christian Reformed Church of North America and focuses primarily on reconciliation with Indigenous Peoples of Canada but also has a focus on climate change and refugees (Centre for Public Dialogue n.d.). The Association for Reformed Political Action (ARPA Canada n.d.) was founded in 2007 to encourage and equip Christian Reformed adherents in public policy advocacy. The office in Ottawa lobbies government and intervenes in court actions on a wide variety of conservative Christian issues (Association for Reformed Political Action n.d.).

Several minority religious groups have advocacy offices in Ottawa. The National Council of Canadian Muslims advocates for the interests of the Muslim communities in Canada (National Council of Canadian Muslims n.d.). As well, the Aga Khan, hereditary imam of Shia Ismaili Muslims, has a significant presence in Ottawa through the Delegation of Ismaili Inamat (Aga Khan n.d.), strategically located close to Global Affairs Canada, and The Global Centre for Pluralism, close to Parliament Hill. The Centre for Israel and Jewish Affairs (CIJA) represents Jewish interests in Ottawa (Centre for Israel Jewish Affairs n.d.). Sikhs interests are ably represented by the World Sikh Organization (World Sikh Organization n.d.).

In addition to the religious advocates in Ottawa, other religious leaders make frequent trips to Ottawa to meet with politicians and government officials. It is clear that there is significant religious input into politics in Canada.

RELIGION AND POLITICS NOW AND THE WAY FORWARD

Over the last 10 years, religious politicians have had some successes in religion-positive politics. The most significant of these issues is religious freedom, particularly internationally. The assassination of Shahbaz Bhatti, Minister for Minorities in Pakistan, in 2011 was the catalyst for several

Canadian Members of Parliament to take action to protect religious freedom internationally. Bhatti had recently visited Canada and met with many politicians, including then Prime Minister Stephen Harper. Harper was motivated to appoint a new Ambassador for Religious Freedom to raise the profile of the issue with Canada's foreign affairs officers.

MPs from across the political spectrum formed a Parliamentary group on international religious freedom (CanFORB). David Anderson, a Christian MP from Saskatchewan, took a leading role in this group. He was also one of the founding members of The International Panel of Parliamentarians for Freedom of Religion or Belief (IPPFoRB). IPPFoRB was formed in 2015 to combat religious persecution and promote freedom of religion or belief. It includes over 300 politicians from 90 countries (IPPFoRB n.d.; Anderson and Mosey 2018). Anderson held seven annual Parliamentary Forums on Religious Freedom, focusing on religious freedom in Canada and internationally. While the political actions on freedom of religion have been by Christians, the advocacy has extended to many religious groups. This includes on behalf of Uyghur Muslims, who have been persecuted in China, and Yizidis being persecuted in Iraq.

When the government changed in 2015, the new Liberal government led by Prime Minister Justin Trudeau appeared less enthusiastic about connection with certain religious groups, particularly Protestant evangelicals. The government canceled the office of the Ambassador for Religious Freedom. Starting in 2018, the government began tying government funding for summer students to adherence to certain ideologies such as pro-choice on abortion and non-discrimination. This made it difficult for Christian camps, which hire on the basis of religion and therefore discriminate, to meet the requirements (Bussey 2021). This government has also been reluctant to condemn the blatant violation of religious freedom perpetrated by the Quebec government with Bill 21.

Governments across Canada, along with those from around the world, have placed significant restrictions on religious gatherings, even closing houses of worship altogether, during the COVID-19 pandemic. Religions are not merely individual preferences but have communal religious practices. Some religions have mandatory weekly religious meetings. More than that, during times of crisis, people turn to religious institutions for understanding and succor, and sometimes practical assistance. Some churches tried alternative meetings such as staying in their cars but holding a worship service in the parking lot but had police ticketing attendees (Lale 2021). Other churches opened in violation of public health restrictions and paid hefty fines (Dawson 2021). One pastor in Alberta was arrested and jailed for refusing to adhere to public health guidelines (Dawson 2021). It has been deeply troubling for religious communities who were restricted from meeting while people could shop in malls and work out in gyms.

Canada has a strong and deep history of religious influence in public policy. Because that was limited to the dominant Roman Catholic and Protestant Christian churches, minority religions were marginalized. Since the 1960s, Canada has experienced significant decline in religiosity with a rise in secularism. Religion has largely been removed from the public square and has been relegated to the private realm. In fact, it is seen as equivalent to a private, voluntary club. This does not mean that there is no religious influence in politics in Canada. Some politicians take their religious beliefs and practices seriously. The multitude of religious organizations engaged in government advocacy are only too happy to work with religiously affiliated politicians to advance policies in Canada and internationally. While many of these organizations are Christian, a significant number represent other faith communities. The influence of religion on politics in Canada is not going away any time soon.

NOTES

1. The statistics for 2021 are all from Statistics Canada 2022. The Canadian Census: A rich portrait of the country's religious and ethnocultural diversity. https://www150.statcan.gc.ca/n1/daily-quotidien/221026/dq221026b-eng.pdf.
2. "Loyalists" were people living in the American colonies who were loyal to Britain.
3. Following 9/11, certain radical Islamic organizations have been designated "listed terrorist entities" in Canada, *Criminal Code of Canada*, RSC 1985, c. 46, s. 83.01.
4. In a string of pivotal cases on religious freedom, the Canadian courts have adopted a "freedom from" rather than "freedom for" approach to public expressions of religion. See, for example, *R. v. Big M Drug Mart*, 1985; *Zylberberg v. Sudbury Board of Education*, 1988; *Canadian Civil Liberties Association v. Ontario (Minister of Education)*, 1990; *Saguenay (Ville de) c. Mouvement laïque québécois*, 2015; *Law Society of British Columbia v. Trinity Western University*, 2018.
5. *Les invasions barbares*, written and directed by Denys Arcand (New York: 2003), film. Quoted in Noll 2006: p. 252.

6. See Conseil Supérieur de l'Éducation 2000, to see the input of Catholics and Protestants on the future of religious education in Quebec.
7. Bill C-233 was introduced by MP Cathay Wagantall in the 43rd Parliament. Wagantall is also the chair of the National Prayer Breakfast.
8. Ontario added s. 18.1 to its Human Rights Code to allow religious officials and sacred spaces an exemption from non-discrimination laws in relation to marriage.
9. This includes Newfoundland, Manitoba, Saskatchewan and Alberta.
10. At most, it has had three elected MPs federally.
11. This includes the Progressive Conservative Party as well as the fledgling Reform Party and its antecedent, the Canadian Alliance.

REFERENCES

Aga Khan Foundation Canada. n.d. Available online: https://www.akfc.ca/about-us/visit-us. Accessed 23 June 2021.

Anderson, D., and J. Mosey. 2018. Legislators lead the way to freedom of religion and belief. *International Journal for Religious Freedom* 11 (1/2): 9–14.

Association for Reformed Political Action. n.d. Available online: https://arpa-canada.ca. Accessed 23 June 2021.

Bélanger, P., and M. Eagles. 2006. The Geography of Class and Religion in Canadian Elections Revisited. *Canadian Journal of Political Science* 39: 591–609.

Berger, T.R. 1982. *Fragile Freedoms: Human Rights and Dissent in Canada, (revised and updated)*. Toronto: Clark, Irwin and Co.

Botting, G. 1993. *Fundamental Freedoms and Jehovah's Witnesses*. Calgary: University of Calgary Press.

Bouchard, G., and C. Taylor. 2008. *Building the Future: A Time for Reconciliation*. Quebec: Government of Quebec.

Brown, D.M. 2000. Freedom From or Freedom For? Religion as a Case Study in Defining the Content of Charter Rights. *UBC Law Review* 33: 551–615.

Buckingham, J.E. 2014. *Fighting over God: A Legal and Political History of Religious Freedom in Canada*. Montreal and Kingston: McGill-Queen's University Press.

Bussey, B., 2021. "That 'Moral Squint' and Canada Summer Jobs," Canadian Council of Christian Charities. https://www.cccc.org/news_blogs/barry/2021/06/14/that-moral-squint-and-canada-summer-jobs/. Accessed 24 June 2021.

Canada. 1966. *Proceedings of the Special Joint Committee the Senate and House of Commons on Divorce*. Ottawa: Government of Canada.

Canadian Association of University Teachers. n.d. "Universities that impose a faith or ideological test." Available online: https://www.caut.ca/latest/publications/academic-freedom/universities. Accessed 30 May 2021.

Canadian Conference of Catholic Bishops. n.d. "History." Available online: https://www.cccb.ca/about/overview/. Accessed 23 June 2021.

Cardus. n.d. Available online: https://www.cardus.ca. Accessed 23 June 2021.

Centre for Israel and Jewish Affairs. n.d. Available online: https://www.cija.ca. Accessed 23 June 2021.

Centre for Public Dialogue. n.d. Available online: https://www.crcna.org/PublicDialogue. Accessed 23 June 2021.

Christian Embassy. n.d. "About". Available online: https://christianembassy.ca/about. Accessed 23 June 2021.

Conseil Supérieur de l'Éducation. 2000. *A New Place for Religion in the Schools*. Quebec: Government of Quebec.

Crowley, T. 1996. The French Regime to 1760. In *A Concise History of Christianity in Canada*, ed. T. Murphy and R. Perin, 1–55. Toronto: Oxford University Press.

Dawson, T. 2021. "The price of worship during COVID: Church fined, pastor in prison." Healthing. Available online: https://www.healthing.ca/news/the-price-of-worship-during-covid-ontario-church-is-fined-and-an-alberta-pastor-sits-in-prison/wcm/4121e657-585f-44a6-a07b-33bcf68ccf3d. Accessed 28 June 2021.

Diefenbaker, J.G. 1985. In *The Personal Letters of a Public Man: The Family Letters of John G. Diefenbaker*, ed. Thad McIlroy. Toronto: Doubleday Canada.

Egerton, G.W. 2000. Trudeau, God and the Canadian Constitution: Religion, Human Rights and Government Authority in the Making of the 1982 Constitution. In *Rethinking Church, State, and Modernity: Canada between Europe and America*, ed. David Lyon and Marguerite Van Die, 90–112. Toronto: University of Toronto Press.

Evangelical Fellowship of Canada. n.d. Available online: https://www.evangelicalfellowship.ca/. Accessed 23 June 2021.

Ferguson, B. 2005. 9.2 Religious Institutions. In *Recent Social Trends in Canada 1960-2000*, ed. L.W. Roberts, R.A. Clifton, B. Ferguson, K. Kampen, and S. Langlois, 359–371. Montreal and Kingston: McGill-Queen's University Press.

Henderson, W. B. n.d. "The Indian Act," *The Canadian Encyclopedia*. Available online: https://www.thecanadianencyclopedia.ca/en/article/indian-act. Accessed 21 May 2021.

Hiemstra, R. and K. Stiller, 2016. "Religious Affiliation and Attendance in Canada," *In Trust Magazine*, New Year 2016. Available online: https://intrust.org/Magazine/Issues/New-Year-2016/Religious-affiliation-and-attendance-in-Canada. Accessed 10 Jun 2022.

IPPFoRB. n.d. Available online: https://www.ippforb.com/. Accessed June 11 2022.

Jenkins, P. 2021. "How Quebec went from one of the most religious societies to one of the least," *The Christian Century*, April 28, 2021.

Lale, B. 2021. "The Church of God in Aylmer went ahead with a drive-in church service for a third straight week Sunday," CTV News. Available online: https://london.ctvnews.ca/the-church-of-god-in-aylmer-went-ahead-with-a-drive-in-church-service-for-a-third-straight-week-sunday-1.4922943. Accessed 24 June 2021.

Lambertson, R. 2005. *Repression and Resistance: Canadian Human Rights Activists, 1930-1960*. Toronto: University of Toronto Press.

Lexier, R., S. Bangarth, and J. Weier. 2018. *The Party of Conscience: The CCF, the NDP, and Social Democracy in Canada*. Toronto: Between the Lines.

Mason, G.W. 1956. *The Legislative Struggle for Church Union*. Toronto: Ryerson Press.

Mendelson, M., and R. Nadeau. 1997. The Religious Cleavage and the Media in Canada. *Canadian Journal of Political Science* 30 (1): 129–146.

Mennonite Central Committee. n.d. Available online: https://mcccanada.ca/get-involved/advocacy/ottawa. Accessed 23 June 2021.

Milloy, J.S. 1999. *A National Crime; The Canadian Government and the Residential School System, 1879 to 1986*. Winnipeg: University of Manitoba Press.

National Council of Canadian Muslims. n.d. Available online: https://www.nccm.ca. Accessed 23 June 2021.

National House of Prayer. n.d. Available online: https://nhop.ca/about-us/history. Accessed 23 June 2021.

Newfoundland and Labrador. 1986. *Education for Self-reliance: A Report on Education and Training in Newfoundland*. St. John's, NL: The Royal Commission on Employment and unemployment.

Noll, M. 2006. What Happened to Christian Canada? *Church History* 75 (2): 245–273.

Penton, J.M. 1976. *Jehovah's Witnesses in Canada: Champions of Freedom of Speech and Worship*. Toronto: Macmillan of Canada.

Quebec, Task Force on the Place of Religion in Schools in Québec. 1999. *L'enseignement culturel des religions. Principes directeurs et conditions d'implantation*. Québec: Government of Quebec.

Robertson, B. 1971. *Wilfrid Laurier: The Great Conciliator*. Toronto: Oxford University Press.

Schull, J. 1965. *Laurier: The First Canadian*. Toronto: Macmillan of Canada.

Skelton, O.D. 1921. *The Life and Letters of Sir Wilfrid Laurier*. Vol. I. Toronto: Oxford University Press.

Snell, J.G. 1991. *In the Shadow of the Law: Divorce in Canada, 1900-1939*. Toronto: University of Toronto Press.

Statistics Canada. 2001. *Religious Groups in Canada*. Ottawa: Government of Canada.

————. 2022. The Canadian Census: A rich portrait of the country's religious and ethnocultural diversity. https://www150.statcan.gc.ca/n1/daily-quotidien/221026/dq221026b-eng.pdf.

Thiessen, J. 2015. *The Meaning of Sunday: The Practice of Belief in a Secular Age.* Montreal and Kingston: McGill-Queen's University Press.

Trudeau, P.E. 1968. *Federalism and the French Canadians.* Toronto: Macmillan of Canada.

Weir, G.M. 1917. *Evolution of the Separate School Law in the Prairie Provinces.* Saskatoon.

Wilkins-LaFlamme, S. 2016. The Changing Religious Cleavage in Canadians' Voting Behaviour. *Canadian Journal of Political Science* 49 (3): 499–518.

World Sikh Organization. n.d. Available online: https://www.worldsikh.org. Accessed 23 June 2021.

World Vision. n.d. Available online: https://www.worldvision.ca/get-involved/advocacy. Accessed 23 June 2021.

LEGISLATION

Act to amend the law concerning education with respect to persons professing the Jewish religion, (1903) 3 Edw. 7, c. 16 (Quebec).

Canadian Charter of Rights and Freedoms, Schedule B to the Canada Act 1982, 1982, c. 11 (U.K.).

Constitution Act, 1867, 30 & 31 Victoria, c. 3 (U.K.).

Constitutional Amendment, 1998 (Newfoundland Act), SI/98-25.

————, 1997 (Québec), SI/97-141 Canada.

Criminal Law Amendment Act, 1968–69, SC 1968–69, c. 38.

Divorce Act, S.C. 1990, c. 46.

LEGAL CASES

A.G. Ontario v. Hamilton Street Railway, [1903] A.C. 524 (JCPC).

Adler v. Ontario, [1996] 3 SCR 609.

Brassard et al, v. Langevin, (1877) 1 SCR 145.

Brophy v. A-G Manitoba, [1895] A.C. 202 (JCPC).

Canadian Civil Liberties Association v. Ontario (Minister of Education) (1990) 71 OR (2d) 341 (Ont. C.A.).

Chabot v. Commissioners of Lamorandiere (1957), 12 DLR (2d) 796 (Que. Q.B.).

City of Winnipeg v. Barrett, [1892] A.C. 445 (JCPC).

Civil Marriage Act, S.C. 2005, c. 33.

Duval v. R. (1938), 64 RJQ 270 (K.B.); leave to appeal dismissed [1938] SCR 390.

Hirsch v. Protestant Board of School Commissioners of Montreal, [1928] AC 200; [1928] 1 DLR 1041 (JCPC).

Hyde v. Hyde and Woodmansee, [L.R.] 1 P. and D. 130 (1866).

In re Legislation Respecting Abstention From Labour on Sunday (1905), 35 SCR 581.

Law Society of British Columbia v. Trinity Western University, [2018] 2 SCR 293.

Loyola High School v. Quebec (Attorney General), [2015] 1 SCR 613.

R. v. Big M Drug Mart, [1985] 1 SCR 295.

R. v. Kinler (1925), 63 RJQ 483 (S.C.).

R. v. Morgentaler, [1988] 1 SCR 30.

Re the Marriage Law of Canada, [1912] AC 880 (JCPC).

Reference Re Same-sex Marriage, [2004] 3 SCR 698.

Roncarelli v. Duplessis [1959] SCR 121.

Saguenay (Ville de) c. Mouvement laïque québécois, [2015] 2 SCR 3.

Trinity Western University v. British Columbia College of Teachers, [2001] 1 SCR 772.

Trinity Western University v. Law Society of Ontario, [2018] 2 SCR 453.

Waldman v. Canada, CCPR/C/67/D/694/1996.

Zylberberg v. Sudbury Board of Education (Director) (1988), 65 OR (2d) 641 (Ont. C.A.).

CHAPTER 29

Religion and Politics in Mexican History

Roberto Blancarte

This text is part of a long-term work that has been growing and transforming. A first version of this work was intended to give a regional vision on the development of secularism in Latin America. It was published as "Laicity and secularism in Latin America," in the Critical Notes section of *Sociological Studies*, Vol. XXVI, no. 76 (January–April, 2008), pp. 139–164. In another article, published in the journal *Civitas*, of the Catholic University of Rio Grande do Sur (Brazil), various perspectives and reflections were added that feed this contribution. The work has been enriched with various contributions to the history of the secular state in Mexico and its relationship with the Catholic Church, published as *Laicidad en México; The construction of the secular Republic in Mexico* (Mexico: IIJ-UNAM, "Collection of Jorge Carpizo Cuadernos." To understand and think about secularism, No. 31, 2013). Also "The religious question and the Constitution of 1917" in *Mexico and the Constitution of 1917; The historical context* (Mexico: Senate of the Republic, LXIII Legislature / Secretariat of Culture / National Institute for Historical Studies of Revolutions in Mexico, Institute of Legal Research, UNAM, 2017). Finally, some reflections were originally made in the book *La República laica en México* (México: Siglo XXI Editores, 2019).

R. Blancarte (✉)
El Colegio De Mexico, Mexico City, Mexico
e-mail: blancart@colmex.mx

S. Holzer (ed.), *The Palgrave Handbook of Religion and State
Volume II*, https://doi.org/10.1007/978-3-031-35609-4_29

689

Although contemporary Mexico is predominantly a Catholic country, it is diverse in its ways of conceiving and practicing Catholicism. The plurality of beliefs, always existing, although legally formalized only since the mid-nineteenth century, is growing. During the first 150 years of its existence as an independent nation, the proportion of members of other Churches and religions was negligible, almost nil. However, as of the 1970s, a significant increase has been observed, both in followers of other Churches, particularly Protestant and Evangelical, and in people who declared themselves "without religion." The 2020 census results of the same confirmed the indicated trend. Exactly 77.7% of the population declared themselves Catholic, while 11.2% declared themselves Protestant or Evangelical Christian. Interestingly enough, 2.5% of Mexicans declared to be believers without having a religious affiliation and 8.1% registered in the category "without religion."[1] In other words, at least 10% of the population in Mexico has not currently an institutional religious affiliation or does not profess any religious belief. Thus, although much of the history in Mexico of the rapport between religion and politics focuses on the relationship between the nascent State and the Catholic Church, it is necessary to understand that much of that which is religious goes beyond the religious institutions and much of that which is political was not necessarily framed in the State.

The concept "Church-State," although important to define the legal frameworks in which the ministers of worship and the faithful of many religious institutions have historically developed, does not succeed in understanding much of what happened in the field of popular beliefs, which commonly escape both State and ecclesial controls. The so-called popular religion, which a good part of the Mexican population lives, although linked to the ecclesial institution in different ways, does not necessarily follow the doctrinal or pastoral norms advocated by the clerical apparatus. Rather, it tends to go its own way, linked to ritual practices and autonomous behaviors that permanently challenge the institution. This is not new. It comes from colonial times, the product of a *sui generis* evangelization, which generated particular religious beliefs and practices.

As the period specialists well affirm, regarding the impact of the Enlightenment on the Catholic Church in New Spain, "the enlightened bishops fought with passion superstitions and popular forms of piety and devotion."[2] On other occasions, the clerical apparatus has embraced some of these practices and devotions, trying to channel them institutionally. The case of the Virgin of Guadalupe is, in this sense, the most representative of this complex relationship. In this regard, the State becomes a distant observer of these internal relationships in the Church and occasionally a facilitator of the conditions for development of such practices (pilgrimages, local festivals). Although it almost always intervenes or has something to say about these behaviors, even taking advantage of them, it is not always a central actor in the daily life of believers. A historical example of the above was the regulation of religious festivals and celebrations of holidays, stipulated in one of the Reform Laws of 1859–1861, which in Mexico established the Church-State separation.[3] The history of these relationships parallels the larger relationship between religion and politics as long as we also understand the social action of communities and society in general. Let us therefore try to keep this framework in mind to understand what happened in this regard in these 200 years of the existence of Mexico as an independent nation.

THE CATHOLIC REPUBLIC

Mexico was born (although not formally) as a Catholic Republic and initially built a State identified with a single religion that was intolerant toward the exercise (public or private) of any other religion. Similar to all the new countries that emerged as a result of the decomposition of the Spanish empire in America, the new empire's rulers tried to inherit the Royal Patronage. In the same logic as the special relationship with the Holy See, the rulers drew up constitutions privileging the Roman Church and did not tolerate the presence of other cults.[4] The Royal Patronage granted by the Holy See through various bulls at the end of the fifteenth and early sixteenth centuries had granted the Catholic kings various rights over ecclesiastical management.

The bull of Alexander VI of May 4, 1493, granted them the dominion of "the indies" and the exclusive privilege of Christianizing the Indians. The same Pope of November 16, 1501, guaranteed the Spanish Crown the tithes and first fruits of the Churches of the Indies. The bull of Julius II of July 28, 1508, granted him the right to universal patronage over the Catholic Church in those lands. Although not everyone would agree in later centuries on the meaning of this concession, regalism assumed that these bulls recognized the authority of the kings of Spain to exercise jurisdiction in all matters related to ecclesiastical government in the Indies. The sovereigns were assumed, in the words of John L. Mecham, as "a species of apostolic vicars with authority over spiritual matters in America."[5]

In other words, by virtue of the Crown taking on all the costs for the expansion of the faith, the Holy See admitted the right of the kings to found Churches, appoint bishops and clergy, helping themselves to sustain it with the tithes. It was not clear (and this would be a source of bitter disputes during the following centuries) whether this was the recognition of an intrinsic right of kings or a revocable concession of the Holy See.

In Mexico, the first insurgents fighting for Independence, many of them priests, stated in their manifestos that the new nation would be Catholic, thus expressing the nation would be protected by the government as well as asserting the exercise of any other religion would not be tolerated. The *Sentiments of the Nation*, by José María Morelos, the *Independence Act of Chilpancingo* of 1813, the *Constitutional Decree of Apatzingán* of 1814, and the *Constitutive Act* of 1823 were antecedents of the first Constitution, which established in 1824 that "the religion of The Mexican nation is and will be perpetually the Roman Catholic, Apostolic. The nation protects it by wise and just laws and prohibits the exercise of any other."[6]

However, the fact that the new governments tried to offer privileged treatment to the Catholic religion did not necessarily translate into submission to the dictates of the Church. On the contrary, it meant in all cases that the State claimed the implicit rights of the Patronage and therefore control over the activities of the clergy and the ecclesiastical institution. This was established by Article 50 of the Mexican Constitution of 1824, which gave Congress powers to exercise the rights of the Patronage and eventually sign a concordat with the Holy See.[7] In other words, the alleged inheritance over the Patronage meant for the governments of the new independent countries of Latin America, including the Mexican one, that the national identity would be Catholic, but that the Church would be, as in the colonial era, under control and jurisdiction of the Crown, or, in this case, the State. There was more continuity than rupture. The regalist tradition, which sought to subject the Church to the ends of kings, had actually been strengthened since the arrival of the Bourbons in Spain in 1700. But, it was mainly from the second half of the eighteenth century, from Carlos III in particular, and the so-called Bourbon Reforms undertaken to streamline the colonial administration and increase the resources that way from America that led to a modification of the relations between the Church and the Crown.

One of the most important measures was the confiscation of ecclesiastical property. The economic doctrine behind this measure assumed that a good part of the lands, real estate, and wealth in general owned by the Church (dead hands) remained out of circulation and impeded economic initiatives. Hence, they suggested confiscating ecclesiastical assets, preventing further depreciation, taking advantage of vacant or unworked lands, and promoting small and medium-sized properties. After the Independence, most of the Spanish-American governments (liberal or conservative), which claimed to be protectors of the Church, would follow the example of the very Catholic kings of Spain, confiscating ecclesiastical property or requesting forced loans from the ecclesiastical institution. All this would weaken the Church at the same time that it partially alienated it from political power as a source of authority for the new States. Religion became an instrument of the State rather than a source of legitimacy.

In the following years, the question of the Patronage was to become an element of contention not only between the new American governments and the Holy See, but also between those who defended the alliance between temporal power and spiritual authority (characteristic of the old regime) and those who were beginning to think of a scheme for the separation of spheres of action. In general terms, while a solution was being sought, through plenipotentiary envoys to Rome, the Congresses established de facto Patronages. However, following the same established practice, none of the new governments dared to appoint bishops for the many vacant diocesan sees, and throughout America, and they had to wait for the arrival of Gregory XVI in 1831 who finally began to appoint bishops.

In the following decades, the power of the Catholic Church in Spanish America would be seriously questioned. At the base of this questioning there was a mixture of political liberalism, jurisdictionalism inherited from regalism and the practice of the Patronage, as well as enormous material needs of the new governments. This existed in those countries (and Mexico was no exception); and since colonial times, the growing conviction of the dominant position of the Church was an obstacle to the economic opportunities of the people and the entire country, as well as to political freedom of individuals.

The Catholic Church and Liberalism

There is an enormous paradox, which in the background hid a possible contradiction in the religious politics of independent Mexico. Mexico was born, de facto, as a Catholic Republic, but with liberal ideals. That would generate irreconcilable contradictions that would mark philosophical debates and political conflicts during the next two centuries; not because there was an intrinsic problem, but because the Holy See clearly and forcefully opposed any compromise with liberalism. Concerned about the absence of integrating elements of the nation, the first Mexican liberals conceived Mexico as a Catholic Republic, even though this distinction was not universally defined. The identification of Mexico as a Catholic Republic (although not formally established as such) granted privileges to Catholicism while being intolerant of the practice of any other religion. Of course, this way of conceiving the Republic directly collided with the principles of freedom and equality, thus establishing a source of contradictions and conflicts between those who still professed a society based on differences and privileges and those who had freedom and equality as an ideal. Thus, during the first decades in the life of Mexico as an independent nation, the debate on the Patronage and the refusal of the Holy See to accept their independence, coupled with the aforementioned contradiction and the growing expansion of liberal ideas, propelled growing discussions and continuous confrontations.

In religious matters, as has been seen, there did not seem to be too many divisions, since most of the independent "criollos" (Americans of Spanish origin) agreed on the idea that the Catholic religion was one of the few elements of national identity, beyond ethnic, regional, and linguistic differences Hence, the protection of Catholicism and its privileges was considered essential. However, the financial needs of the governments and the population also led to confiscation measures such as the nationalization of ecclesiastical property and the elimination of the tithe. Another action aimed at weakening religious power was the abolition of the ecclesiastical jurisdiction. This is the case of Mexico in 1833, Vice President Valentín Gómez Farías tries to start the liberal program, which consists of the prohibition of the dead hands (the Church) from acquiring real estate, the elimination of the tithe (that is, the civil obligation of pay it), the suppression of monastic institutions (in addition to the civil compulsion for the fulfillment of vows) and in general "all the laws that attribute to the clergy the knowledge of civil affairs, such as the marriage contract, etc."[8]

Ecclesiastical authorities are reminded of the observance of the provisions that prohibit secular and regular clergy from dealing or preaching on political matters. Likewise, this program seeks to break the educational monopoly that the Church has from elementary school to the University. The whole system is abolished at the same time that a General Directorate of Public Instruction is established, responsible for teaching in the country. Most of these measures, however, with the exception of the economic, are not implemented and are reversed by successive conservative governments. The same thing happened in 1847. During the Mexican-American War, Gómez Farías tried unsuccessfully to expropriate ecclesiastical property. It will be necessary to wait until the Ayutla Revolution in 1854 for the liberal program to painfully advance. This will be in the midst of riots and wars, such as the Three-Year War (1857–1860) and the French intervention (1862–1867).[9] Finally, after many debates and years of frustration, the idea emerged among the new ruling elite that perhaps the best solution was the separation of ecclesiastical and state businesses.

It could be fairly said that these were ultimately debates and conflicts among the elite. However, the people participated in many ways. The riots, armies, and revolts, as well as the peasant and urban rebellions, could not be understood without popular participation. The alignment with one cause or another did not necessarily respond to an ideological identification. However, the very autonomy of popular religiosity with respect to the institution and the criticism of its (real) wealth and the conflicts that indigenous or mestizo communities sometimes had with the clergy could have contributed to a distancing from conservative positions that were identified in many cases with the Church. Liberalism triumphed in society, but it was defeated within the Catholic Church.

As for the so-called lower clergy, during the first half of the nineteenth century there were not a few clergymen, on both continents, who tried to reconcile liberalism with Catholicism. But, the end result was unfavorable to them. Those who preached an impossible conciliation with new ideas predominated because they were not willing to accept the consequences that liberal reforms entailed for the Church. The Papal States themselves were caught up in the whirlwind of mid-century bourgeois revolutions, which led the Holy See to lock itself in the growing intransigence and condemnation of liberalism and its consequences in matters of religion. But before those events, during the first decades of the independent countries, the members of the clergy were main actors in the various debates, both on the side of the new and old regimes. No one defended a Catholic republicanism and the rights of the Church through the liberal system. Recent studies show that even up to the 1950s many clergymen struggled to demonstrate the compatibility between Catholicism and progress, otherwise understood as the Enlightenment or science. Finally, it must be remembered that many of the men who forged or carried out the liberal reforms were priests.[10] In Mexico, for example, it was the priest José María Luis Mora who, after a first unsuccessful experience to introduce liberal reforms, suggested the need to forget about patronages and concordats, establishing a separation between State businesses and those of Church:

> "From the constitution," he said in 1833, "it is also necessary to make everything in it of concordats and patronage disappear. These voices suppose the civil power invested with ecclesiastical functions, and the ecclesiastical with civil functions, and it is time to make this monstrous mixture, the origin of so many disputes, disappear. The civil authority resumes what belongs to it, abolishing the ecclesiastical jurisdiction, denying the right to acquire by dead hands, disposing of the goods they currently possess, subtracting the civil marriage contract from its intervention, etc., etc., and let it appoint priests and bishops who you like, understanding with Rome as you see fit."[11]

Mora's position, like that of other Catholic priests and parishioners in the world, did not manage to prevail in Mexico until a quarter of a century later. Rather, a reaction was generated from Rome that sought to preserve or recover for the Church a regime of privileges within the framework of a Catholic State. It would be necessary, as we already stated, to wait until the "Ayutla Revolution" in 1854 for the liberal program to begin to painfully advance. The litigation around the Patronage was finally drastically resolved. The liberals realized that this problem had no solution and that perhaps the best thing was a regime of separation, in which the Church (at that time only one was recognized) would take care of its affairs and the State would take care of theirs. By omission, the liberal Constitution of 1857 decreed the separation of Church and State because it did not mention any privileged treatment of the Church or intolerance toward other religions

The Three Years War and the Reform Laws

The opposition by the conservatives and the Church, which would lead to the Three Year War (1857–1860), would radicalize the positions between conservatives and liberals, eventually leading to the enactment of the so-called *Reform Laws.*

Previously, the "Juárez Law," issued on November 22, 1855, by the man who would become the hero of Mexican liberalism, began by timidly extinguishing the ecclesiastical jurisdiction in the civil branch, although leaving it to subsist in criminal matters. It would be the beginning of a series of measures that would allow the establishment of essential civil institutions for the construction of the modern State.[12]

The actions undertaken by Benito Juárez were situated in a general context of regalism and liberalism, which ended up affecting the old power structure that closely united the monarchies and the pontifical see. In both cases, the secular or civil powers were strengthened at the expense of the Church, but this did not always mean the constitution of a secular autonomy—instead, the simple submission of the clergy to the dictates of the civil, monarchical, or republican power. Juarez would pursue the establishment of a republic where there had "more than one and only authority: the civil authority so determined by the national will, without a State religion."[13]

The so-called Reform Laws can be classified as those that were put into effect during the presidencies of Juan Álvarez and Ignacio Comonfort (1854–1857) and those that were promulgated by President Benito Juárez from Veracruz in the middle of the War of Reform, in 1859 and 1860. During the first stage, in addition to the previously mentioned "Juárez Law" of 1855, the better known "Lerdo Law" was added. Miguel Lerdo de Tejada promoted in fact this law in order to confiscate ecclesiastical and military assets. In doing so, he forced the sale of houses and land in the hands of ecclesiastical and military corporations, as well as created limitations on ownership for them.[14] In the letter of that year that the Minister of Finance and Public Credit sent to the state governors, Miguel Lerdo de Tejada justified the confiscation of rustic and urban properties owned by civil and religious corporations, "as an indispensable measure to bypass the main obstacle that has arisen up to now for the establishment of a tax system, uniform and arranged according to the principles of science, mobilizing real estate, which is the natural basis of any good tax system."[15] The idea was to put into circulation a huge mass of real estate that at that time was stagnant and to form a secure base for the establishment of a tax system.

In the same way, the "Iglesias Law," of April 1857, promoted by José María Iglesias, then Minister of "Justice, Ecclesiastical Business, and Public Instruction," regulated the recollection of parochial rights, preventing the priests from demanding them to the poorest and punishing members of the clergy who did not comply with the law.[16]

However, the most important and transcendental "Reform Laws" were those dictated by Juárez from Veracruz, in the midst of the civil war. The justification of the Reform Laws, made "by the constitutional government to the nation" and signed by Juárez, Ruiz, Ocampo, and Lerdo de Tejada, constituted a complete program to transform the country.[17] A profound transformation was required that intertwined productive activities and a new social structure with the libertarian ideals of the independent republic. The program of separation, or "the most perfect independence between State affairs and purely ecclesiastical ones," was announced, implying rather interventionist measures in the life of the Church. These measures include the suppression of corporations of male regulars, the extinction of the brotherhoods (cofradias), or the closure of the novitiates in the nunneries, as well as measures aimed at the creation of a new economic order. The qualities of such an economic order encompass the nationalization of ecclesiastical property of a judicial nature, bearing similarities to the elimination of ecclesiastical jurisdiction, or of enormous political impact, such as letting the cult be supported by the faithful themselves.

However, the set of precepts announced in the Reform Laws did not circumscribe to the religious aspect. It was a comprehensive program of reform of the nation, based on interconnected laws that were to change the face of Mexican society. The separation between the State and the Church, later completed by freedom of worship, would promote both free trade and immigration. The confiscation of ecclesiastical property and the circulation of vacant and national lands would promote industry and the arts. Economic measures, aimed at creating wealth, were intertwined with fiscal and political ones.

Following the liberal plans for the secularization of public life, on July 23, 1859, Juárez promulgated the Civil Marriage Law and the Organic Law of the Civil Registry; and, a week later, the decree by which all cemeteries were secularized. These three measures would establish civil institutions central to the rites of passage of each person (birth, marriage, and death), but above all they allowed the existence of a citizenship independent of religious belief, capable of contracting a marriage contract outside of sacramental rituals of the Catholic Church or of any other religion. This provided cemeteries for all, beyond the beliefs of each individual, which until that moment was not possible, due to the ecclesiastical control of both the records, as well as the matrimonial sacrament and the cemeteries.[18]

On August 11, 1859, Juárez signed a decree on holidays forbidding the official attendance of public servants at religious ceremonies.[19] Rather than establishing a civic calendar, Juarez's decree established which days should be taken as holidays, with the logic of rationalizing the innumerable religious festivals of the communities. The same decree indicated that all laws, circulars, and provisions, whatever they might be, "emanated from the legislator, testamentary institution or simple custom by which the official body [public servants] had to attend the public functions of the Churches" were repealed.[20] Published in December 1860, the Law on Freedom of Worship reiterated that "Although all public officials in their capacity as men will enjoy freedom as much as all men in the country, they do not officially attend the acts of a cult, or as a distinction to their priests, whatever their hierarchy. The troop formed is included in the prohibition." The measure was important because it helped to eliminate the confusion between personal religious beliefs and public function, and avoided forms of religious legitimation of political power.

The aforementioned law on freedom of worship came to close the cycle of the Reform Laws, establishing, in its first article, in a simple and forceful way:

> The laws protect the exercise of Catholic worship and of others that are established in the country, as the expression and effect of religious freedom, which being a natural right of man, does not have and cannot have more limits than the right of a third party and the requirements of public order.[21]

In addition to this, the law ceased in its Article 8 the right of asylum in the temples. More importantly, it established in its Article 11 that no solemn religious act could be carried out outside the temples without written permission granted in each case by the local political authority: "according to the regulations and orders issued by the district and state governors." Article 17 ceased the official treatment that used to be given to various people and ecclesiastical corporations" and Article 24, as indicated, reiterated the prohibition of officials from attending religious ceremonies as such, that is, as functionarys.[22] Finally, upon his return to Mexico City, once the war was over, Juárez complemented the work of secularization by means of a decree on February 2, 1861 by which hospitals and charities were secularized and another on 26 February 1861, which ordered the extinction of religious congregations, except those of the so-called Sisters of Charity.[23]

In sum, the Reform Laws made possible the emergence of a liberal regime and the beginning of the formation of a secular, autonomous, and sovereign State whose institutions no longer depended on religious legitimacy. Hence, many of the laws and decrees insisted both on the new freedoms created and on the various prohibitions that marked a sharp separation not only between the affairs of the State and the Churches, but also between personal beliefs and public function.

These measures, which accompanied those of other liberal states in Europe, did not go unnoticed by the Holy See. In December 1864, Pius IX published the encyclical *Quanta cura* which was accompanied by a catalog of 80 proposals considered unacceptable by the Church's magisterium. This catalog is the famous *Syllabus* or *Compilation that contains the main errors of our time that are noted in the consistorial addresses, encyclicals, and other apostolic letters of our Holy Father Pope Pius IX.* [24]

In spite of everything, the doctrinal positions of the Holy See did not have a major impact on Mexican society. These were published in the midst of the French intervention and Empire of Maximilian (1862–1867), whose liberal spirit did not contribute to the return of conservative positions even though diplomatic relations were established, and a Concordat was considered. None of these efforts, however, were lasting.

State-Churches in the Era of Triumphant Liberalism

The Reform Laws, particularly the law establishing freedom of worship, led to an incipient religious plurality in the country. However, the presence of other religious confessions was more symbolic of the new freedoms rather than a real development of religious pluralism the public sphere. In 1960, one hundred years after the formal establishment of religious freedom only 3.5% of the Mexican population did not declare themselves Catholic. Therefore, the discussion about the role of religion in public affairs continued to revolve around the Catholic Church. After the death of Benito Juárez, which occurred on July 18, 1872, the Liberals tried to consolidate their work of reform. On September 25, 1873, under the government of Sebastián Lerdo de Tejada, the Reform Laws acquired constitutional status when being incorporated into the Constitution of 1857, around five items, in addition to other laws and decrees that remained current:

> Art. 1—The State and the Church are independent of each other. Congress cannot dictate laws—establishing or prohibiting any religion.
> Art. 2—Marriage is a civil contract. This and other acts of civil status of persons, are of the exclusive competence of public servants and officials of the civil order, in the terms considered by the laws, and have the strength and validity that they attribute to them.
> Art. 3—No religious institution can acquire real estate or capital imposed on them, with the sole exception established in the art. 27 of the Constitution.
> Art. 4—The simple promise to tell the truth and to fulfill the obligations that are contracted, will replace the religious oath with its effects and penalties.
> Article 5—No one can be compelled to work without just compensation and without his full consent. The State cannot allow any person to carry any contract, agreement having for its object the restriction, loss or irrevocable sacrifice of the freedom of man, either because of work, education or religious vows. Consequently, the law does not recognize monastic orders, nor can it allow their establishment, whatever the denomination or object with which they intend to be erected. Neither can an agreement be admitted in which the man accepts to his banishment or exile.[25]

One of the consequences of the incorporation of the Reform Laws into the Constitution was the renovated expulsion of the Jesuits and other religious orders from the country. For the liberals of the time, entry through a vow of submission and obedience to a religious or monastic order meant a renunciation or "irrevocable sacrifice" of the freedom of the human being. Therefore, the establishment or existence of these congregations should not be allowed. In fact, this legislation would be ratified in the revolutionary reform of the Constitution of 1917 and would remain in force, although not applied, until 1992. Resistance to these measures and the need to achieve a pacification of the country would lead to Lerdo de Tejada's successor, General Porfirio Díaz, to try a conciliation policy, which would later be questioned.

In practice, however, Porfirio Díaz applied a program that took up the gestures of conciliation that Juárez himself had made upon his triumphant return after the war of French intervention while maintaining the Reform Laws and the spirit of the same. Díaz ended up consolidating a liberal regime, albeit oligarchic, based on an agro-exporter economic model. This model, as much for economic than for political and ideological reasons, sought to impose an order for progress and was supported by an authoritarian government. Although only formally democratic, but enlightened, and influenced by positivism, this government was the scientific ideal of modernity and was based on peace and social order. Politically subdued, the Church nevertheless appeared in this context as a necessary institution for the preservation of the moral and social order. At the same time, however, without domestication, it continued to be an obstacle to progress. It could be said that Díaz tried to achieve both objectives, with some success at least until the end of his last government. Certainly, insofar as his objective was to consolidate peace, from the beginning of his government he promoted the idea that, although the Reform Laws had to be applied, they should not be used as a weapon of persecution against the Church.

Recent investigations in the Secret Archives of the Vatican show, however, that Porfirio Díaz avoided for decades to assume any substantive arrangement with the Holy See.[26] In 1892, for example, the Mexican bishops sent a message to the President, praising the American model of relations, based on religious freedom, to which the general replied clearly marking his idea of the situation and the limits of the action of the Church, much to the chagrin of them and of the pope. He pointed out that: "The country, led by our public men, adopted an entirely civil form of government that dispenses with religion, that considers all denominations equal before the law and that establishes mutual independence between the State and the Church."[27] It added that:

> in order to prevent abuses committed on other occasions, when some ecclesiastical dignitaries became disruptors of public order, the Republic adopted laws and measures to deprive ecclesiastics of those pecuniary riches of which before they had and that they facilitated the interference in political questions foreign to this institution.[28]

The Holy See was not discouraged. In 1896 the pope sent an Apostolic Visitor, Monsignor Nicola Averardi, with the mission of establishing diplomatic ties with the Mexican State; and, if possible, achieving the revocation of the Reform Laws. However, throughout his three years of stay in the country, he did not obtain his objectives. In his private meetings, Díaz pointed out that the political difficulties of the moment prevented him from satisfying the wishes of the Holy See. As Cannelli points out, "the president resorted to sentimental phrases, but devoid of political value, which achieved the objective of arousing an ephemeral illusory effect on the mind of the Vatican prelate."[29] Still, the Apostolic Delegates (representatives of the Holy See before its bishops, but without political representation before the government) tried without luck to advance their positions. In fact, according to the reports of the first Delegate in 1904, General Díaz apparently had not fully appreciated his arrival:

> Don Porfirio avoided any word that might sound like an acknowledgment to the delegate, never mentioned the Pope and reaffirmed the wisdom of the separation between the State and the Church, limiting himself to saying that 'in his mind the separation did not mean opposition and that it would help to the Church, as long as the Laws allow it'.[30]

The balance that can be made of the Díaz regime must therefore be complex and nuanced. Certainly, the general agreed on a policy of conciliation, to promote peace and economic progress. But this never meant, as evidenced by his actions, a surrender of liberal ideals or a revocation of the principles of the Reformation, otherwise sacralized by himself in national public life. Although it relaxed the application of laws regarding tolerance toward male and female religious and convent orders, it never allowed the establishment of diplomatic relations or considered reversing the process of confiscation or nationalization of ecclesiastical property, much less the separation between the State and the Churches or complete freedom of worship. Neither did it favor the public presence of officials in religious ceremonies or religious consecration of public power.

Contrary to the pro-clerical and anti-liberal image that the ideology of the Mexican Revolution created for Díaz, the truth is a larger part of the Catholic clergy considered themselves mistreated by the general and reproached him for his attachment to liberal ideals.

It is clear that the conciliation policy allowed the restructuring of ecclesial power through its social presence more than its political organization. Díaz's tolerance allowed the diffusion of the social doctrine of the Church, the organization of "social journeys," and other religious acts. Many of the regime's critics would come from the conservative sector. After Díaz' fall the members of the National Catholic Party also possessed tragic and questionable roles in the Victoriano Huerta dictatorship. In this sense, one could venture the idea that perhaps Porfirio Díaz, although he remained in power for more than 30 years thanks to positioning himself as a key actor and indispensable character for the maintenance of a conciliatory peace, did not achieve in the long term any of his objectives. Neither did he manage to contain the political reorganization of Catholics in the long term or maintain the support and loyalty of many liberal political groups, who, in the end, felt betrayed and rose up against him.

THE REVOLUTION AGAINST THE CATHOLIC CHURCH

The northern version of the Mexican Revolution had a markedly anticlerical character, a product of both the militant liberal tradition and the reaction to the participation of some members of the Catholic hierarchy and the leadership of the National Catholic Party in the coup d'état against President Francisco I. Madero and the ambiguous role of said social actors during the dictatorship of general Huerta. All this would mark his immediate destiny as well as that of the new Constitution.

The revolutionaries acted as heirs of liberalism, the Constitution of 1857, and the Reform Laws. They assumed the Catholic Church and the Catholic Party were enemies of the revolution, having participated in the fall of Madero and supporting the coup leader, General Huerta. Therefore, the revolutionaries decided to radicalize their positions to eliminate any form of future participation of the clergy in national politics. The diary of debates of the Constituent Congress shows us that there were several currents of thought that converged in this sense. As previously discussed, the first of them thought, to the extent that there had been a way, that the winners of the war had the right to impose their conditions. They would not allow the return of those who were considered counterrevolutionary enemies of the Republic, through democratic instruments.[31] A second current of opinion within the Constituent Congress was influenced by the Enlightenment and positivism ideals and was openly antireligious, insofar as it considered religious beliefs superstitions that should be extirpated, providing the people an outlet by which they could free themselves from ancestral bondage which had them subdued and backward. The third important current in the Constitutional reformers group was formed by the liberal groups who wanted to keep the Church marginalized from public affairs while maintaining the freedom of conscience and religion of the individual. This was the case of the main authors of Article 130 who opposed the prohibition of the sacrament of confession—supported by some—as well as other restrictions that undermined individual freedoms.

There were two characteristics all these currents of opinion had in common. First, those who had fought to restore constitutional order and punish those who betrayed Madero. Second, those who thought that religious beliefs should be a private matter, passing through those who believed it necessary to reach a positivist stage of human development. Both shared a deep anticlericalism and as a consequence, the conviction that it was necessary to limit the capacity for social intervention and the political power of the Catholic Church. This constituent Congress was one formed of triumphant revolutionaries, and members of the Catholic Party or any party with a confessional reference were prevented from participating in it. As a consequence, there was not a single person who defended the positions of the Catholic Church, not for philosophical, religious, historical, or any other reasons.

Thus, the measures imposed in the reformed Constitution of 1917 sought the disappearance of religious power in the new society that it was intended to build; and, anticlericalism, which otherwise had its roots in popular culture, was the prevailing tone in the debates of the Constitution. While many of the prohibitions took up the liberal spirit of the Reform Laws, others went further. In political terms, the most important article was the 130th, due to its recapitulation in its first paragraphs of the essential indications of the Reform Laws as they had been incorporated into the Constitution in 1873.[32] But later several paragraphs were added to limit the political action of the Churches. The main paragraph, in Article 130, was the non-legal recognition of "religious groups called Churches." The legal disappearance of the Churches meant that none of them would have any capacity to defend themselves at courts. The capacity of the federal states to determine the maximum number of ministers of the cults was also added in addition to the obligation that these were Mexican by birth. In the same way, said article established that the ministers of cults could never, "in public or private meetings constituted as a board, nor in acts of worship or religious propaganda, criticize the fundamental laws of the country, of the authorities in particular, or in general of the government." It was added that the ministers of worship would not have the right to an active or passive vote, "nor the right to associate for political purposes."

As if that were not enough, Article 130 stated that for no reason would the decision be revalidated, granted dispensation or determine "any other procedure that has the purpose of giving validity in official courses, to studies carried out in establishments destined for the professional education of ministers of the cults." It was also stated that "periodical publications of a confessional nature, whether due to their program, their title or simply due to their ordinary tendencies, will not be able to comment on national political issues or report on acts of the country's authorities, or individuals, who are directly related to the functioning of public institutions." Likewise, it was strictly forbidden "the formation of all kinds of political groups whose title has any word or any indication that relates it to any religious confession." Nor could political meetings be held in temples.[33]

These and other measures were accompanied by the prohibition for the Churches to possess property, in Article 27, establishing that "religious associations so called churches, whatever their creed, may in no case have the capacity to acquire, possess or administer real estate, nor capital taxes on them." The prohibition on worship outside the temples was also added to Article 24, which, moreover, guaranteed individuals "the freedom to profess the religious belief that pleases them the most and to practice the ceremonies, devotions or acts of the respective cult, in the temples or in their private home, as long as they do not constitute a crime or misdemeanor punishable by law."[34] A separate chapter focused on the establishment of public, secular, and free education, which in Article 3 stated:

> Teaching is free; but that given in official educational establishments will be secular, as well as in primary, elementary and higher education that is imparted in private establishments. No religious corporation, nor minister of any cult, may establish or direct schools of primary instruction. Private elementary schools can only be established subject to official surveillance. Primary education will be given free of charge in official establishments.[35]

This article has undergone several changes. In the 1930s, education went from being secular to socialist and secular again in the following decade. Current Article 3 of the Constitution states that:

> guaranteed by Article 24 freedom of belief, such education shall be secular and, therefore, will remain entirely separate from any religious doctrine; The criteria that will guide this education will be based on the results of scientific

progress, will fight against ignorance and its effects, servitude, fanaticism and prejudice.[36]

In any case, the vast majority of the 1917 reforms were anticlerical rather than antireligious, and their goal was to eliminate the participation of the Catholic Church in the socio-political sphere. It cannot be denied that the revolutionary secularism, much more authoritarian than the liberal, tried to overcome the simple separation and sought the definitive elimination of the Catholic Church as a political and social actor. Therefore, it was not by chance that the hierarchy of the Catholic Church reacted with an unusual firmness and intransigence to the anticlerical measures, opposing the new Constitution and that in subsequent years the positions of radical revolutionaries, as well as Catholic fundamentalists have led to political and armed confrontations, such as the Cristero War (1926–1929). An episode that put to the test not only the relations of the State with the Church, but also those of the hierarchy with their own parishioners, who felt betrayed by the 1929 "arrangements" that ended hostilities.[37]

POST-REVOLUTION AND MODUS VIVENDI

There is no space here to detail the complex events that followed the promulgation of the 1917 Constitution as well as the two decades after. It is worth remembering, however, that, around 1938 and in the following decades, after an implicit agreement (called modus vivendi), based on certain common elements (nationalism, search for social justice, radical antisocialism), what prevailed was a State that preserved the public space for itself, especially in the socio-political field (unions, parties, mass organizations), but allowed the Church greater freedom in the educational field, under various forms of tolerance and dissimulation. Curiously, this agreement, *entente cordiale* or *modus vivendi*, initially established by President Lázaro Cárdenas and the main Catholic leaders in Mexico, closely resembled the agreement Díaz had established with the Church during his successive governments. And in the same way, after several decades, the Catholic Church would have to recompose itself to once again seek a role in the public life of the nation.[38] Thus, as the State of the Mexican Revolution weakened and lost the bases of legitimacy that had given rise to it, the revolutionary governments and later the Institutional Revolutionary Party found it necessary to turn to other sources of legitimacy to stay in power. This, together with other internal phenomena of the Catholic Church, led, among other issues, to a growing public presence of Catholic hierarchs and ministers of worship.

Six decades after the signing of the Constitution, despite its authoritarian features, the Churches, especially the catholic, had substantially ceased to act as political actors. The limitations on the ministers of worship led to a Mexicanization of the clergy and greater participation of Catholic laity in public life, who did not always express the interests and vision of the hierarchy. The health of the various Catholic institutions became apparent upon the pope's visit to Mexico in 1979. In any case, by the late 1980s it was clear the constitutional framework had to adapt to the new perspectives of the contemporary rule of law with particular emphasis on human rights and civil and religious freedoms. Moreover, many of the prohibitions and restrictions established by the 1917 Constituents were not obeyed or tolerated, generating corruption and governmental hypocrisy.

The 1992 Reforms and Populism

It is in this context of decay of the former revolutionary spirit that President Carlos Salinas de Gortari, otherwise questioned for having come to power in highly contested elections and under the shadow of fraud, decided to call for a renewal of the State's public policy in relation to various sectors of society, including the Church. Three years after that convocation, in December 1991, Congress approved a series of reforms to the Constitution regarding religions, ultimately eliminating the additions made in 1917 and returned to the liberal spirit of the nineteenth century.

In reality, the core of the reforms was aimed at recognizing the rights of religious institutions rather than those of believers which in principle had been respected. In other words, the reforms recognized the rights of believers to act, not only as individuals, but also as participants within a larger and organized institution. The Constitution of 1857 and the Reform Laws, incorporated into the Constitution in 1873, had established, precisely within a liberal spirit, freedom of belief and worship, a framework of separation and supremacy of the State over corporations, including the Churches. What the 1917 Constitution had imposed, in the midst of the explicable anticlerical revolutionary radicalism, was the non-legal recognition of the Churches. What the 1992 reforms essentially established was the right of believers to act collectively and in an organized manner. Thus, the new Article 3 allows, for example, the ownership and administration of schools by religious organizations. Article 5 eliminated the prohibition of religious vows and monastic orders, the 24th allows religious acts of public worship to be celebrated "in an extraordinary way" outside the temples, the 27th allows religious associations to acquire, possess or administer "exclusively, the goods that are indispensable for their purpose," and the 130th law restores to the Churches and religious groups their legal personality as religious associations "once they obtain their corresponding registration." However, the 130th law maintains restrictions on the political activities of the ministers of worship and the existence of political parties with confessional references.[39] In sum, the reforms recognize more than anything else the collective, organized, and institutionalized actions of believers. The beneficiaries of these are therefore organized believers, religious institutions, and, to that extent, religious leaderships.

The recognition of legal personality to religious groups by establishing legal rights and obligations for them also modified the type of relationship that Churches and other types of religious groups or communities establish with the State. In this sense, in addition to helping achieve greater transparency in the dealings between governors and governed, the reforms contributed greater visibility to numerous minority Churches and religious groups. With the formal registration as "religious associations," the reforms were able to achieve a public presence they were formerly denied, favoring before only the majority Church due to its social and public presence. Therefore, by granting the reforms legal recognition, the main beneficiaries of the reforms were the minority Churches and marginal religious groups. Around ten thousand religious associations have so far registered before the Interior Ministry in the 30 years since the 1992 reform. In fact, although it was not the original intention when then-President Salinas launched the idea of modernizing relations with "the" Church, as the public debate on the matter developed, it became clear that the reforms could not be exclusively designed for "a" Church but had to consider the wide and growing range of religious preferences of Mexicans. In other words, the reforms should and eventually did consider the growing religious plurality in the country and the need to strengthen a secular state respectful of the diversity of beliefs and impartial in its dealings with the various religious organizations.

The 1992 reforms to the anticlerical articles of the Constitution, undoubtedly important in a framework of growing recognition of freedoms and human rights, would establish the return of the Churches (now in plural) to the public space within a still restrictive legal framework. And although the Constitution would reiterate "the historical principle of separation between the State and the Churches" and the original liberal spirit would be maintained in the Magna Carta, the truth is that, for various reasons, the rules of the game had changed. In other words, the reforms opened new challenges for public management. In the framework of an increasingly democratic society and a State that is more attentive to the existence of different perspectives on the common interest, the Churches, and particularly the Catholic Church, would consider that it was the moment to exert pressure to influence the definition of the laws and public policies of the nation.

The above trend is accentuated with the arrival in power of ideologically conservative governments between 2000 and 2012. The return to power of the Institutional Revolutionary Party in 2012, moreover, didn't mean the return to the previous situation. Rather, ideologically gelatinous governments with populist tendencies would consolidate, producing very ambiguous policies regarding the religious question. As is often the case in populist governments, politicians of various tendencies appealed to religious symbols to legitimize their actions. This made the public actions of religious institutions more complex, as populist politicians tend not only to incorporate elements of popular religiosity (even esoteric or New Age) in his speeches and programs, but also end up trying to replace or supplant religious social organizations. All of this often leads to situations of tension between populist governments and established religions. At the same time, the secularization process itself entails a departure from religious institutions in favor of personal solutions, where beliefs are built and rebuilt many times based on different, if not openly contradictory, traditions. All this leads to a modern paradox from which Mexico cannot escape: the relativization of the role of religious institutions, at the same time, the religious factor reappears and is revalued, but is also used and exploited by political actors. In this sense, the current relations between the State and the Churches diminish in importance, while the nexus between religion and politics acquires new dimensions.

Notes

1. INEGI (National Institute of Statistics and Geography), Press release, number 24/21, January 25, 2021, p. 7. https://www.inegi.org.mx/contenidos/saladeprensa/boletines/2021/EstSociodemo/ResultCenso2020_Nal.pdf.

2. Marta Eugenia García Ugarte (Coordinator), *Catholic Illustration; Episcopal and Episcopate Ministry in Mexico (1758–1829)* Volume I Central Region (Mexico: UNAM, Instituto de Investigaciones Sociales, 2018), p. 12.

3. The Royal Patronage is the legal institution that most impacted the colonial period and the first half of the nineteenth century in Mexico. However, its impact has been little noted. By the Patronage, established by subsequent bulls of the popes, the Holy See admitted the right of the kings to found Churches, to appoint bishops and clergy, helping themselves to sustain them with the tithes. In other words, the Patronage recognized in fact the authority of the kings of Spain to exercise jurisdiction in all matters related to ecclesiastical government in the Indies. John Lloyd Mecham. *Church and State in Latin America; A History of Politico-Ecclesiastical Relations* (Chapel Hill: The University of North Carolina Press, 1934), p. 2.

4. For the case of Mexico, see Oscar Mazín and Francisco Morales, "The Church in New Spain: The years of consolidation," *Great Illustrated History of Mexico*, volume II New Spain from 1521 to 1570 (Mexico: Planeta De Agostini- Conaculta -INAH, 2002), pp. 381–400.

5. John Lloyd Mecham, *op. cit.*, p. 14.

6. Article 3 of the *Federal Constitution of the United Mexican States*, established that "the religion of the Mexican nation is and will be perpetually the Catholic, Apostolic, Roman. The nation protects it by wise and just laws, and prohibits the exercise of any other." See http://www.diputados. gob.mx/biblioteca/bibdig/const_mex/const_1824.pdf.

7. Article XII expressly established that among the powers of the Congress was that of: "Give instructions to celebrate concordats with the apostolic chair, approve them for ratification, and arrange the exercise of patronage throughout the federation." *Federal Constitution of the United Mexican States*, 1824.

8. José María Luis Mora, *Single works*, Volume first. (Paris: Librería de Rosa, 1837, p. XCI. Cited by Jesús Reyes Heroles, *Mexican liberalism*, volume III (Mexico, DF: Fondo de Cultura Económica, 1988), p. 104.

9. Jesús Reyes Heroles, *Mexican liberalism*, volume III (Mexico, DF: Fondo de Cultura Económica, 1988), pp. 69–245.

10. See, for example, the chapter of Brian Connaughton, "The Enemy Within: Independent Catholics and Liberalism in Mexico, 1821–1860," in Jaime E. Rodriguez O. (Editor) The Divine Charter; Constitutionalism and Liberalism in Nineteenth-Century Mexico (Lanham, Boulder, New York, Toronto, Oxford: Rowman & Littlefield Publishers Inc., 2005). Regarding Brazil and other South American countries, see the book by John L. Mecham, *op.cit.*

11. José María Luis Mora, *Mexico and its revolutions*, volume I, pp. 341–342.
12. Consult the full text at: http://www.biblioteca.tv/artman2/publish/1855_150/Ley_Ju_rez.shtml.
13. Benito Juárez, "Communicates to Santacilia the issuance of the first decrees of the Reform Laws," July 12, 1859. *Documents, speeches and correspondence*. Jorge L. Tamayo, selection and notes-Héctor Cuauhtémoc Hernández Silva, digital publishing coordinator (Mexico, DF: Metropolitan Autonomous University-Azcapotzalco/Government of the Federal District, 2006), Document 4, p. 44.
14. "The Law of confiscation of the rustic and urban estates of the civil and religious corporations of Mexico" was issued on June 25, 1856, by President Ignacio Comonfort.
15. Miguel Lerdo de Tejada, Minister of Finance and Public Credit, "Circular addressed to the governors," June 28, 1856, in "150 years of struggle for a secular state." Institutional Revolutionary Party. Organizing Commission of the Commemorations of the Bicentennial of the Start of the Insurgency, the Sesquicentennial of the Reform Laws and the Centennial of the Mexican Revolution (México, DF: 2009), p. 9.
16. The "Law on parochial rights and grants" of April 11, 1857, can be found at: http://www.memoriapoliticademexico.org/Textos/3Reforma/1857LLI.html.
17. "Justification of the Reform Laws; The constitutional government of the nation," July 7, 1859, in *Benito Juárez; Documents, speeches and correspondence*. Jorge L. Tamayo, selection and notes-Héctor Cuauhtémoc Hernández Silva, digital publishing coordinator (Mexico, DF: Universidad Autónoma Metropolitana-Azcapotzalco/Gobierno del Distrito Federal, 2006), volume II, document 1, pp. 12–29.
18. http://memoriapoliticademexico.org/Efemerides/9/25091873.html.
19. With the exception of September 16 and New Year's Day, it included almost exclusively religious dates: Sundays, Thursday and Friday of the Semana Mayor, Corpus Christi Thursday, November 1 and 2, November 12, and December 24. "Decree of the government in which it is declared which days should be taken as holidays and prohibits official attendance at Church functions," August 11, 1859, in *Benito Juárez; Documents, speeches and correspondence*. Jorge L. Tamayo, selection and notes-Héctor Cuauhtémoc Hernández Silva, digital publishing coordinator (Mexico, DF: Universidad Autónoma Metropolitana-Azcapotzalco/Gobierno del Distrito Federal, 2006), volume II, document 11.
20. Ibid.
21. "Law on Freedom of Worship," in *Benito Juárez; Documents, speeches and correspondence*. Jorge L. Tamayo, selection and notes-Héctor Cuauhtémoc

Hernández Silva, digital publishing coordinator (Mexico, DF: Universidad Autónoma Metropolitana-Azcapotzalco/Gobierno del Distrito Federal, 2006), volume III, document 48, pp. 121–127.

22. Ibid.

23. http://memoriapoliticademexico.org/Efemerides/9/25091873.html.

24. Pius IX, Encyclical "Quanta Cura" and "Syllabus", in *Pontifical Encyclicals. Complete collection from 1832 to 1958*, 2nd. Corrected and enlarged edition, volume I (Buenos Aires: Editorial Guadalupe, 1958), pp. 155–168.

25. http://senado2010.gob.mx/docs/cuadernos/documentos Reforma/b17-documentosReforma.pdf.

26. Riccardo Cannelli, *Nazione cattolica e Stato laico; The political-religious conflict in Messico dall'indepe nden za alla rivoluzione: 1821–1914*, (Milano: Guerinit e associati, 2002. Translated and published in Mexico as a *Catholic nation and a secular state*, by the National Institute of Historical Studies of the revolutions of Mexico (Mexico City: Ministry of Education, 2012). Henceforth the Spanish version will be cited.

27. *Ibidem*, p. 93.

28. Ibid.

29. Averardi to Rampolla del Tindaro, 3/10/1899. ASS, AAEESS MESSICO, facs. 71 cited by Cannelli, *Ibidem*, pp. 142–143.

30. Serafini to Merry del Val, 3/26/1904, ASV, ANM, fasc.11. Cited by Cannelli, *Ibidem*, p, 200.

31. Constituent Congress 1916–1917, *Diario de debates* (Mexico, DF: National Institute of Historical Studies of the Mexican Revolution, 1960), 2 vols.

32. The prohibition for the establishment of monastic orders was reiterated in Article 5.

33. The original text of the Political Constitution of the United Mexican States of 1917 can be found at: http://www.juridicas.unam.mx/infjur/leg/conshist/pdf/1917.pdf.

34. Ibid.

35. Ibid.

36. http://www.diputados.gob.mx/LeyesBiblio/pdf/1.pdf.

37. To understand the Cristero war it is essential to read the three volumes of Jean Meyer, *La Cristiada* (México: Siglo XXI Editores, 1973).

38. There is of course a huge bibliography on state-church relations in the post-revolutionary Mexican period. On the basis of modus vivendi, let me suggest reading the first chapters of my book, *History of the Catholic Church in Mexico; 1929–1982* (Mexico, DF: Fondo de Cultura Económica/El Colegio Mexiquense, 1992).

39. There is an abundant bibliography on the 1992 reforms. See for example: Manuel Canto Chac and Raquel Pastor Escobar, *Has God returned to Mexico? The transformation of the Church-State relations*, UAM-Xochimilco, Mexico, 1997 and González Fernández, José Antonio, Ruiz Massieu, José Francisco and Soberanes Fernández, José Luís, *Mexican ecclesiastical law*, UNAM, Editorial Porrúa SA, 2nd Edition, Mexico, 1993.

CHAPTER 30

State, Law, and Religion in Brazil: The Supreme Federal Court Case-Law

Rodrigo Vitorino Souza Alves

The objective of this chapter is to present to the interested public the main topics and cases discussed in the recent case-law of the Brazilian Supreme Federal Court—STF (since 2000)[1]. Before presenting the cases, the main relevant constitutional rules are pointed out, in the light of which cases were generally appreciated:

> Article 5. Everyone is equal before the law, with no distinction whatsoever, guaranteeing to Brazilians and foreigners residing in the Country the inviolability of the rights to life, liberty, equality, security, and property, on the following terms:
> (…)
> VI. freedom of conscience and belief is inviolable, assuring free exercise of religious beliefs and guaranteeing, as set forth in law, protection of places of worship and their rites;
> VII. providing religious assistance at civilian and military establishments for collective confinement is assured, as provided by law;

R. V. S. Alves (✉)
The Brazilian Center of Studies in Law and Religion, Federal University of Uberlândia, Uberlândia, Brazil
e-mail: rodrigo@direitoereligiao.org

S. Holzer (ed.), *The Palgrave Handbook of Religion and State Volume II*, https://doi.org/10.1007/978-3-031-35609-4_30

VIII. no one shall be deprived of any rights because of religious beliefs or philosophical or political convictions, unless invoked in order to be exempted from a legal obligation imposed upon all by one refusing to perform an alternative service established by law;

Article 19. The Union, States, Federal District and Counties are forbidden to:

I. establish religions or churches, subsidize them, hinder their functioning, or maintain dependent relations or alliances with them or their representatives, with the exception of collaboration in the public interest, as provided by law;

Article 150, VI, b. Without prejudice to other guarantees assured the taxpayer, the Union, States, Federal District and Counties are prohibited from: (…) levying taxes on: (…) temples of any religion;

Article 210. §1. Religious education shall be an optional course during normal school hours in public elementary schools.

Article 226. §2. Religious marriage has civil effects, as provided by law.

Article 213. Public funds shall be allocated to public schools, and may be directed to community, religious and philanthropic schools, as defined by law, that: I. prove that they are non-profit and apply their surplus funds in education; II. ensure that their patrimony will be transferred to another community, philanthropic or religious school, or to the Government, in the event they cease their activities.

"UNDER GOD'S PROTECTION": THE INVOCATION OF DIVINITY IN THE CONSTITUTIONAL PREAMBLE

The Direct Action of Unconstitutionality ADI 2076/2002 was presented by the Liberal Social Party, PSL—through which it sought to see recognized offense to the Preamble of the Federal Constitution by the fact that the Constitution of one of the Brazilian States, Acre, omit the expression "under God's protection" from its text.

The Preamble to the Federal Constitution is thus expressed:

We, the representatives of the Brazilian people, gathered in a Constituent National Assembly to establish a democratic state, aimed at ensuring the exercise of social and individual rights, freedom, security, welfare, development, equality and justice as supreme values of a fraternal, pluralistic and unprejudiced society, founded on social harmony and committed, in the internal and international order, with the peaceful settlement of disputes, we promulgate, under God's protection, the following CONSTITUTION OF THE FEDERATIVE REPUBLIC OF BRAZIL.

In turn, it was included in the Preamble of the Constitution of Acre:

Preamble
    The Constituent State Assembly, using the powers that were granted by the Federal Constitution, obeying the democratic ideary, with the thought toward the people and inspired by the heroes of the Acreana Revolution, enacts the following Constitution of the State of Acre.

For the PSL, the discrepancy between the two texts had legal relevance. The preamble would be a normative act constituting a basic supreme principle, with programmatic content and mandatory absorption by States, integrating the constitutional text and being endowed with legal value. In this sense, the omission of the invocation "we promulgate under the protection of God" exclusively in the Preamble of the Constitution of the state of Acre, when compared to the other Brazilian state constitutions, would have violated the Federal Constitution and, additionally, by omitting itself from including such expression, the Constituent State Assembly would have deprived Acre's citizens of being "under God's protection."

In analyzing the case in substance, the STF considered the different doctrinal positions regarding the nature of the constitutional preambles, which can be synthesized in three strands: the positions which consider the preamble to be a textual element without any normative force or obligation and are legally irrelevant, outside the field of law and in the field of policy; the second understandings advocating the full legal effectiveness of the preamble, which would be at the same normative level as the constitutional norms articulated in the form of articles; and the third, intermediate perspective, which considers that there is no normative force in the preamble (it does not create rights or duties), while bearing characteristics that can indirectly interfere in the interpretation and application of the constitutional text—indicating values and aspirations that have informed the adoption of the constitutional text and that can contribute to its interpretation.

Although the STF subsequently appears to have been more inclined to the third strand (see, for example, the opinion of the Justice Rapporteur Cármen Lucia in the Direct Action of Unconstitutionality—ADI 2649/2008), in the case of the Constitution of Acre, the opinion of the Justice Rapporteur Carlos Velloso, followed by the other Justices of the Court participating in the trial, the Court considered that the Preamble is devoid of normative force, being outside the field of law, but in the field of politics, so that there is no mandatory reproduction of its content.

In particular, regarding the expression "under the protection of God," the Justice Rapporteur stressed that the invocation reflected the deist and religious sentiment, which is not inscribed in the Constitution, and that the Brazilian State is secular, enshrining in the Constitution freedom of conscience and belief, and the guarantee that no one will be deprived of rights because of religious belief or philosophical or political conviction. The Constitution protects all, deists, agnostics, or atheists.

In this sense, there would be no unconstitutionality concerning the omission of the expression "under God's protection" by the Acre legislative Assembly, thus remaining defined by the STF:

> Constitutional. Constitution: Central Standards. Constitution of Acre. I.— Central rules of the Federal Constitution: These rules are of compulsory reproduction in the Constitution of the Member State, even because, reproduced or not, they will deal with local order. Claims 370-MT and 383-SP (RTJ 147/404). II.—Preamble to the Constitution: It is not a central rule. Invocation of God's protection: This is not a mandatory reproduction standard in the state constitution, with no normative force. III.—Direct Action of Unconstitutionality deemed unfounded. (ADI 2076, 2002, p. 218)

Although the STF did not, in the end, find any unconstitutionality in this omission, the Acre legislative Assembly promulgated, even before the end of the judgment of the action by the STF, the Constitutional Amendment no. 19/2000, redrafting the Preamble, which now contains the expression "under God's protection."

TAX IMMUNITY

The Federal Constitution provides that the Union, the States, the Federal District, and the Municipalities may institute different types of taxes and fees (Article 145). However, the same Constitution prohibits such taxes from being imposed on "temples of any religion" (Article 150, VI, b), which is known as tax immunity. Different questions concerning the interpretation and application of this immunity have been brought to the STF.

The first involves the extent of immunity, especially if such immunity applies to all the property of a religious institution or strictly to a "temple." In the Extraordinary Appeal—RE 325822/2002, the Diocesan

Miter of Jales sought to recognize the application of immunity to all its assets, including properties given in rent, residences of priests and religious people, pastoral or human-religious formation centers, meeting and administration sites, among others.

For Justice Gilmar Mendes, writer of the STF ruling, tax immunity is not restricted to spaces specifically dedicated to the celebration of religious worship. In the light of paragraph 4 of Article 150 of the Federal Constitution, the immunity must comprise "property, income, and services" that are associated with the essential purposes of religious entities, and that the public authorities are prohibited from imposing taxes in such cases.

Justice Gilmar Mendes also points out that the tax immunity of religious institutions is equivalent to the tax immunity granted to non-profit institutions for education and social assistance, political parties and workers' unions (Article 150, VI, "c" of the Federal Constitution). In this respect, STF had already analyzed different situations (referred to by the Justice Rapporteur Ilmar Galvao), concluding by the recognition of the tax immunity, among which are: tax immunity of the properties that such institutions give in rent to third parties, provided that the rent received is applied for its institutional purposes (Extraordinary Appeal—RE 237718/2001), the extension of immunity to rented properties (Extraordinary Appeal—RE 257700/2000), to property used as the office and residence of members of the entity (Extraordinary Appeal—RE 221395/2000), on the income obtained from the price charged in the parking of vehicles (Extraordinary Appeal—RE 144900/1997) or the provision of services (Instrument Appeal—AI 155822/1995).

In a majority decision, Justice Rapporteur Ilmar Galvao's opinion defeated, the STF, in plenary session, dismissed the appeal, affirming the extension of tax immunity, in the following terms:

> Extraordinary Appeal. 2. Tax immunity of temples of any religion. Prohibition of creating taxes for assets, income and services related to the essential purposes of the entities. Article 150, VI, "b" and § 4 of the Constitution. 3. Religious institution. IPTU on its properties that are rented. 4. The immunity provided for in Article 150, VI, "b", CF, should cover not only buildings intended for worship, but also property, income and services "related to the essential purposes of the entities mentioned therein". 5. The § 4 of the constitutional article serves as an interpretative vector of paragraphs "b" and "c" of Section VI of Section 150 of the Federal

Constitution. Equivalence between the hypotheses of the points referred to. 6. Extraordinary Appeal granted. (RE 325822, 2002, p. 246)

It is also important to note that later, the STF appreciated other related cases, in order to conclude, in particular, that just because the property is vacant does not mean noncompliance with the essential purposes of the religious entity, and it does not authorize the breach of immunity (Regimental Review in the Extraordinary Appeal—AgR ARE 658080/2011) and that it is up to the public authorities, and not to the religious institution, to demonstrate possible deviation of religious purpose in the use of property for the removal of immunity (Regimental Appeal in the Extraordinary Appeal—AgR ARE 800395/2014). See also, in a similar direction: Regimental Review in the Instrument Review—AgR AI 690712/2009 and 389,602/2005.

In another case, the Extraordinary Appeal—RE 578562/2008, the Society of the Church of Saint George and the British Cemetery sought to apply the tax immunity constitutional clause, which protects "temples of any religion" (Article 150, VI, b of the Federal Constitution), to the British Cemetery of the English Colony. Although the Church had received the benefit of tax immunity, the City of Salvador required the payment of the Urban Land and Territorial Tax—IPTU—in relation to the Cemetery, which had been confirmed by the judgment of first instance. Subsequently, the tax collection was authorized by the Court of Justice of the State of Bahia, for not considering that the Cemetery was equivalent to a temple.

In its appeal, the Anglican Society informs the Supreme Federal Court that since the nineteenth century, a chapel for worship in accordance with the Anglican religion and a Cemetery (the "British Cemetery") with hundreds of tombs, being recognized by the State of Bahia as historic and cultural heritage in 1993. The applicant, a philanthropic and non-profit organization, also clarifies that all these facilities are used to promote worship within the Anglican religion, including in the form of funeral religious ceremonies, especially for British citizens.

For Justice Rapporteur Eros Grau, it is necessary to differentiate a Cemetery that is commercially exploited by companies dedicated to this business from a Cemetery that is associated with a religious entity. Even though there may be some religious ceremony, it is not equivalent to a Cemetery that is an extension of a religious entity. In this case, the British Cemetery is an extension of the chapel for worship, according to the

Anglican religion, situated on the same property. Referring to the Extraordinary Appeal—RE 325822/2002, he argued that the tax immunity of religious temples must be interpreted widely, so that the various religious confessions can be covered, being applied not only to their buildings but also to property, income, and services related to the essential purposes of religious entities, in the light of paragraph 4 of Article 150 of the Federal Constitution. Furthermore, he states that the guarantee of tax immunity must be understood based on the interpretation of the entire text of the Constitution and is therefore an unfolding of the constitutional protection of religious freedom, which includes protection of places of worship and their liturgies (Article 5, VI), the safeguard against any embarrassment to its operation (Article 19, I).

By unanimous decision and in accordance with the opinion of the Rapporteur Justice, the STF dismissed the appeal by recognizing that the cemeteries constituting extensions of religious entities are also covered by the protection provided for in Article 150 of the Federal Constitution, the incidence of the tax on its immovable property is impossible.

The third case concerns the Freemasonry claim, in particular the Grande Oriente do Rio Grande do Sul, to be recognized as a religious institution for the purpose of being granted tax immunity, which was brought to STF by means of the Extraordinary Appeal—RE 562351/2012.

In his opinion, the Justice Rapporteur Ricardo Lewandowski fundamentally assessed whether the constitutional reference to "temples of any religion" reaches Freemasonry. For the Justice, it is significant that tax immunity is a development both from the constitutional protection of religious freedom, which includes the free exercise of religious worship, and from the separation between state and religion, because its purpose delimits its field of application, restricted only to religious institutions.

One of the main grounds for the decision was the nature of the Masonic activities carried out by the Grande Loja Maçônica do Estado do Rio Grande do Sul, as described by the entity in its own documents, in which it is emphatically affirmed that Masonry is not a religion, but a private association. By a majority of votes and in accordance with the opinion of the Justice Rapporteur, the STF denies the appeal, not recognizing the extension of tax immunity to Masonry, thus summarizing the judgment:

Constitutional. Extraordinary Appeal. Tax immunity Art. 150, VI, C, from the Federal Charter. Need for review of facts and evidence. Súmula 279 of the STF. Art. 150, VI, B, of the Constitution of the Republic. Scope of the term "temples of any religion." Freemasonry. Not recognized. Extraordinary Appeal known in part and, in what is known, devoid. (RE 562351, 2012, p. 1)

THE TEACHING OF RELIGION IN PUBLIC SCHOOLS

In establishing the fundamental rules for the exercise of the right to education and for the provision of education services, the Federal Constitution defines in Article 210(1) that "religious education, of optional registration, will be a course offered in normal school hours." However, since the promulgation of the Constitution in 1988, the nature of religious education has become a debated topic, especially if public schools could adopt confessional, interfaith, or non-confessional religious teaching models.

Originally, the Law of National Education Guidelines and Bases—LDB (Law no. 9394/1996) expressly provided for the possibility that religious or interfaith education, with the following characteristics, would be offered in public schools:

> Article 33. Religious education, of optional registration, shall be a course offered in the normal hours of public schools of fundamental education, free of charge to public treasury, according to the preferences expressed by the students or their guardians, with one of the following natures:
>
> I—denominational, according to the religious option of the student or his/her parents or tutors, offered by religious teachers or mentors prepared and accredited by their respective churches or religious entities; or
>
> II—interfaith, resulting from agreement between the various religious entities, which will be responsible for the preparation of the respective curriculum.

In 1997, however, this legislation was amended by Law no. 9475/1997, abolishing those categories and granting education systems autonomy to regulate the procedures for defining the content of religious education, in the following terms:

> Article 33. Religious education, of optional registration, is an integral part of the basic formation of the citizen and constitutes a course of the normal hours of public schools of fundamental education, ensuring respect for the religious cultural diversity of Brazil, forbidden any forms of proselytism.

§1 Education systems shall regulate the procedures for the definition of the content of religious education and shall establish the norms for the qualification and admission of teachers.

§2 The education systems will listen to the civil entity, made up of the different religious denominations, for the definition of the content of religious education.

With the new wording, the nature of religious teaching was unclear, and each education system continued to define the mode of teaching, whether confessional/denominational, interfaith, or non-confessional/non-denominational, although it shall always be offered as an elective course (student's constitutional right to opt-out).

A new legislative development took place in 2010, when the Agreement between the Government of the Federative Republic of Brazil and the Holy See on the Legal Status of the Catholic Church in Brazil was signed, then approved by legislative Decree no. 698/2009 and promulgated by Decree no. 7107/2010. In this instrument, it was provided that:

Article 11. The Federative Republic of Brazil, in compliance with the right to religious freedom, cultural diversity and religious plurality of the country, respects the importance of religious education in view of the integral formation of the person.

§1. Religious education, Catholic and of other religious denominations, of optional registration, is a course offered in to the normal hours of public schools of fundamental education, ensuring respect for the religious cultural diversity of Brazil, in accordance with the Constitution and the other laws in force, without any form of discrimination.

This normative provision rekindled the debates on religious education in public schools, giving occasion to at least two lawsuits before the STF.

In the first case, the Direct Action of Unconstitutionality—ADI 4439/2017 was proposed by the Federal Prosecutor General's Office, having as its object Article 33, caput and paragraphs 1 and 2 of Law no. 9392/96 and paragraph 1 of Article 11 of the Agreement between Brazil and the Holy See, especially the provision that religious education will be "Catholic and of other religious denominations." For the Office of the General Prosecutor, these arrangements, analyzed jointly, would allow denominational religious education to be taught in public schools, in violation of the state secularity. Therefore, it sought that the two provisions be interpreted in accordance with the Federal Constitution, so that only the offer of religious education in the non-denominational fashion would be allowed, thus ruling out the possibility of adopting denominational and interfaith models of religious education, with a ban on the admission of teachers as representatives of religious confessions.

Faced with the question, and after hearing the Presidency of the Republic, the Chamber of Deputies, the Federal Senate, the Federal Attorney General, all favorable to the possibility of religious teaching, as well as after a public hearing with representatives from various sectors and social groups (in which most of the groups represented expressed their favor for non-denominational religious education), the Plenary of the STF, in a tight decision of 6 votes to 5, denied the request, affirming the constitutionality of religious education as an optional course of the normal hours of public schools of fundamental education, a decision thus synthesized:

> Religious education in public schools. Denominational content and optional registration. Respect for the secularity of the state/religious freedom. Equal access and equal treatment to all religious denominations. Compliance with article 210, §1, of the constitutional text. Constitutionality of article 33, caput and §§1 and 2, of the Law of National Education Guidelines and Bases, and the Legal Status of the Catholic Church in Brazil promulgated by Decree 7107/2010. Direct Action deemed unfounded. (ADI 4439, 2017, pp. 2–3)

On the grounds for the decision, in a judgment drawn up by Justice Alexandre de Moraes, since Justice Rapporteur Roberto Barroso's opinion was not followed by the majority of the Court, the STF pointed out that the relationship between the State and religions is one of the most important structural themes of the State, the broad religious freedom, which can be perceived in two dimensions, has been ensured throughout the Brazilian republican tradition: The protection of individuals and religious confessions in the face of state interventions or commandments, and the guarantee of the secularity of the State, so that it is free from any religious dogma or principle when defining its activities.

Considering that religious education in public schools of fundamental education is optional to students' participation, the STF considered that the secularity of the State and individual religious freedom are respected even in the face of religious education. Moreover, he stressed that religious freedom is preserved by ensuring that students will not be subjected to any religious education artificially created by public authorities, with the content defined by the State, also prohibiting the favoring of some religious interpretation over others and respecting agnostic and atheistic perspectives.

The second action, the Regimental Review in the Extraordinary Appeal—AG.Reg.RE 1268862/2021, was brought by the Attorney General of the State of Rio de Janeiro, in order to recognize the unconstitutionality of the Rio de Janeiro State Law no. 3280/1999, by providing that the Bible study should integrate religious education, of optional enrollment, into public schools within the state of Rio de Janeiro.

In the judgment of the Appeal, Justice Ricardo Lewandowski reiterated the decision he had taken a few months earlier, when he rejected the Extraordinary Appeal. Referring expressly to the precedent of ADI 4439/2017, to state that denominational or interfaith religious education in public schools is supported by the Constitution, does not violate the duty of state neutrality, and contributes to the construction of a culture of peace and tolerance, as well as to an environment of respect for democratic pluralism and religious freedom. He also points out that ensuring a space to provide the teaching of majority religions in a particular society is not incompatible with the purpose of public education.

THE OBLIGATION TO MAKE BIBLE COPIES AVAILABLE IN SCHOOLS AND LIBRARIES

The Extraordinary Appeal with Review Effect—ARE 1014615/2017 discussed the decision of the Rio de Janeiro Court of Justice, which saw State Law no. 5998/2011 as unconstitutional, by violating the principle of state secularity through the determination to make the Bible available in libraries located in the State of Rio de Janeiro. In the case, by individual decision, the Justice Rapporteur Celso de Melo dismissed the Extraordinary Appeal because he considered that the appeal would be in conflict with the understanding adopted by the STF.

As for the reasoning, both the Court of Justice and the Justice Rapporteur point to two violations arising from the legislation under question: Firstly, a violation in the proposal, since they consider that the legislative Assembly of the State of Rio de Janeiro would have extrapolated its powers, invading the private competence of the Head of the State Executive to define the assignment of state agencies, in which the state's public libraries are inserted, also invading competences of other federal entities when establishing requirements also to federal and municipal libraries, it also encroached on the Union's competence to legislate on civil law by demanding from private libraries compliance with that obligation; secondly, there would be a material violation, by breaching the secularity of the State, which would require separation between political and religious powers.

In this regard, Justice Celso de Melo maintains that the secularity of the State, as a fundamental principle of the Brazilian constitutional order, recognizes to all people the freedom of religious belief (as a projection of freedom of conscience) and the freedom to have or not have any religious faith, it ensures absolute equality of citizens in matters of belief, guarantees full freedom of conscience and worship, protects freedom of religious organizations, demands institutional separation between the State and the Church, differentiates the specific areas or domains of religion and civil power, prohibits the State from exercising its functions based on theological principles or religious reasons, requires the State not to have any denominational interests, and prevents fundamentalist groups from taking ownership of the state apparatus and imposing on other citizens the observance of theological principles and religious guidelines.

In view of this, and considering that the appeal would be in confrontation with the understanding established by the STF, he dismisses the appeal. On the formal issue, the decision is grounded on previous conclusions of the STF, as the Justice's individual decision is based on the case-law of the Court. However, regarding the material issue of the state secularity, no mention is made of the previous case-law of the STF. In this sense, it can be concluded that the dismissal of the appeal, even if considerations have been made about the secularity of the state, is based only on the formal question of the violation in the proposal, since the existence of an understanding established by the Court is essential for the sole decision-making by the Justice Rapporteur to be possible.

It can be observed that another action on the same legal issue was proposed to the STF, the Direct Action of Unconstitutionality—ADI 5248/2018 was considered to be undermined in the light of the decision taken by Justice Celso de Melo, and the proceedings were terminated without judgment on the merits by Justice Alexandre de Moraes.

Approximately four years later, a similar case was faced by the STF, the Direct Action of Unconstitutionality—ADI 5258/2021. In this case, unanimously and in accordance with the opinion of the Justice Rapporteur

Cármen Lucia, the STF has ruled in favor of the request to declare unconstitutional the provisions of Articles 1, 2, and 4 of Law no. 74/2010 of Amazonas, which made it mandatory to maintain at least one copy of the Bible in state schools and public libraries, without restricting the availability of other sacred books from other religious communities. The decision was summarized as follows:

> Direct Action of Unconstitutionality. Constitutional. Law "promulgated" no. 74/2010, of Amazonas. Mandatory maintenance of a copy of the Bible in state schools and public libraries. It offends the principles of isonomy, religious freedom, and state secularity. Caput of article 5 and no. I of article 19 of the Constitution of the Republic. Direct Action of Unconstitutionality upheld. (ADI 5258, 2021, p. 1)

In her opinion, the Justice Rapporteur referred to the individual decision previously mentioned, by Justice Celso de Melo, as well as the judgments on Direct Actions of Unconstitutionality—ADI 5248, 5257 (see below) and 4439, to Brazilian constitutional history, to Decree 119-A of 1890, as well as constitutional arrangements that protect religious freedom, equality, and that require the separation of state and religion to maintain that the specific requirement that a copy of the Bible be made available in public schools and libraries in the State of Amazonas violates the principle of state neutrality, giving unequal treatment among citizens.

For the Justice, state intervention in the religious field, through which measures are promoted that harm or benefit a particular religion to the detriment of others, offends religious freedom, equal treatment, and state secularity. The determination to keep copies of the Bible alone discredits other sacred books and promotes specific cultural values, even if the acquisition of religious books by schools or public libraries is not unlawful.

Finally, the Direct Action of Unconstitutionality—ADI 5256/2021 reinforces the STF's understanding on the subject by recognizing, unanimously and in accordance with the opinion of the Justice Rapporteur Rosa Weber, the unconstitutionality of the Law of the State of Mato Grosso do Sul no. 2902/2004, according to which the State Public Power was obliged to keep copies of the Bible in Catholic and evangelical versions in libraries and school units, without restricting the availability of other sacred books from other religious communities. The decision was summarized as follows:

Direct Action of Unconstitutionality. Law 2902/2004 of the state of Mato Grosso do Sul. Compulsory maintenance of copies of the Holy Bible in the schools of the state education network and in the collection of public libraries of that Unit of the Federation. Violation of the principles of isonomy, religious freedom, and state secularity. Recognition. Precedents. Request upheld. (ADI 5256, 2021, p. 1)

For the Court, the state secularity, although it does not prevent the relationship between state and religions, requires the observance of state impartiality or neutrality in the face of the plurality of religious and non-religious beliefs and orientations of the population. In this sense, the requirement to make copies of the Bible available in schools and state libraries at the expense of the public treasury violates the principles of equality before the law, religious freedom, and state secularity.

BIBLE AS A FOUNDATIONAL BOOK OF RELIGIOUS DOCTRINE

In the Direct Action of Unconstitutionality—ADI 5257/2018, the Prosecutor General of the Republic questioned the constitutionality of Articles 1 and 2 of the Law of the State of Rondonia no. 1864/2008, especially when defining in Article 1 that the Holy Bible, in its various translations into the Portuguese language, is made official in the State of Rondonia as a foundational book of doctrinal source to base the principles, uses, and customs of communities, churches, and groups, and also establishes in Article 2 that such communities, churches, groups, and other social segments may use the Bible as the basis for their decisions and related activities (social, moral, spiritual), with full recognition in the State of Rondonia, in relation to their members and to those requiring their services. In particular, the Office of the Prosecutor General questioned Article 1 and the expression "with full recognition in the State of Rondonia" in Article 2, as it considers that they would violate the constitutional duty of separation between state and religion.

For the STF, the aforementioned provisions of state law, in their entirety, violate the Federal Constitution for the following reasons: An unjustified differential treatment is created between the different religious denominations, the required neutrality of the State is violated, and it implies undue interference by the State in the functioning of religious establishments and in individual religious freedom, because, despite the apparent protection afforded to religious beliefs, it has the implication of transforming the moral obligation of the religious person into a legal obligation to subscribe to religious belief. For these reasons, in a unanimous decision in accordance with the opinion of the Justice Rapporteur Dias Toffoli, the request made in the ADI was upheld and the decision is summarized as follows:

> Direct action of unconstitutionality. State standard that formalizes the bible as a foundational book of doctrinal source. Violation of the principles of state secularity and freedom of belief. Upheld. (ADI 5257, 2018, p. 1)

RITUAL SACRIFICE OF ANIMALS

Through the Extraordinary Appeal—RE 494601/2019, the Prosecutor's Office of the State of Rio Grande do Sul questions the constitutionality of State Law no. 12131/2004, which introduced the single paragraph to Article 2 of State Law no. 11915/2003, to expressly authorize the practice of animal sacrifice by religions of African origin. On the one hand, it questions the fact that state law would be encroaching on Union competence in dealing with criminal matters. On the other hand, on material issues, he argues that the law is abusing the principle of equal treatment by favoring religions of African origin, to the detriment of Jewish and Muslim religions, for example, which would also violate the secular nature of the state.

For the Justice who wrote the decision of the Court, Edson Fachin, the appeal could not prosper. First, because state law does not deal with criminal matters, but only with administrative matters, because it excludes the application of administrative sanction only when the practice of animal sacrifice by followers of African religions takes place. Moreover, regarding the specific mention of "religions of African origin," the specific treatment for them does not imply a breach of equal treatment, given the differentiated historical experience of discrimination and stigmatization faced by religions of African origin in Brazil, while it does not prevent the same treatment to be given to other religions that slaughter animals.

In the ruling, it is also recognized that the practice and rituals related to animal sacrifice are intangible cultural heritage, constituting the ways of creating, making, and living from various religious denominations, particularly those exercising religious freedom in non-institutional forms. These practices are part of the community dimension of religious freedom, which also boasts constitutional protection and does not violate the principle of secularism. For the STF, references to religions of African origin do not offend secularity, since it does not prevent the state from dealing with religious issues but is intended to rule out the invocation of religious motives in the public space as a justification for imposing obligations. In summary:

> Constitutional Law. Extraordinary Appeal with General Repercussion. Environmental protection. Religious freedom. Law 11915/2003 of the state of Rio Grande do Sul. A standard that deals with the ritual sacrifice in the worship and liturgies of religions of African origin. Concurring powers of states to legislate on forests, hunting, fishing, fauna, nature conservation, protection of soil and natural resources, protections of the environment and control of pollution. Sacrifice of animals according to religious precepts. Constitutionality. (RE 494601, 2019, pp. 1–2)

By a majority of votes and in accordance with the opinion of Justice Edson Fachin, drafter of the decision, the STF rejected the appeal of the Prosecutor's Office of the State of Rio Grande do Sul, defining the following thesis of general repercussion: "The animal protection law that allows the ritual sacrifice of animals in the religious services of African origin, in order to safeguard religious freedom, is constitutional."

LIMITS OF THE RELIGIOUS DISCOURSE

Proposed by the Socialist People's Party, or PPS, the Direct Action of Unconstitutionality by Omission—ADO 26/2019 sought to see recognized the alleged inertia of the National Congress in adopting legislative measures to criminalize homophobia and transphobia. In this case, the STF, by majority, upheld the action, recognizing the state of institutional delay, declaring the existence of legislative omission, and informing the National Congress in this regard. Moreover, by applying the technique of interpretation in conformity with the Constitution, it determined that homophobia and transphobia should be framed in the crime of racism, with effect from the conclusion of the trial, and only until the approval by the National Congress of Law that is intended to criminalize homophobia and transphobia.

This same decision, taking into account the particularities of the various religious doctrines, excepts religious discourse, which cannot be considered discriminatory or racist, provided that it does not incite discrimination, hostility, and violence, thus adopting the following thesis of general repercussion on religious freedom defined:

> Criminal repression of homotransphobia does not affect or restrict the exercise of religious freedom, whatever the religious denomination professed, to whose faithful and ministers (priests, pastors, rabbis, Muslim clerics, leaders or celebrants of Afro-Brazilian religions, among others) the right to preach and freely disclose, by word, image or any other means, their thinking and to express their convictions according to what is contained in their books and sacred codes is guaranteed, thus, teaching according to its doctrinal and/or theological orientation, and being able to seek and conquer proselytes and practice the acts of worship and their liturgy, regardless of space, public or private, of their individual or collective action, provided that such manifestations do not configure hate speech, thus those expressions that incite discrimination, hostility or violence against people because of their sexual orientation or gender identity. (ADO 26, 2019, p. 7)

In two other previous cases, ruled respectively by the 1st Chamber and 2nd Chamber of the STF, the limits of religious discourse were discussed in the context of proselytism.

The Ordinary Appeal in Habeas Corpus—RHC 134682/2016 dealt with a religious publication, a book by a Catholic priest, which associates Spiritism with demonic practices and defends the need to rescue its practitioners.

For the 1st Chamber of the STF, following by a majority the opinion of the Justice Rapporteur Edson Fachin, religious freedom and freedom of expression are founding elements of the constitutional order and must be exercised with respect for the other fundamental rights, while the proselytism discourse being essential to its full exercise. The purpose of persuading others is intrinsic to religions of such nature, which may involve comparison between different religions, including by some hierarchization or animosity between them.

In order for a discriminatory speech to be considered criminal, three essential steps must be taken: (1) cognitive judgment of the recognition of differences or inequalities between groups or individuals; (2) evaluative judgment directed to hierarchization, on which is based the supposed relation of superiority between them; and (3) the externalization of the necessity or legitimacy of domination, exploitation, enslavement or elimination of the other.

Thus, criminal practice depends on finding that these three stages are fulfilled. In this case, the text published by the priest is limited to the first two steps (considering the faith inferior to the Catholic and encouraging Spiritist believers to be redeemed), therefore a legitimate practice of proselytism, not fulfilling the third requirement that constitutes discrimination.

By a majority of votes and in accordance with the opinion of the Justice Rapporteur, the 1st Chamber of the STF upheld the ordinary appeal to discontinue the criminal action.

In the second case, the Ordinary Appeal in Habeas Corpus—RHC 146303/2018, ruled by the 2nd Chamber of the STF, the Justice Rapporteur Edson Fachin's opinion was not followed by the Chamber, and the judgment was drawn up by Justice Dias Toffoli. Unlike the previous case, it was not a written publication in which it was argued that practitioners of a religion should be reached or rescued by the message of the Gospel. In this case, the leader of the Church Generation of Jesus Christ propagated an aggressive and severely offensive message against various religions (Catholic, Jewish, Spiritist, Satanic, Wicca, Islamic, Umbandist, and other Evangelical denominations), attacking them and preaching the end of certain religious groups, as well as imputing criminal and offensive acts to their devotees and priests, such as murder, prostitution, theft, manipulation, among others.

For the 2nd Chamber, the right to religious freedom comprises the right to the existence of a multiplicity of religious beliefs and disbelief, which should be harmonized in an environment of religious tolerance, concluding that the discourse that attacks the religion and freedom of religious belief of others, which demeans or belittles its followers, does not deserve protection.

Despite the different positions of the STF Chambers in relation to religious discourse, there are distinctive differences in both the form and content of expression in both cases, which cannot be ignored.

CONSCIENTIOUS OBJECTION AND REASONABLE ACCOMMODATION

In two cases jointly ruled by the STF Plenary in 2020, having Edson Fachin as Justice Rapporteur, the Court recognized the right of civil servants to conscientious objection, so that they may be assured reasonable accommodation for the religious observance of days of rest (such as Saturdays for some religious groups) and festive days, with the possibility of changing working days and times, as well as the right of conscientious objection and reasonable accommodation regarding the stages or procedures of public tenders related to public employment, for people who invoke the impossibility of attending for religious reasons. For the Court, the guarantee of conscientious objection with the consequent reasonable accommodation, besides not violating the state secularity, accomplishes religious freedom and allows for religious pluralism.

In the Extraordinary Appeal with Review Effect—ARE 1099099/2020, which faced the theme of religious observance of days of rest by civil servants, the following thesis of general repercussion was defined by a majority of votes:

> According to Article 5, VIII, of the CRFB [Brazilian Constitution], it is possible for the Public Administration, including in the probationary period, to establish alternative criteria for the regular exercise of the functional duties inherent in public employment, in the face of civil servants that invoke an conscientious objection for reasons of religious belief, provided that the required accommodation is reasonable, the performance of its functions is not distorted and it does not entail a disproportionate burden on the Public Administration, which must decide on a reasoned basis. (ARE 1099099, 2020, p. 2)

In its turn, in the Extraordinary Appeal—RE 611874/2020, the STF discussed the issue of holding stages of public tender at alternative times due to the religious belief of participants, adopting the following thesis of general repercussion, by majority of votes:

> According to Article 5, VIII of the CF [Brazilian Constitution], it is possible to carry out stages of the public tender on different dates and times from those foreseen in the tender announcement by a candidate who invokes conscientious objection on grounds of religious belief, provided that the reasonableness of the amendment is verified, the preservation of equality between all candidates and that it does not entail disproportionate burden on the Public Administration, which must decide in a reasoned manner. (RE 611874, 2020, p. 3)

RELIGION AND HEALTH

In the context of the COVID-19 pandemic, there were two themes related to the harmonization of the exercise of religious freedom with the protection of public health.

In the Extraordinary Appeal with Review Effect—ARE 1267879/2020, by unanimous decision and in accordance with the opinion of the Justice Rapporteur Luis Roberto Barroso, the STF understood that the requirement for vaccination of children does not violate the freedom of conscience and religion of parents, adopting the following thesis of general repercussion:

> It is constitutional the mandatory immunization by means of a vaccine that, registered in a health surveillance agency, (I) has been included in the National Immunizations Program or (ii) has its mandatory application determined by law or (iii) is the subject of a determination of the Union, State, Federal District or Municipality, based on medical-scientific consensus. In such cases, there is no violation of the freedom of conscience and philosophical conviction of parents or guardians, nor of family power. (ARE 1267879, 2020, p. 2)

Among the main grounds mentioned by the Court are the duty of the State to protect people, even if contrary to their will (dignity as a community value), the importance of vaccination for the protection of the whole of society, and illegitimacy of individual choices that seriously harm the rights of third parties (need for collective immunization) and, finally, the limitation of family power, which does not allow parents to jeopardize the health of their children, even if they invoke philosophical conviction (the best interest of the child).

The second most relevant topic was discussed in the context of the Claim for Noncompliance with a Fundamental Precept—ADPF 811/2021. In April 2021, when discussing the case of restrictions imposed on the performance of collective activities in religious temples, for a short period and during one of the most serious phases of the pandemic, by a decree of the State of São Paulo, the STF considered the limits imposed on face-to-face celebrations to be reasonable. Based on the opinion of the Justice Rapporteur Gilmar Mendes and in response to the brief submitted by the Social Democratic Party—PSD, the Court concluded that the core of the freedom of conscience (*forum internum*) was not under discussion, but the constitutionally conferred protection for the freedom to exercise collective worship (*forum externum*), which may be restricted. In this case, the Court, by a majority of votes, stated that the imposition of certain restrictions on the face-to-face collective religious activities during the pandemic of the new coronavirus by the state law of Sao Paulo proved adequate, necessary, and proportionate in strict sense to combat the serious contamination that preceded the adoption of that law.

Final Remarks

Although there have been some cases judged by the Supreme Court in the twentieth century, the period of greater case-law production in the field of freedom of religion or belief began only in the 2000s. Through those landmark rulings, the Supreme Court has affirmed a broad scope of protection for freedom of religion or belief.

In addition to the cases mentioned in this chapter, there are important issues that will still be discussed by the Court in the following months and years, including use of religious clothing (head covering) in identification documents and driver's license (Extraordinary Appeal—RE 859376), presence of religious symbols in public buildings (Extraordinary Appeal with Review Effect—ARE 1249095), refusal to blood transfusion for religious reasons (Claim for Noncompliance with a Fundamental Precept—ADPF 618), payment by the state of a differentiated or alternative medical treatment that is not available in the National Health System due to the religious beliefs of the patient (Extraordinary Appeal—RE 979742 and Extraordinary Appeal—RE 1212272), admission and permanence of religious groups in indigenous lands (Direct Action of Unconstitutionality—ADI 6622), protection of indigenous peoples during the pandemic (Claim for Noncompliance with a Fundamental Precept—ADPF 709), and respect for Sabbath keeping in public tenders as well as in public and private university entrance exams (Direct Action of Unconstitutionality—ADI 3901).

These pending cases refer to some issues that have been debated for decades within Brazilian legal scholarship and they have the potential to bring important contributions for the protection and promotion of freedom of religion or belief for all in Brazil.

NOTE

1. On the topic of freedom of religion or belief in Brazil, see also Alves (2016a, b, c, 2020a, b, c), Alves and Pinto (2020), Alves et al. (2020).

REFERENCES

Alves, Rodrigo Vitorino Souza. 2016a. Brazil. In *Encyclopedia of Law and Religion*, ed. Gerhard Robbers, W. Cole Durham, and Donlu Thayer, vol. v. 2, 42–59. Leiden, Boston: Brill Nijhoff.
———. 2016b. Organization of American States. In *Encyclopedia of Law and Religion*, ed. Gerhard Robbers, W. Cole Durham, and Donlu Thayer, vol. v. 5, 208–216. Leiden & Boston: Brill Nijhoff.
———. 2016c. Separation, Cooperation and Freedom of Religion or Belief: Analyzing the Constitutionality of the Agreements Between the Federal Republic of Brazil and the Holy See. *Revista Latinoamericana de Derecho y Religión* 2 (2): 1–18.
———, ed. 2020a. *Latin American Perspectives on Law and Religion*. Heidelberg, London & New York: Springer.
———. 2020b. Law and Religion in the Encounter of Cultures: The Normative Conflicts Between Freedom of Religion or Belief and the Rights of Indigenous Peoples. In *Latin American Perspectives on Law and Religion*, ed. Rodrigo Vitorino Souza Alves, vol. v. 1, 1st ed., 10–33. Heidelberg & London: Springer.
———. 2020c. The Protection of the Existence and Identity of Religious Minorities Under the United Nations Legal Framework: Between the Group-Centered and Person-Centered Approaches. In *Political and Religious Communities—Partners, Competitors, or Aliens?* ed. Dirk Ehlers and Henning Glaser, 563–591. Baden-Baden: Nomos.
Alves, Rodrigo Vitorino Souza, and Thiago Felipe Alves Pinto. 2020. Investigations on the Use of Limitations to Freedom of Religion or Belief in Brazil. *Religion & Human Rights* 15: 77–95.
Alves, Rodrigo Vitorino Souza, Andréa Letícia Carvalho Guimarães, José Renato Faria Venâncio Prata Resende, and Gabriellen da Silva Xavier do Carmo. 2020. Freedom of Religion or Belief and the Covid-19 Pandemic: An Analysis of the Adoption of Restrictive Measures in Brazil. *Revista general de derecho canónico y derecho eclesiástico del estado* 54: 1–24.
Briefs of the Center to the UN Special Rapporteur on Freedom of Religion or Belief. https://www.ohchr.org/en/issues/freedomreligion/pages/freedomreligionindex.aspx.

Federal Supreme Court Case-Law

Claim for Noncompliance with a Fundamental Precept—ADPF 811/2021 (religious freedom and health issues). http://portal.stf.jus.br/processos/downloadPeca.asp?id=15346816672&ext=.pdf.

Direct Action of Unconstitutionality by Omission—ADO 26/2019 (religion and free speech). http://portal.stf.jus.br/processos/downloadPeca.asp?id=15344606459&ext=.pdf.

Direct Action of Unconstitutionality—ADI 2076/2002 (invocation of God in the Preamble and its legal nature). https://redir.stf.jus.br/paginadorpub/paginador.jsp?docTP=AC&docID=375324.

Direct Action of Unconstitutionality—ADI 2649/2008 (Preamble). http://www.stf.jus.br/portal/inteiroTeor/obterInteiroTeor.asp?id=555517&codigoClasse=504&numero=2649&siglaRecurso=&classe=ADI.

Direct Action of Unconstitutionality—ADI 4439/2017 (religion in public schools). https://redir.stf.jus.br/paginadorpub/paginador.jsp?docTP=TP&docID=15085915.

Direct Action of Unconstitutionality—ADI 5248/2018 (religion in public schools). https://portal.stf.jus.br/processos/downloadPeca.asp?id=313899095&ext=.pdf.

Direct Action of Unconstitutionality—ADI 5256/2021 (religion in public schools). http://portal.stf.jus.br/processos/downloadPeca.asp?id=15348555509&ext=.pdf.

Direct Action of Unconstitutionality—ADI 5257/2018 (Bible as a foundational book of religious doctrine). https://portal.stf.jus.br/processos/downloadPeca.asp?id=15339155696&ext=.pdf.

Direct Action of Unconstitutionality—ADI 5258/2021 (religion in public schools). http://portal.stf.jus.br/processos/downloadPeca.asp?id=15346248154&ext=.pdf.

Extraordinary Appeal with Review Effect—ARE 1014615/2017 (religion in public schools). http://portal.stf.jus.br/processos/downloadPeca.asp?id=311424048&ext=.pdf.

Extraordinary Appeal with Review Effect—ARE 1099099/2020 (conscientious objection and reasonable accommodation). http://portal.stf.jus.br/processos/downloadPeca.asp?id=15346130481&ext=.pdf.

Extraordinary Appeal with Review Effect—ARE 1267879/2020 (religious freedom and health issues). https://redir.stf.jus.br/paginadorpub/paginador.jsp?docTP=TP&docID=755520674.

Extraordinary Appeal—RE 144900/1997 (tax exemption). https://portal.stf.jus.br/processos/detalhe.asp?incidente=1531750.

Extraordinary Appeal—RE 221395/2000 (tax exemption). https://portal.stf.jus.br/processos/detalhe.asp?incidente=1690900.

Extraordinary Appeal—RE 237718/2001 (tax exemption). http://redir.stf.jus. br/paginadorpub/paginador.jsp?docTP=AC&docID=255915.

Extraordinary Appeal—RE 257700/2000 (tax exemption). https://portal.stf.jus. br/processos/detalhe.asp?incidente=1786066.

Extraordinary Appeal—RE 325822/2002 (tax exemption). https://redir.stf.jus. br/paginadorpub/paginador.jsp?docTP=AC&docID=260872.

Extraordinary Appeal—RE 494601/2019 (animal sacrifice). https://redir.stf.jus. br/paginadorpub/paginador.jsp?docTP=TP&docID=751390246.

Extraordinary Appeal—RE 562351/2012 (tax exemption). http://redir.stf.jus. br/paginadorpub/paginador.jsp?docTP=TP&docID=3195619.

Extraordinary Appeal—RE 578562/2008 (tax exemption). https://redir.stf.jus. br/paginadorpub/paginador.jsp?docTP=AC&docID=547393.

Extraordinary Appeal—RE 611874/2020 (conscientious objection and reasonable accommodation). http://portal.stf.jus.br/processos/downloadPeca. asp?id=15346130905&ext=.pdf.

Instrument Appeal—AI 155822/1995 (tax exemption). https://portal.stf.jus. br/processos/detalhe.asp?incidente=1571642.

Ordinary Appeal in Habeas Corpus—RHC 134682/2016 (religion and free speech). https://portal.stf.jus.br/processos/downloadPeca. asp?id=312556698&ext=.pdf.

Ordinary Appeal in Habeas Corpus—RHC 146303/2018 (religion and free speech). https://portal.stf.jus.br/processos/downloadPeca. asp?id=314933571&ext=.pdf.

Regimental Appeal in the Extraordinary Appeal—AgR ARE 800395/2014 (tax exemption). http://redir.stf.jus.br/paginadorpub/paginador.jsp?docTP=TP &docID=7236119.

Regimental Review in the Extraordinary Appeal—AG.Reg.RE 1268862/2021 (religion in public schools). http://portal.stf.jus.br/processos/downloadPeca. asp?id=15346412974&ext=.pdf; https://portal.stf.jus.br/processos/downloadPeca.asp?id=15345591763&ext=.pdf.

Regimental Review in the Extraordinary Appeal—AgR ARE 658080/2011 (tax exemption). http://redir.stf.jus.br/paginadorpub/paginador.jsp?docTP=TP &docID=1738528.

Regimental Review in the Instrument Review—AgR AI 389602/2005 (tax exemption). https://portal.stf.jus.br/processos/detalhe.asp?incidente=2015361.

Regimental Review in the Instrument Review—AgR AI 690712/2009 (tax exemption). https://portal.stf.jus.br/processos/detalhe.asp?incidente=2574029.

SUPREME COURT'S CASES PENDING OF TRIAL

Claim for Noncompliance with a Fundamental Precept—ADPF 618 (refusal to blood transfusion for religious reasons). http://portal.stf.jus.br/processos/detalhe.asp?incidente=5769402.

Claim for Noncompliance with a Fundamental Precept—ADPF 709 and incidental interim relief (protection of indigenous people during the pandemic). http://portal.stf.jus.br/processos/detalhe.asp?incidente=5952986; https://redir.stf.jus.br/paginadorpub/paginador.jsp?docTP=TP&docID=756931172.

Direct Action of Unconstitutionality—ADI 3901 (respect for Sabbath keeping in public tenders as well as in public and private university entrance exams in Pará). http://portal.stf.jus.br/processos/detalhe.asp?incidente=2527365.

Direct Action of Unconstitutionality—ADI 6622 and cautionary measure (admission and permanence of religious groups in indigenous lands and cautionary granted to forbid the entry of new religious missions during the pandemic). http://portal.stf.jus.br/processos/detalhe.asp?incidente=6067929; http://portal.stf.jus.br/processos/downloadPeca.asp?id=15347982643&ext=.pdf.

Extraordinary Appeal with Review Effect—ARE 1249095 (religious symbols in public buildings). http://portal.stf.jus.br/processos/detalhe.asp?incidente=5827249.

Extraordinary Appeal—RE 1212272 (payment by the state of alternative treatment to blood transfusion for religious reasons). http://portal.stf.jus.br/processos/detalhe.asp?incidente=5703626.

Extraordinary Appeal—RE 859376 (use of religious clothing in Identification Document and Driver's License). http://portal.stf.jus.br/processos/detalhe.asp?incidente=4690513.

Extraordinary Appeal—RE 979742 (payment by the state of a differentiated medical treatment that is not available in the National Health System due to the religious beliefs of the patient). http://portal.stf.jus.br/processos/detalhe.asp?incidente=5006128.

CHAPTER 31

God and Communism: Cuba's Constitution, Socialist Construction, and Religion, 1959–1992

Petra Kuivala

INTRODUCTION

Law and legislation have been central to Cuba's revolution and state socialism since 1959. They have served to legitimize Fidel Castro's rule, construct a cohesive nationalistic narrative, and rationalize the use of state power in socialist construction. In all these processes, the role of religion has been relevant, as well, although it is a topic that previous scholarship has neither acknowledged nor discussed.

The central focus of the chapter is a historical and comparative analysis of Cuba's first socialist constitution, established in 1976, and its amended version, introduced in 1992. The chapter concentrates particularly on how religion—freedom of religion, in particular—is framed and discussed in these legal documents. As such, the broader theme addressed in the chapter is the historiographical production of competing, although

P. Kuivala (✉)
Harvard University, Cambridge, MA, USA
e-mail: pkuivala@fas.harvard.edu

S. Holzer (ed.), *The Palgrave Handbook of Religion and State Volume II*, https://doi.org/10.1007/978-3-031-35609-4_31

overlapping, narratives on religion and the revolution, church and state, and socialist construction in Cuba. While religion has been treated in legislation without distinction or preference to creed or denomination, the chapter takes Catholicism as its point of reference, as it is Cuba's historically predominant institutional religious tradition. It is nevertheless important to stress that other Christian denominations, as well as other religious traditions, have existed on the island, hosting varying views on religious presence in socialist society.

The analysis of religion in Cuba's socialist construction draws on legal documents such as the Constitutions of 1976 and 1992 as well as publications and speeches by the state leadership. Additionally, the chapter utilizes documents produced by the Catholic Church and oral history interviews with religious Cubans conducted by the author. They are analyzed as a response and commentary to, first, the legislation and, second, socialist construction founded on legislative transitions. As such, this chapter examines from a comparative perspective the official discourses established by the socialist state and the discourses upheld by the Catholic Church on the social construction of Cuban society.

This research is situated at the intersection of historical and religious studies as well as the multidisciplinary field of Cuban studies. Drawing on the study of legal and political history, the chapter provides an analysis of the development of, first, laws on religious presence and, second, Cuban church-state relations from the perspective of legislation and official socialist politics. By doing so, it engages several relevant discussions in the field and attempts to address some of the remaining lacunae of knowledge regarding legislation and policies on religion in socialist Cuba.

Overall, law, legislation, and legal history remain scarcely utilized perspectives in the study of the Cuban Revolution and socialist society (Grant 2017, p. 81). Similarly, the field of Cuban studies lacks an analysis of the legislation on religion from a broader perspective that situates church-state relations at the intersection of law, Cuban socialism, revolutionary institutions, and state power (Kuivala 2022, pp. 47). Moreover, in previous scholarship, a prevalent emphasis on the 1960s as the decade of revolutionary fervor, national radicalization, and Cold War geopolitics has dominated the field. Historians have produced an extensive body of scholarship that focuses on the first years of post-1959 Cuba from the perspectives of political, social, and cultural history. Much of this work has emphasized bilateral relations between Cuba and the United States, focusing less on Cuba as a part of the Socialist Bloc and the international Left.

With the dominant focus on the early stages of the revolution, scholarship has placed less nuanced and detailed emphasis on the decades following the arguably most radical period of the revolutionary process. Similarly, the prevailing focus on the 1960s has sometimes contributed to a vision of the revolution as being best, or solely, embodied and represented by its earliest stages (Kuivala 2019, p. 102). The 1970s and 1980s, a previously under-researched yet highly interesting epoch of the Cuban Revolution, have attracted increasing scholarly interest in the recent years. This period, characterized by the restructuring of Cuban society by means of institutionalization and collaboration with the Soviet Union, provides important insight into the interplay of state power, political culture, and civil society beyond the focus on Cuba-US relations. The present chapter continues this line of research, further extending its scope of inquiry toward the role of religion in Cuban socialist politics and social order.

The chapter contains three chronologically ordered sections. The first part, focusing on the 1960s, analyzes the evolution of church-state relations during a period characterized by rapid changes in legislative action and the broad restructuring of society and social order as a result of the revolution. The second part examines the 1970s and early 1980s as a period of constitutional reform and consolidation that established socialism as Cuba's official state ideology and introduced the structurally reinforced rule of the Communist Party. The third part, centering on the constitutional amendment of 1992, studies the changes introduced to the constitution as both a mark of a new era in Cuban socialism and a symbol of a long process of transformation in Cuban church-state relations.

The overarching theme of the sections is the chapter's analytical framework: the study of Cuban socialist construction as a narrative of state power and popular participation. This approach allows the chapter to argue that both political culture and legislation were used to construct and maintain a cohesive nationalistic narrative that not only produced popular participation but was also used to demonstrate it. Religion was an area of culture and society that could either consolidate or disrupt this narrative. Therefore, as the chapter shows, controlling and directing religious presence in the public sphere was central to the construction of a unifying narrative on the revolution as the people's shared project.

New Legislation and the Consolidation
of Socialist Construction

Law has played a fundamental, though scarcely discussed, role in Cuba's revolutionary reformation since 1959. Fidel Castro, who personified the revolution both on the island and in international imagination, was a lawyer by education. Moreover, prior to attending university and pursuing legal studies, he had been educated in a Catholic private school by the Jesuit order.

Similarly, as argued by Evenson, law played a crucial role in the creation of Cuban socialism as a transformative tool that allowed the regime to contour and direct acceptable socialist behavior (Evenson 2003, p. 14). Grant states that "at the core of the law's role in this effort has been the concept of socialist legality" (Grant 2017, p. 80). From early on, the revolution employed legislation as a means to fulfill the promises made to the people in order to gain their support and broad popular participation in the revolutionary process. Among the most crucial laws introduced in 1959–1960 were the Agrarian Reform laws, which transformed land ownership on the island by establishing a maximum landholding size and distributing the excess land to previously landless peasants. In turn, the Urban Reform Law cut rental rates, and Cubans owning more than two properties were obliged to surrender their excess real estate, which the state transformed into collectively utilized holdings. As such, the laws reinforced the role of ordinary Cubans as beneficiaries of the new social order, which worked in favor of the revolutionary leadership (Brenner et al. 2008, p. 8; Chase 2015, p. 115; Pérez 2015, pp. 252–253).

The first years of the new revolutionary rule constituted a legislatively unstable period under a fundamental law that was "amended repeatedly as changes in policy required" (Klein 1978, pp. 459–460). The fundamental law provided the basic legal framework for establishing a revolutionary society, and it was modified 19 times between May 1959 and December 1962 (Da Costa and Grant 2017, p. 84). The course of the revolution and its founding political principles were neither linear nor clearly pronounced; rather, new laws and rules were enacted reactively and the Castro regime frequently established new legislation to replace existing laws. Overall, between 1959 and 1963, over 100 new laws were passed (Da Costa and Grant 2017, p. 84).

It is important to note that this changing legislation was also one of the main reasons for the confrontation that emerged between the Catholic

Church and the revolutionary government. Before the revolution and during the consolidation period of the new regime, Catholicism constituted the historically predominant religious tradition in Cuba. Although the church and the state were separated, the Catholic Church enjoyed privileged social status and institutional sway in Cuban society. Moreover, before 1959, the Catholic Church was the dominant provider of private education and healthcare as well as an influential moral agent in Cuban civil society, all of which was dissolved by the new legislation. Because of the loss of these domains of influence, and the episcopate's suspicion of socialist ideas being behind the new legislation, the Church and the revolutionary government clashed on numerous occasions between 1959 and 1961.

Despite the dominance of the Catholic Church, the island contained other Christian denominations, including several Protestant groups, such as Baptists, Methodists, and Adventists. Religion, in general, had already been discussed in the so-called La Yaya Constitution, written in 1897 as the last constitution under the Spanish rule, which contained a bill of individual rights, including freedom of religion and expression (D'Zurilla 1981, p. 1231). In the Constitution of 1940, after which the fundamental law of 1959 was modeled, Cuba was defined as a secular country in which the Church was separated from the state (Constitution of the Republic of Cuba, 1940, article 35).

Through legislative changes and new acts, an early narrative of popular support and mass participation began to legitimize both the leadership's authority and the use of state power over the people. Aside from legislation, ideal revolutionary behavior was constructed and controlled through the public discourses of the state leadership, emerging norms of civic participation, and peer-reinforced social norms. The emerging nationalist narrative privileged revolutionary affiliation and participation as emblematic of an ideal social presence that surpassed other identities such as those of religious individuals. Religious identification was considered a potentially antirevolutionary and therefore unpatriotic attitude (Kuivala 2022, p. 202). As has been argued by Guerra, the shifting definitions of ideal revolutionary identities and participation enabled citizens themselves to act as the judges of such ideals (Guerra 2012, p. 23). This was also reflected in the adoption of varied and often ambiguous stances on religion. The lack of officially pronounced policies allowed local offices and individuals the autonomy to navigate church-state relations in local contexts.

Following the leftward pull and, ultimately, the declaration of the revolution as socialist in 1961, religion was presented in the public political narrative as an outdated cultural expression, a force of opposition, and a source of identity unfitting for true, patriotic revolutionaries. In this environment, Catholics employed the concept of *dentro de los templos* (inside the temples) as an expression of the space they were allowed in society as both religious communities and individual believers (oral history interview by the author, April 2015, Cuba; Kuivala 2022, p. 201). These communities were ordered to limit religious activities and expression to the confines of church buildings and other dedicated gathering spaces approved by state authorities. Similarly, individual Catholics were pressured to consider their religious convictions and beliefs as personal, private matters that belonged primarily to the intimate sphere, not to public life and social presence.

In such ways, religious beliefs and expressions were an area of culture and society that was considered potentially threatening to national cohesion. Other similar elements were the arts and artistic expression. In a speech given in June 1961, Castro noted that the social and economic revolution that had already occurred in Cuba "must inevitably produce a cultural revolution in turn in our country" (*Discurso pronunciado por el Comandante Fidel Castro Ruz como conclusion de las reunions con los intelectuales cubanos*, June 30, 1961). Discussing the role of artists in the construction of revolutionary society, Castro stated:

> The revolutionary puts something above all other matters. The revolutionary puts something above even his own creative spirit. He puts the Revolution above everything else, and the most revolutionary artist will be that one who is prepared to sacrifice even his own artistic vocation for the Revolution.
> *Discurso pronunciado por el Comandante Fidel Castro Ruz como conclusión de las reuniones con los intelectuales cubanos.* (June 30, 1961)

Freedom of artistic expression was tied to being a truly revolutionary artist and representing the revolution's ethos and values through artistic production (*Discurso pronunciado por el Comandante Fidel Castro Ruz como conclusion de las reunions con los intelectuales cubanos*, June 30, 1961). This provides an important point of comparison with religious beliefs, practices, and expression, as the new parameters for social presence entailed accepting the revolution's historiographical claim and the ensuing social norms. Furthermore, arts and cultural life were considered both a means to construct collective social experiences and a reflection of them. Yet they were also both subject to state power as domains that would serve in the social construction and legitimization of revolutionary ideas. Such purposes were presented as a virtuous calling for revolutionary individuals, who were called to construct society by legislation, politics, and the regulation of social norms and behavior alike.

It is important to place religion on the broader map of the revolution's social and cultural effects. Both religion and cultural politics provide a lens to analyze the way Cuba's revolutionary society was constructed: how the state attempted to construct and direct desirable forms of popular expression and how Cubans navigated the contours of such state-imposed restrictions. The comparative perspective suggests that religion, as well as the arts, were situated at the intersection of public political life and discourse as well as the inner world and experience of individuals and communities. As such, a crucial element in Cuban state policies was the construction of a shared sense of belonging and participation through, on the one hand, state-sanctioned narratives that would legitimize the revolution, and, on the other hand, the implementation of cultural politics that would direct the people's responses within the established framework. The law and legislation were key to both of these efforts.

THE FIRST SOCIALIST CONSTITUTION AND THE ATHEIST STATE

The mid-1970s witnessed the introduction of two important pieces of legislation that further defined the role of religion in socialist society: the Cuban Family Code and the first socialist constitution. Overall, the constitution was the culmination of a longer program to introduce a more structural form of socialism in Cuba. The first half of the 1970s marked a period of institutionalization for the Revolution, characterized by a strong Soviet presence in the country and Soviet influence over economic and political modeling (Rojas 2019, p. 43). Soviet influence was also prominent in the concept of socialist legality (Da Costa and Grant 2017, p. 82). Institutionalization was achieved through legislation, including the creation of state structures, offices, and ranks as well as by centralizing authority with the Communist Party (Klein 1978, p. 459; Mesa-Lago 1978, p. 10; Pérez 2015, p. 282). The institutionalization of popular participation also reflected the state's attempts to impose authority and control over civil society (Mesa-Lago 1978, p. 115; Crahan 1985, p. 330).

In 1975, the Cuban Communist Party held its first congress. Among its key outcomes was the resolution to implement an educational policy that would disseminate among the Cuban people the scientific concepts of historical and dialectical materialism, which would serve to help them transcend religious beliefs and dogmas. This would be achieved not by the exclusion of religious Cubans from society but through their inclusion and participation in revolutionary activities (Klein 1978, p. 495). Replacing religious association with participation in the construction of state socialism was also a means to unify the people and further legitimize and uphold the narrative of broad popular consensus and mass support for the state and the political leadership.

Three of the key areas in which the state could provide such inclusion were family, education, and work. The Cuban Family Code, closely related to these opportunities for social construction, was enacted in 1975. It articulated the socialist state's policies on family and education, which were also of crucial interest to religious communities on the island. As has been noted by numerous scholars, both revolutionary and religious cultures shared the conviction that youth and the upcoming generations were essential for transmitting beliefs, values, and ideologies to new members (Casavantes-Bradford 2014, p. 75; Guerra 2012, p. 138; Kuivala 2019, pp. 222–224; Pérez 2015, p. 261). In contrast to the dominant role proposed for the state in education vis-à-vis parental power in the early 1960s, the Family Code emphasized the family as the base unit of society (Smith and Padula 1996, p. 154; Pérez-Stable 2012, p. 117). The family, however, was expected to educate children in a socialist worldview.

As Klein notes, in the Code on Childhood and Youth, the rights to free academic education and to physical education, sports, and recreation were "conditioned on correct political attitudes" (Klein 1978, pp. 491–492). Institutional religious affiliation and active attendance of religious events were usually considered part of the extensive, although sometimes elusive, category of political and revolutionary incorrectness (oral history interview by the author, April 2015, Cuba; oral history interview by the author, September 2015, Cuba). As such, public affiliation to a religious institution, as well as publicly practicing and expressing religion, impeded certain professional and educational trajectories, such as those of an educator or journalist (oral history interview by the author, May 2016, Cuba).

As part of correct social construction, the state encouraged broad popular participation in the arts and cultural life as an antidote to the perceived elitism and potentially counterrevolutionary intellectual life of this domain. Facilitating mass participation through schools, leisure activities, and social organizations (Klein 1978, p. 493) provided a framework for constructing social normativities and ideal affiliation with the revolution. As popular artistic participation was free and supported providing it was not contrary to the Revolution, such forms of mass engagement also offered the state the opportunity to control this potentially critical or subversive area of intellectual activity (Klein 1978, p. 493). Arts and cultural discourses were thus disseminated both through education and via mass organizations and social associations committed to revolutionary ideas.

In this framework, Catholic communities and events represented not only a competing form of social activity but also a potentially threatening form of intellectual life and critique drawn from discourses outside the revolutionary domain. While the Party considered it important to include Christians in the socialist construction of society, membership of the Communist Party and its youth organizations was reserved for individuals subscribing to Marxist-Leninist atheistic doctrine. D'Zurilla notes that the First Congress of the Cuban Communist Party explicitly discussed the atheist programs it planned to launch. While the Party stressed the importance of educating people on atheism, attempts to convince individuals to convert from Christianity to socialism were nonetheless designed to avoid enflaming individuals' sensitivities; rather, the focus was religion's broader sociopolitical function (D'Zurilla 1981, pp. 1257–1258).

The first socialist constitution, enacted in 1976, declared Cuba to be an atheist state, thereby entrenching what was already practiced in religious polity and church-state relations. Nonetheless, scholars such as D'Zurilla (1981) consider the 1976 Constitution vague in its treatment of atheism as a founding state principle: while proclaiming a scientific materialist conception of the universe, the Constitution nevertheless recognized and guaranteed the freedom to profess and practice religion (D'Zurilla 1981, p. 1257).

The Constitution proclaimed the "freedom of conscience and the right of everyone to profess any religion and to practice, within the framework of respect for the law, the belief of his preference" (The Constitution of the Republic of Cuba, 1976, article 54). However, while acknowledging the presence of religion and establishing the freedom of religion for individuals, the Constitution also stressed that the activities of the socialist state were founded on a scientific materialist concept of the universe, about which it sought to educate the Cuban people. Through such a declaration, as is also proposed by Klein, implicit in the text was the continuation of the principle of separation of church and state that had been explicitly stated in all prior constitutions (Klein 1978, p. 494).

Modeled on the 1936 Soviet fundamental law, the Cuban Constitution nevertheless diverged from the laws in the Soviet Union and Eastern Bloc on religious presence in society. In comparison to other constitutions established in socialist states in Europe during the same period, the Cuban Constitution recognized broad freedom of religion; at the other extreme was Albania, which expressly prohibited all religious activities. Nonetheless, the Cuban Constitution maintained more control over the social function of religion than did, for example, the constitution in Poland, whose articles were interpreted as more permissive toward religious education and church-run schools (D'Zurilla 1981, p. 1256).

In practice, the new constitution placed several restrictions on religion in the public sphere. In the hierarchy of duties, the primary duty to work—as another means of socialist construction—precluded the observance of holy days if they coincided with the workweek or revolutionary celebrations. Similarly, the public meetings for religious ceremonies and pilgrimages to shrines were beyond the scope of constitutional protection of the rights of assembly and association. Through such principles, the emphasis on atheism and Marxist-Leninist values was understood to legitimize professional discrimination against religious individuals and their exclusion from public life.

The Constitution also directed the way religion was negotiated in the domestic sphere. Thus, the text stressed the constitutionally imposed duty of the parents to participate in the education and integral development of their children, emblematic of the duty of the entire society to ensure the spirit of communism in education (The Constitution of the Republic of Cuba, 1976, article 38; Klein 1978, p. 492). In such efforts, work, political activities, and military training constituted a part of the curricula in addition to academic subjects. As such, the broad understanding of educational activities further contributed to the exclusion of religion from the public sphere. Politically affiliated mass organizations for the youth and young adults successfully competed with other forms of civic participation, such as participating in religious activities (Kuivala 2019, pp. 222–226).

It is noteworthy that the nexus of religion and family was considered particularly crucial for the education of new revolutionary generations. Therefore, the restrictions on proselytism included not only public spaces but also the domestic sphere, as religious education at home was considered inferior to the duty of parents to advance socialism by educating their children accordingly (Klein 1978, p. 496). In a similar vein, as its broad emphasis, the Constitution stated that the construction of socialism surpassed all other duties and liberties of Cuban individuals:

> None of the freedoms recognized for the citizens can be exercised against what is established in the Constitution and the laws, or against the existence and objectives of the socialist State, or against the decision of the Cuban people to construct socialism and communism. The infraction of this principle is punishable. (The Constitution of the Republic of Cuba, 1976, article 62)

This also included religious expression, particularly at the intersection of religious social ethics and political opinions. Consequently, it directed individuals to consider religion a private, even intimate, matter that was more focused on individual spirituality than public manifestations.

It is important to note that religious communities were not homogeneous in their responses to such use of state power and legislation as a means of socialist construction. The regulation of religious presence provoked a variety of reactions from religious communities on the island. In the Catholic Church, for example, while some considered the separation of church and state, as well as abstinence from political life, a prerequisite for religious survival in Cuban socialist society, others attempted to seek increasing social, even political, influence and visibility from distinctively Christian perspectives (oral history interview by the author, July 2017, Cuba).

D'Zurilla notes that while the Constitution of 1976 established the principle of equality for all citizens and forbade discrimination on the basis of race, color, sex, or national origin, it did not explicitly "prohibit disparate treatment based on religion" (D'Zurilla 1981, p. 1250). Religious Cubans continued to feel they were subjected to discrimination in employment, housing, politics, and education despite the letter of the law. Closely related, despite the constitutional declaration on the freedom of religious beliefs, socialism was considered a higher ideal for which Cuban citizens should strive. Thus, although the Constitution also guaranteed the freedom to practice religion, the state apparatus nonetheless aimed to eradicate religion from Cuban society. At the turn of the 1980s, the Communist Party published a manual for work among religious Cubans, aiming to convert them from Christianity to communism. Developing an approach for promoting socialism and revolutionary participation, the program consisted of "individual work with the believers" and tasked the militant members of the Communist Party with a mission of proselytism (*Trabajo individual con creyentes*, Archivo Histórico de la Arquidiocesis de La Habana).

Despite the ambiguity in implementing the laws on religious freedom, the first socialist constitution was nevertheless received with relative approval by the Catholic Church in Cuba. Because it articulated the official policy on religion in Cuban society, although declaring Cuba an atheist state, the Constitution was received well by the Church from the perspective of coexistence. For the first time since the revolution of 1959 and the restructuring of social order, the new constitution provided a solid reference and an explicit policy on religion in the public sphere, clarifying the position and role of religious institutions. Moreover, at grassroots level, the new constitution made religious communities more secure in their efforts to establish an officially recognized role for religion in Cuban socialist society.

As was discussed in several Catholic communities around the island, the Constitution provided a basis for arguing for religious presence through the representation provided by religious individuals and their multilayered social roles (Prensa Latina/Jaime Ortega Alamino, December 26, 1981, Archivo de la Conferencia de Obispos Católicos de Cuba). The Catholic Church also attempted to encourage individual believers to display their religious affiliation and beliefs in the public sphere. In particular, they sought opportunities to educate the young laity on viewing religious association as a right instead of source of reproach in social and political participation (*Catequesis 10–5 Constitución, Santiago de Cuba, Reflexión Eclesial Cubana*, Archivo Histórico de la Arquidiocesis de la Habana; *Familia 24/2–4 Acción profética, Santiago de Cuba, Reflexión Eclesial Cubana*, Archivo Histórico de la Arquidiocesis de la Habana). The episcopate, as representatives of ecclesial authority, attempted to redirect the narratives of religious presence toward a focus on individual Catholics as contributing and respectable members of society (*Discurso inaugural del ENEC, pronunciado por Mons. Adolfo Rodríguez, presidente de la*

Conferencia Episcopal de Cuba, en nombre de los obispos cubanos, February 17, 1986, Archivo del Obispado de Holguín). As such, the Constitution was used to advocate for the existence and presence of religious communities, since religious freedom was officially declared a constitutional right, as opposed to the previous decade and its more ambiguous policies on religion.

THE CONSTITUTIONAL AMENDMENT OF 1992 AND NEW RELIGIOUS PRESENCE

The first socialist constitution of 1976 was amended in 1992. The substantive changes the amendment introduced were a response to the challenges to Cuba's economy caused by the dissolution of the Soviet Union and the search for a new ideological direction in the wake of the disillusionment experienced after the collapse of the global communist bloc. In reaction to the dramatic decline of the national economy, among the most crucial amendments was the allowing of foreign investment and partnership with the Cuban government and the removal of some of the previously existing restrictions on international economic collaboration. Additionally, all references to the Soviet Union and its legality were removed from the text (Da Costa & Grant 2017, p. 86).

The amendments of 1992 also explicitly dealt with religion as part of Cuba's state socialism. Although the first socialist constitution had defined Cuba as an atheist country and the revolutionary narrative had presented religion as an undesirable element of social construction, this paradigm had already been revised in the late 1980s, when the government had sought to improve its relations with religious groups both on the island and internationally. More broadly, religion, among other previously silenced topics in Cuban society, had already resurfaced in the mid-1980s (Kuivala 2019, pp. 280–282). According to Alonso, as part of the process, the Cuban government had also publicly admitted in the mid-1980s that Cuba represented "a denominationally atheist state" in which "a regime of religious discrimination, incompatible with the socialist ideal, prevailed" (Alonso 2010, p. 153) despite the constitution granting Cubans freedom of religion.

Such considerations were part of a larger project of revising and correcting unsuccessful political, economic, and social trajectories, generally known as the Rectification campaign, launched by the Third Party

Congress in 1986 (LeoGrande 2008, pp. 51–52; Pérez-Stable 2012, pp. 124–127). This rectification process had included a reconsideration of church-state relations and, consequently, the coexistence of religious and revolutionary Cubans. At the same time, the Catholic Church had signaled its intention to contribute to Cuban society through an active presence, although the search for coexistence did not straightforwardly entail the accommodation of socialist ideology.

The reconsideration of religious presence in the public sphere was embodied by the attempts of the state leadership to forge new connections between Christianity and the revolution. In the wake of liberation theology and its nexus with leftist sociopolitical participation, the Cuban government sought to include Christian groups in the social fabric and socialist construction of Cuban society (Kuivala 2019, pp. 239–240). Christian communities on the island held diverse views on social and political integration and accommodation, ranging from support for the state leadership to considering Christianity a force of resistance to socialism (oral history interview by the author, May 2016, Cuba; oral history interview by the author, July 2017, Cuba).

Overall, the mid-1980s was characterized by the government's attempt to revise civic participation and create fora for popular discussion as a response to dissatisfaction and disillusionment among the people (Fernández 2008, pp. 94–95). Coinciding with the religious rapprochement, artistic freedom also increased, and Cuban artists gained more independence vis-à-vis the officially pronounced cultural polities (Padura Fuentes 2008, p. 349). In such ways, similar to the preceding decades, religion was situated in the broader field of civic participation and culture and within the framework of individual expression.

The results of the revision of the boundaries of participation and expression were visible in the amended Constitution of 1992, which proclaimed that the state "recognizes, respects and guarantees freedom of religion." According to the Constitution, Cuba was a secular rather than explicitly atheist country where religious institutions were separated from the state. This articulation marked a significant change: while the Constitution declared the commitment to continuing the construction of a communist state, atheism was no longer an explicit tenet of state ideology. Moreover, the separation of religious institutions from the state echoed previous constitutions spanning back to pre-1959 legislation (Constitution of the Republic of Cuba, 1992, article 8).

Additionally, the text declared that religious freedom included all the different creeds and beliefs present on the island, granting them the same treatment in law (The Constitution of the Republic of Cuba, 1992, article 8). In article 55, this was expanded to the right of every citizen "to change religious beliefs or to not have any, and to profess, within the framework of respect for the law, the religious belief of his preference" (Constitution of the Republic of Cuba, 1992, article 55). As noted by Alonso, the Cuban state explicitly forbade religious discrimination in the Constitution of 1992 in the same way that discrimination on the basis of race and gender was outlawed in the first socialist constitution of 1976 (Alonso 2010, p. 153). This was considered a significant change to the policies implemented and encouraged at the grassroots level. Under the title "Equality," article 42 stated:

> Discrimination because of race, skin color, sex, national origin, religious beliefs and any other form of discrimination harmful to human dignity is forbidden and will be punished by law. (Constitution of the Republic of Cuba, 1992, article 42)

Alonso nevertheless also notes that "making a law is one thing and implementing it another" (Alonso 2010, pp. 153–154). In practice, the ambiguity and local variation in the way religious Cubans were treated and accepted in the public sphere shifted more slowly than the legislative changes introduced by the constitutional amendment.

Whereas, in the earlier constitution, socialist construction had included state-provided education that privileged revolutionary participation and stifled competing forms of identification, the formulation of the Constitution of 1992 implicitly suggested a more moderate approach. The amended text stated that "the institutions of the state educate everyone from the earliest possible age in the principle of equality among human beings" (Constitution of the Republic of Cuba, 1992, article 42). Additionally, article 43 proclaimed that all "citizens, regardless of race, skin color, sex, religious belief, national origin and any situation that may be harmful to human dignity," were to enjoy the same public and social benefits and privileges as other Cubans. For religious individuals, this marked a significant change. For young people practicing religion, particularly important was the statement that they would "have a right to education at all national educational institutions, ranging from elementary schools to the universities, which are the same for all" (Constitution of the Republic of Cuba, 1992, article 43).

Moreover, the amendment enabled practicing Christians to seek membership and positions of power in the Communist Party and for party members to express religious beliefs. Religious orientation no longer impeded merit-based access "to all state, public administration, and production services positions and jobs" or religious Cubans' opportunity to reach "any rank in the Revolutionary Armed Forces and in Security and internal order, in keeping with their merits and abilities" (Constitution of the Republic of Cuba, 1992, article 43).

While the Constitution of 1992 altered the public roles and access to public life of religious Cubans, it nevertheless rested on the precondition that individual freedoms remained linked with the construction of socialism. For example, freedom of speech and press freedom was granted "in keeping with the objectives of socialist society." Similarly, the Constitution stated that the freedoms recognized by the state for citizens could not be "exercised contrary to what is established in the Constitution and by law, or contrary to the existence and objectives of the socialist state, or contrary to the decision of the Cuban people to build socialism and communism" (Constitution of the Republic of Cuba, 1992, article 62). As such, the legal transition of religious presence was again placed within the broader framework of the revolution's historiography, self-articulated narratives, and socialist construction.

Discussion

While much has been written about Cuba's post-1959 political, economic, and social trajectories, these analyses have seldom addressed the role of either law or religion in the restructuring of social order, especially in tandem. This chapter argues, nevertheless, that these two areas were related and pertinent to both the processes of social change and the construction of the revolution's broader historiography: the narrative of widespread popular support and legitimacy obtained from the people that rationalized and consolidated both the revolutionary institutions and state power. As the chapter shows, the intersection of law, legislation, and religion provides an analytical framework to examine, from new perspectives, both Cuban socialism and society and Cuba's international connections and exchanges that shaped Cuban socialism.

An analysis of the legal history of the Cuban Revolution since 1959, particularly the constitutional reforms of 1976 and 1992, shows that law and legislation were foundational to the consolidation and legitimization of revolutionary rule. At the same time, they were used to construct a cohesive historiographical narrative that would sustain state power and rationalize the construction of state socialism. Religion, as the chapter demonstrates, was among the key legislative areas regarding civil society through which the state controlled and managed popular participation and expression.

By escaping the predominant attention on the 1960s as Cuba's decade of revolutionary fervor and transnational connections, a focus on socialist legislation, as well as religion, provides fruitful perspectives for studying Cuba as part of the international Left through the 1990s. The findings of this article suggest that identifying socialist policies on religion as an area of scholarly inquiry provides an opportunity to examine how the Cuban state modeled its polities on civil society and individual rights on the Soviet Union, how it diverged from them, and what was unique to Cuban socialism in these areas. As this chapter shows, religion provides a relevant case and a recurring point of entry to engage in such discussions. As such, the intersection of law, legislation, and religion provides a hitherto missing window on socialist construction in post-1959 Cuba from both national and international perspectives.

BIBLIOGRAPHY

Alonso, Aurelio. 2010. Religion in Cuba's Socialist Transition. *Socialism and Democracy* 24 (1): 147–159.

Brenner, Philip, Marguerite Rose Jiménez, John M. Kirk, and William M. LeoGrande. 2008. Introduction: History as Prologue: Cuba before the Special Period. In *A Contemporary Cuba Reader. Reinventing the Revolution*. Rowman & Littlefield.

Casavantes-Bradford, Anita. 2014. *The Revolution is for the Children. The Politics of Childhood in Havana and Miami, 1959–1962*. The University of North Carolina Press.

Chase, Michelle. 2015. *Revolution within the Revolution. Women and Gender Politics in Cuba, 1952–1962*. The University of North Carolina Press.

Crahan, Margaret. 1985. Cuba: Religion and Revolutionary Institutionalization. *Journal of Latin American Studies* 17 (2): 319–340.

D'Zurilla, William T. 1981. Cuba's 1976 Socialist Constitution and the Fidelista Interpretation of Cuban Constitutional History. *Tulane Law Review* 55: 1223–1283.

Da Costa, Steven Alexandre, and Grant, Julienne E. 2017. Legal System and Government Structure. In *Guide to Cuban Law and Legal Research*, eds. Julienne E. Grant, Marisol Florén-Romero, Sergio D. Stone, Steven Alexandre da Costa, Lyonette Louis-Jacques, Cate Kellett, Jonathan Pratter, Teresa M. Miguel-Stearns, Eduardo Colón-Semidey, Jootaek Lee, Irene Kraft and Yasmin Morais. *International Journal of Legal Information* 45 (2): 76–188.

Evenson, Debra. 2003. *Law and Society in Contemporary Cuba*. Kluwer Law International.

Fernández, Damian. 2008. Society, Civil Society, and the State. An Uneasy Three-Way Affair. In *A Contemporary Cuba Reader. Reinventing the Revolution*. Rowman & Littlefield.

Grant, Julienne E. 2017. Introduction. In *Guide to Cuban Law and Legal Research*, eds. Julienne E. Grant, Marisol Florén-Romero, Sergio D. Stone, Steven Alexandre da Costa, Lyonette Louis-Jacques, Cate Kellett, Jonathan Pratter, Teresa M. Miguel-Stearns, Eduardo Colón-Semidey, Jootaek Lee, Irene Kraft and Yasmin Morais. *International Journal of Legal Information* 45 (2): 76–188.

Guerra, Lillian. 2012. *Visions of Power. Revolution, Redemption, and Resistance, 1959–1971*. The University of North Carolina Press.

Klein, L.B. 1978. The Socialist Constitution of Cuba (1976). *Columbia Journal of Transnational Law* 17: 450–515.

Kuivala, Petra. 2019. *Never a Church of Silence. The Catholic Church in Revolutionary Cuba, 1959–1986*. University of Helsinki, diss.

———. 2022. Rethinking Religion and the Revolution: New Voices and Perspectives. *Cuban Studies* 50: 47–67.

LeoGrande, William M. 2008. 'The Cuban Nation's Single Party.' The Communist Party of Cuba Faces the Future. In *A Contemporary Cuba Reader. Reinventing the Revolution*. Rowman & Littlefield.

Mesa-Lago, Carmelo. 1978. *Cuba in the 1970s. Pragmatism and Institutionalization*. University of New Mexico Press.

Padura Fuentes, Leonardo. 2008. Living and Creating in Cuba. Risks and Challenges. In *A Contemporary Cuba Reader. Reinventing the Revolution*. Rowman & Littlefield.

Pérez, Louis A. 2015. *Cuba. Between Reform and Revolution*. Oxford University Press.

Pérez-Stable, Marifeli. 2012. *The Cuban Revolution. Origins, Course, and Legacy*. Oxford University Press.

Rojas, Rafael. 2019. The New Text of the Revolution. In *The Revolution from Within: Cuba, 1959–1980*, ed. Michael J. Bustamente and Jennifer Lambe. Duke University Press.

Smith, Lois M., and Padula, Alfred. 1996. *Sex and Revolution. Women in Socialist Cuba*. Oxford University Press.

The Constitution of the Republic of Cuba, 1940.

———. 1976.

———. 1992.

Index[1]

[1] Note: Page numbers followed by 'n' refer to notes.

Printed in the United States
by Baker & Taylor Publisher Services